EDITION

7

Marketing Research

EDITION

7

Marketing Research

Alvin C. Burns
Louisiana State University

Ronald F. Bush
University of West Florida

PEARSON

Boston   Columbus   Indianapolis   New York   San Francisco   Upper Saddle River
Amsterdam   Cape Town   Dubai   London   Madrid   Milan   Munich   Paris   Montreal   Toronto
Delhi   Mexico City   São Paulo   Sydney   Hong Kong   Seoul   Singapore   Taipei   Tokyo

Editor-in-Chief: Stephanie Wall
Director of Editorial Services: Ashley Santora
Editorial Assistant: Jacob Garber
Director of Marketing: Maggie Moylan
Executive Marketing Manager: Anne Fahlgren
Senior Managing Editor: Judy Leale
Production Project Manager: Becca Groves
Operations Specialist: Cathleen Petersen
Creative Director: Blair Brown
Senior Art Director: Janet Slowik
Interior and Cover Designer: Wanda Espana
Cover Photo: © peshkova/Fotolia

Senior Editorial Media Project Manager:
  Denise Vaughn
Production Media Project Manager:
  Lisa Rinaldi
Full-Service Project Management:
  S4Carlisle Publishing Services
Composition: S4Carlisle Publishing Services
Printer/Binder: RR Donnelley
Cover Printer: Lehigh-Phoenix Color/
  Hagerstown
Text Font: Times LT Std

Credits and acknowledgments borrowed from other sources and reproduced, with permission, in this textbook appear on the appropriate page within text.

Microsoft® and Windows® are registered trademarks of the Microsoft Corporation in the U.S.A. and other countries. Screen shots and icons reprinted with permission from the Microsoft Corporation. This book is not sponsored or endorsed by or affiliated with the Microsoft Corporation.

Microsoft and/or its respective suppliers make no representations about the suitability of the information contained in the documents and related graphics published as part of the services for any purpose. All such documents and related graphics are provided "as is" without warranty of any kind. Microsoft and/or its respective suppliers hereby disclaim all warranties and conditions with regard to this information, including all warranties and conditions of merchantability, whether express, implied or statutory, fitness for a particular purpose, title and non-infringement. In no event shall Microsoft and/or its respective suppliers be liable for any special, indirect or consequential damages or any damages whatsoever resulting from loss of use, data or profits, whether in an action of contract, negligence or other tortious action, arising out of or in connection with the use or performance of information available from the services.

The documents and related graphics contained herein could include technical inaccuracies or typographical errors. Changes are periodically added to the information herein. Microsoft and/or its respective suppliers may make improvements and/or changes in the product(s) and/or the program(s) described herein at any time. Partial screen shots may be viewed in full within the software version specified.

Library of Congress Cataloging-in-Publication Data

Burns, Alvin C.
 Marketing research / Alvin C. Burns, Ronald F. Bush.—7th ed.
    p. cm.
  ISBN-13: 978-0-13-307467-3
  ISBN-10: 0-13-307467-6
  1. Marketing research. I. Bush, Ronald F. II. Title.
  HF5415.2.B779 2014
  658.8'3—dc23   2012027317

10 9 8 7 6 5 4 3

ISBN 10:   0-13-307467-6
ISBN 13: 978-0-13-307467-3

Only we know how much our wives, Jeanne and Libbo,
have sacrificed during the times we have devoted
to this book. We are fortunate in that, for both of us,
our wives are our best friends and smiling supporters.

Al Burns,
Louisiana State University

Ron Bush,
University of West Florida

Brief Contents

Contents

Preface to *Marketing Research,* Seventh Edition

What's New in the Seventh Edition?

- *New! Reorganization and Reduced Length.* Our adopters have asked for a more concise approach, and we delivered exactly that with this seventh edition. We have reduced the chapters to 16 instead of 20 or more chapters you'll see in many texts. We accomplished this aim by combining some chapters and streamlining the material. For example, we combined the chapter on steps in the research process and determining the problem into one chapter. We combined the chapter on secondary data with packaged (formerly known as standardized) services. We combined the chapters on measurement and questionnaire design. Finally, we combined the chapters on descriptive analysis with tools of parameter estimation. This streamlined approach keeps the focus on the core lessons to be learned.

    Benefit: The book is more synchronized with a 15- or 16-week semester. Students now have a comprehensive learning experience in a more manageable package.

- *New! Updated Integrated Case.* Through our own teaching, we have found that an integrated case is an excellent teaching tool. One case taught throughout the course allows students to see the linkages that exist in the real world all the way from formulating the problem through data analysis. We have made improvements in the case we introduced in the sixth edition. We changed the name of the case to Global Motors (a division of ZEN Motors), but we kept the same characters and the essentials of the 6th edition case: Advanced Automobile Concepts. However, we streamlined the case by reducing some of the issues, and we reduced the number of variables in the case.

    The case focuses on a new manager who must determine the type of automobiles the auto market will demand in the future. Students using this case will learn how to examine attitudes and opinons (for example, attitudes about global warming) that may influence consumer choice, how to determine the most preferred models, and how to identify market segment differences between the different models. Students are shown how SPSS tools can aid them in analyzing case data to make important decisions. We have included one integrated case in every chapter. These appear as the second case at the end of each chapter.

    Benefit: The Global Motors integrated case offers the benefit of allowing students to examine the integrated nature of marketing research projects and to more easily see how data are used to help managers choose from among decision alternatives.

- *New! Influence of Social Media.* We talked to many marketing research professionals to get an understanding of how the industry is adapting to the spread of social media. We immersed ourselves in these new services and listened to dozens of presentations. We selected a representative sampling of these services to include in this new edition. Many of these are highlighted by Social Media Applications in Marketing Research Insights throughout the book.

Benefit: Students have the latest information on industry practices regarding social media. Students will be able to appreciate how an environmental change, such as the rapid rise in social media, provides threats as well as opportunities to an industry.

■ *New! YouTube Examples.* Today, you can find almost anything illustrated by video on YouTube. We didn't want to add YouTube to our book until we saw value in it. That time has come! Today you can find many applications of marketing research on this Internet resource. Our YouTube references in the text provide useful insights ranging from problem definition to statistical analysis to report writing.

Benefit: For students who like video learning, our YouTube references provide different perspectives and how-to insights on topics covered in the text.

■ *New! Mobile Marketing Research.* Another dramatic change in marketing research practice since our sixth edition has been the adoption of mobile technologies. We attended the Mobile Marketing Research Conference in 2011 and gained invaluable insights. We met people who are today's pioneers and tomorrow's leaders in mobile technology. The title of a recent article in *Quirk's Marketing Research Review* puts it this way: "Mobile Research Has Gone Mainstream." We agree, and we have integrated what we have learned about it as well as insights from leaders in this technology into this new edition.

Benefit: Students will be able to appreciate a rapidly expanding technology that is having a major impact on the marketing research industry. Readers will see how mobile research provides fast access to information not easily accessible from traditional methods.

■ *New! International Perspectives.* While there is a focus on U.S. practice, we include new international applications of marketing research throughout this edition. We are pleased to announce that we have established a relationship with ESOMAR, the European Society of Marketing and Opinion Research; the MRIA, the Canadian Marketing Research and Intelligence Association; and the MRS, the United Kingdom's Marketing Research Society. We worked with individuals in these associations to obtain their reports on industry practices as well as insights from practitioners around the world.

Benefit: Students will be able to compare information about the practice of marketing research around the globe.

■ *New! Presentation of Industry Data.* Chapter 2, The Marketing Research Industry, was completely rewritten to provide an international perspective on marketing research practice. New sources of information were obtained, and charts and graphs depict data not previously presented.

Benefit: Students will have a better understanding of the industry structure, practices, and initiatives.

■ *New! New Presentation of Ethical Perspectives.* We decided to treat ethics in this book the way they are treated in the industry. We provide, where appropriate, excerpts from the *Code of Marketing Research Standards* as they are presented by the Marketing Research Association (MRA). We have long had a good relationship with the MRA, which has given us permission present excerpts from the standards. We understand that a textbook cannot teach someone to be ethical. Rather, an effective instructor equipped with a good textbook can teach students the areas of ethical sensitivity in the conduct of marketing research. Of course, we recognize that just presenting codes or standards is not enough to appropriately treat ethics. We also present many research professionals' perspectives on their work in this field. Through these encounters, we can find fascinating insights. An example of an unusual discussion about an ethical issue that most researchers do not discuss is presented in Chapter 2.

Benefit: Students are introduced to areas of ethical sensitivity in the practice of marketing research using the actual codes/standards that practitioners use. As a result, students should have knowledge of potential "ethical dangers," whether as a future buyer or as a supplier of research.

■ *New! Updated Marketing Research Insights.* To help illustrate concepts we discuss in the text or to introduce students to some unique application being used in practice, we provide Marketing Research Insights throughout the book. Virtually all of these features are new and reflect current issues and practice in the industry. These insights generally fit the following categories: practical applications, social media applications, ethical considerations, and global applications.

    Benefit: Students are introduced to real-world applications in the marketing research industry. By focusing on four categories, students see how current issues that are important to the industry are being addressed by today's practitioners.

■ *New! Integration of SPSS 20.0.* This seventh edition is fully integrated with SPSS 20.0. We started this integration in 1995, and we enhance the integration of SPSS by offering your students step-by-step screen captures that help them learn the keystrokes in SPSS. This allows you to spend more time teaching what the analysis technique is, when to use it, and how to interpret it. Illustrated keystrokes for the latest edition of SPSS are presented in this text with clear, easy-to-follow instructions.

    Benefit: Students learn the latest version of SPSS, considered to be the "gold standard" among marketing researchers. By following our step-by-step screen captures, students will see the necessary menu operations and learn how to read SPSS output. Just by reading this book, they can learn a great deal about SPSS by "seeing" it operate before they get to a computer to practice.

■ *New! New End-of-Chapter Cases.* In many chapters, we provide new cases to reflect much of the current material in this seventh edition. We strive to make the cases interesting to the students and illustrate real-world applications.

    Benefit: Students can apply concepts they have just learned in the chapter to a real-world setting. This allows students to see how valuable the information they have learned is in a practical example.

■ *New! Insights from Marketing Research Professionals.* We take pride in the relationships we have developed in the industry. Over the years, we have been able to acquire relationships with practitioners over a wide array of firms. Some of these professionals are CEOs, some are in midmanagement positions, and some are individual entrepreneurs who operate their own firms. Some are with old-line companies that have been around for decades, and some are with new, technology-driven firms. They are located all over the world. We think these relationships give this book a unique perspective over others. We list many of these professionals in the Acknowledgments.

    Benefit: Students get more than an academic perspective of marketing research. They benefit from reading about real practitioners talking about real problems.

The Intended Market for This Book

When we first conceptualized this book back in the early 1990s, we wanted to write it for undergraduate students who were taking marketing research for the first time. We saw other books that were trying to be "all things to all people." Even though they were positioned as research texts for undergraduates, much of the material was advanced. This seventh edition, like its six predecessors, was written specifically for undergraduate students.

Our Approach

Given our intended market, throughout the first six editions we strived to provide instructors with a book designed for undergraduates who wanted to know the "nuts and bolts" of marketing research. For example, our chapter on measurement teaches students the basic question formats, the scales of measurement, the primary uses of each type of scale, and the common methods used to measure popular constructs. It does not dwell on different forms of reliability and validity or the method used to develop valid and reliable multi-item scales. In our analysis chapters, we cover the basic "bread-and-butter" statistical procedures used to analyze data, but we do not cover multivariate techniques or nonparametric statistics in the book itself.

Our approach and writing style have probably been the two main reasons the book has been the market leader for well over a decade. Student evaluations indicate that we deliver on our intent to write at the level that people studying marketing research for the first time understand. We hope your teaching evaluations regarding the textbook will arrive at the same appraisal.

Recommended Prerequisites

To prepare for this course, we feel students should have taken an introductory course in marketing. We assume students know what we mean when we talk about marketing strategy and the elements of the marketing mix. Students having had an introduction to a marketing course will better appreciate the role that marketing research plays in helping managers make better marketing decisions. We also recommend that students take an introductory statistics course prior to taking this course. It helps for them to know concepts such as the area under the normal curve, z scores, and the basics of statistical testing, including interpretation of p values. However, since we both have taught for many years, we are well aware that many students will not recall many of these concepts, and, where necessary, we provide some review of these basics.

AACSB Guidelines

The Association to Advance Collegiate Schools of Business–International (AACSB), our accreditation society, influences us a great deal. We strive to keep current with AACSB's recommendations and guidelines, such as including material that will aid in your course assessment efforts, covering ethical issues, and pointing out global applications.

We include a number of items that should help in assessing your students' understanding of the course content. Each chapter begins with learning objectives. Embedded in each chapter are Active Learning exercises that allow students to apply the knowledge just acquired to some real-world resource. Synthesize Your Learning exercises in this edition require that students revisit chapters to integrate their knowledge from those chapters. For our test bank, Pearson has adopted guidelines established by AACSB. We discuss this in a following section.

Considerations for Planning Your Syllabus

We offer some sample syllabi in the Instructor's Manual. However, some general observations may be helpful in planning a particular syllabus.

- You may not want to cover every chapter. There are typically 15 weeks in a semester and an average of 10 weeks in a quarter, and there are 16 chapters in the book. Some faculty tend not to cover the material in Chapter 5 we refer to as *packaged information*, Chapter 6 on qualitative research, Chapter 15 on regression, or Chapter 16 on the research report. Please understand, we are not recommending you omit any of these chapters; we are simply sharing what we hear from our adopters. This is a personal decision.
- Objective or essay tests? Many factors go into making this decision. However, we have found it useful to use both. We often ask perhaps 35 objective questions worth 2 points each and then three essay questions worth 10 points each. Also, some subjects—sample

size determination, for example—are better treated by giving the students problems to solve.

- Number of tests? We often break the material down into three tests per term. In our experience, students find the first eight chapters to be about equivalent in terms of difficulty. Chapters 9 and 10 on sampling plans and sample size are viewed as more difficult, and the analysis chapters the most difficult.
- Project? Some professors offer a live research project in the course; this requires a heavy time commitment, which should be taken into consideration when writing your syllabus. We offer specific suggestions for conducting a project in our Instructor's Manual.

Other Features in the Seventh Edition

- *Online Link to Careers in Marketing Research.* Some students will be interested in marketing research as a career. Beginning with the sixth edition and continued for the seventh, we provide an online Careers link. This gives us the opportunity to post new happenings in the industry as they occur. Students will find descriptions of positions, salary information, educational requirements, and links to actual position openings.

    There are some excellent masters programs in marketing research. Our Careers link also provides information on these programs. Go to **www.pearsonhighered.com/burns** and click on the link for the Companion Website for Marketing Research, seventh edition. When you open any chapter, you will see the list of links in the left margin. Click on "Careers."

    Benefit: Students have the most up-to-date information about careers.
- *Active Learning Challenges.* We innovated in the sixth edition with the inclusion of short exercises embedded at strategic points in each chapter where students are tasked to use the concept(s) they have just learned to experiment with or apply to some illustrative situation. We believe these exercises serve to solidify learning on the relevant concepts, and we have retained these Active Learning features in the seventh edition.

    Benefit: Active learning allows students to practice or apply some concept or technique they have just read about. Learning is facilitated by reading and then "doing."
- *Synthesize Your Learning.* We have retained this feature from the sixth edition to help students synthesize the knowledge they have gained across several chapters. The exercises require students to go back to previous chapters and integrate material into answers for the exercise. The following Synthesize Your Learning exercises are found at the end of the following chapters: Chapter 5, Drill Bits, Inc.; Chapter 6, Jackie & Adele's Coffee Shop; Chapter 8, Moe's Tortilla Wraps; Chapter 10, Niagara Falls Tourism Association; Chapter 13, Pets, Pets & Pets; and Chapter 15, Alpha Airlines.

    Benefit: This feature allows students to integrate material that is learned in "chunks" to see how the material is related. Students benefit by learning how integrated the marketing research process really is.
- *Guidelines on Reporting Statistical Analyses to Clients.* We have noticed that after teaching our students to properly conduct a statistical analysis using SPSS, they have trouble when it comes to writing down what they have done. In our sixth edition, we added an element in that would address this problem. We believe it is a significant improvement, and we have retained and streamlined it in the seventh edition. In our data analysis chapters, we include information on how to write up the findings for the client. We offer easy-to-follow guidelines and examples.

    Benefit: Most books teach data analysis. Students reading this book will benefit by knowing not only data analysis but also how to report what they find. This should make students better research report writers.

- *The iReportWriting Assistant.* When our students write reports for their marketing research projects, we find ourselves answering the same kinds of questions over and over. "How do you properly reference a journal article?" "What about referencing an online source of information?" "What do you have to reference, and what do you not have to reference?" "When I write the introduction to the research report, what are some of the topics I need to cover, and how do I word them?" We asked a business communications expert, Dr. Heather Donofrio, to develop an online resource that would help students answer these questions. Students can find assistance through the *iReportWriting Assistant*, available online (**www.pearsonhighered.com/burns**) linked to each chapter, in these areas:
  - What to do prior to writing
  - Templates to help students get started writing
  - Help with grammar
  - Help with citations
  - Example reports
    Benefit: In addition to the report writing chapter (Chapter 16), students have an online resource quickly available to them to help with the detailed issues that arise in report writing. This resource will make them better report writers.

- *Advanced Data Analysis Modules.* Even undergraduate students taking their first course in marketing research may need some knowledge of statistical analyses other than those we have provided in the text. Many times these issues arise as a result of a particular need associated with a real-world class project. We wanted to make some of these techniques available to you online, so we have written several additional data analysis modules. The emphasis in these modules is on explaining the basics of the analysis and when it is appropriate. We also provide an example. Topics covered are:
  - When to Use Nonparametric Tests
  - Nonparametric: Chi-square Goodness-of-Fit Test
  - Nonparametric: Mann-Whitney U Test
  - Nonparametric: Wilcoxon Test
  - Nonparametric: Kruskal-Wallis H Test
  - When to Use Multivariate Techniques
  - Factor Analysis
  - Cluster Analysis
  - Conjoint Analysis

     Students can access the modules by going to the textbook website and opening up any chapter. They will see a link to "Online Data Analysis Modules."

- *Online Datasets.* We offer online datasets associated with our cases. Of course, we provide the dataset for our integrated case, Global Motors. We also offer the Hobbit's Choice dataset for professors who wish to use this case. These datasets and the chapter locations of the revelant data analysis cases are as follows:
  - *Global Motors* (Global_Motors.sav)—integrated case dataset used in Chapters 12–16
  - *Hobbit's Choice* (Hobbit.sav)—end-of-chapter case used in Chapters 12–15

To access these datasets, go to www.pearsonhighered.com/burns and click on link for the Companion Website for *Marketing Research*, seventh edition. When you open any chapter, see the list of links in the left margin and click on "SPSS Student Downloads."

Instructor Supplements and Instructional Support

On the basis of our years of experience in teaching, we know that teaching marketing research can be a challenge. We have developed a variety of teaching and learning aids, and adopters of this textbook will receive the following ancillary materials to help them prepare their course and teach it effectively:

- *Companion Website (www.pearsonhighered.com/burns).* Resources for students and instructors may be found at our website. Students may view chapter outlines, chapter objectives, and take sample tests for each chapter. Instructors have access to their online instructional resources. Students and instructors can access databases, the online statistics modules, and the *iReportWriter Assistant* at this website.
- *Instructor's Manual.* The comprehensive instructor's manual offers chapter outlines, key terms, teaching pointers, answers to end-of-chapter questions, and case solutions. The manual may be downloaded from the textbook website.
- *PowerPoint Slides.* We have greatly improved our PowerPoint presentation slides with this edition. The presentations are now more dynamic than ever. The files may be downloaded from the textbook website.
- *Computerized Test Bank.* The supplements package includes a test bank of questions prepared by test-writing professionals. This test bank is available from Pearson Education and can be loaded into Test Generator software. Test Generator allows random selection of test questions, modification of individual questions, or insertion of new questions into a test. For each question in the Test Bank, when possible, we have indicated which AACSB topic is addressed by the question. The AACSB topics are:
  - Communication abilities
  - Ethical understanding and reasoning abilities
  - Analytic skills
  - Use of information technology
  - Dynamics of the global economy
  - Multicultural and diversity understanding
  - Reflective thinking skills

  Also, within the answer line of each question in the Test Bank, AACSB guidelines suggest that we indicate the chapter's learning objective that is covered. We refer you to the start of each textbook chapter for the list of learning objectives.

Student Supplements

SPSS Student Assistant. With previous editions, we created the SPSS Student Assistant, a stand-alone tutorial that teaches students how to use and interpret SPSS. The SPSS Student Assistant may be downloaded from the Companion website. Installation on a personal computer is simple, and the SPSS Student Assistant will reside there for easy, immediate access. The videos show cursor movements and resulting SPSS operations and output. There is a test for each Student Assistant session so that students may assess how well they have learned the material.

Go to www.pearsonhighered.com/burns and click on the link for the Companion Website for *Marketing Research*, seventh edition. When you open any chapter, see the list of links in the left margin and click on "SPSS Student Downloads" for more information.

CourseSmart eTextbooks. Developed for students looking to save on purchasing required or recommended textbooks. Students simply select their eText by title or author and purchase immediate access to the content for the duration of the course using any major credit card. With a CourseSmart eText, students can search for specific key words or page numbers, make notes online, print out reading assignments that incorporate lecture notes, and bookmark important passages for later review. For more information or to purchase a CourseSmart eTextbook, visit www.coursesmart.com.

Acknowledgments

Many people were involved in putting this seventh edition together. We are fortunate to have Pearson as our publisher. Over the years, we have been impressed with the professionalism and dedication of the people at Pearson/Prentice Hall, and the people we worked with on this edition were no exception. We wish to thank our Editor-in-Chief, Stephanie Wall, for her support and leadership. We have worked with Becca Richter Groves, Senior Production Project Manager, on several past editions. This has been another successful collaboration with the Pearson team and we look forward to many more editions!

We have benefited from the input of Heather Donofrio, Ph.D., Business Communications, for several editions. Heather helps us keep the reporting, writing, and presentation chapter current. She also developed the *iReportWriting Assistant*. Ashley Roberts has worked behind the scenes for us on two editions. For this edition, we also benefited from the contributions of Courtney Murphy. Courtney is in the Master of Marketing Research degree program at Southern Illinois University–Edwardsville. We are fortunate to have these bright and enthusiastic people working with us.

We devote a major effort toward developing and maintaining relationships with our colleagues who practice marketing research. Their knowledge and insights are interwoven throughout these pages. Many of these people have been our friends for many years, and we appreciate their contributions. Professionals who contributed to this seventh edition include:

David Almy, CEO, Marketing Research Association

Eduardo Carqueja, NPolls

Kristen Darby, COO, Marketing Research Association

Andrea Fisher, Burke, Inc.

Raleigh Floyd, Nielsen

Chris Forbes, Research Reporter

Steven H. Gittelman, President and CEO, Mktg., Inc.

Erika Harriford-McLaren, Strategic and Corporate Communications Manager, ESOMAR

Lauren Hersch, Client Relationship Manager, IBISWorld

Kees de Jong, Vice Chairman of the Board, Survey Sampling International

Frankie Johnson, Research Arts

Shari Johnson, Business Librarian, University of West Florida

Jackie Lorch, Vice President, Global Knowledge Development, Survey Sampling International

Ramana Madupalli, Director, Master of Marketing Research Program, Southern Illinois University–Edwardsville

Jeff Minier, Co-President, GfK Kynetec

Leonard Murphy, Editor-in-Chief, *Greenbook*

William D. Neal, Founder and Senior Partner, SDR Consulting

Darren Mark Noyce, Founder and Managing Director, SKOPOS Market Insight

Kartik Pashupati, Research Manager, Research Now

Anne Pettit, Vice President, Conversition

Henry Schafer, Executive Vice President, The Q Scores Company

Jessica Smith, Vice President, Offline Client Services, Survey Sampling International

Eelco Snip, Market Intelligence Analyst, ESOMAR

Doss Struse, Managing Partner, Definitive Insights

Naoufel Testaouni, Mirametrix

Liz Tanner, Communications Director, Qualtrics Labs, Inc.

Leslie Townsend, President and Founder, Kinesis

Sima Vasa, Partner and CEO, Paradigm Sample

Mike Webster, Senior Vice President, Research Solutions, Burke, Inc.

Brendan Wycks, Executive Director, Marketing Research and Intelligence Association

Of course, we owe a debt of gratitude to our colleagues in academia who provide reviews of our work. Among the reviewers for the seventh edition were:

Linda Coleman, Salem State University

Michael Pepe, Siena College

Feng Shen, St. Joseph University

Minakshi Trivedi, State University at Buffalo

We also thank those who reviewed the previous six editions of this book. Many of their suggestions and insights are still incorporated in this edition.

Manoj Agarwal, Binghamton University

Linda Anglin, Mankato State University

Silva Balasubramanian, Southern Illinois University

Ron Beall, San Francisco State University

Jacqueline J. Brown, University of Nevada, Las Vegas

Joseph D. Brown, Ball State University

Nancy Bush, Wingate University

E. Wayne Chandler, Eastern Illinois University

Tung-Zong Chang, Metropolitan State University

Kathryn Cort, North Carolina A&T State University

Thomas Cossee, University of Richmond

B. Andrew Cudmore, Florida Institute of Technology

Joshua Fogel, Brooklyn College

Yancy Edwards, University of South Florida

Eric Freeman, Concordia University

Anthony R. Fruzzetti, Johnson & Wales University

Stanley Garfunkel, Queensborough Community College

Corbett Gaulden Jr., University of Texas of the Permian Basin

Ronald Goldsmith, Florida State University

Ashok Gupta, Ohio University

Perry Haan, Tiffin University

Douglas Hausknecht, University of Akron

Stacey Hills, Utah State University

M. Huneke, University of Iowa

Ben Judd, University of New Haven

Karl Kampschroeder, St. Mary's University

James Leigh, Texas A&M University

Aron Levin, Northern Kentucky University

Bryan Lilly, University of Wisconsin

Joann Lindrud, Mankato State University

Subhash Lonial, University of Louisville

Gary McCain, Boise State University

Sumaria Mohan-Neill, Roosevelt University

Thomas O'Conner, University of New Orleans

V. Padmanabhan, Stanford University

Diane Parente, State University of New York, Fredonia

Jean Powers, Ivy Tech Community College

James A. Roberts, Baylor University

Angelina M. Russell, West Virginia University of Technology

Joel Saegert, University of Texas at San Antonio

Don Sciglimpaglia, San Diego State University

Srivatsa Seshadri, University of Nebraska at Kearney

Terri Shaffer, Southeastern Louisiana University

Birud Sindhav, University of Nebraska at Omaha

Bruce L. Stern, Portland State University

John H. Summey, Southern Illinois University

Scott Swain, Boston University

Nicolaos E. Synodinos, University of Hawaii

Peter K. Tat, University of Memphis

William Thomas, University of South Carolina

Paul Thornton, Wesley College

Jeff W. Totten, Southeastern Louisiana State University

R. Keith Tudor, Kennesaw State University

Steve Vitucci, University of Central Texas

Bernard Weidenaar, Dordt College

Carrie White, West Liberty State College

Beverly Wright, East Carolina University

Bonghee Yoo, Hofstra University

Eric Yorkston, Neeley School of Business, Texas Christian University

Charles J. Yoos II, Fort Lewis College

Heiko de B. Wijnholds, Virginia Commonwealth University

Xin Zhao, University of Utah

Finally, we wish to thank our wives, Jeanne and Libbo. Our wives sacrifice much in order to allow us to work on our book. We are fortunate in that, for both of us, our wives are our best friends and smiling supporters.

Al Burns,
Louisiana State University

Ron Bush,
University of West Florida

ABOUT THE AUTHORS

Alvin C. Burns is the Ourso Distinguished Chair of Marketing and Chairperson of Marketing in the E. J. Ourso College of Business Administration at Louisiana State University. He received his doctorate in marketing from Indiana University and an MBA from the University of Tennessee. Professor Burns has taught undergraduate and master's-level courses as well as doctoral seminars in marketing research for over 40 years. During this time, he has supervised a great many marketing research projects conducted for business-to-consumer, business-to-business, and not-for-profit organizations. His articles have appeared in the *Journal of Marketing Research*, *Journal of Business Research*, *Journal of Advertising Research*, and others. He is a Fellow in the Association for Business Simulation and Experiential Learning. He resides in Baton Rouge, Louisiana, with his wife, Jeanne; their purebred Yellow Lab, Shadeaux (it's a Louisiana thing!); and Indy, their mixed-breed rescue dog who wandered into their backyard on a Fourth of July weekend.

Ronald F. Bush is Distinguished University Professor of Marketing at the University of West Florida. He received his B.S. and M.A. from the University of Alabama and his Ph.D. from Arizona State University. With over 35 years of experience in marketing research, Professor Bush has worked on research projects with firms ranging from small businesses to the world's largest multinationals. He has served as an expert witness in trials involving research methods, often testifying on the appropriateness of research reports. His research has been published in leading journals, including the *Journal of Marketing, Journal of Marketing Research, Journal of Advertising Research, Journal of Retailing,* and *Journal of Business,* among others. In 1993, he was named a Fellow by the Society for Marketing Advances. He and his wife, Libbo, live on the Gulf of Mexico, where they can often be found playing "throw the stick" with their Scottish terrier, Maggie.

Introduction to Marketing Research

LEARNING OBJECTIVES

- To know the relationship of marketing research to marketing, the marketing concept, and marketing strategy
- To know how to define marketing research
- To understand the function and uses of marketing research
- To see examples of marketing research for evaluating target markets, product research, pricing research, promotion research, and distribution research
- To describe a marketing information system (MIS) and understand why marketing research occupies a place in an MIS

Welcome to the World of Marketing Research!

Leonard Murphy is the former CEO of the full-service firm *Rockhopper Research* and start-up *BrandScan360*. He is currently Editor-in-Chief of the *GreenBook Blog* and *GreenBook Research Industry Trends Report*. He is a consultant to marketing research firms, keeping them abreast of the many, fast-paced changes occurring in the industry.

Today many managers make decisions related to marketing. One manager needs to determine if Brand A's advertising is effective. Another manager needs to know if funds should be spent to develop a new product proposal. Yet another manager wishes to know how well her brands are performing against competitors' brands in the last six weeks. In some instances, managers can make decisions based on information they already have. But what about all those other decisions? If the wrong choice is made, a bad decision can have a significant negative effect on the company's bottom line. Marketing research plays a useful role in helping managers make the right choices. By providing the information managers need to make more informed decisions, marketing research earns its place in the business world.

In addition, as new technology facilitates the analysis of massive amounts of new data sources as well as those generated by traditional research efforts, marketing researchers are poised to further support the company's performance. This book presents the basics of marketing research. You will also learn that the practice of marketing research is constantly changing as the environments affecting the industry evolve. Just a few years ago, companies had not heard of "social media." Communications about a company or brand were to a large extent controlled by the company, transmitted through the traditional media according to a predetermined schedule. It's a different world today. Consumers set the agenda and effectively control the perception of brands through myriad channels, available anywhere and anytime via socially enabled mobile devices. This new world is both a challenge and an opportunity for marketing organizations, and researchers are at the forefront of learning how to leverage these changes for business impact.

We hope you enjoy learning about marketing research and how the industry is adapting to today's environment!

—*Leonard Murphy*

GREENBOOK.

Text and images: By permission, Leonard Murphy, Greenbook.

Events in the last decade have brought many changes to the world of business. As Leonard Murphy points out, many changes have influenced the marketing research industry. Globalization has added real meaning to the phrase "the business world"! The Internet and many other technological innovations have allowed us to realize the promises of the "information age" in a few short years, and new technologies continue to change the competitive landscape with much greater frequency than ever before. Social media have been adopted at unprecedented rates, allowing people to be "in touch" at a level that is changing human behavior. Widespread adoption of mobile devices and apps put consumers on the information highway 24/7. Significantly, consumers have been given the power, through these online innovations, to generate their own information, creating "consumer-generated media."[1]

These technological changes by themselves challenge managers to keep pace, but they must also understand and respond to a changing world economy. Entire countries grapple with solvency. Political revolution has changed much of the world, and continued unrest threatens more change.[2] As these upheavals continue, businesses cannot stand by and wait for the dust to settle. They must react and even, whenever possible, anticipate what these changes will mean for their markets. Managers must determine what products to make or services to offer, which methods of advertising are most effective, which markets are growing or declining, which prices will help their firm realize its target return on investment (ROI), and which distribution system will add the greatest value to the supply chain. The pace of change means old information is not as useful in making decisions today. As you will learn in the following pages, this is where marketing research plays a role. It provides information to help

Change is occurring at an unprecedented pace in several areas: technology, communications, social relationships, global economy, and politics. Managers need new information to help them make informed decisions more than ever. Marketing research is one source of this information.

Photo: bannosuke/Fotolia

To establish a solid foundation for studying marketing research, you will need to understand its role in and relationship to marketing, along with its definition, uses, forms, and connections to marketing information systems.

Marketing may be thought of as "meeting needs profitably."

decision makers make better decisions. This book will help you learn the process of marketing research so that you will better understand when to use marketing research to make better, more informed decisions as you aim to manage in a world of unprecedented change.

Marketing Research Is Part of Marketing

To fully appreciate the role of marketing research, it is helpful to understand its role in and relationship to marketing. What is **marketing**? A short definition is "meeting needs profitably."[3] When Apple designed the iPad, it met a growing need among those seeking greater computer portability in a tablet format. Amazon has been successful in creating the first generation of online book readers with its Kindle tablets.[4]

The American Marketing Association offers a more detailed definition:

What is marketing? The American Marketing Association defines marketing as the activity, set of institutions, and processes for creating, communicating, delivering, and exchanging offerings that have value for customers, clients, partners, and society at large.

> *Marketing is the activity, set of institutions, and processes for creating, communicating, delivering, and exchanging offerings that have value for customers, clients, partners, and society at large.*[5]

Modern marketing thought holds that firms should *collaborate with* and *learn from* consumers. Social media is facilitating this collaboration, as illustrated in Marketing Research Insight 1.1.

We should also mention that marketing thought evolves and, many believe in the principles espoused by what has become known as the *service-dominant logic for marketing*.[6] Under this philosophy, firms adopt a service-centered view of marketing that (a) identifies core competencies, (b) identifies potential customers who can benefit from these core competencies, (c) cultivates relationships with these customers by creating value that meets their specific needs, and (d) gauges feedback from the market, learn from the feedback, and improve the values offered to the public. Note that this view of marketing implies that firms must be *more* than customer oriented (making and selling what firms think customers want and need). In addition, they must *collaborate with* and *learn from* customers, adapting to their changing needs. A second implication is that products are not viewed as separate from services. "Is General Motors really marketing a service, which just happens to include a by-product called a *car*?"[7] Note that our objective here is not to discuss how marketing thought is evolving but to underscore a crucial point: To practice marketing, marketing decision makers need to make decisions. What are our core competencies? How can we use these core competencies to create value for our consumers? Who are our consumers and how can we collaborate with them? As just one example, social media have created a venue for firms to collaborate with consumers. Marketing Research Insight 1.1 illustrates this use of social media. Managers have always needed information to make better decisions. In our opinion, to practice marketing well in today's environment requires access to more and better information. As you will learn, marketing research provides information to decision makers.

To practice marketing well in today's environment requires more and better information. As you will learn, marketing research provides information to decision makers.

When firms make the right decisions, they produce products and services that their target markets perceive as having value. That value translates into sales, profits, and a positive ROI. However, we see many failures in the marketplace. Consultants Joan Schneider and Julie Hall state that they regularly are contacted by entrepreneurs and brand managers who believe they have come up with a revolutionary product. But Schneider and Hall state that these entrepreneurs almost never have done the research to confirm their grand expectations.[8] As an example, the firm Cell Zones thought it had the answer to cell phone privacy in libraries, restaurants, and so on by creating soundproof booths for private cell phone use. Had the company done the right research and noticed how people were using their new smart phones—texting—managers may have realized that talking in private would not be a big problem for consumers.

See consultants Schneider and Hall at: www.youtube.com. Search "Lessons from New Product Launches—Cell Zone to iPad."

There are many examples of failed products and services. Many of the losses associated with these products could have been avoided if the managers had conducted proper marketing research. Many product extensions—taking a successful brand and attaching it to a different product—have failed. Examples include Life Savers Sodas, Colgate Food Entrees, BIC underwear, Coors Spring Water, and Frito-Lay Lemonade. Negative reactions from consumers were responsible for removing the Ken doll's earring and taking the Cocaine Energy Drink off the market.[9] Could these failures have been avoided with better research information?

MARKETING RESEARCH INSIGHT 1.1   *Social Media Marketing*

Cadbury Chocolates Collaborates with Consumers via Facebook

In 1983 Cadbury Chocolates introduced the Wispa, a chocolate candy bar with the teaser promotional line: "Have you heard the Wispa?" In 2003 Cadbury decided to remove the candy bar from its product line. But the Wispa had many fans, and they had a "voice" through Facebook. About 93 Facebook groups totaling upwards of 14,000 members petitioned Cadbury to relaunch the Wispa. Cadbury listened to these consumers and brought the candy bar back in 2007.[10]

Ray Poynter stated, "In a Web2.0 world, brands have to learn to 'cede control to consumer.'"[11]

Facebook and the other social media give firms the opportunity to collaborate with their consumers. Marketing

Photo: © whiteboxmedia limited/Alamy

research firms are creating products to help firms learn to "listen" and communicate with consumers using social media. In the case of Cadbury, the listening and collaboration paid off. When the company relaunched the product, 41 million bars sold out in just four weeks, and the bar has sold millions more since.[12] Wispa is a prominent part of Cadbury's product line today.

What have we learned so far? To practice marketing correctly, managers must have information to make more informed decisions. This is the purpose of marketing research. This is why we say that marketing research is a part of marketing; it provides the necessary information to enable managers to market ideas, goods, and services *properly*. But how do you market ideas, goods, and services *properly*? You have probably already learned in your studies that you must begin by having the right philosophy, followed by proper marketing strategy. We call that philosophy the *marketing concept*.

THE PHILOSOPHY OF THE MARKETING CONCEPT GUIDES MANAGERS' DECISIONS

A *philosophy* may be thought of as a system of values or principles by which you live. Your values or principles are important because they dictate what you do each day. This is why philosophies are so important; your philosophy affects your day-to-day decisions. For example, you may have a philosophy similar to this: "I believe that higher education is important because it will provide the knowledge and understanding I will need in the world to enable me to enjoy the standard of living I desire." Assuming this does reflect your philosophy regarding higher education, consider what you do from day to day. You are going to class, listening to your professors, taking notes, reading this book, and preparing for tests. If you did not share the philosophy we just described, you would likely be doing something entirely different.

The same connection between philosophy and action holds true for business managers. One of the most important philosophies managers have is that which determines how they view their company's role in terms of what it provides the market. Some managers have a philosophy that "we make and sell product X." A quick review of marketing history will tell us this philosophy is known as a *product orientation*. Another philosophy, known as *sales orientation*, is illustrated by the following statement: "To be successful we must set high sales quotas and sell, sell, sell!"[13] Managers who guide their companies by either of these philosophies may guide them right out of business. A much more effective philosophy—the marketing concept—is defined here by prominent marketing professor, Philip Kotler:

> The **marketing concept** is a business philosophy that holds that the key to achieving organizational goals consists of the company being more effective than competitors in creating, delivering, and communicating customer value to its chosen target markets.[14]

Marketing research firm GfK's NewProductWorks studies product failures and provides clients with information to help them avoid repeating the mistakes of others. NewProductWorks has assembled more than 110,000 products in a display. Go to **www.youtube.com** and search for "NewProductWorks."

Marketing research is a part of marketing; it provides the necessary information to enable managers to market ideas, goods, and services *properly*.

Philosophies are more important to you than you may think; your philosophies dictate how you behave every day.

The marketing concept is often referred to by phrases such as being "market driven" or having a "customer orientation."

It has long been recognized that the philosophy known as the *marketing concept* is the "right" philosophy. Organizations are more likely to achieve their goals if they satisfy consumers' wants and needs.

For many years, business leaders have recognized that this is the "right" philosophy. Although the marketing concept is often used interchangeably with other terms, such as "customer-orientation" or "market-driven," the key point is that this philosophy puts the consumer first.[15]

What does all this mean? It means that having the right philosophy is an important first step in being successful. However, appreciating the importance of satisfying consumer wants and needs is not enough. Firms must also put together the "right" strategy.

THE "RIGHT" MARKETING STRATEGY

Strategy is another name for planning. Firms have strategies in many areas other than marketing. Financial strategy, production strategy, technology strategy, for example, may be key components of a firm's overall strategic plan. Here, we focus on marketing strategy. How do we define marketing strategy?

A marketing strategy consists of selecting a segment of the market as the company's target market and designing the proper "mix" of product/service, price, promotion, and distribution system to meet the wants and needs of the consumers within the target market.

A **marketing strategy** consists of selecting a segment of the market as the company's target market and designing the proper "mix" of product/service, price, promotion, and distribution system to meet the wants and needs of the consumers within the target market.

Because we have adopted the marketing concept, we cannot come up with just any strategy. We have to develop the "right" strategy—the strategy that allows our firm to truly meet the wants and needs of the consumers within the market segment we have chosen. Think of the many decisions we now must answer: What is the market, and how do we segment it? What are the wants and needs of each segment, and what is the size of each segment? Who are our competitors, and how are they already meeting the wants and needs of consumers? Which segment(s) should we target? Which model of a proposed product will best suit the target market? What is the best price? Which promotional method will be the most efficient? How should we distribute the product/service? All these decisions must be answered to develop the "right" strategy. To make the right decisions, managers must have objective, accurate, and timely *information*.

Many decisions must be made to develop the "right" strategy. To make the right decisions, managers must have objective, accurate, and timely *information*.

It is equally important to understand that today's strategy may not work tomorrow because, as we noted at the beginning of this chapter, there is unprecedented change going on in the business environment. What new strategies will be needed in tomorrow's world? As environments change, business decisions must be revised again and again to produce the right strategy for the new environment.

To practice marketing, to implement the marketing concept, and to make the decisions necessary to create the right marketing strategy, managers need information. Now you should see how marketing research is part of marketing; marketing research supplies managers with the information to help them make these decisions.

To practice marketing, to implement the marketing concept, and to make the decisions necessary to create the right marketing strategy, managers need information. Now you should see how marketing research is part of marketing; marketing research supplies managers with the information to help them make these decisions.

What Is Marketing Research?

Now that we have established that managers need information to carry out the marketing process, we need to define marketing research.

Marketing research is the process of designing, gathering, analyzing, and reporting information that may be used to solve a specific marketing problem.

Marketing research is the process of designing, gathering, analyzing, and reporting information that may be used to solve a specific marketing problem.

Thus, marketing research is defined as a *process* that reports information that can be used to solve a marketing problem, such as determining price or identifying the most effective advertising media. The focus then is on a process that results in information that will be used to make decisions. Notice also that our definition refers to information that may be used to solve a *specific* marketing problem. We will underscore the importance of specificity later in this chapter. Ours is not the only definition of marketing research. The American Marketing Association (AMA) formed a committee several years ago to establish a definition of marketing research:

Marketing research is the function that links the consumer, customer, and public to the marketer through information—information used to identify and define marketing opportunities and problems; generate, refine, and evaluate marketing actions; monitor marketing performance; and improve the understanding of marketing as a process.[16]

Each of these definitions is correct. Our definition is shorter and illustrates the *process* of marketing research. The AMA's definition is longer because it elaborates on the function as well as the *uses* of marketing research. In following sections, we will talk more about the function and uses of marketing research.

IS IT MARKET*ING* RESEARCH OR MARKET RESEARCH?

Some people differentiate between market*ing* research and *market* research. Marketing research is defined the way we or the AMA have defined it in previous paragraphs. In fact, the Marketing Research Association (MRA) defines this term similarly as a process used by businesses to collect, analyze, and interpret information used to make sound business decisions and successfully manage the business. In comparison, some define mark*et* research as a subset of market*ing* research, using this term to refer to applying marketing research to a specific market area. The MRA defines **market research** as a process used to define the size, location, and/or makeup of the market for a product or service.[17] Having made this distinction, we recognize that the two names are used interchangeably by many practitioners, publications, organizations serving the industry, and academics.

Some differentiate between market*ing* research and *market* research. Marketing research is the broader of the two terms, whereas *market research* refers to applying marketing research to a specific market. However, in practice, the two names are often used interchangeably.

THE FUNCTION OF MARKETING RESEARCH

The AMA definition states that the **function of marketing research** is to link the consumer to the marketer by providing information that can be used in making marketing decisions. Note that the AMA definition distinguishes between *consumers* and *customers*. The committee intended this differentiation between retail (or b2c) consumers and business (or b2b) customers. Some believe that having the link to the consumer by marketing research is more important today than ever. Having that link with the consumer is crucial if firms are to provide them with the value they expect in the marketplace. Thanks to globalization, online shopping, and social media, consumers today have more choices, more information, and more power to speak to others in the market than ever before.

The function of marketing research is to link the consumer to the marketer by providing information that can be used in making marketing decisions.

What Are the Uses of Marketing Research?

IDENTIFYING MARKET OPPORTUNITIES AND PROBLEMS

The AMA definition also spells out the different uses of marketing research. The first of these uses is the *identification of market opportunities and problems*. It is not easy to determine what opportunities are in the market. We can think of new product or service ideas, but which are feasible? Which ideas can be accomplished, and which will mostly likely generate a good ROI? Often, after someone has found an opportunity by creating a highly successful product or service, managers ask: "Why didn't we see that opportunity?" Some marketing research studies are designed to find out what consumers' problems are and to assess the suitability of different proposed methods of resolving those problems. Consumers wanted complete portability in their music, so Apple developed the iPod. High gasoline prices and concerns about fossil emissions bothered consumers, so Toyota developed the Prius. Consumers wanted increasingly large TV screens to hang on their walls, so Samsung developed an ultra-thin, LED, large-screen TV.

You would think that managers would always know what their problems are. Why would problem identification be a use of marketing research? Problems are not always easy to identify. Managers are more likely to always know the symptoms (sales are down, market share is falling) but determining the cause/s of the symptoms sometimes requires research. The identification of opportunities and problems is discussed in Chapter 3.

Marketing research may be used to generate, refine, and evaluate a potential marketing action.

GENERATE, REFINE, AND EVALUATE POTENTIAL MARKETING ACTIONS

Marketing research can also be used to generate, refine, and evaluate a potential marketing action. Here "actions" may be thought of as strategies, campaigns, programs, or tactics. Barnes & Noble managers felt they had to take some action when their major competitor, Amazon, developed the Kindle and started selling books online. Two years after the Kindle was introduced, the Nook hit the market. "Actions" of Barnes & Noble were: *generating* the basic strategy to compete head-on with their own e-book reader; *refining* the Nook by identifying what features, operating system, apps, and design details it should have; and *evaluating* plans to introduce and market the Nook. Research can be used to help management make better decisions for any and all these actions.

We can think of "actions" as strategies, and strategies involve selection of a target market and designing a marketing mix to satisfy the wants and needs of that target market. Marketing research is conducted in a variety of areas, including determining target markets and conducting product research, pricing research, promotion research, and distribution research. Let's consider some examples:

Selecting Target Markets A great deal of marketing research is conducted to determine the size of various market segments. Not only are managers interested in knowing the size of the market segment that wants an all-electric vehicle but they want to know if that segment is growing or shrinking and how well competitors are fulfilling the wants and needs of that segment. If research shows that a significantly large segment of the market has identifiable needs, the segment is growing; if its needs are either not being met or being met poorly by competition, this segment becomes an ideal candidate for a target market. Now the company must determine how well its core competencies will allow it to satisfy that segment's demand. Nissan very likely looked at the automobile market segments in terms of the number of miles driven in a day (we will consider this factor in the Chapter 5 on secondary data). The company must have found a sizable segment of auto drivers who drive under 90 miles a day, which is the range of its all-electric car, the Leaf.

Product Research Successful companies are constantly looking for new products and services. They know the lesson of the product life cycle: Products will eventually die. As a result, they must have a process in place to identify and test new products. Testing may begin with idea generation and continues with concept tests that allow firms to quickly and inexpensively get consumers' reactions to the concept of a proposed new product. Research studies are conducted on the proposed brand names and package designs of products before commercialization. Maritz Research conducts a *New Vehicle Customer Study*. The company has collected data over several years, and in recent years it has studied hybrids. Its market analysts know why drivers purchase hybrids, what makes them satisfied, what their expectations are for gas mileage and preferences for alternative fuels.[18]

Pricing Research When a revolutionary new product is created, marketers use research to determine the "value" consumers perceive in the new product. When cable TV was introduced, research was conducted to give the early cable providers some clue as to what people would be willing to pay for clear reception and a few additional channels. When cellular phones were introduced, much research was conducted to see what people would be willing to pay for (what was then) a revolutionary "portable" telephone. Marketing research is also conducted to determine how consumers will react to different types of pricing tactics such as "buy one, get one free" versus a "one-half-off" price offer. Using qualitative research in the form of asking potential buyers a series of open-ended questions—a qualitative research technique called "purchase story research"—a researcher found that the way a firm categorized its products negatively affected how b2b buyers had to use their purchase accounts. Once the items were recategorized, sales went up.[19]

Promotion Research As firms spend dollars on promotion, they want to know how effective those expenditures are for the advertising, sales force, publicity/PR, and promotional offers. Firms also conduct research on the effectiveness of different media. Is online advertising more cost-effective than traditional media such as TV, radio, newspaper, and magazine advertising? How can we effectively use social media to "hear" what consumers are saying about our brands and our competitors? As an example of promotion research, the research firm, Marcus Thomas, LLC, conducted research for Akron's Children's Hospital to determine the most effective communication messages to use in a new ad campaign being developed by the hospital.[20]

Distribution Research What are the best channels to get our product to consumers? Where are the best dealers for our product, and how can we evaluate the service they provide? How satisfied are our dealers? Are our dealers motivated? Should we use multichannel distribution? How many distributors should we have? These are but a few of the crucial questions managers may answer through marketing research.

MONITOR MARKETING PERFORMANCE

Control is a basic function of management. To assess performance on some variables, marketing research is often used. Sales by SKU (stock-keeping unit) and by type of distribution, for example, is often gathered through tracking data collected at point-of-sale terminals as consumer packaged goods are scanned in grocery stores, mass-merchandisers, and convenience stores. Such data allow managers to monitor their brands' sales as well as sales of competitors—and thus to monitor their market shares as well. Firms use marketing research to monitor other variables such as their employees' and customers' satisfaction levels. For example, the research firm MSR Group conducted a rolling tracking study measuring drivers of satisfaction of bank customers. The nationwide study allows banks to identify factors that determine advocates and loyal, at-risk, and critical customer relationships.[21] Research firms such as Nielsen and Symphony IRI Group monitor the performance of products in supermarkets and other retail outlets. They track how many units of these products are being sold, through which chains, at what retail price, and so on. You will learn more about tracking studies in Chapter 5. Tracking social media, which has grown quickly the world over, is another means of monitoring market performance. Research firms have developed services that monitor what people are saying about companies, brands, and competitors.

Client firms are interested in "hearing" what consumers on social media such as Facebook and Twitter are saying about their company, brands, and competitors.

Photo: © Scanrail/Fotolia

Though they represent a very small part of the total marketing research studies, another use of marketing research is for studies that are designed to improve our basic understanding of marketing as opposed to solving a particular problem facing a business.

Marketing Research on YouTube™

Marketing research is not always correct. In the classic 1980s movie *Big*, Tom Hanks plays the role of a child in a man's body. He ends up working for a toy company. The company hires a marketing research firm that makes an impressive report on the sales potential of a transformer in the shape of a skyscraper building. While the executives agree fully with the research, Tom Hank's character gives them the insight they really needed—a perspective from that of a kid who finds the toy boring! Go to **www.youtube.com** and enter "Tom Hanks in BIG 'I don't Get it' by Therototube."

IMPROVE MARKETING AS A PROCESS

Improving our understanding of the marketing process entails conducting some marketing research to expand our basic knowledge of marketing. Typical of such research would be attempts to define and classify marketing phenomena and to develop theories that describe, explain, and predict marketing phenomena. Such knowledge is often published in journals such as the *Journal of Marketing Research* or *Marketing Research*. Much of this research is conducted by marketing professors at colleges and universities and by other not-for-profit organizations, such as the Marketing Science Institute.

The latter use could be described as the only part of marketing research that is basic research. **Basic research** is conducted to expand our knowledge rather than to solve a specific problem. For example, research published in the *Journal of Marketing Research* may investigate the psychological process consumers go through in deciding on how long to wait for service to be provided. This basic research is not conducted for any specific company problem but rather to increase our understanding of satisfying consumers of services.[22] However, this basic research could be valuable to Southwest Airlines if the company were conducting an analysis of consumer reactions to different wait times in its telephone reservation system, a specific problem facing Southwest. Research conducted to solve specific problems is called **applied research**, which represents the vast majority of marketing research studies. For the most part, marketing research firms are conducting research to solve a specific problem facing a company. We will revisit the idea that marketing research solves specific problems a little later in this chapter.

MARKETING RESEARCH IS SOMETIMES WRONG

There are plenty of examples of when marketing research didn't provide management with the right answer. General Motors, for example, did research on what was to become the

minivan—a small van that would be suitable for families—but the research did not convince the carmaker to produce a van. Shortly thereafter, Chrysler introduced the Dodge Caravan and Plymouth Voyager minivans, which turned out to be among the most successful models in automotive history.[23] A beer ad in the United Kingdom was deemed by marketing research to be inadequate, but management disagreed. When the ad ran, it was very successful.[24] The marketing research on the pilot of Seinfeld indicated the TV show would be a flop. Six months later, a manager questioned the accuracy of the research and gave the show another try. Seinfeld became one of the most successful shows in television history.[25] When Duncan Hines introduced its line of soft cookies, marketing research studies showed that 80% of customers who tried Soft Batch cookies stated they would buy them in the future. They didn't.[26]

Marketing research is sometimes wrong!

Photo: © auremar/Fotolia

Anyone who observes the marketplace will see products and services introduced and then taken off the market because they do not live up to expectations. Some of these failures are brought to market without any research, which increases their probability of failure. However, as we have learned, even when products are brought to market with the benefit of marketing research, the predictions are not always accurate. But this does not mean that marketing research is not useful. Remember, most marketing research studies are trying to understand and predict consumer behavior, which is a difficult task. The fact that the marketing research industry has been around for many years and is growing means that it has passed the toughest of all tests to prove its worth—the test of the marketplace. If the industry did not provide value, it would cease to exist. For each of the failed examples cited previously, there are tens of thousands of success stories supporting the use of marketing research.

Though marketing research takes on the difficult task of trying to predict consumer behavior—a daunting task, indeed—it has passed the test of the marketplace, and many attest to its value.

The Marketing Information System

Managers have recognized the importance of information as an asset to be managed for many years. The advent of computer technology in the 1960s allowed the dream of information management to become a reality. During the decades since, sophisticated management information systems (MIS) have evolved that attempt to provide the right information at the right time in the right format in the hands of those who must make decisions. Management information systems typically have subsystems to provide the information necessary for a functional area within an organization. Such subsystems are the accounting information system, financial information system, production information system, human resources information system, and marketing information system. Thus far, we have presented marketing research as if it were the only source of information. This is not the case, as you will understand by reading this section on marketing information systems.

So far, we have presented marketing research as if it were the only source of information. This is not the case.

Marketing decision makers have a number of sources of information available to them. We can understand these different information sources by examining the components of the **marketing information system (MIS)**. An MIS is a structure consisting of people, equipment, and procedures to gather, sort, analyze, evaluate, and distribute needed, timely, and accurate information to marketing decision makers.[27] The role of the MIS is to determine decision makers' information needs, acquire the needed information, and distribute that information to the decision makers in a form and at a time when they can use it for decision making. This sounds very much like what we have been saying about marketing research—providing information to aid in decision making. Learning the components of an MIS will help to establish some distinctions.

An MIS is a structure consisting of people, equipment, and procedures to gather, sort, analyze, evaluate, and distribute needed, timely, and accurate information to marketing decision makers.

COMPONENTS OF AN MIS

As noted previously, the MIS is designed to assess managers' information needs, to gather this information, and to distribute the information to the marketing managers who need to make decisions. Information is gathered and analyzed by the four subsystems of the MIS: internal reports, marketing intelligence, marketing decision support, and marketing research. See Figure 1.1. We discuss each of these subsystems next.

A marketing information system (MIS) has four subsystems: internal reports, marketing intelligence, marketing decision support, and marketing research.

Internal Reports System Much information is generated in normal, daily transactions. When you make a purchase at a grocery store, management has a record of the SKUs you purchased, payment method, coupons or special promotions used, store location, and day of week and time of day. When that same grocery store orders supplies of foods, they have a purchase requisition and a shipping invoice when the goods are shipped by the supplier firm. All this information is gathered and serves as a source of information for managers. The **internal reports system** gathers information generated by internal reports, which includes orders, billing, receivables, inventory levels, stockouts, and so on. In many cases, the internal reports

The internal reports system gathers information generated by internal reports, which includes orders, billing, receivables, inventory levels, stockouts, and so on. In many cases, the internal reports system is called the *accounting information system.*

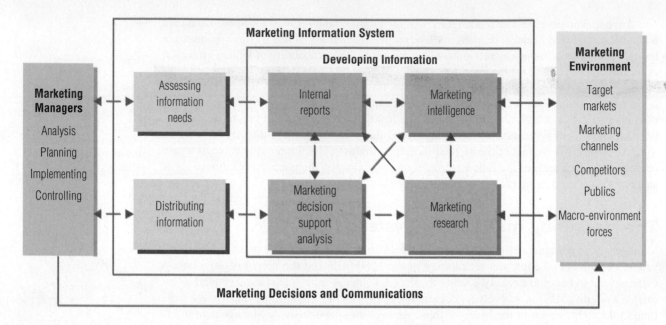

FIGURE 1.1
The Marketing Information System

system is called the *accounting information system*. Although this system produces financial statements (balance sheets and income statements, etc.) that generally contain insufficient detail for many marketing decisions, the internal reports system is a source of extreme detail on both revenues and costs that can be invaluable in making decisions. Other information is also collected, such as inventory records, sales calls records, and orders. A good internal reports system can tell a manager a great deal of information about what has happened within the firm in the past. When information is needed from sources *outside* the firm, marketing researchers must call on other MIS components.

Marketing Intelligence System The **marketing intelligence system** is defined as a set of procedures and sources used by managers to obtain everyday information about pertinent developments in the environment. Consequently, the intelligence system focuses on bringing in information generated outside the firm. Such systems include both informal and formal information-gathering procedures. Informal information-gathering procedures involve activities such as scanning newspapers, magazines, and trade publications. Formal information-gathering activities may be conducted by staff members who are assigned the specific task of looking for anything that seems pertinent to the company or industry. They then edit and disseminate this information to the appropriate members or company departments. Formerly known as "clipping bureaus" (because they clipped relevant newspaper articles for clients), several online information service companies, such as Lexis-Nexis, provide marketing intelligence. To use its service a firm would enter key terms into search forms provided online by Lexis-Nexis. Information containing the search terms appears on the subscriber's computer screen as often as several times a day. By clicking on an article title, subscribers can view a full-text version of the article. In this way, marketing intelligence goes on continuously and searches a broad range of information sources to bring pertinent information to decision makers.

Marketing Decision Support System (DSS) The third component of an MIS is the decision support system. A **marketing decision support system (DSS)** is defined as collected data that may be accessed and analyzed using tools and techniques that assist managers in decision making. Once companies collect large amounts of information, they store this

The marketing intelligence system is defined as a set of procedures and sources used by managers to obtain everyday information about pertinent developments in the environment.

A marketing decision support system (DSS) is defined as collected data that may be accessed and analyzed using tools and techniques that assist managers in decision making.

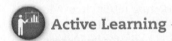 **Active Learning**

Use Google Alerts to Create Your Own Intelligence System

You can create your own intelligence system through Google, which offers a free service called Google Alerts (http://www.googlealerts.com). By entering key words, you will receive emails from Google Alerts whenever something appears with those key words. You can specify searching everything that appears on the Internet or limit results to search only blogs, videos, or books. What value would this be to you? If you have a paper to write for the end of term, this service will allow you to gather information all term as it occurs. Or, if you have an interview coming up, you may want to track the latest information about the company or industry. You will receive email results daily.

information in huge databases that, when accessed with decision-making tools and techniques (such as break-even analysis, regression models, and linear programming), allow companies to ask "what if" questions. Answers to these questions are then immediately available for decision making. For example, salespersons complete daily activity reports showing customers they called on during the day and orders written. These reports are uploaded to the company databases routinely. A sales manager can access these reports and, using spreadsheet analysis, he or she can quickly determine which salespersons are at, above, or below quota for that day of the month.

Marketing Research System Marketing research, which we have already discussed and defined, is the fourth component of an MIS. Now that you have been introduced to the three other components of an MIS, we are ready to address a new question: If marketing research and an MIS are both designed to provide information for decision makers, how are the two different? In answering this question we must see how marketing research differs from the other three MIS components.

First, the **marketing research system** gathers information not gathered by the other MIS component subsystems: Marketing research studies are conducted for a *specific* situation facing the company. It is unlikely that other components of an MIS have generated the particular information needed for the specific situation. When GM was working on changes in the appearance of its new electric car, the Volt, management had several design options available. Could management get information about what today's new car market consumers will most prefer from the internal reports system? No. Could they get useful information from their intelligence system? No. Could they get information from their DSS? You could argue that their DSS has design preference data stored from the past and that this information could be helpful. Yet, when you consider the change in the car-buying public due to a renewed enthusiasm for fuel efficiency, should GM rely on old data on design preferences? Marketing research can provide information to help GM design the Volt for today's consumers.

To consider another example, when *People* magazine wants to know which of three cover stories it should use for this week's publication, can its managers obtain that information from internal reports? No. From the intelligence system or the DSS? No. Filling this information gap is how marketing research plays a unique role in a firm's total information

If marketing research and an MIS are both designed to provide information for decision makers, how are the two different?

By providing information for a *specific* problem at hand, marketing research provides information not provided by other components of the MIS.

Managers can access a DSS and manipulate data using analytical tools such as Excel and SPSS.

Photo: © Yuri Arcurs/Fotolia

system. By providing information for a *specific* problem, marketing research provides information not provided by other components of the MIS. This is why marketing research studies are sometimes referred to as "ad hoc studies." *Ad hoc* is Latin for "with respect to a specific purpose." (Recall that earlier in the chapter when we defined marketing research, we said we would revisit the word *specific*. Now you see why we used that word in our definition.)

There is another characteristic of marketing research that differentiates it from the other MIS components. Though this difference doesn't justify the existence of marketing research in the MIS, it is notable. Marketing research projects, unlike the previous components, are not continuous—they have a beginning and an end. This is why marketing research studies are sometimes referred to as "projects." The other components are available for use on an ongoing basis. However, marketing research projects are launched only when there is a justifiable need for information that is not available from internal reports, intelligence, or the DSS.

> Because marketing research studies are not continuous, they are often referred to as "projects."

Summary

Globalization, the widespread adoption of the Internet, and associated innovations, including the rise of social media such as Facebook and Twitter, have dramatically changed the pace of change in the business world. Yet, managers must still make decisions, and the role of marketing research is to provide information to help managers make better decisions. Because marketing research is part of marketing, to understand marketing research, we must understand the role it plays in marketing. The American Marketing Association (AMA) defines marketing as the activity, set of institutions, and processes for creating, communicating, delivering, and exchanging offerings that have value for customers, clients, partners, and society at large. There are new frameworks for understanding marketing. One such framework is called the "service-dominant logic for marketing," which increases the need for marketers to "hear" their consumers and even to collaborate with them. Marketing research firms are creating products that will allow managers to find out what consumers are saying about them on social media and to help those firms collaborate with their customers using social media. Marketers must "hear the voice of the consumer" to determine how to create, communicate, and deliver value that will result in long-lasting relationships with customers. Some firms "hear" the voice and have success; others do not and experience product and service failures. There are many examples of product failures including Life-Savers sodas, Colgate food entrees, and Frito-Lay Lemonade. In all these cases

managers might have made better decisions with better information.

Because philosophies guide our day-to-day decisions, marketers should follow the philosophy known as the *marketing concept*. The marketing concept states that the key to business success lies in being more effective than competitors in creating, delivering, and communicating customer value to chosen target markets. Companies whose philosophy focuses on products and selling efforts do not tend to stay around long. If a firm's management follows the marketing concept philosophy, they develop the "right" strategies, or plans, to provide consumers with value. In short, to practice marketing as we have described it, managers need information to determine wants and needs and to design marketing strategies that will satisfy customers in selected target markets. Furthermore, environmental changes mean that marketers must constantly collect information to monitor customers, markets, and competition.

One definition of marketing research is that it is the process of designing, gathering, analyzing, and reporting information that may be used to solve a specific problem. The AMA defines marketing research as the function that links the consumer, customer, and public to the marketer through information—information used to identify and define marketing opportunities and problems; generate, refine, and evaluate marketing actions; monitor marketing performance; and improve the understanding of marketing as a process. Some differentiate between market*ing* research and *market* research. Marketing research is the broader of the two names and is used to refer to the process of gathering, analyzing, and reporting information for decision making. Market research refers to applying marketing research to a specific market. However, in practice, the two names are often used interchangeably.

To link the consumer to the marketer by providing information that can be used in making marketing decisions is the function of marketing research. The uses of marketing research are to (1) identify and define marketing opportunities and problems; (2) generate, refine, and evaluate marketing actions; (3) monitor marketing performance; and (4) improve our understanding of marketing. Most marketing research is considered to be applied research in that it is conducted to solve specific problems. A limited number of marketing research studies would be considered basic research in that they are conducted to expand the limits of our knowledge.

If marketing research provides information to make marketing decisions, why should we also have a marketing information system (MIS)? Actually, marketing research is part of an MIS. Marketing research is only one of four subsystems making up an MIS. Other subsystems include internal reports, marketing intelligence, and decision support systems. Marketing research gathers information not available through the other subsystems. Marketing research provides information for the specific problem at hand. Marketing research is conducted on a project basis having a beginning and end. The other MIS components operate continuously, 24/7.

Key Terms

Marketing (p. 3)
Marketing concept (p. 5)
Marketing strategy (p. 6)
Marketing research (p. 6)
Market research (p. 7)
Function of marketing
   research (p. 7)

Basic research (p. 10)
Applied research (p. 10)
Marketing information
   system (p. 11)
Internal reports system (p. 11)

Marketing intelligence system
   (MIS) (p. 12)
Marketing decision support
   system (DSS) (p. 12)
Marketing research system (p. 13)

Review Questions/Applications

1. What is marketing? Explain the role of marketing research in the process of marketing management.
2. Give some examples of products that have failed.
3. Why are philosophies important to decision makers? What is the marketing concept?
4. What is strategy, and why is marketing research important to strategy makers?
5. Define marketing research. Define market research.
6. What is the purpose of marketing research?
7. Name the uses of marketing research.
8. Which use of marketing research is considered basic research?
9. Give your own example to illustrate a marketing research study that may be used in (a) product research, (b) pricing research, (c) promotion research, and (d) distribution research.
10. Distinguish among MIS (marketing information system), marketing research, and DSS (decision support system).

11. Explain why the phrase "specific problem" is important to the definition of marketing research and how this phrase relates to justifying the existence of marketing research in the MIS.
12. Go to your library, either in person or online, and look through several business periodicals such as *Advertising Age, Business Week, Fortune,* and *Forbes.* Find three examples of companies using marketing research.
13. Select a company in a field in which you have a career interest and look up information on this firm in your library or on the Internet. After gaining some knowledge of this company and its products and services, customers, and competitors, list five different types of decisions you believe this company's management may have made within the past two years. For each decision, list the information the company's executives would have needed to make these decisions.

14. In the following situations, what component of the marketing information system would a manager use to find the necessary information?
    a. A manager of an electric utilities firm hears a friend at lunch talk about a new breakthrough in solar panel technology she read about in a science publication.
    b. A manager wants to know how many units of three different products in the company sold during each month for the past three years.
    c. A manager wants to estimate the contribution to company return on investment earned by 10 different products in the company product line.
    d. A manager is considering producing a totally new type of health food. But he would like to know if consumers are likely to purchase the new food, at which meal they would most likely eat the food, and how they would prefer the food to be packaged.

CASE 1.1

Anderson Construction

Larry Anderson is President of Anderson Construction. The firm had been in business for almost five years when the housing industry crashed with the Wall Street debacle of 2008. Anderson had quickly become profitable in the building business, but it was a time when nearly everyone in the business was making profits as the industry was overinflated by a boom based on banking fees rather than real demand. To make a reputation, the company had invested heavily in the selection of a superior construction crew. Larry Anderson had followed a strategy of hiring only personnel with high levels of training and experience. This had given him the ability to be versatile. Anderson had prided itself on quality custom-home construction, but he had a few jobs in large commercial buildings and multifamily, multistory projects. His well-experienced staff of employees gave him the ability to take on a variety of construction projects. By 2012 Anderson was one of the few firms left in town. Most construction firms had gone out of business trying to wait out the housing bust. Anderson remained afloat with a few good employees and very limited demand among a few individuals who were interested in building custom homes. Because Larry had invested in his personnel with better pay and continuous training for them, he still had many employees who stayed in touch with him. These employees were eager to go back to work for Anderson and were biding their time in one or more part-time jobs.

Larry Anderson was not accustomed to doing marketing research. Because he started his business at a time when the artificial building boom was rising, he had what seemed like an endless supply of job opportunities on which to bid. The only research Larry had conducted during those formative years was exploration to find key personnel and to keep up with building materials and building code changes. Now, as Larry had only two custom home jobs in the queue, he began to worry about how he could find more work for his construction crews. He wondered if marketing research would be of any help.

1. Explain why you think Larry Anderson should look into doing marketing research or not doing marketing research?
2. Think about the components of a marketing information system. Which component/s would you suggest Larry Anderson use and why?

CASE 1.2 INTEGRATED CASE

Global Motors

Nick Thomas is a CEO of Global Motors, a new division of a large automobile manufacturer, ZEN Motors. ZEN is a multinational manufacturer headquartered in the United States, which has multiple divisions representing several auto and truck brands. ZEN's divisions have been slowly losing market share to other competitors. Global Motors was created to revive the aging ZEN automobile brands by developing totally new models that are more in tune with today's changing automobile market.

Nick Thomas knows he must come up with some innovations in automobile design and engineering, but he is not certain in which direction he should guide his division. Nick realizes that he needs to find out what consumers' attitudes are toward fuel prices and global warming. This knowledge will help him determine a direction for the company in terms of automobile design. Nick also needs more data on consumer preferences. Will they want to stay with today's standard compacts or hybrids, or might they be interested in radically different models that promise much higher fuel economies?

1. Should Nick Thomas use marketing research?
2. What components of ZEN's MIS will Nick need?

2

The Marketing Research Industry

LEARNING OBJECTIVES

- To learn a brief history of the marketing research industry
- To learn the different types of marketing research firms and the industry structure
- To be aware of criticisms of the industry and the industry's focus on self-improvement
- To appreciate the areas of ethical sensitivity in the marketing research process and to examine the ethical codes and standards developed by professional associations serving the marketing research industry
- To learn about careers in the marketing research industry

A Word from the CEO of the Marketing Research Association

David Almy,
CEO, Marketing
Research
Association

In this chapter you will gain knowledge of the marketing research industry and learn about several professional associations that serve the industry. The Marketing Research Association (MRA) is devoted to improving the quality and ensuring the future of the profession. Founded in 1957, MRA is the leading and largest association of the opinion and marketing research profession, which delivers insights and intelligence to guide the decisions of companies providing products and services to consumers and businesses.

MRA's goal is to encourage high standards within the profession, to raise competency, to establish an objective measure of knowledge and proficiency, to encourage continued advancement, to increase consumer understanding of research, and to foster premiere professional standards in the profession. MRA's **Professional Researcher Certification (PRC)** provides market advantage, confidence, and strength for practitioners. PRCs can demonstrate to their peers, employees, and organization that they have mastered the core PRC principles and are dedicated to staying current in the profession. (You will read more about the PRC in this chapter.) The Review Program for online panel providers brings transparency and quality assurance to the research process.

MRA advocates for a stronger marketing research profession by providing information, education, and networking opportunities that strengthen the industry and ensure the prosperity of the membership. The association works closely with Congress, federal agencies, state legislatures, and regulatory authorities to educate lawmakers and regulatory agents about research, surveys, and privacy issues to lower business costs for research. Enhanced professional credibility and ethical standards are provided through MRA's *Code of Professional Standards*.

MRA pays close attention to the diverse needs of the industry by offering a variety of programs and resources that meet the most rigorous continuing education requirements. Cost-effective and efficient venues for professional education are offered so attendees can gain new ideas, solutions and opportunities to learn with and from colleagues. News and information is continuously provided via MRA's website, monthly magazine, and biweekly newsletter covering research trends, technologies, management, and legal, technical, and business issues.

—David Almy, CEO
Marketing Research Association

Visit the MRA website at
www.MarketingResearch.org

Text and Images: By permission,
David Almy, Marketing Research
Association.

We asked the CEO of the Marketing Research Association (MRA), David Almy, to open this chapter for you because the MRA has become a key professional organization serving the industry. In this chapter we will provide more information about the industry's professional organizations as well as the Professional Researcher Certification (PRC) program, which is sponsored by the MRA. This chapter will introduce several facets of the industry, including a brief history, the different types and sizes of some of the firms, an evaluation of the industry, and methods the industry uses for self-improvement. Finally, we will examine the ethical issues facing the industry. Some of you may have become interested in marketing research as a career. If you want to know more about a career in the industry, including seeking a master's degree in marketing research, we encourage you to go to our website and look under "Careers."

Interested in a career in marketing research? Go to: www.pearsonhighered.com/burns and click on the link for the Companion Website for Marketing Research 7th edition. When you open any chapter, see the list of links in the left margin. Click on "Careers".

EVOLUTION OF AN INDUSTRY

EARLIEST KNOWN STUDIES

People have been gathering information to be used for decision making since the earliest days of recorded history. As Lockley notes, "Even the Children of Israel sent interviewers out to sample the market and produce of Canaan."[1] In the United States, surveys were used in the early 1800s to determine the popularity of political candidates.[2] Political polling is a considerable part of marketing and opinion research today. The first known application of marketing research to a business marketing/advertising problem was conducted by

Industry professional organizations bring practitioners together to improve their skills and to keep them knowledgeable of industry trends.

Photo: Andres Rodriguez/Fotolia

The first known marketing research study conducted to address a marketing/advertising problem was by the advertising agency N. W. Ayer & Son in 1879.

the advertising agency N.W. Ayer & Son in 1879. In trying to put together a schedule of advertisements for its client Nichols-Shepard Company, a manufacturer of agricultural machinery, the ad agency sent a request to state officials and publishers throughout the United States asking for information about grain production.[3]

The first continuous and organized research was started in 1911 by Charles Coolidge Parlin, who was hired by the Curtis Publishing Company to gather information about customers and markets to help Curtis sell advertising space.

Robert Bartels, a marketing historian, writes that the first continuous and organized research was started in 1911 by **Charles Coolidge Parlin**, a schoolmaster from a small city in Wisconsin. Parlin was hired by the Curtis Publishing Company to gather information about customers and markets to help Curtis sell advertising space. Parlin was successful, and the information he gathered led to increased advertising in Curtis's *Saturday Evening Post* magazine. Parlin is recognized today as the "Father of Marketing Research," and the AMA provides an award each year at the annual marketing research conference in his name.[4]

WHY DID THE INDUSTRY GROW?

When the Industrial Revolution led to manufacturers producing goods for distant markets, the need for marketing research emerged.

By the 1920s more marketing research was being practiced in the United States. However, it was not until the 1930s that marketing research efforts became widespread as markets became more geographically diverse. Prior to the Industrial Revolution, businesses were located close to their consumers. In an economy based on artisans and craftsmen involved in barter exchange with their customers, there was not much need to "study" consumers. Business owners saw their customers daily. They knew their needs and wants and their likes and dislikes. However, when manufacturers began producing goods for distant markets, the need for marketing research emerged. Manufacturers in Boston needed to know more about consumers and their needs in "faraway" places such as Denver and Atlanta.

THE 20TH CENTURY LED TO A "MATURE INDUSTRY"

The 1900s saw the marketing research industry evolve. Researcher A. C. Nielsen started his firm in 1923. The Nielsen Company® remains a prominent firm in the industry. In the 1930s colleges began to teach courses in marketing research, and George Gallup was designing surveys that could predict presidential elections. During the 1940s Alfred Politz introduced statistical theory for sampling in marketing research.[5] Also during the 1940s, Robert Merton introduced focus groups, which today represent a large part of what is known as *qualitative marketing research*.

The 1900s saw the marketing research industry move from a few small firms in the 1950s to today's "mature industry" with a global scope. Through the decades, the industry has adopted new statistical methods, qualitative research methods, computerization, and software designed to take advantage of the Internet, all of which provided a continuous stream of new services for clients.

Computers revolutionized the industry in the 1950s.[6] Marketing research in the middle of the 20th century was dominated by small firms.[7] By the 1960s it had not only gained acceptance in business organizations but was also recognized as being crucial to understanding distant and fast-changing markets. The number of marketing research departments grew, as did supplier firms. The 1970s saw the development and adoption of mainframe software to facilitate data analysis, and the introduction of the personal computer in the 1980s meant that even the smallest research firms now had computer capability. Automation meant established services such as "tracking data" could be delivered faster to clients, and new services were created through evolving technology, especially the Internet.

During the 1990s and the early 2000s the industry, taking advantage of the Internet, developed many new online services such as data collection, sampling, analysis, and reporting. Consolidation was driven by the need to globalize. As client firms expanded their operations around the world, U. S. research firms followed their clients by either expanding or merging or acquiring firms in other countries. Likewise, research firms in other countries moved into the United States.

Industry observer Jack Honomichl noted that the industry has "matured" and today is characterized by several professional organizations, a certification program, and many publicly held firms enabling reporting of industrywide revenues, all of which creates a "sense of industry."[8] We will examine how these revenues have changed later in this chapter.

WHO CONDUCTS MARKETING RESEARCH?

INTERNAL SUPPLIERS

Any company seeking to understand its customers, distributors, competitors, or the environments in which they operate may conduct marketing research. Organizations that supply their own marketing research information are called **internal suppliers**, which refers specifically to an entity within the firm that supplies marketing research. Research conducted by internal suppliers is often referred to as **client-side**[9] research. Owner/proprietors of small firms may conduct their own limited marketing research. **DIY**, or do-it-yourself research, has been facilitated by Internet access to secondary data and better knowledge of data analysis software such as SPSS. InCrowd™ is a firm that specializes in creating a DIY platform enabling managers to conduct their own research. DIY research can provide the information needed to make the decision to solve the user's problem in a cost-effective way. In a 2011 survey of marketing research buyers, many stated they planned on using their own internal resources more for conducting online surveys (58%), data mining (40%), and social media monitoring (47%).[10] While DIY has its place, manager/proprietors may not have the time or expertise to feel confident about using DIY for important issues. Consider the example of a business owner who decided he wanted to survey attendees staying at a hotel hosting a business conference. After he spent considerable time developing the questions and printing his questionnaires, he was not allowed to conduct the survey in the lobby by hotel management. When he asked a consultant about this obstacle, the consultant explained that one advantage of outsourcing research is that professionals know how to get the information.[11]

As firm size grows, so does the ability to specialize. Medium-sized firms may assign one or more people responsibility for marketing research. In these cases, the individual or team may actually conduct some of the research, but often their responsibilities lie in helping others in the firm know when to do research and in finding the right supplier firm to help conduct marketing research.

Larger firms, such as those found in the *Fortune 500*, typically have a formal department devoted to marketing research. These departments may appear in organizational charts under a variety of names, such as consumer insights, but they serve the basic function of providing information to decision makers. Industries that tend to rely heavily on marketing research departments include consumer packaged goods (CPG), media and advertising, and pharmaceutical and health care.

EXTERNAL SUPPLIERS

External suppliers are outside firms hired to fulfill a company's marketing research needs. A supplier firm may be referred to as an **agency**.[12] These firms specialize in marketing research and offer their services to buyers needing information to make more informed decisions. In most cases, internal suppliers of marketing research also purchase research from external suppliers. General Motors, for example, while conducting research on electric cars, may hire a research firm in California to provide feedback from consumers who test-drive prototype cars. Large and small firms, for-profit and not-for-profit organizations, and government and educational institutions purchase research information from external suppliers.

> An internal supplier means an entity within the firm supplies marketing research. Research conducted by internal suppliers is often referred to as client-side research.
>
> DIY, or do-it-yourself, research refers to firms conducting their own marketing research. InCrowd™ (www.incrowdnow.com) is a firm that specializes in creating a DIY platform enabling managers to conduct their own research.
>
> While DIY has its place, manager/proprietors may not have the time or expertise to feel confident about using DIY for important issues.
>
> In medium-sized firms, one or more people may be assigned responsibility for marketing research.
>
> Larger firms typically have a marketing research department, especially those in the consumer packaged goods (CPG), media and advertising, and pharmaceutical and health care industries.
>
> External suppliers are outside firms hired to fulfill a company's marketing research needs. A supplier firm may be referred to as an agency.

THE INDUSTRY STRUCTURE

DISTRIBUTION BY SIZE: NUMBER OF EMPLOYEES

The marketing research industry includes a few very large firms with more than 500 employees (1.9%) and several hundred medium-sized firms with 20 to 500 employees (15%), but the vast majority (83.1%) of firms have less than 20 employees. In other words, the marketing

TABLE 2.1 **Distribution of Marketing Research Firms by Number of Employees, United States**

Employer enterprises by employee size (2011)*

No. of Employees	Enterprises	Total (%)
0–4	2,701	61.9
5–9	528	12.1
10–19	398	9.1
20–99	508	11.6
100–499	148	3.4
500+	81	1.9
Total	4,364	100

*Includes only firms with at least one employee

Source: Table supplied by IBISWorld. Copyright © 2012 by IBIS World. Reprinted with permission.

research industry is dominated by "small shops." Table 2.1 shows the distribution of U.S. marketing research firms by employee size.

FIRM SIZE BY REVENUE

Every year the American Marketing Association (AMA) publishes two reports by Jack Honomichl on its website and in the publication *Marketing News*. The *Honomichl Global 25* report ranks the top marketing research firms in the world by revenue earned; these firms include proprietorships as well as international corporations with tens of thousands of employees. Table 2.2 lists the top 10 revenue-producing firms from the 2012 *Honomichl Global 25* report.

> To view the *Honomichl Global 25* or the *Honomichl Top 50* reports, go to the AMA website at www.marketingpower.com and search "Honomichl."

As Table 2.2 indicates, a few firms dominate the industry in terms of size based on employees and revenues; the 25th firm in the Honomichl report has revenues under $100 million. Still, there is extreme competition in the industry. Certainly, the larger firms have advantages, but many small firms develop new approaches and techniques and rely on talented personnel to remain competitive with larger firms. The AMA also publishes the *Honomichl Top 50*

TABLE 2.2 **The Top 10 Marketing Research Firms**

Rank	Company	Parent Country	Website	Employees	Global Revenues
1	Nielsen Holdings N.V. Company	U.S.	Nielsen.com	35,500	$5,353,000,000
2	Kantar	U.K.	Kantar.com	21,900	$3,331,800,000
3	Ipsos SA	France	Ipsos.com	16,659	$2,495,000,000
4	GfK SE	Germany	GfK.com	11,457	$1,914,000,000
5	SymphonyIRI Group, Inc.	U.S.	SymphonyIRI.com	3,928	$764,200,000
6	IMS Health Inc.	U.S.	IMSHealth.com	2,500	$750,000,000
7	Westat, Inc.	U.S.	westat.com	1,947	$506,500,000
8	INTAGE Inc.	Japan	Intage.co.jp	2,153	$459,900,000
9	Arbitron Inc.	U.S.	Arbitron.com	1,205	$422,300,000
10	The NPD Group Inc.	U.S.	NPD.com	1,256	$265,300,000

Source: Honomichl, J. (2012, August 30). "2012 Honomichl Global Top 25 Research Report." *Marketing News*, p. 12 ff. See original article for complete details on revenues and other information. Reprinted with permission.

Eye-tracking can be used by marketing research firms to show clients what parts of an advertisement or web-screen will attract customer attention. In the example shown, the red dots show which parts of the ad attracted attention and the numbers indicate the duration of the fixation. Mirametrix provides an eye-tracking device and software to research firms who offer this service. Visit Mirametrix at www.mirametrix.com.

Photos: By permission, Mirametrix.

listing successful U.S. marketing research firms (report available on the AMA website and published in *Marketing News*).

TYPES OF FIRMS AND THEIR SPECIALTIES

Firms in the research industry can be classified into two main categories: full-service and limited service. **Full-service supplier firms** have the capability to conduct the entire marketing research project for buyer firms. Full-service firms offer clients a broad range of services; they often define the problem, specify the research design, collect and analyze the data, and prepare the final written report. Typically, these are larger firms with the expertise and necessary facilities to conduct a wide variety of research that may range from qualitative studies to large international surveys to modeling effects of a proposed marketing mix. Most of the research firms found in the *Honomichl Global 25* and *Honomichl Top 50* are full-service firms.

Marketing research firms are categorized as either full-service or limited-service firms.

Limited-service supplier firms specialize in one or, at most, a few marketing research activities. Firms can specialize in types of marketing research techniques such as eye-testing (tracking eye movements in response to different promotional stimuli) or mystery shopping (using researchers to pose as shoppers to evaluate customer service); specific market segments such as senior citizens; or certain sports segments such as golf or tennis. The limited-service suppliers can be further classified on the basis of their specialization. These include field services, market segment specialists, sample design and distribution services, data analysis, and specialized research technique service suppliers. Many of these limited-service firms specialize in some form of online research.

A firm that specializes in tracking eye movements of consumers would be considered a limited-service firm.

We can only list a few firm types and examples in Table 2.3. However, you can access industry resources that should provide a better understanding of the many different types of research firms and their specialties. Some professional organizations that provide these listings are *GreenBook*, MRA's *Bluebook*, and *Quirk's*. If you want to see listings of the different types of research firms as well as detailed information on these firms, complete the following "Active Learning" exercise.

TABLE 2.3   **Major Types of Marketing Research Firms**

Type	Description	Example Firms
Syndicated Data Services	Collect information and make it available to multiple subscribers	The Nielsen Co., SymphonyIRI Group, Arbitron
Packaged Services	Use a proprietary process to conduct a service such as test marketing or measuring customer or employee satisfaction	GfK, Video Research LTD, Burke, Inc.
Online Research Specialists	Provide client services associated with measuring online consumer behavior and measurement or online data collection	Comscore, Inc., Harris Interactive, Knowledge Networks, Toluna, Mindfield Internet Panels, FocusVision
Customized Services	Provide services customized to individual client's needs	All of the major firms can do this. Some examples include: Burke, Inc., Kantar, Ipsos SA, Synovate, Maritz
Industry or Market Segment Specialists	Firms specialize in a particular industry or a market segment	IMS Health, Inc., Westat Inc., Latin Facts, Inc., Olson Research Group, Inc.
Technique Specialty		
a. **Eye Movement**	Tracking eye movement to determine better package designs, advertising copy, etc.	The PreTesting Company
b. **Mobile Research**	Conducting research using mobile devices such as iPads or smart phones	Kinesis Survey Technologies, Cint+Mobile, NPolls
c. **Sampling**	Using different sampling methods to draw samples to suit client's research objectives	SSI, uSamp, Research Now, Peanut Labs
d. **Neuroimaging**	Observing brain activity as consumers are exposed to stimuli such as packages or ads	Neurofocus (Nielsen), Sands
e. **Market Segmentation**	Determining firms' target markets, locating these consumers and determining other characteristics of these consumers such as media habits	ESRI, Nielsen Claritas
f. **Social Media Monitoring**	Monitoring for relevant buzz over the social media and attaching meaning for companies and their brands	Decooda, Conversition
g. **Field Services**	Collect data using a variety of methods: telephone, online, person-to-person, mall intercept	MktgInc., Readex Research, I/H/R Research Group, Focus Market Research, Irwin, Fieldwork, Schlesinger Associates

Decooda is a firm that "listens" to the chatter of the social media and interprets its meaning for a company and its brands. Learn more about Decooda by going to **www.youtube.com** and enter: "Decooda Process - Introduction - Social Media Monitoring."

GREENBOOK.

You can learn the different types of marketing research firms by searching The GreenBook. Logo by permission.

   Active Learning

Using the Marketing Research Directories

Let's look at three sources of online information with the purpose of finding out more about the different types of research firms.

Many years ago the New York AMA chapter published a directory of marketing research firms in a book with a green cover. The book became known as "The Green-Book" and remains a key resource of industry information. At www.greenbook.org, you will find several ways to search for marketing research firms. Several specialties are listed, and you can also search by country, state, or metro area. For a comprehensive list of specialties, look at the top left for "Find and compare marketing research firms." From the drop-down menu, click on "Market research specialty." This submenu lists the many types of research and research firms in the industry. Click on a category that interests you to see the information available on each firm.

The Bluebook. This second source is provided by the MRA, available online at www.bluebook.org. You will be able to search by state, by type of data collection, and by several different types of specialties. Spend some time on this website to gain an appreciation for the types of firms in the industry.

Quirk's Researcher SourceBook™. This online directory published by Quirk's Marketing Research Media provides access to more than 7,000 research firms. Go to www.quirks.com and click on "Directories" in the menu bar. You can search by geographical area, specialty, languages spoken, and other factors important to the type of research specialty such as the number of "stations for data collection."

By the time you finish this exercise, you will see that marketing research companies are involved in many areas, including mystery shopping, mock trial juries, advertising effectiveness research, airport interviews, brand/image tracking, copy testing, new product concept testing, competitor analysis, focus groups, opportunity analysis, market forecasting, site selection, and in-store interviewing.

■

INDUSTRY PERFORMANCE

INDUSTRY REVENUES AND PROFITS

How well has the marketing research industry performed in terms of revenues? ESOMAR, an international association of research professionals, estimates worldwide revenues for the marketing research industry at $31.2 billion.[13] This represented a growth of 5.2%, adjusted for inflation, 2.8%, from 2009. Jack Honomichl reports that the top 25 firms brought in more than $18 billion in 2010.[14] Honomichl noted the top 25 firms showed an increase in revenues of 4.9% from 2009 to 2010. This was a 3.2% increase when adjusted for inflation, which still represents real growth and is a healthy increase compared to the 3.1% drop from 2008 to 2009.[15] The 2012 Honomichl Top 50 report ranking the top 50 companies based upon revenues earned in the United States shows an increase in revenues of 5.1% (2.9% after inflation) from 2010 to 2011. The report also showed a 7.9% increase in employees. Figure 2.1 shows the rise and fall of corporate profits. This is a key driver for marketing research revenues. As firms make more profits their research budgets increase. Compared with the growth in GDP for the same time period (1.7%), the research industry was "significantly healthier than the economy in general."[16]

Worldwide revenues for marketing research in 2010 were about $31.2 billion. The industry, like most business sectors, saw a drop during the recent worldwide recession, with an upswing in 2010. Projections are for modest growth during the next several years.

FIGURE 2.1 A Key Driver of Revenues for Marketing Research is Corporate Profits

Source: IBISWorld®, by permission.

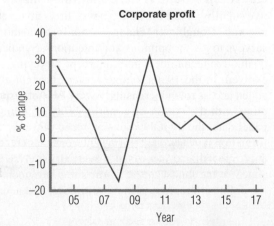

FIGURE 2.2 World Revenues, Market Share, and Growth in the Marketing Research Industry, 2010

Source: ESOMAR Industry Report. (2011). *Global Market Research 2011.* Amsterdam, The Netherlands: ESOMAR, p. 6. By permission.

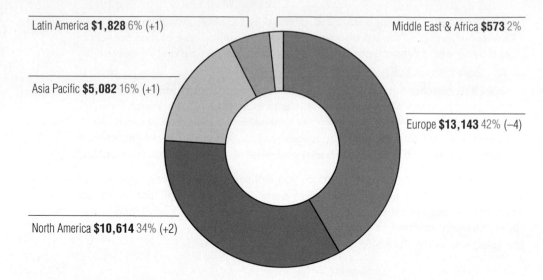

Latin America **$1,828** 6% (+1)

Middle East & Africa **$573** 2%

Asia Pacific **$5,082** 16% (+1)

Europe **$13,143** 42% (−4)

North America **$10,614** 34% (+2)

The marketing research industry relies on derived demand. As its client firms develop new products, expand into new markets, examine new opportunities, and develop and evaluate new promotional campaigns, they need information to guide their decisions. As the world economy continues to improve, client firms' business will grow and so will revenues and profits of the marketing research firms that support them.

Revenues vary around the world. Figure 2.2 shows Europe having the largest market share (42%), followed by North America (34%). The five largest markets by country are: USA (32%), UK (10%), Germany (10%), France (8%), and Japan (6%). Some of the fastest growing countries, in terms of net growth gains from 2009 to 2010, are Austria (11.9%), Poland (11.8%), and Russia (9.1%) in Europe;[17] Vietnam (24.6%), Singapore (15.4%), and Pakistan (12.9%) in Asia;[18] Brazil (27%), Paraguay (15%), and Honduras (14%) in Latin America;[19] and South Africa in Africa.[20]

QUALITATIVE EVALUATIONS OF THE INDUSTRY

Another view of industry performance lies in the qualitative assessments that have been performed over the years. Critical evaluations of the industry have led to an overall assessment that could be summed up in the statement, "The industry is doing a good job but could improve." Constructive criticism has focused on the following areas.

Questions About What Constitutes Marketing Research After many years of relative stability in terms of the types of firms involved in marketing research, the industry today is going through great change. Traditional methods of research included mail and telephone surveys to gather opinions and intentions. Syndicated data, focus groups and a host of other qualitative techniques, mall intercept surveying, and marketing mix/brand equity modeling evolved. In the 1990s, online surveys brought about significant change, and online panels added access to an increasingly wary base of respondents. While the industry has been grappling with the notion of nonprobability sampling and measuring sample quality of online panel data, the digital expansion raced onward.[21] Social media and consumer-generated information mushroomed. Firms emerged quickly to take advantage of the huge new source of data. Specializing in tools to harvest and analyze the information, these firms have now been added to the landscape of information providers. Other examples of the digital revolution are online ethnography, mobile surveys, and neuroscience, to name a few. So significant is

New methods to collect and analyze consumer information, primarily from social media, challenges traditional marketing research information gathering techniques. This has brought controversy as the industry grapples with newcomers. There is some agreement that the industry must adapt and accept new information sources and techniques. Clients will determine their value.

MARKETING RESEARCH INSIGHT 2.1 — *Social Media Marketing*

Types of Social Media[22] and Marketing Research

1. **Blogs**—sharing date-stamped online journal entries in reverse chronological order.
2. **Content Communities**—sharing media content between users. Examples: video, **YouTube**; books, **BookCrossing**; photos, **Flickr**; PowerPoint presentations, **Slideshare**.
3. **Social Networking Sites**—enabling users to connect by creating personal information profiles, inviting friends and colleagues to access those profiles, and sending and receiving emails and instant messages. Examples: **Facebook, LinkedIn, MySpace.**

    Marketing Research Applications: Research firms have developed the ability to "listen" to the millions of conversations and to provide clients with information about their companies and brands as they are being discussed in social media. A number of terms are associated with these applications, such as sentiment, text analytics, brand monitoring, and buzz mining. Decooda, Conversition and BuzzMetrics are examples of marketing research firms providing these services.
4. **Virtual Game Worlds**—platforms that replicate a three-dimensional environment in which users can appear in the form of personalized avatars and interact with each other as they would in real life. Examples: **World of Warcraft** and **EverQuest.**

5. **Virtual Social Worlds**—online communities in which "inhabitants" choose their behavior more freely and essentially live a "virtual life" through avatars. Users interact in a three-dimensional environment with no rules restricting the range of interaction as in virtual games. Example: **SecondLife.**

    Marketing Research Applications: To engage the millions of participants in gamification and social worlds, research firms are innovating to develop marketing research applications. For example, Peanut Labs offers prizes in the form of "Peanut Money" if players complete surveys. Participants can also earn virtual rewards to help them buy products needed in their social worlds.

Photo: © Rafal Olechowski/Fotolia

---

this explosion of technological tools and providers to the industry that the latest ESOMAR report devoted a large section to the topic. Some traditionalists have questioned whether these new supplier firms are even in the marketing research industry. While there is debate, the general conclusion is that the industry has been evolving for decades and clients are less interested in our methods and processes than in the understanding and insights our work may provide. The industry must evolve or die.[23] Marketing Research Insight 2.1 outlines the different types of social media and provides examples of what marketing research firms are doing with them.

Mistreatment of Respondents Too many requests for research, overly long surveys, and breaches of promised anonymity have led to a decrease in the number of respondents willing to take part in research. Some of this was brought on by marketing researchers, but the problems of invasion of privacy and outright unethical practices were exacerbated by telemarketers and other marketers using direct selling. Weary from abuse from telemarketers and other direct marketers, potential respondents have grown resentful of any attempt by others to gather information from them. In the *2007 Confirmit* industry survey of firms in several countries, Wilson and Macer reported that the leading challenge facing the marketing research industry was falling response rates.[24] As telephone survey response rates were lowered to new lows of about 7%, marketing researchers switched to online surveys. However, response rates for online surveys have plummeted as well, and b2b research has experienced a similar decline in response rates.[25] Desperately needing respondents, research firms invested heavily in creating panels of consumers who agree to serve as research respondents.[26] Today, a great deal of data collection occurs through proprietary panels of consumers who have agreed to participate.

Privacy issues continue to be dominant in today's world of "scraping" websites to gather information. (Web scraping is also known as "web harvesting" and uses software to extract information from websites.) The industry has several codes and standards that deal with the ethical treatment of respondents. We will examine some of these standards later in this chapter.

Falling response rates and privacy concerns are major issues facing the marketing research industry.

Marketing Research Is Too Focused on Techniques Over the years marketing practitioners have designed techniques or processes for dealing with certain issues. Critics claim researchers are too quick to identify situations in which they can apply one of their own technique tools. Just because the tool fits the issue doesn't mean the chosen issue deserves attention. Clients may steer clear of companies that promote their standardized technique, preferring to work with firms over a longer time to develop an understanding of their business.[27] Schultz[28] cautioned that too often the research problem is defined in terms of being compatible with an existing tool. Researchers may too readily apply a tool instead of focusing on the more complex strategic issues facing the firm. Other critics have reached similar conclustions.[29]

Clients have complained that research firms are too quick to use one of their standardized techniques.

Marketing Research Viewed as a Commodity Critics claim marketing research is too ofen viewed as supplying routine, low-level reports. Or it may be brought in to assess a new ad campaign or new product idea only *after* the strategic decisions have been made. Mahajan and Wind complain that managers misapply research by not having research professionals involved in high-level, strategic decision making.[30] Marketing research is left to report to lower levels in the firm that are not part of the strategic planning process. This occurs even when marketing research is outsourced to external suppliers. Too many executives view marketing research as providing a commodity to be outsourced to "research brokers," who are hired to conduct a component of the research process when they should be involved in the entire process. Though this criticism focuses on the level of upper management, marketing research professionals must be proactive in demonstrating that the "voice of the consumer" should be included in the development of top-level firm strategy.

Marketing research is too often viewed as a commodity, information needs that can be outsourced when needed. This prevents researchers from being involved in strategic planning.

Other Criticisms Among the other complaints levied against the marketing research industry are a lack of creativity, a failure to understand clients' real problems, a cavalier attitude regarding nonresponse error, the view that research is high-priced relative to its value, and a need for academic marketing research to be more closely related to actual marketing management decisions.[31]

Some earlier criticisms have been resolved or at least lessened. For example, a common complaint for many years was that research took too long. The advent of online techniques has led to faster data collection, analysis, and dissemination. Another criticism was that the industry was "too survey oriented" and that it seemed, no matter what the problem, researchers always recommended a survey. Although surveys remain an important tool in the marketing research toolkit, a variety of alternatives are in use today. Finally, research is much more value-priced today. Many research firms have structured their business plans to gain economies, which they have passed on to client firms.

INDUSTRY SELF-IMPROVEMENT

The marketing research industry has been proactive in terms of self-improvement, largely through industry initiatives, extensive continuing education programs, and certification.

INDUSTRY INITIATIVES

Led by some active professional associations, several initiatives have been undertaken to improve industry performance. We summarize a few of these in following paragraphs.

Best Practices The move toward Total Quality Management in the 1990s spawned an increase in companies' awareness of methods leading to improvement. One such method was spelling out best practices to help companies set benchmarks for performance in key areas. Many of the professional organizations serving the marketing research industry have a program of best practices. The MRA, for example, publishes best practices regarding issues such as privacy, telephone surveying, and online surveying.

Maintaining Public Credibility of Research Researchers are concerned about the general public's trust of research information. Public disgust with telemarketing and political telemarketing known as "push polling"[32] is often inappropriately directed at marketing researchers. Several industry initiatives are directed at keeping the public informed about the value of research, the appropriateness of research methods, and the ethics the industry uses in collecting research information. The industry fought to make **sugging** illegal. This term refers to the practice of "selling under the guise of research"; telemarketers used sugging for years to entice the public into taking what they thought was an opinion survey but actually was a lead-in for a sales pitch. Though not illegal, the industry has fought the use of enticing unknowing consumers into taking a survey when the real intent is to raise funds. This practice is known as **frugging**, for "fund raising under the guise of research."

Sugging, or "selling under the guise of research," is illegal. Frugging, or "fund raising under the guise of research," is unethical but not yet illegal.

The Council of American Survey Research Organizations (CASRO) offers the online guide "Surveys & You" to provide the public with information about the conduct and use of survey research.[33] The American Association for Public Opinion Research (AAPOR) started the **Transparency Initiative** in 2009 to encourage the routine disclosure of methods used in research information released to the public. As you will learn by taking this course, several methods may be used to produce biased information desired by those funding surveys. One way of detecting this bias is to examine the methods used. Several associations have collaborated with AAPOR on this initiative, including CASRO and ESOMAR.[34]

To read about AAPOR's Transparency Initiative, go to www.aapor.org and click on Advocacy & Initiatives.

Monitoring Industry Trends For more than a decade, *GreenBook* has monitored trends in the industry. Published annually as the *GreenBook Research Industry Trends (GRIT)* report, data are provided to the industry in terms of what techniques are being used as well as what drives their use. The report provides insights by contrasting supplier (marketing research firms) views on issues with buyer (clients) views. The report examines perceived threats and attitudes toward changes in the industry, forecasts revenues, and profiles innovations. ESOMAR publishes an annual report, *Global Market Research*, that includes many measures of industry performance. Based in Canada, the Marketing Research and Intelligence Association (MRIA) publishes the annual report *Industry Financial Survey*.

Several professional associations track trends in the marketing research industry.

Improving Ethical Conduct The professional associations serving the marketing research industry have all established rules, standards, or codes of ethical conduct. These associations have been proactive in maintaining and updating these standards. For example, when the Internet made possible online surveys, the industry moved to adopt standards governing

Professional associations for the marketing research industry have all established rules, standards, or codes of ethical conduct.

conduct in this area. Most industry codes of ethics are for the purpose of self-regulating professionals' behavior. In some cases associations may impose penalties, including censure, suspension, or expulsion. Certified professionals may lose their certification if they are found to have violated the granting association's standards. Each organization has it own standards, though some associations coordinate these codes of conduct. There are differences in the codes but also some commonalities among the major associations:

I. Fair Dealings with Respondents
a. Respondents should understand that they may elect to not participate in a research request. Participation is always voluntary and respondents should understand they have the right to withdraw or refuse to cooperate at any stage during the study.
b. Respondent confidentiality must be maintained. Respondent identity should not be revealed without proper authorization.
c. Respondents will be treated professionally. Should respondents be required to use a product or service, researchers will ensure that the product/service will be safe and fit for intended use and labeled in accordance with all laws and regulations.
d. Respondents will not be given dishonest statements to secure their cooperation, and reserachers will honor any promises made to respondents given to secure their cooperation.
e. Special provisions are required for doing research on minors (under 18 years of age).

II. Fair Dealings with Clients and Subcontractors
a. All information obtained from clients shall remain confidential.
b. All research will be carried out according to the agreement with the client.
c. Client identity will not be revealed without proper authorization.
d. Secondary research will not be presented to the client as primary research.
e. Research results are the sole property of the client and will never be shared with other clients.
f. Researchers will not collect information for more than one client at the same time without explicit permission from the clients involved.
g. Clients will be provided the opportunity to monitor studies in progress to ensure research integrity.
h. Researchers will not ask subcontractors to engage in any activity that does not adhere to professional codes, applicable laws, or regulations.

III. Maintaining Research Integrity
a. Data will never be falsified or omitted.
b. Research results will be reported accurately and honestly.
c. Researchers will not misrepresent the impact of the sampling method and its impact on sample data.

IV. Concern for Society
a. Research released for public information will contain information to ensure transparency (i.e., disclosure of method of data collection, the sample frame, sample method, sample size, and margin of error, if appropriate).
b. Researchers will not abuse public confidence in research (e.g., no push polling).
c. Researchers will not represent a nonresearch activity (e.g., sales effort, debt collection) to be research for the purpose of gaining respondent cooperation.

You may want to see the entire standards of ethical conduct of some of these associations:

AAPOR (www.aapor.org): Go to Advocacy & Initiatives.

MRA (www.marketingresearch.org): Go to Standards.

CASRO (www.casro.org): Go to About/Code of Standards.

MRIA (www.mria-arim.ca): Go to Standards.

ESOMAR (www.esomar.org): Go to Knowledge and Standards.

MRS, Marketing Research Society for the United Kingdom (www.mrs.org.uk/): Go to Professional Standards.

We will examine ethical issues in this book by highlighting a particular standard from the MRA's "Code of Marketing Research Standards" where it applies to the subject matter discussed in each chapter. This text also presents *Marketing Research Insights, Ethical Considerations,* such as Marketing Research Insight 2.2.

> We will treat ethical issues in this book by highlighting standards from the MRA's "Code of Marketing Research Standards" where they apply to the subject matter.

MARKETING RESEARCH INSIGHT 2.2 — *Ethical Consideration*

In Marketing Research, Ethics Isn't Just About Methods

Frankie (Francesca) Johnson,
Founder and President of Research Arts

We in the market research industry seem to think about ethics mainly in terms of how we conduct ourselves as we interact with respondents, clients, and field services. We strive to act with integrity and to be honest and worthy of trust. Most people I know in our industry are decent and sincere in their efforts to be ethical as they go about providing the guidance to help their clients succeed. But we don't seem to talk very much about whether some clients are worthy of our help. We seem to spend a lot of time talking about ethical issues involving methods, but very little time talking about the end purpose of the research.

Over the years my company, Research Arts, has avoided working in certain areas. We never accepted assignments from tobacco companies, preferring to focus on food, retail, and finance. That seemed simple enough at one time, but the decision as to what to research, and ultimately help promote, was by no means cut and dried.

Deciding what is acceptable to you is a very personal thing. My own moment of truth, or one moment among many, came when I was asked by a very large global company to conduct a study among 8 to 12 year olds. The goal was to understand how to persuade kids to demand more of their products (soft drinks and junk food snacks) in the vending machines at school. "Micro-marketing" they called it—building sales one school at a time. They paid me very well to moderate the groups and write the report. But I didn't like myself for doing it and still don't. That was the last project I accepted in that category. And from then on, I began to question the ethics of food marketing, especially to vulnerable children.

As a side note, I've never really bought into the idea that one can counterbalance harm with an equivalent amount of good—that the project I did for a nonprofit group working to feed the hungry somehow made up for the one I felt so badly about. Or that the need to earn money to support my children made up for doing work for brands that relied on the cheap labor of someone else's children.

I prefer not to be explicit when I turn down work that I feel contributes to making our world worse rather than better. It seems smug and high-handed. I simply say I am busy. For example, I don't take projects for products that exploit animals for food. I'm not a strict vegan, but I won't work on anything that depends on factory farming. In reality, it's hard to be so absolute about everything. These days, many companies are trying their best to incorporate sustainable practices. And I believe that within these companies, there are many people who care about the same things I do and are working on the inside to implement change.

So it's complicated, and I understand why this subject is rarely discussed professionally. Most of us compartmentalize and compromise, separating our paid work from our work on the causes about which we care most deeply. You are lucky indeed if you work exclusively in an area that feeds your soul. You probably have your own lines. I'm guessing you wouldn't take on a project from a group advocating child pornography or heroin sales. Those are easy black areas. It's the gray areas that are so troubling.

Frankie (Francesca) Johnson is the Founder and President of Research Arts, a leading qualitative market research company since 1984. She has been involved in market research, both as a client and a practitioner, for more than 35 years. Educated at the London School of Economics, Johnson spent her early career as a senior researcher with Quaker and Sears. She was among the first to do online research, both qualitative and quantitative, and keeps current on the new tools and approaches. She is an emeritus member of the American Marketing Association. This article was adapted from her blog at www.researcharts.com.

Text and Images: By permission, Frankie Johnson, Research Arts.

Beyond the general standards, an issue that may pose an ethical problem for researchers is to work on a project in which the outcome may not be in the best interests of society. Imagine, for example, that a client asks a researcher to help identify advertising messages that are persuasive in getting young teens to try their first cigarette. Or, a firm might be asked to develop effective promotions to encourage children to eat more candy. The decisions researchers must make are sometimes difficult. This quandary is rarely discussed professionally. We found a researcher who publicly talked about this decision and asked her to share her thoughts in Marketing Research Insight 2.2.

Certification of Qualified Research Professionals Certification programs assure that those certified have passed some standard(s) of performance. Certification programs in accounting (CPA) and finance (CFA) and other professional areas in business have been in place for many years and give clients confidence in the credibility of those certified professionals. In the United States, professionals may earn the **Professional Researcher Certfication (PRC)**. You can read about the PRC in Marketing Research Insight 2.3. In Canada, the designation of Certified Marketing Research Professional (CMRP) is granted through the MRIA.

Continuing Education The marketing research industry does an exceptional job of providing conferences, workshops, courses, webinars, and many other forms of continuing education for industry professionals. All of the professional organizations listed offer programs

---

MARKETING RESEARCH INSIGHT 2.3　　　　　　*Practical Application*

✓ Professional Researcher Certification

Responding to a need to establish a credentialing program in the industry, several organizations, led by the Marketing Research Association, established a certification program for marketing researchers. The process took several years, and the program started in February 2005. The Professional Researcher Certification program (PRC) is designed to recognize the qualifications and expertise of marketing and opinion research professionals. The goal of PRC is to encourage high standards within the survey profession to raise competency, establish an objective measure of an individual's knowledge and proficiency, and encourage professional development.

Achieving and maintaining PRC validates the knowledge of the market research industry and puts researchers in a select group of like-minded professionals. It's a visible badge of distinction, demonstrating professional skill, commitment, and dedication.

The MRA recently revised the PRC program.[35] The new structure includes two options: *Industry Professional* and *Student*. Individuals can obtain the *Student* PRC designation while they are working on their industry experience and education requirements. Once a *Student* meets the experience, education, and testing requirements, he or she may apply for *Industry Professional* certification.

PRC PROFESSIONAL RESEARCHER CERTIFICATION

Requirements for Professional Researcher Certification
- A minimum of three years of industry experience in the marketing research industry
- 12 hours of PRC-approved training within the last two years
- Passing the PRC exam
- Renewal of the PRC requires 20 hours in PRC-approved training (18 in research; 2 in legal). Certifications must be renewed every two years.

You can read more about the PRC at www.marketingresearch .org/certification

Source: Marketing Research Association, by permission.

MARKETING RESEARCH INSIGHT 2.4   *Practical Application*

The Masters of Marketing Research Program at the University of Southern Illinois-Edwardsville

Ramana Madupalli,
Ph.D., Director of the Master of Marketing Research Program at Southern Illinois University, Edwardsville

The marketing research profession is consistently rated as one of the top 10 careers in the business today. In an ever-changing business world, understanding markets, customers, and competitors has become an essential requirement, and a critical challenge for organizations' success.

Southern Illinois University-Edwardsville's (SIUE) innovative graduate program in marketing research designed to meet the need for skilled marketing research professionals. Our Master of Marketing Research (MMR) program is one of the few specialized programs in the nation that combines practical knowledge with intensive academic training resulting in excellent employment (with a near 100% placement record) and career opportunities in marketing research with leading research agencies and corporations. The MMR program also has an active Advisory Board comprised of marketing research industry leaders representing many of the leading research agencies and Fortune 500 client organizations. The advisory board members regularly interact with the students and faculty and help to keep the curriculum up to date with current industry trends.

SIUE's MMR program is rigorous, high quality, and driven by business practice. Admission is very selective and competitive. The program provides an ideal blend of theoretical and analytical coursework integrated with

marketing research projects and corporate-sponsored graduate internships for qualified students. While providing relevant professional marketing research experience, these internships offer a monthly stipend of $1,000 along with complete tuition waivers. Several leading research agencies and corporations (e.g., Anheuser Busch-InBev, AT&T, Commerce Bank, Covidien, Fleishman Hillard, GFK Kynetec, Hussmann, IPSOS Forward Research, Maritz Research, and Ralcorp) sponsor and support the MMR program and its related internships. Please visit our website (www.siue.edu/mmr) for more information.

We welcome your interest in our program and look forward to your comments and questions.

Text and Images: By permission, Ramana Madupalli, MMR.

designed to keep members up to date on skills needed in the industry. The Burke Institute, a division of Burke, Inc., has been providing high-quality training seminars since 1975. You can see the seminars the institute offers professionals at www.burkeinstitute.com/.

A CAREER IN MARKETING RESEARCH

Perhaps you have developed an interest in marketing research as a career. Recently, ESOMAR hosted an online forum with young researchers with up to six years in their careers. The young researchers were asked about their expectations and experiences in the industry thus far. Despite some negatives brought about by the world recession and changes under way in the industry (discussed earlier in this chapter), the more frequently used terms to describe their work in the industry were: "Never boring," "Fun," and "Cool."[36] You can go directly into marketing research, but a graduate degree is highly desirable. There are some excellent master's degree programs in marketing research. We maintain a "careers" section

The MRIA in Canada certifies researchers through the Certified Marketing Research Professional (CMRP) program. Read about the qualifications for this program at www.mria-arim.ca. Go to the link for Institute for Professional Development/Certification.

Logo by permission, MRIA

for you on this textbook's website. Go to: www.pearsonhighered.com/burns and click on link for the Companion Website for Marketing Research 7th edition. When you open any chapter, see the list of links in the left margin. Click on "Careers". There you will find some good information about careers in the industry as well as links to some master's programs and job descriptions currently available. One of those master's programs is at the University of Southern Illinois-Edwardsville. Read what the director of that program has to say in our Marketing Research Insight 2.4.

WHERE YOU'VE BEEN AND WHERE YOU'RE HEADED!

This concludes our two introductory chapters on marketing research. In Chapter 1 you learned how marketing research is defined and how it fits into a firm's marketing information systems. This chapter provided an overview of the marketing research industry. Now you should be familiar with the types and numbers of firms and the professional organizations that serve the industry. You've learned about issues facing the industry as well as the ethical issues that face all marketing researchers. Now, you are ready to learn about the 11-step process that characterizes marketing research. That process and its first steps are discussed in Chapter 3. Each of the remaining chapters addresses additonal steps in the process.

Summary

Gathering information dates back to the earliest days of recorded history. Early surveys were used for politics in the United States in the early 1800s. The first known application of research to a business/marketing/advertising problem was conducted by an ad agency in 1879, and the first continuous, organized research was started in 1911 by Charles Coolidge Parlin. The industry began to grow in the early 1900s as the Industrial Revolution separated business owners from customers. Many developments occurred during the 20th century that allowed marketing research to evolve into a mature industry.

Research firms may be divided into internal suppliers and external suppliers. Internal suppliers supply research to their own firms (e.g., a marketing research department within a manufacturing firm); this is also known as *client-side research*. External suppliers, sometimes called *agencies*, are outside firms hired to fulfill a firm's marketing research needs. The industry is characterized by a few large firms and many small firms. The largest firms have revenues in the billions of dollars. Firms are classified as full-service or limited-service supplier firms. Several online directories are available to help clients locate marketing research firms.

The industry had total revenues of $31.2 billion in 2010. As did most industries, marketing research firms saw a drop in revenues during the worldwide recession of 2008–2009. Forecasts are for modest revenue and profit growth for the next several years. Europe led the global market with the largest share of revenues (42%) by region, and the United States leads all countries (32%). Some of the fastest growth rates are in South America and Asia.

Challenges facing the marketing research industry include the entry of new firms wielding new technologies, such as tools to harvest data from social media. Marketing researchers are also dealing with lowering response rates and privacy of information laws. Critics of the industry contend that some firms rely too much on techniques that are too standardized instead of focusing on clients' real problems, and some suggest that researchers have allowed their services to be commoditized. The industry strives for self-improvement via efforts to identify and disseminate best practices, maintain public credibility of research, monitor trends, improve ethical conduct of members, support programs to certify professionals, and by offering education programs. Information is provided about careers in the marketing research industry at www.pearsonhighered.com/burns.

Key Terms

Professional Researcher Certification (PRC) (p. 18)
N.W. Ayer & Son (p. 20)
Charles Coolidge Parlin (p. 20)
Internal supplier (p. 21)
Client-side (p. 21)
DIY (p. 21)

External suppliers (p. 21)
Agency (p. 21)
Full-service supplier firms (p. 23)
Limited-service supplier firms (p. 23)
Sugging (p. 29)
Frugging (p. 29)
Transparency Initiative (p. 29)

AAPOR (p. 30)
MRA (p. 30)
CASRO (p. 30)
MRIA (p. 30)
ESOMAR (p. 31)
MRS (p. 31)

Review Questions/Applications

1. Who is known as the "Father of Marketing Research"?
2. Why did marketing research expand by the 1930s?
3. Focus groups are considered to be what type of research?
4. Define *internal suppliers*.
5. What are some advantages of DIY research?
6. Which industries have concentrations of marketing research departments?
7. Define *external suppliers*. What is another name for external suppliers?
8. How many employees do the majority of marketing research firms have?
9. What is a full-service supplier firm? What type of services do they provide?
10. Describe limited-service supplier firms.
11. Explain the meaning of the statement that "marketing research industry thrives off derived demand."
12. What began drastically changing the marketing research industry in the 1990s? Why?
13. What was identified as the leading challenge facing the marketing research industry in the 2007 Confirmit industry survey? Why?
14. Some critics claim marketing research is viewed as a commodity. Why?
15. What movement spawned an increase in company awareness of methods leading to improvement? Describe some of these methods.
16. Define *sugging* and *frugging*.
17. What are some commonalities in the major marketing research associations' code of ethics?
18. What is the PRC, and what is it designed to do?

CASE 2.1

Heritage Research Associates

Tim Colley and John Williams had not been in business long. They started a small marketing research firm in their hometown and had barely made ends meet by taking on very small accounts working mainly with start-up retailers. Their marketing research experience was limited, but they knew the basics. Since they had not taken any specialized training beyond a college course in marketing research, they decided to join the Marketing Research Association. Tim explained their reasoning: "We can tell clients we have the necessary credentials to be members of the most notable marketing research organization in North America." The partners thought this was a good way to persuade clients they knew what they were doing. They added the MRA logo to their promotional materials along with the line: "Heritage is a Certified Member of the MRA." They

used their limited funds to promote Heritage Research Associates and even took out a quarter page ad in a national business magazine.

A phone call early one morning marked a real opportunity for Heritage. The potential client represented his organization as a "privately funded foundation that promoted business rights and the maintenance of a *laissez faire* pro-business environment." They were interested in Heritage doing some research that would disprove some university-sponsored research whose findings had been in the news. The findings were unfavorable toward one of their prominent member industries. The caller stated: "Our patrons are upset that such erroneous information is being fed to the American people, and we are quite prepared to fund additional research to clarify the facts. In fact, we are willing to fund several studies if we get the results we are looking for. Are you up to it?" Tim and John assured the caller that the foundation could be certain that Heritage Research Associates could deliver quality, objective research that would clear up any misconceptions in the minds of the public. The call ended with a promise to send the biased university research reports immediately. A second call was set up to follow in three days.

In the follow-up call the potential client got more specific. His foundation had hired some independent scientists who were willing to testify that certain environmental conditions were not being caused by the concerned industry group. "We have had little problem in getting three scientists, with doctoral degrees from well-known universities, to make statements affirming that firms in one of our major industry groups is not doing any significant harm to our environment." The client went on to say: "What we want now is a study from an independent research firm, such as Heritage, to report attitudes of consumers in terms of whether they are in favor of more industry regulation. We are willing to fund a small pilot study and, if we find Heritage is capable of delivering objective data, we are ready to sign on for a series of perhaps a dozen studies. Furthermore, we are well financed, and I am quite certain we can meet your bid to do this work." The caller went on to ask for a proposal that would outline methods to select the survey sample, research questions, and a sample analysis, including how Heritage would word the report. "Remember, we want this to be an independently prepared project using all your abilities to craft an objective research study," the client stated. Tim and John agreed to deliver a proposal within 10 working days.

Tim and John were thrilled that this opportunity had fallen to them. "Did you hear what he said in terms of 'being certain to accept our bid'?" John exclaimed. "He's telling us he is going to pay whatever we ask. This isn't a penny-pinching client."

Tim said, "Just a minute, though. He's talking about the studies *after* the pilot study. What if they don't like the first study? We won't ever get to the big accounts."

John agreed. "We've got to design a study they will like so we can get the additional work at a premium. This could set our little firm off in a totally new direction!"

"This can make us the most talked-about research firm in the world!" Tim said.

1. Do you think it is ethical to use membership in an association that doesn't require any demonstration of expertise to lead customers into thinking the membership conveys some automatic claim of competency?
2. Consult the MRA Code of Marketing Research Standards. Is the answer to question 1 covered? Explain.
3. What problems do you see in the future for Tim and John and Heritage Research Associates? Do you think they are likely to become the "most talked-about research firm in the world"?
4. Consult the MRA Code of Marketing Research Standards. Are there any standards that back up your answers to question 3?

CASE 2.2   INTEGRATED CASE

Global Motors

Case 1.2 introduced Global Motors, a division of ZEN Motors. You may want to review that case before proceeding here. Nick Thomas, CEO of Global Motors, must try to revitalize the company. After acquainting himself with relevant information from both the ZEN MIS and outside secondary data sources such as trade association and government data about the auto industry, Nick realizes he needs more information. ZEN has a large R&D and engineering staff. A couple of years ago, several initiatives were launched within these groups to explore innovations in auto design and propulsion. Thomas has spent a great deal of time with these scientists and engineers. He regards them to be experts and on the cutting edge of what is capable of being produced. Nick's meetings with the R&D and engineering divisions have revealed some key facts. First, the engineering and production capabilities exist for all electric vehicles as well as hybrids. While a hydrogen engine may be feasible, it is still in the future. Also, though the country has stockpiled vast quantities of compressed natural gas (CNG), the existing infrastructure is just not ready for CNG-powered vehicles in the quantity that would make them profitable. Based on this information, Nick and the staff agree that there are choices to be made among five basic models. Millions of dollars invested in engineering would go into these models. Even the general description such as "all electric" or "hybrid" has been kept top secret in all of ZEN Motors.

Satisfied that he has the engineering and production know-how to produce any one or a combination of these car models, Nick now has an information need: What are car buyers' desires? And who are the car buyers who will want, say, an all-electric model? Can they be described in a way that will allow Global Motors to target them with promotional materials? Nick has several other questions: What are consumer attitudes toward global warming? Are consumers' motives being driven purely by gas prices? Or, are they truly worried about gas emissions and global warming? Global Motors needs help in tracking down information about consumers and their car-buying goals and motivations.

1. Should Nick Thomas use his own internal supplier, ZEN's existing marketing research department, to answer his questions? Are there reasons why he should not use them?

2. If Nick decides to bring in an outside marketing research firm, he will have to reveal proprietary information that is valued at millions of dollars.
A competitor would love to know what ZEN is planning through their new Global Motors division.
Do the MRA's Code of Marketing Research Standards address this issue?

3

The Marketing Research Process and Defining the Problem and Research Objectives

Using Marketing Research to Help Clients Make Decisions

Jeff Minier is Co-President, GfK Kynetec®. Mr. Minier has an MMR, Southern Illinois University-Edwardsville and has almost 20 years of experience in the marketing research industry.

Marketers are faced with many challenges when it comes to managing the brands that fall under their care. One of the most important of these challenges is advertising. Although generally expensive, when marketers get it right, advertising not only makes potential consumers aware of the brand but also shapes perceptions of the brand to match the preferred positioning needed to maximize brand value. Ultimately, advertising helps turn potential buyers into actual buyers, generating increased profit for the brand's manufacturer. Effective advertising can become a bargain regardless of its cost. If you get it wrong, the brand image will suffer, sales won't grow, and the marketer might end up looking for a new job. As such, market research plays a huge role in maximizing the success of advertising investments and minimizing the chance of failure.

Like a lot of marketing components, the advertising process starts as a series of questions deep in the mind of a marketer. The answers to these questions will help narrow down a seemingly endless supply of possible choices in putting together an advertising campaign. What should the ad communicate about the brand? What tone should the ad take? What content should be included in the ad? What images and text should be used? What messages should be conveyed? Who is the audience for our advertising? Where should we advertise? How frequently should we advertise? How much should we spend on advertising? These are decisions all clients must make. A situation analysis, sometimes aided by exploratory-qualitative research, is designed to facilitate these decisions. As you will learn in this chapter, the decisions facing clients drive the research.

To illustrate, let's take the example of a project we recently worked on for a client who needed help with its national advertising campaign. Our client had determined that it needed to create advertising for a health product for horses. Based on qualitative research with horse owners, we had come up with four different ads. However, managers for the client firm could not choose which ad to run because they weren't sure which one of the four would have the most impact with consumers. Because both the benefits of success and the costs of failure are high, they needed to get it right; they needed to pick the right ad for their national campaign. At this point, our client had to choose from among four decision alternatives: ad copy 1, 2, 3, or 4.

Text and images: By permission, Jeff Minier, GfK Kinitec®.

Marketing researchers must choose the type of information to provide clients that will enable them to choose from among the decision alternatives. In this example, what should we measure to allow our client to choose the "right" ad copy? Marketers attribute many constructs to "good" ads: Which one of these ads has the most "stopping power"? In other words, will horse owners even notice the ad among the sea of articles and other ads in a magazine? Which ad is the most relevant to the horse owner? Which is the most believable? Which is the most memorable? Which ad would do the best job in persuading horse owners to try the product? To help our client answer those questions, we also faced decisions to establish our research objectives:

what type of information (construct/s) to measure, from which consumers to obtain information, and how to evaluate the information gathered in the research.

Fortunately, at GfK® we have a proprietary tool for ad testing called Ad Challenger®. This tool helps us ensure that we achieve our research objectives using a procedure that has stood the test of the marketplace and is thoroughly tested.

Once we determined what information we needed to collect, like all market research projects, these questions were transformed into a series of objectives that became the basis for our study. After

Photo: Monkey Business/Fotolia

defining the objectives, a questionnaire was designed to tackle each objective with a complete picture of exactly what the study outputs would look like at the end of the research.

The process of marketing research—the focus of this chapter—provided our client with the information needed to choose from among the four different ads. Ad Challenger® identified the ad with the best scores on several constructs, including recall levels, most liked execution and most appealing, easiest to understand, and the strongest link between product and the main benefit. Access to this information facilitated the client's comparison and ranking of the four decision alternatives. Marketing research made a complex and important decision easy for the client. That is how we provide our clients with the insight they need to solve their problems.

GfK is one of the world's largest research companies, with more than 11,000 experts working to discover new insights about the way people live, think, and shop, in more than 100 markets, every day. GfK is constantly innovating to use the latest technologies and the smartest methodologies to give its clients the clearest understanding of the most important people in the world: their customers. In 2010, GfK's sales amounted to EUR 1.29 billion. To find out more, visit www.gfk.com or follow GfK on Twitter (www.twitter.com/gfk_group).

We could not have a better opening to this foundational chapter than the example provided by marketing research professional Jeff Minier. In the first chapter we introduced the different areas of marketing research such as pricing or distribution research. Minier's example is a perfect illustration of the use of marketing research in the area of promotion, specifically advertising research. The experience he has shared is illustrative of several important concepts you are about to learn. It illustrates how clients' problems are viewed in terms of selecting from among decision alternatives. He also touches on what his firm had to do in terms of research objectives and how his firm moved through the research process. We begin this chapter by introducing this research process. Next, we focus on the first three steps in the process: the decision to conduct marketing research, the decision alternatives, and development of research objectives.

The Marketing Research Process

THE 11-STEP PROCESS

There are many facets to what we call marketing research. Many different research choices come to mind when we think of research: forecasting models that predict sales of new products, measures of customer satisfaction, in-depth interviews to discover consumers' concerns, national polls, and experiments to determine the most eye-catching package design, to name just a few examples. Researchers choose from many, seemingly disorganized sets of alternative approaches in tackling a research project. Fortunately, there is a process, and understanding and adhering to that process provides researchers with direction. Colleen Moore-Mezler, PRC and President of Moore Research Services, stated:

> Here at Moore Research we deal with different types of problems, varying client industries, changes in our clients' markets as their customers and competition adjust to seemingly constant environmental changes. To help us deal with this complexity, researchers have a stabilizing framework upon which we rely to help us sort out each client situation. We do not all share the same framework but many of us agree that there is great value in viewing marketing research as a series of steps making up the process.[1]

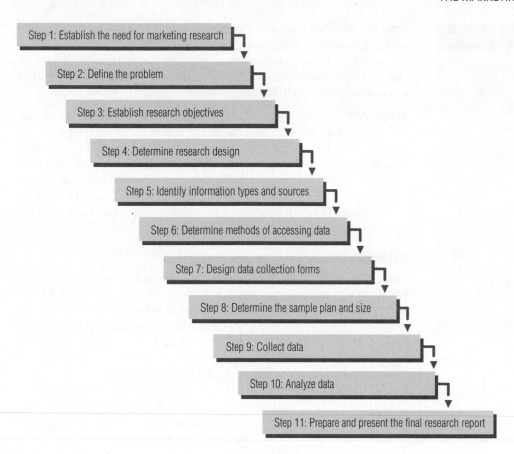

FIGURE 3.1 **11 Steps in the Marketing Research Process**

Step 1: Establish the need for marketing research

Step 2: Define the problem

Step 3: Establish research objectives

Step 4: Determine research design

Step 5: Identify information types and sources

Step 6: Determine methods of accessing data

Step 7: Design data collection forms

Step 8: Determine the sample plan and size

Step 9: Collect data

Step 10: Analyze data

Step 11: Prepare and present the final research report

We, among many, believe the marketing research process should be viewed as a series of steps. As Moore-Mezler states, knowledge of these steps provides a road map for planning a research project. The value in characterizing research projects in terms of successive steps is twofold. First, the steps give researchers and nonresearchers an overview of the process. Second, they provide a procedure in the sense that a researcher knows what tasks to complete and in what order. Our introduction to these steps also provides a preview of what is in store for you in upcoming chapters of this book. We identify the **11 steps in the marketing research process** in Figure 3.1:[2] (1) establish the need for marketing research, (2) define the problem, (3) establish research objectives, (4) determine research design, (5) identify information types and sources, (6) determine methods of accessing data, (7) design data-collection forms, (8) determine the sample plan and size, (9) collect data, (10) analyze data, and (11) prepare and present the final research report. We will discuss each of these steps in the following section, but first we should consider some cautions associated with using a step-by-step approach to the process of marketing research.

CAVEATS TO A STEP-BY-STEP PROCESS

Why 11 Steps? There is nothing sacred about 11 steps. Although we conceptualize the research process as entailing 11 steps, others may present it in fewer or more steps. For example, the process could be distilled into three steps: defining the problem, collecting and analyzing data, and presenting the results. We think this short list oversimplifies the research process. On the other hand, the research process could be set out in 20 or more steps. In our opinion, this provides more detail than is needed. Eleven steps sets out the process explicitly without being overly detailed. But you should know that everyone does not present the research process in the same way we present it here.

"WHERE WE ARE"

1 Establish the need for marketing research.

2 Define the problem.

3 Establish research objectives.

4 Determine research design.

5 Identify information types and sources.

6 Determine methods of accessing data.

7 Design data collection forms.

8 Determine the sample plan and size.

9 Collect data.

10 Analyze data.

11 Prepare and present the final research report.

At the beginning of every chapter, beginning with Chapter 4, the "Where We Are" feature lists the 11 steps of the marketing research process and highlights the step presented in each chapter.

The need for marketing research arises when managers must make decisions and they have inadequate information.

A company's philosophy toward using research will be reflected in the policy regarding use of marketing research.

Not All Studies Use All 11 Steps A second caution is that not all studies follow all 11 steps. Sometimes, for example, a review of secondary research alone may allow the researcher to achieve the research objectives. Our 11 steps assume that the research process examines secondary data and continues on to collect primary data.

Steps Are Not Always Followed in Order Our third and final caution is that most research projects do not follow an orderly, step-by-step process. In fact, the steps are often interrelated. Sometimes, after beginning to gather data, it may be determined that the research objectives should be changed. Researchers do not move robotlike from one step to the next. Rather, as they move through the process, they make decisions on how to proceed in the future, which may involve going back and revisiting a previous step.

INTRODUCING *"WHERE WE ARE"*

Understanding the steps in the marketing research process establishes a foundation for learning to conduct marketing research. As Moore-Mezler stated, knowledge of these steps helps researchers deal with the complex issues that arise in marketing research. We will examine some of those complexities in this text. To provide an aid in dealing with the rest of the course material, we introduce a new section at the beginning of every chapter, beginning with Chapter 4, called "Where We Are." This feature lists the 11 steps, and the step that is presented in the current chapter you are reading will be highlighted. This way, even as you get immersed in the necessary details of marketing research, "Where We Are" is there to show you where the material you are reading fits into the overall framework of marketing research. Now, let's look at our first step!

STEP 1: ESTABLISH THE NEED FOR MARKETING RESEARCH

When managers must make decisions and they have inadequate information, this signals the need for marketing research. Not all decisions will require marketing research. Because research takes time and costs money, managers must weigh the value that may possibly be derived from conducting marketing research and having the information at hand with the cost of obtaining that information. Fortunately, most situations do not require research, because if they did, managers would be mired down in research instead of making timely decisions.

Company Policy Regarding the Use of Marketing Research A company's philosophy toward using research will be reflected in the policy regarding use of marketing research. Management must make a decision about the role they wish marketing research to play in their organization. Some managers simply do not believe in investing time and money conducting research, and they have a *policy of not conducting marketing research*. However, the best of decision makers cannot make good decisions without good information and to rely solely on intuition in today's complex and rapidly changing marketplace is risky business.

For firms that have a policy of using marketing research, several choices must be made as to how much and how often marketing research will be used. First, some companies conduct different types of studies at specified intervals. The major soft drink firms, Coke and Pepsi, for example, conduct regular tracking research on soft drink sales. Conducting marketing research periodically has the advantage of having a recent point of comparison and detecting problems early.

Second, management may adopt a policy to use certain types of studies whenever a particular situation occurs. Many large firms such as Proctor & Gamble and Nabisco, for example, typically conduct a concept test when a new product is being considered.

Third, firms may elect to conduct marketing research on an as-needed basis. The firms adopting this approach regard marketing research as a useful tool, but expenditures on marketing research are only made when management feels the situation justifies gathering additional information. When management cannot decide which ad copy to use in a national campaign, as we saw in our opening vignette, they may acquire the services of a research firm such as GfK.

Finally, company policy regarding marketing research may also show a preference for the type of research management prefers. Some managers use focus groups extensively, whereas others rely on quantitative studies based on large samples.

Even in firms with a proactive policy regarding marketing research, managers may sometimes decide not to use this tool. The following section describes circumstances that indicate research is not needed.

When Is Marketing Research Not Needed?

The Information Is Already Available Managers make many decisions. For routine decisions, most managers have the experience to act without any additional information. Remember, in well-established firms, managers have been intimately involved with their markets for many years. For many decisions, managers can rely on their base of acquired knowledge. When decisions require additional information, other components of the MIS may supply this data. Can the needed information be obtained from the internal reports system? From the marketing intelligence system? From the decision support system? All of these information systems are ongoing sources of information. Marketing managers can quickly and inexpensively (low variable cost) access this information. Coca-Cola, for example, has an extensive database as part of its DSS. Managers at the large soft drink firm have ready access to data needed to forecast the effect on sales if they vary levels of ingredients in their products. When information is *not* available, the researcher should consider conducting marketing research. Marketing Research Insight 3.1 illustrates some examples of firms already having the information they need to make decisions.

The Timing Is Wrong to Conduct Marketing Research In cases when managers decide they need marketing research, time is critical. Consequently, time often plays a critical role in making the decision to use marketing research. Even though online research has sped up the marketing research process considerably, circumstances may dictate there is simply not enough time to conduct marketing research. As an example, let's just assume that an auto manufacturer introduces a hydrogen engine that runs on water, and sales of the car are unprecedented in the history of this mode of transportation. Do other auto firms need to do marketing research to "see" where the market preferences are? Less dramatic examples include a new package design, new flavor, or new ingredient that causes breakthroughs in sales and market shares. Competitive firms need to react quickly.

Time may also be a factor for products that are nearing the end of their life cycle. When products have been around for many years and are reaching the decline stage of their life cycle, it may be too late for research to produce valuable results.

Funds Are Not Available for Marketing Research Especially small firms may not have adequate resources to fund marketing research. Downturns in the general or industry-specific economy may also put marketing research out of reach for some firms.[3] Research, if conducted properly, can be expensive. If shortcuts are taken to save expense, the integrity of the research information gained is questionable.

Conducting the research is one cost but, to be useful, firms must also consider what it may cost to *implement* the research recommendations. The owner of a pizza restaurant saved money for a research project but was then unable to fund any of the recommendations (to build a drive-through and offer delivery service). In this case, the research money was wasted.

Company policy dictates the use of marketing research. In some firms, marketing research is not used. In others, marketing research is used only on an as-needed basis or is conducted periodically or routinely for certain activities such as new product development, advertising effectiveness, or dealer relationship management.

If the market reacts strongly to a competitor's offering, there simply isn't time to conduct a marketing research project.

Small firms or firms that are having cash-flow problems may not conduct marketing research simply because they cannot afford it.

MARKETING RESEARCH INSIGHT 3.1   *Practical Application*

If the Information Is Already Available, Don't Conduct Marketing Research

Marketing researchers John Goodman and David Beinhacker point out that many times companies execute surveys and collect data for information they already have.[4] They suggest clients can save money on research by not doing research to measure variables that are known to be stable and where performance is high. In addition, they recommend not conducting marketing research when internal metrics are already available.

In one financial services firm, management had commissioned research to measure customer satisfaction and quality. Over time the company had developed and was administering 80 different surveys covering all possible customer transactions. Upon examination, it was determined that in about 30 of the 80 transactions, customer expectations were being met from 98% to 99.5% of the time. Should the company use marketing research to measure transactions for which they are consistently near-perfect? The authors conclude that relying on a traditional complaint system would be a wiser method to monitor these transactions.

Goodman and Beinhacker share the story of a major home repair services company that was spending large amounts to survey customers on whether the repair specialist showed up on time. However, the company's call center already had data that tracked how many times customers were calling to complain about repair staff who were either late or didn't show up at all. For a high-involvement event such as having someone in your home, the researchers reported 90% of consumers will call when the repair specialist is late. The researchers ask, why conduct marketing research to collect data when you already have the information needed to make the decision?

In another example, a bank was surveying customers on their satisfaction with the readiness of ATMs, all of which must have some "downtime" for maintenance, repair, and daily cash reloading. The need to survey consumers was questioned when managers noted that the bank already had internal metrics, with data accurate to four decimal places, showing how often the ATMs were down.

If a firm is executing 8 of 10 transactions with little or no error, the authors recommend conducting research only on those transactions where performance is a problem. Neiman Marcus Direct® has a good reputation for handling telephone customer service. However, management has identified two types of transactions that give them problems. Therefore, surveys of customers focus on these two transactions, enabling Neiman to continuously monitor and improve these trouble spots.

A second recommendation is to be certain you don't already have the data before you commission collecting more of the same. The researchers point out that they find many departments operate in silos; other departments in the same company already have internal metrics that will provide the information needed to make an informed decision.

Banks do not need to ask their customers about their attitudes to determine if their ATMs are "down" too much. ATMs automatically record their downtime.

Photo: © ivan_sabo/Fotolia

Costs Outweigh the Value of Marketing Research Managers should always consider the cost of research and the value they expect to receive from conducting it. Although costs are readily estimated, it is much more difficult to estimate the value research is likely to add. Sometimes it is obvious that the value of research is not worth the costs. One researcher reported that he advised his client, a pie manufacturer, not to pursue conducting research on understanding consumer pie buying in convenience stores. Why? The researcher had discovered that only 1% of pie sales were coming through convenience stores.[5]

Some recent work has attempted to generate some heuristics that help determine the value of research. In a collaborative study by *Quirk's Marketing Research Review, Research*

Innovation, and *ROI, Inc.,* 11 methods were developed to determine the return on investment in research. An example of some of commonalities among the methods were:

a. All methods of measuring the value of research should explicitly link the research results to business impacts. In other words, a research study should not just conclude that alternative A produces more consumer satisfaction. Rather, the increase in consumer satisfaction should be linked to impact such as greater customer retention or higher market share.

b. All methods of measuring the value of research should demonstrate that something happened as a result of the research that would not have happened otherwise and quantify the financial value of that difference. Or, the metrics should demonstrate that risk was mitigated and quantify the financial value of that risk reduction.[6]

Although it is difficult to quantify value, some progress is being made among researchers to do a better job of helping clients evaluate research. If a researcher can show the sales volume impact for every 1% increase in consumer awareness, the researcher is in a much better position to help the client determine if research on awareness levels of new package designs is worth the cost.[7] Once a decision is made that research is needed, managers (and researchers) must properly define the problem and the research objectives.

If costs outweigh the value of research, it should not be undertaken.

STEP 2: DEFINE THE PROBLEM—STATING THE DECISION ALTERNATIVES

If a firm decides to conduct marketing research, the second step is to define the problem. This is the most important step, because if the problem is incorrectly defined, all else is wasted effort. As you will see in a later section of this chapter, we prefer to view "the problem" as a statement of decision alternatives. Marketing research should only be conducted when firms need to make a decision and do not have the information available to guide decision making. What do we really mean by "making a decision"? The firm must first identify its decision alternatives and then choose from among them. Revisiting the opening vignette for this chapter, what was GfK's client's problem: trying to choose from among ad copy 1, 2, 3 or 4. Aren't those decision alternatives? If there are no alternatives, no decision is necessary.

A later section of this chapter addresses issues that should be considered to properly define the problem.

The need to make a decision requires decision alternatives. If there are no alternatives, no decision is necessary.

STEP 3: ESTABLISH RESEARCH OBJECTIVES

The achievement of step 3, establishing research objectives, provides the information necessary to choose between the decision alternatives identified in step 2. Research objectives tell the researcher exactly what he or she must do to obtain the information necessary to allow managers to choose between the decision alternatives. For example, if a manager must choose between two proposed ads, A or B, the research objective may be stated along these lines:

A sample of 300 members of our defined target market will be randomly split into two groups. Both groups will be exposed to a 30-minute TV pilot program. For one group the pilot program will have ad A spliced into it, appearing as a regular TV ad; the other group will be exposed to ad B. After the pilot is run, respondents in both groups will be asked "What can you recall about any ads you saw while viewing the pilot program?" A "recall score" will be composed of the percentage of the audience in each group correctly recalling information about the ads, such as the brand and product features and benefits presented in the ad.

Note that the information generated by this research objective will allow the manager to choose between the decision alternatives, A or B. We will revisit research objectives in greater detail later in this chapter.

Research objectives tell the researcher exactly what he or she must do to obtain the information necessary to allow the manager to choose between the decision alternatives.

STEP 4: DETERMINE RESEARCH DESIGN

By *research design* we are referring to the research approach undertaken to meet the research objectives. A decision that is made in determining the research objectives is whether the research will be descriptive, diagnostic, or prescriptive. **Descriptive research** is the most basic objective in that the goal is to *describe* marketing phenomena. A study conducted to measure customer satisfaction on a 10-point scale, for example, will provide a description of satisfaction (e.g., 4.5 on a 10-point scale). Going beyond descriptive research is **diagnostic research**, which is designed to determine *sources* of satisfaction and dissatisfaction, such as a retailer finding out that customers perceive that it carries too little inventory. Finally, **prescriptive research** provides information that allows the manager to best *remedy* the dissatisfaction. For example, prescriptive research would allow the retailer to choose which variety or assortment of merchandise to add to gain the greatest increases in customer satisfaction.

The three widely recognized research designs are exploratory, descriptive, and causal. **Exploratory research**, as the name implies, is a form of casual, informal research that is undertaken to learn more about the research problem, learn terms and definitions, or identify research priorities. Going to the library or exploring the Internet to collect background information on a topic is an example of exploratory research. Often exploratory research is conducted early on to help clients get to the set of decision alternatives. Jeff Minier of GfK illustrates this in the beginning of this chapter. Descriptive research refers to research that describes the phenomena of interest. A marketing executive who wants to know what types of people buy the company's brand is looking for a study *describing* the demographic profile of heavy users of the company brand. Many surveys are undertaken to describe things: level of awareness of advertising, intentions to buy a new product, satisfaction level with service, and so on. The final type of research approach is **causal research** design. Causal studies attempt to uncover what factor or factors *cause* some event. Will a change in the package size of our detergent cause a change in sales? Causal studies are achieved from a class of studies we call experiments. You will learn about these three research designs and when it is appropriate to use each in Chapter 4.

STEP 5: IDENTIFY INFORMATION TYPES AND SOURCES

Since research provides information to help solve problems, researchers must identify the type and sources of information they will use in step 5. There are two types of information: **primary** (information collected specifically for the problem at hand) and **secondary** (information already collected).

Secondary information should always be sought first, since it is much cheaper and faster to collect than primary information. Much secondary information is available in published sources and is either free or available for a small fee. You will learn about *The American Community Survey* in this book. This information source is updated annually and is available free to marketers by the U.S. Census Bureau. Sometimes research companies collect information and make it available to all those willing to pay a subscription. This type of information is referred to as *syndicated data*; Nielsen Media Research's® TV ratings, which report the numbers of persons who watch different TV programs, are an example of syndicated data. Secondary information is discussed further in Chapter 5.

However, sometimes secondary data are not available or are inadequate, outdated, or insufficient. In those situations, primary data must be collected. Beginning with Chapter 6, the rest of this book covers how to gather, analyze, and report primary data.

STEP 6: DETERMINE METHODS OF ACCESSING DATA

Data may be accessed through a variety of methods. While secondary data are relatively easy to obtain, accessing primary data is much more complex. Some data are collected through

---

By *research design* we are referring to the research approach undertaken to meet the research objectives. Three widely recognized research designs are exploratory, descriptive, and causal.

There are two types of information: primary (information collected specifically for the problem at hand) and secondary (information already collected).

observation of consumers. Some data are collected by screening information available online. When the researcher must communicate with respondents, there are four main choices of accessing data: (a) have a person ask questions (i.e., conduct an in-home survey or a telephone survey), (b) use computer-assisted or direct questioning (i.e., computer-assisted telephone interview, or CATI, or an online survey delivered to an email address), (c) allow respondents to answer questions themselves without computer assistance (i.e., mail survey), or (d) use some combination of two more of the previous three modes. Referring to item (d) these are often referred to as *hybrid* or *mixed-mode studies*, one industry survey reported that most of these are a combination of online and CATI data collection.[8]

Marketing Research Insight 3.2 displays the major methods used to access data around the world, as reported by different marketing research organizations. The data show that online use has become the primary method employed by marketing research firms.

The most popular form of accessing data is online surveys. Traditional modes of data collection such as telephone, mail, and face-to-face intercepts still have a place in marketing research.

STEP 7: DESIGN DATA COLLECTION FORMS

Step 7 is designing the form on which we gather data. If we communicate with respondents (ask them questions), the form is called a *questionnaire*. If we observe respondents, the form is called an *observation form*. In either case, great care must be given to design the form properly. Questions must be phrased properly to generate answers that satisfy the research objectives and that can therefore be used to solve the problem. The questions must clear and unbiased. Care must also be taken to design the questionnaire to reduce refusals to answer questions and to get as much information as desired from respondents. Software is available to assist researchers in creating surveys. Most of these programs allow users to post the surveys on the Web, and data are automatically downloaded into software such as Excel or SPSS as respondents complete surveys. One such program is Qualtrics®. You will learn about preparing an objective questionnaire in Chapter 8.

Leslie Townsend is the President and Founder of Kinesis Survey Technologies. You can hear her talk about the future of using mobile surveys in marketing research and the services Kinesis offers to marketing research firms wishing to take advantage of mobile marketing research. Go to www.**youtube.com** and search for "Kinesis Mobile Survey Technologies."

STEP 8: DETERMINE SAMPLE PLAN AND SIZE

In many cases, marketing research studies are undertaken to learn about populations by taking a sample of that population. A population consists of the entire group about which the researcher wishes to make inferences based on information provided by the sample data. A population could be "all department stores within the greater Portland, Oregon, area," or it could be "college students enrolled in the College of Business at XYZ College." Populations should be defined by the research objectives. In our opening vignette, GfK defined the population for its study as "horse owners in the United States." A sample is a subset of the population. **Sample plans** describe how each sample element, or unit, is to be drawn from the total population. The objectives of the research and the nature of the sample frame (list of the population elements or units) determine which sample plan is to be used. The type of sample plan used determines whether the sample is representative of the population.

As you will learn in Chapter 9, sample plans have become more complicated as the world has changed in terms of how to reach people. For example, not many years ago, about 96% of all U.S. households could be reached through a traditional land-line telephone. Today that number has dropped significantly. Researchers must use different methods to reach people who use cell phones exclusively.

Another issue of **sample size**. How many elements of the population should be used to make up the sample? The size of the sample determines how accurately your sample results reflect values in the population. In Chapter 9 you will learn about both sample plans and sample size. Several marketing research firms specialize in helping firms with the sampling process. One such firm is Survey Sampling International®.

Qualtrics is an example of state-of-the-art online surveying software. Visit Qualtrics at www.qualtrics.com

Logo by permission, Qualtrics.

MARKETING RESEARCH INSIGHT 3.2   *Global Application*

How Data Are Collected Around the World

Each year several marketing research professional organizations conduct studies of the industry. While they examine many issues, they typically inquire of member firms as to the methods they have used during the year to access data. GreenBook studies both buyers and suppliers of marketing research. While this sample has an international flavor, most firms (72%) operate entirely in the United States or have offices there.[9] The Canadian-based Marketing Research and Intelligence Association (MRIA) report is a sample of 163 firms that operate in Canada.[10] Finally, the ESOMAR report is based on input from industry associations, leading companies, independent analysts, and ESOMAR representatives.[11] It is probably the best source to reflect a world view.

While the different categories used in these sources make direct comparisons difficult, we can still make some generalizations. The following data indicate that across all three reports, online surveying is the leading form of accessing data (Rank=1).[12] This is followed by the traditional methods, widely used for many years, telephone and face-to-face. Mail

Future-proof market research software for every device.

Capture feedback in the moment, anytime and anywhere.

multimode survey, panel management and community solutions

www.kinesissurvey.com   sales@kinesissurvey.com

GreenBook (Mostly U.S.)	MRIA (Canada)	ESOMAR (World)
Online = 1	Internet/online = 1	Online = 1
Telephone & face-to-face = 2	Telephone = 2	Telephone = 2
Social media monitoring = 3	Mail = 3	Retail audits/Media measurements* = 3
CAPI = 4	Mall intercept = 4	Face-to-face = 4
Mail = 5	Door-to-door = 5	Mail = 5
Mobile/Smart phone/Tablets = 5	Other = 6	
Text analytics = 6		

Mobile devices such as smart phones and tablets make responding to survey requests more convenient, and they reach respondents unavailable through traditional methods of data collection. Kinesis Survey Technologies is a firm that provides a mobile surveying platform for marketing research firms. Visit Kinesis at www.kinesissurvey.com.

Source: Text and images by permission, Kinesis Survey Technologies

surveys are still being used, and new methods of data collection are being used such as mobile (smart phones and portable tablets).

Online research is still a growing method of accessing data by marketing research firms. The data in Table 3.1, provided by ESOMAR, shows the top countries (excluding U.S.) with the highest percentage of spending on online research of total spending. These data exclude online qualitative research and online traffic/audience measurements.

TABLE 3.1   **Countries with the Highest Percentage of Spending for Online Research**

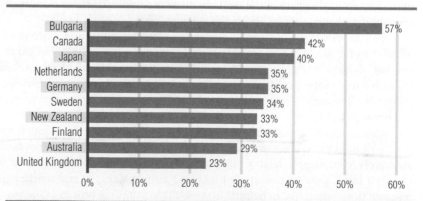

Country	Percentage
Bulgaria	57%
Canada	42%
Japan	40%
Netherlands	35%
Germany	35%
Sweden	34%
New Zealand	33%
Finland	33%
Australia	29%
United Kingdom	23%

Source: ESOMAR Industry Report. (2011). *Global market research 2011*. Amsterdam, The Netherlands: ESOMAR, p. 17. By permission. *This is shown as Automated/Digital/Electronic in the ESOMAR report.

STEP 9: COLLECT DATA

In Chapter 11 you will learn what issues to consider in collecting data in the field to ensure the highest possible data quality. Errors in collecting data may be attributed to fieldworkers or to respondents, and they may be intentional or unintentional. Researchers should know the sources of these errors and implement controls to minimize them. For example, field-workers, those collecting the data, may cheat and make up data they report as having come from a respondent. Researchers aim to minimize this possibility by undertaking a control referred to as *validation*. Validation means that 10% (the industry standard) of all respondents in a marketing research study are randomly selected, re-contacted, and asked if they indeed took part in the study. Companies that specialize in data collection are referred to as **field services firms**.

STEP 10: ANALYZE DATA

Marketing researchers transfer data from the data collection forms and enter the data into software packages that aid them in analyzing the data. In Chapter 12 you will learn how to enter data into and how to conduct data analysis using IBM SPSS, the data analysis software you will be learning in this book. You will learn data analysis, including basic descriptive analysis, to summarize your data in Chapter 12. Also in Chapter 12, you will learn how to generalize values you generate from your sample data to the population, and you will learn how to test hypotheses. In Chapter 13 you will learn how to test for differences between groups. For example, are there differences in intention to buy a new brand between different groups? Determining relationships among variables are covered in Chapter 14. In Chapter 15 you will learn how regression is used to predict a variable given what is known about other variables. The objective of **data analysis** is to use statistical tools to present data in a form that satisfies the research objectives. If the research objective is to determine if there are differences in intention to purchase a new product between four levels of income groups, data analysis would be used to determine if there are any differences in intention to purchase between the income groups and to determine if these differences (based on sample data) actually exist in the population.

STEP 11: PREPARE AND PRESENT THE FINAL RESEARCH REPORT

The final step in the research process is preparing and presenting the marketing research report. The report is essential because it is often the client's only record of the research project. In most cases, marketing research firms prepare a written research report and also make an oral presentation to the client and staff. Marketing researchers follow a fairly standard report-writing format, which is illustrated for you in Chapter 16. Care must be taken to write clearly and to present data accurately using the most appropriate figures and tables. The most important criterion for the report is that it clearly communicates the research findings to the client.

We've just outlined and briefly discussed the steps in the marketing research process. If the researcher and client exercise care, the research process will produce information that can be used to resolve the problem—to choose from among the decision alternatives. The "Where We Are" feature at the beginning of each chapter will help you appreciate marketing research as a process as you delve into the details of each step. We have already discussed step 1 in the marketing research process in the preceding section. In the following sections, we will examine steps 2 and 3.

Defining the Problem

WHAT IS "THE PROBLEM" AND THE "RESEARCH OBJECTIVE"?

The Problem When we refer to "the problem," our focus is on the situation facing the manager or client. **Problems** are situations calling for managers to make choices among decision alternatives. When managers make decisions, they do so to solve a problem. Sometimes these

Survey Sampling International

Visit Survey Sampling International at www.surveysampling.com.

Logo by permission, SSI.

Sample plans describe how each sample element, or unit, is to be drawn from the total population. Sample size refers to the number of elements of the population that are used to make up the sample.

Errors in data collection will occur, so researchers must know the sources of these errors and implement controls to minimize them. Field service firms specialize in data collection.

You will learn IBM SPSS and different types of data analysis in Chapters 12–Chapter 15. The objective of data analysis is to use statistical tools to present data in a form that satisfies the research objectives.

Problems are situations calling for managers to make choices among alternatives.

decisions are so routine and easily made on past experience that we don't think of them as "problems." Nevertheless, choices must be made, and the manager must make the decisions. Managers must choose among alternatives to select new products, choose among advertising copy alternatives, determine the price of their products or services, and select dealers. Managers face a fundamental problem when they must decide what type of business they should pursue! You may have noticed that many of these problems are crucial for the business—and thus often anxiety-provoking for managers. Having the right information to make decisions can reduce this anxiety. As an example, consider the situation shared by the former marketing research director of Betty Crocker®: "Our chefs bring us three new cookie recipes: A, B, and C. It is up to us to determine if any of these recipes are preferred over the other new recipes, and if so, is that most preferred recipe preferred over any of our present cookie recipes for cookies now on the market?"[13] As we noted earlier, a decision consists of decision alternatives, so, assuming the marketing department will pursue only one new recipe at a time, the initial decision alternatives are:

> Proceed with further consumer testing of the new cookie recipe (A, B, or C).

> Do not proceed with further consumer testing of new cookie recipe (A, B, or C).

Recall that marketing research is only conducted when managers do not have the information they need to choose among decision alternatives. Thus in defining the problem, managers must first determine what decisions they must make. Then, they must ask if they have adequate information already available to make the decision. Managers should not conduct marketing research just "to know something" because marketing research takes time and money to conduct.

The Research Objective What is a research objective? Research objectives are totally dependent on the problem, but they state what the researcher must do. Research objectives state specifically what information the research must produce so that the manager can choose the correct decision alternative to solve his or her problem. **Research objectives** are specific and tell the researcher exactly what information must be collected to solve the problem by facilitating selection of a decision alternative. A research objective should should satisfy four criteria: (1) specify from *whom* information is to be gathered, (2) specify *what* information is needed, (3) specify the unit of measurement used to gather the information, and (4) word questions used to gather the information using the respondents' frame of reference. The following research objective fulfills all of these criteria to provide information for the Betty Crocker manager to determine which decision alternative to select:

> Research Objective: Conduct a taste test of 400 persons who have purchased cookies within the last month. Conduct a taste test of new cookie recipes A, B, and C, and following consumption of each, ask: "The next time you decide to buy cookies, how likely are you to buy Brand A? Brand B? Brand C?" Responses are to be measured on a 7-point intensity continuum scale ranging from 1 = Very Unlikely to 7 = Very Likely.

Notice that our research objective specifies from *whom* we gather information (from those who have recently purchased cookies), *what* information (likelihood to purchase), what unit of measurement (a 7-point scale showing different degrees of likelihood), and which information is gathered using the respondent's frame of reference (most consumers will easily understand "how likely are you to buy…?"). We will discuss the criteria for research objectives more thoroughly later in this chapter.

At this point, you should have a good idea about the difference between the problem and the research objective. Later in this chapter we will discuss the process for arriving at the proper problem definition and statement of research objectives.

In defining the problem, managers must first determine what decisions they must make, and they should define those decisions in the form of decision alternatives. Next, they must ask if they have adequate information already available to make the decision.

Research objectives are totally dependent on the problem in that they state specifically what information the research must produce so that the manager can choose the correct decision alternative to solve the problem.

Research objectives should (1) specify from whom information is to be gathered, (2) specify what information is needed, (3) specify unit of measurement used to gather the information, and (4) word questions used to gather the information using the respondents' frame of reference.

THE IMPORTANCE OF PROPERLY DEFINING THE PROBLEM

Marketing research professional Lawrence D. Gibson stated:

> "A problem well defined is a problem half solved" says an old but still valid adage. How a problem is defined sets the direction for the entire project. A good definition is necessary if marketing research is to contribute to the solution of the problem. A bad definition dooms the entire project from the start and guarantees that subsequent marketing and marketing research efforts will prove useless. Nothing we researchers can do has so much leverage on profit as helping marketing define the right problem.[14]

Gibson's statement clearly underscores the importance of properly defining the problem. Other great problem solvers of our time have recognized the need to clearly define the problem. Albert Einstein and Leopold Infield wrote, "The formulation of a problem is often more essential than its solution."[15] The statistician John Tukey, having discussed Type I and Type II errors in statistics, coined *Type III errors* as those made solving the wrong problem![16] Tukey's Type III error illustrates why problem definition is essential. If you define a problem incorrectly, there is nothing you can do in the research process to overcome this error. No matter how well the remainder of the research project is conducted, you solved the wrong problem! If the decision has been made to do research, then properly defining the problem is *the* most important step in the marketing research process.

When you define a problem incorrectly, there is nothing you can do in the research process to overcome this error. This makes defining the problem and research objectives *the* most important step in the marketing research process.

A Process for Defining the Problem and Research Objectives

Lawrence D. Gibson wrote that "defining problems accurately is more an art than science."[17] This section introduces an approach that has been successfully used in the marketing research industry by some practitioners for many years. Figure 3.2 shows the components of this process. Remember, this process assumes management has decided to use marketing research. We will discuss each of these components in the following paragraphs.

Sources of Problems

TWO SOURCES OF PROBLEMS

Failure to Meet an Objective   As Figure 3.2 shows, the first step in this process is recognizing the problem, but we will begin our discussion with the second topic, sources of problems. Once we have a basic understanding of the sources of problems, we will go back to the top of the figure and discuss what we use to recognize these sources.

The two main sources of problems are failure to meet an objective and opportunities. We may recognize we have a problem when there is a gap between what was supposed to happen and what did happen—or when we fail to meet an objective.[18] For example, when our actual sales are below our sales objective, that gap signifies what we normally think of when we use the term *problem*. We must now determine what course of action to take to close the gap between the objective and actual performance.

There are two sources of problems: failures to meet objectives and opportunities.

Opportunity represents what might happen; the problem arises when an opportunity is lost, when there is a gap between what did happen and what could have happened. This situation represents a failure to realize a "favorable circumstance or chance for progress or advancement."

Opportunity   The second source of problems is not often immediately recognized as a "problem." Opportunity represents what might happen; the problem arises when an opportunity is lost, when there is a gap between what did happen and what could have happened. This situation represents a failure to realize a "favorable circumstance or chance for progress or advancement."[19]

More specifically for our purposes, a **marketing opportunity** has been defined as an area of buyer need or potential interest in which a company can perform profitably.[20] Google™, for example, has millions of people using its services daily. There are many opportunities for

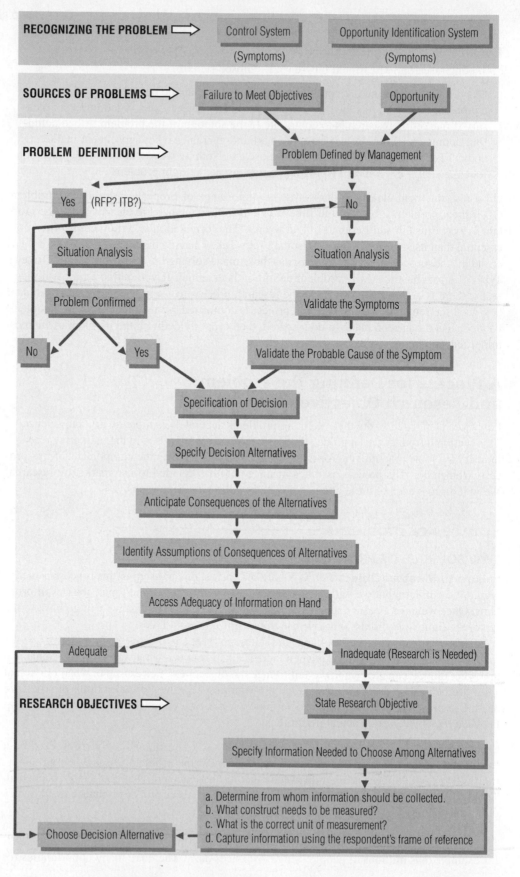

FIGURE 3.2 Defining the Problem and Determining the Research Objectives (Assuming the Use of Marketing Research)

Google to take advantage of this ready market, but the existence of these opportunities does not make the managers' jobs at Google any easier. They still have a problem in that they must make decisions to determine whether and how to take advantage of these opportunities.

Both of these situations—failure to meet an objective and opportunity—have the same consequence for managers: They must make decisions. Hence, we have what was defined earlier as a "problem."

Recognizing the Problem

It is difficult to overstate the importance of recognizing a problem. Managers who do not recognize problems will not be in management for very long. Here we consider two systems to help managers identify problems.

A CONTROL SYSTEM

To help recognize failures to meet objectives, managers must have a control system. In addition, to help recognize opportunities, managers must have a system for identification of opportunities.

For managers to recognize a problem when the source is failure to meet objectives, they must be knowledgeable about objectives and performance. They should be setting objectives and have a control system in place to monitor performance. This is sound management practice. To "control" is a basic function of management. Unless managers have a control system, they will not likely identify problems arising from failure to meet objectives.

OPPORTUNITY IDENTIFICATION SYSTEM

How do managers recognize when they have an opportunity? Unless they have a system for monitoring opportunities, sometimes referred to as a process of **opportunity identification**, managers will not likely identify these problems.[21] Kotler refers to this process as **market opportunity analysis (MOA)**.[22] There is much variability in firms in terms of opportunity identification. Some firms have staffs and formal procedures to ensure that opportunities are found and evaluated. These firms tend to rely on innovations to renew their life cycles and keep them competitive. Other companies only look at opportunities when they seem to "fall in their laps." When that happens, it's likely too late; a competitor may already have an insurmountable head start. We will not discuss MOA in detail, but it is useful to note that if a company wishes to take advantage of opportunities, it must have a system in place to help identify opportunities when they emerge.[23]

THE ROLE OF SYMPTOMS IN PROBLEM RECOGNITION

The classic statement "We have a problem—we are losing money" illustrates why researchers and managers, in properly defining problems, must be careful to avoid confusing symptoms with problems. The problem is not that "we are losing money." Rather, the problem may be found among all those factors that cause us to lose (or make) money; the manager, with help from the researcher, must identify all those possible causes to find the right problem(s). Toward that end, managers must be aware that the symptoms are not the problem but are "signals" that alert us to a problem.

Symptoms are changes in the level of some key monitor that measures the achievement of an objective (e.g., our measure of customer satisfaction has fallen 10% in each of the past two months). The role of a symptom is to alert management to a problem; there is a gap between what should be happening and what is happening. A symptom may also be a perceived change in the behavior of some market factor that implies an emerging opportunity. When sales of portable radios, tape players and TVs took off in the 1980s through the popular Sony® series of Walkman® and Watchman® products, this should have served as a symptom that there was a basic market need for portability. Today that need has resulted in high demand for portability in terms of the many mobile devices available. The key lesson in this example is that symptoms are not problems; their role is as a signal to alert managers to recognize problems.

A function of an internal reports system, part of the firm's MIS, should report alerts when symptoms are emerging. Systems are now available to identify symptoms early. For example, store-level versions of these systems alert managers to potential problems such as stockouts, which often double when stores run promotions. Other alerts make managers aware of promotions that are cannibalizing other products or indicate which geographies are responding or not responding to promotions. Identifying symptoms early can lead to managerial changes that can greatly improve bottom line profits.[24]

Problem Definition—Defining Decision Alternatives

When managers recognize there is a problem, they must define the problem by identifying the decision alternatives. Sometimes management will define the problem *on their own* and realize they need additional information to make the choice among decision alternatives. In these cases, they seek marketing research *after* they have defined the problem. In other cases, managers are aware of the symptoms and call in the researcher to help them define the problem. Whether managers define the problem on their own and then call in marketing research or call in marketing research to help define the problem, in *both cases*, the researcher plays an important role. (Remember, though, that there are many problems for which management defines the problem and selects a decision alternative to solve the problem *without* marketing research.) In the next section we consider the role of the researcher when the problem has been defined by management and when it has not.

THE ROLE OF THE RESEARCHER IN PROBLEM DEFINITION

When Management Has Defined the Problem in Terms of a Decision to Be Made When managers have defined what they think the problem is and the decision that must be made to resolve it, the researcher has an obligation to help managers ensure they are defining the problem correctly. This is particularly true when the researcher is called in by the manager who already has defined a problem in very specific terms. Researchers provide value at this junction in the process by supplying a fresh view, unhindered by biases of recent events, trends, or influences that may have dominated the managers' decision-making process. Think back to the example from GfK that opened this chapter. How did the manager know that the decision alternatives should be ad copy 1, 2, 3, or 4? Researchers are trained to think even broader and should ask: Is advertising copy testing what is really needed to address the problem? Problem definition expert Lawrence D. Gibson wrote: "Researchers must resist the temptation to 'go along' with the first definition suggested. They should take the time to conduct their own investigation and to develop and consider alternative definitions."[25] Look back at Figure 3.2. In the "Yes" section, when management has already defined the problem for the marketing researchers to handle, researchers should conduct an additional preliminary investigation, which may take the form of a type of exploratory research sometimes called a situation analysis. A **situation analysis** is a form of exploratory research undertaken to gather background information and gather data pertinent to the problem area that may be helpful in properly defining the problem decision. A situation analysis may reveal, for example, that the symptom of declining sales is more likely due to a problem with losing distributors than with ad copy. The point is that researchers have a responsibility to ensure they are addressing the right problem, even when the problem has been previously defined by management.

Invitations to bid (ITBs) or **requests for proposals (RFPs)** are often used in the marketing research process. These are routinely used in all business when a firm desires supplier firms to present proposals or bids. In terms of their use in marketing research, both of these represent situations where the manager has predetermined the problem decision and is calling on researchers to present a research proposal to be considered by management. (This is why we place them by the "Yes" in Figure 3.2). This means that much of the dialogue normally necessary between researchers and managers may be circumvented. However, researchers

---

Margin notes:

Whether managers define the problem themselves or call in marketing research to help define the problem, the marketing researcher plays an important role.

When managers have already defined the problem prior to bringing researchers in, researchers must resist the temptation to "go along" with the first definition suggested.

A situation analysis is a form of exploratory research undertaken to gather background information and gather data pertinent to the problem area that may be helpful in properly defining the problem decision.

Invitations to bid (ITBs) or requests for proposals (RFPs) are often used in the marketing research process. These are routinely used in all business sectors when a firm desires supplier firms to present proposals or bids.

still have an obligation to ensure that managers have defined the decision problem correctly even when responding to an RFP or ITB. A firm that sends out phony ITBs or RFPs simply to get ideas for research is practicing highly unethical behavior.

When the problem has been defined by management and after the researcher conducts a situation analysis, the researcher makes a decision as to whether the problem is defined correctly. If, according to the researcher, the problem is confirmed" (see Figure 3.2), the decision to be made is stated and we are now ready to move to the "specification of the decision," which includes stating the decision alternatives ("specify decision alternatives"). Obviously, the researcher has an ethical dilemma if he or she believes the client-manager has defined the problem incorrectly.

When Management Has *Not* Already Defined the Problem in Terms of a Decision to Be Made Sometimes managers call researchers when they sense something is wrong and they need help in diagnosing the situation. They may be aware of symptoms but are not sure what the problem is; hence, they are not sure what decision they should make, if any. Here, the researcher's task is more involved. Again, referring to Figure 3.2, the researcher should also undertake a situation analysis.

CONDUCT A SITUATION ANALYSIS

We have already mentioned that researchers, even when management has previously defined the problem, should conduct a situation analysis, but this analysis is essential when management has not determined the problem. This step may begin with the researcher learning about the industry, the competitors, key products or services, markets, market segments, and so on. The researcher should start with the industry to determine if any symptoms, to be identified later, are associated with the entire industry or only with the client firm. The researcher should then move to the company itself: its history, performance, products/services, unique competencies, marketing plans, customers, and major competitors.

The primary method of conducting a situation analysis is to review both internal and external secondary data. Other methods include conducting experience surveys (discussions with knowledgeable persons inside and outside the firm), case analysis (examples of former, similar situations), pilot studies (mini-studies that may reveal problem areas), and focus groups (small groups discussing topics such as the company's products or services).

VALIDATE THE SYMPTOMS OF THE PROBLEM

Even though Figure 3.2 depicts this component as coming after the situation analysis, the researcher should clarify or validate the symptoms early in the research process. Are we certain the symptoms are true indicators of what they supposedly represent? Companies vary greatly in terms of defining their objectives, monitoring their results, and taking corrective action. Does the company have an adequate control system to identify symptoms? Are there other symptoms not identified? What are they? Are they accurate measures of performance? Are they reported in a timely fashion? Is there adequate screening of the environment to pick up on opportunities?

Next, researchers need to assess the symptoms themselves. Are these symptoms true, or are they artifacts of the control (or opportunity identification) systems in place? Can the symptoms be corroborated by other factors identified in the situation analysis? Are the symptoms aberrant? Are they likely to appear again? You are beginning to realize, no doubt, that the researcher acts much like a detective. It is the researcher's role to explore and to question with the aim of properly defining the problem. Once the researcher has validated the symptoms, he or she is now ready to examine their causes.

DETERMINE THE PROBABLE CAUSE(S) OF THE SYMPTOM

At this point the manager and researcher should be in agreement about which symptom or symptoms are in need of attention. Now it is time to determine what could possibly cause

If, according to the researcher, the "problem is confirmed," the decision to be made is stated and we are now ready to move to the "specification of the decision" which includes stating the decision alternatives ("specify decision alternatives" in Figure 3.2).

The researcher has an ethical dilemma if he or she believes the client-manager has defined the problem incorrectly.

Even when management has previously defined the problem, marketing researchers should conduct a situation analysis, but this analysis is essential when management has not determined the problem.

To assess the veracity of the symptoms, the researcher needs to assess the control (or opportunity identification) system in place as well as the symptoms themselves.

Once the researcher has validated the symptoms, he or she is now ready to examine their causes.

the symptoms. To do this, we must realize that symptoms do not just change. There is always some **cause** or causes for the change. Profits do not go down by themselves. Sales do not drop without customers doing something differently from what they have done in the past. Satisfaction scores do not drop without some underlying cause.

A primary consideration at this stage is the need to determine *all* **possible causes**. If only a partial list of causes is made, it is possible that the real cause will be overlooked, leading ultimately to an incorrect decision. To help you visualize this process, let's look at an example of an apartment complex near your university. Let's assume management has been alerted to symptoms that show the occupancy rate declining from 100% to 80% over the last three semesters. After discussion with the researcher, all possible causes may be grouped in the following categories: (1) competitors' actions, which drew prospective residents away; (2) changes in the consumers (student target population); (3) something about the apartment complex itself; and (4) general environmental factors. The researcher should discuss all these possible causes with management. There may be several possibilities within each of these categories. For example:

> It is crucial to determine *all* possible causes. If only a partial list of causes is made, it is possible that the real cause will be overlooked, leading ultimately to an incorrect decision.

1. Competitors might be reducing rents or "lowering price" by providing free services such as free basic cable TV.
2. The number of students at the university may be declining.
3. The apartment building may not have been adequately maintained and or might appear to be "aging" on the outside.
4. Financial aid may have decreased on campus, so that students are less able to afford off-campus housing.

The situation analysis should have identified these possible causes. After listing all possible causes under each one of the previously identified broad categories, the researcher and manager should narrow down the possible causes to a small set of **probable causes**, defined as the most likely factors giving rise to the symptom(s). In our apartment example, we can assume that the manager and researcher have eliminated many causes for the symptom. For example, there has been no change in financial aid, student enrollment is up, and the apartment building's appearance is on a par with, or even better than, competitors' apartments. After evaluating all the other possible causes, assume the researcher and manager have reduced the probable cause down to competitors offering tenants free cable TV. Notice that something very important has now happened: Management now has a decision to make!

> After listing all possible causes under each of the broad categories identified, the researcher and manager should narrow down the possible causes to a small set of probable causes, defined as the most likely factors giving rise to the symptom(s).

> When the probable cause of the symptom is identified, this triggers a decision to be made by management.

SPECIFICATION OF THE DECISION

The determination that the probable cause of the symptom is competitors offering free cable TV creates a decision for management. In Figure 3.2, we see that we are now ready to specify the decision to be made. Management must decide what to do to win back market share, and as decisions consist of decision alternatives, managers must specify the decision alternatives.

SPECIFY DECISION ALTERNATIVES THAT MAY ALLEVIATE THE SYMPTOM

Essentially, possible **decision alternatives** include any marketing action that the manager thinks may resolve the problem, such as price changes, product modification or improvement, promotion of any kind, or even adjustments in channels of distribution. During this phase the researcher's marketing education and knowledge comes into play fully; often the manager and researcher brainstorm possible decision alternatives that may serve as solutions. It is important for the manager to specify *all* of the decision alternatives needed to address the probable cause of the symptom. As Semon notes, "Unless the entire range of potential solutions is considered, chances of correctly defining the research problem are poor."[26]

> Once the decision alternatives are determined, a manager must try to determine the consequences of choosing each alternative.

Returning to our apartment complex example, assume the manager examines *all* types of television delivery systems. One alternative is to offer what the other apartments are offering; free cable TV. A second alternative is to try to gain a competitive advantage by offering free satellite TV with premium channels. Now the decision alternatives become clear. But what if the manager chooses a decision alternative? What are the consequences?

CONSEQUENCES OF THE ALTERNATIVES

Consequences are the results of marketing actions. To evaluate decision alternatives we must speculate as to the consequences of selecting each alternative. What are the most likely consequences we can anticipate with each decision alternative? Note that we are *anticipating* a consequence. If we *know* the consequence, there is no need for marketing research. Assuming we don't know the consequence, research on each alternative under consideration will help determine which decision alternative is the best choice.

Returning to our apartment complex example, it would seem reasonable for the manager to speculate that if free satellite TV with premium channels is made available for each apartment, the consequence of this alternative would be occupancy rates that are more than enough to offset the cost of providing the service. He makes the same assumption for free basic cable TV. But we must ask: How certain is the manager that this will occur? Hasn't the manager made an *assumption* that by providing satellite TV with premium channels will create a greater demand for our apartment complex?

Decision makers make assumptions when they assign consequences to decision alternatives. **Assumptions** are assertions that certain conditions exist or that certain reactions will take place if the considered alternatives are implemented. Assumptions deserve researcher attention because they are the glue that holds the decision process together. Given a symptom, the manager *assumes* certain causes are at fault. She or he further *assumes* that, by taking corrective actions (alternatives), the problem will be resolved and the symptoms will disappear. In our apartment complex example, the manager's assumption is that free satellite TV with premium channels will be a strong enough incentive to cause current students to switch apartments for the next academic year and strong enough to attract new students to select his apartment over that of competitors who only offer free basic cable TV. Another assumption is that this demand will be so much greater than the demand for apartments with free cable TV that the increase in the demand will more than offset the additional cost of providing the satellite premium channels. As we can see from Figure 3.2, our next step is to determine if we have adequate information on hand to make these assumptions. If we do not feel that information is adequate to support these assumptions, we will likely need new information. The new information will be gathered by conducting marketing research!

If the manager is *completely certain* that he or she has adequate information to support the assumptions, there is no need for research and the decision may be made. The problem may now be resolved by simply choosing the correct decision alternative (See "choose decision alternative" in Figure 3.2). In this case we do not need marketing research, do we? However, if a researcher questions a manager about his or her beliefs regarding the consequences of certain proposed alternatives, it may turn out that the manager is not really as certain as he or she first seemed to be. It is imperative, therefore, that the manager's assumptions be analyzed for validity. To assess validity of the manager's assumptions, the researcher assesses the existing **information state**, which is the quantity and quality of evidence a manager possesses for each of his or her assumptions. During this assessment, the researcher should ask questions about the current information state and determine the desired information state. Conceptually, the researcher seeks to identify **information gaps**, which are discrepancies between the current information level and the desired level of information at which the manager feels comfortable resolving the problem at hand. Ultimately, information gaps are the basis for establishing research objectives. Now let's go back to the apartment complex situation and think about information gaps. Let's assume the manager feels quite confident about the accuracy of his information that competitors are offering free cable TV because they had advertise this new feature and announce it with signs outside their apartment complexes. Plus, we can assume the manager is confident that students are interested in having free basic cable TV because he knows that virtually all of his tenants have basic cable TV in their apartments.

The researcher continues to test assumptions by asking: "How do you know that students will desire the 'premium channels'?" The manager responds: "Because there are great movies on these channels. My wife and I watch a movie almost every night."

What are the most likely consequences we can anticipate with each decision alternative? If we do not know these consequences, marketing research can help us by providing information that allows us to predict the consequences.

Decision makers make assumptions when they assign consequences to decision alternatives. Assumptions are assertions that certain conditions exist or that certain reactions will take place if the considered alternatives are implemented.

If we do not feel that information is adequate to make assumptions about decision alternatives, we will likely need new information. This new information will be gathered by conducting marketing research.

If a researcher questions a manager about his or her beliefs regarding the consequences of certain proposed alternatives, it may turn out that the manager is not really as certain as he or she first seemed to be. It is imperative, therefore, that the manager's assumptions be analyzed for validity.

Information gaps are discrepancies between the current information level and the desired level of information at which the manager feels comfortable resolving the problem at hand. Ultimately, information gaps are the basis for establishing research objectives.

"But, you don't have to study at night, and you are not involved in campus activities and a fraternity or sorority, are you?" the researcher counters. "How do you know that the college students will want the premium channels?"

"I really don't know. I haven't even asked any of my own tenants how many of them subscribe to premium channels," the manager admits.

"Would knowing that information help you make the decision?" the researcher asks. "What if none of them subscribe to premium channels? Is it because they do not want premium channels or because they can't afford them?"

By now the manager realizes that his "certainty" had turned into high "*un*certainty." He has an information gap, and he needs more information to close this gap to make the right decision. This situation is not unusual.

We shouldn't be too hard on our apartment manager. Many people make assumptions and are satisfied with those assumptions until they start asking hard questions. However, when the decision is important, it's wise to make the right decision alternative choice to solve that problem. In our example, the researcher has convinced the manager he needs more information to make sure his assumptions are correct. Exactly what information is needed to close the information gap? Now, we are ready to create our research objectives!

> Exactly what information is needed to close the information gap? Now, we are ready to create our research objectives!

Research Objectives

DEFINING RESEARCH OBJECTIVES

If the manager had the information to close the information gap we just identified, the decision alternative that would best solve the problem could be selected. Remember our discussion of research objectives earlier in this chapter? Recall that research objectives state specifically what information the researcher must produce so that the manager can choose the correct decision alternative to solve his or her problem. It is at this point that the researcher is ready to specify the research objectives. When the manager and researcher agree on what type of information is needed to close the information gap, they can agree on the research objective. Sometimes hypotheses are stated that may be used to guide the development of the research objective. **Hypotheses** are statements that are taken for true for the purposes of argument or investigation. In making assumptions about the consequences of decision alternatives, managers are making hypotheses. For example, a successful restaurant owner uses a hypothesis that he must use X amount of food in an entrée to please his customers. This restaurant owner bases his decisions on the validity of this hypothesis; he makes sure a certain quantity of food is served on every plate regardless of the menu choice. Businesspeople make decisions every day based on statements they believe to be true. They need to have confidence that their most important decisions are based on valid hypotheses. This is similar to our previous discussions about *assumptions*, isn't it? Sometimes the manager makes a specific statement (an assumption) and wants to know if there is evidence to support the statement. In the instances in which a statement is made, we may use the term *hypothesis* to describe this "statement thought to be true for purposes of a marketing research investigation."[27] Note that not all research is conducted through hypotheses. A research question is often used to guide research. In this case, the question, not being a statement, is not considered a hypothesis. You will learn how to test hypotheses using SPSS later in this book. For now, you should understand that when a manager makes a statement he or she assumes to be true and wants the researcher to determine if there is support for the statement, we call these statements *hypotheses*. Since hypotheses are essentially statements of the assumed consequences of a decision alternative, they can be helpful in determining the research objective.

> Hypotheses are statements that are taken for true for the purposes of argument or investigation. In making assumptions about the consequences of decision alternatives, managers are making hypotheses.
>
> Since hypotheses are essentially statements of the assumed consequences of a decision alternative, they can be helpful in determining the research objective.

Stating the research objective is crucial in defining what information will be collected from whom and in what format. The key assessment to be made of the research objective is: If this information, as stated in the research objective, is provided, can a decision alternative be selected? Before we discuss some particulars of defining research objectives, let's look back at our apartment complex example. The researcher and manager agree that they can make the choice in the decision alternatives if they know if students have a greater likelihood of signing a lease with an apartment with free satellite TV with premium channels than an apartment with free basic cable TV. They also agree they want this information to come from a sample of students who are currently enrolled at the university and will be returning next academic year and who intend to rent an off-campus apartment.

An example of a research objective for our apartment complex example is:

> Research Objective: Conduct a survey based on a representative sample of college students who have stated they intend to rent off-campus apartments during the next academic year to determine the likelihood (measured on a 5-point scale ranging from 1 = Very Unlikely to Rent to 5 = Very Likely to Rent) that, given all factors are equal, students will rent from an apartment providing "free basic cable TV" (with channels available clearly stated) or from an apartment complex providing "free satellite TV with premium channels"(with channels available clearly stated).

Is this a good research objective? Recall the previously stated **criteria for writing research objectives**: A research objective should (1) specify from *whom* information is to be gathered, (2) specify *what* information (construct) is needed, (3) specify the unit of measurement used to gather the information, and (4) word questions used to gather the information using the respondents' frame of reference. Let's consider the criteria we should consider in defining research objectives to answer this question.

From Whom Will We Gather Information? Research objectives should address *who has the information we need*. Political pollsters know they must seek information from registered voters. If we are studying factors consumers use in selecting an Internet service provider (ISP), we should seek information from persons who have recently made this decision. In our apartment complex example, the manager and researcher have agreed to seek out information from students "who intend to rent off-campus apartments during the next academic year." Not only should the research objective specify who is to provide the information sought, it should also state *how* these persons are to be included in the sample. Our research objective states that students would be surveyed using a "representative sample." Notice that other decisions are being made when we specify from whom we are gathering the information. We are assuming these persons we have specified will know the information and will provide it to us accurately. Since most students make their own decisions about where they live at college, they should know the information we need. This is not always true. A researcher who asks "anyone in the household" about details of the family's financial plans will find that usually only one person in the household is familiar enough with these plans to answer specific questions. A researcher who asks high school seniors about their preferences for on-campus entertainment when they get to college the next year is asking the wrong people; they do not know because they haven't experienced college campus life yet. Finally, not all respondents are willing to provide the information we seek. Will respondents supply accurate information on such sensitive topics as the number of speeding tickets they've gotten, the amount a family has set aside in a Roth IRA, or a host of other socially or personally sensitive topics? We must make sure we are asking for information that respondents are *willing* to divulge.

What Construct Do We Wish to Measure? Exactly what information do we need to make our choice among the decision alternatives? This chapter opened with the example of managers faced with a decision involving four ads. They needed to choose the best ad, but what do we mean by "best"? It is hard to write a research objective without defining this type of criterion. "What information will tell us which ad is best? Is it the ad that is most memorable? Most relevant? Most believable? Least misinterpreted? Most likable? Most likely to

Stating the research objective is crucial in defining what information will be collected from whom and in what format. The key assessment to be made of the research objective is: If this information, as stated in the research objective, is provided, can a decision alternative be selected?

Memory, relevance, believability, understandability, likability, attitude, and intention to purchase are all examples of constructs—abstract ideas inferred from specific instances that are thought to be related.

produce a favorable attitude? Most likely to produce an intention to buy the advertised product?[28] These questions represent the different types of information we could collect; each is a separate construct. The following constructs have been mentioned: memory, relevance, believability, understandability, likability, attitude, and, intention to purchase. A **construct** is an abstract idea inferred from specific instances that are thought to be related.[29]

For example, marketers refer to the specific instances of someone buying the same brand 9 out of 10 times as a construct referred to as "brand loyalty." Sometimes marketing researchers call the constructs they study *variables*. Variables are simply constructs that can be measured or quantified in some way. They are referred to as variables because they can take on different values—that is, they can vary.[30] (Constants do not vary). A construct provides us with a mental concept that represents real-world phenomena. When a consumer sees an ad for a product and states, "I am going to buy that new product X," marketers would label this phenomenon as the construct called "intention to buy." Marketers use a number of constructs to refer to phenomena that occur in the marketplace. Marketing researchers are constantly thinking of constructs as they go through the problem definition process. Once they know the construct to be measured, they can determine the proper way to measure that construct, which we discuss in the next section.

It is imperative to measure the *right* construct. Can you state the construct we have suggested to measure in the research objective for our apartment complex research project? We could call it "likelihood to rent," which is similar to "intention to rent." To illustrate why the selection of the right construct is important, let's assume we asked a sample of students to tell us what TV channels they currently "most *prefer*" to watch. Note that we would be measuring the construct "current preferences for TV channels." Can we make a decision based on this information? No, we can't because students have only reported what they prefer to watch *from what is currently available* to them. Those who do not have premium TV channels, such as those being considered in our decision, will not list them, so we have no basis for making a decision as to how many students prefer them. Therefore, we can't make a decision because we measured the wrong construct. We really want to know if the presence of free satellite TV with premium channels will affect their *likelihood to rent* our apartment.

What Is the Unit of Measurement? Marketing researchers find constructs helpful because, once it is determined that a specific construct is applicable to the problem, there are customary ways of *operationalizing*, or measuring, these constructs. The research objective should define how the construct being evaluated is actually measured. These definitions are referred to as *operational definitions*. An **operational definition** defines a construct, such as intention to buy or satisfaction, in terms of the operations to be carried out for the construct to be measured empirically.[31]

An operational definition defines a construct, such as intention to buy or satisfaction, in terms of the operations to be carried out for the construct to be measured empirically.

For example, let's take the construct "intention to buy." (This is essentially the same as our "likelihood to rent" example). This construct should represent a person's likelihood to purchase or patronize a particular good or service, such as renting an apartment. We know that since few people know with 100% certainty that they will, or will not, purchase something, we measure this construct using a scaled response format—that is, a scale ranging from 1 to 5, 1 to 7, or 1 to 10. (We are not concerned about the number of scale units here; we are just illustrating that we should measure this construct using a scale of numbers, each representing a different likelihood.) This knowledge becomes useful in properly formulating research objectives. Researchers can access sources of information that provide them with operational definitions needed to measure many constructs.[32]

What is critical in the formulation of research objectives is that the proper unit of measurement be measured for the construct. To answer what is "proper" we could ask: What unit of measurement will allow the manager to choose among decision alternatives? Let's suppose that the researcher and manager have agreed to make a decision based on a statistically significant difference between the *mean* likelihood to rent apartments with cable TV versus satellite TV.

By measuring likelihood to rent on a 1–5 scale for both apartments with free cable TV and satellite TV, we can calculate the mean score for each type of TV service. We can then determine if there is a significant difference between the two means. This should give us the basis for choosing between the two alternatives. What if we had decided to measure "likelihood to rent" by asking students: *If they had a choice between two similar apartments but one offered free satellite TV with premium channels (provide list of channels) and the other offered free basic cable TV (provide list of channels), which would they rent?* Certainly we could do this but we now have "Yes" or "No" answers. We cannot calculate the means we said we needed to make our decision. Whatever the unit of measurement, the researcher and manager must agree on it *before* defining the research objectives to ensure that the choice among alternatives can be made after the research project.

> Whatever the unit of measurement, the researcher and manager must agree on it *before* defining the research objectives to ensure that the choice among alternatives can be made after the research project.

Word the Information Requested of the Respondent Using the Respondent's Frame of Reference Often we use *jargon*, terminology associated with a particular field. Researchers realize that, when they are formulating their research objectives, the information requested of respondents must be *worded using the respondent's frame of reference*. A pharmaceutical manager who is about to initiate a marketing research project with physicians as respondents thinks of a particular drug in terms of dosage, form, differentiating characteristics from the nearest competitor, and so on. On the other hand, the physicians from whom the research must gather information think first in terms of a patient's symptoms, disease severity, possible interaction with other drugs, willingness to comply with treatment, etc. The pharmaceutical manager must think of the information needed in terms of the respondent-physicians' frame of reference, not his or her own.

If we apply this concept to our apartment complex example, we could say that cable and satellite television companies often speak of "basic," "advanced basic," and "premium" channels. Consumers do not think of TV channels in these same terms. Consumers know channels by their names, such as ESPN, CBS, Golf, SHOWTIME, or HBO. This is why it is important in our example to provide consumers with the actual channels provided so that they can make an informed decision without having to guess about what "premium" channels are.

COMPLETING THE PROCESS

Turn back to Figure 3.2. We started this discussion several pages back by addressing different sources of problems (failure to meet objectives and opportunities) and the systems needed to recognize those problems. We then looked at problem definition and stated that problems must be couched in terms of decisions and decisions must be couched in the form of decision alternatives. We addressed two different routes the researcher might take in defining the decision alternatives, depending on whether the manager had already defined the problem. We then discussed how decision alternatives contain assumptions and how managers may be uncertain about these assumptions. Uncertainty of assumptions creates information gaps, and research seeks to fill those gaps. The research objective specifies exactly what information the researcher must collect to fill the information gaps. Once this information is provided, the manager should be able to choose among the decision alternatives. But, exactly how will that decision be made? What must the information look like for a certain alternative to be selected over others? This is the subject of the next section.

Action Standards

We've seen how the problem definition and research objectives development process (Figure 3.2) proceeds using our apartment complex example. However, there is another important element to address. We must specify the action standards. An **action standard** is the predesignation of some quantity of a measured attribute or characteristic that must be achieved for a research objective for a predetermined action to take place. The purpose of the action standard is to define what action will be taken given the results of the research findings.[33] In other words, by specifying the action standard, managers will know, once they

> An action standard is the predesignation of some quantity of a measured attribute or characteristic that must be achieved for a research objective for a predetermined action to take place. The purpose of the action standard is to define what action will be taken given the results of the research findings.

receive the information collected by the researcher, which decision alternative to select. In our apartment complex case, we have determined that one research objective should be to collect information that measures *the likelihood that students will rent an apartment which offers free satellite TV service with premium channels* (alongside the same information for free basic cable TV). Recall that we stated in our research objective that we would measure the construct "likelihood to rent" on a 5-point scale ranging from 1 = Very Unlikely to Rent to 5 = Very Likely to Rent. When we get our research results, how do we know whether to select from our three decision alternatives: (1) offer free satellite TV with premium channels, (2) offer free basic cable TV, or (3) do not offer either TV service?

From the research, we will derive two means, one for premium satellite and one for basic cable. Recall that we are asking respondents to choose an apartment, if all other factors are equal, based on the provision of the two TV options. Let's think about the two means and create a situation in which it is easy to make the decision: The premium satellite mean is 4.8 (high likelihood) and the basic cable is 1.0 (very low likelihood), and the difference between these two means is statistically significant. Clearly, we should select the premium satellite decision alternative.

The manager and researcher should try to determine, prior to collecting the data, at which point they would still make this decision. Let's assume they decide that if the premium satellite mean is above 3.5 and is statistically different from a lower mean for basic cable, they will still go with the decision alternative of premium satellite. In other words, they believe that with any mean of 3.5 or above and with a mean for basic cable significantly (statistically) lower, the demand will be high enough to warrant the extra expense of providing the premium satellite service. A possible action standard that would warrant choosing neither would be two means that are *both below* 2. A possible action standard that would warrant installing basic cable would be a mean for basic cable above 3.5 and either not statistically different from or statistically significant *above* the mean for premium satellite.

Action standards entail making important decisions before you collect information, and they serve as clear guidelines for action once the data has been collection. Ron Tatham, former CEO of Burke, Inc., stated:

> The action standard is an important component of the problem definition and research objective determination process because it requires the client to focus on predetermining what information he or she will need in order to take action. Using action standards helps the researcher determine the appropriate research objective because the specification of the action standards tells the researcher what information and in what format they must provide the client. Secondly, action standards allow clients to take action on research results. Without action standards, managers will often say 'The results of the research are interesting. I learned a lot about the market but I am not sure what to do next.'[34]

Impediment to Problem Definition

As you can now appreciate, the process of defining the problem and research objectives is not simple. It takes time and serious interaction between clients and researchers. This creates a problem because clients are accustomed to dealing with outside suppliers efficiently, making certain not to divulge proprietary information. Some managers, accustomed to dealing with consultants, understand the necessity for serious communications with researchers. However, many managers fall short of appreciating the necessity of frank and detailed discussions during the marketing research process.

Professor Sue Jones wrote:

> It is an accepted wisdom that the stage within a marketing research project of defining the problem is critical; the solution to the research design problem is derived from a full understanding of the marketing problem. Still, it is not uncommon for initial discussions

about a research project to involve relatively superficial dialog between clients and researchers; particularly if the latter are not members of the client organization.[35]

Chet Kane refers to this problem in noting that managers often commission marketing research projects without being involved with them. He states that managers should be involved in designing the research and actually go out into the field and listen to some of the consumer responses' firsthand. Had managers been more involved in the research, they would have known that the positive findings of research for "clear" products (clear beer, clear mouthwash, and clear cola) were based on the novelty or "fad" of the clear products. Had the managers been more involved with the research process, they might not have launched these new products, which failed in the marketplace.[36]

Often, to be effective, the marketing research process is slow and tedious. Managers often are unaware of the required change in their behavior, and this causes difficulties in identifying the real problem. Veteran researchers are well aware of this situation, and it is up to them to properly inform management of their expected role and the importance of this initial step in the research process.

Elements of the Marketing Research Proposal

At some point early in the client–researcher relationship, a contract is prepared. The **marketing research proposal** serves as the basis of a contract as it documents what the marketing researcher proposes to deliver to the client for some consideration, typically a fee. Researchers may work on a *pro bono* basis until it is determined that there is indeed a need for research.

Another model is to use a general research proposal that specifies the work of the researcher until decision alternatives/research objectives may be determined. Otherwise, researchers may work on an hourly basis for, as you have learned, sometimes a great deal of preliminary work must be performed prior to reaching agreement on the decision alternatives and the specific research objectives needed. Generally, the proposal will cover the following elements:

> The marketing research proposal serves as the basis of a contract as it documents what the marketing researcher proposes to deliver to the client for some consideration, typically a fee.

1. *Statement of the problem.* This can range from specifying decision alternatives to identifying the general area in which research is to be conducted (e.g., evaluation of consumer satisfaction).
2. *The research objectives.* If these have not been determined, typically the types of issues to be explored are delineated.
3. *The research method proposed by the researcher to accomplish the research objectives.* This section details topics such as sample size, incidence rates, data collection methods, and any subcontractors to be used and their services. Measures undertaken to reduce nonsampling errors should be enumerated.
4. *Statement of deliverables.* This is typically a research report but may include a presentation(s) and follow-up meetings with clients to discuss implementation issues.
5. *Cost.* If there are expenses to be paid in advance, the exact amounts and dates should be noted. If subcontractors are to be paid directly by the client, this should be noted as well. Clients differ in terms of the detail they prefer in proposals. Some clients will just want to know the major costs, and others will want a detailed proposed budget.[37]
6. *Timetable.* A schedule should be prepared showing dates or date ranges scheduled for the project.

> The marketing research proposal process is an area where clients and researchers should be sensitive to ethical issues.

ETHICAL ISSUES AND THE RESEARCH PROPOSAL

The marketing research proposal process is an area where clients and researchers should be sensitive to ethical issues. Clients should not expect marketing research firms to provide value-added services prior to signing a contract. They should not provide one research company's proposal to other research firms for the purpose of competitive bidding. The research proposal, which may include many hours of work and contain details of proposed methods and cost structures, should be viewed as proprietary information.[38] Finally, some specific codes from the standards of the Marketing Research Association deal with issues related to the proposal:

Section A: All Marketing Research Association Members agree that they:

1. Will ensure that each study is conducted according to the agreement with the client. . . .
4. Will protect and preserve the confidentiality of all research techniques and/or methodologies and of information considered to be confidential or proprietary. (This applies to methods of end-users or other research sub-contractors).

Summary

While there is great variability in marketing research projects, there are enough commonalities among these projects to enable us to characterize them in terms of steps of the research process. The value in characterizing research projects in terms of successive steps is that (1) the steps give researchers and nonresearchers an overview of the entire research process, and (2) they provide a procedure in the sense that a researcher, by referring to the steps, knows what tasks to consider and in what order. The steps are (1) establish the need for marketing research, (2) define the problem, (3) establish research objectives, (4) determine research design, (5) identify information types and sources, (6) determine methods of accessing data, (7) design data collection forms, (8) determine sample plan and size, (9) collect data, (10) analyze data, and (11) prepare and present the final research report.

The first step is determining the need to conduct marketing research. Can the needed information be obtained from the internal reports system? From the marketing intelligence system? From the decision support system? If these ongoing sources of information do not supply the needed data, marketing research may be needed. Sometimes the need to respond quickly to competition means there isn't time to conduct marketing research. Though placing a dollar figure on value is difficult, value *can* be estimated, and a more informed decision may be made justifying or not justifying marketing research.

Problems are situations calling for managers to make choices among alternatives. Research objectives state specifically what information the researcher must produce so that the manager can choose the correct alternative to solve the problem. Figure 3.2 depicts a process that may be used for defining the problem and determining the research objectives. There are two sources of problems. "Failure to meet an objective" arises when there is a gap between what was *supposed* to happen and what *did* happen. "Opportunity" refers to problems that arise when there is a gap between what *did* happen and what *could* have happened. Managers recognize problems either through monitoring

control systems (in the case of failure to meet an objective) or through opportunity identification systems.

Symptoms are changes in the level of some key monitor that measures the achievement of an objective. Symptoms alert managers to both types of problems. The researcher is responsible for ensuring that management has properly defined the problem even in cases when management has already defined the problem through invitations to bid or requests for proposals. In many cases, a situation analysis is required to help define the problem.

When defining the problem, researchers must validate the symptoms that alerted management to the problem to ensure the symptoms are correctly reporting what they portend to report. Researchers should work with managers to determine *all possible causes* for the symptoms.

Researchers should work with managers to reduce all possible causes down to probable causes. The selection of a probable cause creates the decision. The decision itself must specify alternatives that may be used to eliminate the symptom. Researchers must work with managers to clearly state the decision alternatives and to determine the consequences of each alternative. Researchers should assess the assumptions managers have made in determining the consequences of each alternative. If the manager is certain about the assumptions made, a decision alternative may be selected without any further research. However, in most cases, managers are uncertain about their assumptions. Lack of sufficient information creates an information gap, which serves as the basis for establishing research objectives. Sometimes hypotheses are stated to help to guide the development of the research objective.

Research objectives should be specific and address four criteria: (1) specify from *whom* information be gathered, (2) specify *what* information (construct) is needed, (3) specify the unit of measurement used to gather the information, and (4) word questions used to gather the information using the respondents' frame of reference.

Action standards refer to the predesignation of some quantity of a measured attribute or characteristic that must be achieved for a research objective for a predetermined action to take place. Problem definition is sometimes impeded because managers fail to change their normal behavior of dealing with outside suppliers in an efficient manner during problem-solving situations. Marketing research proposals are formal documents prepared by the researcher serving the functions of stating the problem, specifying research objectives, detailing the research method, stating the deliverables and costs, and specifying a timetable. There are ethical issues involved in the research proposal.

Key Terms

11 steps in the marketing research
  process (p. 41)
Descriptive research (p. 46)
Diagnostic research (p. 46)
Prescriptive research (p. 46)
Exploratory research (p. 46)
Causal research (p. 46)
Primary information (p. 46)
Secondary information (p. 46)
Sample plans (p. 47)
Sample size (p. 47)
Field services firms (p. 49)
Data analysis (p. 49)
Problems (p. 49)

Research objectives (p. 50)
Marketing opportunity (p. 51)
Opportunity identification (p. 53)
Marketing opportunity analysis
  (MOA) (p. 53)
Symptoms (p. 53)
Situation analysis (p. 54)
Invitations to bid (ITBs) (p. 54)
Requests for proposals (RFPs)
  (p. 54)
Cause (p. 56)
Possible causes (p. 56)
Probable causes (p. 56)
Decision alternatives (p. 56)

Consequences (p. 57)
Assumptions (p. 57)
Information state (p. 57)
Information gaps (p. 57)
Hypotheses (p. 58)
Criteria for writing research
  objectives (p. 59)
Construct (p. 60)
Operational definition (p. 60)
Action standard (p. 61)
Marketing research proposal
  (p. 63)

Review Questions/Applications

1. What are the steps in the marketing research process?
2. Are all 11 steps in the marketing research process used at all times? Why or why not?
3. Use an example to illustrate that the steps in the marketing research process are not always taken in sequence.
4. How is a company's philosophy toward marketing research reflected in its use of marketing research?
5. Explain why firms may not have a need for marketing research.
6. Why is defining the problem the most important step in the marketing research process?
7. What are some reasons that marketing research is not conducted?
8. Discuss why defining the problem is really stating the decision alternatives.
9. Explain why research objectives differ from the definition of the problem.
10. What are the three widely recognized types of research design?
11. Define primary and secondary information.
12. Which part of the research process ensures that the sample is representative?
13. Which part of the research process ensures the accuracy of the results?
14. What is meant by the *problem*?
15. What is the research objective?
16. What are the two sources of marketing problems?
17. Explain how managers should recognize they have a problem.
18. What is the role of symptoms in problem recognition?
19. What is the role of the researcher when management has already defined the problem?
20. What is a situation analysis, and when would it likely be used when defining the problem?
21. How do ITBs and RFPs influence the problem definition process?
22. What is the role of the researcher when management has *not* already defined the problem?
23. What is meant by the researcher validating the symptoms?
24. What is the difference between "all possible causes" and "probable causes"?
25. What is meant by *consequences* of the decision alternatives?
26. Explain how assumptions play a role in the problem definition process.
27. Use Figure 3.2 and explain what happens when the information on hand is adequate.

28. Explain the information state when there are information gaps.
29. What is needed to close information gaps?
30. What is the role of a hypothesis in defining the problem?
31. What are some relevant factors in determining research objectives?
32. What role do constructs play in the problem definition/research objectives process?
33. What is an operational definition, and where would it likely be used?
34. What is an action standard?
35. Discuss an impediment to problem definition.
36. What are the elements of the marketing research proposal?
37. Search the Internet for marketing research firms. Look through their Web pages. Can you identify examples of what they are presenting to you as relating to steps in the research process?
38. Go to your library's online databases or the Internet and look for examples of firms conducting a marketing research study. There are many examples reported in periodicals such as *Advertising Age, Marketing News, Business Week*, and *Forbes*. Typically, these articles will mention a few details of the research project itself. Identify as many of the steps in the marketing research process as possible that are referred to in the articles you find.
39. Observe a business in your community. Examine what it does, what products or services it provides, how it prices and promotes its products or services, and other aspects of the business. If you managed the business, would you have conducted research to determine the firm's products, design, features, prices, promotion, etc.? If you decide you would not have conducted marketing research on a given area, explain why.
40. Think of what you may imagine as being an opportunity in the marketplace. Explain how Figure 3.2 would help you in conducting or not conducting marketing research.

CASE 3.1

Golf Technologies, Inc.

Golf Technologies, Inc. (GTI) relies on high-level scientific testing to design golf clubs that provide larger "sweet spots," resulting in fewer missed hits and maximum yardage. In the last year, GTI discovered a technical breakthrough. Its newest designed clubs, for the same level of energy, hit the golf ball longer than any existing clubs on the market. CEO Harvey Pennick is very excited about this breakthrough and believes the new clubs will create a new level of excitement and enthusiasm among players. Pennick is well aware that many club manufacturers tout "new, scientific breakthroughs" with each year's new model clubs. He also knows that consumers have become fairly immune to these claims. He believes he must do something different to convince potential buyers that the new line of GTI clubs actually do have a larger, sweeter spot and really do hit the ball farther. Armed with objective tests that prove these claims, Pennick and his marketing staff believe they need a highly credible golfer to be used in their promotional materials (TV ads, magazine ads, infomercials, and special event promotions). The credibility of the message in GTI's promotions will be critical if golfers are to really believe their breakthrough in club design.

Pennick's staff presents the two golfers whom they believe are the best known: Rory McIlroy and Bubba Watson. Both golfers are considered among the best in the world and have very high name recognition. However, both these golfers have current exclusive contracts with other club manufacturers. Both contracts have buyout clauses so if GTI is to hire either one of them, it will be expensive to buy out the existing contract and to offer enough money to attract either of these world-class golfers. GTI will need only one of these golfers to be its new spokesperson.

1. Assuming Pennick agrees with his staff on the choice of McIlroy or Watson, what now is Pennick's decision in terms of decision alternatives?
2. Assuming Pennick is not confident in his assumptions about the consequences of the outcomes associated with your decision alternative, what should Pennick consider doing?
3. Should Pennick decide to conduct marketing research, write the research objective.

CASE 3.2 INTEGRATED CASE

Global Motors

Recall back in Case 1.2 that Nick Thomas has been made CEO of Global Motors, a new division of a large automobile manufacturer, ZEN Motors. ZEN is a multinational manufacturer headquartered in the United States and has multiple divisions representing several auto and truck brands. ZEN's divisions have been slowly losing market share to other competitors. Global Motors was created to bring ZEN Motors back to a highly competitive level in the auto industry by developing new models that are more competitive in today's new car market.

Global Motors now has five different models that are feasible in terms of engineering and production:

1. One-Seat All Electric, mpg-e rating 135; estimated MSRP (manufacturer's suggested retail price) $28,000; range 125 miles.
2. Four-Seat All Electric, mpg-e 99; estimated MSRP $33,000; range 90 miles.
3. Four-Seat Gasoline Hybrid, mpg-e 50; runs on battery for 30 miles and then switches to gas engine; estimated MSRP $38,000.
4. Five-Seat Diesel Hybrid, mpg-e 75; runs on battery for 50 miles and then switches to efficient diesel engine; estimated MSRP $48,000.
5. Five-Seat Standard Gasoline, mpg 26; model is similar to ZEN's newer models; estimated MSRP $22,000.
   Note: mpg-e is a measure of the average distance travelled per unit of energy used. It is the U.S. Environmental Protection Agency's measure of efficiency when alternative fuels (e.g., electricity and gasoline) are used. It allows for a comparison of new energy propulsion with the fuel efficiency in traditional internal combustion engines, mpg.

How will potential auto purchasers in the United States react to these models? Nick needs to know if the level of desirability for these models differs dramatically. Should Global Motors produce one, two, or more of the models?

Nick knows no single model will have universal appeal to a huge market. Rather, different models will appeal to market segments, and Global Motors will be sharing those segments with other able competitors that are working just as hard to develop car models that satisfy consumer needs in those segments. This means Global will not have a model that sells a huge volume, and smaller volume means the carmaker must be efficient in marketing its model(s) to keep operating expenses low and thus turn a profit. One of the most effective ways of keeping marketing costs down is to reach target markets efficiently. In other words, Global Motors wants to reach target markets for whichever models it produces without wasting promotional dollars on those who aren't interested in the model. For example, if the company decides to produce a particular model, a decision must be made in terms of choosing among media types (TV, radio, magazines, newspaper, social media) in which to promote the product. Nick would like to know each market segment's media habits. Which TV show types do most people in each market prefer? Radio genres? Magazine types? Sections of local newspapers? Also, Global's marketing department has moved to spending large sums of the budget on online promotions. Nick wants to know which market segments he can reach through blogs, content communities such as YouTube, social network sites such as Facebook, and online games and virtual worlds.

Knowing that consumers like a particular medium is not enough. For example, Nick may learn that the target market for a particular model prefers one magazine type over another, but there are many choices of magazines within that type. Knowledge of the demographic profiles of the target market segments can be helpful in selecting one newspaper, one magazine, or one dealership for a selected market. Because all media provide information to potential advertisers on the demographics they reach, Global should have a demographic profile of each market segment it attempts to target. To make the most of that information, the carmaker needs information on the demographics of those who most desire each model: gender, age, size of hometown or city, marital status, number of people in family, education, income, and dwelling type.

In terms of positioning the cars, Nick Thomas knows fuel economy will be the key motivator. In addition, he wants to know if appealing to consumers' concerns for global warming will have an impact on sales. Global Motors is making a major effort to reduce carbon emissions by moving to more efficient propulsion systems; should that effort be a prominent part of its positioning statement in promotions? If so, for which models? Nick gets a lot of mixed information in the general information environment about global warming. He wants to know what consumers think about two issues: (1) Are the consumers worried about global warming? (2) Do they believe gasoline emissions contribute to global warming?

Assume that Nick Thomas decides to conduct marketing research and that the marketing researcher agrees with the problems stated in this case.

1. State the problems.
2. Write the research objective for one of your problems defined in your answer to the first question.

4

Research Design

Knowledge of Research Design Is Part of the Researcher's Toolkit

Doss Struse,
Managing Partner,
Definitive Insights®

At Definitive Insights® we are capable of providing virtually any type of research design that will help our clients make better decisions. This may involve exploratory, qualitative research where, for example, we could conduct focus groups to help us learn more about how consumers think about and how they verbalize certain issues. Or, we use quantitative research that helps us actually measure constructs in a way that provides metrics our client can use to choose the best decision alternative.

Once we are familiar with the client's problems, we use our knowledge of research design to help us prepare a master plan that will lead us to our research objective—providing the right information to help our client make the best decision. When we conduct quantitative research, those master plans may be categorized as descriptive research or causal research. In descriptive research we are measuring marketing phenomena needed to achieve a research objective. An example would be a client who has a new product idea but needs information about consumer willingness to buy that product before proceeding further with expensive new product development costs. Our descriptive research design can provide that client with measures of a sample of consumers' "likelihood of buying" the proposed new product. At Definitive Insights we know how to translate these types of metrics into actionable data that allow our clients to make a decision based on high-quality information.

While not used as often, experiments allow researchers to establish causal results. By using an experimental design, researchers can isolate the effects of an independent variable on a dependent variable while controlling for the effects of other variables. For example, if we want to know how a proposed change in package design will affect consumers' awareness of the product sitting on supermarket shelves, we can actually measure that effect. But, to establish causal effects, experiments must be designed properly. In this chapter you will learn what it takes to design an experiment.

An understanding of the different research designs is basic knowledge that all researchers carry in their research "toolkits." That knowledge allows us to make advance decisions for a research project, which translates into a more efficient project in terms of time and costs.

You Gov DefinitiveInsights

Text and images: By permission, Doss Struse, Definitive Insights®.

About Definitive Insights

Definitive Insights, Inc., is a research and consulting company that integrates innovative custom market research with business intelligence and strategy to provide fact-based, research-driven insights that help marketing and business managers support strategic decisions about markets, customers, and offerings. The company offers a full range of cutting-edge research and analytic techniques with an eye for assessing the economic impact of alternative actions and decisions clients can make for their businesses. Definitive Insights, Inc., is headquartered in Portland, Oregon, with an additional office in Seattle, Washington. More information is available at www.definitiveinsights .com

A research design may be developed to determine the best package design needed to attract supermarket shoppers.

Photo: Kadmy/Fotolia

In our opening vignette, Doss Struse, managing partner with Definitive Insights, introduces the basics of research design. Struse mentions different types of designs: exploratory, descriptive, and causal. He also tells us why knowledge of research design is so important to researchers. By the time you finish this chapter, you will have a good grasp of research designs. We will examine the basic three types of research designs and provide you with an understanding of when to use each. You will see, when we explain each type of design, how a researcher can make advance decisions in a research project by knowing the type of research design needed.

Research Design

Marketing research studies are carried out in many different ways. Some projects are experiments of food tasting held in kitchen-like labs; others are focus groups, simulated test markets, or large, nationally representative sample surveys. Some research objectives require only secondary research, whereas others may require thousands of personal interviews. Researchers may observe consumers in convenience stores or conduct two-hour, in-depth, personal interviews in respondents' homes.

Each type of study has certain advantages and disadvantages, and one method may be more appropriate for a given research problem than another. How do marketing researchers decide which method is the most appropriate? After becoming familiar with the problem and research objectives, researchers select a **research design**, which is a set of advance decisions that makes up the master plan specifying the methods and procedures for collecting and analyzing the needed information.

WHY IS KNOWLEDGE OF RESEARCH DESIGN IMPORTANT?

We need to understand why knowledge of research design is important. David Singleton of Zyman Marketing Group, Inc., believes that good research design is the first rule of good research.[1] Why would a practitioner make such a statement? There are reasons to justify the significance placed on research design. First, we need to understand that even though every problem and research objective may seem unique, there are usually enough similarities among problems and objectives to allow us to make some decisions in advance about the best research design to use to resolve the problem. This means we can group or classify seemingly diverse research projects well enough to predetermine the most appropriate research design. So early on in the research process, as the problem and research objectives are forming, researchers can begin to understand which research design will be most appropriate. What allows researchers to do this is the fact that basic research designs available to them can be successfully matched to given problems and research objectives. Once the researcher knows the basic research design, a series of advance decisions may be made to form a framework for the advance planning of the research project. It is at this point that the decisions are made for the project at hand. The research design for the project calls for detailing what will be necessary for a successful project. For example, if a researcher knows that an exploratory research design is called for, he or she can start thinking of the different ways to carry out exploratory research given the unique characteristics of the particular project. A series of focus groups may be needed. Who will participate in the focus groups? How many focus groups will be conducted? What questions will be asked of focus group participants? What should be the outcomes of the focus groups? The research design will lay out these details. Or, perhaps the researcher determines that a causal research design is needed. This sets the researcher off in a completely different direction of thinking about appropriate experimental designs. In this way, identifying the most appropriate basic research design and the characteristics of the design serve the researcher in the same way the blueprint serves the builder. To better understand this analogy, imagine that the researcher has a choice of three basic research designs: exploratory, descriptive, and causal. The builder also has a choice of basic designs in building a house: ranch style, split level, or multistory. Once the builder knows the contract specifies a multistory house, this guides the detailed planning the builder must do to build that house: foundations built to support multiple stories; number, location, and strength of support walls, stairs and stairwells; and type and quantity of building materials. This is exactly how researchers use their knowledge of basic research designs in laying out the detailed design for a research project.

Knowledge of the needed research design allows advance planning so that the project may be conducted in less time and typically at a cost savings due to efficiencies gained in preplanning. Think about taking a long trip. If you have the ability to preplan, you can save

Research design is a set of advance decisions that makes up the master plan specifying the methods and procedures for collecting and analyzing the needed information.

There are enough similarities among problems and objectives that we can group or classify seemingly diverse research projects well enough to predetermine the most appropriate research design.

Identifying the most appropriate basic research design and characteristics of the design serve the researcher in the same way a blueprint serves a builder.

Early in the research process, as the problem and research objectives are forming, researchers can begin to understand which research design will be most appropriate. Their aim is to match basic research designs to given problems and research objectives.

Once the basic research design is identified, the researcher can make a series of advance decisions to form the framework for the advance planning of the research project.

yourself time and money. It works the same way in a research project. This is why all researchers have, as Doss Struse stated in the opening vignette, knowledge of research design in their professional toolkit.

When researchers plan research designs for projects, they must consider relevant ethical issues. Some common ethical considerations are presented in Marketing Research Insight 4.1.

Knowledge of the needed research design allows advance planning so that the project may be conducted in less time and typically at a cost savings due to efficiencies gained in preplanning.

Three Types of Research Designs

Research designs are classified into three traditional categories: exploratory, descriptive, and causal. The choice of the most appropriate design depends largely on the objectives of the research. Three common objectives are (1) to gain background information and to develop hypotheses, (2) to measure the state of a variable of interest (for example, level of brand loyalty), or (3) to test hypotheses that specify the relationships between two or more variables (for example, level of advertising and brand loyalty).

MARKETING RESEARCH INSIGHT 4.1   *Ethical Consideration*

Planning the Research Design: Areas of Ethical Sensitivity

In most cases professionals know more about their fields than the clients who hire them. In fact, this knowledge is the reason we hire professionals. However, that imbalance of knowledge can cause serious ethical issues. In the marketing research industry, these issues may arise in the potential for researchers to take advantage of clients in the research design process.

Recommending a More Costly Design Than Is Needed. Some research designs are simple, efficient, and much less costly than others. Exploratory research, for example, has these characteristics. A researcher could recommend a much more involved research design that takes more time and increases the cost to the client. Why would a researcher do this? If a researcher's fee is based on a percentage of costs of the project, then there is a built-in incentive to boost those costs. Or, if the researcher has an interest in a subcontracting research firm, there is an incentive to use the services of that firm whether needed or not. An egregious example of this ethical lapse is a researcher presenting secondary data as if it were primary data collected by the researcher. The MRA's Code of Marketing Research Standards, Section A 16, states that researchers "will, when conducting secondary research, make the End User aware of the source of the secondary research. At no time will secondary research be presented to the End User as primary data."

Designing a Study in Which Data Are Collected for Multiple Clients. A researcher could save data collection costs by collecting data for multiple clients at the same time. The MRA's Code of Marketing Research Standards, Section A 17, states that researchers "will inform the client if: their work is to be combined or syndicated with other clients' work and/or all or part of their work will be subcontracted outside the researcher's organization."

Using Information Obtained for a Client in Another Research Project. A researcher could design a research project so that a component of the project reflects work already conducted and paid for by a previous client is presented as original work for the present client. The MRA's Code of Marketing Research Standards, Section A 28, provides that researchers "will ensure that the results of the research are the sole property of the End User(s). At no time will results be shared with other clients."

Over- or Underestimating Data Collection Costs. As you will learn, data collection costs are strongly influenced by the incidence rate (the percentage of the population possessing the characteristic(s) required to participate in a study). Incidence rates are high if the research design calls for interviewing "any adult over age 18." Incidence rates are low if the study requires "males, over 65, who take statin drugs but still have high cholesterol counts." The lower the incidence rate, the more persons are required to be contacted to find someone who qualifies for the study. As a result, low incidence rate studies can be very costly. The MRA's Code of Marketing Research Standards, Section A 30, states that researchers "will ensure that all formulas used during bidding and reporting during the data collection process conform with the MRA Incidence Guidelines or with an incidence calculation formula agreed upon between the client and researcher provider(s)."

Wrongfully Gaining Respondent Cooperation to Reduce Costs. A researcher could design a project in which respondent cooperation could be greatly increased by making promises to potential respondents without any intention of fulfilling those promises. The MRA's Code of Marketing Research Standards, Section A 31, requires that researchers "will make factually correct statements, whether verbal or written, to secure cooperation and will honor promises made during the interview to respondents."

Misrepresenting Sampling Methods. Research design will include determining the appropriate sampling plan and sample size. Researchers should not use a sample plan that does not allow achievement of the research objectives of the study. Researchers should inform clients as to how the sample plan will result in a representative sample. Likewise, researchers should inform the client of the effect of sample size on the study's accuracy. Some sample plans are more costly than others, and more sample size means greater costs to clients. The MRA's Code of Marketing Research Standards, Section B 48, requires that researchers "not misrepresent the impact of sample methodology and its impact on survey data."

Adherence to ethical standards applies to many aspects of designing a research project, which is why the MRA and other professional associations develop and maintain codes of ethics and standards of conduct. Professionals who understand and comply with these standards serve their clients' interests fairly and responsibly. Fortunately, 99% of marketing researchers are extremely ethical and follow their association's guidelines. The free market has a wonderful way of ensuring that those who aren't ethical do not stay around for long!

We strongly recommend that you visit the websites of the professional organizations identified in Chapter 2 and read their codes of conduct. The MRA posts its standards at http://www.marketingresearch.org (click the link to Standards).

Designing a research project may involve many ethically sensitive areas. Researchers learn these areas by being familiar with their association's codes and standards.

Photo: StockLite/Shutterstock.com

> Research designs are classified into three traditional categories: exploratory, descriptive, and causal. The choice of the most appropriate design depends largely on the research objectives.

The choice of research design also is dependent on how much we already know about the problem and research objective. The less we know, the more likely it is that we should use exploratory research. Causal research, on the other hand, should only be used when we know a fair amount about the problem and we are looking for causal relationships among variables associated with the problem or research objectives. By reading this chapter you will better understand how different research objectives are best handled by the various research designs.[2]

RESEARCH DESIGN: A CAUTION

Before discussing the three types of research design, a warning may be in order against thinking of research design solely in a step-by-step fashion. The order in which the designs are presented in this chapter—that is, exploratory, descriptive, and causal—is *not* the order in which these designs should be carried out. In some cases, it may be perfectly legitimate to begin with any one of the three designs and to use only that one design. In many cases, however, research is an iterative process: By conducting one research project, we learn that we may need additional research, which may result in using multiple research designs. We could very well find, for example, that after conducting descriptive research, we need to go back and conduct exploratory research.

> It may be perfectly legitimate to begin with any one of the three designs and to use only that one design.

If multiple designs are used in any particular order (if there is an order), it makes sense to first conduct exploratory research, then descriptive research, and finally causal research. The only reason for this order is that each subsequent design requires greater knowledge about the problem and research objectives on the part of the researcher.

EXPLORATORY RESEARCH

Exploratory research is most commonly unstructured, informal research that is undertaken to gain background information about the general nature of the research problem. By unstructured, we mean that exploratory research does not have a predetermined set of procedures. Rather, the nature of the research changes as the researcher gains information. It is informal in that there is no formal set of objectives, sample plan, or questionnaire. Often, small, nonrepresentative, samples are used in exploratory research. Other, more formal, research designs are used to test hypotheses or measure the reaction of one variable to a change in another variable. Yet, exploratory research can be accomplished by simply reading a magazine or even observing a situation. Ray Kroc, the milkshake machine salesman who created McDonald's®, observed that restaurants in San Bernardino, California, run by the McDonald brothers were so busy they burned up more milkshake machines than any of his other customers. Kroc took that exploratory observation and turned it into the world-famous fast-food chain. In another example, an 18-year-old college student sitting in line at a McDonald's drive-through waiting for his cheeseburger saw a dilapidated truck loaded with junk and bearing the sign "Mark's Hauling." This observation set in motion Brian Scudamore's ideas to launch a new type of junk service called 1-800-GOT-JUNK?® Soon he was making so much money he dropped out of college; and before long, the company was grossing revenues near $100 million.[3]

Exploratory research is flexible in that it allows the researcher to investigate whatever sources he or she identifies and to the extent he or she feels is necessary to gain a good feel for the problem at hand. A Wendy's® franchisee went through his restaurant's cash register receipts, which were stamped with dates and times. He observed that early weekday afternoons between 2 and 4:30 p.m. were his slack periods. He then initiated a mobile campaign for a free order of French fries during this time on weekdays. Traffic and sales went up. A University of West Virginia grad, Tom Petrini, attended a conference on sustainability. He noticed almost none of the attendees were drinking water from the reusable containers provided. When he asked them why, they told him there was no place to clean and refill the bottles. He started a company, Evive Station®, that provides free stainless steel containers and followup sterilization and refilling.[4]

Exploratory research is usually conducted when the researcher does not know much about the problem and needs additional information or desires new or more recent information. Often exploratory research is conducted at the outset of research projects. Chapter 3 discussed the use of a situation analysis to help clarify the problem. A situation analysis to help clarify the problem is a form of exploratory research.

Uses of Exploratory Research
Exploratory research is used in a number of situations: to gain background information, to define terms, to clarify problems and hypotheses, and to establish research priorities.

Gain Background Information.
When very little is known about the problem or when the problem has not been clearly formulated, exploratory research may be used to gain much-needed background information. Even the most experienced researchers often undertake some exploratory research to gain current, relevant background information. There is far too much to be gained to ignore exploratory information.

Define Terms.
Exploratory research helps to define terms and concepts. By conducting exploratory research to define a question such as "What is satisfaction with service quality?" the researcher quickly learns that "satisfaction with service quality" is composed of several dimensions—tangibles, reliability, responsiveness, assurance, and empathy. Not only would exploratory research identify the dimensions of satisfaction with service quality, but it could also demonstrate how these components may be measured.[5]

Exploratory research is most commonly unstructured, informal research that is undertaken to gain background information about the general nature of the research problem.

Exploratory research is usually conducted when the researcher does not know much about the problem and needs additional information or desires new or more recent information.

Exploratory research is used in a number of situations: to gain background information, to define terms, to clarify problems and hypotheses, and to establish research priorities.

When very little is known about the problem or when the problem has not been clearly formulated, exploratory research may be used to gain much-needed background information.

Exploratory research helps to define terms and concepts.

Clarify Problems and Hypotheses. Exploratory research allows the researcher to define the problem more precisely and to generate hypotheses for the upcoming study. For example, exploratory research on measuring bank image reveals the issue of different groups of bank customers. Banks have three types of customers: retail customers, commercial customers, and other banks for which services are performed for fees. This information is useful in clarifying the problem of the measurement of bank image because it raises the issue of identifying for which customer group bank image should be measured.

Exploratory research can also be beneficial in the formulation of hypotheses, which are statements describing the speculated relationships among two or more variables. Formally stating hypotheses prior to conducting a research study helps to ensure that the proper variables are measured. Once a study has been completed, it may be too late to state which hypotheses are desirable to test.

Exploratory research allows the researcher to define the problem more precisely and to generate hypotheses for the upcoming study.

Exploratory research can help a firm prioritize research topics.

Establish Research Priorities. Exploratory research can help a firm prioritize research topics.

A summary account of complaint letters by retail store may tell management where to devote their attention. One furniture store chain owner decided to conduct research on the feasibility of carrying office furniture after some exploratory interviews with salespeople revealed that their customers often asked for directions to stores carrying office furniture.

Methods of Conducting Exploratory Research A variety of methods is available to conduct exploratory research. We will cover some of these in the section of this chapter that deals with qualitative research since the methods overlap. In this section we briefly discuss some commonly used methods for conducting exploratory research: secondary data analysis, experience surveys, and case analysis. Other methods common to both exploratory research and qualitative research are discussed in Chapter 6.

A common method of conducting exploratory research is to examine existing information.

For some examples of secondary data often used in marketing research, see www.secondarydata.com, a website developed by Decision Analyst, Inc.

Secondary Data Analysis. The process of searching for and interpreting existing information relevant to the research topic is called **secondary data analysis**. Secondary data are those that have been collected for some other purpose and are almost always a part of a marketing research project. Secondary information is widespread and readily available. Thanks to the Internet and today's sophisticated search engines such as Google®, you can conduct a search for secondary information on virtually any topic quickly and efficiently. Your library and the Internet offer access to large amounts of secondary data, which include information found in books, journals, magazines, special reports, bulletins, and newsletters. An analysis of secondary data is often the core of exploratory research.[6] A search of secondary data or information may come in many forms. Many executives subscribe to journals or trade publications for their particular industry. By reviewing these publications, they are constantly doing a form of exploratory research—looking for trends, innovations, information about current or potential customers and competitors, the general economy, and so on. We devote part of Chapter 5 to analyzing secondary data and some of its sources.

Experience surveys refer to gathering information from those thought to be knowledgeable on the issues relevant to the research problem.

Experience surveys may also be called *key-informant* or *lead-user surveys*.

Experience Surveys. **Experience surveys** refer to gathering information from those thought to be knowledgeable on the issues relevant to the research problem. This technique is also known as the **key-informant technique**; in the technology field, a **lead-user survey** is used to acquire information from lead users of a new technology.[7] A manufacturer of a new building material that provides greater insulation at less cost may call a dozen contractors, describe the new material, and ask them how likely they would be to consider using it on their next building. Design professionals at Volvo™, believing that in the past autos had been designed by and for males, asked 100 women what they wanted in a car. They found some major differences between what women want and what is available, and they used this information in designing vehicles.[8] Experience surveys differ from surveys conducted as part of descriptive research in that there is usually no formal attempt to ensure that the survey results are representative of any defined group of subjects. Nevertheless, useful information can be gathered by this method of exploratory research.

Case Analysis. A review of available information about a former situation(s) that has some similarities to the current research problem is called **case analysis**. Research situations typically have at least some similarities to some past situation.[9] Even when the research problem deals with a radically new product, some similar past experiences may be observed. For example, when Apple introduced the iPad®, this new device may have seemed revolutionary. However, Apple had plenty of experience with examining other new product introductions, such as Amazon's Kindle®. Later, as Apple introduced newer versions of the iPad, it revisited earlier introductions of the same product.

Though often useful, researchers must be cautious in using former case examples for current problems because situations change. For example, consumers are much savvier about buying electronic products than they were even just a few short years ago, and more consumers are gaining information relevant to shopping through their use of the Internet more than ever before.

Focus Groups. Focus groups are small groups brought together and guided by a moderator through an unstructured, spontaneous discussion for the purpose of gaining information relevant to the research problem. (We cover the topic extensively in Chapter 6). Though they are designed to encourage open communication, the moderator's role is to keep the discussion focused on a general topic. A college dean was interested in knowing what students thought about the quality of courses and instruction. She gathered 6 groups of 10 students. Based on the discussions that flowed from the focus groups, she identified commonalities of strengths and weaknesses among some of the courses being taught in the college.

Our concluding word about exploratory research is that some form should be used in almost every research project. Why? Exploratory research, particularly secondary data analysis, is fast. You can conduct quite a bit of exploratory research online in just a few minutes using online databases or a search engine. Second, compared to collecting primary data, exploratory research is cheap. Finally, sometimes exploratory research either provides information to meet the research objective or assists in gathering current information necessary to conduct either a descriptive or causal research design. Therefore, few researchers embark on a research project without doing some exploratory research.

DESCRIPTIVE RESEARCH

Descriptive research is undertaken to describe answers to questions of who, what, where, when, and how. When we wish to know *who* our customers are, *what* brands they buy and in what quantities, *where* they buy the brands, *when* they shop, and *how* they found out about our products, we turn to descriptive research. Descriptive research is also desirable when we wish to project a study's findings to a larger population. If a descriptive study's sample is representative, the findings may be used to predict some variable of interest such as sales.

Classification of Descriptive Research Studies Two basic descriptive research studies are available to the marketing researcher: cross-sectional and longitudinal. **Cross-sectional studies** measure units from a sample of the population at only one point in time. Marketing Research Insight 4.2 provides an example of a descriptive, cross-sectional study.

A study measuring your attitude toward adding a required internship course in your degree program, for example, would be a cross-sectional study. Your attitude toward the topic is measured at *one point in time*. Cross-sectional studies are prevalent in marketing research, outnumbering longitudinal studies and causal studies. Because cross-sectional studies are one-time measurements, they are often described as "snapshots" of the population.

Researchers should use former similar case situations cautiously when trying to apply them to their current research objectives.

To see some focus groups in action, go to **www.youtube.com** and enter "exploratory research." Several examples of this form of exploratory research are depicted, including a focus group sponsored by Coca-Cola (enter "exploratory Research1. mpg" in the search box).

Some form of exploratory research should be used in almost every research project.

Descriptive research is undertaken to describe answers to questions of who, what, where, when, and how.

Two basic descriptive research studies are available to the marketing researcher: cross-sectional and longitudinal. Because cross-sectional studies measure units from a sample of the population at only one point in time, they are often described as "snapshots."

MARKETING RESEARCH INSIGHT 4.2 — *Practical Application*

✓ Descriptive Research Produces Magic Numbers

Eduardo Carqueja, CEO

Magic Numbers® is a magazine that contains the results of many descriptive surveys on topics of interest to much of the population. Data are collected on interesting subjects such as political scandals, use of social media, and household debt. As the accompanying bar chart shows, data are collected in many countries offering readers insights on how populations around the world differ.

Text and images: By permission, Eduardo Carqueja, Magic Numbers®.

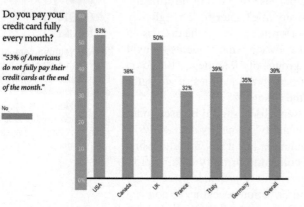

Do you pay your credit card fully every month?

"53% of Americans do not fully pay their credit cards at the end of the month."

No

Source: Saving Habits: Americans: The big spenders. (July/August 2011). *Magic Numbers: Revealing the World's Opinion,* *1*(4), 64. By permission.

Data for *Magic Numbers'* articles are collected by the marketing research firm NPolls®. NPolls has a panel of thousands of consumers all over the world. This study on household debt was conducted in three days in May 2011. The question "Do you pay your credit card fully every month?" and several others were asked of 4,056 people who received and answered the questions on mobile devices, including smart phones, iPads, and iPods. Since the respondents answered these questions at a point in time, this would be classified as a descriptive, cross-sectional study.

As an example, many magazines survey a sample of their subscribers and ask them questions such as their age, occupation, income, and educational level. These sample data, taken at one point in time, are used to describe the readership of the magazine in terms of demographics. Cross-sectional studies normally employ fairly large sample sizes, so many cross-sectional studies are referred to as *sample surveys*.

Sample surveys are cross-sectional studies whose samples are drawn in such a way as to be representative of a specific population. Prior to important elections, many sample surveys ask likely voters: "If the election were held today, which candidate would you vote for?" Such survey results are often featured in the news because they attract a lot of attention. The survey samples are drawn so that the news media may report that the results are representative of the U.S. population and that the results have, for example, a "margin of error of + or − 3%." In other words, sample surveys may be designed so that their results are representative and accurate, within some margin of error, of the true

Sample surveys are cross-sectional studies whose samples are drawn so that they are representative of a specific population.

values in the population. (You will learn how to do this by studying this book.) Sample surveys require that their samples be drawn to a predetermined number according to a prescribed plan. In Chapters 9 and 10, you will learn about these sampling plans and sample size techniques.

Longitudinal studies repeatedly measure the same sample units of a population over a period of time. Because longitudinal studies involve multiple measurements, they are often described as "movies" of the population. Longitudinal studies are employed by almost 50% of businesses using marketing research.[10] To ensure the success of the longitudinal study, researchers must have access to the same members of the sample, called a panel, so as to take repeated measurements. **Panels** represent sample units who have agreed to answer questions at periodic intervals. Maintaining a representative panel of respondents is a major undertaking.

Several commercial marketing research firms develop and maintain consumer panels for use in longitudinal studies. Typically, these firms attempt to select a sample that is representative of some population. Firms such as Knowledge Networks® and Nielsen® have maintained panels consisting of hundreds of thousands of households for many years. In many cases these companies recruit panel members so that the demographic characteristics of the panel are proportionate to the demographic characteristics found in the total population according to Census Bureau statistics. Sometimes these panels will be balanced demographically not only to the United States but more specifically to the various geographical regions. In this way, a client who wishes to get information from a panel of households in the Northwest can be assured that the panel is demographically matched to the total population in the states making up the northwestern region. Many companies maintain panels to target market segments such as "dog owners" or "kids." Paradigm Sample® offers a panel of 18- to 34-year-old smart phone users through its IdeaShifters™ panel. B2B panels are also available allowing researchers to target populations such as building contractors, supermarket owners, physicians, lawyers, university professors, or government workers.

There are two types of panels: continuous panels and discontinuous panels. **Continuous panels** ask panel members the same questions on each panel measurement. **Discontinuous panels** vary questions from one panel measurement to the next.[11] Continuous panel examples include many of the syndicated data panels that ask panel members to record their purchases using diaries or scanners. The essential point is that panel members are asked to record the *same* information (for example, grocery store purchases) over and over.

Discontinuous panels are sometimes referred to as **omnibus panels**. (*Omnibus* means "including or covering many things or classes.") They may be used for a variety of purposes, and the information collected by a discontinuous panel varies from one panel measurement to the next. How longitudinal data are applied depends on the type of panel used to collect the data. Essentially, the discontinuous panel's primary usefulness is that it represents a large group—people, stores, or some other entity—and its members are agreeable to providing marketing research information. Discontinuous panels, like continuous panels, are also demographically matched to some larger entity, implying representativeness as well. Therefore, a marketer wanting to know how a large number of consumers, matched demographically to the total U.S. population, feel about two different product concepts may elect to utilize the services of an omnibus panel. The advantage of discontinuous (omnibus) panels is that they represent a group of persons who have made themselves available for research. In this way, then, discontinuous panels represent existing sources of information that may be quickly accessed for a wide variety of purposes.

Longitudinal studies repeatedly measure the same sample units of a population over a period of time. Panels represent sample units who have agreed to answer questions at periodic intervals. Maintaining a representative panel of respondents is a major undertaking.

Continuous panels ask panel members the same questions on each panel measurement. Discontinuous panels vary questions from one panel measurement to the next.

 **Active Learning**

Omnibus Surveys

Let's learn more about omnibus surveys! Go to www.greenbook.org. At the top left, locate "Find and Compare": "Marketing Research Firms." Under "Select Type of Research," select the drop-down menu and click on "Market Research Specialty" and then "Choose a specialty." Scroll down to "Omnibus Surveys" and click "Find." Other than "consumers," what other types of samples may be accessed using omnibus surveys? Go to some of the firms and read what they have to say about omnibus surveys. How long does it take them to get results back to clients?

The continuous panel is used quite differently. Usually, firms are interested in using data from continuous panels because they can gain insights into *changes in* consumers' purchases, attitudes, and so on. For example, data from continuous panels can show how members of the panel switched brands from one time period to the next. Studies examining how many consumers switched brands are known as **brand-switching studies.** Such studies can be invaluable to brand managers because two cross-sectional studies may show changes in market shares between several brands but they can be misleading. We will illustrate this in Tables 4.1 and 4.2. Table 4.1 shows the results of two separate surveys conducted six months apart. Let's assume you are the brand manager for Famous Amos® chocolate chip cookies. We can see that both studies surveyed 500 families who were purchasers of chocolate chip cookies. In survey 1 Famous Amos had 100 families, and the other two brands had 200 and 200 respectively. (Please note these numbers are for illustration only; they do not reflect the true market shares of these brands.) What can we learn as the brand manager from one cross-sectional study? We now know that we are about 20% of the market and that our two competitors have about equal shares, each about 40% of the market. Now, let's look at another sample of 500 other families six months later as shown in cross-sectional survey 2. What can we learn? First, we see that Famous Amos's share has dropped! A brand manager should be very concerned about a drop in market share. Who is the culprit? If we compare the two cross-sectional studies, we see that Pepperidge Farm® stayed the same at 200 families, but Nabisco® climbed to 225 families. It would be quite natural to assume, "Nabisco is eating our lunch ... er ... cookies!" In this case, the Famous Amos brand manager would start examining Nabisco's marketing mix during the last few months. Has the competitor changed package design? Has it stepped up its promotion? Is it providing retailers with incentives?

Now, let us take a look at a longitudinal study with two waves of measurements, again six months apart. We will assume that the results (total families purchasing each brand) is exactly the same as we have in our two cross-sectional studies. But, what will be different is how each family changed. Remember, with a continuous panel in a longitudinal study we ask the same family the same question with each administration, or wave, of the study. Look at the results in Table 4.2.

Notice that the totals for Wave 1 (green) and Wave 2 (blue) are *exactly the same* as the totals for the two cross-sectional studies shown in Table 4.1. However, the value of longitudinal

TABLE 4.1 **Results of Two Cross-Sectional Studies "Which Brand of Chocolate Chip Cookie Did You Most Recently Purchase?"**

Brand	Cross-Sectional Survey 1	Cross-Sectional Survey 2
Famous Amos	100	75
Pepperidge Farm	200	200
Nabisco	200	225
Total Families	500	500

TABLE 4.2   Results of Two Waves of a Longitudinal Study "Which Brand of Chocolate Chip Cookie Did You Most Recently Purchase?"

Wave 1 Brand	Wave 2 Brand			
	Famous Amos	**Pepperidge Farm**	**Nabisco**	**Totals, Wave 1**
Famous Amos	50	50	0	100
Pepperidge Farm	25	150	25	200
Nabisco	0	0	200	200
Totals, Wave 2	75	200	225	

data is reflected in the tan area inside of Table 4.2. Of the 100 families who bought Famous Amos cookies in Wave 1, 50 of them stayed with Famous Amos in Wave 2. Another 50 families switched to Pepperidge Farm. None of the Famous Amos families switched to Nabisco. Of the 200 Pepperidge Farm families in Wave 1, 25 switched to Famous Amos, 150 stayed with Pepperidge Farm, and 25 switched to Nabisco. Finally, of the 200 Nabisco families in Wave 1, all 200 of them stayed with Nabisco in Wave 2. Are you beginning to see what competition is going on among the brands? It's Pepperidge Farm, not Nabisco, that is interacting with our Famous Amos cookie brand. More detailed data allow us to arrive at a more valid conclusion than we reached by first only considering the cross-sectional studies. This is the value of longitudinal information using continuous panels. We can "see" where the consumers are changing from and to.

Another use of longitudinal data is that of market tracking. **Market-tracking studies** are those that measure some variable(s) of interest—that is, market share or unit sales over time. By tracking sales by SKU over time, managers can learn a great deal about what is happening in the marketplace. We discuss tracking studies in more depth in Chapter 5.

CAUSAL RESEARCH

Causality may be thought of as understanding a phenomenon in terms of conditional statements of the form "If *x*, then *y*." These "if–then" statements become our way of manipulating variables of interest. For example, if the thermostat is lowered, then the air will get cooler. If I drive my automobile at lower speeds, then my gasoline mileage will increase. If I spend more on advertising, then sales will rise. Marketing managers are always trying to determine what will cause a change in consumer satisfaction, a gain in market share, or an increase in sales. In one experiment, marketing researchers investigated how color versus noncolor and different quality levels of graphics in *Yellow Page* ads caused changes in consumers' attitudes toward the ad itself, the company doing the advertising, and perceptions of quality. The results showed that color and high-photographic graphics cause more favorable attitudes. But the findings differ depending on the class of product being advertised.[12] This illustrates how complex cause-and-effect relationships are in the real world. Understanding what causes consumers to behave as they do is extremely difficult. Nevertheless, there is a high "reward" in the marketplace for even partially understanding causal relationships. Causal relationships are determined by the use of experiments, which are special types of studies. Many companies conduct experiments online.[13]

Causal relationships are determined by the use of experiments, which are special types of studies.

Experiments An **experiment** is defined as manipulating an independent variable to see how it affects a dependent variable, while also controlling the effects of additional extraneous variables. **Independent variables** are those variables over which the researcher has control *and* wishes to manipulate. Broadly speaking, you can think of the 4 Ps (product, price, promotion, and place) as independent variables. Some independent variables include level of advertising expenditure, type of advertising appeal (humor, prestige), display location, method of compensating salespersons, price, and type of product. **Dependent variables**, on the other hand, are those variables over which we have little or no direct control but a strong interest

An experiment is defined as manipulating an independent variable to see how it affects a dependent variable, while also controlling the effects of additional extraneous variables.

Independent variables are those variables over which the researcher has control *and* wishes to manipulate. Examples include level of advertising expenditure, type of advertising appeal, display location, method of compensating salespersons, price, and type of product.

Dependent variables are those variables over which we have little or no direct control but a strong interest in changing. Examples include sales, market share, customer satisfaction, sales force turnover, and net profits.

Extraneous variables are those that may have some effect on a dependent variable but yet are not independent variables.

in changing. Common dependent variables include sales, market share, customer satisfaction, sales force turnover, net profits, and RONW (return on net worth). Certainly, marketers are interested in changing these variables. But because they cannot change them directly, they attempt to change them through the manipulation of independent variables. To the extent that marketers can establish causal relationships between independent and dependent variables, they enjoy some success in influencing the dependent variables. Consider an analogy familiar to students: If you want to change your GPA (dependent variable), you must change certain independent variables such as amount of time devoted to study, class attendance, devotion to reading your textbook, and listening habits in the lecture hall.

Extraneous variables are those that may have some effect on a dependent variable but yet are not independent variables. To illustrate, let's say you and your friend wanted to know if brand of gasoline (independent variable) affected gas mileage in automobiles (dependent variable). Your "experiment" consists of each of you filling up your two cars, one with Brand A, the other with Brand B. At the end of the week, you learn that Brand A achieved 18.6 miles per gallon and Brand B achieved 26.8 miles per gallon. Does Brand B cause better gas mileage than Brand A? Or could the difference in the dependent variable (gas mileage) be due to factors *other* than gasoline brand (independent variable)? Let's take a look at what these extraneous variables may be: (1) One car is an SUV, and the other is a small compact. (2) One car was driven mainly on the highway, and the other was driven in the city in heavy traffic. (3) One car has properly inflated tires, whereas the other car does not. All these extraneous variables could have caused the difference in the dependent variable.

Let's look at another example. Imagine that a restaurant chain conducts an experiment to determine the effect of supplying nutritional information on menu items (independent variable) on restaurant sales (dependent variable).[14] Management has a record of restaurant sales without menu-supplied nutritional information and then changes the menus (manipulates the independent variable) to include the nutritional information and measures sales once again. The experiment is conducted in one of the chain's restaurants. Assume sales increased. Does this mean that if the chain changes the menu information, then sales will increase in all its restaurants? Might other extraneous variables have affected sales? Could the following two variables have affected the restaurant's sales: (1) the restaurant selected for the experiment is located in a high income area in California known for health spas and workout gyms; and (2) just prior to changing the menus, the FDA announced a study that caloric content for the same type of food had wide variation depending on the restaurant (coffee ranges in calories from 80 to 800 per cup; hamburgers range from 250 to over 1,000). Yes, the clientele for the restaurant selected for the experiment could be unique, and a new, highly publicized study about nutritional information from a respected source, the FDA, could certainly have had an effect on the acceptance of the new menu information. In fact, it could have helped create "buzz" or positive WOM (word-of-mouth) influence. Both these possible influences are likely extraneous variables that have an effect on the dependent variable, yet themselves not defined as independent variables. As this example illustrates, it would be difficult to isolate the effects of independent variables on dependent variables without controlling for the effects of the extraneous variables. Unfortunately, it is not easy to establish causal relationships, but it can be done. In the following section, we will see how the design of an experiment allows us to assess causality. Marketing Research Insight 4.3 illustrates how an experiment was conducted to show a causal relationship between store layout and sales of salted snacks in convenience stores.

An experimental design is a procedure for devising an experimental setting so that a change in a dependent variable may be attributed solely to the change in an independent variable.

Experimental Design   An **experimental design** is a procedure for devising an experimental setting so that a change in a dependent variable may be attributed solely to the change in an independent variable. In other words, experimental designs are procedures that allow experimenters to control for the effects on a dependent variable by any extraneous variable. In this way, the experimenter is assured that any change in the dependent variable was due only to the change in the independent variable.

MARKETING RESEARCH INSIGHT 4.3   *Practical Application*

TNS Global Uses Experiments to Increase Client's Sales in Convenience Stores

Herb Sorensen,
Ph. D., Scientific Director, TNS Global, Retail & Shopper Practice and Adjunct Senior Researcher, University of South Australia

A salty snack brand manufacturer thought there was a potential for increased sales in the convenience store channel. In this case, two chains of stores, widely dispersed geographically, were selected to represent the channel, nationally. Obviously, there would be many variables across all the chains nationally, but understanding what drove sales in two chains could provide valuable insight for the channel. The basic experimental design here is referred to as a *controlled store test*, since two panels of matched stores were selected in each chain: Experimental A vs. Control A; Experimental B vs. Control B, where A and B are the chains. In this chapter you will learn about the importance of having equivalent experimental and control groups in an experiment.

The study began with tracking shopper behavior in stores, and interviewing them to learn more about their habits and practices in convenience stores *before* suggestions were made in terms of store design, layout, and merchandising.

The PathTracker® study of where shoppers went in a few stores, how long they spent there, and what categories they visited, in combination with interviews at the exits, revealed that those who buy snacks on impulse are usually coming to the store to pay for gas. The primary path in a convenience store goes from the entrance to the checkout and or cold vault. This is an example of doing some preliminary exploratory research before the experiment.

Review of all the data from the exploratory research suggested that successful snack aisles will be located on the primary path to the checkout and beverages and will vertically divide chips and other salty snacks (e.g., nuts, seeds). Salty snacks will be grouped by product type and within each type items will be brand blocked.

For the experiment, all of the experimental stores had the recommended new shelf location and merchandise configuration installed. These changes constituted manipulation of the independent variable. As you will also learn in this chapter, we kept the control stores in their pretest conditions. The dependent variable was sales, which were recorded for both experimental and control stores, on a week-by-week basis, for the entire prior year, plus the 12 weeks of the experiment, and 4 weeks of post-test. Not only did having pretest and post-test measures allow us to calculate the experimental effect (E), we also obtained a good understanding of other variables such as seasonality, local neighborhood, and store-specific extraneous variables.

The net result of this project was that sales of chips, nuts, and seeds increased with the new independent variable. Other salty snacks increased only slightly. Of great interest was that although the brand manufacturer's product sales increased significantly, from the retailer's point of view, more importantly, the sales of all the category brands increased.

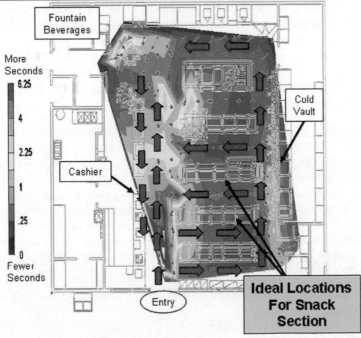

C-Store Shopper Seconds and Primary Path

Fountain Beverages

More Seconds
6.25
4
2.25
1
.25
0
Fewer Seconds

Cashier

Cold Vault

Entry

Ideal Locations For Snack Section

Text and images: By permission, Herb Sorensen, TNS Global.

Herb Sorensen is a preeminent authority on observing and measuring shopping behavior and attitudes within the four walls of the store. He has worked with Fortune 100 retailers and consumer packaged goods manufacturers for more than 35 years, studying shopper behavior, motivations, and perceptions at the point of purchase. Sorensen's patented shopper tracking technology PathTracker® is helping to revolutionize retail marketing strategies from a traditional "product-centric" perspective to a new "shopper-centric" focus.

Herb has conducted studies in North America, Europe, Asia, Australia, and South America. His research has been published in AMA's Marketing Research, The Journal of Advertising Research, FMI Advantage Magazine, Progressive Grocer, *and* Chain Drug Review, *and he has served as an expert source for* The Wall Street Journal, Supermarket News, *and* BusinessWeek. *Additionally, he is currently a panelist of Retail Wire's "Brain Trust."*

Herb was named one of the top 50 innovators of 2004 by Fast Company Magazine *and shared the American Marketing Association's 2007 EXPLOR Award for technological applications that advance research, with Peter Fader and his group at the Wharton School of Business of the University of Pennsylvania. Herb has a Ph.D. in Biochemistry.*

Let's look at how experimental designs work. First, we list the symbols of experimental design:

O = The measurement of a dependent variable

X = The manipulation, or change, of an independent variable

R = Random assignment of subjects (e.g., consumers, stores) to experimental and control groups

E = Experimental effect—that is, the change in the dependent variable due to the independent variable

When a measurement of the dependent variable is taken *prior to* changing the independent variable, the measurement is sometimes called a **pretest**. When a measurement of the dependent variable is taken *after* changing the independent variable, the measurement is sometimes called a **posttest**.

A **"true" experimental design** isolates the effects of the independent variable on the dependent variable while controlling for effects of any extraneous variables.

Designs that do not properly control for the effects of extraneous variables on our dependent variable are known as **quasi-experimental designs**. Control of extraneous variables is typically achieved by the use of a second group of subjects, known as a control group. By **control group**, we mean a group whose subjects have not been exposed to the change in the independent variable. The **experimental group**, on the other hand, is the group that has been exposed to a change in the independent variable. By having these two groups as part of our experimental design, we can overcome many of the problems associated with quasi-experimental designs. We shall use the following true experimental design to illustrate the importance of the control group.

> A "true" experimental design isolates the effects of the independent variable on the dependent variable while controlling for effects of any extraneous variables.

Before-After with Control Group. The **before-after with control group** design may be achieved by randomly dividing subjects of the experiment into two groups: the control group and the experimental group. If we assume that our restaurant chain has 100 restaurants spread around the country, we could easily randomly divide them into two groups of 50 restaurants each. Management already has a pretest measurement of the dependent variable on both groups by virtue of knowing sales volume prior to changing the menus. Next, the independent variable, adding the nutritional information to the menus, is changed only in the experimental group (50 restaurants). Finally, after some time period, posttest measurements are taken of the dependent variable in both groups of restaurants. This design may be diagrammed as follows:

$$\text{Experimental group } (R) \quad O_1 \, X \, O_2$$
$$\text{Control group } (R) \qquad\quad O_3 \quad O_4$$

where $\qquad E = (O_2 - O_1) - (O_4 - O_3).$

By randomly (R) dividing our 100 restaurants into two groups—50 in the experimental group and 50 in the control group—the groups should be equivalent. That is, both groups should be as similar as possible, each group having an equal number of restaurants in high income, middle income, and low income areas, and an equal number of restaurants in locales favoring exercising and nutrition concern. In fact, the average age of the restaurants should be equal, the average square footage should be equal, the average number of employees should be equal, and the average sales should be equal. In other words, randomization should yield two groups of restaurants that are *equivalent* in all respects. An experimenter should take whatever steps are necessary to meet this condition if he or she uses this design. There are other methods for gaining equivalency besides randomization. Matching on criteria thought to be important, for example, would aid in establishing equivalent groups. When randomization or matching on relevant criteria does not achieve equivalent groups, more complex experimental designs should be used.[15]

Looking back at our design, the *R* indicates that we have randomly divided our restaurants into two equal groups—one a control group, the other an experimental group. We also see that pretest measurements of our dependent variable, restaurant sales, were recorded for both groups of restaurants, as noted by O_1 and O_3. Next, we see by the *X* symbol that only in the experimental group of restaurants were the menus changed to add the nutritional information for the menu items. Finally, posttest measurements of the dependent variable were taken at the same time in both groups of restaurants, as noted by O_2 and O_4.

Now, what information can we gather from this experiment? First, we know that $(O_2 - O_1)$ tells us how much change occurred in our dependent variable during the time of the experiment. But was this difference due solely to our independent variable, *X*? No, $(O_2 - O_1)$ tells us how many dollars in sales may be attributed to (1) the change in menu information *and* (2) other extraneous variables, such as the FDA publicizing the wide variation in nutritional values obtained in restaurant meals or just that more people decided to eat in restaurants during this time interval. Now, let us look at what is measured by the differences in sales among our control restaurants $(O_4 - O_3)$. Because it cannot account for changes in restaurant sales due to a change in menu information (the menus were not changed), then any differences in sales as measured by $(O_4 - O_3)$ must be due to the influence of all extraneous variables on restaurant sales. Therefore, the *difference* between the experimental group and the control group, $(O_2 - O_1) - (O_4 - O_3)$, results in a measure of *E*, the "experimental effect."

We now know that if we change menu information, then restaurant sales will change by an amount equal to *E*. We have, through experimentation using a proper experimental design, made some progress at arriving at causality. However, we should point out here, though we have established causality, it did not come without cost and complexity. Notice our experiment went from changing menus in 1 store to 50 stores, and our total experiment involved 100 stores!

As we noted earlier, there are many other experimental designs, and of course, there are almost limitless applications of experimental designs to marketing problems. Although we have demonstrated how valuable experimentation can be in providing knowledge, we should not accept all experiments as being valid. How we assess the validity of experiments is the subject of our next section.

How Valid Are Experiments? How can we assess the validity of an experiment? An experiment is valid if: (1) the observed change in the dependent variable is, in fact, due to the independent variable, and (2) the results of the experiment apply to the "real world" outside the experimental setting.[16] Two forms of validity are used to assess the validity of an experiment: internal and external.

Internal validity is concerned with the extent to which the change in the dependent variable was actually due to the independent variable. This is another way of asking if the proper experimental design was used and if it was implemented correctly. To illustrate an

Internal validity is concerned with the extent to which the change in the dependent variable was actually due to the independent variable.

experiment that lacks internal validity, let us return to our change in menu information example. Recall that we took the effort to expand our restaurants to 100 and randomly divided them into two groups, to ensure that the experimental group and control group were, in fact, equivalent. What would happen if the researcher did not ensure the equivalency of the groups? Our experimental effect, E, could be due to the differences in the two groups (e.g., one group of restaurants was located in areas with clientele sensitive to nutrition). This difference in the groups, then, would represent an extraneous variable that had been left uncontrolled. Such an experiment would lack internal validity because it could not be said that the change in the dependent variable was due solely to the change in the independent variable. Experiments lacking internal validity have little value because they produce misleading results.

External validity refers to the extent that the relationship observed between the independent and dependent variables during the experiment is generalizable to the "real world."[17] In other words, can the results of the experiment be applied to all the restaurants in the chain? There are several threats to external validity. How representative is the sample of test units? Is this sample really representative of the population? Additionally, there exist many examples of the incorrect selection of sample units for testing purposes. For example, some executives, headquartered in large cities in cold winter climates, have been known to conduct "experiments" in warmer, tropical climes during the winter. Although the experiments they conduct may be internally valid, it is doubtful that the results will be generalizable to the total population.

External validity refers to the extent that the relationship observed between the independent and dependent variables during the experiment is generalizable to the "real world."

Another threat to external validity is the artificiality of the experimental setting itself. To control as many variables as possible, some experimental settings are far removed from real-world conditions.[18] If an experiment is so contrived that it produces behavior that would not likely be found in the real world, then the experiment lacks external validity.

Types of Experiments We can classify experiments into two broad classes: laboratory and field. **Laboratory experiments** are those in which the independent variable is manipulated and measures of the dependent variable are taken in a contrived, artificial setting for the purpose of controlling the many possible extraneous variables that may affect the dependent variable.

Laboratory experiments are those in which the independent variable is manipulated and measures of the dependent variable are taken in a contrived, artificial setting for the purpose of controlling the many possible extraneous variables that may affect the dependent variable.

To illustrate, let us consider a study whereby subjects are invited to a theater and shown test ads, copy A or copy B, spliced into a TV pilot program. Why would a marketer want to use such an artificial, laboratory setting? Such a setting is used to control for variables that could affect the purchase of products other than those in the test ads. By bringing consumers into a contrived laboratory setting, the experimenter is able to control many extraneous variables. For example, you have learned why it is important to have equivalent groups (the same kind of people watching copy A as those watching copy B commercials) in an experiment. By inviting preselected consumers to the TV pilot showing in a theater, the experimenter can match (on selected demographics) the consumers who view copy A with those who view copy B, thus ensuring that the two groups are equal. By having the consumers walk into an adjoining "store," the experimenter easily controls other factors such as the time between exposure to the ad copy and shopping, as well as the consumers' being exposed to other advertising by competitive brands. As you have already learned, any one of these factors, left uncontrolled, could have an impact on the dependent variable. By controlling for these and other variables, the experimenter can be assured that any changes in the dependent variable were due solely to differences in the independent variable, ad copy A and copy B. Laboratory experiments, then, are desirable when the intent of the experiment is to achieve high levels of internal validity.

There are advantages to laboratory experiments. First, they allow the researcher to control for the effects of extraneous variables. Second, compared to field experiments, lab experiments may be conducted quickly and with less expense. Obviously, the disadvantage is the lack of a natural setting, and therefore, there is concern for the generalizability of the findings to the real world. **Field experiments** are those in which the independent variables are manipulated and the measurements of the dependent variable are made on test units in their natural setting. Many marketing experiments are conducted in natural settings, such as in supermarkets, malls, retail stores, and consumers' homes. Let us assume that a marketing manager conducts a *laboratory* experiment to test the differences between ad copy A, the company's existing ad copy, and a new ad copy, copy B. The results of the laboratory experiment indicate that copy B is far superior to the company's present ad copy A. But, before spending the money to use the new copy, the manager wants to know if ad copy B will really create increased sales in the real world. She elects to actually run the new ad copy in Erie, Pennsylvania, a city noted as being representative of the average characteristics of the U.S. population. By conducting this study in the field, the marketing manager will have greater confidence that the results of the study will actually hold up in other real-world settings. Note, however, that even if an experiment is conducted in a naturalistic field setting to enhance external validity, the experiment is invalid if it does not also have internal validity.

The primary advantage of the field experiment is that of conducting the study in a naturalistic setting, thus increasing the likelihood that the study's findings will also hold true in the real world. Field experiments, however, are expensive and time consuming. Also, the experimenter must always be alert to the impact of extraneous variables, which are difficult to control in the natural settings of field experimentation.

The example we just cited of using Erie, Pennsylvania, for a field experiment would be called a "test market." Much of the experimentation in marketing, conducted as field experiments, is known as *test marketing,* which is discussed in the following section.

Test Marketing

Test marketing is the phrase commonly used to indicate an experiment, study, or test that is conducted in a field setting. Companies may use one or several test-market cities, which are selected geographical areas in which to conduct the test. There are two broad classes of uses of test markets: (1) to test the sales potential for a new product or service, and (2) to test variations in the marketing mix for a product or service.[19]

Although test markets are very expensive and time consuming, the costs of introducing a new product on a national or regional basis routinely amount to millions of dollars. The costs of the test market are then justified if the results of the test market can improve a product's chances of success. Sometimes the test market results will be sufficient to warrant further market introductions. Sometimes the test market identifies a failure early on and saves the company huge losses. The GlobalPC™, a scaled-down computer targeted for novices, was tried in test markets. The parent company, MyTurn™, concluded that the test market sales results would not lead to a profit, and the product was dropped before the company experienced further losses.[20]

Test markets are conducted not only to measure sales potential for a new product but also to measure consumer and dealer reactions to other marketing-mix variables. A firm may use only department stores to distribute the product in one test-market city and only specialty stores in another test-market city to gain some information on the best way to distribute the product. Companies can also test media usage, pricing, sales promotions, and so on through test markets. Products and services in both the consumer (B2C) and industrial (B2B) markets may be test marketed. Marketing Research Insight 4.4 describes some current test markets.

TYPES OF TEST MARKETS

Test markets have been classified into four types: standard, controlled, electronic, and simulated.[21] The **standard test market** is one in which the firm tests the product or marketing mix variables through the company's *normal* distribution channels. A negative of this type of test market is that competitors are immediately aware of the new product or service. However,

Field experiments are those in which the independent variables are manipulated and the measurements of the dependent variable are made on test units in their natural setting.

Test marketing is the phrase commonly used to indicate an experiment, study, or test that is conducted in a field setting.

Test markets have been classified into four types: standard, controlled, electronic, and simulated.

MARKETING RESEARCH INSIGHT 4.4 *Practical Application*

Test Marketing New Product and Service Ideas

Is TV Going to the Dogs?

Dog TV® is testing a cable channel designed for dogs. The test was run in San Diego, California, and piped into the homes of about 1 million cable subscribers. *Dog TV* has been researched for over four years. Former TV signals appeared as just a flickering screen to dogs, but today's digital TV systems allow dogs to see images. Colors in the new system will appear "off" to humans as the signal is designed for a dog's vision, sporting hues of blue and yellow. Veterinary-approved music is to provide a soothing background; there will be little barking! The philosophy is to provide programming that, instead of having dogs focus on some event, is soothing and relaxing. Studies have shown dogs seem to like it. The test market is to determine if human owners will pay the $4.99 a month to have the channel.[22] Take a look at *Dog TV* on www.youtube.com.

Photo: 3dfoto/Shutterstock.com

Brush Away Those Cavities!

Nanova, Inc.®, scientists announced that they are test-marketing a new plasma toothbrush designed to eliminate drilling for cavities. Testing began early in 2012. The plasma brush uses chemical reactions to disinfect and clean out cavities for fillings within 30 seconds.[23]

Want a Burger and Fries with that Bordeaux?

White Castle®, the hamburger chain based in Columbus, Ohio, is test marketing the sales of beer and wine in Latvia,

Indiana. Alcohol will be sold in restaurants that combine the burger chain with the company's new blaze modern BBQ. Burger King is also test marketing the sale of alcohol in its restaurants in Miami.[24]

Slimmer Sodas?

Having promising results with its Dr. Pepper Ten®, a low-calorie drink, Dr. Pepper Snapple Group, Inc.®, is test-marketing five other drinks, including Sunkist Ten®, Canada Dry Ten®, and 7Up Ten® in the slimmer 10-calorie versions. Test markets are in Columbus, Ohio; Des Moines, Iowa; and central Pennsylvania.[25]

---

standard test markets are good indicators as to how the product will actually perform because they are conducted in real settings.

Controlled test markets are conducted by outside research firms that guarantee distribution of the product through prespecified types and numbers of distributors.

Electronic test markets are those in which a panel of consumers has agreed to carry identification cards that each consumer presents when buying goods and services.

Controlled test markets are conducted by outside research firms that guarantee distribution of the product through prespecified types and numbers of distributors. Companies specializing in providing this service provide dollar incentives for distributors to provide them with guaranteed shelf space. Controlled test markets offer an alternative to the company that wishes to gain fast access to a distribution system set up for test-market purposes. The disadvantage is that this distribution network may or may not properly represent the firm's actual distribution system. **Electronic test markets** are those in which a panel of consumers has agreed to carry identification cards that each consumer presents when buying goods and services. These tests are conducted only in a small number of cities in which local retailers have agreed to participate. The advantage of the card is that as consumers buy (or do not buy) the test product, demographic information on the consumers is automatically recorded. In some cases, firms offering electronic test markets may also have the ability to link media viewing habits to panel members as well. In this way, firms using the electronic test market also know how different elements of the promotional mix affect purchases of the new product. Obviously, the electronic test market offers speed, greater confidentiality, and less cost than standard or controlled test markets. However, the disadvantage is that the test market is one more step removed from the real market.[26]

Simulated test markets (STMs) are those in which a limited amount of data on consumer response to a new product is fed into a model containing certain assumptions regarding planned marketing programs, which generates likely product sales volume.[27]

There are many advantages to STMs. They are much faster and only cost 5% to 10% of the cost of a standard test market. STMs are confidential; competitors are less likely to know about the test. The primary disadvantage is that STMs are not as accurate as full-scale test markets as they are dependent on the assumptions built into the models.[28]

SELECTING TEST-MARKET CITIES

Three criteria are useful for selecting test-market cities: **representativeness, degree of isolation**, and **ability to control distribution and promotion**. Because one of the major reasons for conducting a test market is to achieve external validity, the test-market city should be representative of the marketing territory in which the product will ultimately be distributed. Consequently, a great deal of effort is expended to locate the "ideal" city in terms of comparability with characteristics of the total U.S. (or other country) population. The "ideal" city is, of course, the city whose demographic characteristics most closely match the desired total market. For instance, R. J. Reynolds® chose Chattanooga, Tennessee, to test-market its Eclipse® "smokeless" cigarette because Chattanooga has a higher proportion of smokers than most cities, and R. J. Reynolds needed to test Eclipse with smokers.[29]

When a firm test-markets a product, distribution of the product and promotion of the product are isolated to a limited geographical area, such as Tulsa, Oklahoma. If the firm advertises in the *Tulsa World* newspaper, the newspaper not only covers Tulsa but also has very little "spillover" into other sizable markets. Therefore, the company, along with its dealers, competitors, and so on, is not likely to get many calls from a nearby city wanting to know why it cannot buy the product. Distribution has been restricted to the test market, Tulsa. Some markets are not so isolated. If you were to run promotions for a product test in the *Los Angeles Times*, you would have very large spillover of newspaper readership outside the Los Angeles geographical area. Note that this would not necessarily be a problem as long as you wanted to run the test in the geographical area covered by the *Los Angeles Times* and you also had arranged for the new product to be distributed in this area.

The ability to control distribution and promotion depends on a number of factors. Are distributors in the city available and willing to cooperate? If not, is a controlled-test-market service company available for the city? Will the media in the city have the facilities to accommodate your test-market needs? At what costs? All of these factors must be considered before selecting the test city. Fortunately, because city governments often consider it desirable to have test markets conducted in their city because it brings in additional revenues, they and local media typically provide a great deal of information about their city to prospective test marketers.

PROS AND CONS OF TEST MARKETING

The advantages of test marketing are straightforward. Testing product acceptability and marketing-mix variables in a field setting provides the best information possible to the decision maker prior to actually going into full-scale marketing of the product. Test marketing allows for the most accurate method of forecasting future sales, and it allows firms the opportunity to pretest marketing-mix variables. On the con downside, first, test markets do not yield infallible results. Second, competitors may intentionally try to sabotage test markets. For example, firms may flood a test market with sales promotions if they know a competitor is test-marketing a product.[30] Another problem with test markets is their cost. The costs of test markets involving several test cities and various forms of promotion can easily run in the millions. Third, test

Simulated test markets (STMs) are those in which a limited amount of data on consumer response to a new product is fed into a model containing certain assumptions regarding planned marketing programs, which generates likely product sales volume.

Three criteria are useful for selecting test-market cities: representativeness, degree of isolation, and ability to control distribution and promotion.

markets bring about exposure of the product to the competition. Competitors get the opportunity to examine product prototypes and to see the planned marketing strategy for the new product via the test market.

Finally, test markets may create ethical problems. Companies routinely report test-marketing results to the press, which allows them access to premarket publicity. But are negatives found in the test market always reported, or do we hear only the good news? Companies eager to get good publicity may select test-market cities that they feel will return favorable results. Perhaps the company already has a strong brand and market power in the market. Is this method of getting publicity ethical? There have been efforts to make reporting of test markets more candid.[31]

Summary

Research design refers to a set of advance decisions made to develop the master plan to be used in the conduct of the research project. There are three general research designs: exploratory, descriptive, and causal. The significance of studying research design is that, by matching the research objective with the appropriate research design, a host of research decisions may be predetermined. Therefore, a research design serves as a "blueprint" for researchers. Research designs are not carried out in a particular order; in fact, some projects may require only one form of research. But research is often an iterative process in which initial research indicates the need for additional studies, often of a different design.

As a rule, researchers are much more knowledgeable of the marketing research process than managers. This imbalance of knowledge, which is not unique to marketing research, may lead to serious ethical issues. Ethical codes and standards developed by professional organizations prohibit such practices as designing research that is much more complex and expensive than needed.

Selecting the appropriate research design depends, to a large extent, on the research objectives and existing information about the problem. If very little is known, exploratory research is appropriate. Exploratory research is unstructured, informal research undertaken to gain background information; it is helpful for more clearly defining the research problem. Exploratory research is used in a number of situations: to gain background information, to define terms, to clarify problems and hypotheses, and to establish research priorities. Reviewing existing literature, surveying individuals knowledgeable in the area to be investigated, relying on former similar case situations, or conducting focus groups are methods of conducting exploratory research. Exploratory research should almost always be used because it is fast and inexpensive; sometimes it resolves the research objective or is helpful in carrying out descriptive or causal research.

If concepts, terms, and so on are already known and the research objective is to describe and measure phenomena, then descriptive research is appropriate. Descriptive research measures marketing phenomena and answers the questions of who, what, where, when, and how. Descriptive studies may be conducted at one point in time (cross-sectional), or several measurements may be made on the same sample at different points in time (longitudinal). Longitudinal studies are often conducted using panels. Panels represent sample units who have agreed to answer questions at periodic intervals. Continuous panels are longitudinal studies in which sample units are asked the same questions repeatedly. Brand-switching tables may be prepared based on data from continuous panels. Market-tracking studies may be conducted using data from continuous panels.

The second type of panel used in longitudinal research is the discontinuous panel. Discontinuous panels, sometimes called omnibus panels, are those in which the sample units are asked different questions. The main advantage of the discontinuous panel is that research firms have a large sample of persons who are willing to answer whatever questions they are asked.

Causal relationships provide relationships such as "If *x*, then *y*." Causal relationships may be discovered only through special studies called experiments. Experiments allow us to determine the effects of a variable, known as an independent variable, on another variable, known as a dependent variable. Experimental designs are necessary to ensure that the effect we observe in our dependent variable is due to our independent variable and not to other variables known as extraneous variables. The validity of experiments may be assessed by internal validity and external validity.

Laboratory experiments are particularly useful for achieving internal validity, whereas field experiments are better suited for achieving external validity. Test marketing is a form of field experimentation. Various types of test markets exist (standard, controlled, electronic, and simulated).

Although test markets garner much useful information, they are expensive and not infallible. Test-market cities are selected on the basis of their representativeness, isolation, and the degree to which market variables such as distribution and promotion may be controlled.

Key Terms

Research design (p. 70)
Exploratory research (p. 73)
Secondary data analysis (p. 74)
Experience surveys (p. 74)
Key-Informant Technique (p. 74)
Lead-user survey (p. 74)
Case analysis (p. 75)
Focus groups (p. 75)
Descriptive research (p. 75)
Cross-sectional studies (p. 75)
Sample surveys (p. 76)
Longitudinal studies (p. 77)
Panels (p. 77)
Continuous panels (p. 77)
Discontinuous panels (p. 77)
Omnibus panels (p. 77)

Brand-switching studies (p. 78)
Market-tracking studies (p. 79)
Causality (p. 79)
Experiment (p. 79)
Independent variables (p. 79)
Dependent variables (p. 79)
Extraneous variables (p. 80)
Experimental design (p. 80)
Pretest (p. 82)
Posttest (p. 82)
"True" experimental design (p. 82)
Quasi-experimental designs (p. 82)
Control group (p. 82)
Experimental group (p. 82)
Before-after with control group (p. 82)

Internal validity (p. 83)
External validity (p. 84)
Laboratory experiments (p. 84)
Field experiments (p. 84)
Test marketing (p. 85)
Standard test market (p. 85)
Controlled test markets (p. 86)
Electronic test markets (p. 86)
Simulated test markets (STMs) (p. 87)
Representativeness (p. 87)
Degree of isolation (p. 87)
Ability to control distribution and promotion (p. 87)

Review Questions/Applications

1. What is research design?
2. Explain why it is significant for marketing researchers to be knowledgeable of research design.
3. Discuss how research design can lead to ethically sensitive situations.
4. Provide an example of exploratory research.
5. In which type of research design would the key-informant technique be used?
6. What is the difference between longitudinal studies and cross-sectional studies?
7. In what situation would a continuous panel be more suitable than a discontinuous panel? In what situation would a discontinuous panel be more suitable than a continuous panel?
8. What type of panel is an omnibus panel?
9. Explain why studies of the "if–then" variety are considered to be causal studies.
10. Define each of the following types of variables and give an example of each in an experiment designed to determine the effects of an advertising campaign: independent, dependent, extraneous, control group, and experimental group.
11. Explain the two types of validity in experimentation and also explain why different types of experiments are better suited for addressing one type of validity versus another.

12. Distinguish among the various types of test marketing.
13. Think of a past job you have held. List three areas in which you, or some other person in the organization, could have benefited from having information generated by research. What would be the most appropriate research design for each of the three areas of research you have listed?
14. You are no doubt familiar with Internet search engine companies that find online sources pertaining to words, phrases, or questions entered by users. Can you identify research problems likely to be addressed by a search engine company such as Google? What type of research design would you recommend for these problems?
15. Design an experiment. Select an independent variable and a dependent variable. What are some possible extraneous variables that may cause problems? Explain how you would control for the effects these variables may have on your dependent variable. Is your experiment a valid one?
16. The Maximum Company has invented an extra-strength, instant coffee brand to be called "Max-Gaff" and positioned to be stronger tasting than any competing brands. Design a taste-test experiment that compares Max-Gaff to the two leading instant coffee brands to determine which brand consumers consider to taste the strongest. Identify and diagram your experiment. Indicate how the

experiment is to be conducted, and assess the internal and external validity of your experiment.

17. Coca-Cola® markets PowerAde® as a sports drink that competes with Gatorade®. Competition for sports drinks is fierce where they are sold in the coolers of convenience stores. Coca-Cola is thinking about using a special holder that fits in a standard convenience-store cooler but moves PowerAde to eye level and makes it more conspicuous than Gatorade. Design an experiment that determines whether the special holder increases the sales of PowerAde in convenience stores. Identify and diagram your experiment. Indicate how the experiment is to be conducted and assess the internal and external validity of your experiment.

18. SplitScreen is a marketing research company that tests television advertisements. SplitScreen has an agreement with a cable television company in a medium-sized city in Iowa. The cable company can send up to four different television ads simultaneously to different households. SplitScreen also has agreements with the three of the largest grocery store chains, which will provide scanner data to SplitScreen. About 25% of the residents have SplitScreen scan cards that are scanned when items are bought at the grocery store and that allow SplitScreen to identify who bought which grocery products. For allowing SplitScreen access to their television hookups and their grocery-purchase information, residents receive bonus points that can be used to buy products in a special points catalog. Identify and diagram the true experimental design possible using the SplitScreen system. Assess the internal and external validity of SplitScreen's system.

CASE 4.1

Memos from a Researcher[32]

John Daniel, a researcher at Georgia Metro Research, made the following notes about several of his clients to you, a newly hired trainee who had just graduated from college:

Client A is a consumer packaged goods manufacturer with a well-established brand name. The client has focused on manufacturing and distribution for years while the marketing program has been set on "auto pilot." All had worked fine, though there was a hint of emerging problems when, in the preceding year, market share had fallen slightly. Now, our client has just reviewed the current market share report and notices that over the previous 12 months, their share has gradually eroded 15%. When market share falls, clients are eager to learn why and to take corrective action. In these situations we know immediately the problem is that we don't know what the problem is. There are many possible causes for this slippage. We need to determine the research design needed.

Second, Client B is a manufacturer of several baked goods products sold in grocery stores throughout the country. Marketing is divided into five regional divisions in the United States. The five divisions have had total autonomy over their advertising though all of them have used TV advertising almost exclusively. Each division has tried several different TV ad campaigns; some were thought to be successful and others not as successful, but no one had ever formally evaluated the ad expenditures. A new Marketing VP now wants to evaluate the advertising. She's interested in knowing not only the sales of the client's products sold during the different campaigns but also what happened to sales of competitors' brands. In this case, the client needs us to *describe* sales by SKU in the client's product category for each TV market and for each time period associated with each ad campaign. What research design do you recommend?

Finally, Client C is in a very competitive category with equal market share of the top three brands. Our client is convinced that they have changed every marketing mix variable possible except for package design. Since the three competitive brands are typically displayed side-by-side, they want us to determine what factors of package design (e.g., size, shape, color, texture) cause an increase in awareness, preference for, and intention to buy the brand. What do you recommend for the appropriate research design?

1. Describe what research design you would recommend for each client.
2. For each research design you selected for the three clients, discuss *why* you believe your choice of design is the correct choice.

CASE 4.2 INTEGRATED CASE

Global Motors

Nick Thomas has been considering some of the issues identified in Case 3.2. He is considering different directions to take. First, he is a little concerned that most of the information on which Global Motors has based its decisions thus far is derived from either industry reports or opinions of company managers, designers, and engineers. Granted, these persons are quite knowledgeable of the automobile industry. But Nick is concerned that neither he nor the company have input from consumers.

First, Nick wants some consumer feedback on the different models proposed. He would like to have some consumer input on what prospective customers think of the proposed models. Will they think they are too radically different or embrace them as the future in autos? Will they think the fuel-efficient cars are too light and less safe? Will they miss the luxury options? Nick wants a little input from consumers to give him confidence the company is on the right track with these proposed models.

Second, assuming consumers believe the proposed models are appropriate, Nick wants to know the level of desirability among the U.S. car-buying public for each of the models. For the model or models Global Motors may produce, how can he determine which types of consumers will want them? For example, will higher, middle, or lower income consumers have different model preferences? Will gender, age, or education explain differences in preferences for the different models? With access to this information, Nick knows he can develop a good description of the target market for the proposed models, and this data will be invaluable in helping Global Motors market the model(s) efficiently. Also, Nick wants to know the media preferences of consumers. If he can determine that consumers who desire a particular model have preferences for types of TV programs, radio stations, magazines, or newspaper sections, this information will facilitate more efficient marketing.

Finally, Nick is interested in a study that will help determine how much consumers will be willing to pay for each 5 mpg increase in fuel economy. He knows consumers will be willing to pay more for more fuel-efficient vehicles, but he hopes to be able to quantify the connection between lower fuel consumption and model price.

1. To deal with the first set of issues—determining how consumers feel about the proposed models—what research design would you suggest? Why?
2. Consider the second set of issues in the case. Nick needs to know the level of desirability among U.S. car buyers for each of the proposed models. He also needs to know the demographic characteristics of car buyers as well as their media habits. What research design would you suggest? Why?
3. The final issue concerns determining how much more consumers will be willing to pay for each 5 mpg incremental increase in fuel economy Global Motors can offer. What research design would you suggest? Why?

Secondary Data and Packaged Information

The Evolution of Secondary Data

Shari Johnson, Business Librarian, University of West Florida. Ms. Johnson has a BS from the University of Delaware and holds the MLIS from the University of Texas, Austin.

Text and photo: By permission.

Marketing researchers make heavy use of secondary data or information. The cost and effort of performing primary research through surveys and other means make secondary data even more valuable. Population and income alone are two of the key ingredients used in determining the size of a market. Dozens of other types of information are available in secondary data sources, which is why students of marketing research need to devote special attention to secondary data.

Secondary data are widely available today, much of it retrievable over the Internet. In the United States we have been blessed for many decades with good secondary data. Fortunately, the Founding Fathers of the United States stipulated in the Constitution that a census be taken every ten years to determine appropriate representation in Congress, votes in the Electoral College, and funding of government programs. The United Kingdom and most developed countries have good secondary data. Yet, in many parts of the world, including China and developing countries in Asia and Africa, secondary data are lacking or, if available, are unreliable or dated.

The decennial census in the United States has been the "grandfather" of secondary data since it began in 1790. The creation of the U.S. Census was a key event in the evolution of secondary data for marketing researchers. Yet, census data alone was not enough for business use as business evolved and became more complex. Also, as business cycles evolved more quickly, waiting ten years for new census data was not practical. As a result, private firms filled the gap and provided information not available through the Census Bureau. For example, the *Sales & Marketing Management's Survey of Buying Power* (SBP) provided marketing managers with updated data on metropolitan statistical areas (MSAs) and every county in the United States each year. Plus value was added by putting data together in a way that represented the buying power of a geographical market area in terms of a four-digit index number known as the *Buying Power Index*. This data was useful to managers who were trying to determine new markets, create sales territories, select dealers, or allocate promotional dollars to the different markets. Many other private firms, basing their services on the census every ten years, offered value-added products. This same cycle has occurred in the area of *geodemography*. The U.S. government created the Topologically Integrated Geographic Encoding and Referencing (TIGER) database in the early 1980s, and many private firms have used this technology to create services providing usable secondary data to managers. Examples include Esri's service Tapestry™ Segmentation, Nielsen's Claritas™ segmentation service, and even the GPS in your car!

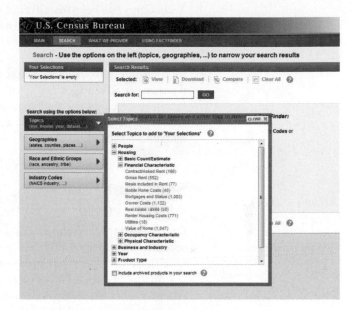

Photo: U.S. Census Bureau, Public Information Office

We are now going through another major event change in the area of secondary data. The U.S. government took a major leap forward beginning in 1996 by creating the American Community Survey (ACS). The ACS has a major advantage over the census in that it is updated annually, a key weakness of census data. It has taken several years, but the ACS is now in full swing, ready for marketing managers, marketing researchers, and you to use. It is free and is available 24/7. Already we have seen several of the private information providers disappear (the most notable is the SBP). But, if the cycle continues, we will continue to see gaps in the ACS filled by private firms. For example, buying power trends are now tracked by patterns in credit card purchases and sold by private firms to market researchers. I would predict secondary data will play a larger role in tomorrow's marketing research industry.

Photo: Chad McDermott/Fotolia

W̶e open this chapter with Ms. Johnson's comments not only because she is an expert in secondary data but also because she worked in marketing research for a large financial services firm. She understands how marketing researchers can use secondary information. Her comments point out that secondary data is an evolving field. Technology has been the driver of advances in the last couple decades. This chapter explores changes in the collection and provision of secondary data, but you will want to keep up with continued shifts in this area, as you will likely be using these information sources in your career. Fortunately, you live in a world where secondary data are readily available and easily accessed. This chapter explores how secondary data are used,[1] how we classify different types, what advantages and disadvantages these information sources offer, and where marketing researchers can find significant sources of secondary data. In addition, we introduce another type of information we call *packaged information* and examine its applications in marketing research.

Secondary Data

PRIMARY VERSUS SECONDARY DATA

Data needed for marketing management decisions can be grouped into two types: primary and secondary. **Primary data** refers to information that is developed or gathered by the researcher specifically for the research project at hand.

In this chapter we focus on secondary data and a form of it we call *packaged information*. After this chapter, much of the remainder of this text is devoted to teaching you how to collect and analyze primary data.

Secondary data have previously been gathered by someone other than the researcher and/or for some other purpose than the research project at hand.

As commercial firms, government agencies, or community service organizations record transactions and business activities, they are creating a written record of these activities in the form of secondary data. When consumers fill out warranty cards or register their boats, automobiles, or software programs, this information is stored in the form of secondary data. It is available for someone else's *secondary* use. The Internet provides an incredible stock of free secondary data, and this online data access will likely continue to grow and become more and more important.

USES OF SECONDARY DATA

There are so many uses of secondary data that it is rare for a marketing research project to be conducted without including some of this information. Some projects may be based exclusively on secondary data. The applications of secondary data range from predicting broad changes in a culture's "way of life" to specific applications, such as selecting a street address location for a new car wash. Decision Analyst, Inc., a marketing research firm, has a Web site entirely devoted to secondary data. Suggested applications include economic-trend forecasting, corporate intelligence, international data, public opinion, and historical data, among others. Marketers are interested in knowing secondary data in terms of demographic data to help them forecast the size of the market in a newly proposed market territory. A researcher may use secondary data to determine the population and growth rate in almost any geographical area. Government agencies are interested in knowing secondary data to guide public policy decisions. The Department of Education needs to know how many five-year-olds will enter the public school system each year. Health care planners need to know how many senior citizens will be eligible for Medicare during the next decade. Sometimes secondary data can be used to evaluate market performance. For example, since gasoline and fuel taxes collected per gallon are available in public records, petroleum marketers can easily determine the volume

---

Primary data refers to information that is developed or gathered by the researcher specifically for the research project at hand.

Secondary data have previously been gathered by someone other than the researcher and/or for some other purpose than the research project at hand.

The applications of secondary data range from predicting broad changes in a culture's "way of life" to specific applications, such as selecting a street address location for a new car wash.

Decision Analyst, Inc., a marketing research firm, has a website (www.secondary.com) devoted to secondary data. Suggested applications include economic-trend forecasting, corporate intelligence, international data, public opinion, and historical data.

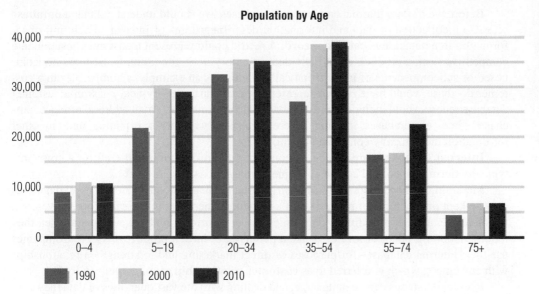

Population by Age

FIGURE 5.1
Census Data May Be Used to Assess Changes in Age Distributions for a Market

Source: A Summary of the 2010 Census: Selected Population, Demographic and Housing Characteristics (2011, June). Hayward, CA: City of Hayward.

of fuels consumed in a county, thus making market share calculations easy and reliable. Articles are written on virtually every topic, and this storehouse of secondary data is available to marketers who want to understand a topic more thoroughly even though they themselves may not have firsthand experience. A wealth of secondary data is available concerning the lifestyles and purchasing habits of demographic groups. Since the people in these demographic groups tend to make similar purchases and have similar attitudes, they have been scrutinized by marketers. The most significant of these demographic groups for decades has been the baby-boomer population, defined as those born between 1946 and 1964.[2] As boomers enter middle- and senior-age status, other demographic groups, such as the Gen Xers (generally defined as people born between 1965 and 1979) and Gen Yers (with birth dates generally between 1977 and 1994), are also studied by marketers.[3] Tootelian and Varshney provided research on "grandparents." This demographic group represents one-fourth of the U.S. population and spends about $55 billion a year on their grandchildren, which represents a growing market.[4] Secondary data may be used to assess how a geographical area is changing. Figure 5.1 shows the number of inhabitants of Hayward, California, and population changes from the 1990 census to the 2010 census. Notice the large increase in the age 35–54 population since 1990.

CLASSIFICATION OF SECONDARY DATA

Internal Secondary Data Secondary data may be broadly classified as either internal or external. **Internal secondary data** are data that have been collected *within* the firm.

Such data include sales records, purchase requisitions, and invoices. Obviously, a good marketing researcher always determines what internal information is already available. You may recall from Chapter 1 that we referred to internal data analysis as being part of the internal reports system of a firm's marketing information system (MIS). Today a major source of internal data is databases that contain information on customers, sales, suppliers, and any other facet of business a firm may wish to track. Kotler and Keller define **database marketing** as the process of building, maintaining, and using customer (*internal*) databases and other (*internal*) databases (products, suppliers, and resellers) to contact, transact, and build customer relationships.[5]

Internal secondary data are data that have been collected *within* the firm.

Database marketing is the process of building, maintaining, and using customer (*internal*) databases and other (*internal*) databases (products, suppliers, and resellers) to contact, transact, and build customer relationships.

Before we discuss internal and external databases, we should understand that a **database** refers to a collection of data and information describing items of interest.[6] Each unit of information in a database is called a **record**. A record could represent a customer, a supplier, a competitive firm, a product, or an individual inventory item, for example. Records are composed of subcomponents of information called **fields**. As an example, a company with a customer database would have *records* representing each customer. Typical *fields* in a customer database record would include name, address, telephone number, email address, products purchased, dates of purchases, locations where purchased, warranty information, and any other information the company considered useful.

Internal databases are databases consisting of information gathered by a company, typically during the normal course of business transactions.

Marketing managers normally develop internal databases about customers, but databases may be kept on any topic of interest, such as products, members of the sales force, inventory, maintenance, and supplier firms. Companies gather information about customers when they inquire about a product or service, make a purchase, or have a product serviced. Companies use their internal databases for purposes of direct marketing and to strengthen relationships with customers, which is referred to as **customer relationship management (CRM)**.[7]

Internal databases can be quite large, and dealing with the vast quantities of data they contain can be a problem. **Data mining** is the name for software that helps managers make sense out of seemingly senseless masses of information contained in databases.[8] **Micromarketing** refers to using a differentiated marketing mix for specific customer segments, sometimes fine-tuned for the individual shopper.[9] Databases and data mining make micromarketing possible. An example is the pop-up ads you may see online after searching for a product.

However, even simple databases in small businesses can be invaluable. Kotler and Keller describe five ways that companies use their databases:

1. To *identify prospects*, such as sorting through replies to company ads to identify customers who can be targeted with more information
2. To decide *which customers should receive a particular offer*, such as sending a cross-selling suggestion two weeks after a sale
3. To *deepen customer loyalty* by remembering customer preferences and sending appropriately customized materials reflecting those preferences
4. To *reactivate customer purchases*, such as automatically sending out a birthday card
5. To avoid serious customer mistakes, such as charging a fee to one of the firm's largest customers[10]

Databases can tell managers which products are selling, report inventory levels, and profile customers by SKU. Coupled with geodemographic information systems (GIS), databases can provide maps indicating ZIP codes in which the most profitable and least profitable customers reside. Internal databases, built with information collected during the normal course of business, can provide invaluable insights for managers.

What companies do with information collected for their internal databases can present ethical problems. Should your credit card company share the information on what types of goods and services you bought with anyone who wants to buy that information? Should your Internet service provider be able to store information on which Internet sites you visit? As more consumers have grown aware of these privacy issues, more companies have adopted privacy policies.[11] Marketing Research Insight 5.1 illustrates how collecting data on consumers can raise ethical concerns.

External Secondary Data

Published Sources **External secondary data** are data obtained from *outside* the firm. We classify external data into three sources: (1) *published*, (2) *syndicated services data*, and (3) *databases*.

Sidebar notes:

Internal databases consist of information gathered by a company, typically during the normal course of business transactions.

Companies use their internal databases for customer relationship management (CRM).

Data mining software helps managers make sense out of seemingly senseless masses of information contained in databases.

Micromarketing employs a differentiated marketing mix for specific customer segments, sometimes fine-tuned for the individual shopper.

What companies do with information collected for their internal databases can present ethical problems.

Marketing Research on YouTube™ Want to see an example of consumer information taken "too far"? Go to **www.youtube.com** and enter "ordering pizza in the future." You may get a laugh out of it, but you will also see what disturbs those who are interested in protecting consumer privacy!

MARKETING RESEARCH INSIGHT 5.1   *Ethical Consideration*

Target Targets Pregnant Female Customers

Photo: © bociek666/Fotolia

Target®, like most retailers, knows that most consumers do not buy everything they need at one store. Rather, they buy groceries at the grocery store and toys at the toy store, and they visit Target when they need items they associate with Target, such as cleaning supplies or new socks. Understandably, one of the successful chain's goals is convincing customers that the only store they need is Target. But because consumers' shopping habits are so ingrained, it's difficult to change them.

There are certain critical points in our lives when old routines suddenly diminish and we are likely to adopt new buying habits. Target's marketing staff believed that one of those moments is right around the birth of a child, when parents are exhausted and overwhelmed and their shopping patterns and brand loyalties are up for grabs. Because birth records are usually public, the moment a couple have a new baby, they are almost instantaneously bombarded with offers, incentives, and advertisements from all sorts of companies. To get a jump on that competition, Target looked for a way to reach couples early—before other retailers know a baby is on the way. Marketers wanted to send specifically designed ads to women as early as their second trimester, which is when most pregnant women begin buying prenatal vitamins and maternity clothing. The goal was to progress from these items to baby supplies— from formula and diapers to clothing, toys, and nursery furnishings—and then to other household items so that Target would eventually become the family's one-stop shopping destination. How could the retailer achieve this aim?

Target collects data on every person who shops at its stores, assigning a unique code known as the guest ID number. If a shopper uses a credit card or coupon, fills out a survey, mails in a refund form, calls the customer help line, or opens an email, Target links that interaction to the guest ID. The company also collects demographic information, such as age, marital status, number of kids, place of residence, and estimated salary, and it can buy additional data. To make sense of all this information, Target, like many firms, relies on marketing research and predictive analysis software. One aim of these analyses is to connect with consumers during major life events, like graduating from college or moving to a new city, when their shopping habits became flexible. Among these life events, none are more significant than having a baby. At that moment new parents' habits are more flexible than almost any time in their adult lives.

How does Target identify pregnant customers before all the other retailers? A researcher used Target's baby registry to identify customers who used it and then backtracked to see what products they had purchased early in their pregnancy. He identified unique patterns: Pregnant women bought a lot of unscented lotions in their second trimester, and in the first 20 weeks, they bought supplements such as calcium, magnesium, and zinc. As they got close to delivery, pregnant women bought soap, cotton balls, hand sanitizers, and washcloths. All in all, the researcher identified 25 products that allowed him to calculate a "Pregnancy Prediction Score." Target applies this scoring system to all customers; those who score high enough are assumed to be pregnant and receive targeted promotions on products Target predicts they will need.

Like many marketers, Target is honing its ability to micromarket—targeting each consumer with promotional materials designed for that individual. Though there were some glitches that Target continues to improve, its sales of mom and baby products have increased. Do you think these practices are ethical?

Source: Information was adapted from Charles Duhigg, "How Companies Learn Your Secrets," *New York Times*, February 16, 2012.

Published sources are those sources of information that are prepared for public distribution and are normally found in libraries or through a variety of other entities, such as trade associations, professional organizations, and companies. Many published sources are now being made available via the Internet. Published sources of secondary information come from governments, nonprofit organizations such as chambers of commerce, colleges and universities, trade and professional associations, and for-profit entities (e.g., Pearson Prentice Hall,

External secondary data are data obtained from three main sources outside the firm: (1) published, (2) syndicated services data, and (3) databases.

Examples of external secondary data include the white papers marketing research firms post on their websites.

McGraw-Hill, and research firms). Many research firms publish secondary information in the form of books, newsletters, white papers, special reports, magazines, or journals. Marketing research firms may post white papers on many topics on their websites. For example, see www.burke.com and go to "Literature Library."

Syndicated services data are provided by firms that collect data in a standard format and make them available to subscribing firms.

Syndicated Services Data Firms that collect data may make it available in a standard format subscribing firms as **syndicated services data**. Such data are typically highly specialized and are not available in libraries for the general public.

External databases are databases supplied by organizations outside the firm. Online information databases are sources of secondary data searchable by search engines online.

External Databases **External databases** are databases supplied by organizations outside the firm. They may be used as sources for secondary data. **Online information databases** are sources of secondary data searchable by search engines online.

Some online databases are available free of charge and are supplied as a service by a host organization. However, many online information databases are available from commercial sources that provide subscribers password (or IP address identification) access for a fee. Different databases are often packaged together by vendors that produce the software that retrieves the information. Sometimes called *aggregators* or *data banks*, these services or vendors may offer a wide variety of indexes, directories, and statistical and full-text files all searched by the same search logic. Such services include IBISWorld, Factiva, Ebsco, and ProQuest. Business databases make up a significant proportion of these data banks.

ADVANTAGES OF SECONDARY DATA

The five advantages of secondary data are that secondary data can be obtained quickly and inexpensively, are usually available, enhance primary data collection, and can sometimes achieve the research objective.

The advantages of secondary data are, for the most part, readily apparent. There are five main advantages of using secondary data: (1) It can be obtained quickly; (2) compared to collecting primary data, secondary data are inexpensive; (3) for almost any application, some secondary data are readily available; (4) secondary data may enhance primary data by providing a current look at issues, trends, yardsticks of performance, and so on that may affect what primary data should be collected; and (5) secondary data may be all that is needed to achieve the research objective. For example, a supermarket chain marketing manager wants to allocate TV ad dollars to the 12 markets in which the chain owns supermarkets. A quick review of secondary data shows that retail sales on food is available by TV market area. Allocating the TV budget based on the percentage of food sales in a given market would be an excellent way to solve the manager's problem and satisfy the research objective.

DISADVANTAGES OF SECONDARY DATA

Five of the problems associated with secondary data include incompatible reporting units, mismatch of the units of measurement, differing definitions used to classify the data, timeliness of the secondary data, and lack of information needed to assess data credibility.

Although the advantages of secondary data almost always justify a search of this information, there are caveats associated with secondary data. Five of the problems associated with secondary data include incompatible reporting units, mismatch of the units of measurement, differing definitions used to classify the data, timeliness of the secondary data, and lack of information needed to assess the credibility of the data reported. These problems exist because secondary data have not been collected specifically to address the problem at hand but have been collected for some other purpose.

These problems exist because secondary data have not been collected specifically to address the problem at hand but have been collected for some other purpose.

Incompatible Reporting Units Secondary data are provided in reporting units, such as county, city, metro area, state, region, ZIP code, or core-based statistical areas. **Core-based statistical areas (CBSAs)** are geographic reporting units used by the Census Bureau. CBSAs are made up of two smaller units, metropolitan and micropolitan statistical areas (SAs). **Metropolitan SAs** are defined by the Office of Management and Budget (OMB) as having at least one urbanized area of 50,000 or more population, plus adjacent territory that has a high degree of social and economic integration with the core as measured by commuting ties. **Micropolitan SAs** are a new set of statistical areas that have at least one urban cluster of at least 10,000 but less than 50,000 population, plus adjacent territory that has a high degree of social and economic integration with the core MSA as measured by commuting ties. A researcher's use of secondary data often depends on whether the reporting unit matches the researcher's need. For example, a researcher wishing to evaluate market areas for the purpose of consideration for expansion may be pleased with data reported at the county level. A great deal of secondary data is available at the county level. But what if another marketer wishes to evaluate a two-mile area around a street address that is proposed as a site location for a retail store? County data would hardly be adequate. Another marketer wishes to know the demographic makeup of each ZIP code in a major city in order to determine which ZIP codes to target for a direct mail campaign. Again, county data would be inappropriate. While inappropriate reporting units are often problems in using secondary data, more and more data are available today in multiple reporting units. Data at the ZIP + 4 level are becoming more widely available. **Geodemographics** is the term used to describe the classification of arbitrary, usually small, geographic areas in terms of the characteristics of their inhabitants. Aided by computer programs called *geodemographic information systems* (GIS), geodemographers can access huge databases and construct profiles of consumers residing in geographic areas determined by the geodemographer. Instead of being confined to fixed geographic reporting units such as a city, county, or state, geodemographers can produce this information for geographic areas thought to be relevant for a given marketing application (such as our previous two-mile-radius example).

Measurement Units Do Not Match Sometimes secondary data are reported in measurement units that do not match the measurement unit the researcher needs. Available studies of income may measure income in several ways: total income, income after taxes, household income, and per-capita income. Consider a research project that seeks to categorize businesses by size in terms of square footage but data are available based only on sales volume, number of employees, and annual profits.

Class Definitions Are Not Usable The class definitions of the reported data may not be usable to a researcher. Secondary data are often reported by breaking a variable into different classes and reporting the frequency of occurrence in each class. For example, suppose a source of secondary data reports the variable of household income in three classes. The first class reports the percentage of households with income from $20,000 to $34,999, and the third class reports the percentage of households with incomes of $50,000 and over. For most studies, these classifications are applicable. However, imagine you are a manufacturer of high-end plumbing fixtures looking to expand the number of distributorships. You have learned that your dealers are most successful in geographical areas with average household incomes above $80,000. You need another source of information as the available source of secondary data only reports household incomes of $50,000 and over. What would a researcher do in this situation? Typically, if you keep looking, you can find what you need. There may be other sources of secondary data in other categories.

Data Are Outdated Sometimes a marketing researcher will find information reported with the desired unit of measurement and the proper classifications; however, the data may be out of date and no longer reliable. Some secondary data are published only once. However, even for secondary data published at regular intervals, the time that passed since the last publication can be a problem when applying the data to a current problem. The researcher must assess the usefulness of the available data.

EVALUATING SECONDARY DATA

The advice that you can't believe everything you read holds true for marketing research. You must carefully assess the quality and validity of secondary data in deciding whether to use it as a basis for making decisions. Caution is especially in order with Internet sources

To determine the reliability of secondary information, marketing researchers must evaluate it.

because few quality standards are applied to most Internet sites. To determine the reliability of secondary information, marketing researchers must evaluate it. The following paragraphs offer five questions that are useful in evaluating secondary data.

What Was the Purpose of the Study? Studies are conducted for a purpose, and sometimes readers do not know the true purpose. Some studies are conducted to "prove" some position or to advance the special interest of those conducting the study. In the 1980s environmentalists became concerned over the growing mountains of disposable plastic diapers that had all but replaced cloth diapers. More than a dozen state legislatures were considering various bans, taxes, and even warning labels on disposable diapers. Then "research studies" were produced whose "purpose" was to evaluate the environmental effects of disposable versus cloth diapers. The "new" research purported to "prove" that cloth diapers, by adding detergent by-products to the water table, were more harmful to the environment than the ever-lasting plastic disposables. Soon after several of these studies were made available to legislators, the movement against disposables was dead. However, further scrutiny might have called these findings into question. Procter & Gamble, which owned the lion's share of the market for disposable diapers, commissioned the consulting firm of Arthur D. Little, Inc., to conduct one of the studies. Another study that favored disposables was conducted by Franklin Associates, whose research showed disposables were not any more harmful than cloth diapers. But who sponsored this study? The American Paper Institute, an organization with major interests in disposable diapers.

Not all "scientific" studies touted in this debate supported the use of disposable diapers. A 1988 study characterized disposable diapers as "garbage" contributing to massive buildups of waste that was all but impervious to deterioration. Who sponsored this study? The cloth diaper industry![12]

Users of secondary data should try to understand the true purpose of a study they are using as secondary data.

Another example of the need to consider the source of data involves a "study" reported by the news media citing the terrible condition of roads and bridges in the United States. Who sponsored the study? An organization representing road and bridge construction companies. It may well be that the study was objective and accurate. However, users of secondary information should be well aware of the *true purpose* of the study and evaluate the information accordingly.

Not all research studies that are available sources of secondary data are conducted in an objective manner. You must ask who conducted the study.

Who Collected the Information? Even when you are convinced that there is no bias in the purpose of the study, you should question the competence of the organization that collected the information. Organizations differ in terms of the resources they command and their quality control. How can you evaluate the competency of the organization that collected the data? First, ask others who have more experience in a given industry. Typically, credible organizations are well known in those industries for which they conduct studies. Second, examine the report itself. Competent firms almost always provide carefully written and detailed explanations of the procedures and methods used in collecting the information cited in the report. Third, contact previous clients of the firm. Have they been satisfied with the quality of the work performed by the organization? Be wary of using information just because it is available on the Internet. The "information superhighway" is a rich source of all sorts of information, but, as we have noted previously, the objectivity and reliability of all these data is not guaranteed. Always check for the original source of the information if it is available.

It may be crucial to know exactly what was measured in a report before using the results.

What Information Was Collected? Many studies are available on topics such as economic impact, market potential, and feasibility.

But what exactly was measured in these studies that constitute impact, potential, or feasibility? Studies may claim to provide information on a specific subject but, in fact, measure something quite different. Consider the example of two studies offering differing results on the number of businesses in each county as a basis for projecting sales for a B2B service. A key question in evaluating the differing data was how the number of businesses was measured. In one report, each existing business location counted as a business, resulting in a high count, as one business may have had a dozen distribution outlets. In another report, only the business and not its outlets was counted. This resulted in a low count of "number of businesses." Is this distinction important? It may or may not be, depending on how the study's user intends to use the information. B2B service providers would need to assess if their service could be sold to each individual distribution outlet or only to the parent company. The important point is that users should discover exactly what information was collected!

How Was the Information Obtained? You should be aware of the methods used to obtain information reported in secondary sources.

What was the sample? How large was the sample? What was the response rate? Was the information validated? As you will learn throughout this book, there are many alternative ways of collecting primary data, and each may have an impact on the information collected. Remember that, even though you are evaluating secondary data, this information was gathered as primary data by some organization. Therefore, the alternative ways of gathering the data had an impact on the nature and quality of the data. It is not always easy to find out how the secondary data were gathered. However, as noted previously, most reputable organizations that provide secondary data also provide information on their data collection methods.

How Consistent Is the Information with Other Information? In some cases, the same secondary data are reported by multiple, independent organizations, which provides an excellent way to evaluate secondary data sources. Ideally, if two or more independent organizations report the same data, you can have greater confidence in the validity and reliability of the data. Demographic data for metropolitan areas (MAs), counties, and most municipalities are widely available from more than one source. If you are evaluating a survey that is supposedly representative of a given geographic area, you may want to compare the characteristics of the sample of the survey with the demographic data available on the population. If you know, based on U.S. census data, that there are 45 percent males and 55 percent females in a city and a survey, which is supposed to be representative of that city, reports a sample of 46 percent males and 54 percent females, then you can be more confident in the survey data.

It is rare that two organizations will report exactly the same results. In assessing differing data, the magnitude of the differences is a good place to start. If all independent sources report very large differences of the same variable, then you may not have much confidence in any of the data. You should look carefully at what information was collected and how it was collected for each reporting source.

> Evaluate the method used to collect the primary data now available to you as secondary data. You will be much better at doing this when you finish this course.

> If two or more sources of secondary data differ, you should investigate why. Did they measure the same entity? Did they use different methods to collect their data?

KEY SOURCES OF SECONDARY DATA FOR MARKETERS

By now it should be clear that there are thousands of sources of secondary data that may be relevant to business decisions. Table 5.1 lists some of the major sources that are useful in marketing research. Many of these resources are available in print, but the trend has been to offer them online.

THE AMERICAN COMMUNITY SURVEY

The taking of a census of the U.S. population began in 1790. Prior to 1940, everyone had to answer all the questions the census used. In 1940, the long form—a longer questionnaire that goes out to only a sample of respondents—was introduced as a way to collect more data more rapidly and without increasing the burden of all respondents. By 2000, the long form went to one in six housing units. As a result, much of the census data are based on statistical sampling.[13] The 2010 Census departed from tradition and only collected data using the short form. This was done in an effort to get more accurate counts, and we now know that the 2010 Census was very accurate.[14] The short form asks only for name, sex, age,

TABLE 5.1 Secondary Information Sources for Marketing

I. Reference Guides

Encyclopedia of Business Information Sources

Detroit: Gale Group, Annual. For the researcher, this guide lists marketing associations, advertising agencies, research centers, agencies, and sources relating to various business topics. It is particularly useful for identifying information about specific industries.

II. Indexes

ABI/INFORM Global

Ann Arbor, MI: ProQuest, 1971–. Available online, this database indexes and abstracts major journals relating to a broad range of business topics. Electronic access to many full-text articles is also available. ABI/INFORM Global may be complemented by ABI/INFORM Archive, ABI/INFORM Dateline, and ABI/INFORM Trade & Industry and may be searched alone or in tandem with any or all of these databases at subscribing libraries.

Business Source Complete

Ipswich, MA: Ebsco, 1926–. Available online, this database provides abstracts and full text of thousands of scholarly journals and trade magazines and makes available SWOT analyses, marketing research reports, and country condition reports.

Business File ASAP

Detroit: Gale Group, 1980–. Available online, this index covers primarily business and popular journals and includes some full-text articles.

Wilson Business Full Text

Ipswich, MA: Ebsco, 1995–. Available online, this basic index is useful for indexing the major business journals.

III. Dictionaries and Encyclopedias

Dictionary of Marketing Terms

Hauppauge, NY: Barron's, 4th ed., 2008. Prepared by Jane Imber and Betsy Ann Toffler, this dictionary includes brief definitions of popular terms in marketing.

American Buyers: Demographics of Shopping

Detroit: Gale, 2010. Available online in Gale's Virtual Reference Library. *American Buyers* is based on unpublished data collected by the Bureau of Labor Statistics' Consumer Expenditure Survey, an ongoing, nationwide survey of household spending.

Brands and Their Companies

Detroit: Gale, 2012. Available online in Business and Company Resource Center and Gale Directory Library. Lists manufacturers and distributors from small to large corporations, from both public and private sectors, covering hundreds of thousands of consumer brands and companies.

Encyclopedia of Consumer Brands

Detroit: St. James Press, 2005. For consumable products, personal products, and durable goods, this source provides detailed descriptions of the history and major developments of major brand names.

IV. Directories

Bradford's Directory of Marketing Research Agencies and Management Consultants in the United States and the World

Middleberg, VA: Bradford's, Biennial. Indexed by type of service, this source gives scope of activity for each agency and lists names of officers.

Broadcasting and Cable Yearbook

New Providence, NJ: R. R. Bowker, Annual. A directory of U.S. and Canadian television and radio stations, advertising agencies, and other useful information.

Directories in Print

Detroit: Gale Research, Annual. Available online in Gale Directory Library. Provides detailed information on business and industrial directories, professional and scientific rosters, online directory of databases, and other lists. This source is particularly useful for identifying directories associated with specific industries or products.

Gale Directory of Publications and Broadcast Media

Detroit: Gale Research, Annual. Available online in Gale Directory Library. A geographic listing of U.S. and Canadian newspapers, magazines, and trade publications as well as broadcasting stations. Includes address, edition, frequency, circulation, and subscription and advertising rates.

TABLE 5.1 Secondary Information Sources for Marketing (continued)

V. Statistical Sources

Datapedia of the United States, 1790–2005

Lanham, MD: Bernan Press, 2001. Based on the *Historical Statistics of the United States from Colonial Times* and other statistical sources, this volume presents hundreds of tables reflecting historical and, in some cases, forecasting data on numerous demographic variables relating to the United States.

Editor and Publisher Market Guide

New York: Editor and Publisher, Annual. Provides market data for more than 1,500 U.S. and Canadian newspaper cities covering facts and figures about location, transaction, population, households, banks, autos, etc.

Market Share Reporter

Detroit: Gale Research, Annual. Available online in Gale Directory Library and Business and Company Resource Center (Gale). Provides market share data on products and service industries in the United States.

Standard Rate and Data Service

Des Plaines, IL: SRDS, Monthly. In the SRDS monthly publications (those for consumer magazine and agrimedia, newspapers, spot radio, and spot television), marketing statistics are included at the beginning of each state section.

---

date of birth, race, ethnicity, relationship, and housing tenure. Data from the long form is still needed but is now collected through the *American Community Survey*. For many years the census has been the backbone of secondary data in the United States. Marketers use the information in many ways, and marketing research firms have developed many products to aid in the use of census data. You can learn more about 2010 Census at the official website: http://2010.census.gov.

The **American Community Survey (ACS)** may represent the most significant change in the availability of secondary data to be used for marketing research purposes in several decades. The U.S. Census Bureau created the ACS in 1996 to collect economic, social, demographic, and housing information as part of the Decennial Census Program. The survey is designed to help update Decennial Census data by collecting information on a small percentage of the population in all counties, American Indian Areas, Alaska Native Areas, and Hawaiian Home Lands on a rotating basis using a sample. The main advantage is that the ACS will provide data annually instead of once every 10 years. Since these data will have the U.S. Census Bureau's "high marks" for reliable data *and* will be current, the ACS is likely to become a major secondary data resource for marketing researchers.

In addition to providing new data each year, the ACS will offer a measure of accuracy of the yearly estimates. To do this, the ACS relies on a sampling plan that involves surveying about 3 million Americans every year. Because a sample is used, data are reported with a margin of error, which is an estimate of the accuracy of the data. (You will learn about margin of error in Chapter 10.)

Learning How to Use the ACS The following pages introduce and explore the ACS and the **American Factfinder**, which is the tool used for searching data collected by the ACS. To begin this exploration, go to www.census.gov and hover on the *Data* link. You will see a menu that includes *American Factfinder*. There are several ways you can enter your search criteria, and you can

Learn more about the 2010 Census at the official website: http://2010.census.gov. Several interactive resources are available there.

The 2010 Census had one of the shortest forms in history. It was just 10 questions and took only about 10 minutes to complete. The 2010 census has been determined to very accurate.

Photo: U.S. Census Bureau, Public Information Office.

To see how important the American Community Survey is to businesses, go to **www.youtube.com** and enter: "Target and the American Community Survey."

The ACS provides current data about communities every year, rather than once every 10 years. Visit the ACS at www.census .gov.

access much more than the ACS in *American Factfinder*. For example, if you search under "industry codes," much of the information will be derived from the Economic Census or related databases, such as County Business Patterns. The Economic Census is conducted every five years. On the other hand, the ACS collects information about the population. Table 5.2 lists the general types of information available in the ACS. Look around the website and you will see "QuickFacts" that offer instant basic information about the population, business, and geography for the country and for each state.

Now, let's explore how to use the *American FactFinder* by searching for specific information. The basic search logic is that you select the type of information you need (e.g., per-capita income) and then select the geographical area for which you wish the information to be reported (e.g., nation, a state, or CBSA). As you enter these search criteria, the applicable tables will appear on the screen. Close your search window and open the top table. Be sure to review all tables returned on your search to find all applicable data.

TABLE 5.2 Subject Coverage in the American Community Survey

Social Characteristics	Economic Characteristics
Educational attainment	Income
Field of degree	Benefits
Grade in which enrolled	Food stamps benefit
Marital status and history	Employment status
Fertility	Period of military service
Grandparents as caregivers	Health insurance status
Veterans	Occupation
Disability status	Industry
Place of birth	Place of work
Citizenship status	Commuting to work
Year of entry	Means of transportation to work
Language spoken at home	Time leaving home to go to work
Ancestry and tribal affiliation	Travel time to work
	Work experience

Housing Characteristics	Demographic Characteristics
Tenure	Sex
Occupancy and structure	Age
Home owner and rental vacancy rate	Race
Housing value	Hispanic origin
Taxes and insurance	Nativity of parent
Utilities	Place of birth
Mortgage or monthly rent	Persons in household
Poverty status of households	Persons in family
Group quarters status: institutional or noninstitutional	
Vehicles available	
Kitchen and plumbing facilities	
Telephone service available	
Farm residence	

Let's consider the example of researching the feasibility of opening a home management service in which your company manages the care and maintenance of homes, yards, and automobiles. Based on past experience, you know the market for this type of service is the upscale consumer with a housing value of $500,000 and above. You want to know which MSAs have the greatest number of homes valued in the $500,000-plus category. According to Table 5.2, housing value is included in the ACS under housing characteristics. First, go the *American Factfinder*. Click on Topics, and you will see a menu that includes housing. Open it and search for "Value of home" (see Figure 5.2). When you click on this entry, notice that it appears in the upper left-hand corner under "Your Selections." Now select the geographic locations for which you wish home values to be reported. A "Select Geographies" dialog box appears. The drop-down menu offers a number of options. By selecting "Metro statistical area/micro," you will have access to all the MSAs or each one individually. Since you want to compare MSAs, select "all…" Once you select your geographical area, you can close the dialog box. Now your results appear as a list of tables. You will see the first few are identical except that some are based one, three, or five years of sample data. (As a rule, the more sampling that has been done, the smaller the margin of error will be in the estimates.) Open one of the tables and scroll down until you find "Value" (of home). You can scroll across the top to examine each MSA. The files are downloadable in comma delimited, Excel™, PDF™, or Rich Text formats. Now, with the data in Excel, you can combine the categories of housing values $500,000 or above and get a distribution of the households in the MSAs rank ordered. This is just a simple example of how useful this data can be for business decisions. We will take a look at one more example that is applicable to the integrated case featuring Global Motors in Marketing Research Insight 5.2.

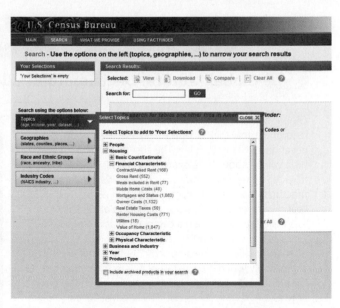

Photo: U.S. Census Bureau, Public Information Office.

FIGURE 5.2

Searching Topics Allows You to Select the Type of Information You Seek

FINAL WORDS ON SECONDARY INFORMATION

Knowing where to find information is a valued skill in the workplace. Take the opportunity you have in college to develop this skill. We have just scratched the surface in terms of introducing you to secondary data sources that will be beneficial to you in your career. Can secondary information help you get that career position? You bet! If you are not aware of what is going on in the industry and within the firm that interviews you, you will be behind others who have taken the time to gain that knowledge. They will most likely get the second interview. A good place to start learning about an industry is *IBISWorld Industry Reports*. Ask your librarian how you can gain access to IBISWorld.

What is Packaged Information?

We are now ready to turn to a special form of secondary data. **Packaged information** is a type of secondary data in which the data collected and/or the process of collecting

IBISWorld publishes a comprehensive collection of up-to-date Industry Research Reports covering more than 700 industries at the five-digit North American Industry Classification System (NAICS) codes. By offering concise, factual, and easy-to-use reports, IBISWorld provides information on key statistics, industry conditions, market characteristics and drivers, and historical and forecast analysis. By permission.

Photo: Copyright © 2012 by IBISWorld. Reprinted with permission.

MARKETING RESEARCH APPLICATION 5.2   *Practical Application*

Global Motors: Decision to Build a Totally Electric Car

Global Motors is considering adding a car model to its product mix that will be totally electric. Buyers will never have to buy gasoline. The cost to operate this vehicle will be about $.02 per mile versus about $.12 per mile for a gasoline vehicle. Global knows some manufacturers have an all-electric car, such as the Nissan Leaf. However, designers and managers at Global Motors believe they can gain a competitive advantage over these vehicles by building a car surface that is made of solar panels. Unlike other competitive vehicles that charge only when plugged into an electrical outlet, a car with a solar panel "skin" can absorb additional energy as long as the sun is out. This innovation is significant for another reason: If electric car owners charge their vehicles with electricity from a coal-powered electric plant (which powers the dominant percentage of U.S. power plants), the greenhouse gas emissions are still 0.8 lbs per mile driven. While this is better than the 1 lb per mile for gasoline-powered emissions, it means the gas-free vehicles are far from "emission free."[15] A solar panel skin would help reduce the gas emissions, and the Global car would not only have greater range but also come closer to a truly emission-free vehicle. However, the range of electric cars is still a major concern even with the ability of a constant charge using the solar panels. While the solar panels will help, they cannot keep up with the energy needed to propel the car even on a very sunny day. It is estimated that the range of this new car will be 125 miles, an improvement over other cars with a range of 60 to 100 miles. Before proceeding with design, Global managers want to know if this car will suffice for the bulk of commuter travel to and from work each day and still have sufficient range to run errands. If the majority of workers commute under 30 minutes each way to work, then the new car would have adequate range to get owners to and from work and run a few errands. Before going further with the concept of the new vehicle, secondary data may be assessed to answer the question, "What is the mean travel time, one way, for Americans to travel to work?" By retrieving ACS data via *American Factfinder*, managers quickly learn that the average time, in minutes, driven by Americans to work is 25.3. This is sufficient for them to continue with development plans for the new car.

After several months of concept testing using focus groups, a prototype vehicle is developed. The prototype meets all engineering and design expectations. Cost estimates for full-scale production put the cost of the car above a typical compact

Commute time is available in the ACS.

Photo: U.S. Census Bureau, Public Information Office

sedan, but the major selling point is that this pricetag would be offset by reduced operating costs. Now Global would like to test-market 20 of the vehicles in a metropolitan statistical area selected based, in part, on the percentage of the MSA's population who commute less than 30 minutes. You can conduct this research yourself by using the following steps to access ACS data to evaluate one MSA, Jacksonville, Florida, on this criterion.

1. Go to www.census.gov and hover on "Data."
2. From the menu, select *American Factfinder* and then "Topics."
3. In the dialog box that appears, select "People" and then "Employment." (You may want to experiment with different topics until you become acquainted with the data available to you).
4. From the next menu that appears, select the item "Commuting (journey to work)." It should appear as one of "Your Selections" in the upper left window.
5. To select the Jacksonville, Florida, MSA, go to "geographies" and select Metro/Micro statistical areas and scroll down until you find Jacksonville, Florida. Once you add this geography, close the dialog box and view the tables. Again, you will notice that you have several available to you.
6. Select the top table, and find information about the "mean travel time to work under 30 minutes." Does Jacksonville, Florida, qualify for the test market based on this criterion?

the data are prepackaged for all users. There are two broad classes of packaged information: syndicated data and packaged services.

Syndicated data are collected in a standard format and made available to all subscribers.

For example, Marketing Evaluations, Inc., offers several *Q Scores*® services. They measure the familiarity and appeal of performers in categories such as actors, actresses, authors, athletes, and sportscasters. This information is used by companies to help them choose the most appropriate spokesperson for their company and by producers for casting television shows and movies. **Performer Q**® is the service for ratings of approximately 1,800 performers. Data are available by demographic groups, and the company offers trends for many more personalities going back to 1964.[16] Betty White and Tom Hanks, for example, are performers who have high *Q Scores*. The company even maintains ratings of deceased performers called *Dead Q*.[17] Data for performers studied are the same and are bought as a package by subscribers who typically include advertisers, TV and movie production companies, licensing companies, and talent and public relations companies. Data are collected two times a year for all performers based on a sample of nearly 2,000 persons.

Another example of syndicated data is the Nielsen Ratings service, which measures TV audience size and viewer demographics for TV programs.[18] This information is packaged and made available to subscribers who typically include advertisers, ad agencies, TV production companies, networks, and cable companies.

On the other hand, the term **packaged services** refers to a prepackaged marketing research *process* that is used to generate information for a particular user. Note that, unlike syndicated data, the data from a packaged service will differ for each client. **Esri's Tapestry™ Segmentation** is such a service that uses a ready-made, prepackaged process to profile residential neighborhoods. This information is purchased by clients with the aim of better understanding who their customers are, where they are located, how to find them, and how to reach them. Whereas the data will differ for each client, Esri's process for generating the data is the same for all clients.[19] We discuss both of these types of information next.

Syndicated data are a form of external, secondary data that are supplied from a common database to subscribers for a service fee. Such information is typically detailed information that is valuable to firms in a given industry and is not available in libraries. Firms supplying syndicated data follow standard research formats that enable them to collect the same data over time. These firms provide specialized, routine information needed by a given industry in the form of ready-to-use, packaged data to subscribing firms. We mentioned the Nielsen Ratings of TV programming earlier. As another example, Arbitron supplies syndicated data on the number and types of listeners to the various radio stations in each radio market. This package of information helps advertising firms reach their target markets; it also helps radio stations define audience characteristics by providing an objective, independent measure of the size and characteristics of their audiences. With syndicated data, both the process of collecting and analyzing the data and the data themselves are not varied for the client.[20] Each subscriber to Arbitron buys the same "book" for each radio market. On the other hand, packaged services rarely provide clients with the same data. Rather, it is the *process* they are marketing. The application of that process will result in different data for each client. For example, a packaged service may measure customer satisfaction. Instead of a client firm trying to "reinvent the wheel" by developing its own process for measuring customer satisfaction, it may elect to use a packaged service to accomplish this aim. This is also true for several other marketing research services, such as test marketing, naming new brands, pricing a new product, or using mystery shoppers. Why would they want to use a packaged service instead of a service customized for their firm? We cover this in the next section.

The recognized industry standard for measuring consumer appeal of personalities, characters, licensed properties, programs and brands

Logo: By permission, Q Scores.

Packaged information is a type of secondary data in which the data collected and/or the process of collecting the data are prepackaged for all users. Two broad classes of packaged information are syndicated data and packaged services.

As opposed to customized services where a new research process is developed to meet a client's research objectives, packaged services use the same process for each buyer.

Syndicated data are collected in a standard format and made available to all subscribers.

Go to www.qscores .com and visit Marketing Evaluations, Inc., site. Learn about the different Q Score studies that are available.

Packaged services refer to a prepackaged marketing research *process* that is used to generate information for a particular user.

Esri's Tapestry Segmentation is a packaged service that uses a process to profile residential neighborhoods. This information is purchased by clients desiring to better understand who their customers are, where they are located, how to find them, and how to reach them.

With syndicated data, the data and the process used to generate the data are not varied for the client. With packaged services, the process of collecting data is the same across all users.

 Active Learning

Use Esri's *Tapestry Segmentation* to Learn About Your Neighborhood

Go to www.esri.com and click on the link to Products/Data/Demographic, Consumer and Business Data/Lifestyles. There you will find the website for the Tapestry Segmentation program, which has categorized every ZIP code according to the prevalence of one or more of the 65 different consumer types. Find out about your neighborhood by entering your own ZIP code. Does the description fit your perceptions of the types of people in your neighborhood?

ADVANTAGES AND DISADVANTAGES OF PACKAGED INFORMATION

Advantages of syndicated data are shared costs, high-quality data, and speed with which data are collected and made available for decision making.

Syndicated Data   One of the key advantages of syndicated data is *shared costs*. Many client firms may subscribe to the information; thus, the cost of the service is greatly reduced to any one subscriber firm. Second, because syndicated data firms specialize in the collection of standard data and because their long-term viability depends on the validity of the data, the quality of the data collected is typically very high. One final advantage of syndicated data is that the information is normally disseminated very quickly to subscribers; the more current the data, the greater their usefulness.

Disadvantages of syndicated data are that there is little control over what data are collected, buyers must commit to long-term contracts, and competitors have access to the same information.

A primary disadvantage of syndicated data is that buyers have little control over what information is collected. Are the units of measurement correct? Are the geographical reporting units appropriate? A second disadvantage is that buyer firms often must commit to long-term contracts when buying syndicated data. Finally, there is no strategic information advantage in purchasing syndicated data because all competitors have access to the same information. However, in many industries, firms would suffer a serious strategic disadvantage by not purchasing the information.

Advantages of packaged services are the experience of the firm offering the service, reduced cost, and increased speed of conducting the service.

Packaged Services   The key advantage of using a packaged service is taking advantage of the experience of the research firm offering the service. Imagine a firm setting out to conduct a test market for the very first time. It would take the firm several months to gain the confidence needed to conduct the test market properly. Taking advantage of others' experiences with the process is a good way to minimize potential mistakes in carrying out the research process. When a firm offers a packaged service, it has spent a great deal of time and effort in ensuring the process effectively delivers the information needed. In other words, it has worked out all the "bugs." A second advantage is the reduced cost of the research. Because the supplier firm conducts the service for many clients on a regular basis, the procedure is efficient and far less costly than if the buyer firm tried to conduct the service itself. A third advantage is the speed of the research service. The efficiency gained by conducting your service over and over translates into reduced turnaround time from start to finish of a research project. These are all reasons why client firms are interested in packaged services, and because of these advantages, many marketing research firms offer packaged services.

Disadvantages of packaged services are the inability to customize services and the service firm not being knowledgeable about the client's industry.

One disadvantage of using packaged services is the inability to customize aspects of a project when using a packaged service. Second, the company providing the packaged service may not know the idiosyncrasies of a particular industry; therefore, there is a greater burden on the client to ensure that the packaged service fits the intended situation. Client firms, being fully aware of the idiosyncrasies of their markets, need to be familiar with the service provided, including what data are collected on which population, how the data are collected, and how the data are reported before they purchase the service.

Applications of Packaged Information   Packaged information may be applied to many marketing research decisions, such as measuring consumer attitudes and opinions; defining market segments; monitoring media usage and promotion effectiveness; and conducting market-tracking studies. In the following section we illustrate these applications with examples of firms that provide the service.

Measuring Consumer Attitudes and Opinions. Marketers are always interested in consumer attitudes and opinions. At one time, the American public frowned on buying on credit. That attitude has certainly changed as credit card ownership surged beginning in the 1970s. Marketers are interested in consumers' attitudes toward private brands versus national brands, the quality of products made in America and elsewhere, and claims of health benefits. Defense contractors are interested in the public's attitude toward war. Universities are interested in consumers' attitudes about the value of higher education. Manufacturers are interested in prevailing attitudes about pollution and government regulation. Research firms supply packaged services that measure and report attitudes and opinions on these issues and many more. One of the oldest of these firms is Gallup, which has been tracking attitudes and opinions for many decades.

Gallup (www.gallup .com) has been tracking consumers' attitudes and opinions for many decades.

Market Segmentation. There are several marketing research firms that offer a packaged service of providing client firms with sophisticated methods of identifying members of their target market, locating these members, and providing information that will help develop promotional materials to efficiently reach these target markets. At the base of many of these services is geodemographics linking marketing information, such as consumer demographics, to specific geographical locations (latitude and longitude coordinates). Esri's Tapestry Segmentation and Nielsen's Claritas allow users to access to information at any geographical location specified.

Monitoring Media Usage and Promotion Effectiveness. We have already mentioned the Nielsen Ratings for measuring TV audiences and Arbitron's service of measuring radio listenership. Two other examples are measuring "buzz" and print media promotional impact.

> **Monitoring consumer buzz. Buzz or consumer-generated media (CGM)** is content created by consumers on blogs, discussion boards, forums, user groups, and other social media platforms. Opinions, comments, and personal experiences are posted and made publicly available on a wide range of issues, including products and brands. Buzz is also referred to as online consumer **word of mouth (eWOM).** As we have previously noted, buzz has experienced an extremely fast growth rate around the world in the last few years, and increasing mobile connectivity is projected to keep growth rates high. Consumers who value nonmarketer-controlled sources of information often seek out opinions, recommendations, and product reviews. Companies desiring to keep track of the buzz about their own brands and those of their competitors may purchase a packaged service from a marketing research firm. Several firms offer such a packaged service, including Nielsen's BuzzMetrics, SKOPOS ChatBack, Decooda, and Conversition.

Replikator is a packaged service offered by SKOPOS that allows clients to measure the effectiveness of promotional material in print media.

Photo and logo: By permission, SKOPOS.

> **Monitoring and effectiveness of print media.** When promotional materials are placed in a newpaper, direct mail piece, website, or magazine or on the package itself, marketers want to know what gets consumers' attention and what they think of the message. Packaged services are available to monitor the effectiveness of print media promotional messages. To measure reaction to print media, the SKOPOS service RepliKator™ allows consumers to electronically flip through the pages of a magazine or other printed material to resemble as close as possible reading

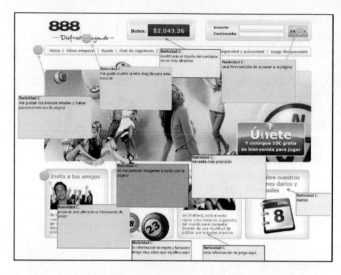

SKOPOS SketchPad™ is a packaged service designed to help clients understand consumers' reactions to promotional messages. In this example Spanish speaking consumers have made notes on areas of the ad shown.

Photo: By permission.

Logo: By permission, Nielsen.

through a magazine. Then SKOPOS can measure what the reader recalled from having read the magazine.

SKOPOS has two other packaged services for assessing promotional materials. SketchPad™ allows consumers to view a print message and to place emoticons on the message and add their comments of likes/dislikes/improvements. HeetSeeker™ is used in conjunction with SketchPad™ and allows for interpretation of the areas of the promotional piece that got the most attention.

Market Tracking Studies Nielsen is the leader in the industry in terms of analysis of consumer purchase behavior. Nielsen **tracking studies** are longitudinal studies that monitor a variable such as sales or market share over time. Nielsen has two different methods of tracking the movement of goods at the retail level. First, consumers participating in a large panel group use a wand supplied by Nielsen to swipe the UPC barcode on goods they bring home. Data are uploaded to a Nielsen database. Second, Nielsen has agreements with many retailers to purchase data as it is scanned at checkout. The company augments these methods with in-store auditors to ensure they have a sample of stores that are representative. These methods give Nielsen the ability to offer a packaged service of key information to marketing managers. They can purchase tracking data for their category and get up-to-date information about what brands are selling at which retailers at the SKU level, and they can learn what their competitors are selling, which is key strategic information.

 Synthesize Your Learning

This exercise will require you to take into consideration concepts and material from the following chapters:

Chapter 1	Introduction to Marketing Research
Chapter 2	The Marketing Research Industry
Chapter 3	The Marketing Research Process and Defining the Problem and Research Objectives
Chapter 4	Research Design
Chapter 5	Secondary Data and Packaged Information

Drill Bits, Inc.

Bob Douglass owns a machine shop. Most of his work is local business as machine shop work is labor intensive, and it is difficult to obtain large-quantity orders. Bob is considering branching out. For many years he has observed a couple of local manufacturers whose processes require them to make highly precise drills in metal. For example, the engine block cylinders they produce must be extremely precise for the engines to run at the required compression standards. To make such a precise drill, the drill bits can be used only a few times before they lose their original specifications. Then these expensive drill bits must be thrown away. Bob's customers have complained about this for years, and Bob has been working on a process to refurbish these throwaway bits back to their original specifications.

Finally, Bob has perfected this process. His local customers try out the refurbished bits and are ecstatic with the results. They can now get double life or even more out of a drill bit. Bob knows his machine shop will soon be very busy from these two local customers.

To expand his business to accommodate a large volume of refurbishment business, he knows he will have to invest a large sum of money in expanding the building and the machinery needed for the process to accommodate new customers. But he has no idea of the volume of business to expect.

1. Looking back at Chapter 1, how would you describe the purpose of marketing research in terms of Bob's situation?

2. If Bob is interested in finding a marketing research firm in his state, describe how he might find marketing research firms by states using information contained in Chapter 2.

3. In Chapter 3 we discussed what the "problem" really is. What is Bob's problem?

4. If Bob just wants to know how many firms made engine blocks in the United States, what type of research design would best describe this activity?

5. What secondary source of information would Bob want to seek to achieve his goal stated in question 4?

Summary

Data may be grouped into two categories: primary and secondary. Primary data are gathered specifically for the research project at hand. Secondary data have been previously gathered for some other purpose. There are many uses of secondary data in marketing research, and sometimes secondary data are all that is needed to achieve the research objectives. Secondary data may be internal, previously gathered *within* the firm for some other purpose. Examples include data collected and stored from sales receipts, such as types, quantities, and prices of goods or services purchased; customer names; delivery addresses; shipping dates; and salespeople making the sales. Storing internal data in electronic databases has become increasingly popular and may be used for database marketing. Databases are composed of records, which contain subcomponents of information called *fields*. Companies use information recorded in internal databases for purposes of direct marketing and to strengthen relationships with customers. The latter is a process known as *customer relationship management* (CRM). External secondary data are obtained from sources outside the firm. These data may be classified as (1) published, (2) syndicated services data, and (3) databases. There are different types of published secondary data, such as reference guides, indexes and abstracts, bibliographies, almanacs, manuals, and handbooks. Syndicated services data are provided by firms that collect data in a standard format and make them available to subscribing firms. Online information databases are sources of secondary data searchable by search engines online. Examples include Factiva, IBISWorld, LexisNexis, and ProQuest.

Secondary data have the advantages of being quickly gathered, readily available, and relatively inexpensive; they may add helpful insights should primary data be needed, and sometimes secondary data are all that is needed to achieve the research objective. Disadvantages are that the data are often reported in incompatible reporting units (e.g., county data are reported when ZIP code data are needed), measurement units do not match researchers' needs (e.g., household income is reported when per-capita income is needed), class definitions are incompatible with the researchers' needs (e.g., income is reported in classes up to $50,000 but the researchers need to know what percent of the population earns $75,000 or more), and secondary data may be outdated. Evaluation of secondary data is important; researchers must ask certain questions to ensure the integrity of the information they use. The ACS may represent the most significant change in the availability of secondary data to be used for marketing research purposes in several decades. The ACS makes data available on an annual basis instead of the 10-year interval required in the past to update census data.

Packaged information is a type of secondary data in which the data collected and/or the process of collecting the data is the same for all users. There are two classes of packaged information. Syndicated data are collected in a standard format and made available to all subscribing users. An example would be the Nielsen TV ratings. Packaged services offer a standardized marketing research process that is used to generate information for a particular user. Esri's Tapestry Segmentation is a system of classifying residential neighborhoods into 65 different segments. That process is standardized; it is the same for all Tapestry users. The information from the process is then applied to generate different data for each user. With syndicated data, the data are the same for each user, and with packaged services, the process of generating data for each user is the same.

Syndicated data have the advantages of shared costs of obtaining the data among all those subscribing to the service, high data quality, and the speed with which data are collected and distributed to subscribers. Disadvantages are that buyers cannot control what data are collected, must commit to long-term contracts, and gain no strategic information advantage in buying syndicated data because the information is available to all competitors.

Packaged services have the advantage of use of the supplier firm's expertise in the area, reduced costs, and speed with which supplier firms can conduct the service. The disadvantages of packaged services are that the process cannot be easily customized and the supplier firm may not know the idiosyncrasies of the industry in which the client firm operates.

Four major areas in which packaged information sources may be applied are measuring consumers' attitudes and opinions, defining market segments, monitoring media usage and promotion effectiveness, and conducting market-tracking studies.

Key Terms

Primary data (p. 94)
Secondary data (p. 94)
Internal secondary data (p. 95)
Database marketing (p. 95)
Database (p. 96)
Record (p. 96)
Fields (p. 96)
Internal databases (p. 96)
Customer relationship management (CRM) (p. 96)
Data mining (p. 96)
Micromarketing (p. 96)

External secondary data (p. 96)
Published sources (p. 97)
Syndicated services data (p. 98)
External databases (p. 98)
Online information databases (p. 98)
Core-based statistical areas (CBSAs) (p. 98)
Metropolitan SAs (p. 98)
Micropolitan SAs (p. 98)
Geodemographics (p. 99)
American Community Survey (ACS) (p. 103)

American Factfinder (p. 103)
IBISWorld Industry Reports (p. 105)
Packaged information (p. 105)
Syndicated data (p. 107)
Performer Q (p. 107)
Packaged Services (p. 107)
Esri's Tapestry Segmentation (p. 107)
Buzz (p. 109)
Consumer-generated media (CGM) (p. 109)
Word of mouth (eWOM) (p. 109)

Review Questions/Applications

1. Briefly describe the history of secondary data in the United States.
2. Describe where the material in this chapter falls within the steps of the marketing research process.
3. What are secondary data, and how do they differ from primary data?
4. Describe some uses of secondary data.
5. Take a look at Figure 5.1, which is an example of the use of census data. If you had only these data to review, which type of business do you think would be better suited to the market area represented by these data: a child care center or a retirement home? Why?
6. Describe the classifications of secondary data.
7. What is a database, and what are the components of a database?
8. Describe a database that would be useful to a local pizza restaurant.
9. What is meant by CRM?

10. What is the difference between data mining and micromarketing?
11. Give an example of micromarketing.
12. Describe five ways in which companies may use a database.
13. Explain why you think Target's use of its database information in Marketing Research Insight 5.1 is ethical or not ethical.
14. Briefly explain the three different types of external secondary data discussed in the chapter.
15. Name three external databases and identify other external databases available to you at your school.
16. What are the five advantages of secondary data?
17. Discuss the disadvantages of secondary data.
18. Which disadvantage of secondary data is resolved by geodemographics and why?
19. How would you go about evaluating secondary data? Why is evaluation important?

20. Describe the *ACS* in terms of the advantage it offers as well as how to retrieve data.
21. Explain why information such as that contained in *IBISWorld Industry Reports* would be beneficial to you for an upcoming interview.
22. What is meant by *packaged information*?
23. What is syndicated data? Give an example of a company that supplies syndicated data and describe the information it provides.
24. What are *packaged services*? Give an example of a company that supplies a packaged service and describe the type of information it provides.
25. Esri's market segmentation service, Tapestry Segmentation, would be classified as which type of packaged information? Why?
26. What are the advantages and disadvantages of syndicated data?
27. What are the advantages and disadvantages of packaged services?
28. Describe some areas in which packaged information may be applied.
29. Access your library's online databases. Describe how your library helps categorize the many databases to guide in your selection of sources appropriate for business.
30. Go online to your library's website. Can you locate a database that would be a good choice to find publications such as journal articles, trade publications, or newspapers? What are they?
31. Take a look at the sources of secondary data for marketing decisions in Table 5.1. Use your library's resources and find at least four of these sources. Examine them and write down the types of information available in the source and describe where the source is located in your library.
32. Find your library's online databases and check to see if any of them have the ability to automatically put an article you retrieve in a format suitable for citing (e.g., MLA or APA).
33. Refer back to Table 5.2, which describes the subjects of information covered in the *ACS*. Imagine that you are thinking about locating very upscale restaurants in 10 different areas of the country and you want to use ACS data to help you rank different cities in terms of their market potential for an upscale restaurant. What factors would you consider using and why? (It will be helpful for you to access the website and actually view some of the information under the different subjects.)
34. Refer back to Marketing Research Insight 5.2. Would Jacksonville, Florida, actually meet the criterion to be a test market? Cite the information on which you base your decision.
35. In the chapter we used an example of going to the Esri Tapestry Segmentation website for an "active learning" exercise. Go to those instructions. Enter your residence ZIP code and describe the inhabitants in terms of the one or more 65 consumer types available in the software.

CASE 5.1

Open Doors: Using NAICS and the American Community Survey

Laurie Fulkerson and a furniture sales representative at market.

Text and images: By permission, Laurie Fulkerson, Open Doors.

Laurie Fulkerson is the owner of Open Doors, a furniture store in Birmingham, Alabama. Laurie has been very successful in operating the store primarily because she has excellent skills at understanding her market's preferences. When she is at market, she is constantly asking herself, "Will my customers buy this?" As a result, she rarely has to take markdowns.

For many years, operating the one store was all Laurie could handle as she also ran a household with a husband and three children. Now, all the children have graduated from college and have careers of their own. Laurie and her husband, Vance, have discussed expanding the business. Profits, while very good at the one store, are limited by one location. The couple are considering either a new location in Birmingham or expanding to another city that is near enough to limit transportation costs. At the same time, Laurie and Vance agree they don't want to discount a location that may be very profitable because it is a couple of more hours away than another location.

In addition to Birmingham-Hoover, other metropolitan statistical areas that are within reasonable distance are Auburn-Opelika, Huntsville, Mobile, Montgomery, and Tuscaloosa, Alabama; Baton Rouge, Louisiana; and Pensacola-Ferry Pass-Brent, Florida. Laurie and Vance realize they need some data to make a sound business decision. One major concern they have is "retail saturation."

That is, is an MSA "overretailed"? How many furniture stores already exist in each MSA? To determine an answer, Vance suggests they get the North American Industry Classification System (NAICS) code for "furniture stores." The NAICS code is a useful "key" for searching for information about that particular group of firms.

Follow these steps to search for the data:

a. Enter www.census.gov to go to the Census Bureau's NAICS website.
b. In the "Downloads/Reference Files/Tools" area, click on "2012 NAICS." This will take you to a listing of different industries and their respective codes.
c. Click on "44-45 Retail Trade." "Furniture Stores" is the most appropriate match for Open Doors. Click on the six-digit code (442110), and you will see a definition of the types of stores included in this code number:
This industry comprises establishments engaged primarily in retailing new furniture, such as household furniture (e.g., baby furniture box springs and mattresses) and outdoor furniture, office furniture (except those sold in combination with office supplies and equipment), and/or furniture sold in combination with major appliances, home electronics, home furnishings, or floor coverings.
d. Go to www.census.gov and then the Data/American Factfinder to use this tool to search the *ACS* for the information Laurie and Vance will need to narrow down their choices of MSAs where they might locate a second store.
e. Go to "Industry Data" and enter the NAICS code 442110 in the search box. When the search results appear, click on the box on the left and then click "add." This will add the NAICS code to "Your Selections."
f. To select MSAs, go to "Geographies" and in the "Select geographic type" drop-down menu, select "Metro Statistical Areas/Micro Statistical Areas." You will need to "Add to Your Selections" to each one of the MSAs being considered. Note that when you do this, the *American Factfinder* add this selection to "Your Selections." Now Laurie and Vance, by clicking on the top table in the output, have their information.

Geographic area name	2007 North American Industry Classification System (NAICS) code	Meaning of 2007 North American Industry Classification System (NAICS) code	Year code	Number of establishments	Paid employees for pay period including March 12 (number)	Noise range for paid employees for pay period including March 12 (%)	First-quarter payroll ($1,000)	Noise range for first-quarter payroll (%)	Annual payroll ($1,000)	Noise range for annual payroll (%)
Auburn-Opelika, AL Metro Area	442110	Furniture stores	2009	12	70	G	390	G	1,716	G
Baton Rouge, LA Metro Area	442110	Furniture stores	2009	63	738	G	6,029	G	23,813	G
Birmingham-Hoover, AL Metro Area	442110	Furniture stores	2009	119	971	G	6,878	G	27,646	G
Huntsville, AL Metro Area	442110	Furniture stores	2009	52	358	G	2,299	G	9,562	G
Mobile, AL Metro Area	442110	Furniture stores	2009	49	428	G	3,146	G	12,071	G
Montgomery, AL Metro Area	442110	Furniture stores	2009	28	218	G	1,577	G	6,418	G
Pensacola-Ferry Pass-Brent, FL Metro Area	442110	Furniture stores	2009	36	233	H	1,730	G	6,546	G
Tuscaloosa, AL Metro Area	442110	Furniture stores	2009	27	158	G	1,192	G	3,573	G

1. Based on the output from their data search, the Fulkersons have a number of variables that can be used to assess the market potential for furniture stores in each market. What are these variables?
2. What is wrong with evaluating the MSAs based on the number of furniture stores already existing in those geographical areas? What additional information could the Fulkersons use as a better metric for determining "retail saturation" for furniture stores in each MSA?
3. Find the information you proposed in question 2 and enter the data in an Excel spreadsheet. Create the formula to calculate your "Index of Retail Furniture Store Saturation."
4. Based on your results in question 3, which MSA should the Fulkersons select to open the next Open Doors?

CASE 5.2 INTEGRATED CASE

Global Motors

Nick Thomas is an authority on automobile manufacturing. Like many good managers, he also knows he doesn't know everything. A number of issues may influence consumers' decisions regarding the cars they will demand in the future. Certainly, the general level of the economy, as measured by GDP, unemployment rate, and average incomes, affect the number and types of vehicles purchased. Also, experience shows that specific issues are closely tied to automobile demand. Gasoline prices have always impacted market demand for various types of vehicles. Nick also knows consumers' perceptions and expectations about future gasoline prices are as important as the actual prices when it comes to car sales.

A disturbing topic on which Nick has little real knowledge is global warming. He has read articles in the newspaper about climate change, and he knows it has become a target of political debate. So far, he doesn't sense great concern among the public, but he knows that if evidence of global warming continues to grow and if consumers come to believe that gasoline emissions contribute to climate change, these trends will impact the automotive industry like nothing we've seen before. To Nick, global warming is the "800-pound gorilla in the room" that most people are ignoring or discounting. He hopes that global warming will not occur and what warming we do experience will ultimately be attributed to a normal change in climate that the Earth experiences from time to time. But Nick knows he cannot rely on his hopes; he needs better information if he is to plan for the future properly.

1. Go to secondary data sources such as your university's online databases. You may want to talk to your librarian or search online for the most appropriate databases for this topic. Search for some articles on "global warming" or "climate change." Take notes on the topics that are covered in the titles or abstracts and create an outline of the topics covered. This will help you become familiar with subject in greater detail.
2. Scan several of the articles you've found and outline key points made in the articles. Organize the articles based on the topics covered and write a five-page paper on the topic using subheadings to cover the different issues you've discovered.
3. Evaluate the sources you've used in your paper according to the criteria outlined in this chapter. Do you believe some sources of information are more trustworthy than others? How would you determine trustworthiness?
4. If Nick Thomas wants to learn how consumers' attitudes toward global warming are related to car-buying intentions, where might he find this data?

Qualitative Research Techniques

Turning Qualitative Buzz into Business Insights

Annie Pettit, PhD, Chief Research Officer, Conversition. A Research Now partner company.

If you have a Facebook, Twitter, YouTube, or LinkedIn account, you are already contributing to the billions of new social media data points that are created every year. Millions of websites allow users to formally discuss the perceived pros and cons of specific features of individual brands, as well as to make casual, off the cuff, silly, and random remarks about brands, products, and people. But whether it's a well-thought-out essay or a phrase jotted in haste, these opinions are a treasure trove of instantly available data ready to be mined and measured.

Social media research offers many advantages to researchers. Because historical data is readily available, researchers can access pre/post measurement data even if an event was discovered after the fact. And, though surveys have been and continue to be extremely popular for eliciting opinions, social media offers people a place to share their unstructured and unelicited opinions, perhaps, at times, in ways that are more honest and heartfelt than surveys. Further, where traditional research methods must work under responder time and fatigue constraints, social media research has no similar barriers. When millions of people talk about a brand, they invariably touch on thousands of topics, something no survey or focus group can manage without causing undue strain on their respondents.

Fortunately, many companies with social media expertise have made the process of collecting and coding these millions of records much easier. Basic products are available that allow you to read, monitor, and track opinions, while more advanced products align themselves with traditional market research processes, including sampling, weighting, scaling, and coding. The key to success with this methodology is the same as any other: Begin with a research objective and the results will follow.

Conversition is a market research company that specializes in social media listening. It applies proven research principles to the collection and analysis of social media data, including Twitter tweets, Facebook status updates, Wordpress blogs, and more. Through a multi-stage process, brand opinions are collected, cleaned of spam and irrelevant data, scored into a 5-point sentiment scale, coded into category-relevant variables, and made available in an easy-to-use web portal. Our listening and survey tools are complementary to traditional market research methodologies and will help you develop a well-rounded view of consumer conversations about your client's product, service, or brand.

Visit Conversition at www.conversition.com

Text and images: By permission, Annie Pettit, Conversition.

Qualitative research methods are sometimes referred to as the "soft side" of marketing research simply because the findings typically are not quantitative. Most recently, however, marketing researchers have learned how to use tools such as neuroimaging, eye tracking, and facial expression recognition to understand marketing phenomena, so newer qualitative research techniques are based on medical or other such science. As you will learn, qualitative research is an important tool that provides clients with insights not found in quantitative research. This chapter discusses how to distinguish between qualitative and quantitative research as well as the various methods used in conducting qualitative research. Each qualitative method has its place in the marketing research process, and each has its unique advantages and disadvantages as well. Because focus groups are a popular qualitative marketing research technique, an in-depth discussion of them is included. We begin with a discussion of quantitative, qualitative, and pluralistic research.

Photo: kbuntu/Fotolia

117

Quantitative, Qualitative, and Pluralistic Research

The means of data collection during the research process can be classified into two broad categories: quantitative and qualitative.

There are vast differences between these two methods, and it is necessary to understand their special characteristics to make the right selection. To start, we briefly define these two approaches, and then we describe pluralistic research.

Quantitative research is the traditional mainstay of the research industry, and it is sometimes referred to as "survey research." For our purposes, **quantitative research** is defined as research involving the administration of a set of structured questions with predetermined response options to a large number of respondents. When you think of quantitative research, you might envision a panel company whose members complete an online survey. That is, quantitative research often involves a sizable representative sample of the population and a formalized procedure for gathering data. The purpose of quantitative research is specific, and this research is used when the manager and researcher have agreed that precise information is needed. Data format and sources are clear and well defined, and the compilation and formatting of the data gathered follows an orderly procedure that is largely numerical in nature.

Qualitative research, in contrast, involves collecting, analyzing, and interpreting data by observing what people do and say. Observations and statements are free form or nonstandardized because questions and observations are open ended. Qualitative data can be quantified, but only after a translation process has taken place. For example, if you asked five people to express their opinions on a topic such as gun control or promoting alcoholic beverages to college students, you would probably get five different statements. But after studying each response, you could characterize each one as "positive," "negative," or "neutral." This translation step would not be necessary if you instructed them to choose predetermined responses such as "yes" or "no." Any study that is conducted using an observational technique or unstructured questioning can be classified as qualitative research, which is becoming increasingly popular in a number of research situations.[1]

Why would you want to use such a "soft" approach? Occasionally, marketing researchers find that a large-scale survey is inappropriate. For instance, Procter & Gamble™ may be interested in improving its Ultra Tide laundry detergent, so it invites a group of homemakers to brainstorm how Ultra Tide could perform better or how its packaging could be improved or discuss other features of the detergent. These ideas may have been the origins of Tide Stain Release or Tide To Go. Listening to the market in this way can generate excellent packaging, product design, or product positioning ideas. As another example, if the P&G marketing group were developing a special end-of-aisle display for Tide, it might want to test one version in an actual supermarket environment. It could place one in a Safeway grocery store in a San Francisco suburb and videotape shoppers as they encountered the display. The videos would then be reviewed to determine what types of responses occurred. For instance, did shoppers stop there? Did they read the copy on the display? Did they pick up the displayed product and look at it? Qualitative research techniques afford rich insight into consumer behavior.[2] An example of an application of qualitative research with a global market segment, namely, China, is offered in Marketing Research Insight 6.1.

With the rush to online quantitative research that produces huge amounts of data, qualitative research is sometimes overlooked.[3] However, it is our goal in this chapter to emphasize the value of qualitative research techniques and the need for qualitative research and quantitative research to work hand in hand.

Although there are proponents of both types of research, many marketing researchers have adopted **pluralistic research**, which is defined as the combination of qualitative and quantitative research methods with the aim of gaining the advantages of both. With pluralistic research, it is common to begin with exploratory qualitative techniques as, for example, in-depth interviews of selected dealers or a series of focus group discussions with customers to

The means of data collection during the research process can be classified into two broad categories: quantitative and qualitative.

Quantitative research is defined as research involving the administration of a set of structured questions with predetermined response options to a large number of respondents.

Qualitative research involves collecting, analyzing, and interpreting data by observing what people do and say.

Qualitative research techniques afford rich insight into consumer behavior.

Pluralistic research is defined as the combination of qualitative and quantitative research methods to gain the advantages of both.

MARKETING RESEARCH INSIGHT 6.1 *Global Application*

Using Photo-Elicitation to Understand Global Markets

Photo-elicitation is a qualitative research technique where people are instructed to take photographs of a consumption experience, and they are later engaged in an in-depth interview to find out their feelings, thoughts, and actions for each picture. It is a way to construct the complete consumption experience because the informant identifies what scenes or activities are significant by deciding to take the pictures. The researcher is then assured that there is some meaningfulness to each picture. With careful and skillful probes, the researcher encourages the informant to divulge the underlying meaning. Venkatraman and Nelson describe the method this way: "Photo-elicitation also elicits rich descriptions of the physical layout and emotional reactions to the servicescape by facilitating deep dives by the informants or helping them go below conscious, surface-level observations to connect to deeper, submerged feelings, symbols, myths, and metaphors."[4] Photo-elicitation is an especially easy-to-implement research technique because of the widespread adoption of digital photography technology.

These authors point out that a great many food companies such as Starbucks™, McDonald's®, or Kentucky Fried Chicken® are rapidly penetrating global markets such as China. It is important that these companies truly understand how their global markets are experiencing their products and services because when a product from one culture is introduced to another culture, the consumer experience is often surprisingly different for consumers in the second culture. Thus, these authors conducted a photo-elicitation of the experiences of young urban Chinese consumers with Starbucks. Coffee is not a typical Chinese drink, and coffee shops are a new phenomenon in China. In addition, the Chinese culture discourages sharing feelings and opinions with strangers. So, the photographs became focal activities that the Chinese informants could talk about without violating cultural norms. The findings of this study paints a picture of the Chinese Starbucks experience, which is outlined in the following bullets.

- Starbucks is a safe haven from the chaos and noise of crowds in the streets; it provides warmth, security, and privacy.
- Starbucks is like home; it is attractive and charming.

With photo-elicitation people talk about the photos they took of a recent consumption experience.

Photo: Kzenon Shutterstock.com

- Starbucks is a place to relax; the seating and décor is inviting and calming.
- Starbucks is a private, yet social, place where young Chinese people can gather with their close friends and chat.
- Starbucks is romantic; the furniture arrangement allows for couples to have intimate "happy chats."
- Starbucks is a way to learn more about America, which is an interesting observation because Starbucks is supposed to embody Italian espresso bars.
- Starbucks is exotic. It is very different to Chinese because the coffee and other offerings are new and strange to them.

That final point has important implications for Starbucks because the Chinese informants expressed that their initial encounter with Starbucks was bewildering and frustrating. They did not know how to order, what to order, how to drink the coffee, or what to do with the sugar and milk. They had to seek advice from their friends or watch the behavior of other Starbucks customers. Fortunately for Starbucks, its other aspects were strong attractions that countered these negatives of these initial encounters.

understand how they perceive your product and service as compared with those of competitors. Even an observational study could be used if it is helpful in understanding the problem and bringing to the surface issues in the research project. These activities often help crystallize the problem or otherwise highlight factors and considerations that might be overlooked if the researcher had rushed into a full-scale survey. The qualitative phase serves as a foundation for the quantitative phase of the research project because it provides the researcher with firsthand knowledge of the research problem. Armed with this knowledge, the researcher's design and execution of the quantitative phase are invariably superior to what they might have been without the qualitative phase. With pluralistic research, the qualitative phase serves to frame the subsequent quantitative phase, and in some cases, a qualitative phase is applied after a quantitative study to help the researcher understand the findings in the quantitative phase.[5] As an example, *The Arizona Republic* newspaper has used online focus groups for brainstorming, and the outcomes of these sessions are then used to devise online surveys. Through this pluralistic approach, the Showtime network investigated different lifestyle types of its *Nurse Jackie* show viewers: those who watch on demand, those preferring to watch live, those who use DVRs, and those using a combination of the viewing platforms.[6] The on-demand and DVR viewers really valued the ability to pause, rewind, and reexperience; the live watchers eagerly anticipated the premiere shows; the DVR users had constraints and needed the convenience of recorded episodes; and the combination viewers had complicated schedules and used whatever platform worked that week.

OBSERVATION TECHNIQUES

One qualitative method is to observe phenomena. Researchers observe behavior and record what they see.

We begin our description of qualitative research techniques with **observation methods**, which are techniques in which the researcher relies on his or her powers of observation to obtain information. Observation requires something to observe, and researchers typically use video or audio recorders, photographs, handwritten notes, or some other tangible record of what is observed. As we describe each observation technique, you will see that each is unique in how it obtains observations.

Four general ways of organizing observations are (1) direct versus indirect, (2) covert versus overt, (3) structured versus unstructured, and (4) in situ versus invented.

Types of Observation   At first glance, it may seem that observation studies can occur without any structure; however, it is important to adhere to a plan so that the observations are consistent and comparisons or generalizations can be made without worrying about any conditions of the observation method that might confound the findings. There are four general ways of making observations: (1) direct versus indirect, (2) overt versus covert, (3) structured versus unstructured, and (4) in situ versus invented.

Observing behavior as it occurs is called direct observation.

Direct Versus Indirect   Observing behavior as it occurs is called **direct observation**.[7] For example, if we are interested in finding out how much shoppers squeeze tomatoes to assess their freshness, we can observe people actually picking up the tomatoes. Direct observation has been used by Kellogg to understand breakfast rituals, by a Swiss chocolate maker to study the behavior of "chocoholics," and by the U.S. Post Office's advertising agency to come up with the advertising slogan "We Deliver."[8] It has also been used by General Mills to understand how children eat breakfast, leading to the launch of Go-Gurt, a midmorning snack for schoolchildren.[9]

With indirect observation, the researcher observes the effects or results of the behavior rather than the behavior itself. Types of indirect observations include archives and physical traces.

Some behaviors, such as past actions, cannot be directly observed. In those cases, we must rely on **indirect observation**, which involves observing the effects or results of the behavior rather than the behavior itself. Types of indirect observations include archives and physical traces.

Archives   **Archives** are secondary sources, such as historical records, that can be applied to the present problem. These sources contain a wealth of information and should not be overlooked or underestimated. Many types of archives exist. For example, records of sales calls may be inspected to determine how often salespeople make cold calls. Many companies mine scanner data for insight on the effects of price changes, promotion campaigns, or package size changes. Scanner data is an archive of the purchasing behaviors of consumers.

Physical Traces   **Physical traces** are tangible evidence of some past event. For example, we might turn to "garbology" (observing the trash of subjects being studied) as a way of finding out how much recycling of plastic milk bottles occurs. A soft drink company might do a litter audit to assess how much impact its aluminum cans have on the countryside. A fast-food company such as Wendy's might measure the amount of graffiti on buildings located adjacent to prospective location sites as a means of estimating the crime potential for each site.[10]

Covert Versus Overt With **covert observation**, the subject is unaware that he or she is being observed. An example is a "mystery shopper" who is hired by a retail store chain to record and report on sales clerks' assistance and courtesy. One-way mirrors and hidden cameras are a few of the other ways used to prevent subjects from becoming aware that they are being observed. The aim of this approach is to observe typical behaviors; if the subjects were aware they were being watched, they might change their behavior, resulting in observations of atypical behavior. If you were a store clerk, how would you act if the department manager told you he would be watching you for the next hour? You would probably be on your best behavior for those 60 minutes. Covert observation has proved illuminating in studies of parents and children shopping together in supermarkets.[11] With direct questions, parents might feel compelled to say that their children are always on their best behavior while shopping.

Sometimes it is impossible for the respondent to be unaware that someone is watching. Examples of **overt observation**, all of which require the subjects' knowledge, include laboratory settings, recordings of sales calls, People Meters (Nielsen Media Research's device that is attached to a television set to record when and to what station a set is tuned), and Arbitron's Personal Portable Meter. Because people might be influenced by knowing they are being observed, it is wise to always minimize the presence of the observer to the maximum extent possible.

> When the respondent knows he or she is being observed, this form of research is known as overt observation.

Structured Versus Unstructured When using **structured observation** techniques, the researcher identifies beforehand which behaviors are to be observed and recorded. All other behaviors are "ignored." Often a checklist or a standardized observation form is used to isolate the observer's attention to specific factors. These highly structured observations typically require a minimum of effort on the part of the observer.

> The researcher identifies beforehand which behaviors are to be observed and recorded in structured observation.

Unstructured observation places no restriction on what the observer notes. All behavior in the episode under study is monitored. The observer watches the situation and records what he or she deems interesting or relevant. Of course, the observer is thoroughly briefed on the area of general concern. This type of observation is often used in exploratory research. For example, Black & Decker® might send someone to observe carpenters working at various job sites as a means of better understanding how the tools are used and to help generate ideas as to how to design the tools for increased safety.

> In using unstructured observation, there are no predetermined restrictions on what the observer records.

In Situ Versus Invented With **in situ observation**, the researcher observes the behavior exactly as it happens. For instance, a mother and small daughter are observed in a store buying sandals for the daughter or a family meal is observed from start to finish as it takes place in that family's home. Mystery shopping is done in situ. Midas improved its service quality by having customers make videos of themselves as they made car service appointments.[12] **Invented observation** occurs when the researcher creates the situation. For example, a researcher might ask people to make a video as they try out a new toilet bowl cleaner. A pharmaceutical company that asked osteoporosis sufferers to make collages describing their feelings about taking their medications found that patients are reluctant to question their doctors about prescribed medications.[13]

APPROPRIATE CONDITIONS FOR THE USE OF OBSERVATION

Certain conditions must be met before a researcher can successfully use observation as a marketing research tool: The event must occur during a relatively short time interval, and the observed behavior must occur in a public setting. In addition, observation is typically used when the possibility of faulty recall rules out collecting information by asking the subject.

Short time interval means that the event must begin and end within a reasonably short time span. Examples include a shopping trip in a supermarket, waiting in a teller line at a

Observation is used with behaviors that take place over a short time interval, such as shopping in a supermarket and waiting in a bank teller line.

Public behavior refers to behavior that occurs in a setting the researcher can readily observe such as shopping in a grocery store or with children in a department store.

Observations should be used when consumers cannot recall their behaviors, such as knowing how many different web pages they accessed while shopping online. Inability to recall such behaviors is known as *faulty recall*.

Observation research has the advantage of seeing what consumers actually do instead of relying on their self-report of what they think they do.

bank, purchasing a clothing item, or observing children as they watch a television program. Some decision-making processes can take a long time (for example, buying a home), and it would be unrealistic to observe the entire process. As a result, observational research is usually limited to scrutinizing activities that can be completed in a relatively short time or to observing certain phases of those activities with a longer time span.

Public behavior refers to behavior that occurs in a setting the researcher can readily observe. Actions such as cooking, playing with one's children at home, or private worship are not public activities and are therefore are not usually suitable for observational studies such as those described here.

Faulty recall occurs when actions or activities are so repetitive or automatic that the observed person cannot recall specifics about the behavior under question. For example, people cannot recall accurately how many times they looked at their wristwatch while waiting in a long line to buy a ticket to a best-selling movie or which brands of cookies they looked at while grocery shopping. Observation is necessary under circumstances of faulty recall to fully understand the behavior at hand. Faulty recall is one of the reasons that companies have experimented for many years with mechanical devices to observe these behaviors.[14]

ADVANTAGES OF OBSERVATIONAL DATA

Observation of humans in their natural context is the approach that has been used by anthropologists for more than 100 years and is an accepted method of conducting marketing research.[15] Typically, the subjects of observational research are unaware they are being studied. Because of this, they react in a natural manner, giving the researcher insight into actual, not reported, behaviors. As previously noted, observational research methods also mean that there is no chance for recall error. The subjects are not asked what they remember about a certain action. Instead, they are observed while engaged in the act. In some cases, observation may be the only way to obtain accurate information. For instance, children who cannot yet verbally express their opinion of a new toy will do so by simply playing or not playing with the toy. Retail marketers commonly gather marketing intelligence about competitors and about their own employees' behaviors by hiring the services of mystery shoppers who pose as customers but who are actually trained observers.[16] Of course, mystery shopping should be conducted in an ethical manner, as described in the MRA code of ethics excerpt in Marketing Research Insight 6.2. In some situations, data can be obtained with better accuracy and less cost by using observational methods as opposed to other means. For example, counts of in-store traffic can often be made by means of observational techniques more accurately and less expensively than by using survey techniques. Also, pluralistic researchers will use observation techniques to supplement and complement other techniques.[17]

LIMITATIONS OF OBSERVATIONAL DATA

One disadvantage of observational research is that few persons are normally observed. Researchers must be concerned about the issue of how accurately those observed represent all consumers in the target population.

The limitations of observation reflect the limitations of qualitative research in general. With direct observation, typically only small numbers of subjects are studied and usually under special circumstances, so their representativeness is a concern.[18] This factor, plus the subjective interpretation required to explain the observed behavior, usually forces the researcher to consider his or her conclusions to be tentative. Certainly, the greatest drawback of all observational methods is the researcher's inability to pry beneath the behavior observed and to interrogate the person on motives, attitudes, and all of the other unseen aspects of why what was observed took place.

To recap, a limitation of observation is that motivations, attitudes, intentions, and other internal conditions cannot be observed. Only when these feelings are relatively unimportant or are readily inferred from the behavior is it appropriate to use observational research methods. For example, facial expression might be used as an indicator of a child's attitudes or

MARKETING RESEARCH INSIGHT 6.2 *Ethical Consideration*

Marketing Research Association Code of Ethics

Mystery Shopping

Mystery shopping is a long-established research technique used by a wide variety of commercial, governmental, and other organizations. Its purpose is to help such groups to assess and improve the standards of service they provide to their customers by comparing their achieved performance against their own targets and against the standards provided by competitors and other organizations. The approach involves the use of evaluators who are specially trained to observe and measure the nature and quality of the services being offered to customers. These mystery shoppers pose as consumers and chronicle

detailed information about their mystery shopping experience using questionnaires or narrative reports.

MRA considers mystery shopping a legitimate form of marketing research when it is employed for customer satisfaction purposes—that is, to determine likely customer perceptions and needs. It is not considered marketing research when it is used for nonresearch purposes such as identifying individuals for disciplinary actions, falsely elevating sales by creating a demand for products or services that does not really exist in the current marketplace, or obtaining personal information for nonresearch purposes.

---

preferences for various types of fruit drink flavors because children often react with conspicuous physical expressions. But adults and even children usually conceal their reasons and true reactions in public, and this fact necessitates a direct questioning approach because observation alone cannot give a complete picture of why and how people act the way they do.

> The major disadvantage of observation research is the inability to determine consumers' motives, attitudes, and intentions.

Focus Groups

A popular qualitative research technique is **focus groups**, which are small groups of people brought together and guided by a moderator through an unstructured, spontaneous discussion for the purpose of gaining information relevant to the research problem.[19] Although focus groups should encourage openness on the part of the participants, the approach ensures that discussion is "focused" on some general area of interest. For example, the Piccadilly Cafeteria chain periodically conducted focus groups all around the country. The conversation may seem "freewheeling," but the purpose of the focus group may be to learn what people think about some specific aspect of the cafeteria business, such as the perceived quality of cafeteria versus traditional restaurant food.

> Focus groups are small groups of people brought together and guided through an unstructured, spontaneous discussion for the purpose of gaining information relevant to the research problem.

Focus groups represent a useful technique for gathering information from a limited sample of respondents. The information can be used to generate ideas, to learn the respondents' "vocabulary" when relating to a certain type of product, or to gain some insights into basic needs and attitudes.[20] Focus groups may represent 85% to 90% of the total money spent on qualitative research.[21] They have become so popular in marketing research that every large city has a number of companies that specialize in performing focus group research. You will most certainly encounter focus group research if you become a practicing marketing manager. "Almost nothing gets done without them," says Bill Hillsman, a successful advertising executive whose campaigns have promoted the Minnesota Twins, the Dales shopping centers, and Arctic Cat® snowmobiles.[22] Focus groups are an invaluable means of regaining contact with customers when marketers have lost touch, and they are helpful in learning about new customer groups.

> Information from focus groups can be used to generate ideas, to learn the respondents' "vocabulary" when relating to a certain type of product, or to gain some insights into basic needs and attitudes.

HOW FOCUS GROUPS WORK

Focus groups are of two basic types. **Traditional focus groups** select about 6 to 12 persons who interact in a dedicated room, with a one-way mirror for client viewing, for about two

Traditional focus group facilities have a one-way mirror or cameras, which allow clients in an adjoining room to watch the focus group without influencing what its members say and do.

Focus group participants' comments are encouraged and guided by moderators.

hours. In recent years, **contemporary focus groups**[23] have emerged that differ in that they are online and the client can observe the online activity from any remote location.

Focus group participants are guided by **moderators**. The training and background of the moderator is extremely important for the success of the focus group.[24] Focus group moderators are responsible for creating an atmosphere that is conducive to openness, yet they must make certain the participants do not stray too far from the central focus of the study. Good moderators have excellent observation, interpersonal, and communication skills to recognize and overcome threats to a productive group discussion. They are prepared, experienced, and armed with a detailed list of topics to be discussed.[25] It is also helpful if focus group moderators can eliminate any preconceptions on discussion topics from their minds. The best moderators are experienced, enthusiastic, prepared, involved, energetic, and open minded.[26] With an incompetent moderator, the focus group can become a disaster.

Focus group company principals are sometimes referred to as qualitative research consultants (QRCs). The QRC prepares a **focus group report** that summarizes the information provided by the focus group participants relative to the research questions. Two factors are crucial when analyzing the data. First, some sense must be made by translating the statements of participants into categories or themes and then reporting the degree of consensus apparent in the focus groups.[27] Second, the demographic and buyer behavior characteristics of focus group participants should be judged against the target market profile to assess to what degree the groups represent the target market.

The focus group report reflects the qualitative aspect of this research method. It lists all themes that have become apparent, and it notes any diversity of opinions or thoughts expressed by the participants. It will also have numerous verbatim excerpts provided as evidence.[28] In fact, some reports include complete transcripts or video recordings of the focus group discussion. This information is then used as the basis for further research studies or even for more focus groups. If the information is used for subsequent focus groups, the client uses the first group as a learning experience, making any adjustments to the discussion topics as needed to improve the research objectives. Although focus groups may be the only type of research used to tackle a marketing problem or question, they are also used as a beginning point for quantitative research efforts; that is, a focus group phase may be used to gain a feel for a specific survey that will ultimately generate standardized information from a representative sample.

Marketing Research on YouTube™ | YouTube Logo: Learn about Focus Groups with YouTube by going to **www.youtube.com** and search for "Focus Group Research: Premium Salad Dressing Packaging."

 Active Learning

Learn More About Qualitative Research

Go to the Qualitative Research Consultants Association website (www.qrca.com). Click on "About Research," then "What Is Qualitative Research," to access the "When to Use Qualitative Research" page. Now let's consider the example of recommendations made by a university's faculty senate to the administration. For each of these recommendations, indicate whether qualitative research should be used to evaluate students' opinions. What are the pros and cons of using this form of research in each case?

1. Require all students to park at a central parking lot two miles from campus and take shuttle buses to campus.
2. Increase tuition by 10%.
3. Schedule classes on Monday/Wednesday or Tuesday/Thursday, leaving Friday for student organization meetings and group project work.
4. Require students to take at least 18 hours of course work during summer school.
5. Require every student to purchase and bring an iPad to class.

ONLINE FOCUS GROUPS

The **online focus group** is a form of contemporary focus group in which respondents communicate via an Internet forum, which clients can observe. Typically, online focus groups allow the participants the convenience of being seated at their own computers, while the moderator operates out of his or her office. The online focus group is "virtual" in that it communicates electronically and does not have face-to-face contact. For example, FocusVision World-wide® (www.focusvision.com) has an online focus group system using webcams and voice communication that connect the moderator and focus group members in real time while clients can observe and send chat messages to the moderator during the discussion if they wish. Online focus groups have the following advantages over traditional focus groups: (1) no physical setup is necessary, (2) transcripts are captured on file in real time, (3) participants can be in widely separated geographic locations, (4) participants are

Online focus group participants are relaxed, but they can become bored or distracted.

Photo. AZP Worldwide/Shutterstock

comfortable in their home or office environments, and (5) the moderator can exchange private messages with individual participants. Innovative approaches are possible, as some researchers combine online with telephone communications for maximum effectiveness.[29] Nonetheless, there are some disadvantages to online focus groups: (1) observation of participants' body language is not possible, (2) participants cannot physically inspect products or taste food items, and (3) participants can lose interest or become distracted.[30]

> Respondents to an online focus group communicate via the Internet, and clients may observe the virtual chat.

A variation of the online focus group is conducted in a traditional setting, but the client watches online. With the use of streaming media and high-speed Internet connections, ActiveGroup has pioneered this research technique. For example, ActiveGroup (www.activegroup.net) offers clients the ability to view focus groups online using streaming video. The focus group is conducted at a traditional focus group facility with the participants seated with the moderator. This type of online focus group allows several members of the client firm to observe the focus group at their own location. This saves the client firm travel expense and time. ActiveGroup operates in more than 1,000 focus group locations in 45 countries.

Since their entry into the research industry a few years ago, online focus groups have grown in popularity. While they will not replace traditional focus groups, they offer a viable research method.[31] A recent article compared traditional in-person focus groups, videoconferencing focus groups, online focus groups, and "telepresence" focus groups using large high-definition screens to create a focus group appearance and experience when participants are in diverse remote locations. Table 6.1 reveals how these four types compare on various factors.

ADVANTAGES OF FOCUS GROUPS

The four major advantages of focus groups are that (1) they generate fresh ideas; (2) they allow clients to observe their participants; (3) they may be directed at understanding a wide variety of issues, such as reactions to a new food product, brand logo, or television ad; and (4) they allow fairly easy access to special respondent groups, such as lawyers or doctors (whereas it may be very difficult to find a representative sample of these groups).

> Focus groups generate fresh ideas, allow clients to observe them, are applicable to a wide variety of issues, and allow researchers to obtain information from "hard-to-reach" subpopulations.

DISADVANTAGES OF FOCUS GROUPS

There are three major disadvantages to focus groups: (1) They do not constitute representative samples; therefore, caution must be exercised in generalizing findings; (2) success is greatly dependent on the ability of the moderator; and (3) it is sometimes difficult to interpret the results of focus groups (the moderator's report is based on a subjective evaluation of participants' statements and interactions).

> Focus groups are not representative, and it is sometimes difficult to interpret the research results.

TABLE 6.1 Comparisons of Traditional and Contemporary Focus Groups[32]

Factor	In-Person Focus Group	Video Streaming	Online Focus Group	Telepresence
Reduced travel for clients		√	√	√
Reduced travel for moderators			√	√
Increased global diversity without additional travel			√	√
Available in desired locations	√	√	√	
Real-time client viewing	√	√	√	√
High-quality viewing experience	√			√
Full view of body language/facial expressions	√			√
High quality audio-video recording	√	√		
Video accessibility (e.g., archiving, clipping, replay)	√	√		
Simultaneous translations	√	√		

WHEN SHOULD FOCUS GROUPS BE USED?

Focus groups should be considered when the research question requires something to be explored or described.

When the research objective is to explore or describe rather than predict, focus groups may be an alternative. They work well for the following situations: A company wants to know "how to speak" to its market; what language and terms do its customers use? What are some new ideas for an ad campaign? Will a new service we are developing have appeal to customers, and how can we improve it? How can we better package our product?[33] In all these cases, focus groups can describe the terms customers use; their reactions and ideas for ads; the reasons why service, product, or package features are appealing; and suggestions for improving the company's delivery of benefits. Refer to the following section, "Some Objectives of Focus Groups," for elaboration on when focus groups are particularly useful.

WHEN SHOULD FOCUS GROUPS NOT BE USED?

Focus groups should not be used when the research questions require a prediction or when a major decision affecting the company's livelihood rests on the research results.

Because focus groups are based on a small number of persons who are not representative of some larger population, care must be exercised in using focus groups. If the research objective is to predict, focus groups should not be used. For example, if we show 12 persons in a focus group a new product prototype and 6 say they will buy it, it is not defensible to predict that 50% of the population will buy it. Likewise, if the research will dictate a major, expensive decision, the company should not rely solely on the use of focus groups. If a high-stakes decision is at hand, research that is representative of some population and that has some known margin of error (quantitative research) should be used.

SOME OBJECTIVES OF FOCUS GROUPS

There are four main objectives of focus groups: (1) to generate ideas; (2) to understand consumer vocabulary; (3) to reveal consumer needs, motives, perceptions, and attitudes about products or services; and (4) to understand findings from quantitative studies.

Focus groups generate ideas for managers to consider.

Focus groups *generate ideas* for managers to consider. Krispy Kreme has conducted focus groups to help design new product choices and stores. If managers consistently hear that their customers prefer their doughnuts but go elsewhere for gourmet coffees, this gives Krispy Kreme management ideas for changing their product mix to include gourmet coffee. Mothers talking about the difficulties in strapping children in car restraint seats give designers of these products ideas. Consumers discussing the difficulties of moving furniture give rise to innovations in furniture designed for portability.

To *understand consumer vocabulary* entails using a focus group to stay abreast of the words and phrases consumers use when describing products to improve communications about those products or services. Such information may help in advertising copy design or in the preparation of an instruction pamphlet. This knowledge refines research problem definitions and also helps structure questions for use in later quantitative research.

The third objective—to *reveal consumer needs, motives, perceptions, and attitudes* about products or services—involves using a focus group to refresh the marketing team's understanding of what customers really feel or think about a product or service. Alternatively, managers may need early customer reactions to changes being considered in products or services.[34] Focus groups are commonly used during the exploratory phase of research.[35] This application is useful in generating objectives to be addressed by subsequent research.

Finally, to *understand findings from quantitative studies* requires using focus groups to better comprehend data gathered from other surveys. Sometimes a focus group can reveal why the findings came out a particular way. For example, a bank image survey showed that a particular branch consistently received lower scores on "employee friendliness." Focus group research identified the problem as being several frontline employees who were so concerned with efficiency that they appeared to be unfriendly. The bank revised its training program to remedy the problem.

Warner-Lambert is one company that has successfully used focus groups to accomplish all four of these objectives. Its consumer health products group, which markets over-the-counter health and beauty products as well as nonprescription drugs, uses focus groups extensively.[36] In fact, Warner-Lambert uses a combination of qualitative research techniques to gain background information, to reveal needs and attitudes related to health and beauty products, to interpret the results of qualitative studies, and to stimulate brainstorming new ideas. Focus groups have been useful in understanding basic shifts in consumer lifestyles, values, and purchase patterns.

> Focus groups may be used to understand the consumers' vocabulary, needs and motives, and attitudes.

> Focus groups may be used to better understand findings of quantitative studies.

OPERATIONAL ASPECTS OF TRADITIONAL FOCUS GROUPS

Before a traditional focus group is conducted, certain operational questions should be addressed. It is important to decide how many people should take part in a focus group, who they should be, how they will be selected and recruited, and where they should meet. General guidelines exist for answering these questions. A discussion of each follows.

How Many People Should Be in a Focus Group? According to standard industry practice, the optimal size of a traditional focus group is 6 to 12 people. A small group (fewer than six participants) is not likely to generate the energy and group dynamics necessary for a truly beneficial focus group session. A small group will often result in awkward silences and force the moderator to take too active a role in the discussion just to keep the discussion alive. Similarly, a group with more than a dozen participants may prove too large to be conducive to a natural discussion. As a focus group becomes larger in size, it tends to become fragmented. Those participating may become frustrated by the inherent digressions and side comments. Conversations may break out among two or three participants while another is talking. This situation places the moderator in the role of disciplinarian, in which he or she is constantly calling for quiet or order rather than focusing the discussion on the issues at hand.

Unfortunately, it is often difficult to predict the exact number of people who will attend the focus group interview. Ten may agree to participate, and only 4 may show up; 14 may be invited in hopes that 8 will show up, and all 14 may arrive. Of course, if this occurs, the researcher faces a judgment call as to whether or not to send some home. There is no guaranteed method to ensure a successful participation ratio. Incentives (which will be discussed later) are helpful but definitely not a certain way of gaining acceptance. Although 6 to 12 is the ideal focus group size range, because of the uncertainty of participation, focus groups with fewer than 6 or more than 12 do take place.

> The optimal size of a focus group is 6 to 12 people.

Ideally, focus group members should be homogeneous.

Who Should Be in the Focus Group?   It is generally believed that the best focus groups are composed of participants who share homogeneous characteristics. This requirement is sometimes automatically satisfied by the researcher's need to have particular types of people in the focus group. For instance, the focus group may be comprise executives who use satellite phones, building contractors who specialize in building homes over $500,000 in value, or salespeople who are experiencing some common customer service difficulty. With consumer products, the focus group's common trait may just be that everyone buys salsa.

The need for similar demographic or other relevant characteristics in focus group members is accentuated by the fact that participants are typically strangers. In most cases, they are not friends or even casual acquaintances, and many people feel intimidated or at least hesitant to voice their opinions and suggestions to a group of strangers. But participants typically feel more comfortable once they realize they have similarities such as their age (they may all be in their early 30s), job situations (they may all be junior executives), family composition (they may all have preschool children), purchase experiences (they may all have bought a new car in the past year), or even leisure pursuits (they may all play tennis). Furthermore, by conducting a group that is as homogeneous as possible with respect to demographics and other characteristics, the researcher is assured that differences in these variables will be less likely to confuse the issue being discussed.

Selection of focus group members is determined by the purpose of the focus group.

How Should Focus Group Participants Be Recruited and Selected?   As you can guess, the selection of focus group participants is determined largely by the purpose of the focus group. For instance, if the purpose is to generate new ideas on GPS system improvements, the participants must be consumers who own a GPS system. If the focus group is intended to elicit building contractors' reactions to a new type of central air-conditioning unit, it will be necessary to recruit building contractors. It is not unusual for companies to provide customer lists or for focus group recruiters to work from secured lists of potential participants. For instance, with building contractors, the list might come from the local Yellow Pages or a building contractor trade association membership roster. In any case, it is necessary to initially contact prospective participants by telephone to qualify them and then to solicit their cooperation in the focus group. Occasionally, a focus group company may recruit by requesting shoppers in a mall to participate, but this approach is rare.

As we noted earlier, "no-shows" are a problem with focus groups, and researchers have at least two strategies to entice prospective participants. Incentives are used to encourage recruits to participate in focus groups. These range from monetary compensation for the participant's time to free products or gift certificates. Many focus group companies use callbacks, email, or text messages during the day immediately prior to the focus group to remind prospective participants they have agreed to take part. If one prospective participant indicates that some conflict has arisen and he or she cannot be there, it is then possible to recruit a replacement. Neither approach works perfectly, as we indicated earlier, and anticipating how many participants will show up is always a concern. Some focus group companies have a policy of overrecruiting, and others have lists of people they can rely on to participate, given that they fit the qualifications.

Focus group facilities should be comfortable, allow interaction, and not have distractions.

Where Should a Focus Group Meet?   Since the focus group discussion will last 90 minutes or more, it is important that the physical arrangement of the group be comfortable and conducive to group discussion. Focus groups ideally are conducted in large rooms set up in a format suitable given the research objective. In some cases, in which it is important to have face-to-face interaction, a round table format would be ideal. Other formats are more suitable for tasting foods or beverages or for viewing video. The overriding consideration is that the moderator has good eye contact with every participant.[37] Focus groups are held in a variety of settings. An advertising company conference room, a moderator's home, a respondent's home, the client's office, hotels, and meeting rooms at churches are all locations in which focus groups can be held. Aside from a seating arrangement in which participants can all see one another, the second critical requirement in selecting a meeting place is to find one quiet enough to permit an intelligible audiotaping of the sessions. Marketing research firms with focus group facilities similar to those we described at the beginning of this section offer ideal settings for focus groups.

When Should the Moderator Become Involved in the Research Project? Moderators should not be viewed as robots needed to lead a discussion who may be hired at the last minute to run the focus groups. The focus group's success depends on the participants' involvement in the discussion and in their understanding of what is being asked of them. Productive involvement is largely a result of the moderator's effectiveness, which in turn is dependent on his or her understanding of the purpose and objectives of the interview. Unless the moderator understands what information the researcher is after and why, he or she will not be able to phrase questions effectively. It is good policy to have the moderator contribute to the development of the project's goals to guide the discussion topics. By aiding in the formation of the topics (questions), he or she will be familiar with them and will be better prepared to conduct the group. It is important when formulating questions that they be organized into a logical sequence and that the moderator follow this sequence to the furthest extent possible. The moderator's introductory remarks are influential; they set the tone for the session. All subsequent questions should be prefaced with a clear explanation of how the participants should respond, for example, how they really feel personally, not how they think they should feel. This allows the moderator to establish a rapport with participants and to lay the groundwork for the interview's structure.

Moderators should not be hired at the last minute to run focus groups. They should thoroughly understand the research objectives.

How Are Focus Group Results Reported and Used? As we noted earlier, focus groups report some of the subtle and obscure features of the relationships among consumers and products, advertising, and sales efforts. They furnish qualitative data on things such as consumer language; emotional and behavioral reactions to advertising; lifestyle; relationships; the product category and specific brand; and unconscious consumer motivations relative to product design, packaging, promotion, or any other facet of the marketing program under study. However, focus group results are qualitative and not perfectly representative of the general population.

What Other Benefits Do Focus Groups Offer? The focus group approach is firmly entrenched in the marketing research world as a mainstay technique. Because they are of reasonable total cost when compared with large-scale quantitative surveys involving a thousand or more respondents, adaptable to managers' concerns, and capable of yielding immediate results, focus groups are an appealing qualitative research method. Moreover, face-to-face focus groups are becoming common worldwide, and online focus groups are boosting the popularity of focus groups with new capabilities.[38] They are a unique research method because they permit marketing managers to see and hear the market. Managers become so engrossed in their everyday problems and crises that they find it refreshing to see their customers in person. It is common for marketing managers to come away from a focus group session observation stimulated and energized to respond to the market's desires.

Use of focus group is growing worldwide.

Other Qualitative Research Techniques

Although the focus group is clearly the most popular, it is not the only qualitative research technique available to marketing researchers. Other such methods include in-depth interviews, ethnographic research, protocol analysis, various projective techniques, and physiological measurement.

IN-DEPTH INTERVIEWS

An **in-depth interview**, commonly referred to as an IDI, is defined as a set of probing questions posed one on one to a subject by a trained interviewer to gain an idea of what the subject thinks about something or why he or she behaves in a certain way. It is sometimes conducted in the

An in-depth interview involves a set of probing questions posed one on one by a trained interviewer about what the subject things about something or why he or she behaves in a certain way.

respondent's home or possibly at a central interviewing location, such as a mall-intercept facility, where several respondents can be interviewed in depth in a relatively short time. The objective is to obtain unrestricted comments or opinions and to ask questions that will help the marketing researcher better understand the various dimensions of these opinions as well as the reasons for them. Of primary importance is the compilation of the data into a summary report so as to identify common themes. New concepts, designs, advertising, and promotional messages can arise from this method.[39] Compared to a focus group, an IDI is better at investigating complex interrelationships, needs, and motivations for purchasing behaviors.[40] When IDIs are conducted over the telephone, they are referred to as "tele-depth interviews" (TDIs). Some companies use the Internet as a way to display visuals, in which case the approach is referred to as *Web-TDI*.[41]

> When IDIs are conducted using the telephone they are called "tele-depth interviews or TDIs. When visuals are added by the web, they are called Web-TDIs.

There are advantages and disadvantages to in-depth interviewing. Interviewers have the ability to probe by asking many additional questions based on a subject's responses. This enables the research technique to generate rich, deep responses. In-depth responses may be more revealing in some research situations than responses to predetermined, yes–no questions typical of a structured survey. If used properly, IDIs can offer great insight into consumer behavior.[42,43] However, this advantage also leads to the major disadvantage of in-depth interviewing, which is the lack of structure in the process. Unless interviewers are well trained, the results may be too varied to give sufficient insight to the problem. IDIs are especially useful when the researcher wants to understand decision making on the individual level, details about how products are used, or the emotional and sometimes private aspects of consumers' lives.[44,45]

In-depth interviews should be conducted by a trained fieldworker who is equipped with a list of topics or, perhaps, open-ended questions. The interviewee is not provided a list of set responses and then instructed to select one from the list. Rather, the interviewee is encouraged to respond in his or her own words, and the interviewer is trained in asking probing questions such as "Why is that so?" "Can you elaborate on your point?" and "Would you give me some specific reasons?" These questions are not intended to tap subconscious motivations; rather, they simply ask about conscious reasons to help the researcher form a better picture of the respondent's thoughts. The interviewer may record responses or take detailed notes. Although it is typical to do face-to-face IDIs, as we noted with TDIs, they can be done over the telephone when interviewees are widely dispersed.[46] In-depth interviews are versatile, but they require careful planning, training, and preparation.[47]

> **Marketing Research on YouTube™** | Learn about Consumer In-Depth Interviews with YouTube by going to **www.youtube.com** and search for "In Depth Interview – Primary Research."

Laddering is a technique used in in-depth interviews in an attempt to discover how product attributes are associated with desired consumer values. Essentially, values that are important to consumers are determined, such as "good health." Next, researchers determine which routes consumers take to achieve their values, such as exercise, eating certain foods, stress reduction, and so on. Finally, researchers attempt to determine which specific product attributes are used as a means of achieving the end that is the desired value. Through in-depth interviews researchers may learn that low-sodium foods or "white meats" are instrumental in achieving "good health."[48] The term *laddering* comes from the notion that the researcher is trying to establish the linkages, or steps, leading from product attributes to values. We asked Professor Philip Trocchia to provide some additional insights on laddering; his overview is featured in Marketing Research Insight 6.3.

The summary report for the in-depth interview will look very similar to one written for a focus group study; that is, the analyst looks for common themes across several in-depth interview transcripts, and these are noted in the report. Verbatim responses are included in the report to support the analyst's conclusions, and any significant differences of opinion that are found in the respondents' comments are noted as well. Again, it is vital to use an analyst who is trained and experienced in interpreting the qualitative data gathered during in-depth interviews.

PROTOCOL ANALYSIS

> Protocol analysis places people in a decision-making situation and asks them to verbalize everything they considered.

Protocol analysis involves placing a person in a decision-making situation and asking him or her to verbalize everything he or she considers when making a decision. This special-purpose qualitative research technique has been developed to peek into the consumer's

MARKETING RESEARCH INSIGHT 6.3   *Practical Application*

The Laddering Interview

Philip Trocchia
Associate Professor of Marketing, University of South Florida, St. Petersburg

Laddering is a type of one-on-one in-depth interview technique that seeks to reveal how individuals relate the features of products they purchase to their personally held beliefs. In laddering interviews, consumers are asked to describe why they purchased a particular good or service. After uncovering relevant product attributes or features influencing their purchase decisions, the interviewer probes further with the aim of guiding consumers to reveal what benefits they associate with the product feature(s) identified earlier. The interviewer then attempts to uncover why those product benefits are of importance to the consumer subjects. In this portion of the interview, consumers' personal values are revealed.

The term *laddering* refers to the series of linkages described above: Relevant features of the consumer's described product purchase are related to the perceived benefits of the product. Product benefits are then linked to the individual's personal set of values. For example, suppose a consumer regularly purchases a particular cereal. The interviewer would ask her why she buys that specific cereal. She might respond that it is high in fiber, a brand attribute. The consumer would then be asked why high fiber is important, and the respondent may express health reasons as a benefit of fiber. Finally, the interviewer would ask the consumer why good health is important to her, and the respondent might indicate that she associates good health with some personal value(s), such as happiness, freedom, or pleasure. The summary ladder for this consumer would be: high fiber (attribute or feature) → good health (benefit or consequence) → freedom (value). A typical report for the series of laddering interviews would contain a summary of the common attribute–benefit–value linkages among the respondents, along with demographic characteristics of the consumers who possess common linkage patterns. This information helps marketing managers make decisions such as "Ensure that our cereal has high fiber" and "Develop promotional messages linking freedom derived from good health derived from high fiber diets." Demographic profiles of this target market could be used to buy media targeting this demographic group.

Professor Philip Trocchia is Associate Professor of Marketing, University of South Florida, St. Petersburg. He has employed qualitative research techniques for such organizations as The Poynter Institute, Computer Renaissance, and The Honda Grand Prix of St. Petersburg. He has also written an article on the laddering technique in the Journal of Management Education.

Text and images by permission.

decision-making processes. Often an audio recorder is used to maintain a permanent record of the person's thinking. After several people have provided protocols, the researcher reviews them and looks for commonalities, such as evaluative criteria used, number of brands considered, types and sources of information used, and so forth.

Protocol studies are useful in two different purchase situations. First, they are helpful for purchases involving a long time frame in which several decision factors must be considered, such as when buying a house. By having people verbalize the steps they went through; a researcher can piece together the whole process. Second, when the decision process is very short, recall may be faulty, and protocol analysis can be used to slow down the process. For example, most people do not give much thought to buying chewing gum, but if Dentyne wanted to find out why people buy Spearmint gum, protocol analysis might provide some important insights regarding this purchasing behavior.

PROJECTIVE TECHNIQUES

Projective techniques involve situations in which participants are placed in (projected into) simulated activities in the hopes that they will divulge things about themselves that they might not reveal under direct questioning. Projective techniques are appropriate in situations in

> Projective techniques involve situations in which participants are placed in (projected into) simulated activities in the hopes that they will divulge things about themselves that they might not reveal under direct questioning.

which the researcher is convinced that respondents will be hesitant to relate their true opinions. Such situations may include behaviors such as tipping waitstaff, socially undesirable behaviors such as smoking or road rage, questionable actions such as littering, or even illegal practices such as betting on football games.

Five common projective techniques are used by marketers: the word-association test, the sentence completion test, the picture test, the cartoon or balloon test, and role-playing activity. A discussion of each follows.

Word-Association Test A **word-association test** involves reading words to a respondent who then answers with the first word that comes to his or her mind. These tests may contain over 100 words and usually combine neutral words with words being tested in ads or words involving product names or services. The researcher then looks for hidden meanings or associations between responses and the words being tested on the original list. This approach is used to uncover people's real feelings about these products or services, brand names, or ad copy. The time taken to respond, called "response latency," and/or the respondents' physical reactions may be measured and used to make inferences. For example, if the response latency to the word "duo" is long, it may mean that people do not have an immediate association with the word.

Decision Analyst, Inc., uses word-association tests in its battery of qualitative online research services. Anywhere from 50 to 75 words are given to online respondents as stimuli. Respondents then type the first word, association, or image that comes to mind. Sample sizes are typically 100 to 200 persons, and the entire process lasts about 30 minutes. Decision Analyst states that this projective technique is helpful in determining awareness or exploring the imagery or other associations that are linked to brands.[49]

Sentence-Completion Test With a **sentence-completion test**, respondents are given incomplete sentences and asked to complete them in their own words. The researcher then inspects these sentences to identify themes or concepts. The notion here is that respondents will reveal something about themselves in their responses. For example, suppose that Lipton® Tea is interested in expanding its market to teenagers. A researcher might recruit high school students and instruct them to complete the following sentences:

Someone who drinks hot tea is _____.

Tea is good to drink when _____.

Making hot tea is _____.

My friends think tea is _____.

The researcher examines the written responses and attempt to identify central themes. For instance, the theme identified for the first sentence might be "healthy," which would signify that tea is perceived as a drink for those who are health conscious. The theme for the second sentence might be "hot," indicating that tea is perceived as a cold-weather drink, whereas the theme for the third sentence may turn out to be "messy," denoting the students' reaction to using a tea bag. Finally, the last sentence theme might be "okay," suggesting there are no peer pressures working to cause high school students to avoid drinking tea. Given this information, Lipton might deduce that there is room to capitalize on the hot-tea market with teens.

Decision Analyst, Inc., also conducts sentence-completion tests online. Its service provides 50 to 75 respondents 50 to 60 incomplete sentences.[50]

Picture Test With a **picture test**, sometimes called a "thematic apperception test," a picture is provided to participants, who are instructed to describe their reactions by writing a short story about the picture. The researcher analyzes the content of these stories to ascertain feelings, reactions, or concerns generated by the picture. Such tests are useful when testing pictures being considered for use in brochures and advertisements and on product packaging. For example, a test advertisement might depict a man holding a baby, and the ad headline might

A word-association test involves reading words to a respondent who then answers with the first word that comes to his or her mind.

With a sentence-completion test, respondents are given incomplete sentences and asked to complete them in their own words. The researcher then inspects these sentences to identify themes or concepts.

With a picture test, a picture is provided to participants who are instructed to describe their reactions by writing a short story about the picture.

say, "Ford includes driver and passenger air bags as standard equipment because you love your family." A picture test may well divulge something about the picture that is especially negative or distasteful. Perhaps unmarried male respondents cannot relate to the ad because they do not have children and have not experienced strong feelings for children. On the other hand, it may turn out that the picture has a much more neutral tone than Ford's advertising agency intended. It may be that the picture does not generate feelings of concern and safety for the family in married respondents with young children. In any case, without the use of a picture test, it would be difficult to determine the audience's reactions.

Cartoon or Balloon Test   With a **balloon test**, a line drawing with an empty "balloon" above the head of one of the actors is provided to subjects who are instructed to write in the balloon what the actor is saying or thinking. The researcher then inspects these thoughts to find out how subjects feel about the situation described in the cartoon. For example, when shown a line drawing of a situation in which one of the characters is making the statement, "Ford Explorers are on sale with a discount of $4,000 and 0% interest for 48 months," the participant is asked how the other character in the drawing would respond. Feelings and reactions of the subject are judged based on their answers.

> With a balloon test, a line drawing with an empty "balloon" above the head of one of the actors is provided to subjects who are instructed to write in the balloon what the actor is saying or thinking.

Role-Playing Activity   With **role playing**, participants are asked to pretend they are a "third person," such as a friend or neighbor, and to describe how they would act in a certain situation or to a specific statement. By reviewing their comments, the researcher can spot latent reactions, positive or negative, conjured up by the situation. It is believed that some of the respondents' true feelings and beliefs will be revealed by this method because they can pretend to be another individual. For example, if Ray-Ban® is developing a new "Astronaut" sunglasses model with superior ultraviolet light filtration, space-age styling, and a cost of about $200, role playing might be used to fathom consumers' initial reactions. In this use of role playing, subjects could be asked to assume the role of a friend or close workmate and to indicate what they would say to a third person when they learned that their friend had purchased a pair of Astronaut sunglasses. If consumers felt the Astronaut model was overpriced, this feeling would quickly surface. On the other hand, if the space-age construction and styling were consistent with these consumers' lifestyles and product desires, this fact would be divulged in the role-playing comments.

> With role playing, participants are asked to pretend they are a "third person," such as a friend or neighbor, and to describe how they would act in a certain situation or to a specific statement.

These projective techniques were adapted from psychology by marketing researchers many years ago. They remain in use today, although some marketing researchers have developed new projective techniques, many of which are proprietary. Table 6.2 provides information on five such projective techniques that were developed and are used by Talking Business (www.TalkingBusiness.net), a qualitative research firm that specializes in innovative research and strategic brand development.

As with in-depth interviews, all of these projective techniques require highly qualified professionals to interpret the results. This increases the cost per respondent compared with other survey methods. Because of this aspect, projective techniques are not used extensively in commercial marketing research, but each one has value in its special realm of application.[51]

ETHNOGRAPHIC RESEARCH

Ethnographic research is an approach borrowed from anthropology; it is defined as a detailed, descriptive study of a group and its behavior, characteristics, culture, and so on.[52] *Ethno* refers to people, and *graphy* refers to a field of study. Anthropologists have gained insights into human behavior by living with or among their subjects, called *immersion*, for prolonged periods to study their emotions, behaviors, and reactions to the demands of everyday events. Ethnography uses several different types of research, including immersion, participant observation, and informal and ongoing in-depth interviewing. Ethnographers pay close attention to words, metaphors, symbols, and stories people use to explain their lives and communicate with one another.[53] Marketers have increasingly used ethnographic research to

> Ethnographic research is a term borrowed from anthropology to describe a detailed, descriptive study of a group and its behavior, characteristics, culture, and so on.

TABLE 6.2   Projective Techniques That Can Be Used with Focus Groups[54]

Technique Name	Description	Application
Sort Me Up™	Respondents are given products (or cards with product names) and asked to sort them into groups and then to provide a descriptive name for each group	Reveals competitive sets of products and brands Offers segmentation implications Shows how consumers perceive products and brands
Sort Me Straight™	For each attribute, respondents rank cards with brand names from most to least	Identifies how the target brand performs on specific attributes with respect to competing brands
Picture This, Picture That™	Respondents are given several pictures that represent a wide range of emotions and asked to select pictures that represent specific brand/category/situations	Reveals images and emotions that are associated with specific brand/category/situations
Color My World™	Respondents are given several color swatches (paint chips) and asked to select color(s) that represent specific brand/category/situations	Offers insight into positive and negative imagery and associations for specific brand/category/situations
Dot, Dot, Dot™	Respondents are given 10 dot-shaped stickers or tokens and asked to allocate them across flavors, brands, advertisements, etc.	Provides a relative ranking for each of the alternatives. Follow-up probing reveals why certain alternatives are favored

Marketing **Research** on YouTube™ | Learn about Consumer In-Depth Interviews with YouTube by going to **www.youtube.com** and search for "IMG Ethnography sample."

study consumer behavior, such as how subjects act during "shop-alongs" or in restaurants.[55] One interesting finding of ethnographic research is that American consumers are transforming their kitchens into HIVEs (highly interactive + virtual environments), offering significant opportunities for electronics companies.[56]

Here are some examples of ethnographic marketing research provided by the Qualitative Research Consultants Association:[57]

- Moms at home making dinner for the household
- Men at breakfast to observe what they eat and why
- Shopping with people at supermarkets and retail stores to observe how they shop and how they make brand decisions
- "Hanging out" with teen girls as they shop and socialize in the mall
- Walking with seniors in their walking groups and listening to them discuss their hopes, fears, worries, health, and family/friends
- Watching people use a product they have been given days ago to find out how it fit into their routine (test product or a competitive product)
- Observing the "before and after" someone takes a medication and how it makes or does not make a difference in his or her life

THE "NEW" QUALITATIVE RESEARCH TECHNIQUES

There are many new qualitative research techniques in addition to those we have identified in this chapter.

The various techniques described thus far are in no way a complete list. Other techniques are used to study human behavior, and there are promising analytical techniques for interpreting the marketing strategy implications of qualitative data.[58] However, each qualitative research technique that is new to marketing research brings with it a need to understand the theoretical and practical aspects of that technique to apply it properly, so it is best to hire a specialist with expertise in the particular qualitative research technique. As you would expect, computer technology and Internet access have allowed a number of companies, such as Good Karma Consulting, to adapt projective and qualitative research techniques so that subjects can do them quickly and easily online.[59] Finally, the rapidly growing social media marketing phenomenon is an especially active area where innovative qualitative research techniques are being developed and used. Marketing Research Insight 6.4 reports on the emergence of digital journals as a means of gathering qualitative data from online community members.

MARKETING RESEARCH INSIGHT 6.4   *Social Media Marketing*

Using Digital Diaries in Marketing Research: From "Dear Diary" to "Hey, Check Me Out!"

Before the advent of social media, some people meticulously and routinely wrote personal and private thoughts in their diaries that they locked away from prying eyes. In the social media era, people think nothing of divulging all kinds of trivial and significant information about themselves and their thoughts to complete strangers. Burt Leiman, managing director of Firefly Millward Brown, believes that digital diaries have immense potential as marketing research tools.[60]

With the incredible popularity of social media such as Facebook, Twitter, Orkut, and Mixi, consumers—especially younger consumers—almost obsessively post views and divulge their behaviors on mundane and seriously personal topics to friends and strangers. Moreover, the concept of "private" topics is shifting so that illnesses, body functions, sexual performance, and even criminal behavior are now public knowledge in some social networks. The opportunity to digitally journal is omnipresent with mobile apps and automatic posting of all kinds of information, including pictures and video, to social media.

The door is open, according to Mr. Leiman, for marketing researchers to capitalize on the new comfort levels evident in social media exchanges. He has four recommendations:

- Don't hesitate to ask consumers to tweet or post their reflections about mundane or personal habits.
- Create an affinity group social network so that new digital journal users will feel immediately comfortable with sharing information.
- Use technology to build a platform for rich digital journaling, such as pictures, video, and so on, and encourage frequent and spontaneous use of it.
- Be aware that unless agreements are in place, consumers who participate in a marketing research social digital journal study may share these experiences with their other social media outlets and thus alert competitors to the client's activities.

PHYSIOLOGICAL MEASUREMENT

Physiological measurement involves studying an individual's involuntary responses to marketing stimuli via the use of equipment that monitors eye dilation, respiration, voice pitch, brain waves, or some other body processes. We asked Courtney Murphy, Master of Marketing Research candidate, Southern Illinois University, Edwardsville, and a former student of one of the textbook authors, to describe brain wave research, which she is studying. Her description is featured in Marketing Research Insight 6.5.

The notion behind neuromarketing research is that physiological reactions cannot be consciously controlled, so they possibly reveal reactions that the individual is unaware of or unwilling to divulge. With most physiological measures, people who are monitored find the situation strange, and they may experience uneasiness during the monitoring. Because of this factor and the necessary equipment, these techniques are rarely used in marketing research.

We briefly describe two physiological measures to round out this chapter on qualitative research: the pupilometer and the galvanometer. The **pupilometer** is a device that attaches to a person's head and determines interest and attention by measuring the amount of dilation in the pupil of the eye. It actually photographs the movement of a person's pupil when he or she views different pictures. Theoretically, a person's pupil enlarges more with an interesting image than when an uninteresting one is viewed. **Eye tracking** is a technique for measuring where the eyes are looking. Which parts of an ad "catches the consumer's eye?" For example, AT&T™ has begun to use eye tracking coupled with in-depth interviewing to understand how its customers interact with its customer service website.[61] Eye tracking is especially useful in analyzing how consumers process advertisements.[62]

The **galvanometer** is a device that determines excitement levels by measuring the electrical activity in the respondent's skin. It requires electrodes or sensing pads to be taped to a person's body to monitor this activity. When a person encounters an interesting stimulus, the electrical

Physiological measurement involves monitoring a respondent's involuntary responses to marketing stimuli via the use of equipment that monitors body processes.

The pupilometer is a device that attaches to a person's head and determines interest and attention by measuring the amount of dilation in the pupil of the eye.

Qualitative Research Can Involve Observing Brain Activity!

Courtney Murphy
Master of Marketing Research Candidate, Southern Illinois University, Edwardsville

In this chapter you are learning about qualitative research. While quantitative research primarily involves asking consumers questions, qualitative research relies on observing consumers. One qualitative technique is called *neuroimaging*, which uses several techniques to measure brain activity. Neuroscience helps us to understand what it means when different parts of the brain show activity. The medial prefrontal cortex, for example, controls higher-level cognitive processing such as brand associations. By showing a consumer a stimulus such as an ad or a brand name, and then observing where brain activity occurs, marketing researchers can gain insights about what is going on in the subconscious mind.

Sometimes the interpretation of the subconscious differs from what consumers tell us when we ask them direct questions. Traditional methods of data collection rely on the consumer's conscious recollections. Yet, while the brain spends 2% of its energy on conscious activity, the remaining 98% is largely devoted to unconscious processing. Neuroimaging allows us to "see" the subconscious brain activity, which can provide additional insights into consumer behavior. The integration of neuroscience and marketing is often called *neuromarketing*. Dr. A. K. Pradeep of Neurofocus®, a neuromarketing research firm in Berkeley, California, describes his work as the "comput[ing] the deep subconscious response to stimuli."[63]

As an example of neuromarketing, neuroscientist Read Montague was interested in knowing why Pepsi did not have a dominant market share over Coke because Pepsi constantly promotes taste tests showing that, in a blind test, most

consumers prefer Pepsi over Coke. His research concluded that there was more activity in the medial prefrontal cortex, a portion of the brain that controls higher-level cognitive processing like brand association, when participants knew they were drinking Coke.[64] He concluded that consumers have a strong brand relationship with Coke. Another experiment confirms this strong brand linkage to preference. When consumers were given an unlabeled cup of Coke and a labeled cup of Coke, the majority preferred the labeled cup of Coke. A consumer's relationship with a brand can override true taste preferences.[65]

Neuromarketing research is constantly evolving, and several different approaches are used to observe the consumer's brain activity. The brain functions through the transmission of electrical impulses, and this electrical activity can be measured. Electroencephalography (EEG) measures the changes in electrical activity at the scalp. Consumers wear a device similar to a headband, and researchers can determine exactly when brain activity begins after exposure to a stimulus. By taking many samples, researchers can determine exactly which part of the brain is "firing" due to the stimulus. Knowledge of that brain part's function allows for better interpretation of the meaning of the brain activity.[66]

Functional magnetic resonance imaging (fMRI) is another method of neuromarketing research. Because active brain cells require more oxygen and glucose than less active brain cells, fMRI tracks blood flow to determine which parts of the brain are most active in reacting to a certain stimulus. Just like a normal MRI scan, the participant must be lying down on or sitting up in the fMRI machine. Unlike the EEG, fMRI can locate almost exactly *where* neural activity is taking place within a millimeter of its actual location.[67]

SOUTHERN ILLINOIS UNIVERSITY
EDWARDSVILLE
SCHOOL OF BUSINESS

MMR
Master of Marketing Research

A Nielsen Company

Neurofocus is a wholly owned subsidiary of The Nielsen Company and is recognized as the global leader in neuromarketing.

By permission.

Several *biometric techniques* may be used in neuromarketing research. *Eye-tracking* is used to allow researchers to know exactly what stimulus the consumer is viewing to associate brain activity with the correct stimulus. *Automatic facial expression recognition* is being used to help interpret emotions. Facial recognition software compiles hundreds and even thousands of facial expressions to recognize the expression of the consumer being observed. The algorithms used in these software programs can be extremely complex, matching up the exact emotion expressed by the consumer according to the relative size, location, and position of a consumer's cheekbones, eyes, nose, and jaw. Other measures of emotion such as *electrocardiography* to measure heartbeat and measures of respiration and *GSR* (galvanic skin response) are used to measure anxiety.

Neuromarketing is still in its early stages. However, if using neuromarketing research can help us gain only small incremental increases in our understanding of consumer behavior, that knowledge can be valuable. Though some critics would have us believe marketers have the ability to train consumers as robots, marketers know there is far more about consumers we don't understand than we understand.

Text and images: By permission, Courtney Murphy, MMR.

impulses in the body become excited. Physiological measures are useful under special circumstances, such as testing sexually oriented stimuli about which many people are embarrassed or may not tell the truth, and they require special skills to be administered correctly. There are two disadvantages to using physiological measurement techniques. First, the techniques are unnatural, and subjects may become nervous and emit false readings. Second, even though we know that the respondent reacted to the stimulus, we do not know if the response was positive or negative.[68]

Eye tracking and galvanometers are now considered "old" methods as marketing research is moving into neuroscience techniques with difficult-to-pronounce names, such as electroencephalography and topography.[69] However, these techniques suffer from the same interpretation difficulties as the old methods.

As you learned in Marketing Research Insight 6.5, **neuroimaging**, or viewing brain activity, may aid marketing researchers to better understand consumers' unconscious activity when they are being tested. By using neuroimaging and understanding the neuroscience behind it, marketing researchers may be able to more accurately posit what consumers really want (which can be different from what they say they want), what appeals to them, and what drives them to buy. For example, suppose an advertising company wants to observe a college student's responses to energy drink displays at a grocery store during finals. The student could be fit with an EEG device before walking through the store; the device might be hidden beneath a hat so that other shoppers will not react to the device and make the student insecure or nervous. While the student is exploring the various displays, data collected from the EEG device could measure variables such as happiness, confusion, anger, and other emotional responses.[70]

The galvanometer is a device that determines excitement levels by measuring electrical activity in the respondent's skin.

 Synthesize Your Learning

This exercise will require you to take into consideration concepts and material from the following chapters:

| Chapter 5 | Second Data and Packaged Information |
| Chapter 6 | Qualitative Research Techniques |

Lucy Betcher had worked as a consultant for the Small Business Administration for a number of years. Her old high school classmates and their spouses gather at least once a year to renew friendships. Judy Doyle, Mike Fuller, Adele Smith, Nancy Egolf, Joy Greer, and Jackie Reynolds had different careers and several were retiring. At their last reunion, Jackie mentioned to Lucy that she was interested in doing something else after retiring from teaching. Adele overheard this conversation and said she was interested in trying something new as well. Could Lucy, with all her years of helping others get started in business, assist her friends?

The next morning, while sitting on Todd and Joy's comfortable balcony overlooking boats in a canal, Lucy asked the entire group: "Jackie and Adele are interested in getting into some sort of business opportunity. Do any of you have any thoughts on this?"

Mike, having spent a successful career in pharmaceutical sales, said, "There are opportunities for services for senior citizens in terms of prescription drug management and administration." Mike noted that many older people still in their homes or living in retirement centers had difficulty keeping track of getting their prescriptions filled and taking their medications on schedule.

"It's a real problem when people get to be 85 and over," Mike said. "I see a growing need for a personal service that would provide this type of care."

Nancy and Judy talked about a unique coffee shop they had patronized. Not only was the staff knowledgeable about different types of coffees and helpful in guiding customers to sample different flavors, but the shop also sold a variety of coffee markers and tea makers and books on coffee and teas. However, what they really liked was the atmosphere. Instead of the placid and contemplative ambience that most coffee shops offer, this shop featured different "learning" exhibits where you could interact and discover something new. The topics changed weekly—local history, coffee making, art, music, and readings by authors.

The two women were fascinated with the shop and had talked to the owner about franchising the concept so they could each start one in their home towns in Pennsylvania and New York. The owner told them he had several successful franchises operating. The biggest challenge the prospective coffee shop owners would face initially would be in finding a location that would attract the clientele who would embrace the product and atmosphere and return regularly. The owner obviously couldn't help them make those decisions in their home towns, so they would need help finding the best locations there.

1. Looking back at Chapter 5, what secondary data could identify the number of persons in different age-groups in each CBSA?

2. Based on what you learned in Chapter 5, identify a packaged services firm that would be helpful in locating a successful coffee shop in different locales. Assume that since the coffee shop owner has several successful coffee shops, he has a database of current customer information.

3. Considering either the prescription service or the coffee shop venture, what qualitative research techniques would you now recommend that the prospective business owners use? Why would you recommend these qualitative techniques?

Summary

This chapter described the various qualitative research techniques used by marketing researchers. Quantitative research uses predetermined structured questions with predetermined structured response options. It is also normally characterized by the use of large samples. Qualitative research is much less structured than quantitative approaches. Qualitative research involves collecting, analyzing, and interpreting data by observing what people do or say. The observations and statements are in an unstructured, nonstandardized form. The advantage of qualitative research is that it allows researchers to gather deeper, richer information from respondents. Pluralistic research involves using both qualitative and quantitative research methods.

Observation is a qualitative research technique in which researchers observe what consumers do rather than communicate with them. Observation techniques can be direct or indirect, covert or overt, structured or unstructured, and in situ or invented. Circumstances most suited to observational studies involve a (1) short time interval, (2) public behavior, and (3) the likelihood of faulty recall if respondents are asked about previous experiences. The primary advantage of observation is that researchers record what respondents actually do instead of relying on their recall of what they think they do. The limitations of observation studies are that they often rely on small samples, so representativeness is a concern. Another disadvantage is the subjective interpretation required to explain the behavior observed. Researchers do not know consumers' motives, attitudes, or intentions.

Focus groups, or moderated small-group discussions, are a popular form of qualitative research. The major task of the moderator is to ensure freewheeling and open communication that stays focused on the research topic. Traditional focus groups use about 6 to 12 persons in a dedicated room, with a one-way mirror for client viewing. Recent innovations in contemporary focus groups include online focus groups in which clients may observe from a distant location via video streaming over the Internet. Another form of online focus group allows people to participate from their homes or any remote location where they observe and respond to other participants via chat rooms. Focus groups have the following advantages: (1) they generate fresh ideas; (2) they allow clients to observe their participants; and (3) they may be directed at understanding a wide variety of issues. Disadvantages include lack of representativeness, subjective evaluation of the meaning of the discussions, and high costs per participant. Focus groups should be used when there is a need to describe marketing phenomena. They should not be used when there is a need to predict a phenomenon such as projecting sales for a new product evaluated by a focus group. Four main objectives of focus groups are to generate ideas; to understand consumer vocabulary; to reveal consumer needs, motives, perceptions, and attitudes on products or services; and to better understand findings from quantitative studies.

To convene a focus group, marketing researchers should have 6 to 12 participants. sharing similar characteristics and come up with a plan for potential "no shows." Focus group facilities exist in most major cities, but any large room with a central table can be used. The moderator's role is key to a successful focus group, and he or she should become involved early on in the research project.

Another qualitative technique involves in-depth interviews (IDIs) to examine consumer motivations and hidden concerns. Protocol analysis induces participants to "think aloud" so the researcher can map the decision-making process a consumer uses in making a purchase decision. Projective techniques, such as word association, sentence completion, or role playing, are also useful in unearthing motivations, beliefs, and attitudes that subjects may not be able to express well verbally. Ethnographic research involves observing consumers in near-natural settings to monitor their behaviors, relations with others, and emotions.

New qualitative research techniques have emerged with advances in computer, Internet, and communications technologies. Some physiological measurements, such as pupil dilation or eye movement and electrical activity in the skin or brain, may also offer clues to consumer reactions to products and messages. Neuromarketing is an emerging field that may offer additional qualitative insights into consumer behavior.

Key Terms

Quantitative research (p. 118)
Qualitative research (p. 118)
Pluralistic research (p. 118)
Observation methods (p. 120)
Direct observation (p. 120)
Indirect observation (p. 120)
Archives (p. 120)
Physical traces (p. 120)
Covert observation (p. 121)
Overt observation (p. 121)
Structured observation (p. 121)
Unstructured observation (p. 121)

In situ observation (p. 121)
Invented observation (p. 121)
Focus groups (p. 123)
Traditional focus group (p. 123)
Contemporary focus group (p. 124)
Moderators (p. 124)
Focus group report (p. 124)
Online focus group (p. 125)
In-depth interview (p. 129)
Laddering (p. 130)
Protocol analysis (p. 130)
Projective techniques (p. 131)

Word-association test (p. 132)
Sentence-completion test (p. 132)
Picture test (p. 132)
Balloon test (p. 133)
Role playing (p. 133)
Ethnographic research (p. 133)
Physiological measurement (p. 135)
Pupilometer (p. 135)
Eye Tracking (p. 135)
Galvanometer (p. 135)
Neuroimaging (p. 137)

Review Questions/Applications

1. Define quantitative research. Define qualitative research. List the differences between these two research methods. What is pluralistic research?

2. What is meant by an "observation technique"? What is observed, and why is it recorded?

3. Indicate why covert observation would be appropriate for a study on how parents discipline their children when dining out.

4. Describe a traditional focus group.

5. Describe two formats of online focus groups.

6. Describe at least three different uses of focus groups.

7. How are focus group participants recruited, and what is a common problem associated with this recruitment?

8. Should the members of a focus group be similar or dissimilar? Why?

9. Describe what a focus group setting looks like and how a focus group would take place in one.

10. Should the marketing manager client be a focus group moderator? Why or why not?

11. Indicate how a focus group moderator should handle each of the following cases: (a) a participant is loud and dominates the conversation; (b) a participant is obviously suffering from a cold and goes into coughing fits every few minutes; (c) two participants who, it turns out, are acquaintances persist in a private conversation about their children; and (d) the only minority representative participant in the focus group looks uncomfortable with the group and fails to make any comments.

12. What should be included in a report that summarizes the findings of a focus group?

13. Indicate the advantages and disadvantages of client interaction in the design and execution of a focus group study.

14. What is laddering? Discuss how it may be used in marketing research.

15. What is protocol analysis?

16. What is meant by the term *projective*, as in *projective techniques*?

17. Describe (a) sentence completion, (b) word association, and (c) balloon test. Create one of each of these that might be used to test the reactions of parents whose children are bed wetters to absorbent underpants that their children would wear under their nightclothes.

18. What is ethnographic research? Discuss how a marketing researcher could get into an ethically sensitive situation using the technique.

19. What is physiological measurement? Give examples of two techniques.

20. Associated Grocery Stores (AGS) has always used paper bags for sacking groceries in its chain of retail supermarkets. Management has noticed that some competitors are offering reusable bags to their customers. AGS management isn't certain just how strongly consumers in its markets feel about having to bring the reusable bags every time they visit the supermarket. Select two projective techniques. First, defend your use of a projective technique. Second, describe in detail how your two chosen techniques would be applied to this research problem.

21. Your university is considering letting an apartment management company build an apartment complex on campus. To save money, the company proposes to build a common cooking area for every four apartments. This area would be equipped with an oven, stove-top burners, microwave oven, sink, food preparation area, garbage disposal, and individual minirefrigerators with locks on them for each apartment. Two students would live in each apartment, so eight students would use the common cooking area. You volunteer to conduct focus groups with students to determine their reactions to this concept and to brainstorm suggestions for improvements. Prepare the topics list you would have as a guide in your role as moderator.

CASE 6.1

The College Experience

Dr. Daniel Purdy,
Western Washington
University

This case was provided by Professor Daniel Purdy, Assistant Director of the MBA Program, and Professor Wendy Wilhelm, Professor of Marketing, both of Western Washington University.

The College of Business at Western Washington University is a full-service business school at a midsized regional university. The College of Business specializes in undergraduate business education with selected graduate programs. While the College emphasizes mostly professional education, it does so within a liberal arts context. Business majors range from standards such as Accounting, Marketing, and Finance to more unique

offerings, such as the highly successful Manufacturing and Supply Chain Management degree.

The College is committed to a student-centered style of education that emphasizes the students not as customers but as equal stakeholders in the process of education. As part of its commitment to involving the students as true partners, the College has recently begun the process of conducting focus groups of undergraduate and graduate students. The objective of these focus groups is to identify negative and positive attitudes about the College and develop new ideas to improve the College.

Dr. Wendy Wilhelm,
Western Washington
University

The following is an excerpt from the transcript of the first undergraduate focus group. This group included 14 students with the following makeup: 50% male and 50% female; 93% work part-time or more, and 7% do not work; and 29% management majors, with other majors no more than 15%.

Moderator: So what do you guys think are some ways that the College (not the University) can be improved?

Jeff: I really like the fact that professors are accessible, willing to help and a lot of them let us call them by their first name. Something that I think could be better is that we don't spend enough time learning how to do things but instead professors spend too much time talking about theory.

Sarah: Yea, Yea, I agree totally. It seems like most of the time we aren't learning practical skills but just talking about what we "should" do, not really learning how to do it.

Moderator: Interesting points, how would you suggest the College try to increase the amount of practical learning?

Todd: It would really be cool if we could do more real-life professional work in our classes. Things like skill-based projects that focus on doing what we would really do in our profession.

Tim: I think we should all have to do a mandatory internship as part of our major. Right now, some majors let you do it as an elective but they are really hard to find and get.

Moderator: Good ideas. Are there other things you think we could improve?

Rhonda: I agree that the professors try really hard to be open to students but the advising is really not very good, I don't know how to fix it but I know my advisor is pretty much useless.

Ariel: I know, I know. It is so frustrating sometimes. I go to my advisor and she tells me to just fill in my degree planning sheet and she'll sign it. It's like they don't even know what I should be taking or why.

Jon: My advisor is kind of funny, he just tells me that he doesn't really know that much about classes he doesn't teach and my guess is as good as his. At least he's honest anyway.

Moderator: Ok, Ok, so the advising you are getting from the faculty leaves a little to be desired. What do you guys do to figure out how to plan your degrees if your advisors aren't helping much?

Sarah: I just ask my friends who are further along in the major than I am.

Mark: Yea, me too. In the Student Marketing Association we all give each other advice on what professors are good, what classes go good together, which have prerequisites and stuff like that. It would be cool if we could have something like that for the whole college.

Moderator: Don't you think CBE could be improved if we developed some sort of Peer-Advising Program?

Using these excerpts as representative of the entire focus group transcript, answer the following questions:

1. Do you think focus groups were the appropriate research method in this case, given the research objectives? What other type(s) of research might provide useful data?
2. Evaluate the questions posed by the moderator in light of the research objectives/question: (a) Are any of them leading or biased in any way? (b) Can you think of any additional questions that could/should be included?
3. Examine the findings. How is CBE perceived? What are its apparent strengths and weaknesses?
4. Can we generalize these findings to all of the College's students? Why or why not?

Text and images: By permission, Drs. Daniel Purdy and Wendy Wilhelm, Western Washington University.

CASE 6.2 INTEGRATED CASE

Global Motors

Nick Thomas, CEO of Global Motors, has begun formulating some concepts in terms of the types of car models to pursue to bring the ZEN Motors product line back to life. He has been using a cross-functional approach to new product development involving finance, production, R&D, marketing, and advertising in his planning. Ashley Roberts, from advertising, is discussing some of the general plans for the new car models with Nick. He tells Ashley Global Motors needs more marketing research information about customer preferences for different types of cars. However, he notes that the broad choices will come down to different-sized vehicles with some much smaller than ZEN has ever built. One model being considered is a small, almost scooterlike car. Other models are larger but still much smaller than ZEN's traditional line of cars to obtain suitable mpg ratings. Ashley

knows this is a big change for ZEN and the way it has advertised for years. She wonders if the customers who prefer the new, smaller models possess different sets of salient values. Perhaps those who prefer the scooterlike model would value excitement and entertainment in their lives while those expressing a preference for the larger-sized, high-mpg models would place a higher priority on social recognition or harmony with the environment or some other value. If differences are found, the agency can alter the values emphasized in the ad's visuals and copy (e.g., depicting an exciting life, thrill of the drive or sense of accomplishment or recognition of contributing to environmental problems, and so on) to suit the model of the car being promoted.

What technique identified in this chapter would help Ashley Roberts with this advertising task? Why?

Evaluating Survey Data Collection Methods

LEARNING OBJECTIVES

- To learn the four basic alternative modes for gathering survey data
- To understand the advantages and disadvantages of each of the various data collection modes
- To become knowledgeable about the details of different types of survey data collection methods, such as personal interviews, telephone interviews, and computer-administered interviews, including online surveys
- To comprehend the factors researchers consider when choosing a particular survey method

"WHERE WE ARE"

1 Establish the need for marketing research.

2 Define the problem.

3 Establish research objectives.

4 Determine research design.

5 Identify information types and sources.

6 Determine methods of accessing data.

7 Design data collection forms.

8 Determine the sample plan and size.

9 Collect data.

10 Analyze data.

11 Prepare and present the final research report.

Mobile Data Collection

Leslie Townsend, President, Kinesis Survey Technologies LLC

Mobile data collection is but the newest part of an evolving mix of data collection modes that began more than a century ago and gathered impetus as new forms of communication—— telephone, radio, television, computers, and most recently mobile devices—entered people's lives. These devices not only brought entertainment and enrichment of daily routines, but have each in turn served to influence commerce through the use of advertising. All have been, at one time or another, disruptive technologies.

New research data collection modes are adopted when they can deliver one of three unique advantages to the market research industry:

- A more cost-effective solution
- A faster delivery time
- A unique capability that has not existed in the past

Quantitative data collection began with pen and paper, and even today this mode persists. For example, in the U.S. health care industry, there is currently regulation requiring the utilization of this mode for specific types of data collection. Many U.S. Census forms are still completed on paper, mailed in, and scanned (or manually entered when data cannot be scanned accurately). Paper-based data collection is used today by organizations that require full representation of the underlying population, including that very small percentage that does not have access to telephones or computers.

Most paper-based data collection was displaced when nationwide calling became affordable, which occurred when competition was introduced into the telecommunications networks and drove long-distance rates down. Telephone-based data collection, in turn, provided impetus to automated dialers and the emergence of computers, which created the CATI (computer-assisted telephone interviewing) market. CATI systems greatly improved the productivity of telephone interviewers through automated dialing, tracking performance statistics that could be reported back to management, and enabling the programming of skip patterns and other logic.

Visit www.kinesissurvey.com

Text and images: By permission, Leslie Townsend, Kinesis Survey Technologies LLC.

Yet no matter how automated, CATI systems still require an interviewer. As the online population increased over the past two decades, a tremendous cost component of market research was able to be eliminated through the online administration of surveys with no "read-aloud" element. This capability also reduced some inherent biases, in that the interviewer's tone or manner of questioning could not "lead" the respondent to a specific response, and respondents were not somehow encouraged to please the interviewer. There is greater bias in the online population, however, because the penetration of households with access to online computing remains lower than the penetration of households with telephones.

Is mobile data collection the latest disruptor? In many ways it is, and in other ways it is a merely a continuation of previous online data collection practices, both qualitative and quantitative, that began a generation ago. There is no denying that today's smart phones, often coupled with social media, are fundamentally changing the manner in which generations across the globe communicate and interact. The mobile phone has been credited with everything from improving the economies of rural areas in remote regions by introducing e-commerce and lending to generating the "crowd voicing" that has led to political uprisings. If it is transforming political processes and economies, it cannot help but impact the market research industry.

Mobile data collection offers fielding times that are at least as fast, and often faster, than traditional online surveys because the mobile device is a personal one that is typically with the respondent at all times. Today additional costs are associated with mobile data collection simply because it is a new technology to adopt, but in the longer run, mobile data collection should be no more expensive than other types of online surveys. Most importantly, however,

Taking online surveys on an iPad or other tablet computer is becoming a common practice.

mobile data collect offers the ability to collect situational and new types of data. It is the first data collection mode that can be utilized at the point of sale and consumption. It also offers important new forms of metadata—most significantly, location-based data, both at a point in time and potentially on a tracking basis. Because mobile phones have a camera, incoming media are easily incorporated into data collection; with the ability to scan barcodes, reporting accuracy of purchases can be improved. (Marketing Research Insight 7.1, included later in this chapter, expands on Ms. Townsend's observations on mobile data collection.)

About Kinesis

Kinesis is the industry leader for future-proof market research solutions. Offering powerful and cutting-edge survey software and panel management software, Kinesis is committed to advancing innovation in both desktop and mobile research. Kinesis was founded in June 2003 to capitalize on the capabilities of wireless devices to fill critical technology gaps within the market research industry. Since that time, the company has been at the forefront of exploration and innovation in mobile market research and today is the world leader in mobile survey software. Kinesis is headquartered in Austin, Texas, and has a European office in London. With clients and partners located across the globe, Kinesis proudly supports next-generation market research worldwide.

Surveys involve interviews with a large number of respondents using a predesigned questionnaire.

A s you are learning in this course, there are many different ways of conducting marketing research studies. In previous chapters, we discussed different forms of research, such as focus groups, experiments, and surveys. There are many ways of gathering information among these various types of studies. In this chapter, our attention is on surveys. A **survey** involves interviews with a large number of respondents using a predesigned questionnaire.[1] Communication is necessary to learn what respondents are thinking—their opinions, preferences, or planned intentions. Large numbers of respondents may be required to collect a large enough sample of important subgroups or to ensure that the study accurately represents some larger population. In this chapter we focus on the various methods used to collect data for surveys.

This chapter begins with a short discussion on why surveys are popular and advantageous. Next, it describes basic survey modes: (1) person-administered surveys, (2) computer-assisted surveys, (3) computer-administered surveys, (4) self-administered surveys, and (5) mixed-mode, sometimes called "hybrid," surveys.

Key advantages of surveys include standardization, ease of administration, ability to tap the "unseen," suitability to tabulation and statistical analysis, and sensitivity to subgroup differences.

We discuss the advantages and disadvantages of each of these modes and present the various alternative methods of collecting data within each of three basic data collection modes. For example, person-administered surveys may be conducted through mall intercepts or telephone. Finally, we discuss factors a market researcher should consider when deciding which data collection method to use.

Basic survey modes include person-administered surveys, computer-assisted surveys, self-administered surveys, and mixed-mode, or "hybrid," surveys.

Advantages of Surveys

Compared to observation or other qualitative methods, survey methods allow the collection of significant amounts of data in an economical and efficient manner, and they typically involve large sample sizes. There are five advantages of using survey methods: (1) standardization, (2) ease of administration, (3) ability to tap the "unseen," (4) suitability to tabulation and statistical analysis, and (5) sensitivity to subgroup differences (see Table 7.1).

TABLE 7.1   Five Advantages of Surveys

Advantage	Description
Provides standardization	All respondents react to questions worded identically and presented in the same order. Response options (scales) are the same, too.
Easy to administer	Interviewers read questions to respondents and record their answers quickly and easily. In many cases, the respondents read and respond to the questionnaires themselves.
Gets "beneath the surface"	While not as detailed as in-depth interviews or focus groups, it is common to ask questions about motives, circumstances, sequences of events, or mental deliberations, none of which are available in observation studies.
Easy to analyze	Standardization and computer processing allow for quick tallies, cross tabulations, and other statistical analyses despite large sample sizes.
Reveals subgroup differences	Respondents can be divided into segments or subgroups (e.g., users vs. nonusers or age-groups) for comparisons in the search for meaningful differences.

 Active Learning

Experience the Advantages of Surveys

To experience the advantages of surveys firsthand, administer the following survey to four friends, two males and two females. You can either (1) write or type the questions on paper and hand them to each friend or (2) read each question and record the answers of each friend separately. However, in the second option, you should keep each friend's answers separate from the others.

1. Did you watch television last night?
    _____ Yes _____ No
2. (If yes) For about how many hours did you watch television last night?
    _____ Less than 1 _____ Between 1 and 2
    _____ Between 2 and 4 _____ More than 4
3. Why do you usually watch television? (Select only one)
    _____ Entertainment (variety, humor, drama, sports, talk)
    _____ Education (science, news, history, cooking)
    _____ Escape (science fiction, action, reality, travel)
4. What is your gender?
    _____ Male _____ Female

Now that you have administered the survey, let's consider each advantage.

Standardization. How have the response options for questions 2 and 3 standardized the survey? In other words, what answers might have come about if you did not give your respondents these specific response categories from which to pick?

Ease of Analysis. What percent of your friends who took part in the survey watched television last night? What percent of them watched TV four or more hours? To answer these questions, how long did it take for you to tabulate the findings? Also, since the respondents checked off or voiced the answers, how did this make your analysis task easy?

Ease of Administration. How difficult was it for you to administer the survey? One way to answer this is to estimate how long it took for you, on average, to obtain each respondent's answers.

Get Beneath the Surface. Do your friends watch television mostly for entertainment, education, or escape? Tabulate the answers to question 3 to find out. Notice that with a single question, you have discovered the reasons, or motivations, for your friends' television viewing.

Subgroup Differences. Do the two males differ from the two females? Do separate percentage tabulations for each gender and compare the percentages. In a matter of a few minutes, you can spot whether or not differences exist in the subgroups and what the differences are.

Modes of Data Collection

THE DATA COLLECTION DILEMMA AND IMPACT OF TECHNOLOGY

Before we begin this section, we must alert you to the fact that the data collection step in the marketing research process is in the midst of great change. There are two reasons for this change. First, in recent decades, there has been a dramatic decline in the willingness of the general public to take part in surveys, and, second, computer and telecommunications technology has advanced significantly and opened new, efficient ways for marketing researchers to collect data. With respect to declining survey response rates, Roger Tourangeau[2] has identified the major reasons for this trend. The factors underlying a growing unwillingness in the U.S. public to take part in surveys are use of "gatekeepers," such as answering machines, caller ID, and call blocking (for example, it is estimated that over 25% of American homes have moved exclusively to mobile phones[3]); reduced amounts of free time; decline in the public's engagement with important issues; rising percent of foreign-born Americans who are not fluent in English; and increases in the number of elderly who have comprehension and expression difficulties. There is also a growing desire for privacy among Americans. Indeed, the declining cooperation rates are being experienced worldwide, not just in the United States. These rising nonresponse rates have caused marketing researchers to rethink the use of traditional data collection methods.

Thus, technology has opened doors to new methods, although it has not solved the nonresponse problem. Two primary reasons for the technology push are rising costs of data collection and consumers' adoption of new communication systems.[4] The cost of doing research has increased along with rising prices of energy, personnel, and support functions. To remain competitive and, in some cases, to remain in business, marketing research companies have sought out data collection cost-saving alternatives of many types. At the same time, consumers have integrated personal, laptop, and handheld computers into their lives, and many have adopted mobile communication systems. To stay relevant, marketing research companies have necessarily adapted to these new communication systems.

The rise of technology and the rapid adoption of sophisticated personal communication systems by consumers underlie the troublesome data collection dilemma faced by marketing researchers all over the globe. In particular, the response rate—the percent of individuals asked to participate in a survey who actually take part in that survey—is low and declining yearly.[5] At the same time, a "squeeze" is apparent in the rising percent of noncontacts, or the percent of those individuals who researchers attempt to contact to ask to take part in a survey who cannot be reached. The problem is especially significant with telephone interviewing, as telephone users have effectively blocked marketing researchers with caller ID, answering devices, and the like.

Surely, you have personally experienced the wave of technological advances in communications. In the case of data collection, where the marketing research industry is completely

TABLE 7.2   Data Collection and Computer Technology

	No Computer	Computer
Interviewer	**Person administered** Interviewer reads questions and records the answers on paper.	**Computer assisted** Interviewer reads the questions and uses computer technology to record the answers and/or otherwise assist in the interview.
No interviewer	**Self-administered** Respondent reads the questions on a page and responds by writing on the questionnaire.	**Computer administered** Computer communicates the questions and records the respondent's answers.

dependent on communications, profound shifts have taken place and continue to take place. These shifts are partly due to changes in the communication preferences of consumers. For example, mobile telephones with caller identification and conference calling capabilities are the communication standard of many consumers. At the same time, these changes are due to technological advances that make the data collection process faster, simpler, more secure, and even less expensive.

Data collection is currently a blend of traditional, or low-technology, methods and contemporary, or high-technology, approaches. As noted in Table 7.2, the four possible types of data collection are characterized by (1) whether an interviewer is used and (2) whether computer technology is employed. Thus, data collection can be person administered, computer assisted, computer administered, or self-administered. We will describe each form of administration in detail. Each data collection mode has special advantages and disadvantages that we describe in general before discussing the various types of surveys found within each category. Specific advantages and disadvantages on these various types are discussed later in the chapter.

PERSON-ADMINISTERED SURVEYS

In a **person-administered survey**, an interviewer reads questions, either face-to-face or over the telephone, to the respondent and records his or her answers without the use of a computer. This was the primary administration mode for many years. However, its popularity has fallen off as costs have increased and as computer technology has advanced. Nevertheless, person-administered surveys are still used, and we describe the advantages and disadvantages associated with these surveys next.

In a person-administered survey, an interviewer reads questions, either face-to-face or over the telephone, to the respondent and records his or her answers without the use of a computer.

Advantages of Person-Administered Surveys   Person-administered surveys have four unique advantages: They offer feedback, rapport, quality control, and adaptability.[6] They also tend to have higher response rates than methods without interviewers, permit a variety of techniques (such as card sorting) that are cumbersome with other data collection methods, and overcome illiteracy or poor reading ability of the language.[7]

1. Feedback   Interviewers often must respond to direct questions from respondents during an interview. Sometimes respondents do not understand the instructions, they may not hear the question clearly, or they might become distracted during the interview. A human interviewer may be allowed to adjust his or her questions according to verbal or nonverbal cues. When a respondent begins to fidget or look bored, the interviewer can say, "I have only a few more questions." Or if a respondent makes a comment, the interviewer may jot it down as a side note to the researcher.

Without a personal interviewer, a respondent may fail to understand survey questions.

Photo: Yuri Arcurs/Shutterstock

2. Rapport Some people distrust surveys in general, or they may have some suspicions about the survey at hand. It is often helpful to have another human being present to develop some rapport with the respondent early on in the questioning process. A person can create trust and understanding that nonpersonal forms of data collection cannot achieve.

3. Quality Control An interviewer sometimes must select certain types of respondents based on gender, age, or some other distinguishing characteristic. Personal interviewers may be used to ensure that respondents are selected correctly. Using a personal interviewer ensures that every question will be asked of the respondent. Additionally, some researchers feel that respondents are more likely to be truthful when they respond face-to-face.

4. Adaptability Personal interviewers can adapt to respondent differences. It is not unusual, for instance, to find an elderly person or a very young person who must be initially helped step-by-step through the answering process to understand how to respond to questions. Interviewers are trained to ensure that they do not alter the meaning of a question by interpreting the question to a respondent. In fact, interviewers should follow precise rules on how to adapt to different situations presented by respondents.

Personal interviewers can build rapport with respondents who are initially distrustful or suspicious.

Personal interviewers can adapt to differences in respondents, but they must be careful not to alter the meaning of a question.

The disadvantages of person-administered surveys are human error, slow data collection, high cost, and interview evaluation apprehension among respondents.

Disadvantages of Person-Administered Surveys The drawbacks to using human interviewers are human error, slowness, cost, and interview evaluation.

1. Humans Make Errors Human interviewers may ask questions out of sequence, or they may change the wording of a question, which may change the meaning of the question altogether. Humans can make mistakes recording the information provided by the respondent. Human interviewers may make any number of errors when they become fatigued or bored from repetition.

While not an "error" in the sense we are discussing, another danger of using personal interviewers is the potential for "cheating," such as trying to steer survey participants to certain responses or purposefully recording answers that do not reflect the participants' responses.

2. Slow Speed Collecting data using human interviewers is slower than other modes because of necessary sequential interviewing. Although pictures, videos, and graphics can be handled by personal interviewers, they cannot accommodate them as quickly as, say, computers. Often personal interviewers simply record respondents' answers using pencil and paper, which necessitates a separate data-input step to build a computer data file. For this reason, increasing numbers of data collection companies have shifted to the use of laptop computers that immediately add the responses to a data file.

3. High Cost Naturally, the use of a face-to-face interviewer is more expensive than, say, mailing the questionnaire to respondents. Typically, personal interviewers are highly trained and skilled, which explains the expense factor. Of course, a telephone personal interviewer is less expensive, but this method is still more costly than mail or online surveys.

Interview evaluation occurs when the interviewer's presence creates anxieties in respondents that may cause them to alter their normal responses.

4. Fear of Interview Evaluation Another disadvantage of person-administered surveys is that the presence of another person may create apprehension,[8] called *interview evaluation*, among certain respondents. **Interview evaluation** may occur when another person is involved in the interviewing process and some respondents are apprehensive that they are answering "correctly." Even when responding to questions from a perfect stranger, some people become anxious about the possible reaction of the interviewer to their answers. They may be concerned as to how the interviewer evaluates their responses, especially on personal topics, such as personal hygiene, political opinions, financial matters, and age. The presence of a human interviewer may cause survey respondents to answer differently than they would in a nonpersonal data collection mode. Some respondents, for example, try to please the interviewer by saying what they think the interviewer wants to hear.

COMPUTER-ASSISTED SURVEYS

Computer technology represents an attractive, efficient, and flexible option with respect to survey mode, and new developments occur almost every day. While person-administered surveys were the industry mainstay, computer-assisted survey methods have grown to a dominant position in developed countries. In this mode, a telephone interviewer may read questions and record answers on a computer screen. In a **computer-assisted survey**, the interviewer basically verbalizes the questions while relying to some degree on computer technology to facilitate the interview work. Here the computer accommodates the interview process by, for example, showing the questions to read, allowing storage of the answers, or, perhaps, even demonstrating some product feature with a video or pictures. Computer technology assists the interviewer by making the interview process more efficient and effective. As you would expect, computer-assisted surveys have many advantages and a few disadvantages.

Technology plays a support role in the interviewer's work in a computer-assisted survey.

Advantages of Computer-Assisted Surveys There are variations of computer-assisted surveys. The interviewer may be calling on a phone or interacting with respondents face-to-face. The computer may provide and record all questions and answers, say on a pad or tablet, or it may be used to cryptically record answers. Regardless of which variation is considered, at least four advantages of computer-assisted surveys are evident: speed; relatively error-free interviews; use of pictures, videos, and graphics; and quick capture of data. Of course, because a trained interviewer is present, computer-assisted data collection automatically garners the benefits of person-administered data collection.

1. Speed Perhaps the greatest single advantage of computer-assisted data collection is its ability to gather survey data very quickly. The computer-assisted approach is much faster than the purely human interview approach. A computer does not become fatigued or bored, and it does not make human errors. The speed factor translates into cost savings.

Computer-assisted surveys are fast, error free, capable of using pictures or graphics, able to capture data in real time, and less threatening for some respondents.

2. Relatively Error-Free Interviews Properly programmed, the computer-assisted approach guarantees zero computer errors, although it cannot prevent interviewer errors, such as inadvertently skipping questions, asking inappropriate questions based on previous responses, misunderstanding how to pose questions, or recording the wrong answer.

3. Use of Pictures, Videos, and Graphics Computer graphics can be integrated into questions as they are viewed on a computer screen. Rather than having an interviewer pull out a picture of a new type of window air conditioner, for instance, computer graphics can show it from various perspectives. High-quality streaming video may be programmed so that the respondent can see the product in use or can be shown a wide range of visual displays.

4. Quick Capture of Data At the end of the interviewer's day, he or she typically conveys the respondents' data into the central office. This can be done by modem, by downloading via cable, or any other computer media transfer method.

The quick capture of data by computer-administered surveys is an important advantage of this data collection mode.

With computer-assisted telephone interviews, responses can be stored immediately because a central computer system is used, while in other cases the responses are periodically loaded to a master data file.

Disadvantages of Computer-Assisted Surveys The primary disadvantages of computer-assisted surveys are that they require some level of technical skill and setup costs may be significant.

1. Technical Skills May Be Required A wide range of computer-assisted methods is available to marketing researchers. While the simplest options require minimal technical skills and even interviewers with low computer skills can master them quickly, more sophisticated versions (such as CATI, to be described later) require considerable skill to master the computer interfaces.

2. Setup Costs Can Be High While computer technology can result in increases in productivity, there can be high setup costs associated with getting some of these systems in place and operational. Computer-assisted systems, such as electronic notebooks or tablets, incur initial purchase costs. With the most sophisticated computer-assisted survey types, programming and debugging must take place with each survey. One software evaluator has estimated that two days of setup time by an experienced programmer was fairly efficient.[9] Depending on what type of computer-assisted survey is under consideration, these costs, including the associated time factor, can render computer-assisted delivery systems for surveys less attractive relative to other data collection options.

SELF-ADMINISTERED SURVEYS

In a **self-administered survey**, the respondent completes the survey on his or her own with no agent—human or computer—administering the interview.[10] We are referring to the prototypical "paper-and-pencil" survey here where the respondent reads the questions and responds directly on the questionnaire. Normally, the respondent goes at his or her own pace, and often he or she selects the place and time to complete the survey. He or she also may decide when the questionnaire will be returned. In other words, responding to the questions is entirely under the control of the respondent.

Advantages of Self-Administered Surveys Self-administered surveys have three important advantages: reduced cost, respondent control, and no interviewer-evaluation apprehension.

1. Reduced Cost Eliminating the need for an interviewer or an administering device such as a computer program can result in significant cost savings.

2. Respondent Control Respondents can control the pace at which they respond, so they may not feel rushed. Ideally, a respondent should be relaxed while responding, and a self-administered survey may effect this relaxed state.

3. No Interviewer-Evaluation Apprehension As we noted earlier, some respondents feel apprehensive when answering questions, or the topic may be sensitive, such as gambling,[11] smoking, or personal hygiene. The self-administered approach takes the administrator, whether human or computer, out of the picture, and respondents may feel more at ease. Self-administered questionnaires have been found to elicit more insightful information than face-to-face interviews.[12]

Disadvantages of Self-Administered Surveys The disadvantages of self-administered surveys are respondent control, lack of monitoring, and high questionnaire requirements.

1. Respondent Control Because self-administration places control of the survey in the hands of the prospective respondent, this type of survey is subject to the possibilities that

---

Disadvantages of computer-assisted data collection are the requirement of technical skills and high setup costs.

Some types of computer-assisted surveys incur relatively high setup costs.

In a self-administered survey, the respondent completes the survey on his or her own; no human or computer agent administers the interview.

Self-administered surveys have three important advantages: reduced cost, respondent control, and no interviewer-evaluation apprehension.

The disadvantages of self-administered surveys are respondent control, lack of monitoring, and high questionnaire requirements.

If respondents misunderstand or do not follow directions, they may become frustrated and quit.

respondents will not complete the survey, will answer questions erroneously, will not respond in a timely manner, or will refuse to return the survey.

2. Lack of Monitoring With self-administered surveys, there is no opportunity for the researcher to monitor or interact with the respondent during the course of the interview. A monitor can offer explanations and encourage the respondent to continue. But with a self-administered survey, respondents who do not understand the meaning of a word or who are confused about how to answer a question may answer improperly or become frustrated and refuse to answer at all.

3. High Questionnaire Requirements Because of the absence of the interviewer or an internal computer check system, the burden of respondent understanding falls on the questionnaire itself. Not only must it have perfectly clear instructions, examples, and reminders throughout, the questionnaire must also entice the respondents to participate and encourage them to continue answering until all questions are complete. Questionnaire design is important regardless of the data collection mode. However, with self-administered surveys, clearly the questionnaire must be thoroughly reviewed and accurate before data collection begins. You will learn more about designing questionnaires in Chapter 9.

> With self-administered surveys, the questionnaire must be especially thorough and accurate to minimize respondent errors.

COMPUTER-ADMINISTERED SURVEYS

In a **computer-administered survey**, a computer plays an integral role in posing the questions and recording respondents' answers. The prototypical computer-administered survey is an online survey in which respondents are directed to a website that houses the questionnaire. Amazingly sophisticated web-based questionnaire design systems can easily qualify respondents, skip questions that should not be asked based on previous answers, include randomly administered stimuli, use quota systems for sample sizes, display a range of graphics and video, and accomplish a large variety of tasks that just a few years ago required the presence of a human interviewer. Computer-administered surveys are not bound to the Internet, as they can be adapted for telephone delivery, similar to "robo-calls" but more sophisticated to allow respondents to answer questions either verbally or with phone buttons.

Advantages of Computer-Administered Surveys

1. Breadth of User-Friendly Features A great many online questionnaire design systems are available, and the large majority of them are easy to learn as long as the user has modest computer skills. Many have built-in question libraries, simple skip logic, and copy-and-paste features. They easily accommodate graphics and video snippets of almost any type. Some have respondent-interactive features such as drag-and-drop, sliding scales, constant sum scales, graphic rating scales, and more. Most have annotated screen captures and/or videos help systems. Many are linked to online panel companies so the researcher can access practically any typical respondent group almost immediately (for a price). They host the online questionnaires, collect the data, offer simple statistical and graphical analyses, and afford downloads of the data into multiple formats such as Excel or SPSS.

2. Relatively Inexpensive Many of these systems are designed for the DIY (do-it-yourself) marketing researcher, so they have free trial versions and graduated pricing systems that make them affordable. Of course, the most sophisticated systems are expensive, although not on a per-survey basis for marketing research companies that perform many surveys annually.

3. Reduction of Interview Evaluation Concern in Respondents Concerns among respondents that they should give the "right" or "desirable" answers tend to diminish when they interact with a computer. In such cases, some researchers believe that respondents will provide more truthful answers to potentially sensitive topics. A related emerging advantage of online surveys is that when they are coupled with opt-in or "permission marketing," they are becoming known for their high response rates. That is, where a panel or database of a firm's customers has agreed to respond to online survey requests from a research firm or the company, studies have shown that respondents are more cooperative and more actively involved in the survey, and response inducements such as prenotifications and personalization are unnecessary.[13]

Disadvantage of Computer-Administered Surveys
Requires Computer-Literate and Internet-Connected Respondents Whereas this requirement is typically a low hurdle, there are instances where the respondents do not qualify—for example, some children, senior citizens, or disadvantaged socioeconomic groups. Many foreign countries have low computer and Internet penetration levels that discourage the use of computer-administered surveys.

Computer-administered data collection is similar to but not the same as web-based data collection. While the Internet has its own unique aspects that facilitate the collection of both qualitative and quantitative data, researchers are moving rapidly into mobile data collection. Marketing Research Insight 7.1 identifies various mobile-based approaches to the collection of survey data.

MARKETING RESEARCH INSIGHT 7.1 *Practical Application*

Comparisons of Different Mobile Data Collection Modes

Note: This Marketing Research Insight was provided by Leslie Townsend, President, Kinesis Survey Technologies, LLC, who also wrote the opening vignette for this chapter.

Mobile data collection began during the late 1990s, mostly on an experimental basis, although it is only now reaching a "tipping point." There have been four primary means of data collection using mobile devices:

Offline: Data is collected in a software application and uploaded and synchronized with any previously uploaded data. Offline data collection has historically been most popular for mall and street intercept interviewing, as well as for rural and lesser developed regions where online communications are less common.

SMS: Data collection via SMS (short message service text messages) is typically used for very short surveys consisting of one to four questions. Questions and their responses are relayed back and forth via text messaging in disconnected sessions. Typically, if a question is not answered, it is assumed to be a "dropout" for administrative purposes, and any subsequent questions are not relayed. A variation of this mode is to use MMS, or multimedia messaging service. While this mode may be used in the future, MMS is not currently considered a cost-effective solution.

Browser-based: Surveys are administered in the same manner as other online surveys, with respondents using online sessions to input responses. Historically, any mobile phone with a browser and an online connection can be supported, but the browsing experience varies by device. The respondent experience continues to improve rapidly, however, and is best supported with the latest generation of HTML5 browsers.

"Apps": So prolific and popular that they are denoted by slang, downloadable applications have also become a common means of mobile data collection, particularly when used to collect media such as digital images and video recordings. App is a generic term that is used to indicate a downloadable application for a smart phone. Apps can be offline or online, but most smart phone apps allow respondents to input data in either mode. There is little current differentiation between apps and previous offline data collection applications; most offline data collection is facilitated by older, more rudimentary apps that were in use prior to the evolution of smart phones.

The advantages and disadvantages to these modes are summarized in the following table but are more often than not intuitively apparent based on in situ requirements. The exception falls to the use of browser-based solutions versus apps, where the majority of discussion will be focused.

Comparison of Costs and Relative Advantages Disadvantages of Mobile Data Collection Modes

Data Collection Mode	Relative Costs	Advantages	Disadvantages
Offline	*Investment in the device is usually required, and some companies lease devices on a project basis. As of this writing, the iPad has become the de facto device for mall and street intercepts in developed regions.*	*Data can be collected in any region of the world.*	*Devices can be lost or stolen, and in these instances, data is lost. Quotas cannot be easily administered.*
	Most offline data collection utilizes an interviewer, which increases data collection costs significantly.	*There is no need to worry about respondents absorbing data collection costs.*	*Reporting will lag data collection activity significantly.*
SMS MMS	*High. There is a per-message fee for every question sent, as well as every response received. If respondents do not answer a question, there is also a per-message fee associated with any reminder messages.*	*Respondents use their own devices; no interviewer required. Virtually every mobile device worldwide supports SMS as a single global standard. Usability is intuitive.*	*Logic cannot easily be incorporated. Surveys are severely limited in length. Intrusion level is high. Opt-in requirements are stringent. Respondents may bear significant costs in some regions. Sending practices vary worldwide.*
Browser based	*Typically low for respondents as well as researchers, but data plans vary globally.*	*Respondents use their own devices; no interviewer required. All types of logic and quotas easily supported. Applications can support any type of device for more similar experience across devices. Real-time reporting easily supported. Media easily supported.*	*Some specific types of data, such as location-based information and bar code scans, are more easily captured via apps that collect data in the background.*
		Can easily support multi-mode/device-agnostic solutions.	
Apps	*Typically low to no charge for a download; for respondents, costs are approximately equivalent to a browser-based experience since an Internet connection is required to transmit data. Costs to develop and maintain the app can be high relative to other modes, however.*	*Respondents use their own devices; no interviewer required.*	*Must be developed for each operating system.*
			Cannot easily control whether or not respondents will accept software updates. The majority of downloaded apps are never used.

Offline data collection modes via mobile devices are used almost exclusively in regions and situations in which network availability (a cellular carrier, Wi-Fi, or satellite) is not ensured or cannot be utilized for security or other reasons. This can include shopping malls and hospitals but could also include a remote village in the Himalayas. Mobile devices are transforming the market research landscape, and no more so than in developing regions where paper-based surveys collected by on-site interviewers were previously the only data collection option. The use of a device that eliminates the risk associated with shipping collected data, as well as the time and resources spent inputting it, have made mobile devices, especially tablet PCs, the devices of choice in remote regions.

SMS surveys are far and away the most expensive and most intrusive of mobile survey solutions, yet they remain popular. In the United States and Europe, mobile carriers use them as a means to conduct customer satisfaction surveys after the activation process and when visiting the carrier's retail site. Other types of businesses may use them as well, but only with permission, and most regions have stricter laws associated with sending. Therefore, there is generally a close relationship between the sender and message recipient. Due to per-message costs, surveys must be brief, usually no more than four questions in length. Media cannot be incorporated as sending and receiving costs would become more than respondents would be willing to bear. Perhaps the biggest disadvantage is the potential disruption for the respondent; an alert message might be sent to a personal device at an inconvenient or disruptive time, such as when the respondent is traveling in another time zone. SMS surveys are used successfully in some developing regions where respondents often have mobile devices but do not have computers. In these regions, compensation (incentive) plans must be carefully considered, because personal income may be too low for respondents to affordably participate. (In developed regions, respondents are generally not concerned with messaging costs.)

Browser-based surveys offer an extremely cost-effective means to support mobile respondents, with little additional

(continued)

development effort over traditional online data collection, by detecting the type of device and browser in use and rendering content accordingly. By far the greatest advantage of browser-based surveys is that there is no disruption to the survey-taking methods with which respondents are already familiar—those of receiving invitations via email, clicking on a link, and taking a survey. Because of the rapid growth in the use of smart phones and other mobile devices for both checking email and browsing websites, researchers can no longer control the type of device that a respondent will use when entering a research exercise, and attempting to control it will only result in a bias of research data. Thus, a browser-based mobile approach lowers overall development costs, provides a smooth transition to multimode research without increasing data bias, and still enables the other benefits of online research, including low-cost data collection, real-time reporting, easily programmed advanced logic and quota administration, easy implementation of consistent branding across devices and browsers, and rapid time to market.

With the advent of HTML5, mobile browsers will be increasingly powerful and will replace the need for the majority of apps. As of this writing, downloadable applications must be developed independently for each platform (iOs, Android, Blackberry, Windows), creating the need to develop the same app functionality across multiple devices, at least for research situations in which respondents use their own devices. As has been evidenced historically, the status and popularity of a device can drive rapid adoption, so at any point in time the need to develop to a new platform could arise. More importantly, however, are the extra steps entailed to get the respondent to download the app as well as any functional updates, especially in the researcher's desired time frame.

Additionally, today we see a wide abundance of apps being developed, which may result in oversaturation. Some support specific regions and languages only. Some are for projects of short-term duration, while other are associated with panel membership and longer-term trackers. It remains to be seen what the tolerance will be among mobile respondents: How many different research apps will they be willing to download and use? The most successful apps have been those that are used on a daily basis and enhance communications, productivity, and entertainment to their user base. Early research suggests that respondents reach a limit on the number of apps they will download and use, and it is unlikely that research apps will be viewed as highly desirable by a majority of mobile users. Respondents might download an app to participate in a specific project or join a panel, but continuous use will require continuous development to maintain the engagement factor—and there is no assurance that respondents will feel motivated to download the updates.

Research apps also present a controlled experience. In today's online environment, so-called DIY (do-it-yourself) models are increasingly common. Enterprises select software tools for their own use to program surveys and invite panelists. It is common to select a multivendor approach with multiple panels to fill a survey, which may be programmed in house or by a third vendor. The app is disruptive to this business model.

As previously stated, mobile browser-based solutions are superior for the majority of data collection needs. But since HTML5 has not been fully realized in its development vision and it may take another four years before its complete feature set is available, it is a data collection mode still building toward its full potential. Still, even under development, HTML5.1 offers benefits of lower battery consumption and development costs, while still providing geolocation, animation, and other functionality that takes place today largely inside the app.

MIXED-MODE SURVEYS

Mixed-mode surveys, sometimes referred to as *hybrid surveys*, use multiple data collection modes. It has become increasingly popular to use mixed-mode surveys in recent years. Part of this popularity is due to the increasing use of online survey research. As more and more respondents have access to the Internet, online surveys, a form of computer-administered surveys, are often combined with some other method, such as telephone surveying, a form of person-administered surveying. Another reason for the popularity of mixed-mode surveys is the realization by marketing researchers that respondents should be treated like customers.[14] Basically, this realization translates into the need to match data collection mode with respondent preferences insofar as possible so as to foster respondent goodwill[15] and maximize the quality of data collected.[16]

Mixed-mode surveys, sometimes referred to as hybrid surveys, use multiple data collection modes.

With a mixed-mode approach, a researcher may use two or more survey data collection modes to access a representative sample,[17] or modes may be used in tandem such as use of the Internet to solicit respondents who agree to a face-to-face interview.[18] Some companies are experimenting with multiple mobile media modes to match up with mobile, social media-using consumers.[19] Also, as in the case of eBay's use of hybrid research,[20] these surveys may facilitate the use of both quantitative and qualitative techniques to do "deep dives" into understanding buyer-seller trust relationships.

Advantage of Mixed-Mode Surveys

1. Multiple Avenues to Achieve Data Collection Goal The main benefit of mixed-mode surveys is that researchers can take advantage of each of the various modes to achieve their data collection goals. For example, one quarterly administered panel of households uses a randomly selected sample of about 800 households. Since 50% of these households have Internet service, they may be surveyed each quarter via an online survey. This gives the panel administrators the advantages associated with online surveys; they may access all the panel households with the touch of a computer key. Also, as respondents open their emailed questionnaires and answer, their responses are automatically downloaded to the panel's statistical package for analysis. To achieve a representative sample, households without Internet service must be included. Households without Internet service typically have telephones, so these panel members are contacted each quarter via telephone surveys. With this mixed-mode approach, the panel administrators can take advantage of the speed and low cost of online surveying and the advantage of reaching the total household population using telephone surveys.[21]

> The advantage of mixed-mode surveys is that researchers can take the advantage of each of the various modes to achieve their data collection goals.

Disadvantages of Mixed-Mode Surveys   There are two primary disadvantages of using hybrid data collection modes.

1. The Survey Mode May Affect Response   One reason for researchers' past reluctance to use mixed modes for gathering data is concern that the mode used may affect responses given by consumers. Will consumers responding to an in-home interview with a personal interviewer respond differently than those responding to an impersonal, online survey? This disparity has been shown in comparing an online survey to a telephone survey.[22] Studies have been conducted to assess differences between data collection methods in mixed-mode applications.[23] The results of studies addressing the question of survey mode effects on respondents are not entirely consistent, so our warning is that the researcher must assess differences in data collected to determine if the data collection mode explains any disparities.

> A disadvantage of the mixed-mode survey is that the researcher must assess the effects the mode may have on response data.

2. Additional Complexity   Multiple modes add to the complexities of data collection.[24] For example, if you are conducting a survey online and by telephone, the wording of the instructions must be different to accommodate those reading instructions they themselves are to follow (for online respondents) versus a telephone interviewer reading the instructions to the respondent. Further, data from the two sources will need to be integrated into a single data set, so much care must be taken to ensure data are compatible. Even within a particular data collection method, there can be a mixture of different types of information, which increases the complexity of marketing research. Read Marketing Research Insight 7.2 for examples of how Coca-Cola® and Nokia® use mobile research texting, digital photos, and blogs.

> Multiple modes add to the complexities of data collection such as differences in instructions and integration of data from different sources.

MARKETING RESEARCH INSIGHT 7.2   *Practical Application*

How Coca-Cola and Nokia Use Mobile Research[25]

Mobile marketing research is the use of surveys where the respondents participate by using their mobile phones via web, SMS, or MMS. This is the communication mode of choice for most young consumers—a prime target market for soft drink companies such as Coca-Cola. The benefits of mobile marketing research are (1) convenience for participants, (2) improved participation rates, (3) proximity to the "moment," and (4) access to more of the population. Ancillary benefits include lower cost, faster turnaround, and the possibility of geolocational data.

A research project conducted for Coca-Cola recruited a panel of respondents who first answered an online survey about competing soft drink brands. Then, the respondents were instructed to text whenever they encountered one of these brands over the next seven days. They used a special code system to indicate where they saw the brand, how they felt about the brand, and how likely they were to purchase the brand at that time. They also took digital photos and sent them in. This research gave Coca-Cola an "in the moment" understanding of how target customers relate to Coca-Cola and its competitors. In another application of mobile marketing research, Nokia gave mobile phones to respondents and asked them to video-record themselves interacting with the brands they love. The "moblog" of video and pictures was then uploaded to the researchers' site and participants later discussed their experiences and feelings as they reviewed the visuals. While mobile research is just arriving on the scene, it is an exciting approach that fits the mobile lifestyle of younger consumers.

Descriptions of Data Collection Methods

Now that you have an understanding of the pros and cons of person-administered, self-administered, computer-assisted, and computer-administered surveys, we can describe the various interviewing techniques used in each mode. Not including mixed-mode surveys, several data collection methods are used by marketing researchers (Table 7.3):

Person-administered/computer-assisted (if computer is used to facilitate) surveys:

1. In-home survey
2. Mall-intercept survey
3. In-office survey
4. Telephone survey

Computer-administered surveys:

5. Fully automated survey
6. Online survey

Self-administered surveys:

7. Group self-administered survey
8. Drop-off survey
9. Mail survey

Marketing Research on YouTube™ To learn more about conducting a survey, go to www.youtube.com and search for "Quantitative Surveying Methods."

PERSON-ADMINISTERED INTERVIEWS

To recap, person-administered interviews use human interviewers who may rely on computer assistance. The critical feature is that a human is conducting the interview. There are four common variations of person-administered interviews, and their differences are based largely on the location of the interview. These methods include the in-home interview, the mall-intercept interview, the in-office interview, and the telephone interview.

TABLE 7.3 Various Ways to Gather Data

Data Collection Method	Description
In-home interview	The interviewer conducts the interview in the respondent's home. Appointments may be made ahead by telephone.
Mall-intercept interview	Shoppers in a mall are approached and asked to take part in the survey. Questions may be asked in the mall or in the mall-intercept company's facilities located in the mall.
In-office interview	The interviewer makes an appointment with business executives or managers to conduct the interview at the respondent's place of work.
Telephone interview	Interviewers work in a data collection company's office using cubicles or work areas for each interviewer, usually reading questions on a computer monitor. Often the supervisor has the ability to "listen in" to interviews and to check that they are being conducted correctly.
Fully automated interview	A computer is programmed to administer the questions. Respondents interact with the computer and enter in their own answers by using a keyboard, by touching the screen, or by using some other means.
Online survey	Respondents answer a questionnaire that resides on the Internet.
Group self-administered survey	Respondents take the survey in a group context. Each respondent works individually, but they meet as a group, which allows the researcher to economize.
Drop-off survey	Questionnaires are left with the respondent to fill out. The administrator may return at a later time to pick up the completed questionnaire, or it may be mailed in.
Mail survey	Questionnaires are mailed to prospective respondents who are asked to fill them out and return them by mail.

In-Home Surveys As the name implies, an **in-home survey** is conducted by an interviewer who enters the home of the respondent. In-home interviews take longer to recruit participants, and researchers must travel to and from respondents' homes. Therefore, the cost per interview is relatively high. Two factors justify the high cost of in-home interviews. First, the marketing researcher must believe that personal contact is essential to the success of the interview. Second, the researcher must be convinced that the in-home environment is conducive to the questioning process. In-home interviews are useful when the research objective requires a respondent's physical presence to see, read, touch, use, or interact with the research object, such as a product prototype. In addition, the researcher may believe that the security and comfort of respondents' homes are important elements affecting the quality of the data collected. For example, the Yankelovich Youth MONITOR conducts in-home interviews of children who are age 6 and older so that both parents and children are comfortable with the interviewing process.[26]

Some research objectives require the respondents' physical presence to interact with the research object. A company develops a new type of countertop toaster oven that is designed to remain perfectly clean. However, to get the benefit of clean cooking, it must be set up according to different cooking applications (pizza versus bacon, for example), and the throwaway "grease catch foil" must be placed correctly at the bottom of the unit to work properly. Will consumers be able to follow the setup instructions? This is an example of a study that would require researchers to conduct surveys in respondents' home kitchens. Researchers would observe as respondents open the box, unwrap and assemble the device, read the directions, and cook a meal. All of this may take an hour or more. Again, respondents may not be willing to travel somewhere and spend an hour on a research project. They may be more likely to do this in their own home.

Mall-Intercept Surveys Although the in-home interview has important advantages, it has the significant disadvantage of cost. The expense of in-home interviewer travel is high, even for local surveys. Patterned after "man-on-the-street" interviews pioneered by opinion-polling companies and other high-traffic surveys conducted in settings where crowds of pedestrians pass by, the **mall-intercept survey** is one in which the respondent is encountered and questioned while he or she is visiting a shopping mall. A mall-intercept company generally has offices in a large shopping mall, usually one that draws from a regional rather than a local market area. Typically, the interview company negotiates exclusive rights to do interviews in the mall and, thus, forces all marketing research companies that wish to do mall intercepts in that area to use that interview company's services. In any case, the travel costs are eliminated because respondents incur the costs themselves by traveling to the mall. Mall-intercept interviewing has acquired a major role as a survey method because of its ease of implementation,[27] and it is available in many countries.[28] Shoppers are intercepted in the pedestrian traffic areas of shopping malls and either interviewed on the spot or asked to move to a permanent interviewing facility located in the mall office. Although some malls do not allow marketing research interviewing because they view it as a nuisance to shoppers, many permit mall-intercept interviews and may rely on these data themselves to fine-tune their own marketing programs. Mall-intercept companies are adopting high-tech approaches, such as iPads and other mobile devices, and they are experimenting with kiosks to attract respondents.[29]

In addition to low cost, mall interviews have many of the benefits associated with in-home interviewing. As we noted earlier, the most important advantage is the presence of an interviewer who can interact with the respondent.[30] However, a few drawbacks are specifically associated with mall interviewing. First, sample representativeness is an issue, for most malls draw from a relatively small area in close proximity to their location. If researchers are looking for a representative sample of some larger area, such as the county or MSA, they should be wary of using the mall intercept. Some people shop at malls more frequently than others and therefore have a greater chance of being interviewed.[31] Recent growth of nonmall retailing concepts, such as catalogs and stand-alone discounters such as Walmart, mean that more

In-home interviews are used when the survey requires respondents to see, read, touch, use, or interact with a product prototype and when the researcher believes the security and comfort of respondents' homes are important in affecting the quality of the data collected.

In-home interviews facilitate interviewer–interviewee rapport.

Mall-intercept interviews are conducted in large shopping malls, and they are less expensive per interview than are in-home interviews.

The representativeness of mall interview samples is always an issue.

The representativeness of mall interview samples is always an issue.

Photo: Maksim Shmeljov/Shutterstock

mall visitors are recreational shoppers rather than convenience-oriented shoppers, resulting in the need to scrutinize mall-intercept samples as to what consumer groups they actually represent.[32] Also, many shoppers refuse to take part in mall interviews for various reasons. Nevertheless, special selection procedures called *quotas*, which are described in Chapter 9, may be used to counter the problem of nonrepresentativeness.

A second shortcoming of mall-intercept interviewing is that a shopping mall does not have a comfortable home environment that is conducive to rapport and close attention to details. The respondents may feel uncomfortable because passersby stare at them; they may be pressed for time or otherwise preoccupied by various distractions outside the researcher's control. These factors may adversely affect the quality of the interview. Some interview companies attempt to counter this problem by taking respondents to special interview rooms located in the interview company's mall offices. This procedure minimizes distractions and encourages respondents to be more relaxed. Some mall interviewing facilities have kitchens and rooms with one-way mirrors.

Mall interview companies use rooms in their small headquarters areas to conduct private interviews in a relaxed setting.

In-Office Surveys   Although the in-home and mall-intercept interview methods are appropriate for a wide variety of consumer goods, marketing research conducted in the business-to-business or organizational market typically requires interviews with business executives, purchasing agents, engineers, or other managers. Normally, **in-office surveys** take place in person while the respondent is in his or her office or perhaps in a company lounge area. Interviewing businesspeople face-to-face has essentially the same advantages and drawbacks as in-home consumer interviewing. For example, if Knoll, Inc., wants information regarding user preferences for different adjustment features that might be offered in an ergonomic office chair designed for business executives, it would make sense to interview prospective users or purchasers of these chairs. It would also be logical that these people would be interviewed at their places of business.

In-office interviews are conducted at executives' or managers' places of work because they are the most suitable locations.

As you might imagine, in-office personal interviews incur relatively high costs. Those executives qualified to give opinions on a specific topic or individuals who would be involved in product purchase decisions must first be located. Sometimes names can be obtained from sources such as industry directories or trade association membership lists. More frequently, screening must be conducted over the telephone by calling a particular company that is believed to have executives of the type needed. However, locating those people within a large organization may be time consuming. Once a qualified person is located, the next step is to persuade that person to agree to an interview and then set up a time for the interview. This may require a sizable incentive. Finally, an interviewer must go to the particular place at the appointed time. Even with appointments, long waits are sometimes encountered, and cancellations are not uncommon because businesspeople's schedules sometimes shift unexpectedly. Added to these cost factors is the fact that interviewers who specialize in businesspeople interviews are more costly in general because of their specialized knowledge and abilities. They have to navigate around gatekeepers such as secretaries, learn technical jargon, and be conversant on product features when the respondent asks pointed questions or even criticizes questions as they are posed to him or her.

In-office personal interviews incur costs because of difficulties in accessing qualified respondents.

Telephone Surveys As we have mentioned previously, the need for a face-to-face interview is often predicated on the necessity of the respondent's actually seeing a product, advertisement, or packaging sample. On the other hand, it may be vital that the interviewer watch the respondent to ensure that correct procedures are followed or otherwise to verify something about the respondent or his or her reactions. However, if physical contact is not necessary, telephone interviewing is an attractive option. There are a number of advantages as well as disadvantages associated with telephone interviewing.[33]

Advantages of telephone interviews are cost, quality, and speed.

The advantages of telephone interviewing are many, and they explain why phone surveys are common in marketing surveys. First, the telephone is a relatively inexpensive way to collect survey data. Long-distance telephone charges are much lower than the cost of a face-to-face interview. A second advantage of the telephone interview is that it has the potential to yield a high-quality sample. If the researcher employs random dialing procedures and proper callback measures, the telephone approach may produce a better sample than any other survey procedure. However, as noted previously in this chapter, a significant percentage of households are dropping wire-line phone service in favor of mobile phones. This trend is more prevalent in younger populations, so researchers must consider this issue when selecting an access mode. A third important advantage is that telephone surveys have quick turnaround times. Most telephone interviews are of short duration anyway, but a good interviewer may complete several interviews per hour. Conceivably, a study could have the data collection phase executed in a few days with telephone interviews. In fact, in the political polling industry in which real-time information on voter opinions is essential, it is not unusual to have national telephone polls completed in a single night.

Unfortunately, the telephone survey approach has several shortcomings. First, the respondent cannot be shown anything or physically interact with the research object. This shortcoming ordinarily eliminates the telephone survey as an alternative in situations requiring that the respondent view product prototypes, advertisements, packages, or anything else. A second disadvantage is that the telephone interview does not permit the interviewer to make the various judgments and evaluations that can be made by the in-person interviewer. For example, judgments regarding respondent income based on their home and other outward signs of economic status cannot be made. Similarly, the telephone does not allow for the observation of body language and facial expressions, nor does it permit eye contact. On the other hand, some may argue that the lack of face-to-face contact is helpful. Self-disclosure studies have indicated that respondents provide more information in personal interviews, except when the topics are threatening or potentially embarrassing. Questions on alcohol consumption, contraceptive methods, racial issues, or income tax reporting will probably generate more valid responses when asked in the relative anonymity of the telephone than when administered face-to-face.[34] A review article concluded that, compared to face-to-face interviews, telephone interviews elicit more suspicion and less cooperation, generate more "no opinions" and socially desirable answers, and foster more dissatisfaction with long interviews.[35]

The telephone is a poor choice for conducting a survey with many open-ended questions.

A third disadvantage of the telephone interview is that marketing researchers are more limited in the quantity and types of information they can obtain. Very long interviews are inappropriate for the telephone, as are questions with lengthy lists of response options that respondents will have difficulty remembering when they are read over the telephone. Respondents short on patience may hang up during interviews, or they may utter short and convenient responses just to speed up the interview. Obviously, the telephone is a poor choice for conducting an interview with many open-ended questions where respondents make comments or give statements as the interviewer will have great difficulty recording these remarks.

The final—and perhaps and most significant—problem with telephone surveys is the growing threat to its existence as a result of increased noncooperation by the public. This situation is compounded by consumers' use of answering machines, caller recognition, and call-blocking devices.[36] The industry reacted to these gatekeeping methods by developing many panels as a way to gain access to different populations.[37] Another difficulty is that legitimate telephone interviewers must contend with the negative impression people have of telemarketers.[38]

Telephone interviewers must contend with the negative impression people have of telemarketers.

Central location interviewing is the current telephone survey standard because it affords efficient control of interviewers.

Despite their shortcomings and declining response rates, telephone surveys remain popular. In fact, when monetary incentives, assurance that it is not a sales call, and a promise of a short survey are involved, response rates are quite good according to one study conducted in New Zealand.[39]

Central location telephone surveying involves a field data collection company installing several telephone lines at one location from which interviewers make calls. Usually, interviewers have separate enclosed work spaces and lightweight headsets that free both hands so they can record responses. Everything is done from this central location. Obviously, there are many advantages to operating from a central location. For example, resources are pooled, and interviewers can handle multiple surveys, such as calling plant managers in the afternoon and households in the evening hours. The reasons accounting for the prominence of the central location phone interview are efficiency and control. Efficiency is gained when everything is performed at a single location and further acquired by the benefit that multiple telephone surveys can be conducted simultaneously.

Apart from cost savings, perhaps the most important reason for the popularity of central location interviewing is quality control. Recruitment and training are performed uniformly at this location. Interviewers can be oriented to the equipment, study the questionnaire and its instructions, and practice the interview among themselves over their phone lines. Also, the actual interviewing process can be monitored. Most telephone interviewing facilities have monitoring equipment that permits a supervisor to listen in on interviewing as it is being conducted. Interviewers who are not doing the interview properly can he spotted and the necessary corrective action taken. Ordinarily, each interviewer will be monitored at least once per shift,[40] but the supervisor may focus attention on newly hired interviewers to ensure they are doing their work correctly. The fact that interviewers never know when the supervisor will listen in tends to ensure more diligence. Also, completed questionnaires are checked on the spot as a further quality control check. Interviewers can be immediately informed of any deficiencies in filling out the questionnaire. Finally, there is control over interviewers' schedules. That is, interviewers report in and out and work regular hours, even if they are evening hours, and make calls during the time periods stipulated by the researcher as appropriate interviewing times.

With CATI, the interviewer reads the questions on a computer screen and enters respondents' answers directly into the computer program.

The most advanced telephone interview companies have computerized the central location telephone interviewing process with systems called **computer-assisted telephone interviews (CATI)**. Although each system is unique and new developments occur regularly, we can describe a typical setup. Each interviewer is equipped with a hands-free headset and is seated in front of a computer screen that is driven by the company's computer system. Often the computer dials the prospective respondent's telephone automatically, and the computer screen provides the interviewer with the introductory comments. As the interview progresses, the interviewer moves through the questions by pressing a key or a series of keys on the keyboard. Some systems use light pens or pressure-sensitive screens.

The questions and possible responses appear on the screen one at a time. The interviewer reads the questions to the respondent and enters the response codes, and the computer moves on to the next appropriate question. For example, an interviewer might ask if the respondent owns a dog. If the answer is "yes," there could appear a series of questions regarding what type of dog food the dog owner buys. If the answer is "no," these questions would be inappropriate. Instead, the computer program skips to the next appropriate question, which might be "Do you own a cat?" In other words, the computer eliminates the human error potential that would exist if this survey were done in non-CATI interviewing. The human interviewer is just the "voice" of the computer, but because telephone communication is used, the respondent usually does not have any clue that a computer is involved.

With CATI, the computer can be used to customize questions. For example, in the early part of a long interview, the interviewer might ask a respondent the years, makes, and models of all cars he or she owns. Later interview questions might focus on each vehicle. The question might come up on the interviewer's screen as follows: "You said you own a Lexus. Who in your family drives this car most often?" Other questions about this car and others owned would appear in similar fashion. These questions are handled much more efficiently in the computerized version because the interviewer does not need to physically flip questionnaire pages back and forth or remember previous responses.

The CATI approach also eliminates the need for editing completed questionnaires and creating computer data files by later manually entering every response with a keyboard. There is no checking for errors in completed questionnaires because there is no physical questionnaire. More to the point, most computerized interview systems do not permit users to enter an "impossible" answer. For example, if a question has three possible answers with codes A, B, and C and the interviewer enters a D by mistake, the computer will ask for the answer to be reentered until an acceptable code is entered. If a combination or pattern of answers is impossible, the computer will not accept an answer, or it may alert the interviewer to the inconsistency and move to a series of questions that will resolve the discrepancy. Data entry for completed questionnaires is eliminated because data are entered directly into a computer file as the interviewing is completed.

This second operation brings to light another advantage of computer-administered interviewing. Tabulations may be run at any point in the study. Such real-time reporting is impossible with paper-and-pencil questionnaires in which there can be a wait of several days following interviewing completion before detailed tabulations of the results are available. Instantaneous results available with CATI provide some real advantages. Based on preliminary tabulations, certain questions may be dropped, saving time and money in subsequent interviewing. If, for example, more than 90% of those interviewed answered a particular question in the same manner, there may be no need to continue asking the question.

Tabulations may also suggest the addition of questions to the survey. If an unexpected pattern of product use is uncovered in the early interviewing stages, questions can be added to further delve into this behavior. The computer-administered telephone survey affords an element of flexibility unavailable in the traditional paper-and-pencil survey methods. Finally, managers may find the early reporting of survey results useful in preliminary planning and strategy development. Sometimes survey project deadlines run very close to managers' presentation deadlines, and advance indications of the survey's findings permit managers to organize their presentations in advance rather than all in a rush the night before. The many advantages and quick turnaround of CATI and CAPI (computer-assisted personal interviewing) make them mainstay data collection methods for many syndicated omnibus survey services.[41,42]

With CATI, the interviewer is the "voice" of the computer.

Most CATI systems are programmed to reject wrong answers.

CATI systems permit tabulation in midsurvey.

 Active Learning

Setting Up Controls for a Telephone Interview

For this active learning exercise, assume your marketing research course requires team projects and your team decides to research why students at your university chose to attend it. Your five-member team will conduct telephone interviews of 200 students selected at random from your university's student directory with each team member responsible for completing 40 interviews by calling from his or her apartment or dorm room. You have volunteered to supervise the telephone interviewing. You have read about the tight controls in effect with central telephone interview companies, and you realize that quality assurance procedures should be in place with your student team member telephone interviewers. To satisfy each of the following telephone quality issues, what procedure would you propose to use?

Quality Assurance Procedure	Write your proposed procedures here
The student team member interviewers should call the right students at the proper times of the day.	
They must conduct the interviews correctly by reading the instructions and "skipping" questions as required by the respondent's answers.	
The 40 interviews should be conducted on schedule.	
Interviewers should be instructed on how to handle "no answers" and answering machines.	
A mechanism should be in place to detect bogus interview data in case some interviewers decide to submit false results.	

You may want to review the descriptions of how central location telephone surveys are conducted to see if your answers to these questions about your team research project are consistent with standard practices in marketing research described in this chapter. After you complete this exercise, write about how control of telephone interviews would be easier if done in a central location telephone facility.

COMPUTER-ADMINISTERED INTERVIEWS

Computer technology has had a significant impact on the data collection phase. There are two variations of computer-administered interview systems. In one, a "synthetic" human interviewer is used, meaning that the questions are prerecorded or a computer "voice" is generated. Thus, it may sound as if a human interviewer is doing the questioning, but it is really a machine. Second, the Internet-based interview has charged to the forefront of survey techniques, and we describe online surveys in this section as well.

Fully Automated Survey   Some companies have developed **fully automated surveys**, in which the survey is administered by a computer but not online. With one such system, a computer dials a phone number, and a recording is used to introduce the survey. The respondent then uses the push buttons on his or her telephone to make responses, thereby interacting directly with the computer. In the research industry, this approach is known as **completely automated telephone survey (CATS)**. CATS has been successfully employed for customer satisfaction studies, service quality monitoring, election day polls, product/warranty

 Marketing Research on YouTube™ To see how to set up a completely automated telephone system, go to **www.youtube.com** and search for "Learn About PrecisionPolling.com."

registration, and even in-home product tests with consumers who have been given a prototype of a new product.[43]

In another system, the respondent sits or stands in front of the computer unit and reads the instructions from the screen. Each question and its various response options appear on the screen, and the respondent answers by pressing a key or touching the screen. For example, the respondent may be asked to rate how satisfied, on a scale of 1 to 10 (where 1 is very unsatisfied and 10 is very satisfied), he or she was the last time he or she used a travel agency to plan a family vacation. The instructions would instruct the respondent to press the key with the number appropriate to his or her degree of satisfaction. The respondent might press a 2 or a 7, depending on his or her experience and expectations. However, if the respondent presses 0 or a letter key, the computer could be programmed to beep, indicating that the response was inappropriate, and instruct the respondent to make another entry.

All of the advantages of computer-driven interviewing are found in this approach. In addition, the interviewer expense or extra cost of human voice communication capability for the computer is eliminated. Because respondents' answers are saved in a file during the interview itself, tabulation can take place on a daily basis, and it is a simple matter for the researcher to access the survey's data at practically any time.[44]

Online surveys allow respondents to participate in relaxed and comfortable surroundings.

Photo: Dmitriy Shironosov/Shutterstock

Online Interviews The **Internet-based questionnaire** in which the respondent answers questions online has become the industry standard for surveys in virtually all high-Internet-penetration countries. Internet-based online surveys are fast, easy, and inexpensive.[45] The questionnaires accommodate all of the standard question formats, and they are very flexible, including the ability to present pictures, diagrams, or displays to respondents. Internet-based or web surveys have earned varying levels of popularity around the world. Read Marketing Research Insight 7.3 to learn about the similarities and differences in favored data collection methods across global regions.

Online data collection has profoundly changed the marketing research landscape,[46] particularly in the case of online panels.[47] For instance, using such a panel, a company could conduct "episodic" research of customer satisfaction instead of one large study per year, facilitating "continuous market intelligence" through a survey posted permanently on the web and modified as the company's strategies are implemented. Company managers can click up tabulated customer reactions on a daily basis.[48] Some researchers refer to this advantage of online surveys as *real-time research*.[49] The speed, convenience, and flexibility of online surveys make them very attractive.[50] Online surveys are generally believed to generate response quality equal to telephone or mail surveys, although research on this assumption is only now becoming evident.[51] One serendipitous aspect of online surveys is that because the researcher can monitor survey response progress on a continual basis, it is possible to spot problems with the survey and to make adjustments to correct these problems.

Returning to the topic at hand, the online survey is no cure-all for a marketing researcher's data collection woes, as the marketing research industry quickly learned that its honeymoon with Internet surveys was short. Their novelty soon wore off, and Internet surveys quickly began exhibiting symptoms of low cooperation rates that diminish the quality of telephone and mail surveys. Marketing researchers were quick to realize that online surveys presented design challenges and opportunities related to fostering cooperation in potential respondents.

Marketing Research on YouTube™ | If you want to learn how to do an online survey using Google Docs, go to **www.youtube.com** and search for "Create a Free Online Survey Using Google Docs (Free Online Survey Tool)."

MARKETING RESEARCH INSIGHT 7.3   *Global Application*

How Research Modes Differ by World Region

An annual survey of marketing research companies conducted by the London-based company, Meaning Ltd presents data for three global regions: North America, Europe, and Asia-Pacific.[52] The survey touches on a great many aspects of marketing research, including data collection modes. The following table shows the currently used data collection modes based on volume of surveys.

Web-based surveys are dominant, accounting for almost half of all surveys worldwide. However, a regional comparison shows that reliance on web surveys is most common in North America (53%) and least common in the Asia-Pacific region (37%). Internet technology has not penetrated Asia-Pacific countries to the same extent as in North American and

European countries; this observation is supported by the relatively heavy use of "paper-and-pencil" or "hard-copy" questionnaires in Asia-Pacific data collection at 22%, compared to Europe with 13% and North America with 9%. In another table, the Meaning report contained information on predicted growth of data collection modes. The interesting finding is that Asia-Pacific research companies expect laptop or tablet computer-assisted personal interview (CAPI) to grow significantly, whereas North American companies project slower growth and European companies expect CAPI to diminish. North American companies have significantly higher expectations that data collection via mobile devices will increase in the future.

Data Collection Modes by World Region, 2010

2010	Total	North America	Europe	Asia-Pacific
CATI (single mode)	27%	25%	27%	28%
Laptop or tablet CAPI	3%	1%	4%	6%
CAPI on handled or mobile devices	2%	2%	1%	2%
Web surveys (self-completion)	47%	53%	45%	37%
SMS text messaging (self-completion)	*	*	*	*
Other self-completion on mobile (not SMS)	1%	1%	2%	0%
IVR (interactive voice response)	1%	1%		1%
Paper	13%	9%	13%	22%
Mixed mode CATI and web	4%	4%	5%	4%
Any other mixed mode	2%	2%	3%	*

*Less than .5%

Online surveys have important advantages of speed and low cost, plus real-time access of data; however, there are drawbacks of sample representativeness, respondent validation, and difficulty in asking probing types of questions.

 Active Learning

Learn About Online Marketing Research Software Systems

Several companies have developed online questionnaire design and hosting systems. A quick search using Google will likely turn up 20 or more competitors. Practically all of these companies allow you to use their systems on a trial basis. Select one and download or otherwise gain access to the online survey system. Now answer each of the following questions:

1. How do you create the following question and answers on this system: *Have you purchased something at a Best Buy store in the past month?*
   Yes   No
2. What is skip logic, and how does it work on this system if you want the respondents who did purchase something at Best Buy to indicate whether they bought a 3-D HDTV?
3. Is the system user-friendly? Why or why not?
4. What feature best demonstrates that this system is using sophisticated computer and/or Internet technology?

SELF-ADMINISTERED SURVEYS

Recall that a self-administered survey is one where the respondent is in control, often deciding when to take the survey, where to take it, and how much time and attention to devote to it. With a self-administered survey, the respondent always decides what questions he or she will or will not answer. That is, the respondent fills in answers to a static copy of the questionnaire, which is what we have referred to as a paper-and-pencil questionnaire in previous descriptions. Probably the most popular type of self-administered survey is the mail survey; however, researchers may consider two other variations from time to time: the group self-administered survey and the drop-off survey.

Before continuing, let's address why Internet-based interviews are not categorized as self-administered. They do not fall into this category because the sophistication of Internet-based questionnaire design software does not allow respondents to avoid answering key questions. For example, the program may be set up to remind a respondent that a certain question was not answered. This prompt continues until the respondent answers the question. In addition, online questionnaire systems usually have skip logic, meaning that questions that are not appropriate to ask based on previous answers (e.g., Do you own a car? If no, do not ask questions about the car; if yes, do ask questions about the car) are not seen by the respondent. Because we consider the ability of Internet surveys to stop respondents from "opting out" of questions and skip logic to be significant quality control features, we have not included Internet-based interviews in the self-administered group.

Group Self-Administered Survey Basically, a **group self-administered survey** entails administering a questionnaire to respondents in groups rather than individually for convenience and to gain economies of scale. For example, 20 or 30 people might be recruited to view a TV program sprinkled with test commercials. All respondents would be seated in a viewing room facility, and a video would run on a large television projection screen. Then they would be given a questionnaire to fill out regarding their recall of test ads, their reactions to the ads, and so on. As you would suspect, it is handled in a group context primarily to reduce costs and to provide the ability to interview a large number of people in a short time.

> Group self-administered surveys economize in time and money because a group of respondents participates simultaneously.

Variations for group self-administered surveys are limitless. Students can be administered surveys in their classes; church groups can be administered surveys during meetings; and social clubs and organizations, company employees, movie theater patrons, and other groups can be administered surveys during meetings, work, or leisure time. Often the researcher will compensate the group with a monetary payment as a means of recruiting the support of the group's leaders. In all of these cases, each respondent works through the questionnaire at his or her own pace. Granted, a survey administrator may be present, so there is some opportunity for interaction concerning instructions or how to respond, but the group context often discourages the respondents from asking all but the most pressing questions.

Drop-Off Survey Another variation of the self-administered survey is the **drop-off survey**, sometimes called "drop and collect," in which the survey representative approaches a prospective respondent, introduces the general purpose of the survey to the prospect, and leaves it with the respondent to fill out on his or her own. Essentially, the objective is to gain the prospective respondent's cooperation. The respondent is told that the questionnaire is self-explanatory and that it will be left with him or her to fill out at leisure. Perhaps the representative will return to pick up the questionnaire at a certain time, or the respondent may be instructed to complete and return it by prepaid mail. Normally, the representative will return on the same day or the next day to pickup the completed questionnaire. In this way, a representative can cover a number of residential areas or business locations in a single day with an initial drop-off pass and a later pick-up pass. Drop-off surveys are especially appropriate for local market research undertakings in which travel is necessary but limited. They have been reported to have quick turnaround, high response rates, minimal interviewer influence on answers, and good control over how respondents are selected; plus, they are inexpensive.[53] Studies have shown the drop-off survey improves response rates with business or organizational respondents.[54]

> Drop-off surveys must be self-explanatory because they are left with the respondents who fill them out without assistance.

Variations of the drop-off method include handing out the surveys to people at their places of work, asking them to fill them out at home, and then to return them the next day. Some hotel chains have questionnaires in their rooms with an invitation to fill them out and turn them in at the desk on checkout. Restaurants sometimes ask customers to fill out short questionnaires before they leave. Stores sometimes have short surveys on customer demographics, media habits, purchase intentions, or other information that customers are asked to fill out at home and return on their next shopping trip. A gift certificate drawing may even be used as an incentive to participate. As you can see, the term *drop-off* can be stretched to cover any situation in which the prospective respondent encounters the survey as though it were "dropped off" by a research representative.

Mail Survey A **mail survey** is one in which the questions are mailed to prospective respondents who are asked to fill them out and return them to the researcher by mail.[55] Part of its attractiveness stems from its self-administered aspect: There are no interviewers to recruit, train, monitor, and compensate. Similarly, mailing lists are readily available from companies that specialize in this business, and it is possible to access specific groups of target respondents. For example, it is possible to obtain a list of physicians specializing in family practice who operate clinics in cities larger than 500,000 people. Also, one may opt to purchase computer files, printed labels, or even labeled envelopes from these companies. In fact, some list companies will even provide insertion and mailing services. A number of companies sell mailing lists, and most, if not all, have online purchase options. On a per-mailed respondent basis, mail surveys are inexpensive. But mail surveys incur all of the problems associated with not having an interviewer present that were discussed earlier in this chapter.

> Mail surveys suffer from nonresponse and self-selection bias.

Despite the fact that the mail survey is described as "powerful, effective, and efficient"[56] by the American Statistical Association, this research vehicle is plagued by two major problems. The first is **nonresponse**, which refers to questionnaires that are not returned.[57] The second is **self-selection bias**, which means that those who do respond are probably different from those who do not fill out the questionnaire and return it; therefore, the sample gained through this method is nonrepresentative of the general population. Research shows that self-selected respondents can be more interested and involved in the study topic.[58] To be sure, the mail survey is not the only survey method that suffers from nonresponse and self-selection bias.[59] Failure to respond is found in all types of surveys, and marketing researchers must be constantly alert to the possibilities that their final samples are somehow different from the original set of potential respondents because of some systematic tendency or latent pattern of response. Whatever the survey mode used, those who respond may be more involved with the product, they may have more education, they may be more or less dissatisfied, or they may even be more opinionated in general than the target population of concern.[60]

> Self-selection bias means respondents who return surveys by mail may differ from the original sample.

Before we leave this section describing various ways of performing a survey, we want to remind you that the Marketing Research Association Code of Ethics explicitly addresses ethical standards for all and specific forms of surveys. When you read the MRA Code excerpts included in Marketing Research Insight 7.4, you will see that the code has standards for the professional treatment of respondents, the requirement for detailed instructions of interviewers, the prohibition of using a respondent for multiple surveys at the same time, and the requirement to obey laws of various types regarding the recruitment of Internet respondents.

Choice of the Survey Method

How does a marketing researcher decide what survey method to use? Since you have read our descriptions, you now know that each data collection method has unique advantages, disadvantages, and special features. As a quick reference tool, we have summarized these for you in Table 7.4. As you can see by reviewing this table, there is no "perfect" data collection method. The marketing researcher is faced with the problem of selecting the one survey mode that is most suitable in a given situation.

MARKETING RESEARCH INSIGHT 7.4 — *Ethical Consideration*

Marketing Research Association Code of Ethics: Respondent Participation

9. **Will treat respondents in a professional manner.** *Those engaged in any phase of the research process will maintain high standards of personal conduct in their interaction with respondents.*

20. **Will provide detailed written or verbal study instructions to those engaged in the data collection process.** *To ensure the success of the research, detailed instructions are to be provided prior to the start of any project. These instructions must be confirmed for understanding, ability of the agency to implement and agreement to comply.*

34. **Will ensure that companies, their employees and subcontractors involved in the data collection process adhere to reasonable precautions so that multiple surveys are not conducted at the same time with a specific respondent without explicit permission from the sponsoring company or companies.**

Company policies or procedures must prohibit the practice of multiple screening or interviewing of a single respondent during any one interview. Any deviation of this policy will require the permission and mutual consent of both Client and Data Collector. Primary specifications must be adhered to within any study. No demographic or screening information that may be used for future or additional studies will be collected.

41. **For Internet research, will follow all federal, state and local laws regarding internet/online communications. This takes into account all opt-in/opt-out requests.** *Internet research is subject to many laws and regulations at both the state and federal level. It is incumbent upon all members to be familiar with all laws and regulations applicable to their business and ensure that all such laws and regulations are followed exactly.*

How does a researcher decide which is the best survey mode for a particular research project? When answering this question, the researcher should always have the overall quality of the data collected as a foremost concern. Even the most sophisticated techniques of analysis cannot make up for poor data. The researcher must strive to choose a survey method that achieves the highest quality of data allowable with the time, cost, and other special considerations[61] involved with the research project at hand. We wish we could provide a set of questions about these considerations that, when answered, would point to the single most appropriate data collection method. However, this is not possible because situations are unique and researchers have to apply good judgment to narrow down the many candidate data collection methods to one that best fits the circumstances. In some cases, these judgments are quite obvious, but in others, they require some careful thinking. Also, as we have indicated in our descriptions, new data collection methods have emerged[62] and improvements in existing methods have come about, so the researcher must constantly update his or her knowledge of these data collection methods. Nonetheless, time, cost, need for respondent interaction, the incidence rate, and special circumstances are prime considerations in the data collection method decision.

In selecting a data collection mode, the researcher balances quality against cost, time, and other considerations.

HOW MUCH TIME IS THERE FOR DATA COLLECTION?

Sometimes data must be collected quickly. There are many reasons for tight deadlines. A national campaign is set to kick off in four weeks, and one component needs testing. A trademark infringement trial, set to begin in four weeks, needs a survey of the awareness of the company's trademark. An application for a radio license with the FCC is due in six weeks, and a listenership study of other stations in the area must be conducted. These are just a few time constraints in data collection. The traditional choice in projects with a short time horizon is a telephone survey. Today, online surveys are exceptionally fast data collection alternatives. Magazine ads, logos, and other marketing stimuli may be evaluated in online surveys. Poor choices under the condition of short time horizon would be in-home interviews or mail surveys because their logistics require long time periods.

A short deadline may dictate which data collection method to use.

TABLE 7.4 **Major Advantages and Disadvantages of Common Data Collection Methods**

Method	Major Advantages	Major Disadvantages	Comment
In-home interview	Conducted in privacy of the home, which facilitates interviewer–respondent rapport	Cost per interview can be high; interviewers must travel to respondent's home	Often much information per interview is gathered
Mall-intercept interview	Fast and convenient data collection method	Only mall patrons are interviewed; respondents may feel uncomfortable answering questions in the mall	Mall-intercept company often has exclusive interview rights for that mall
In-office interview	Useful for interviewing busy executives or managers	Relatively high cost per interview; gaining access is sometimes difficult	Useful when b2b respondents must examine prototypes or samples of products
Telephone interview	Fast turnaround; good quality control; reasonable cost. CATI eliminates human interviewer error; simultaneous data input to computer file; good quality control	Restricted to telephone communication; CATI setup costs can be high	Long-distance calling is not a problem
Fully automated interview	Respondent responds at his or her own pace; computer data file results	Respondent must be willing to respond to a "robo-call" format	Many variations are emerging
Online survey	Ease of creating and posting; fast turnaround; computer data file results	Respondent must have access to the Internet	Fastest-growing data collection method; very flexible; online analysis available
Group self-administered survey	Cost of interviewer eliminated; economical for assembled groups of respondents	Must find groups and secure permission to conduct the survey	Prone to errors of self-administered surveys; good for pretests or pilot tests
Drop-off survey	Cost of interviewer eliminated; appropriate for local market surveys	Generally not appropriate for large-scale national surveys	Many variations exist with respect to logistics and applications
Mail survey	Low cost per respondent	Slow and suffers from nonresponse and self-selection	Probably the least used data collection method

HOW MUCH MONEY IS THERE FOR DATA COLLECTION?

With a generous budget, any appropriate data collection method can be considered, but with a tight budget, the more costly data collection methods must be eliminated from consideration. With technology costs dropping and Internet access becoming more and more common, online survey research options have become attractive when the data collection budget is austere. For example, some online survey companies allow their clients to design the questionnaire and select the target sample type and number from their panels. Here, surveys can be completed for a few hundred or a few thousand dollars, which, most researchers would agree, is a small data collection budget. Of course, the researcher must be convinced that the panel members are those he or she desires to survey. Other considerations include respondent interaction, incidence rate, or any other "cultural" factors that have a bearing on the selection of the data collection method.

WHAT TYPE OF RESPONDENT INTERACTION IS REQUIRED?

Most certainly, the data collection method selection may be influenced by any special requirements that are a vital part of the survey. That is, there might be a requirement that the respondent inspect an advertisement, package design, or logo. Or the researcher may want respondents to handle a prototype product, taste formulations, or watch a video. Typically, when requirements such as these are built into the survey, the researcher has discussed data collection issues early on with the client and agreed on a data collection mode that accommodate the client's time, cost, and other requirements.

For example, if the respondent needs to view photos of a logo or magazine ad, mail surveys or online surveys may be considered. If the respondent needs to observe a short video or moving graphic, online surveys may be considered. If the respondent needs to watch a 20-minute infomercial, mailed videos (with a considerable incentive!), mall intercepts, or special online systems can be considered. If the respondent is required to handle, touch, feel, or taste a product, mall intercept company services are reasonable. If a respondent is required to actually use a product in a realistic setting, in-home interviews may be the only data collection method that will work.

> If respondents need to see, handle, or experience something, the data collection mode must accommodate these requirements.

WHAT IS THE INCIDENCE RATE?

By **incidence rate** we are referring to the percentage of the population that possesses some characteristic necessary to be included in the survey. Rarely are research projects targeted to "everyone." In most cases, there are qualifiers for being included in a study. Examples are registered voters, persons owning and driving their own automobile, and persons age 18 and older. Sometimes the incidence rate is very low. A drug company may want to interview only men above 50 with medicated cholesterol above the 250 level. A cosmetics firm may only want to interview women who were planning facial cosmetic surgery within the next six months. In low-incidence situations such as these, certain precautions must be taken in selecting the data collection method. In the examples of people with a specific medical condition or interest in cosmetic surgery, it would be foolishly time consuming and expensive to send out interviewers door-to-door looking for members who have the qualifications to participate in the study. A data collection method that can easily and inexpensively screen respondents, such as with telephone or Internet modes, is desirable with a low-incidence-rate situation because a great many potential respondents must be contacted, but a large percentage of these would not qualify to take the survey. Of course, the marketing research industry has worked with low-incidence populations for a long time, and online panels that are maintained by research providers are often touted as affordable ways for researchers to access the low-incidence panel members who are preidentified.[63]

> The incidence rate, the percentage of the population that possesses some characteristic necessary to be included in the survey, affects the decision about data collection mode.

ARE THERE CULTURAL AND/OR INFRASTRUCTURE CONSIDERATIONS?

Finally, on occasion, data collection method choice is shaped by cultural norms and/or communication or other systems that are in place. These considerations have become more of an issue as more and more marketing research companies operate around the globe. For example face-to-face is the preferred mode for Spaniards. However, in Scandinavia, residents are uncomfortable allowing strangers in their homes. Therefore, telephone and online surveying is more popular than door-to-door interviewing. On the other hand, in India, less than 10% of residents have a telephone, and online access is very low; as a result, door-to-door interviewing is used often.[64] In Canada, where incentives are typically not offered to prospective respondents, there is heavy use of telephone surveys.

Online research is growing.[65] A firm conducting a study in a culture about which researchers are unfamiliar needs to consult the services of local research firms before making the data collection method decision. A good example of special considerations are the Millennials, a generation of frequent electronic social media users who are a prime target for many food, clothing, and high-tech companies; by reading Marketing Research Insight 7.5, you will see that the only practical way to do research with these respondents is with some online-based data collection method.

> Cultural norms and/or limitations of communications systems may limit the data collection mode choice.

MARKETING RESEARCH INSIGHT 7.5   *Social Media Marketing*

Maintaining a MROC for Millennials

The Millennial Generation includes anyone born in the past 30 years, and it represents the first generation to be completely digital. The Millennial lifestyle includes constant communication using social and mobile media: blogging, tweeting, texting, and posting on Facebook are their vehicles of choice. Millennials represent millions of dollars of buying power, and a great many companies compete for this market. StrategyOne, a marketing research company located in Washington, D.C., has created a unique approach to doing marketing research on Millennials.[66] StrategyOne created a marketing research online community (MROC) called 8095 Live, which is consistent with the fact that many Millennials join online brand communities. The 8095 Live MROC is a ready-made online panel of about 500 Millennials that StrategyOne can access at any time to perform research for its clients seeking to understand the needs and preferences of this generation.

MROCs are very different from online panels where respondents are specifically recruited and compensated for participating in surveys. These groups are more organic because responding to surveys is only one aspect of online community participation. StrategyOne discovered that it is necessary to develop subcommunities about topics and issues that are foremost in Millenials' minds and to use "community managers" who stimulate and facilitate discussion on the manager's topic. Because 8095 Live members are not compensated for participating in surveys, the community managers build relationships with their community members, and they use these relationships to urge the members to participate in surveys.

What are some distinguishing characteristics of the Millennials according to StrategyOne? From a white paper posted on StrategyOne's website,[67] here are some interesting facts about the Millennials:

- Almost 90% share their brand preferences online.
- Six in ten are willing to share personal information with trusted brands.
- Family and friends are top sources of information.
- A slight majority of Millennials consults four or more information sources when choosing which product or service to purchase.
- Nine in ten Millennials take action weekly on behalf of a brand.
- A majority have joined multiple brand-sponsored online communities.
- Almost one-half write about positive experiences with products or companies online, while almost 40% write about negative experiences.
- In the 30 days before they were surveyed, one-third or more Millennials have recommended that a friend or family member purchase a specific product in one or more of the following categories: food, electronics, personal care products, beauty product, or clothing.

Summary

The data collection step in the marketing research process is accomplished via five basic survey modes: (1) person-administered surveys, (2) computer-assisted surveys, (3) computer-administered surveys, (4) self-administered surveys, and (5) mixed-mode, sometimes called *hybrid*, surveys. Person-administered survey modes are advantageous because they allow feedback, permit rapport building, facilitate certain quality controls, and capitalize on the adaptability of a human interviewer. However, they are slow, prone to human error, and costly, and they sometimes produce respondent apprehension known as *interview evaluation*. Computer-assisted interviews have all the person-administered survey advantages and disadvantages, with added advantages of less error, more efficiency, and use of computer media.

Computer-administered interviews, on the other hand, are faster and error free; they may include pictures or graphics capabilities, allow for real-time capture of data, and make respondents feel more at ease because another person is not listening to their answers. Disadvantages are that technical skills are sometimes required, and high set-up costs may be required if users are not computer literate. Self-administered survey modes have the advantages of reduced cost, respondent control, and no interview evaluation apprehension. The disadvantages are that respondents may not complete the task or complete the task in error, there is no monitor to guide respondents, and the questionnaire must be "perfect" to facilitate self-administration.

Finally, mixed-mode or hybrid surveys use multiple data collection methods. The advantage of mixed-mode surveys is that researchers can take the advantages of each of the various modes to achieve their data collection goals. Disadvantages are that different modes may produce different responses to the same research question, and researchers must evaluate these differences. In addition, multimode methods result in greater complexities, as researchers must design different questionnaires and be certain that data from different sources all come together in a common database for analysis.

Nine survey data collection methods may be used: (1) in-home interviews, which are conducted in respondents' homes; (2) mall-intercept interviews, conducted by approaching shoppers in a mall; (3) in-office interviews, conducted with executives or managers in their places of work; (4) telephone interviews, either from central location telephone interviews conducted by workers in a telephone interview company's facilities or using a CATI system; (5) computerized, fully automated surveys; (6) online surveys; (7) group self-administered surveys, in which the questionnaire is handed out to a group for individual responses; (8) drop-off surveys, in which the questionnaire is left with the respondent to be completed and picked up or returned at a later time; and (9) mail surveys, in which questionnaires are mailed to prospective respondents who are requested to fill them out and mail them back. The specific advantages and disadvantages of each data collection mode were discussed.

Researchers must take into account several considerations when deciding on a survey data collection mode: (1) the survey time horizon, (2) the survey data collection budget, (3) the type of respondent interaction required, (4) incidence rate, and (5) cultural and infrastructure considerations. All should be considered, but one or more factors may be paramount because each data collection situation is unique. Ultimately, the researcher will select a data collection mode with which he or she feels comfortable and one that will result in the desired quality and quantity of information without exceeding time or budget constraints.

Key Terms

Survey (p. 144)
Person-administered survey (p. 147)
Computer-assisted survey (p. 149)
Self-administered survey (p. 150)
Computer-administered survey (p. 151)
Mixed-mode survey (p. 154)
In-home survey (p. 157)
Mall-intercept survey (p. 158)

In-office survey (p. 160)
Central location telephone survey (p. 160)
Computer-assisted telephone interviews (CATI) (p. 162)
Fully automated survey (p. 163)
Completely automated telephone survey (CATS) (p. 162)

Internet-based questionnaire (p. 165)
Group self-administered survey (p. 165)
Drop-off survey (p. 166)
Mail survey (p. 166)
Nonresponse (p. 166)
Self-selection bias (p. 166)
Incidence rate (p. 167)

Review Questions/Applications

1. List the major advantages of survey research methods over qualitative methods. Can you think of any drawbacks, and, if so, what are they?
2. What aspects of computer-administered surveys make them attractive to marketing researchers?
3. What are the advantages of person-administered over computer-administered surveys?
4. What would be the motivation for a researcher to consider a mixed-mode survey?
5. Indicate the differences between (a) in-home surveys, (b) mall-intercept surveys, and (c) in-office surveys. What do they share in common?
6. Why are telephone surveys popular?
7. Indicate the pros and cons of self-administered surveys.
8. What advantages do online surveys have over various types of self-administered surveys?

9. What are the major disadvantages of a mail survey?
10. How does a drop-off survey differ from a regular mail survey?
11. How does the incidence rate affect the choice of a data collection mode?
12. Is a telephone interview inappropriate for a survey that has as one of its objectives a complete listing of all possible advertising media a person was exposed to in the last week? Why or why not?
13. NAPA Auto Parts is a retail chain specializing in stocking and selling both domestic and foreign automobile parts. It is interested in learning about its customers, so the marketing director sends instructions to all 2,000 store managers telling them that whenever a customer makes a purchase of $150 or more, they are to write down a description of the customer who made that purchase. They are to do this just for the second

week in October, writing each description on a separate sheet of paper. At the end of the week, they are to send all sheets to the marketing director. Comment on this data collection method.

14. Discuss the feasibility of each type of survey mode for each of the following cases:
    a. Fabergé wants to test a new fragrance called "Lime Brut."
    b. Kelly Services needs to determine how many businesses expect to hire temporary secretaries for those who go on vacation in the summer.
    c. The Britannica Online for Kids requires information on the degree to which parents of elementary school-aged children see encyclopedias as worthwhile purchases for their children.
    d. AT&T is considering a television screen phone system and wants to know people's reaction to it.

15. With a telephone survey, when a potential respondent refuses to take part or is found to have changed his or her telephone number or moved away, it is customary to simply try another prospect until a completion is secured. It is not standard practice to report the number of refusals or noncontacts. What are the implications of this policy for the reporting of nonresponse?

16. Compu-Ask Corporation has developed a stand-alone computerized interview system that can be adapted to almost any type of survey. It can fit on a handheld tablet computer, and the respondent directly answers questions using a stylus once the interviewer has turned on the tablet and started up the program. Indicate the appropriateness of this interviewing system in each of the following cases:
    a. A survey of plant managers concerning a new type of hazardous waste disposal system
    b. A survey of high school teachers to see if they are interested in a company's videos of educational public broadcast television programs
    c. A survey of consumers to determine their reactions to a nonrefrigerated variety of yogurt

17. A researcher is pondering what survey mode to use for a client who markets a home security system for apartment dwellers. The system comprises sensors that are pressed onto all of the windows and magnetic strips that are glued to each door. Once plugged into an electric socket and activated with a switch box, the system emits a loud alarm and simulates a barking guard dog when an intruder trips one of the sensors. The client wants to know how many apartment dwellers in the United States are aware of the system, what they think of it, and how likely they are to buy it in the coming year. Which consideration factors are positive and which are negative for each of the following survey modes: (a) in-home interviews, (b) mall intercepts, (c) online survey, (d) drop-off survey, and (e) CATI survey?

CASE 7.1

Machu Picchu National Park Survey

In Peru, there are many ruins of the temples and palaces of the Inca Indians, who attained what some historians consider to be the highest accomplishments in the Americas for agriculture, engineering, monument building, and craftsmanship. Unfortunately, the Incas were no match for the Spanish, who, with firearms and horses, defeated the entire Incan Empire in a matter of a few years in the 1560s.

In 1913, Hiram Bingham discovered the Incan complex called Machu Picchu, which was not plundered by the Spanish Conquistadors. It is the best-preserved Incan ruin of its type. Located at 8,000 feet above sea level on a mountain at the border of the Andes Mountains and the Peruvian jungle, Machu Picchu is still very difficult to access, as it requires a three-hour mountain train ride to reach from Cusco, Peru, the closest city. Normally, tourists board the train very early in the morning in Cusco and arrive at the Machu Picchu village train station around 10 a.m. They then board buses that take 30 minutes that climb up the 6-mile switchback dirt road to the entrance of Machu Picchu. With guides or on their own, tourists wander the expansive Machu Picchu ruins, have lunch at the Machu Picchu lodge located at the top of the mountain, and hurry to catch the bus down the mountain so they will not miss the one train that leaves around 3 p.m. to return to Cusco. Some tourists stay overnight at the Machu Picchu Lodge or in one of the six hotels located at the base in Machu Picchu village. At peak season, approximately 1,000 tourists visit Machu Picchu daily.

Machu Picchu is a Peruvian national park, and since it is the one of the top tourist attractions in the world, the national park department wishes to conduct a survey to research the satisfaction of tourists with the park's many features and with their total experience on their visit to Peru. With the help of a marketing researcher who specializes in tourism research, the park department officials have created a self-administered questionnaire for its survey. Now they must choose from several alternatives for gathering the data. Using concepts in this chapter and your knowledge of data collection methods and issues, answer the following questions.

1. If the questionnaire is an online survey, would it be successful? Why or why not?
2. If the park department uses a mail survey, what issues must be resolved? Would it be successful? Why or why not?
3. If the seven hotels in the Machu Picchu area each desired to know how its customers felt about the hotel's

services, prices, and accommodations, how might both the park department and the hotels work together on data collection to effect a mutually beneficial survey?
4. Using the knowledge that the Peruvian national park department has meager resources for marketing research, suggest a different method (not online, not mail, and not partnering with the local hotels) with the potential of effecting a high response rate and high-quality responses.

CASE 7.2 INTEGRATED CASE

Global Motors

Global Motors hired CMG Research to perform research, and Cory Rogers, vice president of CMG, presents his interpretations of the focus groups he had subcontracted for Nick Thomas, CEO of Global Motors. Nick is impressed with the amount of information that was collected from just a few focus groups. "Of course," Cory notes, "we have to take all of this information as tentative because we talked with so few folks, and there is a good chance that they are just a part of your target market. But we do have some good exploratory research that will guide us in the survey." Nick agrees with Cory's assessment and asks, "What's next?" Cory says, "I need to think about how we will gather the survey data. That is, in order to make an informed decision as to the type(s) of new automobile models to manufacture and market, it is important to understanding the worries and preferences of potential automobile buyers. We need to survey prospective automobile purchasers, and it is time to start thinking about the method of data collection."

While specifics are still to be hammered out, Global Motors executives and the marketing research team agree that the survey should reach 1,000 to 2,000 American households. Again, with the details to come, the survey will include 30 to 40 questions on a variety of topics, including household demographics, beliefs about global warming and gasoline's contribution to global warming, reactions to the various "new technology" automobiles, and any other questions identified in the research project objectives. The survey will be directed to either the male or the female head of the household, aiming for equal gender representation. Other than this factor, the overriding objective of the survey

method decision is to choose a method that will ultimately yield a respondent profile that reflects the demographic and automobile ownership profile of the American public. It is possible to purchase lists of American households in just about any quantity desired—hundreds, thousands, or even tens of thousands. These lists can be in the form of mailing addresses, email addresses, telephone numbers, or any combination. Here are some of the questions Cory Rogers must answer:

1. If a mail survey is used, what would be the pros, cons, and special considerations associated with achieving the overriding objective of the survey?
2. Many telephone data collection companies offer national coverage. Some have centralized telephone interview facilities, and some offer CATI services. If one of these companies is selected to conduct a telephone survey, what would be the pros, cons, and special considerations associated with achieving the overriding objective of the survey?
3. The following data collection methods are not likely to achieve the overriding objective. For each one, indicate why not.
   a. Drop-off survey
   b. Group-administered survey
   c. Mall-intercept survey
4. Compare the use of an in-home method to the use of an online method for Global Motors survey. What are the relevant pros and cons of each one? Indicate which one you would recommend and why.

Understanding Measurement, Developing Questions, and Designing the Questionnaire

"WHERE WE ARE"

Knowledge of Measurement Options and Design

Darren Mark Noyce, FMRS MCIM, Founder & Managing Director, SKOPOS Insight Group, United Kingdom.

Evidence is everything. Reliable evidence is everything plus the kitchen sink with correct plumbing and no dripping taps that provides hot or cold water whenever you need it in the right quantities.

At SKOPOS we have a mantra: *Take client problems, turn them into questions, to generate answers that form solutions.* This is a perfect blend of empathy and authority, art and science, structure and free choice, creativity and dependability. For example, after a series of open-ended, less-structured focus groups with customers, we may determine that a client's dropping market share or profits is caused by growing customer dissatisfaction. We then must devise questions (usually in the form of a structured questionnaire) that consumers can understand and that actually measure satisfaction from a customer perspective in a way that we can appropriately analyze, synthesize, and then decipher and diagnose, so we can accurately advise our client. Not only must we be sure that our questions are really measuring customer satisfaction (or maybe dissatisfaction, delight, etc.), but we must ask the questions using the desired type and level of measurement.

Let's look at how we can measure customer satisfaction for one of our large retail clients. We could just ask consumers: Are you satisfied with company X? Yes (1) or No (2). By wording the question this way, we have determined the level of measurement. In this case we would call it a *nominal* type of measurement as we have nominally assigned a name to a number code (and vice versa) to represent each possible answer to the question. This level of measurement will allow us to determine what percent of our sample is satisfied and what percent isn't. But this is hardly sufficient to help our client!

What if we want to diagnose the sources of low or high satisfaction scores? We need to measure satisfaction with all the different dimensions making up consumer satisfaction such as satisfaction with store cleanliness, employee courtesy, product selection, or waiting time. Going further, we need to provide actionable results to provide our clients with real value. We have models that will tell us which area(s) of dissatisfaction create the greatest likelihood that customers will switch brands (shop at competitors' stores). This information would be invaluable to our client in that managers would know that store cleanliness, for example, is three times more important than product display in keeping loyal customers. Our client would know immediately where to invest resources.

But our models require that we be able to calculate, say, means and standard deviations in our data to achieve a more precise and higher level of mathematical solidity. Put another way, for such a study we have design choices for the level (or precision or sensitivity) of measurement we use that will dictate whether we can, say, calculate means and standard deviations—and hence input into our models. As you will learn in this chapter, these higher levels of measurement are referred to as *scale*. This example should illustrate why marketing researchers need to understand the basics of measurement and question selection/design. Had we measured customer satisfaction by just asking the question: Are you satisfied/not satisfied with company X? we would have done our client a disservice. Because we understand measurement concepts and how these are composed, we can ask questions that generate answers that form solutions.

This is what our clients expect of us at SKOPOS. Everything and the kitchen sink.

The SKOPOS Insight Group is headquartered in Cologne, with offices around Europe and the world. SKOPOS delivers actionable customer insight generated from precision market research (using traditional methods as well as more modern online/mobile surveys and qualitative techniques). Applications include website and SEO evaluation, customer satisfaction, market sizing/profiling, and e-mail marketing campaign evaluation, all from a customer/user perspective with the strongest analysis, interpretation and holistic market knowledge.

Visit SKOPOS Insight Group at www.SKOPOS.info

Text and images: By permission, Darren Mark Noyce, SKOPOS Insight Group, UK.

Photo: EuToch/Fotolia

Basic Concepts in Measurement

Measurement is determining a description or amount of some property of an object that is of interest to the researcher.

As this chapter's opening remarks by Mr. Noyce reveal, marketing research relies heavily on **measurement**, which is defined as determining a description or the amount of some property of an object that is of interest to the researcher. For instance, a marketing manager may want to determine what brand a person typically purchases or how much of the product he or she uses in a certain time period. This information, once compiled, can help answer specific research objectives such as determining product opinions and usage.

But what are we really measuring? We are measuring properties—sometimes called characteristics, attributes, or qualities—of objects. Objects include consumers, brands, stores, advertisements, or whatever construct is of interest to the researcher working with a particular manager. **Properties** are the specific features or characteristics of an object that can be used to distinguish it from another object. For example, assume the object we want to research is a consumer. As depicted in Figure 8.1, the properties of interest to a manager who is trying to define who buys a specific product are a combination of demographics, such as age and gender, as well as buyer behavior, which includes such things as the buyer's preferred brand and perceptions of various brands. Once the object's designation on a property has been determined, we say that the object has been measured on that property. Measurement underlies marketing research to a great extent because researchers are keenly interested in describing marketing phenomena. Furthermore, researchers are often given the task of finding relevant differences in the profiles of various customer types, and measurement is a necessary first step in this task.

Measurement is a simple process as long as we are measuring **objective properties**, which are physically verifiable characteristics such as age, income, number of bottles purchased, store last visited, and so on. They are observable and tangible. Typically, objective properties such as gender are preset as to appropriate response options, such as "male" or "female." However, marketing researchers often desire to measure **subjective properties**, which cannot be directly observed because they are mental constructs such as a person's

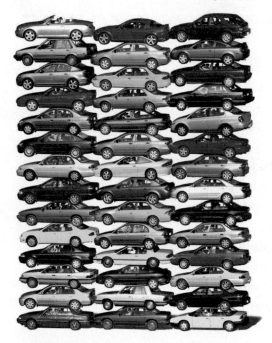

Regardless of make or model, automobiles have several properties that can be measured.

Photo: Edwin Verin/Shutterstock

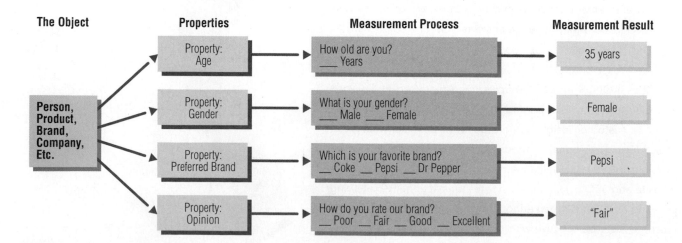

The Object	Properties	Measurement Process	Measurement Result
Person, Product, Brand, Company, Etc.	Property: Age	How old are you? ___ Years	35 years
	Property: Gender	What is your gender? ___ Male ___ Female	Female
	Property: Preferred Brand	Which is your favorite brand? ___ Coke ___ Pepsi ___ Dr Pepper	Pepsi
	Property: Opinion	How do you rate our brand? ___ Poor ___ Fair ___ Good ___ Excellent	"Fair"

FIGURE 8.1 How Measurement Works in Marketing Research

attitude or intentions. Subjective properties are unobservable and intangible. In this case, the marketing researcher must ask a respondent to translate his or her feelings or opinions onto a measurement continuum, which is not an easy task. To do this, the marketing researcher must adapt or develop rating scale formats that are very clear and used identically by respondents. This process is known as **scale development**, which is designing questions and response formats to measure the subjective properties of an object.[1] Our exploration of this process begins with introducing some basic measurement concepts.

Types of Measures

Marketing researchers describe measures in several different ways. In this section we describe the three measures used by SPSS: nominal, ordinal, and scale. This approach will facilitate your future use of SPSS because it will link your questionnaire design knowledge with the concepts used in SPSS.

NOMINAL MEASURES

Nominal measures are defined as those that use only labels; that is, they possess only the characteristic of description. Examples include designations as to race, religion, type of dwelling, gender, brand last purchased, and buyer/nonbuyer. Answers involve yes–no, agree–disagree, or any other instance in which the descriptors cannot be differentiated except qualitatively. If you describe respondents in a survey according to their occupation—banker, doctor, computer programmer—you have used a nominal scale. Note that these examples of a nominal scale only label the consumers. They do not provide other information such as "greater than," "twice as large," and so forth. Examples of nominal-scaled questions are found in Table 8.1A.

Nominal scales label objects.

ORDINAL MEASURES

Ordinal measures permit the researcher to rank order the respondents or their responses. For instance, if the respondent is asked to indicate his or her first, second, third, and fourth choices of brands, the results are ordinally scaled. Similarly, if one respondent checks the category "Commute regularly" on a travel-frequency scale and another checks the category "Commute infrequently," the result is an ordinal measurement because we know that the first respondent commutes more than the second one, but not by how much. Ordinal scales indicate only relative size differences among objects: greater than, less than, or equal to. See some examples of ordinal measures in Table 8.1B.

Ordinal scales indicate only relative size differences between objects.

SCALE MEASURES

Scale measures are those in which the distance between each level is known. There are two types of scale measures. **Ratio scale** measures are ones in which a true zero origin exists—such as an actual number of purchases in a certain time period, dollars spent, miles traveled, number of children in the household, or years of college education. As you can see, ratio scales are easy for respondents to understand as they are in dollars, times, years, or some other familiar denomination. The ratio characteristic allows us to construct ratios when comparing results of the measurement. One person may spend twice as much as another or travel one-third as far. Refer to Table 8.1D for examples.

Ratio scales have a true zero point.

Interval scale measures are rating scales for subjective properties where, for adjacent levels, the distance is normally defined as one scale unit. For example, a coffee brand rated 3 in taste is one unit away from one rated 4. Implicitly, equal intervals exist between the level descriptors. That is, if you are asked to evaluate a store's salespeople by selecting a single designation from a list of "extremely friendly," "very friendly," "somewhat friendly," "somewhat unfriendly," "very unfriendly," or "extremely unfriendly," the researcher probably assumes that each designation is one unit away from the preceding one. In these cases, we say that the

TABLE 8.1   Examples of the Use of Different Types of Measures

A. Nominal Measure Questions

1. Please indicate your gender. _____ Male _____ Female
2. Are you planning on purchasing a new automobile in the next six months?
   _____ Yes _____ No _____ Unsure
3. Do you recall seeing a Delta Airlines advertisement for "carefree vacations" in the past week?
   _____ Yes _____ No

B. Ordinal Measure Questions

1. Please rank each brand in terms of your preference. Place a "1" by your first choice, a "2" by your second choice, and so on.
   _____ 3 Musketeers
   _____ Baby Ruth
   _____ Milky Way
2. For each pair of grocery stores, circle the one you would be more likely to patronize.
   Kroger versus Publix
   Publix versus A&P
   A&P versus Kroger
3. In your opinion, would you say the prices at Walmart are
   _____ Higher than Sears,
   _____ About the same as Sears, or
   _____ Lower than Sears?

C. Interval Scale Measure Questions

1. Please rate each of the following in terms of your overall performance.

Brand	Not Enjoyable							Very Enjoyable		
Game of Thrones	1	2	3	4	5	6	7	8	9	10
Mad Men	1	2	3	4	5	6	7	8	9	10
The Borgias	1	2	3	4	5	6	7	8	9	10

2. Indicate your degree of agreement with the following statements by circling the appropriate number.

Statement	Strongly Disagree				Strongly Agree
a. I always look for bargains.	1	2	3	4	5
b. I enjoy being outdoors.	1	2	3	4	5
c. I love to cook.	1	2	3	4	5

3. Please rate the **Chevrolet Camaro** by checking the line that best corresponds to your evaluation of each item listed.
   Slow pickup _____ _____ _____ _____ _____ _____ _____ Fast pickup
   Good design _____ _____ _____ _____ _____ _____ _____ Bad design
   Low price   _____ _____ _____ _____ _____ _____ _____ High price

D. Ratio Scale Measure Questions

1. Please indicate your age.
   _____ Years
2. Approximately how many times in the last month have you purchased something over $5 in price at a 7-11 store?
   0 1 2 3 4 5 More (specify:_____)
3. How much do you think a typical purchaser of a $250,000 term life insurance policy pays per year for that policy?
   $_____

scale is an *assumed interval*. Interval scales, such as those in Table 8.1C, may be intuitive for respondents, but they always measure subjective properties, and as you will soon learn, they require careful judgment on the part of the marketing researcher when used.

Because most subjective, or psychological, properties exist on a continuum ranging from one extreme to another in the mind of the respondent, it is common practice to use interval scale questions to measure them. Sometimes numbers are used to indicate a single unit of distance between each position on the scale. Usually, but not always, the scale ranges from an extreme negative through a neutral and to an extreme positive designation. The neutral point is not considered zero, or an origin; instead, it is considered a point along the continuum. In the examples in Table 8.2, you will see that all of them span a continuum ranging from extremely negative to extremely positive with a "no opinion" position in the middle of the scale. As shown in Tables 8.1C and 8.2, these descriptors are evenly spaced on a questionnaire; as such, the labels connote a continuum and the check lines are equal distances apart. By wording or spacing the response options on a scale so they appear to have equal intervals between them, the researcher achieves a higher level of measurement than ordinal or nominal, and a higher level measure allows the researcher to see finer distinctions among respondents' properties.

Marketing researchers often rely on the standard measures known as *workhorse scales*.

Photo: Becky Swora/Shutterstock

Interval Scales Commonly Used in Marketing Research

It is not good practice to invent a novel scale format with every questionnaire. Instead, marketing researchers often fall back on standard types used by the industry. By now you know that marketing researchers often measure subjective properties of consumers. There are various terms and labels given to these constructs, including attitudes, opinions, evaluations, beliefs, impressions, perceptions, feelings, and intentions. Because these constructs are unobservable, the marketing researcher must develop some means of allowing respondents to express the

Marketing researchers use standard scales rather than inventing new ones for each research project.

TABLE 8.2   The Intensity Continuum Underlying Scaled-Response Question Forms

Extremely Negative			Neutral			Extremely Positive
Strongly Disagree	Disagree	Somewhat Disagree	Neither Agree nor Disagree	Somewhat Agree	Agree	Strongly Agree
1	2	3	4	5	6	7
Extremely Dissatisfied	Very Dissatisfied	Somewhat Dissatisfied	No Opinion	Somewhat Satisfied	Very Satisfied	Extremely Satisfied
1	2	3	4	5	6	7
Extremely Unfavorable	Very Unfavorable	Somewhat Unfavorable	No Opinion	Somewhat Favorable	Very Favorable	Extremely Favorable
1	2	3	4	5	6	7

Interval scales are used to measure unobservable constructs.

direction and intensity of their impressions in a convenient and understandable manner. To do this, the marketing researcher uses interval scales. In this section, we will describe the basic interval scale formats that are most common in marketing research practice. You will find these scale formats time and again on questionnaires; hence, we refer to them as **workhorse scales** because they do the bulk of the measurement work in marketing research.

THE LIKERT SCALE

The Likert scale format measures intensity of agreement or disagreement.

An interval scale commonly used by marketing researchers[2] is the **Likert scale**, in which respondents are asked to indicate their degree of agreement or disagreement on a symmetric agree–disagree scale for each of a series of statements. That is, the scale captures the intensity of their feelings toward the statement's claim or assertion because respondents are asked how much they agree or disagree with the statement. With this scale, it is best to use "flat" or plain statements and let the respondent indicate the intensity of his or her feelings by using the agree–disagree response continuum position. Table 8.3 presents an example of its use in an online survey.

The Likert type of response format, borrowed from a formal scale development approach introduced by Rensis Likert, has been extensively modified and adapted by marketing researchers, so much, in fact, that its definition varies from researcher to researcher. Some assume that any intensity scale using descriptors such as "strongly," "somewhat," and "slightly" is a Likert variation. Others use the term only for questions with agree–disagree response options. We tend to agree with the second opinion and prefer to refer to any scaled measurement other than an agree–disagree dimension as a "sensitivity" or "intensity" scale. But this convention is only our preference, and you should be aware that different researchers embrace other designations.

A lifestyle inventory measures a person's activities, interests, and opinions with a Likert scale.

A special application of the Likert question form called the **lifestyle inventory** takes into account the values and personality traits of people as reflected in their unique activities, interests, and opinions (AIOs) toward their work, leisure time, and purchases. Examples of lifestyle statements are: "I shop a lot for specials," "I prefer to pay for purchases with my debit card," or "My children are an important part of my life." Lifestyle questions measure consumers' unique ways of living. These questions can be used to distinguish among types of purchasers such as heavy versus light users of a product, store patrons versus nonpatrons, or other customer types. They can assess the degree to which a person is, for example, price-conscious, fashion-conscious, an opinion giver, a sports enthusiast, child oriented, home centered, or financially optimistic. The technique was originated by advertising strategists who wanted to obtain descriptions of groups of consumers as a means of establishing more effective advertising. The underlying belief is that knowledge of consumers' lifestyles, as opposed to just demographics, offers direction for marketing decisions. Many companies use psychographics as a market targeting tool.[3]

Marketing Research on YouTube™ | To see a "cute" presentation on the Likert scale, launch www.youtube.com, and search for "Using the Likert Scale to evaluate a kid's halloween party."

TABLE 8.3   Example of a Likert Scale

Indicate the degree to which you agree or disagree with each of the following statements.

Statement	Strongly Agree	Agree	Neutral	Disagree	Strongly Disagree
Levi's Engineered jeans are good looking.	◎	◎	◎	◎	◎
Levi's Engineered jeans are reasonably priced.	◎	◎	◎	◎	◎
Your next pair of jeans will be Levi's Engineered jeans.	◎	◎	◎	◎	◎
Levi's Engineered jeans are easy to identify on someone.	◎	◎	◎	◎	◎
Levi's Engineered jeans make you feel good.	◎	◎	◎	◎	◎

 **Active Learning**

Construct a College Student Lifestyle Inventory

As a college student yourself, you can easily relate to the dimensions of college student lifestyle. In this active learning exercise, take each of the following college student activities and write the Likert scale statement that could appear on a college student lifestyle inventory questionnaire. Be sure to model your statements as recommended in our descriptions of the Likert scale workhorse scale format.

College Lifestyle Dimension	Write Your Statement Below	Strongly Disagree	Disagree	Neither Disagree nor Agree	Agree	Strongly Agree
Studying		1	2	3	4	5
Going out		1	2	3	4	5
Working		1	2	3	4	5
Exercising		1	2	3	4	5
Shopping		1	2	3	4	5
Dating		1	2	3	4	5
Spending money		1	2	3	4	5

The Likert 5-point scale is flexible when it comes to measuring constructs or concepts. It is also amenable to sophisticated statistical analysis that has the potential to reveal important relationships or associations among constructs.

THE SEMANTIC DIFFERENTIAL SCALE

A specialized interval scale format that has sprung directly from the problem of translating a person's qualitative judgments into metric estimates is the **semantic differential scale**. Like the Likert scale, this one has been borrowed from another area of research, namely, semantics. The semantic differential scale contains a series of bipolar adjectives for the various properties of the object under study, and respondents indicate their impressions of each property by indicating locations along its continuum. The focus of the semantic differential is on the measurement of the meaning of an object, concept, person, or experience.[4] Because many marketing stimuli have meaning, mental associations, or connotations, this type of synthetic scale works well when the marketing researcher is attempting to determine brand, store, or other images.[5]

> The semantic differential is a good way to measure a brand, company, or store image.

The construction of a semantic differential scale begins with the determination of a concept or object to be rated, usually a brand or company. The researcher then selects bipolar pairs of words or phrases that could be used to describe the object's salient properties. Depending on the object, some examples might be "friendly–unfriendly," "hot–cold," "convenient–inconvenient," "high quality–low quality," or "dependable–undependable." The opposites are positioned at the endpoints of a continuum of intensity, and it is customary to use five or seven separators between each point. The respondent then indicates his or her evaluation of the performance of the object, say, a brand, by checking the appropriate line. The closer the respondent checks to an end point on a line, the more intense is his or her evaluation of the object being measured.

When using a semantic differential scale, you should control for the *halo effect*.

Table 8.4 shows a semantic differential scale for a survey for Red Lobster. The respondents also rated Jake's Seafood Restaurant on the same survey. You can see that each respondent has been instructed to indicate his or her impression of various restaurants such as Red Lobster by clicking on the appropriate circle between the several bipolar adjective phrases. As you look at the phrases, you should note that they have been randomly flipped to avoid having all of the "good" ones on one side. This flipping procedure is used to avoid the **halo effect**,[6] which is a general feeling about a store or brand that can bias a respondent's impressions on its specific properties.[7] For instance, let's say respondents who are big fans of Red Lobster complete a survey with all the positive items on the right-hand side and all the negative on the left-hand side; they might click on the answers on the right-hand side without reading each characteristic carefully. But it is entirely possible that some specific aspects of the Red Lobster dining experience might not be as good as others. Perhaps the restaurant is not located in a convenient place, or the menu is not as broad as some might like. Randomly flipping

TABLE 8.4 Example of a Semantic Differential Scale

Indicate your impression of *Red Lobster* restaurant by checking the bubble corresponding to your opinion for each pair of descriptors.

High prices	○ ○ ○ ○ ○ ○ ○	Low prices
Inconvenient location	○ ○ ○ ○ ○ ○ ○	Convenient location
For me	○ ○ ○ ○ ○ ○ ○	Not for me
Warm atmosphere	○ ○ ○ ○ ○ ○ ○	Cold atmosphere
Limited menu	○ ○ ○ ○ ○ ○ ○	Wide menu
Fast service	○ ○ ○ ○ ○ ○ ○	Slow service
Low-quality food	○ ○ ○ ○ ○ ○ ○	High-quality food
A special place	○ ○ ○ ○ ○ ○ ○	An everyday place

Presentation of the Results

High prices	○ ● ○ ● ○ ○ ○	Low prices
Inconvenient location	○ ○ ● ○ ● ○ ○	Convenient location
Not for me	○ ● ● ○ ○ ○ ○	For me
Cold atmosphere	○ ○ ● ● ○ ○ ○	Warm atmosphere
Limited menu	○ ● ○ ● ○ ○ ○	Wide menu
Slow service	○ ○ ○ ● ● ○ ○	Fast service
Low-quality food	○ ○ ● ● ○ ○ ○	High-quality food
An everyday place	○ ● ○ ○ ● ○ ○	A special place

●————● Red Lobster
●·········● Jake's Seafood Restaurant

favorable and negative ends of the descriptors in a semantic differential scale minimizes the halo effect.[8] Also, there is some evidence that when respondents are ambivalent about the survey topic, it is best to use a balanced set of negatively and positively worded questions.[9]

One of the most appealing aspects of the semantic differential scale is the ability of the researcher to compute averages and then to plot a "profile" of the brand or company image. Each check line is assigned a number for coding. Usually, the numbers 1, 2, 3, and so on, beginning from the left side, are customary. Then, because a metric scale is used, an average may be computed for each bipolar pair. The averages are plotted as you see them, and marketing researchers have a nice graphical communication vehicle with which to report the findings to their clients.

With a semantic differential scale, a researcher can plot the average evaluation on each set of bipolar descriptors.

THE STAPEL SCALE

A Stapel scale relies not on bipolar terms but on positive and negative numbers, typically ranging from +5 to –5. The scale may or may not have a neutral zero. The Stapel scale is easier to construct than a semantic differential scale because the researcher does not need to come up with bipolar adjectives for each attribute. It is also flexible to administer as respondents do not need to "see" the scale the way they do when responding to a semantic differential scale. However, to use a Stapel scale properly, respondents must feel comfortable with the use of negative numbers.

A Stapel scale is easily recognized as it has numbers that range from a minus end to a corresponding plus end, with or without a zero as the midpoint.

More on Interval Scales Used in Marketing Research Briefly, we will describe two issues in the use of interval scales. The first issue is whether to include the middle, neutral response option. Our Likert scale, lifestyle, and semantic differential examples all have a neutral point, but some researchers prefer to leave out the neutral option on their scales. Valid arguments exist for both options.[10] Those arguing for the inclusion of a neutral option believe that some respondents do not have opinions formed on that item, and they must be given the opportunity to indicate their ambivalence. Proponents of not including a neutral position, however, believe that respondents may use the neutral option as a dodge or a method of hiding their opinions.[11] Eliminating the neutral position forces these respondents to indicate their opinions or feelings.

Use a neutral response option when you think respondents have a valid "no opinion" response.

The second issue concerns whether to use a symmetric or a nonsymmetric scale. A **symmetric interval scale** is "balanced," as it has equal amounts of positive and negative positions, and typically it has "no opinion" or "neutral" separating the negative and positive sides. But not all constructs have counter opposing ends. That is, a **nonsymmetric interval scale**, which has mainly degrees of positive positions, would be more appropriate because most people do not think in degrees of negative importance.

Sometimes, common sense causes the researcher to conclude that only the positive side is appropriate.[12] For example, suppose you were asked to indicate how important having jail bail bond protection was for you as a feature when you purchased automobile insurance. It is doubtful that you would differentiate between "extremely unimportant," "very unimportant," or "somewhat unimportant," but you could indicate how important it was to you with the response options of "not important" to "somewhat important," "very important," and "extremely important." In fact, for many constructs, symmetric scales are awkward or nonintuitive and should not be used.[13] Consequently, some scales contain only the positive side, because very few respondents would make use of the negative side. When in doubt, a researcher can pretest both complete and one-sided versions to see whether respondents will use the negative side. As a general rule, it is best to pretest a sensitivity scale to make sure it is being used in its entirety. Some individuals, such as Hispanics, have tendencies to use only one end of a scale,[14] and pretests should be used to find a scale that will used appropriately.

Use common sense in deciding whether to have a completely symmetric scale.

It has been our experience that when you study each workhorse scale and the other scaled-response question formats described in this chapter, each one makes sense. However, when faced with the actual decision as to what scale to recommend in a given situation, it is difficult for neophyte marketing researchers to sort these scales out. As we indicated in Chapter 3, the mind set of marketing researchers is geared toward the actual survey steps, and questionnaire design is a vital step that they must think about when formulating marketing research proposals. In those situations, researchers rely on "constructs," or standard marketing concepts, and develop a mental vision of how each construct will be measured. This mental vision, which we defined in Chapter 3, is called an *operational definition.*

Table 8.5 offers a quick reference to appropriate scales pertaining to the constructs most often measured by marketing researchers. You will notice that the scales in this table are interval scaled because most of the constructs are attitudinal or intensity scales, and the general recommendation is to use the highest level scale possible.[15] Of course, this is not a complete list of marketing constructs, but the constructs in Table 8.5 are often involved in marketing research undertakings.

TABLE 8.5   Commonly Used Interval Scales for Selected Constructs

Construct	Response Scale
Brand/Store Image	Semantic differential (with 5 or 7 scale points) using a set of bipolar adjectives Example: *Refer to example on page 182.*
Frequency of use	Labeled (Never, Rarely, Occasionally, Often, Quite Often, Very Often) OR # times per relevant time period (e.g., month) Example: *How often do you buy takeout Chinese dinners?*
Importance	Labeled (Unimportant, Slightly Important, Important, Quite Important, Very Important) OR numbered rating using 5 scale points Example: *How important is it to you that your dry cleaning service has same-day service?*
Intention to purchase	Labeled (Unlikely, Somewhat Likely, Likely, Quite Likely, Very Likely) OR 100% probability Example: *The next time you buy cookies, how likely are you to buy a fat-free brand?*
Lifestyle/Opinion	Likert (Strongly Disagree–Strongly Agree with 5 scale points) using a series of lifestyle statements Example: *Indicate how much you agree or disagree with each of the following statements.* 1. *I have a busy schedule.* 2. *I work a great deal.*
Performance or Attitude	Labeled (Poor, Fair, Good, Very Good, Excellent) OR numbered rating scale using 5 scale points OR Stapel scale using –3 to +3 Example: *Indicate how well you think Arby's performs on each of the following features.* 1. *Variety of items on the menu* 2. *Reasonable price* 3. *Location convenient to your home*
Satisfaction	Labeled (Not at All Satisfied, Slightly Satisfied, Somewhat Satisfied, Very Satisfied, Completely Satisfied) OR 10-point satisfaction scale where 1 = "not at all satisfied" and 10 = "completely satisfied" Note: If there is reason to believe that an appreciable number of respondents are not satisfied, the recommendation is for a symmetric balanced scale to measure the degree of dissatisfaction (Completely Dissatisfied; Slightly Dissatisfied; Neither Dissatisfied nor Satisfied; Slightly Satisfied; Completely Satisfied) Example: *Based on your experience with Federal Express, how satisfied have you been with its overnight delivery service?*

A great many variations of interval scales are used in marketing research. If you choose a career in the marketing research business, you will come to realize that each marketing research company or marketing research department tends to rely on "tried-and-true" formats that they apply from study to study. There are good reasons for this practice of adopting a preferred question format. First, it expedites the questionnaire design process. That is, by selecting a standardized scaled-response form that has been used in several studies, there is no need to be creative and invent a new form. This saves both time and costs.[16] A valuable byproduct of using the same scale in global marketing research is that cultural response biases can be identified and adjustments can be made. To learn about cultural response bias, read Marketing Research Insight 8.1. Second, testing a synthetic scaled-response format across several studies offers the opportunity to assess its reliability as well as its validity. Both of these topics are discussed in detail in the next sections of this chapter, which introduce the basic concepts involved with reliability and validity of measurements and illustrate the methods used to assess reliability and validity.

Researchers tend to rely on "tried-and-true" scale formats.

MARKETING RESEARCH INSIGHT 8.1 — *Global Application*

Global Marketing Research

Challenges of Question Design in Global Marketing Research

Many companies operate in global markets, meaning that their products and services are used in a variety of cultural settings. A marketing researcher attempting to do research in a foreign country is faced with respondents who are different in many respects, including language, religion, food, holidays, transportation, values, government, and entertainment. Various cultures also exhibit differing response biases. Some cultures avoid extremes, while others embrace them. Some cultures demand opinions to be aired, while others expect them to be tempered.

Rating scales are commonly used in global marketing research; however, it has been shown that cultural differences, rather than true differences in opinions or attitudes, sometimes result in different responses from country to country. The following graph vividly illustrates how cultural differences can affect responses to a purchase intentions scale.[17]

The figure shows that Chinese and Brazilian respondents are more inclined to respond in the affirmative and "maybe," while Italian and Japanese respondents are more likely to respond in the negative and "maybe." U.S., U.K., and Mexican respondents are more inclined to respond in the negative. Marketing research companies that perform a great deal of global marketing research are able to detect these cultural response biases across many, many studies and make appropriate adjustments. But companies with less global marketing research experience are likely to err in their conclusions about differences between global markets because they are unaware of these biases or otherwise unable to make such adjustments.

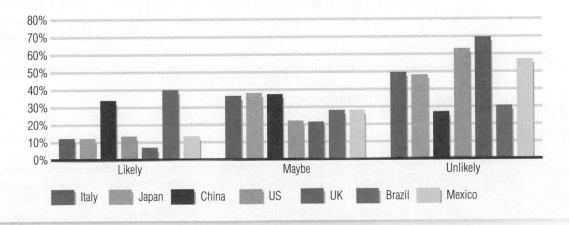

Figuring out what scale to use and when is challenging for a neophyte marketing researcher.

Photo: Masson/Shutterstock

Reliable measures obtain identical or very similar responses from the same respondent.

Validity is the truthfulness of responses to a measure.

Reliability and Validity of Measurements

Ideally, a measurement used by a marketing researcher should be reliable and valid. With a **reliable measure**, a respondent responds in the same or very similar manner to an identical or near-identical question. Obviously, if a question elicits wildly different answers from the same person and you know the person is unchanged between administrations of the question, something is very wrong with the question. It is unreliable.[18]

Validity, on the other hand, refers to the accuracy of the measurement: It is an assessment of the exactness of the measurement relative to what actually exists. A **valid measure** is truthful. To illustrate this concept and its difference from reliability, think of a respondent who is embarrassed by a question about his income. This person makes under $20,000 per year, but he does not want to share that with the interviewer. Consequently, he responds with the highest category, "Over $100,000." In a retest of the questions, the respondent persists in his lie by stipulating the highest income level again. Here, the respondent has been perfectly consistent (that is, reliable), but he has also been completely untruthful (that is, invalid). Of course, lying is not the only reason for invalidity. The respondent may have a faulty memory, may have a misconception, or may even be a bad guesser, which causes his responses to be inexact from reality.[19]

Designing a Questionnaire

A questionnaire presents the survey questions to respondents.

A **questionnaire** is the vehicle used to present the questions the researcher desires respondents to answer. A questionnaire serves six key functions: (1) It translates the research objectives into specific questions asked of respondents. (2) It standardizes those questions and the response categories so that every participant responds to identical stimuli. (3) By its wording, question flow, and appearance, it fosters cooperation and keeps respondents motivated throughout the interview. (4) It serves as an enduring record of the research. (5) Depending on the data collection mode used, such as online, a questionnaire can speed up the process of data analysis. (6) Finally, it contains the information on which reliability and validity assessments may be made. In other words, questionnaires are used by researchers for quality control.

Given that it serves all of these functions, the questionnaire is at the center of the research process. In fact, studies have shown that questionnaire design directly affects the quality of the data collected. Even experienced interviewers cannot compensate for questionnaire defects.[20] The time and effort invested in developing a good questionnaire are well spent.[21] Designing a questionnaire requires the researcher to go through a series of interrelated steps.

THE QUESTIONNAIRE DESIGN PROCESS

Questionnaire design is a systematic process that requires the researcher to go through a series of considerations.

Questionnaire design is a systematic process in which the researcher contemplates various question formats, considers a number of factors characterizing the survey at hand, ultimately words the various questions carefully, and organizes the questionnaire's layout.

Figure 8.2 offers a flowchart of the various phases in a typical questionnaire design process. As you can see, a significant part of questionnaire design involves the development of individual questions in the survey, identified as "Question Development" in the figure. We have expanded and highlighted the question development steps so you can see that the researcher must execute some specific activities before any question is acceptable. As you

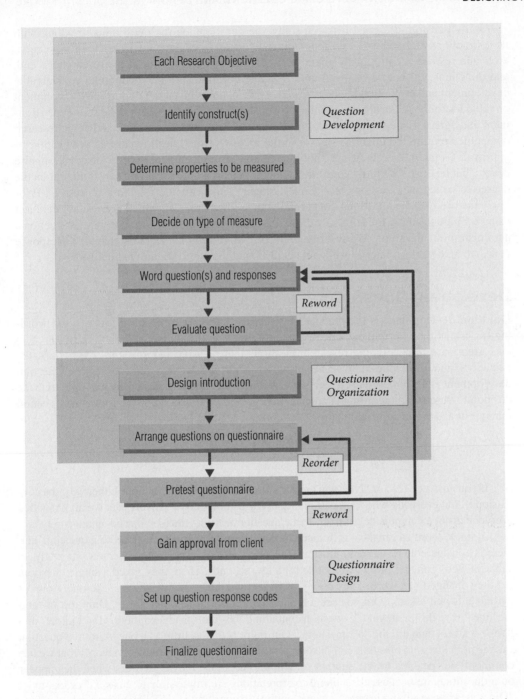

FIGURE 8.2 Question Development and Questionnaire Design Process

can see in Figure 8.2, a question will ordinarily go through a series of drafts before it is in acceptable final form. In fact, even before the question is constructed, the researcher mentally reviews alternative question response scale formats to decide which ones are best suited to the survey's respondents and circumstances. As the question begins to take shape, the researcher continually evaluates the question and its response options. Changes are made, and the question's wording is reevaluated to make sure that it is asking what the researcher intends. Also, the researcher strives to minimize **question bias**, defined as the ability of a question's wording or format to influence respondents' answers.[22] Question development takes place for every question pertaining to each research objective. We elaborate on question development and the minimization of question bias in the following sections.

Question bias occurs when the question's wording or format influences the respondent's answer.

To watch a presentation on effective online questionnaire design, launch **www.youtube .com**, and search for "Online Survey Design – Importance of Good Online Survey Questionnaire Design."

With a custom-designed research study, the questions on the questionnaire, along with its instructions, introduction, and general layout, are all systematically evaluated for potential error and revised accordingly. Generally, this evaluation takes place at the researcher's end, and the client will not be involved until after the questionnaire has undergone considerable development and evaluation by the researcher. The client is given the opportunity to comment on the questionnaire during the client approval step, in which the client reviews the questionnaire and agrees that it covers all appropriate issues. This step is essential, and some research companies require the client to sign or initial a copy of the questionnaire as verification of approval. Granted, the client may not appreciate all the technical aspects of questionnaire design, but he or she is vitally concerned with the research objectives and can comment on the degree to which the questions on the questionnaire appear to address these objectives. Prior to client approval, the questionnaire normally undergoes a pretest, which is an actual field test using a limited sample to reveal any difficulties that might still lurk in wording, instructions, administration, and so on. We describe pretesting more fully later in this chapter.[23] Response codes, to be described later as well, are decided, and the questionnaire is finalized.

Developing Questions

Question development is the practice of selecting appropriate response formats and wording questions that are understandable, unambiguous, and unbiased.

Question development is the practice of selecting appropriate response formats and wording questions that are understandable, unambiguous, and unbiased. Marketing researchers take great care in developing research questions that measure (1) attitudes, (2) beliefs, (3) behaviors, and (4) demographics[24] because they desire reliable and valid responses. Question development is absolutely vital to the success of the survey. Here is a corny example to make our point that question wording is crucial. How would you respond to the following question that might appear on a questionnaire?

> *Are you trying to control your compulsive gambling?*
>
> ___ *Yes* ___ *No*

If you answer "Yes" or "No," you are admitting to a gambling addiction. Either way, the conclusion is that everyone who took part in the survey gambles compulsively. But we all know that everyone is not a compulsive gambler, so the question wording must be flawed, and it surely is.[25]

A single word can make a difference in how study participants respond to a question, and there is considerable research to illustrate this point. For example, researchers in one study let subjects view a picture of an automobile for a few seconds. Then, they asked a single question, but they changed one word. They asked, "Did you see the broken headlight?" to one group of participants and asked, "Did you see a broken headlight?" to another group. Only the "a" and the "the" were different, yet the question containing the "the" produced more "don't know" and "Yes" answers than did the "a" question.[26] Our point is that as little as a one word in a question can result in question bias that will distort the survey findings. Unfortunately, words that we use commonly in speaking to one another sometimes encourage biased answers when they appear on a questionnaire because their literal interpretations are impossible to answer. For example, "Did you ever use a Laundromat?" means anytime in your lifetime; "Did you have any concerns about your cell phone's reception?" means absolutely even the tiniest concern, and "Do you always buy Bose products?" means every time without fail. These commonly used words are *extreme absolutes*, meaning that they place respondents in a situation where they must either agree fully or they must completely disagree with the extreme position in the question.

Some words, when taken literally, introduce question bias.

FOUR DOS OF QUESTION WORDING

Question evaluation amounts to scrutinizing the wording of a question to ensure that question bias is minimized and that the question is worded so that respondents understand it and can respond to it with relative ease. As we noted earlier, question bias occurs when the phrasing of a question influences a respondent to answer wrongly or with other than perfect accuracy. Ideally, every question should be examined and tested according to a number of crucial factors known to be related to question bias. To be sure, question evaluation is a judgment process, but we can offer four simple guidelines, or "dos," for question wording.[27] We strongly advise ensuring that the question is: (1) focused, (2) simple, (3) brief, and (4) crystal clear. A discussion of these four guidelines follows.

The researcher uses question evaluation to scrutinize a possible question for its question bias.

The Question Should Be Focused on a Single Issue or Topic To the greatest extent possible, the researcher must stay focused on the specific issue or topic.[28] For example, take the question "What type of hotel do you usually stay in when on a trip?" The focus of this question is hazy because it does not narrow down the type of trip or when the hotel is being used. For example, is it a business or a pleasure trip? Is the hotel at a place en route or at the final destination? A more focused version is "When you are on a family vacation, what type of destination hotel do you typically use?" As a second example, consider how "unfocused" the following question is: "When do you typically go to work?" Does this mean when do you leave home for work or when do you actually begin work once at your workplace? A better question would be "At what time do you ordinarily leave home for work?"

A question should be focused.

The Question Should Be Brief Unnecessary and redundant words should always be eliminated. This requirement is especially important when designing questions that will be administered verbally, such as over the telephone. Brevity will help the respondent to comprehend the central question and reduce the distraction of wordiness. Here is a question that suffers from a lack of brevity: "What are the considerations that would come to your mind while you are confronted with the decision to have some type of repair done on the automatic icemaker in your refrigerator assuming that you noticed it was not making ice cubes as well as it did when you first bought it?" A better, brief form would be "If your icemaker was not working right, how would you correct the problem?" One source recommends that a question should be no more than 20 words long.[29]

A question should be brief.

The Question Should Be Grammatically Simple A simple sentence is preferred because it has only a single subject and predicate, whereas compound and complex sentences are busy with multiple subjects, predicates, objects, and complements. The more complex the sentence, the greater the potential for respondent error. With more conditions to remember, the respondent's attention may wane, or he or she may concentrate on only one part of the question. To avoid these problems, the researcher should strive to use only simple sentence structure[30]—even if two separate sentences are necessary to communicate the essence of the question. Take the question "If you were looking for an automobile that would be used by the head of your household who is primarily responsible for driving your children to and from school, music lessons, and friends' houses, how much would you and your spouse discuss the safety features of one of the cars you took for a test drive?" A simple approach is "Would you and your spouse discuss the safety features of a new family car?" followed by (if yes) "Would you discuss safety 'very little,' 'some,' 'a good deal,' or 'to a great extent'?"

A question should be grammatically simple.

The Question Should Be Crystal Clear[31,32] Forgive us for stealing a line uttered by actor Tom Cruise in one of his movies, but it is essential that all respondents "see" the question identically. It is best to avoid words that are vague or open to misinterpretations. For example, the question "How many children do you have?" is unclear because it can be interpreted in various ways. One respondent might think of only those children living at home, whereas another might include children from a previous marriage. A better question is "How many children under the age of 18 live with you in your home?" To develop a crystal-clear question, the researcher may be forced to slightly abuse the previous guideline of simplicity, but with a bit of effort, question clarity can be obtained with an economical number of words.[33] One author has nicely summarized this guideline: "The question should be simple, intelligible, and clear."[34]

A question should be crystal clear.

FOUR DONT'S OF QUESTION WORDING

In four situations question bias is practically assured. An awareness of these problem areas can help avoid them or spot them when you are reviewing a questionnaire draft. Specifically, the question should not be (1) leading, (2) loaded, (3) double-barreled, or (4) overstated. Before we describe each instance of a poorly worded question, we wish to point out that if any one of them is used intentionally by a researcher, it is a violation of the Marketing Research Association's Code of Ethics. Marketing Research Insight 8.2 states simply that any "framing," or wording of questions that influences a respondent's answer, is wrong.

Do Not "Lead" the Respondent to a Particular Answer A **leading question** gives a strong cue or expectation as what answer to provide.[35] Therefore, it biases responses. Consider this question: "Don't you worry when using your credit card for online purchases?" The respondent is being led because the question wording insinuates that one should worry. Therefore, the question "leads" respondents to the conclusion that there must be some worries, and, therefore, they will likely agree with the question, particularly respondents who have no opinion. Rephrasing the question as "Do you have concerns when using your credit card for online purchases?" is a much more objective request of the respondent. Here the respondent is free—that is, not led—to respond "yes" or "no." Examine the following questions for other forms of leading questions:

As a Cadillac owner, you are satisfied with your car, aren't you?	This is a leading question because the wording presupposes that all Cadillac owners are satisfied. It places the respondent in a situation where disagreement is uncomfortable and singles him/her out as an outlier.
Have you heard about the satellite radio system that everyone is talking about?	This is a leading question because it conditions the respondent in terms of answering in a socially desirable manner. In other words, few people would want to admit they are clueless about something "everybody is talking about."[36]

Do not use leading questions that have strong cues on how to answer.

While you may think that leading questions are easy to identify and that they do not trick any intelligent person into a biased answer, we have just scratched the surface of this form of bias. Read Marketing Research Insight 8.3 to gain an understanding the various forms of leading questions.

Do Not Use "Loaded" Wording or Phrasing Whereas leading questions are typically obvious, loaded questions are stealthy. That is, a **loaded question** has buried in its wording elements a sneaky presupposition, or it might make reference to universal beliefs or rules of

---

MARKETING RESEARCH INSIGHT 8.2   *Ethical Consideration*

Marketing Research Association Code of Ethics: Respondent Participation

1. Will treat the respondent with respect and not influence a respondent's opinion or attitude on any issue through direct or indirect attempts, including the framing of questions.

Interviewers should not ask questions in a way that leads or influences respondents' answers, nor can they provide their own opinions, thoughts or feelings that might bias a respondent and therefore have an impact on the answers given.

MARKETING RESEARCH INSIGHT 8.3 *Practical Application*

The Many Ways That a Question Can Be Leading

Questions can lead respondents in a variety of ways. The following table lists six different types of leading questions and provides examples.[37]

As can be seen in these examples, questions may lead respondents to answer in a particular way with both subtle and obvious cues.

Assumptive questions *ask questions with a built-in assumption or expectation.*

Example: "Do you think that prices will continue climbing?"	*Bias: Has built in assumption that prices will rise.*

Linked statements *pose an emotional or evaluative condition and then ask the question.*

Example: The 2010 BP oil spill caused havoc in the Gulf of Mexico. How do you feel about BP's ability to prevent a similar disaster?	*Bias: Sets up BP as the culprit for the devastating oil spill and "contaminates" the respondent.*

Implication questions *link two events with an inescapable chain of events.*

Question: If you do not renew your automobile inspection, what will happen?	*Bias: Hardly anything good can come from failing to do something that is supposed to be done.*

Ask for agreement *questions explicitly asks for agreement or disagreement as opposed to asking if the respondent agrees or disagrees.*

Example: To what extent do you agree that Las Vegas is a gambling paradise?	*Bias: Assumes that the respondent agrees, but some respondents may not.*

Tag questions *are short questions posed after a statement that disguise a command and make it look like a question.*

Example: Many people think that the price of a Lexus is unaffordable. Don't you?	*Bias: The "tag" strongly implies agreement with the statement.*

Coercive questions *have some sort of threat in them.*

Example: Don't you agree with patriotic Americans that buying foreign automobile models hurts the U.S. economy?	*Bias: threatens the respondent with be labeled as un-American if he or she does not agree.*

behavior. It may even apply emotionalism or touch on a person's inner fears. Our compulsive gambling question was loaded because it presupposes that respondents have a gambling problem. Some researchers refer to a loaded question simply as a "biased question."[38] Identifying bias in a question requires thoughtful judgment. For example, a company marketing mace for personal use may use the question, "Should people be allowed to protect themselves from harm by using a Taser in self-defense?" Obviously, most respondents will agree with the need to protect oneself from harm, and self-defense is acceptable, but these are loaded concepts because no one wants to be harmed and self-defense is only legal if one is attacked. Eliminating the loaded aspect of this question would result in the question, "Do you think carrying a Taser is acceptable for someone who believes it is needed?" As you can see, the phrasing of each question should be examined thoroughly to guard against the various sources of question bias error. With the new wording of the question in our example, we do not load it by mentioning harm or self-defense.

Do not use loaded questions with emotional overtones.

Do Not Use a "Double-Barreled" Question A **double-barreled question** is really two different questions posed in one question.[39] With two questions posed

"Don't you think fast foods have too many calories?" is a leading question.

Photo: Peter Kim/Shutterstock

Do not use double-barreled questions that ask two questions at the same time.

together, it is difficult for a respondent to answer either one directly.[40] Consider a question asked of patrons at a restaurant, "Were you satisfied with the restaurant's food and service?" How do respondents answer? If they say "yes," does it mean they were satisfied with the food? The service? Both? The survey would be much improved by asking two questions: one about the food and another about service.

Do Not Use Words That Overstate the Case An **overstated question** places undue emphasis on some aspect of the topic. It uses what might be considered "dramatics" to describe the topic. Here is an example that might be found in a survey conducted for Ray-Ban sunglasses: "How much do you think you would pay for a pair of sunglasses that will protect your eyes from the sun's harmful ultraviolet rays, which are known to cause blindness?" As you can see, the overstatement concerns the effects of ultraviolet rays, and because of this overstatement, respondents may be compelled to think about how much they would pay for something that can prevent blindness and not about how much they would really pay for sunglasses. A more toned-down and acceptable question wording would be, "How much would you pay for sunglasses that will protect your eyes from the sun's glare?" Avoid using words that overstate conditions. It is better to present the question in a neutral tone rather than in a strong positive or negative tone.

Do not use overstated questions with wording that overemphasizes the case.

To be sure, there are other question wording pitfalls.[41] For example, it is nonsensical to ask respondents about details they don't recall ("How many and what brands of aspirin did you see last time you bought some?"), to pose questions that invite guesses ("What is the price per gallon of premium gasoline at the Exxon station on the corner?"), or to ask respondents to

---

MARKETING RESEARCH INSIGHT 8.4　　　*Practical Application*

More Dos and Don'ts for the Development of Questions

Developing questions is a bit more complicated and challenging than remembering four dos and four don'ts. Additional guidance is useful in wording questions and creating a questionnaire. Marketing research practitioner Brett Plummer recently issued his own list of dos and don'ts.[42] Of course, some of Plummer's recommendations overlap with those presented previously in this chapter, but he suggests additional considerations that are essential to the design of good questions.

Dos include:

1. Keep your research objectives in mind. After drafting all the questions, go back and make sure that every objective has all of the necessary questions.
2. Consider which question type is best for each question. The options are open ended, which are difficult to analyze; single or multiple choice, which are quick and easy for respondents; ranking, which are somewhat confusing to respondents; and rating, which requires selection of the appropriate rating scale.
3. Take into account how the data will be analyzed. Nominal and ranking measures must be analyzed with percentages. Rating scales can be analyzed with averages and advanced statistical techniques.

4. Include all valid response options. With a multiple choice question, be sure to list all reasonable answers along with "other" and "none of the above."
5. Consider where your question falls in the flow of the survey. Group similar items together, ask important questions fairly early on, and consider if earlier questions might bias answers to later ones.

Don'ts include:

6. Don't create confusing or ambiguous questions. Avoid jargon, technical wording, and pretest the questions to make sure they are understandable to prospective respondents.
7. Don't forget to carefully review response options for appropriateness and overlap. Whether the question is a "choose one" or "choose all that apply," type, the choices should be mutually exclusive.
8. Don't lead respondents toward anwers. A good marketing researcher will study the more subtle types of leading questions and avoid them.
9. Don't ask redundant questions. Respondents are especially likely to stop responding if they believe the survey is wasting their time with repetitive questions.

 **Active Learning**

Identify and Reword 'Bad' Questions

Can you identify what is "bad" about a question and correct it? Here are some questions that might appear on a questionnaire. Each violates at least one of the dos-and-don'ts question wording presented in this chapter. For each question, write a short description about what makes it problematic, identify the "do" or "don't" it violates, and suggest a better version.

Question	What's the Problem?	What's a Better Question?
How do you feel about car seats for infants?		
When your toddler wants to ride in the car with you when you run errands or pick up your older children at school, practice, or some friend's home, do you use an infant car seat?		
If using an infant car seat is not convenient for you to use, or when you are in a hurry and your toddler is crying, do you still go ahead and use the infant car seat?		
How much do you think you should have to pay to for an infant seat that restrains and protects your toddler in case someone runs into your car or you lose control of your car and run into a light post or some other object?		
Shouldn't concerned parents of toddlers use infant car seats?		
Since infant car seats are proven to be exceptionally valuable, do you agree that infant car seats be used for your loved ones?		
Do you think parents who are responsible citizens and who are aware of driving dangers use infant car seats?		
If you had an accident with your toddler on board, do you believe an infant car seat could protect your child from being maimed?		

predict their actions in circumstances they cannot fathom ("How often would you frequent this new, upscale restaurant that will be built 10 miles from your home?"). Marketing Research Insight 8.4 lists more dos and don'ts of question development. Using common sense in developing questions for your questionnaire will help to avoid most sources of question wording bias.

Table 8.6 summarizes guidelines for question wording and applies the dos and don'ts discussed thus far to a survey on automobile global positioning systems (GPS). This table provides examples of problematic questions that violate the associated question wording recommendation along with improved examples that abide by the recommendations. Use Table 8.6 as a handy study guide and a reference to keep our question wording recommendations foremost in your mind when you are involved in question development.

Adhering to these guidelines is standard operating procedure for seasoned researchers, but slips do occur occasionally even for the most experienced professionals. This potential for

TABLE 8.6   Examples of Dos and Don'ts for Question Wording

Do-or-Don't Guideline	Problematic Question	Improved Question
Do: Be focused	How do you feel about your automobile's GPS system?	Please rate your automobile's GPS system of each of the following features. (Features are listed.)
Do: Be brief	When traffic conditions are bad, do you or do you not rely on your automobile's GPS system to find the fastest way to work?	Does your automobile GPS system help you arrive at work on time?
Do: Be simple and structured	If you needed to find your child's best friend's house that was over 10 miles from your house for your child to attend a birthday party, would you rely on your automobile GPS system to get you there?	To what extent would you rely on your automobile GPS system to find a friend's house?
Do: Be crystal clear	Is your automobile GPS system useful?	How useful is your automobile GPS system for each of the following occasions? (Occasions are listed.)
Don't: Lead	Shouldn't everyone have a GPS system in their automobile?	In your opinion, how helpful is an automobile GPS system?
Don't: Load	If GPS systems were shown to help us decrease our depletion of world oil reserves, would you purchase one?	How much do you think an automobile GPS system might save you on gasoline?
Don't: Double-barrel	Would you consider purchasing an automobile GPS system if it saved you time, money, and worry?	Would you consider buying an automobile GPS system if you believed it would reduce your commuting time by 10%? (Separate questions for money and worry savings.)
Don't: Overstate	Do you think an automobile GPS system can help you avoid traffic jams that may last for hours?	To what extent do you believe an automobile GPS system will help you avoid traffic congestion?

mistakes explains why many researchers use "experts" to review drafts of their questionnaires. For example, it is common for the questionnaire to be designed by one employee of the research company and then given to colleague who understands questionnaire design for a thorough inspection for question bias as well as **face validity**—that is, if the questions "look right."

Questionnaire Organization

Now that you have learned about question development, we can turn to the organization of the questionnaire. Normally, the researcher creates questions by starting with each research objective in turn and developing the questions that relate to each objective. In other words, the questions are developed but not arranged on the questionnaire. **Questionnaire organization** is the sequence of statements and questions that make up a questionnaire. Questionnaire organization is a critical concern because the questionnaire's arrangement and the ease with which respondents complete the questions have potential to affect the quality of the information that is gathered. Well-organized questionnaires motivate respondents to be conscientious and complete, while poorly organized surveys discourage and frustrate respondents and may even cause them to stop answering questions in the middle of the survey. As a guide to good question development and questionnaire design, we have prepared Marketing Research Insight 8.5, which lists 10 best practices of questionnaire design. We will describe two critical aspects of questionnaire organization: the introduction and the actual flow of questions in the questionnaire body.

Questionnaire organization pertains to the introduction and actual flow of questions on the questionnaire.

MARKETING RESEARCH INSIGHT 8.5   *Practical Application*

Best Practices for Questionnaire Design

Some researchers claim that questionnaire design is the most critical phase of the marketing research process, and there is ample evidence to support that point of view. If the questionnaire does not include questions related to research objectives, the marketing research project is doomed to failure. However, even if the questionnaire does include questions for all research objectives, it can still fail on various levels. A poorly designed questionnaire can fatigue, confuse, bore, overtax, or even insult respondents—and result in their refusal to answer the questions. Marketing research practitioners who have been successful in questionnaire design recently identified what they believe are best practices of this critical step in the marketing research process.[43] Following is a compilation of their recommendations.

1. If appropriate, use scales that are longer than five items; 7- and 10-point scales will yield data that facilitates sophisticated statistical analysis.
2. When using a number scale, use verbal labels on some scale items such as the ends or every other one to ensure that respondents understand the differences between the numbers.
3. Catch "straight-liners," or respondents who do not read the questions and just give the same answer (such as "no opinion"), with something clever such as a question like "Check 5 as the answer to this question."
4. Do not overwhelm respondents. For example, do not ask them to rank several brands, which requires significant mental effort. Instead, have them rate them on a simple scale. Do not use a huge rating matrix on an online survey. Instead, break it down into manageable pages.
5. Do not use complicated, technical, abstract, or biased wording. If respondents cannot relate to the words in a question, they will lose interest in the survey.
6. Ensure that questions follow a logical sequence respondents can perceive and thus understand why the questions are being asked.
7. Do not ask open-ended questions unless they are absolutely necessary. When respondents are asked to write answers, they tend to be brief, particularly if they have answered several open-ended questions earlier in the survey.
8. Use "not applicable," "does not apply," or "cannot assess" to allow respondents without the relevant experience or information to quickly move on to the next question. Asking respondents to comment on something with which they are unfamiliar makes them feel uneasy.
9. Use neutral points on symmetric rating scales unless there are compelling reasons to omit them.
10. For online and self-administered surveys, use a pleasing visual layout. Online surveys, in particular, should use pages, skip logic, interactive features, and other elements that engage the respondent appropriately and reduce the burden of answering questions.

THE INTRODUCTION

The introduction is crucial in questionnaire design.[44] The **introduction** sets the stage; it is what a potential respondent reads or hears before he or she begins answering survey questions.

Of course, each survey and its target respondent group are unique, so a researcher cannot use a standardized introduction. In this section, we discuss five functions that are accomplished by the introduction.

First, it is common courtesy that the interviewer introduces him/herself at the beginning of a survey. Additionally, the sponsor of the survey may be identified. There are two options with respect to sponsor identity. With an **undisguised survey**, the sponsoring company is identified, but with a **disguised survey**, the sponsor's name is not divulged to respondents. The choice of which approach to take rests with the survey's objectives or with the researcher and client who agree whether disclosure of the sponsor's name or true intent can in some way influence respondents' answers. Another reason for disguise is to prevent alerting competitors to the survey.

The decision about whether to use a disguised survey depends on the survey's objectives, possible undue influence with knowledge of the client, or desire not to alert competitors of the survey.

Second, the general purpose of the survey should be described clearly and simply. By simply, we mean that the purpose may be expressed generically in one or two sentences. Typically, respondents are not informed of the several specific purposes of the survey as it would be boring and perhaps intimidating to list all the research objectives. Consider a bank hiring a marketing research firm to conduct a survey. The actual purpose of the survey is to determine the bank's image relative to that of its competitors. However, researchers conducting the survey need only say, "We are conducting a survey on customers' perceptions of financial institutions in this area." This satisfies the respondent's curiosity and does not divulge the name of the bank.

Third, prospective respondents must be made aware of how and why they were selected. Just a short sentence to answer the respondent's mental question of "Why me?" will suffice. Telling respondents that they were "selected at random" usually is sufficient. Of course, you should be ethical and tell them the actual method that was used. If their selection wasn't random, you should inform them as to which method was used but in a nontechnical manner.

The introduction should indicate to respondents how they were selected.

Fourth, prospective respondents must be asked for their participation in the survey. If you are conducting a personal interview or a telephone interview, you might say something like "I would now like to ask you a few questions about your experiences with automotive repair shops. OK?" You should be as brief as possible yet let the respondent know you are getting ready for him or her to participate by answering questions. This is also the appropriate time to offer an incentive to participate. **Incentives** are offers to do something for the respondent to increase the probability that the respondent will participate in the survey. Researchers may use various incentives to encourage participation. As consumers have become more resistant to telemarketers and marketing researchers' pleas for information, researchers are reporting they must offer increased incentives. Offering a monetary incentive, a sample of a product, or a copy of study results are examples. Other incentives encourage respondent participation by letting them know the importance of their participation: "You are one of a select few, randomly chosen, to express your views on a new type of automobile tire." Or the topic itself can be highlighted for importance: "It is important that consumers let companies know whether they are satisfied."

Other forms of incentives address respondent anxieties concerning privacy. Two methods tend to reduce these anxieties and, therefore, increase participation. The first is ensuring **anonymity**, in which the respondent is not known and therefore is assured that neither the respondent's name nor any identifying designation will be associated with his or her responses. The second method is **confidentiality**,[45] which means the respondent's name is known by the researcher but is not divulged to a third party, namely, the client. Anonymous surveys are most appropriate in data collection modes where the respondent responds directly on the questionnaire. Any self-administered survey qualifies for anonymity as long as the respondent does not indicate his or her identity and provided the questionnaire does not have any covert identification tracing mechanism. However, when an interviewer is used, appointments and/or callbacks are usually necessary, so there typically is an explicit designation of the respondent's name, address, telephone number, and so forth associated with the responses. In this case, confidentiality may be required.

Anonymity means the respondent is not known and, therefore, may not be identified, while confidentiality means the respondent's identity is not to be divulged to a client or any other third party.

A fifth and final function of the introduction is to qualify prospective respondents if they are to be screened for their appropriateness to take part in the survey. **Screening questions** are used to ferret out respondents who do not meet qualifications necessary to take part in the research study.[46] Whether you screen respondents depends on the research objectives. If the survey's objective is to determine the factors used by consumers to select an automobile dealer for the purpose of purchasing a new car, you may want to screen out those who have never purchased a new car or those who have not purchased a new car within the last, say, two years. For those who answer "no" to the question "Have you purchased a new car within the last two years?" the survey is terminated with a polite "Thank you for your time." Some would argue that you should put the screening question early on so as to not waste the time of the researcher or the respondent. This should be considered with each survey. We place screening questions as last in the introduction because we have found it awkward to begin a

Screening questions are used to identify respondents who do not meet qualifications necessary to take part in the research study.

conversation with a prospective respondent without first taking care of the first four items we just discussed.

The creation of the introduction should entail just as much care and effort as the development of the questions on the questionnaire. The first words heard or read by prospective respondents will largely determine whether they will take part in the survey. It makes sense, therefore, for the researcher to labor over an invitation or opening until it has a maximum chance of eliciting the respondents' cooperation to take part in the survey.[47] If the researcher is unsuccessful in persuading prospective respondents to take part in the survey, all of his or her work on the questionnaire will have been in vain.[48]

QUESTION FLOW

Question flow pertains to the sequencing of questions or blocks of questions, including any instructions, on the questionnaire. Each research objective gives rise to a question or a set of questions. As a result, as indicated in Figure 8.2, questions are usually developed on an objective-by-objective basis. However, to facilitate respondents' ease in answering questions, the organization of these sets of questions should follow some understandable logic much as possible. A commonly used sequence of questions is presented in Table 8.7. Questions should be organized in a logical or commonsense progression.[49] Of course, it should be obvious that an objective is to keep the questionnaire as short as possible as long questionnaires have a negative effect on the response rate.[50] If necessary, the first few questions are normally screening questions, which will determine whether the potential respondent qualifies to participate in the survey based on certain selection criteria the researcher has deemed essential.

Once the individual qualifies to take the survey, the next questions may serve a "warm-up" function. **Warm-up questions** are simple and easy-to-answer questions that are used to get the respondents' interest[51] and to demonstrate the ease of responding to the research request. Ideally, warm-up questions pertain to the research objectives, but the researcher may opt for a few quick and easy superfluous questions to heighten the respondent's interest so that he or she will be more inclined to deal with the harder questions that follow.

Transitions are statements or questions used to let the respondent know that changes in question topic or format are about to happen. A statement such as "Now, I would like to ask you a few questions about your family's TV viewing habits" is an example of a transition statement. Such statements aid in making certain that the respondent understands the line of questioning. Transitions include "skip" questions. The response to a **skip question** affects which question will be answered next. An example is the question "When you buy groceries, do you usually use coupons?" If the person responds in the negative, questions asking the details of coupon usage are not appropriate, and the questionnaire will instruct the respondent (or the interviewer, if one is being used) to skip over or to bypass those questions. If the researcher has a great number of transition and skip questions, he or she may consider making a flowchart of the questions to ensure there are no errors in the instructions.[52]

As Table 8.7 reveals, it is good practice to "bury" complicated and difficult-to-answer questions deep in the questionnaire. Scaled-response questions, such as semantic differential scales, Likert-type response scales, or other questions that require some degree of mental activity, such as evaluating choices, voicing opinions, recalling past experiences, indicating intentions, or responding to "what if" questions, are found here. There are two main reasons for this placement. First, by the time the respondent has arrived at these questions, he or she has answered several relatively easy questions and is now caught up in a responding mode in which he or she feels some sort of commitment. Thus, even though the questions in this section require more mental effort, the respondent will feel more compelled to complete the questionnaire than to break it off. Second, if the questionnaire is self-administered, the respondent will see that only a few sections of questions remain to be answered. The end is in sight, so to speak. If the survey is being administered by an interviewer, the questionnaire will typically have prompts included for the interviewer to notify the respondent that the interview

Warm-up questions are used near the beginning of the survey to get the respondent's interest and demonstrate the ease of responding to the research request.

Transitions are statements made to let the respondent know that changes in question topic or format are forthcoming.

Attention should be given to placing the questions developed into a logical sequence to ease respondent participation.

TABLE 8.7 **Logical Sequence of Survey Questions**

Question Type	Order	Examples	Rationale
Screens	First questions asked	"Have you shopped at Old Navy in the past month?" "Is this your first visit to this store?"	Used to select the respondent types desired by the researcher to be in the survey
Warm-ups	Immediately after any screens	"How often do you go shopping for casual clothes?" "On what days of the week do you usually shop for casual clothes?"	Easy to answer; shows respondent that survey is easy to complete; generates interest
Transitions (statements and questions)	Prior to major sections of questions or changes in question format	"Now, for the next few questions, I want to ask about your family's TV viewing habits." "Next, I am going to read several statements and, after each, I want you to tell me if you agree or disagree with this statement."	Notifies respondent that the subject or format of the following questions will change
Complicated and difficult-to-answer questions	Middle of the questionnaire; close to the end	"Rate each of the following 10 stores on the friendliness of their salespeople on a scale of 1 to 7." "How likely are you to purchase each of the following items in the next three months?"	Respondent has committed himself or herself to completing the questionnaire; can see (or is told) that there are not many questions left
Classification and demographic questions	Last section	"What is the highest level of education you have attained?"	Questions that are "personal" and possibly offensive are placed at the end of the questionnaire

The more complicated and difficult-to-answer questions are placed deep in the questionnaire.

For some people, age is a personal question, so it is best to ask about it at the end of the interview.

Photo: Janina Dierks/Shutterstock

is in its final stages. Also, experienced interviewers can sense when respondents' interest levels sag, and they may voice their own prompts, if permitted, to keep respondents on task. Online surveys often have a "% complete" bar or indication that the survey is close to completion.

The final section of a questionnaire is traditionally reserved for classification questions. **Classification questions**, which almost always include demographic questions, are used to classify respondents into various groups for purposes of analysis. For instance, the researcher may want to classify respondents into categories based on age, gender, and income level. The placement of classification questions such as these at the end of the questionnaire is useful because some respondents will consider certain demographic questions "personal," and they may refuse to give answers to questions about the highest level of education they attained, their age, their income level, or marital status.[53] In these cases, if a respondent refuses to answer, the refusal comes at the very end of the questioning process. If it occurred at the beginning, the interview would begin with a negative tone, perhaps causing the person to think that the survey will

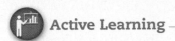 **Active Learning**

Decide on Questionnaire Order in a Questionnaire

For a survey to determine the attractiveness of a possible new restaurant, the following table identifies each of the research objectives as well as a possible measurement scale to be used with each research objective. Using your newly acquired knowledge of question flow and questionnaire organization, for each objective, indicate where on the questionnaire you recommend to place the question(s) pertaining to that research objective. Jot down your reasoning for your recommendation on question order as well.

Research Objective and Description	How to Measure?	Order in the Questionnaire and Reason(s) for This Order
Will the restaurant be successful? Will a sufficient number of people patronize the restaurant?	Describe the restaurant concept and ask intentions to purchase there on a scale.	
How should the restaurant be designed? What about décor, atmosphere, specialty entrées and desserts, wait staff uniforms, reservations, special seating, and so on?	Determine respondents' preferences for each of the several possible design features on a preference scale.	
What should be the average price of entrées? How much are potential patrons willing to pay for the entrées as well as for the house specials?	Describe standard entrées and possible house specials and identify how much respondents are willing to pay using price ranges.	
What is the optimal location? How far from patrons' homes are patrons willing to drive, and are there any special location features (such as waterfront deck seating, free valet parking, no reservations, etc.) to take into consideration?	Determine furthest driving distance respondents are willing to drive to the new restaurant for each location feature.	
What is the profile of the target market?	Ask for demographics of the respondents.	
What are the best promotional media? What advertising media should be used to best reach the target market?	Determine normal use of various local media, such as newspaper, radio, and television, and identify specifics, such as what newspaper sections are read, what radio programming respondents prefer, and what local television news times are watched.	

be asking any number of personal questions, and the respondent may very well object to taking part in the survey at that point.[54]

Computer-Assisted Questionnaire Design

Computer-assisted questionnaire design refers to software that allows users to use computer technology to develop and disseminate questionnaires and to retrieve and analyze data gathered by the questionnaire. Computer-assisted questionnaire design software packages

Demographics questions, sometimes called *classification questions*, are used to classify respondents into various groups for purposes of analysis.

Computer-assisted questionnaire design is easy, fast, friendly, and flexible.

offer several advantages: Compared to using a word processor, they are easier, faster, friendlier, and provide significant functionality.[55] In this section, we discuss the functionality of computer-assisted questionnaire design programs.

QUESTION CREATION

The typical questionnaire design program will query the user on, for example, what type of question to use, how many response categories to include, whether multiple responses are permitted, and how response options will appear on the questionnaire. Usually, the program offers a selection list of question types such as closed-ended, open-ended, numeric, or scaled-response questions. The program may even have a question library[56] feature that provides "standard" questions on constructs that researchers often measure, such as demographics, importance, satisfaction, performance, or usage. Plus, the researcher can upload graphics files of various types if these are part of the research objectives. Most computer-assisted questionnaire design programs are quite flexible and allow the user to modify question formats, build blocks or matrices of questions with the identical response format, include an introduction and instructions to specific questions, and move the location of questions with great ease. Often, the appearance can be modified to the designer's preferences for font, background, color, and more.

SKIP AND DISPLAY LOGIC

Skip logic lets the questionnaire designer direct the online survey to ask questions based on previous answers. For instance, with the question, "Did you order a Papa John's Pizza delivery for your family in the past month?" if the answer is "Yes," the respondent will be directed to several questions about Papa John's Pizza, but if the answer is "No," these questions will be skipped. That is, the "No" respondent will not see these questions. **Display logic** is similar to skip logic, and the survey displays or asks questions that are appropriate based on the respondent's prior answers. With display logic, there can be a list of companies with a question, such as "Check all the pizza delivery companies you have used in the past month." Then, the program asks, or displays, only those questions pertaining to the company or companies indicated.

DATA COLLECTION AND CREATION OF DATA FILES

Computer-assisted questionnaire design programs create online survey questionnaries. Once online, the survey is ready for respondents who are alerted to the online survey with whatever communication methods the researcher wishes to use. Normally, a data file is built as respondents take part—that is, in real time. To elaborate, each respondent accesses the online questionnaire, registers responses to the questions, and, typically, clicks on a "Submit" button at the end of the questionnaire. The submit signal prompts the program to write the respondent's answers into a data file, so the data file grows in direct proportion to and at the same rate as respondents submit their surveys. Features such as requesting an email address are often available to block multiple submissions by the same respondent. The data file can be downloaded at the researcher's discretion, and several different formats, including SPSS-readable files, are usually available.

DATA ANALYSIS AND GRAPHS

Many of the software programs for questionnaire design have provisions for data analysis, graphic presentation, and report formats of results. Some packages offer only simplified graphing capabilities, whereas others offer different statistical analysis options. It is useful to researchers to monitor the survey's progress with these features. The graph features vary, and some of these programs enable users to create professional-quality graphs that can be saved and/or embedded in word processor report files.

Computer-assisted questionnaire design programs have question types, question libraries, real-time data capture, and downloadable data sets.

Marketing Research on YouTube™ To learn about one company's survey software, launch **www.youtube.com** and search for "Survey Software: What Is Snap Survey Software?"

Coding the Questionnaire

A final task in questionnaire design is **coding**, or using numbers associated with question response options to facilitate data analysis after the survey has been conducted. The logic of coding is simple once you know the ground rules. The primary objective of coding is to represent each possible response with a unique number because numbers are easier and faster to use in computer tabulation programs. Online questionnaires typically do coding automatically.

Here are the basic rules for questionnaire coding:

- Every closed-ended question should have a code number associated with every possible response.
- Use single-digit code numbers, beginning with "1," incrementing them by 1 and using the logical direction of the response scale.
- Use the same coding system for questions with identical response options regardless of where these questions are positioned in the questionnaire.
- Remember that a "check all that apply" question is just a special case of a "yes" or "no" question, so use a 1 (= yes) and 0 (= no) coding system for each response option.
- Whenever possible, set up the coding system before the questionnaire is finalized.

For a hard copy questionnaire, codes are normally placed in parentheses beside the answers. In an online questionnaire, the codes are set up internally and not displayed. For labeled scales, it is recommended that the numbers match the direction of the scale. For example, the codes 1–5 would match a Poor-Fair-Good-Very Good-Excellent scale. If we happened to have a 5-point Likert scale with Strongly Disagree to Strongly Agree response options in our questionnaire, the codes would be 1–5. For any interval scale questions in which numbers are used as the response categories, the numbers are already on the questionnaire, so there is no need to use codes for these questions.

Finally, occasionally a researcher uses an **"all that apply" question** that asks respondents to select more than one item from a list of possible responses.[57] With "all that apply" questions, the standard approach is to have each response category option coded with a 0 or a 1. The designation 0 will be used if the category is not checked, whereas a 1 is used if it is checked by a respondent. It is as though the researcher asked each item in the list with a yes/no response.

Codes are numbers associated with question responses to facilitate data entry and analysis.

The codes for an "all that apply" question are set up as though each possible response was answered with "yes" or "no."

Pretesting the Questionnaire

Refer back to Figure 8.2, and you will find that as part of the questionnaire design process, a pretest should be made of the entire questionnaire.[58] A **pretest** involves conducting a dry run of the survey on a small, representative set of respondents to reveal questionnaire errors before the survey is launched.[59] Pretest participants should be representative of the target population under study. Before the questions are administered, participants are informed of the pretest, and their cooperation is requested in spotting words, phrases, instructions, question flow, or other aspects of the questionnaire that appear confusing, difficult to understand, or otherwise problematic. Normally, from 5 to 10 respondents are involved in a pretest, and the researcher looks for common problem themes across this group.[60] For example, if only one pretest respondent indicates some concern about a question, the researcher probably would not attempt modification of its wording, but if three mention the same concern, the researcher would be alerted to the need to undertake a revision. Ideally, when making revisions, researchers ask the following questions from a respondent's point of view: Is the meaning of the question clear? Are the instructions understandable? Are the terms precise? Are there any loaded or charged words?[61] However, because researchers can never completely replicate the respondent's perspective, a pretest is extremely valuable.[62]

A pretest is a dry run of a questionnaire to find and repair difficulties that respondents encounter while taking the survey.

Synthesize Your Learning

This exercise will require you to take into consideration concepts and material from these two chapters.

Chapter 7	Evaluating Survey Data Collection Methods
Chapter 8	Understanding Measurement, Developing Questions, and Designing the Questionnaire

Moe's Tortilla Wraps

Moe's is a sandwich shop that sells wraps, which are sandwiches made with tortillas rather than regular sandwich bread. Seven Moe's units are located in the greater San Diego, California, area, and Moe is thinking about setting up a franchise system to go "big time" with statewide coverage. Moe hires a marketing strategy consultant who recommends that he conduct a baseline survey of his seven San Diego units to better understand his customers and to spot strengths and weaknesses he might not be aware of. The consultant recommends that Moe also do a survey of consumers in the San Diego area who are not Moe's Tortilla Wraps customers or who are infrequent customers to see if there are weaknesses or factors that are preventing them from being loyal customers. Finally, the consultant recommends that surveys be done in three of the possible expansion metropolitan areas of San Francisco, Sacramento, and Los Angeles to ascertain the attractiveness of and market potential for Moe's Tortilla Warps to sandwich shop users in these cities. The consultant mentions that, ideally, the three surveys would have some equivalent or highly similar questions to facilitate comparisons of the findings among the surveys.

Together Moe and the consultant agree on the following research objectives.

Research Objectives for Users of Moe's Tortilla Wraps Survey in San Diego, California

1. How often do users purchase a sandwich at Moe's?
2. Overall, how satisfied are users with Moe's Tortilla Wraps?
3. How do they rate the performance of Moe's Tortilla Wraps on the following aspects?
   a. Competitive price
   b. Convenience of locations
   c. Variety of sandwiches
   d. Freshness of sandwich fillings
   e. Speed of service
   f. Taste of wraps
   g. Uniqueness of sandwiches
4. Obtain a demographic profile of the sample.

Research Objectives for Nonusers of Moe's Tortilla Wraps Survey in San Diego, California

1. How often do people purchase sandwiches from sandwich shops?
2. Overall, how satisfied are they with the sandwich shop they use most often?
3. Have they heard of Moe's Tortilla Wraps?
4. If so, have they used Moe's in the past six months?
5. If so, how do they rate Moe's Tortilla Wraps performance on the following various aspects?
   a. Competitive price
   b. Convenience of locations
   c. Variety of sandwiches
   d. Freshness of sandwich fillings
   e. Speed of service

  f. Taste of wraps

  g. Uniqueness of sandwiches

6. Obtain a demographic profile of the sample.

Research Objectives for Potential Users of Moe's Tortilla Wraps Survey in San Francisco, Sacramento, and Los Angeles, California

1. How often do people purchase sandwiches from sandwich shops?

2. How do they rate the sandwich shop they use most often on the following various aspects?

   a. Competitive price

   b. Convenience of locations

   c. Variety of sandwiches

   d. Freshness of sandwich fillings

   e. Speed of service

   f. Taste of wraps

   g. Uniqueness of sandwiches

3. Given the following description...

   A sandwich shop that uses tortillas rather than bread for its sandwiches. It specializes in Southwest-flavored beef, chicken, ham, or processed-meat sandwiches dressed with cheese, chopped lettuce, tomato, onions, and/or peppers and topped with salsa or a spicy chipotle dressing, all priced at about the same you would pay for a sandwich at Jack in the Box.

4. What is their reaction to the use of tortilla in place of bread in a sandwich?

5. How likely are they to use this sandwich shop if it was at a convenient location in their city?

6. Obtain a demographic profile of the sample.

   For each set of objectives associated with each target group of consumers, decide and justify a data collection method. Given your chosen data collection method, design the full questionnaire, including: selecting measurement scales, developing questions, and finalizing the appearance of the questionnaire for each of the three Moe's Tortilla Wraps surveys. In your deliberations, keep in mind that cost is a concern as Moe does not have deep pockets to finance this research. However, his expansion plans are not on a fast timetable, so the completion time of the surveys is not especially critical. Of course, it is important to have survey findings that are representative of the respective target consumers for each survey.

Summary

This chapter discussed the concepts involved in measurement of the subjective properties of marketing phenomena. The three types of measures used in marketing research are (1) nominal or simple classifications, (2) ordinal or rank order, and (3) scale measures that include ratio scales using real numbers with a true zero and interval scales using equal-appearing spaced gradations. Marketing researchers commonly use interval scales to measure subjective properties of objects. First, the Likert scale appears as an agree–disagree continuum with five to seven positions. Lifestyle questions use a Likert approach to measure people's attitudes, interests, and opinions. Second, the semantic differential scale uses bipolar adjectives to measure the image of a brand or a store. Third, the Stapel scale uses a symmetric + and − number system. Some constructs are measured with a symmetric interval scale, while others, which do not have gradations of negativity, are commonly measured with a nonsymmetric interval scale.

Finally, reliability and validity of measurement were described. Reliability is the degree to which a respondent is consistent in his or her answers. Validity, on the other hand, is the accuracy of responses. It is possible to have reliable measures that are inaccurate, and therefore, not valid.

The questionnaire design process involves question development to ensure unbiased questions and question organization, or sequencing, on the questionnaire. We advocate that the designer follow a step-by-step development process that begins with question development and proceeds through question evaluation, client approval, and a pretest to ensure that the questions and instructions are understandable to respondents. The objective of question development is to create questions that minimize question bias and to ensure that questions are focused, simple, brief, and crystal clear. Question bias is most likely to occur when question wording is leading, loaded, double-barreled, or overstated.

The organization of questions on the questionnaire is critical, including the first statements, or introduction to the survey. The introduction should identify the sponsor of the survey, relate its purpose, explain how the respondent was selected, solicit the individual's cooperation to take part, and, if appropriate, qualify him/her for taking part in the survey. The order and flow of questions on the questionnaire relates to the roles of screens, warm-ups, transitions, "difficult" questions, and classification questions.

Survey questions are typically coded with numbers corresponding to all possible responses to facilitate analysis. Marketing researchers may use software systems that perform online questionnaire design; we briefly described the features of these programs. This chapter concluded with a discussion of the function of and details for pretesting a questionnaire.

Key Terms

Measurement (p. 176)
Properties (p. 176)
Objective properties (p. 176)
Subjective properties (p. 176)
Scale development (p. 176)
Nominal measures (p. 177)
Ordinal measures (p. 177)
Scale measures (p. 177)
Interval scale (p. 177)
Ratio scale (p. 177)
Workhorse scales (p. 180)
Likert scale (p. 180)
Lifestyle inventory (p. 180)
Semantic differential scale (p. 181)
Halo effect (p. 182)
Symmetric interval scale (p. 183)
Nonsymmetric interval scale (p. 183)

Reliabile measure (p. 186)
Valid measure (p. 186)
Questionnarie (p. 186)
Questionnaire design (p. 186)
Question bias (p. 187)
Question development (p. 188)
Question evaluation (p. 188)
Leading question (p. 190)
Loaded question (p. 190)
Double-barreled question (p. 191)
Overstated question (p. 192)
Face validity (p. 194)
Questionnaire organization (p. 194)
Introduction (p. 195)
Undisguised survey (p. 195)
Disguised survey (p. 195)
Incentives (p. 196)

Anonymity (p. 196)
Confidentiality (p. 196)
Screening questions (p. 196)
Question flow (p. 197)
Warm-up questions (p. 197)
Transitions (p. 197)
Skip question (p. 197)
Classification questions (p. 198)
Computer-assisted questionnaire design (p. 199)
Skip logic (p. 200)
Display logic (p. 200)
Coding (p. 201)
"All that apply" question (p. 201)
Pretest (p. 201)

Review Questions/Applications

1. What is measurement? In your answer, differentiate an object from its properties, both objective and subjective.
2. Distinguish the three measures used in marketing research.
3. How does an interval scale differ from a ratio scale?
4. Explain what is meant by a continuum along which a subjective property of an object can be measured.
5. What are the arguments for and against the inclusion of a neutral response position in a symmetric scale?

6. Distinguish among a Likert scale, a lifestyle scale, and a semantic differential scale.
7. What is the halo effect, and how does a researcher control for it?
8. Provide questions that would measure each of the following constructs:
   a. Brand loyalty
   b. Intentions to purchase
   c. Importance of "value for the price"
   d. Attitude toward a brand

e. Recall of an advertisement

f. Past purchases

9. How does reliability differ from validity? In your answer, define each term.

10. What is a questionnaire, and what are the functions of a questionnaire?

11. What is meant by the statement that questionnaire design is a systematic process?

12. What are the four guidelines or "dos" for question wording?

13. What are the four "don'ts" for question wording. Describe each.

14. What is the purpose of a questionnaire introduction, and what should it accomplish?

15. Indicate the functions of (a) screening questions, (b) warm-ups, (c) transitions, (d) "skip" questions, and (e) classification questions.

16. What is coding and why is it used? Relate the special coding need with "all that apply" questions.

17. Mike, the owner of the convenience store Mike's Market, is concerned about low sales. He reads in a marketing textbook that the image of a store often has an impact on its ability to attract its target market. He contacts the All-Right Research Company and commissions it to conduct a study that will shape his store's image. You are charged with the responsibility of developing the store image part of the questionnaire. Design a semantic differential scale that will measure the relevant aspects of Mike's Market's image. In your work on this scale, you must do the following: (a) brainstorm the properties to be measured, (b) determine the appropriate bipolar adjectives, (c) decide on the number of scale points, and (d) indicate how the scale controls for the halo effect.

18. Each of the following examples involves a market researcher's need to measure some construct. Devise an appropriate scale for each one. Defend the scale in terms of its scaling assumptions, number of response categories, use or nonuse of a "no opinion" or neutral response category, and face validity.

    a. Mattel wants to know how preschool children react to a sing-along video game in which they must sing along with an animated character and guess the next word in the song at various points in the video.

    b. TCBY is testing five new flavors of yogurt and wants to know how its customers rate each one on sweetness, flavor strength, and richness of taste.

    c. A pharmaceutical company wants to find out how much a new federal law eliminating dispensing of free sample prescription drugs by doctors will affect their intentions to prescribe generic versus brand-name drugs for their patients.

19. Harley-Davidson is the largest American motorcycle manufacturer, and it has been in business for several decades. Several years ago, Harley-Davidson expanded into "signature" products such as shirts that prominently display its logo. Some people have a negative image of Harley-Davidson because it was the motorcycle favored by the Hell's Angels and other motorcycle gangs. There are two research questions here. First, do consumers have a negative feeling toward Harley-Davidson, and, second, are they disinclined toward the purchase of Harley-Davidson signature products such as shirts, belts, boots, jackets, sweatshirts, lighters, and key chains? Design a Likert measurement scale that can be used in a nationwide telephone study to address these two issues.

20. Listed here are five different aspects of a questionnaire to be designed for the crafts guild of Maui, Hawaii. It is to be administered by personal interviewers who will intercept tourists as they are waiting at the Maui Airport in the seating areas of their departing flight gates. Indicate a logical question flow on the questionnaire using the guidelines in Table 8.3.

    a. Determine how they selected Maui as a destination.

    b. Discover what places they visited in Maui and how much they liked each one.

    c. Describe what crafts they purchased, where they purchased them, when they bought them, how much they paid, who made the selection, and why they bought those particular items.

    d. Specify how long they stayed and where they stayed while on Maui.

    e. Provide a demographic profile of each tourist interviewed.

21. Using the Internet, find a downloadable trial version of a computer-assisted questionnaire design program and become familiar with it. With each of the following possible features of computer-assisted questionnaire design programs, briefly relate the specifics on how the program you have chosen provides the feature.

    a. Question-type options

    b. Question library

    c. Font and appearance

    d. Web uploading (sometimes called "publishing")

    e. Analysis, including graphics

    f. Download file format options

22. Panther Martin invents and markets various types of fishing lures. In an effort to survey the reactions of potential buyers, it hires a research company to intercept fishermen at boat launches, secure their cooperation to use a Panther Martin lure under development sometime during their fishing trip that day, meet them when they return, and verbally administer questions

to them. As an incentive, each respondent will receive three lures to try that day, and five more will be given to each fisherman who answers the questions at the end of the fishing trip.

What opening comments should be verbalized when approaching fishermen who are launching their boats? Draft a script to be used when asking these fishermen to take part in the survey.

CASE 8.1

Extreme Exposure Rock Climbing Center Faces The Krag

For the past five years, Extreme Exposure Rock Climbing Center has enjoyed a monopoly. Located in Sacramento, California, Extreme Exposure was the dream of Kyle Anderson, who has been into freestyle extreme sports of various types, including outdoor rock climbing, hang gliding, skydiving, mountain biking, and snowboarding. Now in his mid-30s, Kyle came to realize in the year of his 30th birthday that after three leg fractures, two broken arms, and numerous dislocations, he could no longer participate regularly on the extreme edge. So, he found an abandoned warehouse, recruited two investors and a friendly banker, and opened up Extreme Exposure.

Kyle's rock-climbing center has over 6,500 square feet of simulated rock walls to climb, with about 100 different routes up to a maximum of 50 vertical feet. Extreme Exposure's design permits the four major climbing types: top-roping, where the climber climbs up with a rope anchored at the top; lead-climbing, where the climber tows the rope that he or she fixes to clips in the wall while ascending; bouldering, where the climber has no rope but stays near the ground; and rappelling, where the person descends quickly by sliding down a rope. Climbers can buy day or monthly passes or annual memberships. Shoes and harnesses can be rented cheaply, and helmets are available free of charge as all climbers must wear protective helmets. In addition to individual and group climbing classes, Extreme Exposure has several group programs, including birthday parties, a kids' summer camp, and corporate team-building classes.

Kyle notices a newspaper article about another rocking climbing center, to be called The Krag, that will be built in Sacramento in the next six months. He notes the following items about The Krag that are different from Extreme Exposure: (1) The Krag will have climbs up to a maximum 60 vertical feet, (2) it will have a climber certification program, (3) there will be day trips to outdoor rock-climbing areas, (4) there will be group overnight and extended-stay rock-climbing trips to the Canadian Rockies, and (5) The Krag's annual membership fee will be about 20% lower than Extreme Exposure's.

Kyle chats with Dianne, one of his Extreme Exposure members who is in marketing, during a break in one of her climbing visits. Dianne summarizes what she believes Kyle needs to find out about his current members:

1. What is demographic and rock-climbing profile of Extreme Exposure's members?
2. How satisfied are members with Extreme Exposure's climbing facilities?
3. How interested are its members in: (a) day trips to outdoor rock-climbing areas, (b) group overnight and/or extended-stay rock-climbing trips to the Canadian Rockies, and (c) a rock-climber certification program?
4. What are members' opinions of the annual membership fee charged by Extreme Exposure?
5. Will members consider leaving Extreme Exposure to join a new rock-climbing center with climbs that are 10 feet higher than the maximum climb at Extreme Exposure?
6. Will members consider leaving Extreme Exposure to join a new rock-climbing center with higher climbs and a lower annual membership fee?

For each of Dianne's questions, identify the relevant construct and indicate how it should be measured.

CASE 8.2 INTEGRATED CASE

Global Motors

Cory Rogers, Vice President of CMG Research, now feels he has a good grasp of the research objectives needed to conduct the research study for Nick Thomas of Global Motors. Furthermore, he has taken some time to write operational definitions of the constructs, so he has done most of the preliminary work on the questionnaire. The next step is questionnaire design. Cory and Nick have decided that the most reasonable approach to the survey is to use an online panel. This alternative, while somewhat expensive, will guarantee that the final sample is representative of the market. That is, companies that operate such panels assure buyers of their services that the sample will represent any general target market that a buyer may desire to have represented. In the case of Global Motors, the market of interest is "all automobile owners," meaning that practically all adults qualify.

Consequently, it is time to design a questionnaire suitable for administration to an online panel of adult consumers. The survey objectives relevant to questionnaire design for this phase of the research project include:

1. What are (prospective) automobile buyers' attitudes toward
   a. Gasoline use contribution to global warming
   b. Global warming
2. Do attitudes related to global warming vary by market segment? Market segments are defined by
   a. Demographics
      i. Age
      ii. Income
      iii. Education
      iv. Gender
      v. Family size
      vi. Home town size
      vii. Dwelling type
3. What are consumer preferences and intentions for various types of fuel-efficient automobiles?
   a. One-seat, all-electric
   b. Four-seat, all-electric
   c. Four-seat gasoline hybrid
   d. Five-seat diesel hybrid
   e. Five-seat standard size gasoline
4. What are media habits of those who prefer the new automobile types?
   a. Reading newspapers (local, state, national, etc.)
   b. Watching TV (comedy, drama, sports, reality, etc.)
   c. Listening to FM radio (easy listening, country, top 40, oldies, etc.)
   d. Reading magazines (general interest, business, science, sports, etc.)
5. What are the social media usage profiles of these consumers with respect to how often they engage in
   a. Online blogging
   b. Content communities
   c. Social network sites
   d. Online games
   e. Virtual worlds

If necessary, go over the needed integrated case facts and information imparted to you in previous chapters, and design an online survey questionnaire for Global Motors. Aim for proper construct measurement, clear question wording, appropriate question flow, and all other principles of good questionnaire design.

Selecting the Sample

LEARNING OBJECTIVES

- To become familiar with sample design terminology
- To understand the differences between probability and nonprobability sampling methods
- To learn how to take four types of probability samples: simple random samples, systematic samples, cluster samples, and stratified samples
- To learn how to take four types of nonprobability samples: convenience samples, purposive samples, referral samples, and quota samples
- To acquire the skills to administer different types of samples, including online samples
- To be able to develop a sample plan

"WHERE WE ARE"

Change in the Sampling Industry

Kees de Jong,
Vice Chairman,
Board of Directors,
SSI

The sampling and research industries are in a time of unprecedented change and transformation. Globalization, the promise of technology, the variety of research techniques available today and the rapid pace of change all combine to make this one of the most exciting times ever to work in market research. Many of the changes influencing sampling and research are being driven by major global trends in society and technology:

- Urbanization continues at a rapid pace. The urban center of gravity is moving South and East, and the global consumer class is growing at lightning speed so businesses need access to opinions from more people in more different places than ever before.

- Technology allows us to easily and cheaply gather and store huge amounts of information, so basic information is easily available and researchers today are looking to precisely target rare populations for their primary research.

- In times of economic austerity, businesses demand more than just research results: They expect research to provide real-time insights and to have a measurable impact on their business. Therefore it's more important than ever to access the right people to answer our questions.

- In many parts of the world, mobile phones are the only way to access the Internet, so researchers cannot field the long, grid-heavy questionnaires of the past and are forced to rethink how to effectively collect opinions.

- The empowerment of consumers through the Internet means people expect to give their opinions on their own terms, not ours. Social media sites are the best examples. Sample providers and researchers are focusing more on providing a good experience for the participant than they did in the past. If we do not provide a survey-taking experience that fits people's lifestyle and preferred mode of communication, more and more people will choose not to participate.

- Because people are busier than ever and can guard their privacy with technology like caller IDs, they are more difficult to reach than ever before, so sample providers are turning to multimode samples, using combinations of mobile texts, email, landline and wireless calls, social media messaging, and more to reach a diverse, representative population.

Text and images: By permission, SSI.

Survey Sampling International® (SSI) has experienced many changes as well. Twenty years ago SSI had just one office in Connecticut, with a small local staff doing business only in the United States. Today, SSI provides sampling across 72 countries to over 2,000 companies from 30 offices spanning every time zone and with staff fluent in 36 languages.

SSI's products have changed dramatically as well. SSI has long been a pioneer in sampling for research: first by inventing random digit telephone sampling in the 1970s, then introducing online samples in the '90s, and in 2010 creating a fully dynamic sampling platform (SSI Dynamix™), which integrates survey participants from all areas of the Internet, including SSI's own global panels, social media, websites, affiliate partnerships, mobile participants, and more, using psychographic profiling to keep the samples consistent.

Looking to the future, we expect to see even more change. Will questionnaires as we know them even exist in future decades? Or will we ask just one or two in-the-moment questions to supplement passively collected data? Will researchers be replaced by businesspeople doing their own research using easily available do-it-yourself software packages? How will mobile devices evolve, and how will practical considerations like screen size affect our ability to ask questions and hear opinions?

Young people with a variety of interests and experience are entering the profession: anthropologists, storytellers, analysts, writers, gaming entrepreneurs, mobile device experts, and social media pioneers. Their energy and diversity of talent will surely help the industry prosper in these changing times.

Photo: Ints Vikmanis/Fotolia

Amid all this change, the underlying principles of sound sampling haven't changed since SSI was founded nearly 40 years ago: To be confident that our research data is reliable, we must gather opinions from a broad, diverse sampling frame; we must use randomization to minimize the risk of bias; and we must respect research participants' time by providing them with a satisfying opinion-giving experience so they will want to keep sharing their thoughts with us in the future.

—*Kees DeJong*
Vice Chairman, Board of Directors, SSI

International markets are measured in hundreds of millions of people, national markets comprise millions of individuals, and even local markets may constitute hundreds of thousands of households. To obtain information from every single person in a market is usually impossible and obviously impractical. For these reasons, marketing researchers make use of a sample. This chapter describes how researchers go about taking samples. As can be seen in our SSI vignette, both technology and globalization have combined to make taking a sample a complicated process. We begin with definitions of basic concepts, such as population, sample, and census. Then we discuss the reasons for taking samples. From here, we distinguish the four types of probability sampling methods from the four types of nonprobability sampling methods. Because online surveys are popular, we discuss sampling aspects of these surveys. Finally, we present a step-by-step procedure for taking a sample, regardless of the sampling method used.

Basic Concepts in Samples and Sampling

Sampling has its own basic terminology: population, census, sample, sample unit, sample frame, sample frame error, and sample error. As we describe these concepts, it will be useful to refer to Figure 9.1, which depicts them in a way that conveys how they relate to one another.

POPULATION

The population is the entire group under study as defined by research objectives.

A **population** is defined as the entire group under study as specified by the objectives of the research project. As can be seen in Figure 9.1, the population shape is the largest and most encompassing entity. Managers tend to have a less specific definition of the population than do researchers. This is because the researcher must use the description of the population precisely, whereas the manager uses it in a more general way.

For instance, let us examine this difference for a research project performed for Terminix Pest Control. If Terminix were interested in determining how prospective customers were combating roaches, ants, spiders, and other insects in their homes, the Terminix manager would probably define the population as "everybody who might use our services." However, the researcher in charge of sample design would use a definition such as "heads of households in those metropolitan areas served by Terminix who are responsible for insect pest control." Notice that the researcher has converted "everybody" to "households who are responsible for insect pest control." and has indicated more precisely who the respondents will be in the form of "heads of households." The definition is also made more specific

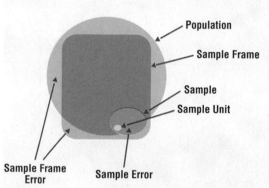

Labels: Population, Sample Frame, Sample, Sample Unit, Sample Frame Error, Sample Error

FIGURE 9.1 Basic Sampling Concepts

by the requirement that the household be in a metropolitan Terminix service area. Just as problem definition error can be devastating to a survey, so can population definition error because a survey's findings are applicable only to the population from which the survey sample is drawn. For example, if the Terminix population is "everybody who might use our services," it would include industrial, institutional, and business users as well as households. If a large national chain such as Hilton Hotels or Olive Garden Restaurants were included in the survey, then the findings could not be representative of households alone.

The population is the entire group under study.

Photo: Robert F. Balazik/Shutterstock

CENSUS

A **census** is defined as an accounting of the complete population. In other words, if you wanted to know the average age of members of a population, you would have to ask each and every population unit his or her age and compute the average. Surely, you can see the impracticalities associated with a census, particularly when you think about target markets encompassing millions of consumers.

A census requires information from everyone in the population.

Perhaps the best example of a census is the U.S. census taken every 10 years by the U.S. Census Bureau (**www.census.gov**). The target population in the case of the U.S. census is all households in the United States. In truth, this definition of the population constitutes an "ideal" census, for it is virtually impossible to obtain information from every single U.S. household. At best, the Census Bureau can reach only a certain percentage of households, obtaining a census that provides information within the time period of the census-taking activity. Even with a public awareness promotional campaign budget of several hundred thousand dollars that covered all of the major advertising media forms, such as television, newspaper, and radio, and an elaborate follow-up procedure, the Census Bureau admits that its numbers are not 100% accurate.[1]

The difficulties encountered by U.S. census takers are identical to those encountered in marketing research. For example, there are instances of individuals who are in transition between residences, without places of residence, illiterate, incapacitated, illegally residing in the United States, or unwilling to participate. Marketing researchers undertaking survey research face all of these problems and a host of others. In fact, researchers long ago realized the impracticality and outright impossibility of taking a census of a population. Consequently, they turned to the use of subsets, or samples, which were chosen to represent the target population.

SAMPLE AND SAMPLE UNIT

Both a sample and a sample unit are depicted in Figure 9.1. A **sample** is a subset of the population that suitably represents that entire group.[2] Once again, there are differences in how the manager and the researcher use this term. The manager will often overlook the "suitably" aspect of this definition and assume that any sample is a representative sample. However, the researcher is trained in detecting sample errors and is careful in assessing the degree of representativeness of the subgroup selected to be the sample.

The sample is a subset of the population, and the sample unit pertains to the basic level of investigation.

A **sample unit** is the basic level of investigation. That is, in the Terminix example, the unit is a household. For a WeightWatchers survey, the unit would be one person, but for a survey of hospital purchases of laser surgery equipment, the sample unit would be hospital purchasing agents because hospital purchases are being researched.

A sample frame is a master source of sample units in the population.

Marketing Research on YouTube™ To learn about sample frame, launch **www.youtube .com** and search for "Sample source and sampling frames."

SAMPLE FRAME AND SAMPLE FRAME ERROR

You should notice in Figure 9.1 that the sample and sample unit exist within the area called the *sample frame*. A **sample frame** is a master source of sample units in the population. You can see in Figure 9.1 that the sample frame shape does not take in all of the population shape; further, it takes in some area that is outside the population's boundary. In other words, the sample frame does not always correspond perfectly to the population.

For instance, if a researcher has defined a population to be all automobile dealers the state of Wyoming, she would need a master listing of these establishments as a frame from which to sample. Similarly, if the population being researched were certified public accountants (CPAs), a sample frame for this group would be needed. In the case of automobile dealers, a list service such as American Business Lists of Turnersville, New Jersey, which has compiled its list of automobile dealers' Yellow Pages listings, might be used. For CPAs, the researcher could use the list of members of the American Institute of Certified Public Accountants, located in New York City, which contains a listing of all accountants who have passed the CPA exam. Sometimes the researcher cannot find a list, and the sample frame becomes a matter of whatever access to the population the researcher can conceive, such as "all shoppers who purchased at least $50 worth of merchandise at a Radio Shack store in March."

A sample frame invariably contains **sample frame error**, which is the degree to which the sample frame fails to account for all of the population. From the figure, you can see that a sample frame may be incomplete, meaning it might omit some units, or it might be inaccurate, meaning it may have units that are not actually in the population. A way to envision sample frame error is by comparing the list with the population and seeing to what degree the list adequately matches the targeted population. What do you think is the sample frame error in our Wyoming autmobile dealers sample? The primary error involved lies in using only Yellow Pages listings. Not all shops are listed in the Yellow Pages, as some have gone out of business, some have come into being since the publication of the Yellow Pages, and some may not be listed at all. The same type of error exists for CPAs, and the researcher would have to determine how current the list is that he or she is using.[3]

To illustrate the impact of the sample frame on survey results, Table 9.1 summarizes points made by Steve Gittelman and Elaine Trimarchi[4] of Mktg. Inc. These authors use extensive research to determine differences in samples drawn from various sources. The table notes three different sample frames: in-store shopper who use credit cards, in-store shoppers who do not use credit cards, and online shoppers who use credit cards. Notice that the consumer behaviors (use of the Internet, use of credit cards, etc.) are very different for each of the three sample frames, and if any of these five consumer behavior characteristics was a research objective, the findings would be dramatically different as a function of the sample frame used.

As you would expect, the booming social media marketing phenomenon has given marketing researchers immense challenges because users of social media are difficult to identify. However, a progressive company called Peanut Labs has come up with an innovative approach

> A listing of the population may be incomplete and/or inaccurate and thus contain sample frame error.

TABLE 9.1 The Same Frame Can Greatly Affect the Findings of a Survey

Sample Frame	Use of the Internet	Use of Credit Cards	Price Sensitivity	Use of Online Banking	Shopping in Stores
People who purchase in stores using credit cards	Very low	Very high	Low	Very low	Very high
People who shop in stores but don't use credit cards	Very low	Very low	High	Very low	High
People who buy online and use credit cards	Very high	Very high	Moderate	Low	Moderate

MARKETING RESEARCH INSIGHT 9.1 — *Social Media Marketing*

Noman Ali, CEO and Co-Founder, Peanut Labs

Peanut Labs is a company that was created by developing a means to access the growing number of people attracted to social media sites and engage them in ways that benefit third parties such as marketing research companies. The founders' ingenious idea was to create a system to reward (monetize) users of social media communities to be involved in third-party tasks. For example, Farmville game players could be rewarded with an in-game item they needed to play (fertilizer) if they took a short survey provided by the marketing research firm for a client. Peanut Labs is widely recognized as an innovative firm fulfilling a fast-growing need in the marketing research industry. CEO and Co-founder Noman Ali explains his company's model.

When we were initially building out the monetization idea for Peanut Labs, there were two clear goals to accomplish. The first was to bridge the gap between consumers on social media sites and market researchers wanting to leverage social media traffic by gaining access to those consumers. The second was to generate a new monetization channel for today's most popular online destinations. We wanted to create a model that was complementary to a social media user experience and also solved the demanding needs of third-party aspects. The result was a win-win situation for all involved.

One of the unique by-products of our monetization cycle is the opportunity for Peanut Labs to connect marketing researchers to the enormous population of social media users, a demographic that is oftentimes hard to reach via more traditional research methods. In the past, marketing research has been narrow in scope in terms of the different channels offered to access consumers. With the adoption of social media and the freedom to access a nearly unlimited number of possible respondents, we are now witnessing major innovations in marketing research. The effects of social media will only continue to increase with time, as every day it gets further embedded into our daily lives. The time to embrace this change has arrived, and we are honored and excited to be at the research industry forefront.

Peanut Labs is the largest social media and gaming sample provider in the United States, leading the industry in online market research by means of monetizing the most popular social media destinations. By creating a seamless interaction between marketing researchers and social media users, Peanut Labs has created a new conduit enabling effective marketing research without disrupting the overall online experience.

Text and images: By permission, Noman Ali, Peanut Labs.

---

to tap into social media user populations. We asked Noman Ali, CEO and Co-Founder, Peanut Labs®, to describe his company's approach in Marketing Research Insight 9.1.

SAMPLING ERROR

Sampling error is any error in a survey that occurs because a sample is used.[5] Sampling error is caused by two factors. First, there is the method of sample selection, which, as you will learn later in this chapter, includes sample frame error. In Figure 9.1, the sample shape is inside the sample frame shape, but it includes some area outside the population shape. This type of sample error results when the sample frame is not completely faithful to the population definition. You will learn in this chapter that some sampling methods minimize this error factor, whereas others do not control it adequately.

The second factor is the size of the sample. We discuss the relationship between sample size and sampling error in the following chapter, Chapter 10.

> Whenever a sample is taken, the survey will reflect sampling error.

Reasons for Taking a Sample

By now you may have surmised at least two general reasons why a sample is almost always more desirable than a census. First, there are practical considerations, such as cost and population size, that make a sample more desirable than a census. Taking a census is expensive, as

> Taking a sample is less expensive than taking a census.

consumer populations may number in the millions. Even if the population is restricted to a medium-sized metropolitan area, hundreds of thousands of individuals can be involved.

Second, typical research firms or the typical researcher cannot analyze the huge amounts of data generated by a census. Although computer statistical programs can handle thousands of observations with ease, they slow down appreciably with hundreds of thousands, and most are unable to accommodate millions of observations. In fact, even before researchers consider the size of the computer or tabulation equipment to be used, they must consider the various data preparation procedures involved in just handling the questionnaires or responses and transferring these responses into computer files. If "hard-copy" questionnaires are to be used, the sheer physical volume can easily overwhelm the researcher's capabilities.

Defending the use of samples from a different tack, we can turn to an informal cost–benefit analysis to defend the use of samples. If the project director of our Terminix household survey had chosen a sample of 500 households at a cost of $10,000 and had determined that 20% of those surveyed "would consider" switching to Terminix from their current pest control provider, what would be the result if a completely different sample of the same size were selected in identical fashion to determine the same characteristic? For example, suppose the second sample resulted in an estimate of 22%. The project would cost $10,000 more, but what has been gained with the second sample? Common sense suggests very little additional information has been gained, for if the project director combined the two samples, he would come up with an estimate of 21%. In effect, $10,000 more has been spent to gain 1% more of information. It is extremely doubtful that this additional precision offsets the additional cost. We will develop this notion in more detail in the following chapter on sample size determination.

Probability Versus Nonprobability Sampling Methods

With probability sampling, the chances of selection are known; with nonprobability sampling, they are not known.

All sample designs fall into one of two categories: probability or nonprobability. **Probability samples** are samples in which members of the population have a known chance (probability) of being selected into the sample. **Nonprobability samples**, on the other hand, are samples where the chances (probability) of selecting members from the population into the sample are unknown. Unfortunately, the terms *known* and *unknown* are misleading; to calculate a precise probability, one would need to know the exact size of the population, and it is impossible to know the exact size of the population in most marketing research studies. If we were targeting, for example, readers of *People* magazine, the exact size of the population changes from week to week as a result of new subscriptions, old ones running out, and fluctuations in sales as a function of whose picture is on the cover. It is hard to think of cases in which the population size is known and stable enough to be associated with an exact number.

The essence of a known probability rests in the sampling method rather than in knowing the exact size of the population. Probability sampling methods are those that ensure that, if the exact size of the population were known for the moment in time that sampling took place, the probability of any member of the population being selected into the sample could be calculated. In other words, this probability value is really never calculated in actuality, but we are assured by the sample method that the chances of any one population member being selected into the sample could be computed. This is a important theoretical notion underlying probability sampling.

With probability sampling, the method determines the chances of a sample unit being selected into the sample.

With nonprobability methods there is no way to determine the probability even if the population size is known because the selection technique is subjective. As one author has described the difference, nonprobability sampling uses human intervention, whereas probability sampling does not.[6] Nonprobability sampling is sometimes called "haphazard sampling" because it is prone to human error and even subconscious biases.[7] The following descriptions underscore that the sampling method determines probability or nonprobability sampling.

PROBABILITY SAMPLING METHODS

There are four probability sampling methods: simple random sampling, systematic sampling, cluster sampling, and stratified sampling. Table 9.2 introduces each of these methods.

Simple Random Sampling With **simple random sampling**, the probability of being selected into the sample is equal for all members of the population. This probability is expressed by the following formula:

Formula for simple random sample selection probability

$$\text{Probability of selection} = \text{sample size/population size}$$

With simple random sampling, if the researcher is surveying a population of 100,000 recent Kindle Fire buyers with a sample size of 1,000 respondents, the probability of selection on any single population member into this sample would be 1,000 divided by 100,000, or 1 out of 100, calculated to be 1%.

Examples of simple random sampling include the random device method and the random numbers method.

The Random Device Method. The **random device method** involves using an apparatus of some sort to ensure that every member of the population has the same chance of being selected into the sample. Familiar examples of the random device method include the flipping of a coin to decide heads or tails, lottery numbers selected by numbered ping pong balls, a roulette wheel in a casino, and a hand dealt in a poker game. In every case, every member of the population has the same probability of being selected as every other member of that population: 1/2 for the coin toss, 5/55 lottery balls, 1/37 roulette numbers, or 5/52 cards. Applied to sampling, you can create a device for randomly choosing participants by their names or some

With simple random sampling, the probability of selection into the sample is "known" for all members of the population.

The "random device" is a form of simple random sampling.

TABLE 9.2   Four Different Probability Sampling Methods

Simple Random Sampling

The researcher uses random numbers from a computer, random digit dialing, or some other random selection procedure that guarantees each member of the population in the sample frame has an identical chance of being selected into the sample.

Systematic Sampling

Using a sample frame that lists members of the population, the researcher selects a random starting point for the first sample member. A constant *skip interval*, calculated by dividing the number of population members in the sample frame by the sample size, is then used to select every other sample member from the sample frame. A skip interval must be used so that the entire list is covered, regardless of the starting point. This procedure accomplishes the same end as simple random sampling, and it is more efficient.

Cluster Sampling

The sample frame is divided into groups called clusters, each of which must be considered to be similar to the others. The researcher can then randomly select a few clusters and perform a census of each one (one stage). Alternatively, the researcher can randomly select more clusters and take samples from each one (two stage). This method is desirable when highly similar clusters can be easily identified, such as subdivisions spread across a wide geographic area.

Stratified Sampling

If the population is believed to have a skewed distribution for one or more of its distinguishing factors (e.g., income or product usage), the researcher identifies subpopulations in the sample frame called *strata*. A simple random sample is then taken of each stratum. Weighting procedures may be applied to estimate population values, such as the mean. This approach is better suited than other probability sampling methods for populations that are not distributed in a bell-shaped pattern (i.e., skewed).

other unique designation. For example, suppose you wanted to determine the attitudes of students in your marketing research class toward a career in marketing research. Assume that the class you have chosen as your population has 30 students enrolled. To do a **blind draw**, you write the name of every student on a 3-by-5 index card and put all the cards and inside a container. Next, you place a top on the container and shake it vigorously. This procedure ensures that the names are thoroughly mixed. You then ask some person to draw the sample. This individual is blindfolded so that he or she cannot see inside the container. You would instruct him or her to take out 10 cards as the sample. In this sample, every student in the class has an equal chance of being selected with a probability of 10/30 or 33%—a 1 in 3 chance of being selected into that sample.

The Random Numbers Method All of our random device examples involve small populations that are easily accommodated by the physical aspects of the device. With large populations, random devices become cumbersome (just try shuffling a deck of 1,000 playing cards). A tractable and more sophisticated application of simple random sampling is to use computer-generated numbers based on the concept of **random numbers**, which are numbers whose chance nature is assured. Computer programs can be designed to generate numbers without any systematic sequence to the numbers whatsoever—that is, they are random. A computer easily handles data sets of hundreds of thousands of individuals; it can quickly label each one with a unique number or designation, generate a set of random numbers, and match the random numbers with the unique designations of the individuals in the data set to select or "pull" the sample. Using random numbers, a computer system can draw a huge random sample from a gigantic population in a matter of minutes and guarantee that every population member in the computer's files has the same chance of being selected in the sample.

Marketing Research Insight 9.2 shows the steps involved in using random numbers generated by a spreadsheet program to select students from this 30-member population. Beginning with the first generated random number, you would progress through the set of random numbers to select members of the population into the sample. If you encounter the same number twice within the same sample draw, the number is skipped over because it is improper to collect information twice from the same person.

A random number embodies simple random sampling assumptions.

Games of chance such as bingo, lottery, or roulette are based on random selection, which underlies random sampling.

Photo: Elaine Barker/Shutterstock

 Active Learning

Are Random Numbers Really Random?

Some people do not believe that random numbers are actually random. These individuals sometimes point out that certain numbers seem to repeat more frequently than other numbers in lotteries, or they may claim to have a "favorite" or "lucky" number that wins for them when gambling or taking a chance of some sort. You can test the randomness of random numbers by creating an Excel spreadsheet and using its random number function. Use the following steps to perform this test.

MARKETING RESEARCH INSIGHT 9.2 — *Practical Application*

How to Use Random Numbers to Select a Simple Random Sample

Step 1: Assign a unique number to each member of the population.

Name	Number
Adams, Bob	1
Baker, Carol	2
Brown, Fred	3
Chester, Harold	4
Downs, Jane	5
...	↓
Zimwitz, Roland	30

23	12	8	4	22	17	6	23	14	2	13

Select the first random number and find the corresponding population member. In the following example, number 23 is the first random number.

Step 3: Select the person corresponding to that number into the sample.
#23—Stepford, Ann

Step 4: Continue to the next random number and select that person into the sample.
#12—Fitzwilliam, Roland

Step 2: Generate random numbers in the range of 1 to N (30 in this case) by using the random number function in a spreadsheet program such as Microsoft Excel.[8] Excel generates random numbers from 0.0 to 1.0, so if you multiply the random number by N and format the result as an integer, you will have random numbers in the range of 1 to N. The following set of random numbers was generated this way.

Step 5: Continue on in the same manner until the full sample is selected. If you encounter a number selected earlier such as the 23 that occurs at the eighth random number, simply skip over it because you have already selected that population member into the sample. (This explains why eleven numbers were drawn.)

1. First, open Excel and place numbers 1–100 in cells A2–A101 with 1 in A2, 2 in A3, 3 in A4, etc. up to 100 in A101.
2. Place numbers 1–100 in cells C1–CX1, respectively.
3. Next, in cells C3–CX101, enter the Excel function =INT(RAND()*100)+1. (Note: you can enter this formula into cell C3, then copy it and paste the copy into cells C4–CX101. You should see numbers that are whole integers ranging from 1 to 100 in cells C3–CX101.)
4. Next in cell B1, enter =COUNTIF(C2:CX2,A2). Copy this formula and paste it into cells B2–B101. You will now see integers such as 0, 1, 2, 3, etc. in column B2–B101.
5. Finally, in cell B102, enter in the formula =AVERAGE(B2:B101). Format Cell B102 to be a Number with 1 decimal place.
6. Cell B102 is the average number of times the number in column A2–A101 appears in the corresponding row, meaning row C2–CX2 for A2 or 1, C3–CX3, for A3 or 2, and so on.

What is in cell B102? It is the average number of times out of 100 times that each number from 1 to 100 appeared in its respective row. In other words, if the average in cell B102 is 1, then every number from 1 to 100 had an equal chance of being in its respective row. Stated differently, B102 is the number of chances out of 100 for any number from 1 to 100 to be selected by Excel's random number function.

You can "redraw" all 1,000 random numbers in Excel by simply entering in a blank-Return anywhere in the spreadsheet. Try this with cell A1 several times, and you will see that the average changes slightly, but it will tend to "hover" around 1.0.

You can test the "lucky number" theory by copying row 101 into rows 105–114 and placing the lucky number into cells A105–A114. Create an average of cells B105:B114 in cell B115. Then do several repetitions by entering in a blank-Return and keep track of the numbers that appear in cell B115. You will find that it is typically 1, meaning that the lucky number has no more chance of being drawn than any of the 99 other random numbers.

Now that you know how to draw a random sample from a finite population, we can describe the use of this sampling technique. Marketing Research Insight 9.3 recaps how researchers drew simple random samples of the messages issued by major corporations in the United States and Australia on Twitter in an attempt to identify the companies' marketing strategies in connecting with customers via this form of social media.

Advantages and Disadvantages of Simple Random Sampling Simple random sampling is an appealing sampling method simply because it embodies the requirements necessary to obtain a probability sample and, therefore, to derive unbiased estimates of the population's characteristics. This sampling method guarantees that every member of the population has an equal chance of being selected into the sample; therefore, the resulting sample, no matter what the size, will be a valid representation of the population.

However, there are some slight disadvantages associated with simple random sampling. To use either the random device or the random numbers approach, it is necessary to predesignate each population member. In the blind draw example, each student's name was written on

MARKETING RESEARCH INSIGHT 9.3 — *Social Media Marketing*

Random Samples Reveal Corporations' Twitter Marketing Strategies

Many companies are using social media such as Facebook and Twitter to communicate with current and prospective customers. Because of its length constraint, micro-blogging, an emerging social media marketing tool, is closely associated with Twitter. Two Australian market researchers[9] recently noted that because of the newness of this social media marketing phenomenon, there is very little theoretical guidance available for its use, nor is there a storehouse of practical wisdom for companies to tap when formulating their Twitter marketing strategies. The researchers noted that there is a great need to examine Twitter marketing strategies because 60% of Fortune 500 companies had a Twitter account in 2010, a rate that had advanced 35% over 2009. These researchers selected 10 successful and well-known companies, such as Microsoft, Qantas, Domino's Pizza, and *Cosmopolitan* magazine, with separate headquarters in both Australia and the United States.

They downloaded all tweets sent by these accounts over a recent 18-month period and then used simple random sampling to select 200 random tweets per company/headquarters. The focus of the research was to study the interactivity fostered by each company's tweets. Tweets with a hashtag (#) were coded as highly interactive because Twitter allows users to follow discussion threads with hashtagged tweets. Retweets or "mentions" were considered moderately interactive, and replies to tweets were considered lowly interactive. A separate consideration was whether a tweet contained a hyperlink; hyperlinks to internal company sites were deemed highly interactive. The findings were quite surprising:

- Almost no consistency in Twitter strategy was found across the several companies under study.
- There was great inconsistency within companies across countries. For example, Qantas Australia issued about 60% hashtags, while Qantas USA issued only 5% hashtags. Similarly, only 3% of Microsoft USA tweets were replies, but 77% of Microsoft Australia were replies.
- There was great inconsistency in the use of hyperlinks across companies and within companies across countries. For instance, Qantas USA issued 21% internal links, while Qantas Australia issued 42% internal links.

Thus, it appears that the use of Twitter is highly idiosyncratic. This finding suggests that companies are in the trial-and-error stage of understanding how Twitter can be useful. No company appears to have mastered the use of Twitter as an effective means of communicating with its customers.

an index card, and in the random numbers example, every population member was assigned a unique label or number. In essence, simple random sampling necessarily begins with a complete listing of the population, and current and complete listings are sometimes difficult to obtain. Incomplete or inaccurate listings of populations, of course, contain sample frame error. If the sample frame does not exist as an electronic list, we indicated that it can be cumbersome to manually provide unique designations for each population member.

Using random numbers to draw a simple random sample requires a complete accounting of the population.

Simple Random Sampling Used in Practice There are two practical applications in which simple random sample designs are employed quite successfully: random digit dialing and computer-based random samples. In fact, these two general cases constitute the bulk of the use of simple random sampling in marketing research.

One instance in which simple random sampling is commnly employed is through the use of random digit dialing. **Random digit dialing (RDD)** is used in telephone surveys to overcome the problems of unlisted and new telephone numbers. Unlisted numbers are a growing concern not only for researchers in the United States but in all industrialized countries, such as those in Europe, as well.[10,11] A current challenge to random digit dialing is cell phone ownership.[12]

Random digit dialing overcomes problems of unlisted and new telephone numbers.

In random digit dialing, telephone numbers are generated randomly with the aid of a computer. Telephone interviewers call these numbers and administer the survey to the respondent once the person has been qualified.[13] However, random digit dialing may result in a large number of calls to nonexisting telephone numbers. A popular variation of random digit dialing that reduces this problem is the **plus-one dialing procedure**, in which numbers are selected from a telephone directory and a digit, such as a "1," is added to each number to determine which telephone number is then dialed. Alternatively, the last digit can be substituted with a random number.[14]

Plus-one dialing is a convenient variation of random digit dialing.

While random digit dialing was the marketing research industry's first wholesale incorporation of random sampling, with current computer technology, it is feasible to use random sampling in a wide variety of situations. For example, often companies possess computer lists, company files, or commercial listing services that have been converted into databases. Practically every database software program has a random number selection feature, so simple random sampling is easy to achieve if the researcher has a computerized database of the population. The database programs can work with random numbers of as many digits as are necessary, so even Social Security numbers with nine digits are no problem. Companies with credit files, subscription lists, or marketing information systems have the greatest opportunity to use this approach, or a research company may turn to a specialized sampling company such as SSI to have it draw a random sample of households or businesses in a certain geographic area using its extensive databases.

In our chapter on the marketing research industry, we made note of the many companies that maintain consumer and business panels of various types, and practically every one of these companies sells access to random samples of their panels. That is, their panels, which sometimes numbers in the tens of thousands of individuals, are really megasamples of various types of populations. These panels operate as sample frames from which the panel company draws smaller random samples according to the specifications of their clients.

Systematic Sampling In the special situation of a large population list that is not in the form of a computer database, such as a telephone book or a directory, the time and expense required to use simple random sampling are daunting. Fortunately, an economical alternative probability sampling method can be used. At one time, **systematic sampling**, which is a way to select a random sample from a directory or list that is much more efficient (uses less effort) than with simple random sampling, was the most prevalent type of sampling technique used. However, its popularity has fallen as computerized databases and generated random number features have become widely available. However, in the special case of a physical listing of the population, such as a membership directory or a telephone book, systematic sampling is often chosen over simple random sampling based primarily on the economic efficiency it represents. In this instance, systematic sampling can be applied with less difficulty and accomplished in a shorter time than can simple random sampling. Furthermore, in these instances,

Systematic sampling is more efficient than simple random sampling.

systematic sampling has the potential to create a sample that is almost identical in quality to samples created from simple random sampling.

One must calculate a "skip interval" to use systematic sampling.

To use systematic sampling, it is necessary to obtain a hard-copy listing of the population. As noted earlier, the most common listing is a directory of some sort. The researcher decides on a **skip interval**, which is calculated by dividing the number of names on the list by the sample size, as can be seen in the following formula:

Formula for skip interval

Skip interval = population list size/sample size

Names are selected based on this skip interval. For example, if one calculated a skip interval of 250, every 250th name would be selected into the sample. The use of this skip interval formula ensures that the entire list will be covered. Marketing Research Insight 9.4 shows how to take a systematic sample.

Why Systematic Sampling Is Efficient Systematic sampling is probability sampling because it employs a random starting point, which ensures there is sufficient randomness in the systematic sample to approximate an equal probability of any member of the population being selected into the sample. In essence, systematic sampling envisions the list as made up of the skip interval number of mutually exclusive samples, each one of which is representative of the listed population. The random starting point guarantees that the selected sample is selected randomly.

How does the random starting point take place? With a directory or physical list as the sample frame, the efficient approach is to first generate a random number between 1 and the number of pages to determine the page on which you will start. Suppose page 53 is drawn. Another random number would be drawn between 1 and the number of columns on a page to decide the column on that page. Assume the third column is drawn. A final random number between 1 and the number of names in a column would be used to determine the actual starting position in that column. Let's say the 17th name is selected. From that beginning point, the skip interval would be employed. The skip interval would ensure that the entire list would be covered, and the final name selected would be approximately one skip interval before the starting point. It is convenient to think of the listing as circular, so that A follows Z if the list were alphabetized, and the random starting point determines where the list "begins."

MARKETING RESEARCH INSIGHT 9.4   *Practical Application*

 How to Take a Systematic Sample

Step 1: Identify a listing of the population that contains an acceptable level of sample frame error.
Example: the telephone book for your city

Step 2: Compute the skip interval by dividing the number of names on the list by the sample size.
Example: 25,000 names in the phone book, sample size of 500, so skip interval = every 50th name

Step 3: Using random number(s), determine a starting position for sampling the list.
Example: *Select*: random number for page number
Select: random number for the column on that page

Select: random number for name position in that column (say, Jones, William P.)

Step 4: Apply the skip interval to determine which names on the list will be in the sample.
Example: Jones, William P. (skip 50 names) Lathum, Ferdinand B.

Step 5: Treat the list as "circular." That is, the first name on the list is now the initial name you selected, and the last name is now the name just prior to the initially selected one.
Example: When you come to the end of the phone book names (Zs), just continue on through the beginning (As).

The essential difference between systematic sampling and simple random sampling is apparent in the use of the words *systematic* and *random*. The system used in systematic sampling is the skip interval, whereas the randomness in simple random sampling is determined through the use of successive random draws. Systematic sampling skips its way through the entire population list from random beginning point to end, whereas random sampling guarantees that the complete population will be covered by successive random draws. The efficiency in systematic sampling is gained by two features: (1) the skip interval aspect and (2) the need to use random number(s) only at the beginning.

Systematic sampling is more efficient than simple random sampling because only one or a very few random numbers need to be drawn at the beginning.

 Active Learning

Take a Systematic Sample Using Your Telephone Book

This Active Learning Exercise will give you experience in taking a systematic sample from a hard copy list, such as a telephone book. For this exercise, you will use the telephone book for your locality, and you will apply systematic sampling steps as though you were selecting a sample of 1,000 households. Use the following steps:

1. Estimate the total number of households listed in the telephone book. To arrive at this estimate:
   a. Determine the total number of pages of household listings:
      _____ pages
   b. Determine the number of columns of numbers per page:
      _____ columns
   c. Determine the average number of households listings per column (Note: if there business telephone numbers mixed with the households ones, you will need to make an adjustement for this factor.):
      _____ household listings
   d. Determine the estimated total number of households in your sample frame (the telephone book) by mutiplying the number of pages by the number of columns and again by the number of household listings per column.
      _____ Household numbers
   e. Determine the skip interval by dividing the number of household numbers by the sample size, 1,000.
      _____ Skip interval
   f. Now, using some sort of random number generator such as an Excel function or a table of random numbers (typically found in a statistics textbook), select a random starting point either of two ways:
      1. Select a random numbers between 1 and the total number of households in your sample frame, or
      2. Select a random page from 1 to the number of pages in the telephone book and turn to that page. Then select a random column from 1 to the number of columns per page and go to that column. Finally, select a random household in that column with a random number from 1 to the number of households per column.
   g. Using your skip interval, you can now select the 1,000 household telephone listings.
   h. The procedure you have used here assumes that every one of your 1,000 randomly selected households will particpate in the survey (100% response rate); however, this assumption is unrealistic. Assume that you expect a 50% response rate. What adjustment to the skip interval calculation can you make to accommodate the fact every other prospective respondent will refuse to take part in the survey when asked?

With systematic sampling, the small loss in sampling precision is counterbalanced by its economic savings.

Disadvantage of Systematic Sampling. The greatest danger in the use of systematic sampling lies in the listing of the population (sample frame). Sample frame error is a major concern for telephone directories because of unlisted numbers. It is also a concern for lists that are not current. In both instances, the sample frame will not include certain population members, and these members have no chance of being selected into the sample because of this fact.

Cluster Sampling Another form of probability sampling is known as **cluster sampling**, in which the population is divided into subgroups, called "clusters," each of which could represent the entire population. Note that the basic concept behind cluster sampling is similar to the one described for systematic sampling, but the implementation differs. The procedure uses some convenient means that identifies clusters that are theoretically identical, such as the pages of listings in a hard-copy directory. Any one cluster or page, therefore, could be a representation of the population. Cluster sampling can even be applied to an electonic database (The clusters can be everyone whose name begins with A, B, C, etc.). It is easy to administer, and cluster sampling goes a step further in striving to gain economic efficiency over systematic sampling by simplifying the sampling procedure used.[15] We illustrate cluster sampling by describing a type of cluster sample known as area sampling.

A cluster sampling method divides the population into groups, any one of which can be considered a representative sample.

Area Sampling as a Form of Cluster Sampling In **area sampling**, the researcher subdivides the population to be surveyed into geographic areas, such as census tracts, cities, neighborhoods, or any other convenient and identifiable geographic designation. The researcher has two options at this point: a one-step approach or a two-step approach. In the **one-step area sample** approach, the researcher may believe the various geographic areas (clusters) to be sufficiently identical to allow concentrating his or her attention on just one area and then generalizing the results to the full population. But the researcher would need to select that one area randomly and perform a census of its members. Alternatively, he or she may employ a **two-step area sample** approach to the sampling process. That is, for the first step, the researcher could select a random sample of areas, and then for the second step, he or she could decide on a probability method to sample individuals within the chosen areas. The two-step area sample approach is preferable to the one-step approach because there is always the possibility that a single cluster may be less representative than the researcher believes. But the two-step method is more costly because more areas and time are involved. Marketing Research Insight 9.5 illustrates how to take an area sample using subdivisions as the clusters.[16]

Area sampling employs either a one-step or two-step approach.

Area grid sampling is a variation of the area sampling method. To use it, the researcher imposes a grid over a map of the area to be surveyed. Each cell within the grid then becomes a cluster. The difference between area grid sampling and area sampling lies primarily in the use of a grid framework, which cuts across natural or artificial boundaries, such as streets, rivers, city limits, or other separations normally used in area sampling. Geodemography has been used to describe the demographic profiles of the various clusters.[17] Regardless of how the population is sliced up, the researcher has the option of a one-step or a two-step approach.[18]

Disadvantage of Cluster (Area) Sampling The greatest danger in cluster sampling is cluster specification error that occurs when the clusters are not homogeneous. For example, if a subdivision association used area sampling to survey its members using its streets as cluster identifiers, and one street circumnavigated a small lake in the back of the subdivision, the "Lake Street" homes might be more expensive and luxurious than most of the other homes in the subdivision. If, by chance, Lake Street was selected as a cluster in the survey, it would most likely bias the results toward the opinions of the relatively few wealthy subdivision residents. In the case of one-step area sampling, this bias could be severe.

Stratified Sampling All of the sampling methods we have described thus far implicitly assume that the population has a normal, or bell-shaped, distribution for its key properties. That is, every potential sample unit is assumed to have a fairly good representation of the population, and any who are extreme in one way are perfectly counterbalanced by opposite extreme

MARKETING RESEARCH INSIGHT 9.5   *Practical Application*

How to Take a Two-Step Area Sampling Using Subdivisions

Step 1: Determine the geographic area to be surveyed and identify its subdivisions. Each subdivision cluster should be highly similar to all others.
Example: 20 subdivisions within 5 miles of the proposed site for our new restaurant; assign each a number.

Step 2: Decide on the use of one-step or two-step cluster sampling.
Example: Use two-step cluster sampling.

Step 3: (assuming two-step): Using random numbers, select the subdivisions to be sampled.

Example: Select four subdivisions randomly, say, numbers 3, 15, 2, and 19.

Step 4: Using some probability method of sample selection, select the members of each chosen subdivision to be included in the sample.
Example: Identify a random starting point; instruct fieldworkers to drop off the survey at every fifth house (systematic sampling).

potential sample units. Unfortunately, it is common to work with populations in marketing research that contain unique subgroupings; you might encounter a population that is not distributed symmetrically across a normal curve. With this situation, unless you make adjustments in your sample design, you will end up with a sample described as "statistically inefficient"—that is, inaccurate. One solution is **stratified sampling**, which separates the population into different subgroups and then samples all of these subgroups.

Working with Skewed Populations A **skewed population** has a long tail on one side and a short tail on the opposite end. As such, it deviates greatly from the bell-shaped distribution that is assumed to be the case in the use of simple random, systematic, or cluster

With stratified sampling, the population is separated into different strata, and a sample is taken from each stratum.

Our area sampling example uses subdivisions as clusters.
Photo: Condor 36/Shutterstock

sampling. If any of these methods is used to draw the sample from a skewed distribution, it most certainly would be inaccurate.

For example, let's take the case of a college that is attempting to assess how its students perceive the quality of its educational programs. A researcher has formulated the question, "To what extent do you value your college degree?" The response options are along a 5-point scale where 1 equals "not valued at all" and 5 equals "very highly valued." The population of students is stratified or divided by year: freshman, sophomore, junior, and senior. That is, the researcher identifies four strata that comprise the complete population of the college's students. We would expect the response to differ by stratum (the respondent's year classification) because seniors probably value a degree more than do juniors, who value a degree more than do sophomores and so on. At the same time, you would expect that seniors would be more in agreement (have less variability) than would underclass students. This belief is due to the fact that freshmen are students who are trying out college, some of whom are not serious about completing it and do not value it highly but some of whom are intending to become doctors, lawyers, or professionals whose training will include graduate degree work as well as their present college studies. The serious freshmen students would value a college degree highly, whereas their less serious peers would not. Thus, we would expect much variability in the freshmen students, less in sophomores, still less in juniors, and the least with seniors. The situation might be something similar to the distributions illustrated in Figure 9.2. Note that this figure portrays the four class strata distributions as normal curves, whereas the entire college population of all four classes is a skewed curve.

With stratified random sampling, one takes a skewed population and identifies the subgroups, or **strata**, contained within it. Simple random sampling, systematic sampling, or some other type of probability sampling procedure is then applied to draw a sample from each stratum because we typically believe that the individual strata have bell-shaped distributions. In other words, it is a "divide and conquer" approach to sampling.

Accuracy of Stratified Sampling How does stratified sampling result in a more accurate overall sample? This accuracy is achieved in two ways. First, stratified sampling allows for explicit analysis of each stratum. Our college degree example (Figure 9.2) illustrates why a

> Stratified sampling is appropriate when we expect that responses will vary across strata, or groups in the population.

FIGURE 9.2
Stratified Simple Random Sampling

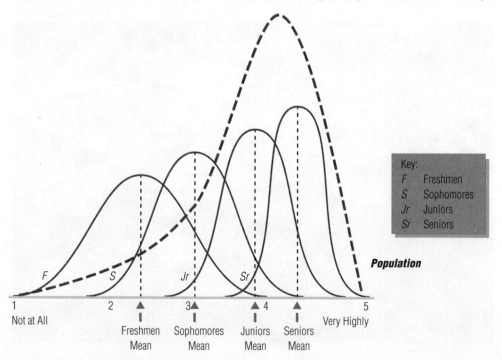

Key:
F Freshmen
S Sophomores
Jr Juniors
Sr Seniors

"To what extent do you value a college degree?"

researcher would want to know about the distinguishing differences between the strata to assess the true picture. Each stratum represents a different response profile, and by recognizing this, stratified sampling is a more accurate sample design.

Second, there is a procedure that allows the estimation of the overall sample mean by use of a **weighted mean**, whose formula takes into consideration the sizes of the strata relative to the total population size and applies those proportions to the strata's means. The population mean is calculated by multiplying each stratum by its proportion and summing the weighted stratum means. This formula results in an estimate that is consistent with the true distribution of the population. This formula is used for two strata:

Formula for weighted mean

$$\text{Mean}_{\text{population}} = (\text{mean}_A)(\text{proportion}_A) + (\text{mean}_B)(\text{proportion}_B)$$

where A signifies stratum A, and B signifies stratum B.

Here is an example of the use of weighted mean. A researcher separates a population of households that rent DVDs on a regular basis into two strata. Stratum A is families without young children, and stratum B is families with young children. When asked to use a scale of 1 = poor, 2 = fair, 3 = good, 4 = very good, and 5 = excellent to rate their video/DVD rental store on its DVD selection, the means were computed to be 2.0 (fair) for the families with young children stratum B sample and 4.0 (very good) for the families without young children stratum A sample. The researcher knows from census information that families without young children account for 70% of the population, whereas families with young children accounted for the remaining 30%. The weighted mean rating for video selection is then computed as (.7)(2.0) + (.3)(4.0) = 2.6 (between fair and good).

How to Apply Stratified Sampling Marketing researchers find stratified sampling especially useful when they encounter skewed populations. Prior knowledge of populations under study, augmented by research objectives sensitive to subgroupings, sometimes reveals that the population is not normally distributed. Under these circumstances, it is advantageous to apply stratified sampling to preserve the diversity of the various subgroups. Usually, a **surrogate measure**, which is some observable or easily determined characteristic of each population member, is used to help partition or separate the population members into their various subgroupings. For example, in the instance of the college, the year classification of each student is a handy surrogate. Researchers may divide the population into as many relevant strata as necessary to capture different subpopulations. For instance, the college might want to further stratify on college of study or grade-point average (GPA) ranges. Perhaps professional school students value their degrees more than do liberal arts students or high GPA students more than average GPA or failing students. The key issue is that researchers should use some basis for dividing the population into strata that results in different responses across strata. Also, there should be some logic or usefullness to the stratification system.

If the strata sample sizes are faithful to their relative sizes in the population, the research design reflects a **proportionate stratified sample**. Here you do not need to use the weighted formula because each stratum's weight is automatically accounted for by its sample size. But think for a moment about proportionate sampling: It erroneously assumes that the variability of each stratum is related to its size. Larger strata have more variability than small ones, but a large stratum could be composed of homogeneous individuals, translating to a relatively small stratum sample size, while a small stratum could be composed of very different individuals, translating to a relative large stratum sample size. As a result, some researchers opt to use the stratum relative variability rather than the relative size, as a factor in deciding stratum sample size. That is, if a stratum has low variability, precise estimates of that stratum may be obtained with a small sample size, and the "extra" sample saved could be allocated to strata with high variance. This provides for **statistical efficiency** meaning, for the same sample size researchers

Stratified sampling is used when the researcher is working with a "skewed" population divided into strata and wishes to achieve high statistical efficiency.

A stratified sample may require the calculation of a weighted mean to achieve accuracy.

Researchers should select a basis for stratification that reveals different responses across the strata.

 To learn about stratified sampling, launch **www** **.youtube.com** and search for "Stratified sampling by maysterchief."

SPSS Student Assistant
About your SPSS Student Assistant

MARKETING RESEARCH INSIGHT 9.6   *Practical Application*

How to Take a Stratified Sample

Step 1: Be certain that the population's distribution for some key factor is *not* bell-shaped and that separate subpopulations exist.
Example: Condominium owners differ from apartment dwellers in their homeowners' insurance needs, so stratify by condo ownership and apartment dwelling.

Step 2: Use this factor or some surrogate variable to divide the population into strata consistent with the separate subpopulations identified.
Example: Use a screening question on condo ownership/apartment dwelling. This may require a screening survey using random digit dialing to identify respondent pools for each stratum.

Step 3: Select a probability sample from each stratum.
Example: Use a computer to select simple random samples for each stratum.

Step 4: Examine each stratum for managerially relevant differences.
Example: Do condo owners differ from apartment dwellers in the value of the furniture they own (and need covered by insurance)? Answer: Condo owners average $15,000 in owned furniture value; apartment dwellers average $5,000 in owned furniture value.

Step 5: If stratum sample sizes are not proportionate to the stratum sizes in the population, use the weighted mean formula to estimate the population value(s).
Example: If condo owners are 30% and apartment dwellers are 70% of the population, the estimate of the average is ($15,000)(.30) + ($5,000)(.70) = $8,000 owned furniture value.

With nonprobability sampling, there is a good possibility that nonrepresentative sample units will be selected. (New Orleans Saints fan Scott McGowan, dressed as the Joker. *Photo:* Julia Morgan Photography)

With nonprobability sampling methods, some members of the population do not have any chance of being included in the sample.

may obtain equivalent precision among the strata. This approach is called **disproportionate stratified sampling**, and a weighted formula needs to be used because the strata sizes do not reflect their relative proportions in the population. We have provided a step-by-step description of stratified sampling in Marketing Research Insight 9.6.

NONPROBABILITY SAMPLING METHODS

All of the sampling methods we have described thus far embody probability sampling assumptions. In each case, the probability of any unit being selected from the population into the sample is known, even though it cannot be calculated precisely. The critical difference between probability and nonprobability sampling methods is the mechanics used in the sample design. With a nonprobability sampling method, selection is not based on chance or randomness. Instead, a nonprobability sample is based on an inherently biased selection process, typically to reduce the cost of sampling.[19] With a nonprobability sample, the reseacher has some savings but at the expense of using a sample that is not truly representative of the population.[20] There are four nonprobability sampling methods: convenience samples, purposive samples, referral samples, and quota samples (Table 9.3). A discussion of each method follows.

Convenience Samples Samples drawn at the convenience of the interviewer are called **convenience samples**. Accordingly, the most convenient areas to a researcher in terms of reduced time and effort turn out to be high-traffic areas, such as shopping malls or busy pedestrian intersections. The selection of the place and, consequently, prospective respondents is subjective rather than objective. Certain members of the population are automatically eliminated from the sampling process.[21] For instance, people who may be infrequent or even nonvisitors of the particular high-traffic area being used would not be included. In the absence of strict selection procedures, some members of the population may be omitted because of their physical appearance, general demeanor, or the fact that

TABLE 9.3   Four Types of Nonprobability Sampling Methods

Convenience Sampling

The researcher or interviewer uses a high-traffic location, such as a busy pedestrian area or a shopping mall as the sample frame from which to intercept potential respondents. Sample frame error occurs in the form of members of the population who are infrequent or nonusers of that location. Other error may result from any arbitrary way the interviewer selects respondents from the sample frame.

Purposive Sampling

The researcher uses his or her judgment or that of some other knowledgeable person to identify who will be in the sample. Subjectivity and convenience enter in here; consequently, certain members of the population will have a smaller chance of selection than will others.

Referral Sampling

Respondents are asked for the names or identities of others like themselves who might qualify to take part in the survey. Members of the population who are less well known or disliked or whose opinions conflict with the selected respondents have a low probability of being selected.

Quota Sampling

The researcher identifies quota characteristics, such as demographic or product use factors, and uses these to set up quotas for each class of respondent. The sizes of the quotas are determined by the researcher's belief about the relative size of each class of respondent in the population. Often, quota sampling is used as a means of ensuring that convenience samples will have the desired proportion of different respondent classes.

they are in a group rather than alone. One author states, "Convenience samples … can be seriously misleading."[22] The Active Learning exercise convenience sampling demonstrates these drawbacks.

Convenience samples may misrepresent the population.

 Active Learning

Assess the Representativeness of Various Convenience Samples

Suppose the Athletic Department at your university is disappointed about student attendance of its "minor" collegiate sports events such as wrestling, cross country, and softball. The athletic director wants to learn why students do not attend these events. Listed below are possible locations for a convenience sample. With each one, indicate what types of students would be overrepresented in the sample and what types would be underrepresented versus the population of students at your university for each case.

Convenience sample location	What students would be overrepresented?	What students would be underrepresented?
The University Recreation Center		
The University Commons		
The Library		
Physics 401 (Advanced class for physics majors)		

It should be obvious that mall-intercept companies use convenience sampling to recruit respondents. For example, shoppers are encountered at large shopping malls and quickly qualified with screening questions. For those satisfying the desired population characteristics, a questionnaire may be administered or a taste test performed. Alternatively, the respondent may be given a test product and asked if he or she would use it at home. A follow-up

Mall intercepts are convenience samples.

telephone call some days later solicits his or her reaction to the product's performance. In this case, the convenience extends beyond easy access of respondents into considerations of setup for taste tests, storage of products to be distributed, and control of the interviewer workforce. Additionally, large numbers of respondents can be recruited in a matter of days. The screening questions and geographic dispersion of malls may appear to reduce the subjectivity inherent in the sample design, but in fact the vast majority of the population was not there and could not be approached to take part. There are ways of reducing convenience sample selection error using a quota system, which we discuss shortly.

By now you are well aware that convenience samples disallow members of the population from being represented in the sample. Read Marketing Research Insight 9.7 to see how much of the population of India was not represented in a sample that some researchers drew in their survey to assess the level of satisfaction of owners of the Tata Indian brand of automobile.

With a purposive sample, one "judges" the sample to be representative.

Purposive Samples Unlike convenience samples, **purposive samples** require a judgment or an "educated guess" as to who should represent the population. Often the researcher or some individual helping the researcher who has considerable knowledge about the population will choose those or those types of individuals who he or she feels constitute the sample. This practice is sometimes called a *judgment sample* or an *exemplar sample*. It should be apparent that purposive samples are highly subjective and, therefore, prone to much error.

Focus group studies use purposive sampling rather than probability sampling. In a recent focus group concerning the likely demand for low-fat, nutritious snacks, 12 mothers of preschool children were selected as representative of the present and prospective market. Six of the woman also had school-age children, while the other six had only preschoolers. That is, the researcher purposely included the two types of focus group participants because in his judgment, these 12 women represented the population adequately for the purposes of the research. It must be quickly pointed out, however, that the intent of this focus group was far different from the intent of a survey. Consequently, the use of a purposive sample was considered satisfactory for this particular phase in the research process for the snacks. The focus group findings served as the foundation for a large-scale regional survey conducted two months later that relied on a probability sampling method.

As you would expect, there are grave ethical considerations attached to sample method decisions in marketing research. The relevant sections in the Marketing Research Association (MRA) Code of Ethics that pertain to sample methods are presented in Marketing Research Insight 9.8. The MRA states that researchers must "follow scientifically sound sampling methods consistent with the purpose of the research," and it specifically warns researchers not to mislead clients into believing the sample is adequate when it is not. It also holds that the sample selection should be disclosed, particularly if requested by a third party, and specifically as to how the sample method enables the accomplishment of the survey objectives. Item 56, in particular, calls for full disclosure in this regard.

Marketing Research on YouTube™ | To learn about nonprobability sampling methods, launch www.youtube.com and search for "Examples of nonprobability sampling methods."

A referral sample asks respondents to provide the names of additional respondents.

Referral Samples Sometimes called "snowball samples," **referral samples** require respondents to provide the names of prospective respondents. Such samples begin when the researcher compiles a short list of possible respondents that is smaller than the total sample he or she desires for the study. After each respondent is interviewed, he or she is queried about the names of other possible respondents.[23] In this manner, additional respondents are referred by previous respondents. Or, as the informal name implies, the sample grows just as a snowball grows when it is rolled downhill.

Referral samples are most appropriate when there is a limited or disappointingly short sample frame and when respondents can provide the names of others who would qualify for the survey. The nonprobability aspects of referral sampling come from the selectivity used throughout. The initial list may also be special in some way, and the primary means of adding people to the sample is by tapping the memories of those on the original list. While they rely heavily on social networks,[24] referral samples are often useful in industrial marketing research situations.[25]

MARKETING RESEARCH INSIGHT 9.7   *Global Application*

Indian Researchers Use Convenience Sampling to Investigate Satisfaction with the Tata Automobile

In India, the largest domestic automobile company is Tata Motors, headquartered in Mumbai. Tata Motors has a long history; it was established in 1945 and is the market leader in at least three different car sizes: compact, mid-sized, and utility vehicle. However, Tata Motors has faced increased foreign automobile competition, especially from Suzuki, Hyundai, General Motors, and Ford. Three market researchers[26] recently undertook a study to examine the degree of satisfaction with Tata owners for various aspects of Tata Motors, such as affordable prices, attractive discounts, knowledge ability of salespersons, and availability and variety of models. They also investigated owners' overall opinion of Tata Motors.

These researchers chose to perform the survey in Jaipur, Rajasthan, located in north-central India, with a population of more than 3 million. India has 45 cities with populations of 1 million and more, and Jaipur is ranked 10th in this list. Rajasthan is the eighth largest state in India with a population of about 67 million and accounting for less than 6% of the total population of India. India has a population of about 1.2 billion people, so the city of Jaipur accounts for 0.2% of the total Indian population. The researchers chose five different areas in Rajasthan and interviewed 20 Tata owners at each location. The areas were chosen in "a scattered manner" to obtain a more "effective result."

With respect to overall satisfaction, the researchers found the patterns depicted in the figure developed from a table in the report.

These findings suggest that Tata Motors has a high vote of consumer satisfaction in total and across all three owner age groups. The authors conclude that "overall, customers are satisfied"; however, because the sample was a convenience sample taken in a specific city in India, this conclusion cannot be defended. At best, the researchers have found that with certain Tata Motors automobile owners in Jaipur, there is a fairly high degree of overall satisfaction. That is, if we assume that Tata ownership is spread evenly across the Indian population, because of the nature of the convenience sample used in this study, more than 99.8% of Tata owners were omitted from the sample frame.

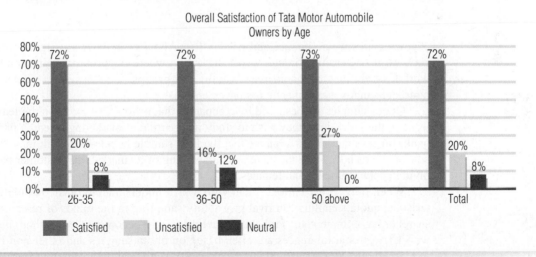

Overall Satisfaction of Tata Motor Automobile Owners by Age

Quota Samples Specified percentages of the total sample for various types of individuals to be interviewed constitute a **quota sample**. For example, a researcher may desire the sample to be 50% males and 50% females. As we indicated earlier, quota samples are commonly used by marketing researchers who rely on mall intercepts, a convenience sample method. The quotas are determined through application of the research objectives and are defined by key characteristics used to identify the population. In the application of quota sampling, a fieldworker is provided with screening criteria that will classify the potential respondent into a particular quota group. For example, if the interviewer is assigned to obtain a sample quota of 50 each for black females, black males, white females, and white males, the qualifying

Quota samples rely on key characteristics to define the composition of the sample.

MARKETING RESEARCH INSIGHT 9.8 — *Ethical Consideration*

Marketing Research Association Code of Ethics: Sampling Method

48. Will not misrepresent the impact of sample methodology and its impact on survey data.
Fair and honest information as to how sample methodology will affect survey data must be available to sample purchasers. This information must accurately represent likely outcomes and results as opposed to other available methodologies.

49. Will, upon request, disclose practices and methods used for generating, stratifying and selecting specific samples.
Information on how certain samples are created must be made available to researchers so that they can make informed decisions about sample purchase and use.

50. Will, upon request, identify the appropriateness of the sample methodology itself and its ability to accomplish research objectives.
Information as to the appropriateness of the sample methodology must be made available to sample

purchasers. This information must accurately portray the sample's ability to attain the buyer's research objectives. As a research partner, the sampling provider must be prepared to advise about alternative sampling methods if appropriate.

56. Will, to the fullest extent possible on each project, counsel End Users as to the appropriateness of the sample methodology being employed. Ultimately, communication of critical information resides with the Research Provider working with the End User.
If it is the responsibility of the Research Provider to procure sample, it is also the responsibility of the Research Provider to ensure that any and all pertinent information about the sample that will affect the outcome of the study or its results be conveyed to the End User (e.g., sample derivation, use and effect).

Quota samples are appropriate when researchers have a detailed demographic profile of the population on which to base the sample.

SPSS Student Assistant
SPSS Quick Tour: Part I

characteristics would be race and gender. If our fieldworkers were assigned mall intercepts, each would determine through visual inspection where the prospective respondent falls and work toward filling the quota in each of the four groups. A quota system reduces some of the nonrepresentativeness inherent in convenience samples.

Quota samples are best used by companies that have a firm grasp on the features characterizing the individuals they wish to study in a particular marketing research project. A large bank, for instance, might stipulate that the final sample be one-half adult males and one-half adult females because in the bank's understanding of its market, the customer base is equally divided between males and females.

When done conscientiously and with a firm understanding of the population's characteristics, quota sampling can rival probability sampling in the minds of researchers. One researcher has commented, "Probability sampling is the recommended method, but in the 'real world,' statistical inferences are often based on quota samples and other non-random sampling methods. Strangely, these heretical uses of statistical theory, in my experience, seem to work just as well as they do for 'purist' random samples."[27]

Online Sampling Techniques

Sampling for Internet surveys poses special opportunities and challenges, but most of these issues can be addressed in the context of our probability and nonprobability sampling concepts.[28] The trick is to understand how the online sampling method in question works and to interpret the sampling procedure correctly with respect to basic sampling concepts.[29] Unfortunately, these sampling procedures are often "behind the scenes" or not obvious until one delves into the mechanics of the sample selection process. Basically, three types of samples are used with online surveys: (1) online panels, (2) river samples, and (3) list samples.

ONLINE PANEL SAMPLES

Online panels, as we have described and alluded to in various places in this textbook, are large numbers of individuals who have agreed to participate in online surveys. Normally, they have registered with a panel company and have agreed to participate in surveys with some sort of compensation, such as points that can be redeemed for products and services. Panel members have divulged large amounts of information about themselves to the panel company, so it is easy for the company to select panelists who satisfy population membership criteria specified by clients, such as age range, education level, and household size. Panel companies have hundreds of thousands of prospective respondents, and they select them based on any such criteria and/or sampling requirements specified by their clients. Online panel samples are popular, but there are lingering concerns about the true representativeness of samples provided by panel companies.

RIVER SAMPLES

A **river sample** is created via the use of banners, pop-ups, or other online devices that invite website visitors to take part in the survey. The "river" is the steady stream of website visitors, and these invitations figuratively dip respondents out of the Internet river. Of course, the online questionnaire may have screening questions so that only qualified prospects are allowed to take part in the survey. The sample frame of a river sample is the stream of visitors visiting the site issuing the invitation, and river samples are considered random samples of these sample frames as long as the invitations are not unusual in duration, appearance, or relevance.

EMAIL LIST SAMPLES

Email list samples are those purchased or otherwise procured from someone or some company that has compiled email addresses of opt-in members of the population of interest. The vendor company can pull random samples and may have the ability to satisfy selection criteria specified by the client company. The list company may sell the list, or it might issue email invitations to maintain the propriety of email adresses on the list. Obviously, the master source list is the sample frame, so if the list company has been diligent, the email list sample will be a good representation of the population. However, if the list company has not done due diligence, there will be sample frame error in the email list.

Developing a Sample Plan

Up to this point, we have discussed various aspects of sampling as though they were discrete and seemingly unrelated decisions. However, they are logically joined in a definite sequence of steps, called the **sample plan**, which the researcher goes through to draw and ultimately arrive at the final sample.[30] These steps are listed and described in Table 9.4.

SPSS®

SPSS Student Assistant
SPSS Quick Tour: Part II

TABLE 9.4 Steps in a Sample Plan

Step	Action	Description
1	Define the population	Create a precise description of the group under investigation using demographics, buyer behavior, or other relevant constructs
2	Obtain a sample frame	Gain access to some master source that uniquely identifies all the units in the population with minimal sample frame error
3	Decide on the sample method	Based on survey objectives and constraints, endeavor to select the best probability sample method, or alternatively, if appropriate, select the best nonprobability sample method
4	Decide on the sample size	If a probability sampling plan is selected, use a formula; to be covered in the following chapter
5	Draw the sample	Using the chosen sample method, apply the necessary steps to select potential respondents from the sample frame
6	Validate the sample	Inspect some relevant characteristics of the sample (such as distribution of males and females, age ranges, etc.) to judge how well it matches the known distribution of these characteristics in the population

Summary

Sampling methods facilitate marketing research without requiring a census of an entire population. Marketing researchers aim to avoid sample frame error, which includes omissions and inaccuracies that will adversely affect the sample drawn from it.

A sample is taken because it is too costly to perform a census and there is sufficient information in a sample to allow it to represent the population. We described four probability sampling methods in which there is a known chance of a member of the population being selected into the sample. Simple random sampling uses devices or aids, such as random numbers, to ensure that every member of the population has the same chance of being selected into the sample. Systematic sampling uses a random starting point and "skips" through a list. Cluster sampling can be applied to areas such as subdivisions so that only a few areas are selected and canvassed or sampled. Stratified sampling is used when different strata are apparent in the population and each stratum is randomly sampled.

We also described four nonprobability sampling methods that contain bias because all members of the population do not have a fair chance of being selected into the sample. Convenience sampling uses high-traffic locations, such as a malls, to make it easy for an interviewer to intercept respondents. Purposive sampling rests on someone's subjective judgement as to who should be in the sample. Referral sampling relies on respondents to give up names of friends to be asked to take part in the survey, and quota sampling is convenience sampling with quotas or limits on the numbers of respondents with specific characteristics. Finally, we described six steps needed to develop a sample plan: (1) define the relevant population, (2) obtain a sample frame, (3) decide on the sample method, (4) decide on the sample size, (5) draw the sample, and (6) validate the sample.

Key Terms

Population (p. 210)
Census (p. 211)
Sample (p. 211)
Sample unit (p. 211)
Sampling error (p. 213)
Sample frame (p. 212)
Sample frame error (p. 212)
Sampling error (p. 213)
Probability samples (p. 214)
Nonprobability samples (p. 214)
Simple random sampling (p. 215)
Random device method (p. 215)
Blind draw method (p. 216)

Random numbers (p. 216)
Random digit dialing (p. 219)
Plus-one dialing procedure (p. 219)
Systematic sampling (p. 219)
Skip interval (p. 220)
Cluster sampling (p. 222)
Area sampling (p. 222)
One-step area sample (p. 222)
Two-step area sample (p. 222)
Stratified sampling (p. 223)
Skewed population (p. 223)
Strata (p. 224)
Weighted mean (p. 225)

Surrogate measure (p. 225)
Proportionate stratified sample (p. 225)
Statistical efficiency (p. 225)
Disproportionate stratified sampling (p. 226)
Convenience samples (p. 226)
Purposive samples (p. 228)
Referral samples (p. 228)
Quota sample (p. 229)
Online panels (p. 231)
River sample (p. 231)
Email list samples (p. 231)
Sample plan (p. 231)

Review Questions/Applications

1. Distinguish a nonprobability from a probability sampling method. Which one is the preferable method and why? Indicate the pros and cons associated with probability and nonprobability sampling methods.
2. List and describe briefly each of the probability sampling methods described in the chapter.
3. What is meant by the term *random*? Explain how each of the following embodies randomness: (a) blind draw, (b) use of random digit dialing, and (c) use of a computer to generate random numbers.
4. In what ways is a systematic sample more efficient than a simple random sample? In what way is systematic sampling less representative of the population than simple random sampling?
5. Distinguish cluster sampling from simple random sampling. How are systematic sampling and cluster sampling related?
6. Differentiate one-step from two-step area sampling and indicate when each one is preferred.
7. What is meant by a *skewed* population? Describe a skewed population distribution variable and provide an example.

8. What are some alternative online sampling methods? Describe each one.

9. Briefly describe each of the four nonprobability sampling methods.

10. Why is quota sampling often used with a convenience sampling method such as mall intercepts?

11. Provide the marketing researcher's definitions for each of the following populations:
   a. Columbia House, a mail-order house specializing in movie and television DVDs and music CDs, wants to determine interest in a 12-for-1 offer on its CDs to new members.
   b. The manager of your student union is interested in determining if students desire a "universal" debit ID card that will be accepted anywhere on campus and in many stores off campus.
   c. Joy Manufacturing Company decides to conduct a survey to determine the sales potential of a new type of air compressor used by construction companies.

12. Here are four populations and a potential sample frame for each one. With each pair, identify (1) members of the population who are not in the sample frame and (2) sample frame items that are not part of the population. Also, for each one, would you judge the amount of sample frame error to be acceptable or unacceptable?

Population	Sample Frame
a. Buyers of Scope mouthwash	Mailing list of *Consumer Reports* subscribers
b. Listeners of a particular FM radio classical music station	Telephone directory in your city
c. Prospective buyers of a new day planner and prospective clients tracking kit	Members of Sales and Marketing Executives International (a national organization of sales managers)
d. Users of weatherproof decking materials (to build outdoor decks)	Individuals' names registered at a recent home and garden show

13. A market researcher is proposing a survey for the Big Tree Country Club, a private country club that is contemplating several changes in its layout to make the golf course more championship caliber. The researcher is considering three different sample designs as a way to draw a representative sample of the club's golfers. The three alternative designs are:
   a. Station an interviewer at the first hole tee on one day chosen at random, with instructions to ask every 10th golfer to fill out a self-administered questionnaire.
   b. Put a stack of questionnaires on the counter where golfers check in and pay for their golf carts. There would be a sign above the questionnaires, and there would be an incentive for a "free dinner in the clubhouse" for three players who fill out the questionnaires and whose names are selected by a lottery.
   c. Use the city telephone directory to conduct a plus-one dialing procedure. With this procedure, a random page in the directory would be selected, and a name on that page would be selected, both using a table of random numbers. The plus-one system would be applied to that name and every name listed after it until 1,000 golfers are identified and interviewed by telephone.

   Assess the representativeness and other issues associated with this sample problem. Be sure to identify the sample method being contemplated in each case. Which sample method do you recommend using and why?

14. A researcher has the task of estimating how many units of a revolutionary new photocopy machine (it does not require ink cartridges and it is guaranteed not to jam) will be purchased among businesses in Cleveland, Ohio, for the coming annual sales forecast. Her plan is to ask the likelihood that they will purchase the new device, and for those who are "very likely" to purchase, she wants respondents to estimate how many machines their company will buy. She has data to divide the companies into small, medium, and large firms based on number of employees at the Cleveland office.
   a. What sampling plan should be used?
   b. Why?

15. Honda USA is interested in learning what its 550 U.S. dealers think about a new service program the carmaker provided to dealers at the beginning of last year. Honda USA wants to know if the dealers are using the program and, if so, their likes and dislikes about it. The carmaker does not want to survey all 550 dealers but hopes to ensure that the results are representative of all dealers.
   a. What sampling plan should be used?
   b. Why?

16. Applebee's Restaurants has spent several tens of thousands dollars advertising the restaurant during the last two years. Marketing executives want to measure what effect the advertising has had, and they decide to measure top of mind awareness (TOMA). A TOMA score for such a restaurant is the ranking a firm has as a result of asking a representative sample of

consumers in the service area to "name a non-fast-food restaurant." The restaurant that is named by the most persons has the top TOMA score. It is important that Applebee's management conduct the TOMA survey on a representative sample in the metropolitan area.
a. What sampling plan should be used?
b. Why?

17. Belk has a chain of department stores across the South. Top management requires that each store manager collect, maintain, and respond to customer complaint letters and calls. Each store keeps a file of complaint letters that have been received. Top management is considering establishing a more formalized method of monitoring and evaluating the response managers give to the complaint letters. They want some information that will tell them whether they need to develop such a formalized program or whether they can leave well enough alone and allow managers to use their discretion in handling the complaints. They want to review a sample of these complaint letters and the response to them.
a. What sampling plan should be used?
b. Why?

18. Jetadiah Brown wants to establish a pet store called Jet's Pets. Jet thinks there is an opportunity in the south side of the city because he knows that many new subdivisions have been built; and many families have bought homes there. Plus, he knows there are no pet stores located on the south side. This growth in the number of families and the lack of competitors strongly suggest a marketing opportunity for Jet's Pets.

Jet wants to survey the families in two ZIP code areas. Of course, he cannot survey all of them, so he must use a sample. For each of the following possible ways of selecting a sample of the families living in several subdivisions in two ZIP code areas: (1) identify the type of sample method; (2) identify the sample frame; (3) indicate what, if any, sample frame error there is; and (4) indicate the degree to which the resulting sample will be representative of all families living in the two ZIP code areas.
a. Place questionnaires in veterinarian clinics located in the two ZIP code areas for pet owners to fill out while they are waiting for the doctor to examine their pet.
b. Select every 100th name in the city telephone book; call and interview only those who live in the two ZIP code areas.
c. Use a random number system to select a single subdivision located somewhere in the two ZIP code areas, and then place questionnaires in the mailboxes of every home in the selected subdivision.
d. Announce in the local newspaper a "Cutest Dog Contest" with contestants sending in a photo and address information. Use the contestants who live in the two zip code areas as the sample.
e. Go to the local animal shelter and get the addresses of the past pet adopters who live in the two ZIP code areas. Send a mail survey to the nearest neighbor's address for each of the addresses obtained from the animal shelter. For example, if the adopter lives at 1 Green Street, send the mail questionnaire to the occupants at 2 Green Street.

CASE 9.1 PEACEFUL VALLEY

Subdivision: Trouble in Suburbia

Located on the outskirts of a large city, the suburb of Peaceful Valley comprises approximately 6,000 upscale homes. The subdivision came about 10 years ago when a developer built an earthen dam on Peaceful River and created Peaceful Lake, a meandering 20-acre body of water. The lake became the centerpiece of the development, and the first 1,000 half-acre lots were sold as lakefront property. Now Peaceful Valley is fully developed with 50 streets, all approximately the same length with about 120 houses on each street. Peaceful Valley's residents are primarily young, professional, dual-income families with one or two school-age children.

Peaceful Valley has not been living up to its name in recent months. The Suburb Steering Committee has recommended that the community build a swimming pool, tennis court, and meeting room facility on four adjoining vacant lots in the back of the subdivision. Construction cost estimates range from $1.5 million to $2 million, depending on the size of the facility. Currently, every Peaceful Valley homeowner is billed $100 annually for maintenance, security, and upkeep of the development. About 75% of residents pay this fee. To finance the proposed recreational facility, every Peaceful Valley household would be expected to pay a one-time fee of $500, and annual fees would increase to $250 based on facility maintenance cost estimates.

Objections to the recreational facility come from various quarters. For some, the one-time fee is unacceptable; for others, the notion of a recreational facility is not appealing. Some residents have their own swimming pools, belong to local tennis clubs, or otherwise have little use for a meeting room facility. Other Peaceful Valley homeowners see the recreational facility as a wonderful addition where their children could learn to swim, play tennis, or just hang out under supervision.

The president of the Peaceful Valley Suburb Association has decided to conduct a survey to poll the opinions and preferences of Peaceful Valley homeowners regarding the swimming pool, tennis court, and meeting room facility concept. Review the following possible sample methods. Indicate your reactions and answers to the questions associated with each possible method.

1. There is only one street into/out of the subdivision. The president is thinking of paying his teenage daughter to stand at the stop light at the entrance to Peaceful Valley next week between the hours of 7 and 8:30 a.m. to hand out questionnaires to exiting drivers while they wait for the red light to change. The handouts would include addressed, postage-paid envelopes for returns. Identify what sample method the president would be using, list its pros and cons, and indicate how representative a sample would result.

2. The chairperson of the Suburb Steering Committee thinks the 1,000 homeowners whose houses are on the waterfront properties of Peaceful Lake are the best ones to survey because they paid more for their lots, their houses are bigger, and they tend to have lived in Peaceful Valley longer than other residents. If these 1,000 homeowners are used for the sample, what sample method would be involved, what are its pros and cons, and how representative a sample would result?

3. Assume that the Steering Committee chairperson's point that the 1,000 waterfront owners are not the same as the other 5,000 Peaceful Valley Subdivision homeowners is true. How should this fact be used to draw a representative sample of the entire subdivision? Identify the probability sampling method that is most appropriate, and indicate, step-by-step, how it should be applied here.

4. How would you select a simple random sample of those Peaceful Valley homeowners who paid their subdivision association dues last year? What, if any, sample bias, might result from this approach?

5. How could a two-step cluster sample be used here? Identify this sample method and describe how it could be used to select a representative sample of Peaceful Valley households?

CASE 9.2 INTEGRATED CASE

Global Motors

After some deliberation, Cory Rogers of CMG Research and Nick Thomas of Global Motors are now confronted with the data collection method for the Global Motors survey down to the use of an online panel. With the data collection method and questionnaire design settled, Global Motors are now confronted with the data collection step in the marketing research process. While the size of the sample is not precisely known, it is understood that it will be "quite large." However, the principals involved realize that a large sample size will be useless if the sample selection process fails to garner a representative sample.

With some thought and a bit of discussion, the principals have come to agreement that the population is all households in the United States. The major issue to resolve in these population definition debates was whether to include individuals who do not own vehicles. Eventually, it was decided to include the nonowners, as the development and ultimate manufacture of the new models has a five-year horizon, and it is possible that in that time period, nonowners could move into the vehicle owner category. At the same time, the attractiveness of electric and/or hybrid vehicles may be great for vehicle nonowners, and it did not seem prudent to leave out this possibly significant segment of the potential vehicle-buying public. Recent census estimates place the number of U.S. households to be approximately 115 million units.

1. Specify the population definition.
2. If a probability sampling method is to be used, what would be a reasonable sample frame for
   a. A telephone survey
   b. A mail survey
   c. An online survey
3. What are the practical problems involved with drawing a simple random sample of American households (regardless of the survey method)?
4. If random digit dialing was used for the sample plan, what are the advantages and disadvantages of this sample method?
5. Should Global Motors use a probability online panel of U.S. households such as the one maintained by Knowledge Networks, Inc.? With respect to sample design, what are the advantages and disadvantages involved with using this approach? (You may want to review Knowledge Networks, Inc., services by visiting its website at www.knowledgenetworks.com.)

Determining the Size of a Sample

Doing a Telephone Survey? How Many Phone Numbers Will You Need?

Jessica Smith, Vice President, Offline Services, SSI.

In this chapter you will learn how to determine an appropriate sample size, *n*. If you are doing a telephone survey, how many numbers will you need in order to obtain your desired *n*? To answer this question, we asked an expert, Jessica Smith, at Survey Sampling International, to tell you how it's done at the leading sample provider in the world.

You will learn how to calculate the size of a sample in this chapter. Here's a related question: For a given sample size, *n*, how many telephone numbers will you need? This may seem like a difficult task to determine, but by following a few basic rules, it can become quite simple. To start, two pieces of information are required. The first is an estimate of the incidence of qualified individuals in the particular geographic frame you've selected. The second is an idea of how many qualified individuals contacted will actually complete the interview. We call these two pieces of information the *incidence rate* and the *completion rate*. It's useful to be somewhat conservative in projecting these rates, since these figures are rarely known as facts until the survey has been completed.

Next, you must know the number of completed interviews required, or the *n*. Then, it's necessary to have information on what we call the *working phones rate*. The working phones rate varies with the type of sample being used.

The equation we use to calculate the number of phone numbers needed for a project starts with the number of completed interviews required, *n*, divided by the working phones rate. That result is then divided by the incidence rate. Then, that quotient is divided by the contact and cooperation rates to determine the total number of numbers you will need for your project.

SSI's Formula for Determining the Number of Telephone Numbers Needed

$$\text{Number of telephone numbers needed} = \frac{\text{complete interviews}}{\text{working phone rate} \times \text{incidence} \times \text{completion rate}}$$

Where:

Completed Interviews = Number of interviews required for a survey (n).

Completion Rate = Percent of qualified respondents who complete the interview (taking into account circumstances such as refusals, answering machines, no answers, and busy signals).

Working Phone Rate = Percent of working residential telephone numbers for the entire sample. Rate varies by country and also depends on the selection methodology. Typically, in the United States, working phone rate ranges from 23% to 53%.

Incidence = The percent of a group that qualifies to be selected into a sample (to participate in a survey). Qualification may be based on one or many criteria, such as age, income, product use, or place of residence. The incidence varies depending on the factors specified by the client.
Incidence = product incidence × geographic incidence × demographic incidence

Product Incidence = Percentage of respondents who qualify for a survey based on screening for factors like product use, ailments, or a particular behavior.

Geographic Incidence = Likelihood of a respondent living in the targeted geographic area, expressed as a percentage.

Demographic Incidence = Percentage of respondents who qualify for a survey based on demographic criteria. The most common targets include age, income, and race.

Photo: Kurhan/Fotolia

For example, if 800 completed interviews are needed, the working phone rate is 50%, the incidence is 70%, and the completion rate is estimated to be 25%, 9,143 numbers should be ordered (800 / 0.50 / 0.70 / 0.25).

Text and images: By permission, SSI.

Science. People. Innovention

Marketing managers typically confuse sample size with sample representativeness.

In the previous chapter, you learned that the method of sample selection determines its representativeness. Unfortunately, many managers falsely believe that sample size and sample representativeness are related, but they are not. By studying this chapter, you will learn that the size of a sample directly affects its degree of accuracy or error, which is completely different from representativeness.

Consider this example to demonstrate that there is no relationship between the size of a sample and its representativeness of the population from which it is drawn. Suppose we want to find out what percentage of the U.S. workforce dresses "business casual" most of the workweek. We take a convenience sample by standing on a corner of Wall Street in New York City, and we ask everyone who will talk to us about whether they come to work in business casual dress. At the end of one week, we have questioned more than 5,000 respondents in our survey. Are these people representative of the U.S. workforce population? No, of course, they are not. In fact, they are not even representative of New York City workers because a nonprobability sampling method was used. What if we asked 10,000 New Yorkers with the same sample method? No matter what its size, the sample would still be unrepresentative for the same reason.

The selection method, not the size of the sample, determines a sample's representativeness.

There are two important points. First, only a probability sample, typically referred to as a *random sample*, is truly representative of the population, and, second, the size of that random sample determines the sample's accuracy of findings.[1] **Sample accuracy** refers to how close a random sample's statistic (for example, percent of yes answers to a particular question) is to the population's value (that is, the true percent of agreement in the population) it represents. Sample size has a direct bearing on how accurate the sample's findings are relative to the true values in the population. If a random sample has 5 respondents, it is more accurate than if it had only 1 respondent; 10 respondents are more accurate than 5 respondents and so forth. Common sense tells us that larger random samples are more accurate than smaller random samples. But, as you will learn in this chapter, 5 is not 5 times more accurate than 1, and 10 is not twice as accurate as 5. The important points to remember at this time are that (1) sample method determines a sample's representativeness, while (2) sample size determines a random sample's accuracy. Precisely how accuracy is affected by the size of the sample constitutes a major focus of this chapter.

The accuracy of a sample is a measure of how closely it reports the true values of the population it represents.

We are concerned with sample size because a significant cost savings occurs when the correct sample size is calculated and used. To counter the high refusal rate that marketing research companies encounter when they do surveys, many companies have created respondent panels, as described earlier in this textbook. Tens and hundreds of thousands of consumers have joined these panels with the agreement that they will respond to survey requests quickly, completely, and honestly. These panels are mini-populations that represent consumer markets of many types. The panel companies sell random access to their panelists for a fee per respondent, typically based on the length of the survey. If a marketing research project director requests a sample size of 10,000 respondents and the panel company charges $5 per respondent, the sample cost is 10,000 times $5, or $50,000. A sample size of 1,000 respondents would cost 1,000 times $5, or $5,000. Thus, if 1,000 is the "correct" sample size, there would be a $45,000 savings in the marketing research project cost. When marketing research proposals are submitted, the cost or price is included. The 10,000 sample size bid would be significantly higher in price than would be the 1,000 sample size bid, and it would probably not be competitive for that reason.

Accordingly, this chapter is concerned with random sample size determination methods. To be sure, sample size determination can be a complicated process,[2,3,4] but our aim in this chapter is to simplify the process and make it more intuitive. To begin, we share some axioms about sample size. These statements serve as the basis for the confidence interval approach, which is the best sample size determination method to use; we describe its underlying notions of variability, allowable sample error, and level of confidence. These are combined into a simple formula to calculate sample size, and we give some examples of how the formula works. Next, we describe four other popular methods used to decide on a sample's size that have important limitations. Finally, we briefly review some practical considerations and special situations that affect the final sample size.

Sample Size Axioms

How to determine the number of respondents in a particular sample is actually one of the simplest decisions in the marketing research process,[5] but it may appear bewildering because formulas are used. A sample size decision is usually a compromise between what is theoretically perfect and what is practically feasible. This chapter presents the fundamental concepts that underlie sample size decisions.[6]

There are two good reasons a marketing researcher should have a basic understanding of sample size determination. First, many practitioners have a **large sample size bias**, which is a false belief that sample size determines a sample's representativeness. This bias is represented by a common question: "How large a sample should we have to be representative?" We have already established that there is no relationship between sample size and representativeness, so you already know one of the basics of sample size determination. Second, a marketing researcher should have a basic understanding of sample size determination because sample size is often a major cost factor, particularly for personal interviews but even with telephone and online surveys. Consequently, understanding how sample size is determined will enable researchers to help managers better manage their resources.

Table 10.1, which lists eight axioms about sample size and accuracy, should help to contradict the large sample size bias among many marketing research clients. An axiom is a universal truth, meaning that the statement will aways be correct. However, we must point out that these axioms pertain only to probability samples, so they are true only as long as a random sample is being used. Remember, no matter how astonishing one of our statements might seem, it will always be true when dealing with a random sample. As we describe the confidence interval method of sample size determination, we will refer to each axiom in turn and help you understand the axiom.

> The size of a sample has nothing to do with its representativeness. Sample size affects the sample accuracy.

TABLE 10.1 The Axioms of Random Sample Size and Sample Accuracy

1. The only perfectly accurate sample is a census.
2. A random sample will always have some inaccuracy, which is referred to as *margin of sample error* or simply *sample error*.
3. The larger a random sample is, the more accurate it is, meaning the less margin of sample error it has.
4. Margin of sample error can be calculated with a simple formula and expressed as a ±% number.
5. You can take any finding in the survey, replicate the survey with a random sample of the same size, and be "very likely" to find the same finding within the ±% range of the original sample's finding.
6. In almost all cases, the margin of sample error of a random sample is independent of the size of the population.
7. A random sample size can be a tiny percent of the population size and still have a small margin of sample error.
8. The size of a random sample depends on the client's desired accuracy (acceptable margin of sample error) balanced against the cost of data collection for that sample size.

The Confidence Interval Method of Determining Sample Size

The most correct method of determining sample size is the **confidence interval approach**, which applies the concepts of accuracy (margin of sample error), variability, and confidence interval to create a "correct" sample size. This approach is used by national opinion polling companies and most marketing researchers. To describe the confidence interval approach to sample size determination, we first must describe the four underlying concepts.

SAMPLE SIZE AND ACCURACY

The first axiom, *"The only perfectly accurate sample is a census,"* is easy to understand. You should be aware that a survey has two types of error: nonsampling error and sampling error.

Nonsampling error pertains to all sources of error other than the sample selection method and sample size, including problem specification mistakes, question bias, data recording errors, or incorrect analysis. Recall from Chapter 9 that sampling error involves both sample selection method and sample size.[7] With a census, every member of the population is selected, so there is no error in selection. Because a census accounts for every single individual, and if we assume there is no nonsampling error, it is perfectly accurate, meaning that it has no sampling error.

However, a census is almost always infeasible due to cost and practical reasons, so we must use some random sampling technique. This fact brings us to the second axiom, *"A random sample will always have some inaccuracy, which is referred to as 'margin of sample error' or simply 'sample error.'"* This axiom emphasizes that no random sample is a *perfect* representation of the population. However, it is important to remember that a random sample is nonetheless a *very good* representation of the population, even if it is not perfectly accurate.

The third axiom, *"The larger a random sample is, the more accurate it is, meaning the less margin of sample error it has"* serves notice that there is a relationship between sample size and accuracy of the sample. This relationship is presented graphically in Figure 10.1. In this figure, margin of sample error is listed on the vertical axis, and sample size is noted on the horizontal axis. The graph shows the sample error levels for samples ranging in size from 50 to 2,000. The shape of the graph is consistent with the third axiom because margin of sample error decreases as sample size increases. However, you should immediately notice that the graph is not a straight line. In other words, doubling sample size does not result in halving the sample error. The relationship is an asymptotic curve that will never achieve 0% error.

There is another important property of the sample error graph. As you look at the graph, note that at a sample size of around 1,000, the margin of sample error is about ±3% (actually ±3.1%), and it decreases at a very slow rate with larger sample sizes. In other words, once a sample is greater than, say, 1,000, large gains in accuracy are not realized even with large

FIGURE 10.1
The Relationship Between Sample Size and Sample Error

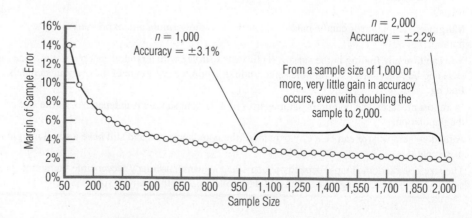

increases in the size of the sample. In fact, if it is already ±3.1% in accuracy, little additional accuracy is possible.

With the lower end of the sample size axis, however, large gains in accuracy can be made with a relatively small sample size increase. You can see this vividly by looking at the sample errors associated with smaller sample sizes in Table 10.2. For example, with a sample size of 50, the margin of sample error is ±13.9%, whereas with a sample size of 200 it is ±6.9%, meaning that the accuracy of the 200 sample is roughly double that of the 50 sample. But as was just described, such huge gains in accuracy are not the case at the other end of the sample size scale because of the nature of the curved relationship. You will see this fact if you compare the sample error of a sample size of 2,000 (±2.2%) to that of a sample size of 10,000 (±1.0%): with 8,000 more in the sample, we have improved the accuracy only by 1.2%. So, while the accuracy surely does increase with greater and greater sample sizes, there is only a minute gain in accuracy when these sizes are more than 1,000 respondents.

The sample error values and the sample error graph were produced via the fourth axiom:[8] *"Margin of sample error can be calculated with a simple formula, and expressed as a ±% number."* The formula follows:

Margin of sample error formula

$$\pm \ \text{Margin of Sample Error} = 1.96 \times \sqrt{\frac{p \times q}{n}}$$

Yes, this formula is simple; "n" is the sample size, and there is a constant, 1.96. But what are p and q?

p and q: THE CONCEPT OF VARIABILITY

Let's set the scene. We have a population, and we want to know what percent of the population responds "yes" to the question, "The next time you order a pizza, will you use Domino's?" We will use a random sample to estimate the population percent of "yes" answers. What are the possibilities? We might find 100% of respondents answering "yes" in the sample, we might find 0% of yes responses, or we might find something in between, say, 50% "yes" responses in the sample.

When we find a wide dispersion of responses—that is, when we do not find one response option accounting for a large number of respondents relative to the other items—we say that the results have much variability. **Variability** is defined as the amount of dissimilarity (or similarity) in respondents' answers to a particular question. If most respondents indicate the same answer on the response scale, the distribution has little variability because respondents are highly similar. On the other hand, if respondents are evenly spread across the question's response options, there is much variability because respondents are quite dissimilar. So, the 100% and the 0% agreement cases have little variability because everyone answers the same, while the 50% in-between case has a great deal of variability because with any two respondents, one answers "yes", while the other one answers "no".

The sample error formula pertains only to nominal data, or data in which the response items are categorical. We recommend that you always think of a yes/no question; the greater the similarity, meaning that the more you find people saying yes in the population, the less the variability in the responses. For example, we may find that the question "The next time you order a pizza, will you use Domino's?" yields a 90% to 10% distribution split between "yes" versus "no". In other words, most of the respondents give the same answer, meaning that there is much similarity in the responses and the variability is low. In contrast, if the question results

TABLE 10.2   Sample Sizes and Margin of Sample Error

Sample Size (n)	Margin of Sample Error (Accuracy Level)
10	±31.0%
50	±13.9%
100	±9.8%
200	±6.9%
400	±4.9%
500	±4.4%
750	±3.6%
1,000	±3.1%
1,500	±2.5%
2,000	±2.2%
5,000	±1.4%
10,000	±1.0%

With a sample size of 1,000 or more, very little gain in accuracy occurs even with doubling or tripling the sample.

Variability refers to how similar or dissimilar responses are to a given question.

The less variability in the population, the smaller will be the sample size.

Photo: Nomad_Soul/Shutterstock

A 50/50 split in response signifies maximum variability (dissimilarity) in the population, whereas a 90/10 split signifies little variability.

in a 50/50 split, the overall response pattern is (maximally) dissimilar, and there is much variability. You can see the variability of responses in Figure 10.2. With the 90/10 split, the graph has one high side (90%) and one low side (10%), meaning almost everyone agrees on Domino's. In contrast, with disagreement or much variability in people's answers, both sides of the graph are near even (50%/50%).

The Domino's Pizza example relates to p and q in the following way:

p = percent saying yes
q = 100% − p, or percent saying no

In other words, p and q are complementary numbers that must always sum to 100%, as in the cases of 90% + 10% and 50% + 50%. The p represents the variable of interest in the population that we are trying to estimate.

In our sample error formula, p and q are multiplied. The largest possible product of p times q is 2,500, or 50% times 50%. You can verify this fact by multiplying other combinations of p and q, such as 90/10 (900), 80/20 (1,600), or 60/40 (2,400). Every combination will have a result smaller than 2,500; the most lopsided combination of 99/1 (99) yields the smallest product. If we assume the worst possible case of maximum variability, or 50/50 disagreement, the sample error formula becomes even simpler and can be given with two constants, 1.96 and 2,500, as follows:

Sample error formula with $p = 50\%$ and $q = 50\%$

$$\pm \text{ Margin of Sample Error } \% = 1.96 \times \sqrt{\frac{2{,}500}{n}}$$

This is the **maximum margin of sample error** formula we used to create the sample error graph in Figure 10.1 and the sample error percentages in Table 10.2. To determine how much sample error is associated with a random sample of a given size, all you need to do is to plug in the sample size in this formula.

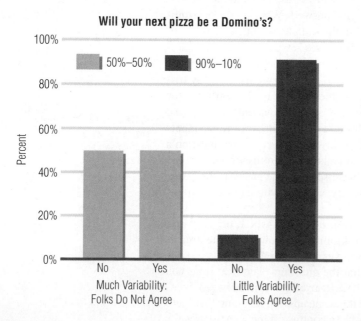

Will your next pizza be a Domino's?

FIGURE 10.2

THE CONCEPT OF A CONFIDENCE INTERVAL

The fifth sample size axiom states, *"You can take any finding in the survey, replicate the survey with a random sample of the same size, and be "very likely" to find the same finding within the ±% range of the original sample's finding."* This axiom is based on the concept of a confidence interval.

A **confidence interval** is a range whose endpoints define a certain percentage of the responses to a question. A confidence interval is based on the normal, or bell-shaped, curve commonly found in statistics. Figure 10.3 reveals that the properties of the normal curve are such that 1.96 multiplied by the standard deviation theoretically defines the end points for 95% of the distribution.

The theory called the **central limit theorem** underlies many statistical concepts, and this theory is the basis of the fifth axiom. A replication is a repeat of the original, so if we repeated our Domino's survey a great many times—perhaps 1,000—with a fresh random sample of the same size and we made a bar chart of all 1,000 percents of "yes" results, the central limit theorem holds that our bar chart would look like a normal curve. Figure 10.4 illustrates how the bar chart would look if 50% of our population members intended to use Domino's the next time they ordered a pizza.

Figure 10.4 reveals that 95% of the replications fall within ±1.96 multiplied by the sample error. In our example, 1,000 random samples, each with sample size (n) equal to 100, were taken; the percent of yes answers was calculated for each sample; and all of these were plotted in line chart. The sample error for a sample size of 100 is calculated as follows:

Sample error formula with $p = 50\%$, $q = 50\%$, and $n = 100$

$$
\begin{aligned}
\pm \text{ Margin of Sample Error \%} &= 1.96 \times \sqrt{\frac{2,500}{n}} \\
&= 1.96 \times \sqrt{\frac{2,500}{100}} \\
&= 1.96 \times \sqrt{25} \\
&= 1.96 \times 5 \\
&= \pm 9.8
\end{aligned}
$$

which means that the limits of the 95% confidence interval in our example is 50% ± 9.8%, or 40.2% to 59.8%.

The confidence interval is calculated as follows:

Confidence interval formula

Confidence interval = $p \pm$ margin of sample error

How can a researcher use the confidence interval? This is a good time to leave the theoretical and move to the practical aspects of sample size. The confidence interval approach allows the researcher to predict what would be found if a survey were replicated many times. Of course, no client would agree to the cost of 1,000 replications, but the researcher can say, "I found that 50% of the sample intends to order Domino's the next time. I am very confident that the true population percent is between 40.2% and 59.8%; in fact, I am confident that

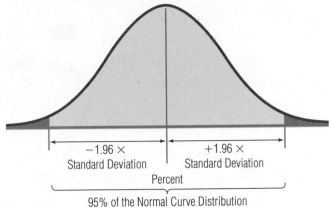

−1.96 × Standard Deviation +1.96 × Standard Deviation

Percent

95% of the Normal Curve Distribution

FIGURE 10.3 Normal Curves with its 95% Properties

A confidence interval defines end points based on knowledge of the area under a bell-shaped curve.

To learn about the central limit theorem, launch **www.youtube.com** and search for "The Central Limit Theorem."

The confidence interval gives the range of findings if the survey were replicated many times with the identical sample size.

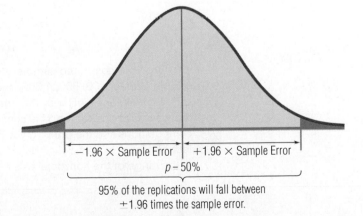

−1.96 × Sample Error +1.96 × Sample Error

p − 50%

95% of the replications will fall between +1.96 times the sample error.

FIGURE 10.4 Plotting the Findings of 1,000 Replications of the Domino's Pizza Survey

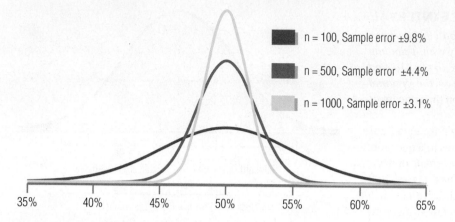

FIGURE 10.5 **Sampling Distributions Showing How the Sample Error Is Less with Larger Sample Sizes**

if I did this survey over 1,000 times, 95% of the findings will fall in this range." Notice that the researcher never does 1,000 replications; she just uses one random sample, uses this sample's accuracy information from p and q, and applies the central limit theorem assumptions to calculate the confidence intervals.

What if the confidence interval was too wide? That is, what if the client felt that a range from about 40% to 60% was not precise enough? Figure 10.5 shows how the sample size affects the shape of the theoretical sampling distribution and, more important, the confidence interval range. Notice in Figure 10.5 that the larger the sample, the smaller the range of the confidence interval. Why? Because larger sample sizes have less sample error, meaning that they are more accurate, and the range or width of the confidence interval is the smaller with more accurate samples.

 Active Learning

How Does the Level of Confidence Affect the Sample Accuracy Curve?

Thus far, the sample error formula has used a z value of 1.96, which corresponds to the 95% level of confidence. However, marketing researchers sometimes use another level of confidence—the 99% level of confidence with the corresponding z value of 2.58. For this Active Learning exercise, use the sample error formula with $p = 50\%$ and $q = 50\%$ but use a z value of 2.58 and calculate the sample error associated with sample sizes of the following:

Sample Size (n)	Sample Error (e)
100	±_____%
500	±_____%
1,000	±_____%
2,000	±_____%

Plot your computed sample error ± numbers that correspond to 99% confidence level sample sizes of 100, 500, 1,000, and 2,000 in Figure 10.1. Connect your four plotted points with a curved line similar to the one already in the graph. Use the percents in Table 10.2 to draw a similar line for the 95% confidence level sample sizes sample error values. Using your computations and the drawing you have just made, write down two conclusions about the effect of a level of confidence different from 95% on the amount of sample error with samples in the range of the horizontal axis in Figure 10.3.

1. _____

2. _____

HOW POPULATION SIZE (*N*) AFFECTS SAMPLE SIZE

Perhaps you noticed something that is absent in all of these discussions and calculations, and that element is mentioned in the sixth sample size axiom, *"In almost all cases, the margin of sample error of a random sample is independent of the size of the population."* Our formulas do not include *N*, the size of the population! We have been calculating sample error and confidence intervals without taking the size of the population into account. Does this mean that a sample of 100 will have the same sample error and confidence interval of ±9.8% for a population of 20 million people who watched the last SuperBowl, 2 million Kleenex tissue buyers, and 200,000 Scottish Terrier owners? Yes, it does. The only time the population size is a consideration in sample size determination[9] is in the case of a "small population," and this possibility is discussed in the final section in this chapter.

Because the size of the sample is independent of the population size, the seventh sample size axiom, *"A random sample size can be a very tiny percent of the population size and still have a small margin of sample error,"* can now be understood. National opinion polls tend to use sample sizes ranging from 1,000 to 1,200 people, meaning that the sample error is around ±3%, or highly accurate. In Table 10.2, you will see that a sample size of 5,000 yields an error of ±1.4%, which is a very small error level, yet 5,000 is less than 1% of 1 million, and a great many consumer markets—cola drinkers, condominium owners, debit card users, allergy sufferers, home gardeners, Internet surfers, and so on—each comprise many millions of customers. Here is one more example to drive our point home: A sample of 500 is just as accurate for the entire population of China (1.3 billion people) as it is for the Montgomery, Alabama, area (375,000 people) as long as a random sample is taken in both cases. In both cases, the sample error is ±4.4%.

With few exceptions, the sample size and the size of the population are not related to each other.

To learn about sample size, launch **www.youtube.com** and search for "How sample size is determined."

SPSS®

SPSS Student Assistant: Milk Bone Biscuits: Setup Basics for Your SPSS Dataset

The Sample Size Formula

You are now acquainted with the basic concepts essential to understanding sample size determination using the confidence interval approach. To calculate the proper sample size for a survey, only three items are required: (1) the variability believed to be in the population, (2) the acceptable margin of sample error, and (3) the level of confidence required in your estimates of the population values. This section will describe the formula used to compute sample size via the **confidence interval method**. As we describe the formula, we will present some of the concepts you learned earlier a bit more formally.

To compute sample size, only three items are required: variability, acceptable sample error, and confidence level.

DETERMINING SAMPLE SIZE VIA THE CONFIDENCE INTERVAL FORMULA

As you would expect, there is a formula that includes our three required items.[10] When considering a percentage, the formula is as follows:[11]

Standard sample size formula

$$n = \frac{z^2(pq)}{e^2}$$

where

   n = the sample size

   z = standard error associated with the chosen level of confidence (typically, 1.96)

   p = estimated percent in the population

   $q = 100 - p$

   e = acceptable margin of sample error

The standard sample size formula is applicable if you are concerned with the nominally scaled questions in the survey, such as yes or no questions.

Variability: _p_ x _q_ This sample size formula is used if we are focusing on some nominally measured question in the survey. For instance, when conducting our Domino's Pizza survey, our major concern might be the percentage of pizza buyers who intend to buy Domino's. If no one is uncertain, there are two possible answers: those who do and those who do not. Earlier, we illustrated that if our pizza buyers' population has little variability—that is, if almost everyone, say, 90%, is a Domino's Pizza-holic—this belief will be reflected in the sample size formula calculation. With little variation in the population, we know that we can take smaller samples because this is accommodated in the formula by $p \times q$. The estimated percent in the population, p, is the mechanism that performs this translation along with q, which is always determined by p as $q = 100\% - p$.

Managers sometimes find it unbelievable that a sample can be small yet highly accurate.

Photo: Andresr/Shutterstock

In marketing research, a 95% or 99% level of confidence is standard practice.

Acceptable Margin of Sample Error: _e_ The formula includes another factor—acceptable margin of sample error. **Acceptable margin of sample error** is the term, e, which is the amount of sample error the researcher will permit to be associated with the survey. Notice that since we are calculating the sample size, n, the sample error is treated as a variable, meaning that the researcher (and client) will decide on some desirable or allowable level of sample error and then calculate the sample size that will guarantee that the acceptable sample error will be delivered. Recall that sample error is used to indicate how closely to the population percentage you want the many replications, if you were to take them.

That is, if we performed any survey with a p value that was to be estimated—who intends to buy from Walmart, IBM, Shell, Allstate, or any other vendor versus any other vendor—the acceptable sample error notion would hold. Small acceptable sample error translates into a low percent, such as ±3% or less, whereas high acceptable sample error translates into a large percent, such as ±10% or higher.

Level of Confidence: _z_ Finally, we need to decide on a level of confidence, or, to relate to our previous section, the percent of area under the normal curve described by our calculated confidence intervals. Thus far, we have used the constant 1.96 because 1.96 is the z value that pertains to 95% confidence intervals. Marketing researchers typically worry only about the 95% or 99% level of confidence. The 95% level of confidence is by far the most commonly used one, so we used 1.96 in the examples earlier and referred to it as a constant because it is the chosen z in most cases.

Actually, any level of confidence ranging from 1% to 100% is possible, but you would need to consult a z table to find the corresponding value. Market researchers almost never deviate from 95%, but if they do, 99% is the likely level to be used. We have itemized the z values for the 99% and 95% levels of confidence in Table 10.3 for easy reference.

We are now finally ready to calculate sample size. Let us assume there is great expected variability ($p = 50\%$, $q = 50\%$) and we want ±10% acceptable sample error at the 95% level of confidence ($z = 1.96$). To determine the sample size needed, we calculate as follows:

Sample size computed with _p_ = 50%, _q_ = 50%, and _e_ = ±10%

$$
\begin{aligned}
n &= \frac{1.96^2 (50 \times 50)}{10^2} \\
&= \frac{3.84(2,500)}{100} \\
&= \frac{9,600}{100} \\
&= 96
\end{aligned}
$$

TABLE 10.3   Values of _z_ for 95% and 99% Level of Confidence

Level of Confidence	z
95%	1.96
99%	2.58

For further validation of the use of the confidence interval approach, recall our previous comment that most national opinion polls use sample sizes of about 1,100, and they claim about ±3% accuracy (allowable sample error). Using the 95% level of confidence, the computations would be:

Sample size computed with $p = 50\%$, $q = 50\%$, and $e = 3\%$

$$n = \frac{1.96^2(50 \times 50)}{3^2}$$
$$= \frac{3.84(2,500)}{9}$$
$$= \frac{9,600}{9}$$
$$= 1,067$$

In other words, if these national polls were to be ±3% accurate at the 95% confidence level, they would need to have sample sizes of 1,067 (or about 1,100 respondents). The next time you read in the newspaper or see on television a report on a national opinion poll, check the sample size to see if there is a footnote or reference on the "margin of error." It is a good bet that you will find the error to be somewhere close to ±3% and the sample size to be in the 1,100 range.

What if the researcher wanted a 99% level of confidence in estimates? The computations would be as follows:

99% confidence interval sample size computed with $p = 50\%$, $q = 50\%$, and $e = 3\%$

$$n = \frac{2.58^2(50 \times 50)}{3^2}$$
$$= \frac{6.66(2,500)}{9}$$
$$= \frac{16,650}{9}$$
$$= 1,850$$

 Marketing Research on YouTube™ To learn about sample size using proportions, launch **www.youtube.com** and search for "How to calculate sample size proportions."

Thus, if a survey were to have ±3% allowable sample error at the 99% level of confidence, it would need to have a sample size of 1,850, assuming the maximum variability (50%).

Active Learning

Sample Size Calculations Practice

While you can mentally follow the step-by-step sample size calculations examples we have just described, it is always more insightful for someone just learning about sample size to perform the calculations themselves. In this Active Learning exercise, refer back to the standard sample size formula, and use it to calculate the appropriate sample size for each of the following six cases. Each case represents a different question on a survey.

Case	Confidence Level	Value of p	Allowable Error	Sample Size (write your answer below)
Alpha	95%	65%	±3.5%	_____
Beta	99%	75%	±3.5%	_____
Gamma	95%	60%	±5%	_____
Delta	99%	70%	±5%	_____
Epsilon	95%	50%	±2%	_____
Zeta	99%	55%	±2%	_____

MARKETING RESEARCH INSIGHT 10.1 *Practical Application*

Determining Sample Size Using the Mean: An Example of Variability of a Scale

We have presented the standard sample size formula in this chapter, which assumes that the researcher is working with a case of percentages (p and q). However, there are instances when the researcher is more concerned with the mean of a variable, in which case the percentage sample size formula does not fit. Instead, the researcher must use a different formula for sample size that includes the variability expressed as a standard deviation. That is, this situation calls for the use of the standard deviation, instead of p and q, to indicate the amount of variation. In this case, the sample size formula changes slightly to be the following:

Sample size formula for a mean

$$n = \frac{s^2 z^2}{e^2}$$

where

- n = the sample size
- z = standard error associated with the chosen level of confidence (typically, 1.96)
- s = variability indicated by an estimated standard deviation
- e = the amount of precision or allowable error in the sample estimate of the population

Although this formula looks different from the one for a percentage, it applies the same logic and key concepts.[12] As you can see, the formula determines sample size by multiplying the squares of the variability (s) and level of confidence values (z) and dividing that product by the square of the desired precision value (e).

First, let us look at how variability of the population is a part of the formula. It appears in the form of s, or the estimated standard deviation of the population. This means that, because we are estimating the population mean, we need to have some knowledge of or at least a good guess at how much variability there is in the population. We must use the standard deviation because it expresses this variation. Unfortunately, unlike our percentage sample size case, there is no "50% equals the most variation" counterpart, so we have to rely on some prior knowledge about the population for our estimate of the standard deviation. That prior knowledge could come from a previous study on the same population or a pilot study.

If information on the population variability is truly unknown and a pilot study is out of the question, a researcher can use a range estimate and knowledge that the range is approximated by the mean ±3 standard deviations (a total of 6). On occasion, a market researcher finds he or she is working with metric scale data, not nominal data. For instance, the researcher might have a 10-point importance scale or a 7-point satisfaction scale that is the critical variable with respect to determining sample size. Finally, we must express e, which is the acceptable error around the sample mean when we ultimately estimate the population mean for our survey. In the formula, e must be expressed in terms of the measurement units appropriate to the question. For example, on a 1–10 scale, e would be expressed as, say .25 scale units.

Suppose, for example, that a critical question on the survey involved a scale in which respondents rated their satisfaction with the client company's products on a scale of 1 to 10. If respondents use this scale, the theoretical range would be 10, and 10 divided by 6 equals a standard deviation of 1.7, which would be the variability estimate. Note that this would be a conservative estimate as respondents might not use the entire 1–10 scale, or the mean might not equal 5, the midpoint, meaning that 1.7 is the largest variability estimate possible in this case.[13]

SPSS®

SPSS Student Assistant: Milk Bone Biscuits: Modifying Variables and Values

When estimating a standard deviation, researchers may rely on (a) prior knowledge of the population (previous study) or (b) a pilot study or (c) divide the range by 6.

A researcher can calculate sample size using either a percentage or a mean. We have just described (and you have just used in the Active Learning exercise) the percentage approach to computing sample size. Marketing Research Insight 10.1 describes how to determine sample size using a mean. Although the formulas are different, the basic concepts involved are identical.

Practical Considerations in Sample Size Determination

Although we have discussed how variability, acceptable sample error, and confidence level are used to calculate sample size, we have not discussed the criteria used by the marketing manager and researcher to determine these factors. General guidelines follow.

HOW TO ESTIMATE VARIABILITY IN THE POPULATION

When using the standard sample size formula using percentages, there are two alternatives: (1) expect the worst case or (2) guesstimate what is the actual variability. We have shown that with percentages, the **worst case**, or most, **variability** is 50%/50%. This assumption is the most conservative one, and it will result in the calculation of the largest possible sample size.

On the other hand, a researcher may want to use an educated guess about p, or the percentage, in order to lower the sample size. Remember that any *p/q* combination other than 50%/50% will result in a lower calculated sample size because *p* times *q* is in the numerator of the formula. A lower sample size means less effort, time, and cost, so there are good reasons for a researcher to try to estimate *p* rather than to take the worst case.

Surprisingly, information about the target population often exists in many forms. Researchers can estimate variance in a population by seeking prior studies on the population or by conducting a small pilot study. Census descriptions are available in the form of secondary data, and compilations and bits of information may be gained from groups such as chambers of commerce, local newspapers, state agencies, groups promoting commercial development, and a host of other similar organizations. Moreover, many populations under study by firms are known to them either formally through prior research studies or informally through business experiences. All of this information combines to help the research project director to grasp the variability in the population. If the project director has conflicting information or is worried about the timeliness or some other aspect of the information about the population's variability, he or she may conduct a pilot study to estimate *p* more confidently.[14,15]

HOW TO DETERMINE THE AMOUNT OF ACCEPTABLE SAMPLE ERROR

The marketing manager intuitively knows that small samples are less accurate, on average, than are large samples. But it is rare for a marketing manager to think in terms of sample error. It is up to the researcher to educate the manager on what might be acceptable or "standard" sample error.

Translated in terms of accuracy, the more accurate the marketing decision maker desires the estimate to be, the larger must be the sample size. It is the task of the marketing research director to extract from the marketing decision maker the acceptable range of allowable margin of error sufficient to make a decision. As you have learned, the acceptable sample error is specified as a plus or minus percent. That is, the researcher might say to the marketing decision maker, "I can deliver an estimate that is within ±10% of the actual figure." If the marketing manager is confused at this, the researcher can next say, "This means that if I find that 45% of the sample is thinking seriously about leaving your competitors and buying your brand, I will be telling you that I estimate that between 35% and 55% of your competitors' buyers are thinking about jumping over to be your customers." The conversation would continue until the marketing manager feels comfortable with the confidence interval range.

HOW TO DECIDE ON THE LEVEL OF CONFIDENCE

All marketing decisions are made under a certain amount of risk, and it is mandatory to incorporate the estimate of risk, or at least some sort of a notion of uncertainty, into sample size determination. Because sample statistics are estimates of population values, the proper approach is to use the sample information to generate a range in which the population value is anticipated to fall. Because the sampling process is imperfect, it is appropriate to use an estimate of sampling error in the calculation of this range. Using proper statistical terminology, the range is what we have called the confidence interval. The researcher reports the range and the confidence he or she has that the range includes the population figure.

As we have indicated, the typical approach in marketing research is to use the standard confidence interval of 95%. This level translates to a *z* of 1.96. As you may recall from your statistics course, any level of confidence between 1% and 99.9% is possible, but the only other level of confidence that market researchers usually consider is 99%. With the 99% level of confidence, the corresponding *z* value is 2.58. The 99% level of confidence means that if the survey were replicated many times with the sample size determined by using 2.58 in the sample size formula, 99% of the sample *p*'s would fall in the sample error range, or *e*.

By estimating p to be other than 50%, the researcher can reduce the sample size and save money.

Researchers can estimate variability by (a) assuming maximum variability ($p = 50\%$, $q = 50\%$), (b) seeking previous studies on the population, or (c) conducting a small pilot study.

Marketing researchers often must help decision makers understand the sample size implications of their requests for high precision, expressed as acceptable sample error.

Use of 95% or 99% level of confidence is standard in sample size determination.

However, since the z value is in the numerator of the sample size formula, an increase from 1.96 to 2.58 will increase the sample size. In fact, for any given sample error, the use of the 99% level of confidence will increase sample size by about 73%. In other words, using the 99% confidence level has profound effects on the calculated sample size. Are you surprised that most marketing researchers opt for a z of 1.96?

HOW TO BALANCE SAMPLE SIZE WITH THE COST OF DATA COLLECTION

The researcher must take cost into consideration when determining sample size.

Perhaps you thought we had forgotten to comment on the final sample size axiom, ***"The size of a random sample depends on the client's desired accuracy (acceptable margin of sample error) balanced against the cost of data collection for that sample size."*** This is a crucial axiom, as it describes the reality of almost all sample size determination decisions. In a previous chapter, we commented on the cost of the research versus the value of the research and that there is always a need to make sure that the cost of the research does not exceed the value of the information expected from that research. In situations where data collection costs are significant, such as with personal interviews or in the case of buying access to online panel respondents, cost and value issues come into play vividly with sample size determination.[16] Because using the 99% level of confidence impacts sample size considerably, market researchers almost always use the 95% level of confidence.

To help you understand how to balance sample size and cost, let's consider the typical sample size determination case. First, 95% level of confidence is used, so $z = 1.96$. Next, the $p = q = 50\%$ situation is customarily assumed as it is the worst possible case of variability. Then, the researcher and marketing manager decide on a *preliminary* acceptable sample error level. As an example, let's take case of a researcher and a client initially agreeing to a ±3.5% sample error.

Using the sample size formula, the sample size, n, is calculated as follows.

Sample size computed with $p = 50\%$, $q = 50\%$, and $e = 3.5\%$

$$n = \frac{1.96^2(50 \times 50)}{3.5^2}$$

$$= \frac{3.84(2,500)}{12.25}$$

$$= \frac{9,00}{12.25}$$

$$= 784 \text{ (rounded up)}$$

A table that relates data collection cost and sample error is a useful tool when deciding the survey sample size.

If the cost per completed interview averages around $20, then the cost of data collection for a sample size is 784 times $20, which equals $15,680. The client now knows the sample size necessary for a ±3.5% sample error and the cost for these interviews. If the client has issues with this cost, the researcher may create a table with alternative accuracy levels and their associated sample sizes based on his or her knowledge of the standard sample size formula. The table could also include the data collection cost estimates so that the client can make an informed decision on the acceptable sample size. While not every researcher creates a table such as this, the acceptable sample errors and the costs of various sample sizes are most certainly discussed to come to an agreement on the survey's sample size. In most cases, the final agreed-to sample size is a trade-off between acceptable error and research cost. Marketing Research Insight 10.2 presents an example of how this trade-off occurs.

Other Methods of Sample Size Determination

In practice, a number of different methods are used to determine sample size, including some that are beyond the scope of this textbook.[17] The more common methods are described briefly in this section. As you will soon learn, most have limitations that makes them undesirable, even though you may find instances in which they are used and proponents who argue for

MARKETING RESEARCH INSIGHT 10.2   *Practical Application*

How Clients and Marketing Researchers Agree on Sample Size

In this fictitious example, we describe how sample size is determined for a survey for a water park owner who is thinking about adding an exciting new ride to be called "The Frantic Flume."

Larry, our marketing researcher, has worked with Dana, the water park owner, to develop the research objectives and basic research design for a survey to see if there is sufficient interest in the Frantic Flume ride. Yesterday, Dana indicated she wanted to have an accuracy level of ±3.5% because this was "just a little less accurate than your typical national opinion poll."

Larry did some calculations and created a table that he faxed to Dana. The table looks like this.

The Frantic Flume Survey Sample Size, Sample Error, and Sample Data Collection Cost

Sample Size	Sample Error	Sample Cost*
784	±3.5%	$15,680
600	±4.0%	$12,000
474	±4.5%	$9,480
384	±5.0%	$7,680
317	±5.5%	$6,340
267	±6.0%	$5,340

*Estimated at $20 per completed interview

The following phone conversation now takes place.

LARRY: "Did the fax come through okay?"

DANA: "Yes, but maybe I wish it didn't."

LARRY: "What do you mean?"

DANA: "There is no way I am going to pay over $15,000 just for the data collection."

LARRY: "Yes, I figured this when we talked yesterday, but we were talking about the accuracy of a national opinion poll then. Now we are talking about your water park survey. So, I prepared a schedule with some alternative sample sizes, their accuracy levels, and their costs."

DANA: "Gee, can you really get an accuracy level of ±6% with just 267 respondents? That seems like a very small sample."

LARRY: "Small in numbers, but it is still somewhat hefty in price as the data collection company will charge $20 per completed telephone interview. You can see that it will still amount to over $5,000."

DANA: "Well, that's nowhere near $15,000! What about the 384 size? It will come to $7,680 according to your table, and the accuracy is ±5%. How does the accuracy thing work again?"

LARRY: "If I find that, say, 70% of the respondents in the random sample of your customers want the Frantic Flume at your water park, then you can be assured that between 65% to 75% of all of your customers want it."

DANA: "And with $7,680 for data collection, the whole survey comes in under $15,000?"

LARRY: "I am sure it will. If you want me to, I can calculate a firm total cost using the 384 sample size."

DANA: "Sounds like a winner to me. When can you get it to me?"

LARRY: "I'll have the proposal completed by Friday. You can study it over the weekend."

DANA: "Great. I'll set up a tentative meeting with the investors for the middle of next week."

their use. Since you are acquainted with the eight sample size axioms and you know how to calculate sample size using the confidence interval method formula, you should comprehend the limitations as we point out each one.

ARBITRARY "PERCENT RULE OF THUMB" SAMPLE SIZE

Arbitrary sample size approaches rely on erroneous rules of thumb.

The **arbitrary approach** may take on the guise of a "percent rule of thumb" statement regarding sample size: "A sample should be at least 5% of the population in order to be accurate." In fact, it is not unusual for a marketing manager to respond to a marketing researcher's sample size recommendation by saying, "But that is less than 1% of the entire population!"

You must agree that the arbitrary percentage rule of thumb approach certainly has some intuitive appeal in that it is very easy to remember, and it is simple to apply. Surely, you will not fall into the seductive trap of the percent rule of thumb, for you understand that sample size is not related to population size. Just to convince yourself, consider these sample sizes.

If you take 5% samples of populations with sizes 10,000, 1 million, and 10 million, the n's will be 500, 50,000, and 500,000, respectively. Now, think back to the sample accuracy graph (Figure 10.1). The highest sample size on that graph was 2,000, so obviously the percent rule of thumb method can yield sample sizes that are absurd with respect to accuracy. Further, you have also learned from the sample size axioms that a sample can be a very small percent of the total population and have great accuracy.

In sum, arbitrary sample sizes are simple and easy to apply, but they are neither efficient nor economical. With sampling, we wish to draw a subset of the population in a thrifty manner and to estimate the population values with some predetermined degree of accuracy. "Percent rule of thumb" methods lose sight of the accuracy aspect of sampling; they certainly violate some of the axioms about sample size, and, as you just saw, they certainly are not cost effective when the population under study is large.

> *Arbitrary sample sizes are simple and easy to apply, but they are neither efficient nor economical.*

CONVENTIONAL SAMPLE SIZE SPECIFICATION

The **conventional approach** follows some "convention" or number believed somehow to be the right sample size. Managers who are knowledgeable of national opinion polls may notice that they are often taken with sample sizes of between 1,000 and 1,200 respondents. They may question marketing researchers whose sample size recommendations vary from this convention. On the other hand, a survey may be one in a series of studies a company has undertaken on a particular market, and the same sample size may be applied each succeeding year simply because it was used last year. The convention might be an average of the sample sizes of similar studies, it might be the largest sample size of previous surveys, or it might be equal to the sample size of a competitor's survey the company somehow discovered.

> *Using conventional sample size can result in a sample that may be too small or too large.*

The basic difference between a percent rule of thumb and a conventional sample size determination is that the first approach has no defensible logic, whereas the conventional approach appears logical. However, the logic is faulty. We just illustrated how a percent rule of thumb approach such as a 5% rule of thumb explodes into huge sample sizes very quickly; conversely, the national opinion poll convention of 1,200 respondents would be constant regardless of the population size. Still, this characteristic is one of the conventional sample size determination method's weaknesses, for it assumes that (1) the manager wants an accuracy of around ±3% and (2) there is maximum variability in the population.

> *Conventional sample sizes ignore the special circumstances of the survey at hand.*

> *Sometimes the researcher's desire to use particular statistical techniques influences sample size.*

Adopting past sample sizes or taking those used by other companies can be criticized as well, for both approaches assume that whoever determined sample size in the previous studies did so correctly—that is, not with a flawed method. If a flawed method was used, you simply perpetuate the error by copying it, and if the sample size method used was not flawed, the circumstances and assumptions surrounding the predecessor's survey may be very different from those encompassing the present one. The conventional sample size approach ignores the circumstances surrounding the study at hand and may well prove to be much more costly than would be the case if the sample size were determined correctly.

STATISTICAL ANALYSIS REQUIREMENTS SAMPLE SIZE SPECIFICATION

On occasion, a sample's size will be determined using a **statistical analysis approach**, meaning that the researcher wishes to perform a particular type of data analysis that has sample size requirements.[18] In truth, the sample size formulas in this chapter are appropriate for the simplest data analyses.[19] We have not discussed statistical procedures as yet in this text, but we can assure you that some advanced

The conventional approach wrongly uses a "cookie cutter" resulting in the same sample size for every survey.

Photo: Ar2r/Shutterstock

techniques require certain minimum sample sizes to be reliable or to safeguard the validity of their statistical results.[20] Sample sizes based on statistical analysis criteria can be quite large.[21]

Sometimes a research objective is to perform subgroup analysis,[22] which is an investigation of subsegments within the population. As you would expect, the desire to gain knowledge about subgroups has direct implications for sample size.[23] It should be possible to look at each subgroup as a separate population and to determine sample size for each subgroup, along with the appropriate methodology and other specifics to gain knowledge about that subgroup. That is, if you were to use the standard sample size formula described in this chapter to determine the sample size and more than one subgroup was to be analyzed fully, this objective would require a total sample size equal to the number of subgroups multiplied by the standard sample size formula's computed sample size.[24] Once this is accomplished, all subgroups can be combined into a large group to obtain a complete population picture. If a researcher is using a statistical technique, he or she should have a sample size large enough to satisfy the assumptions of the technique. Still, a researcher needs to know if that minimum sample size is large enough to give the desired level of accuracy.

COST BASIS OF SAMPLE SIZE SPECIFICATION

Sometimes termed the **"all you can afford" approach**, this method uses cost as an overriding basis for sample size. Returning to the eighth sample size axiom, managers and marketing research professionals are vitally concerned with the costs of data collection because they can mount quickly, particularly for personal interviews, telephone surveys, and even mail surveys in which incentives are included in the envelopes. Thus, it is not surprising that cost sometimes becomes the only basis for sample size.

Exactly how the "all you can afford" approach is applied varies a great deal. In some instances, the marketing research project budget is determined in advance, and set amounts are specified for each phase. Here, the budget may have, for instance, $10,000 for interviewing, or it might specify $5,000 for data collection. A variation is for the entire year's marketing research budget amount to be set and to have each project carve out a slice of that total. With this approach, the marketing research project director is forced to stay within the total project budget, but he or she can allocate the money across the various cost elements, and the sample size ends up being whatever is affordable within the budget.

Specifying sample size based on a predetermined budget is a case of the tail wagging the dog. That is, instead of establishing the value of the information to be gained from the survey as the primary consideration in determining sample size, the focus is on budget factors that usually ignore the value of the survey's results to management. In addition, this approach certainly does not consider sample accuracy at all. In fact, because many managers harbor a large sample size bias, it is possible that their marketing research project costs are overstated for data collection when smaller sample sizes could have sufficed quite well. As can be seen in our Marketing Research Insight 10.3, the Marketing Research Association Code of Ethics excerpt warns that marketing researchers should not misrepresent sample methodology; the code labels as unscrupulous taking advantage of any large sample size biases in clients as a means of charging a high price or inflating the importance of the findings.

Still, as the final sample size axiom advises, marketing researchers and their clients cannot decide on sample size without taking cost into consideration. The key is to remember *when* to consider cost. In the "all you can afford" examples we just described, cost drives the sample size determination completely. When we have $5,000 for interviewing and a data collection company tells us it charges $25 per completed interview, our sample is set at 200 respondents. However, the correct approach is to consider cost relative to the value of the research to the manager. If the manager requires extremely precise information, the researcher will surely suggest a large sample and then estimate the cost of obtaining the sample. The manager, in turn, should then consider this cost in relation to how much the information is actually worth. Using the cost schedule concept, the researcher and manager can then discuss alternative sample sizes, different data collection modes, costs, and other considerations. This

Using cost as the sole determinant of sample size may seem wise, but it is not.

The appropriateness of using cost as a basis for sample size depends on when cost factors are considered.

is a healthier situation, for now the manager is assuming some ownership of the survey and a partnership arrangement is being forged between the manager and the researcher. The net result will be a better understanding on the part of the manager as to how and why the final sample size was determined. This way cost will not be the only means of determining sample size, but it will be given the consideration it deserves.

Two Special Sample Size Determination Situations

In concluding our exploration of sample size, let's take up two special cases: sample size when sampling from small populations and sample size when using a nonprobability sampling method.

SAMPLING FROM SMALL POPULATIONS

Implicit to all sample size discussions thus far in this chapter is the assumption that the population is very large. This assumption is reasonable because there are multitudes of households in the United States, millions of registered drivers, millions of persons over the age of 65, and so forth. It is common, especially with consumer goods and services marketers, to draw samples from very large populations. Occasionally, however, the population is much smaller. This is not unusual in the case of B2B marketers. This case is addressed by the condition stipulated in our sixth sample size axiom, "In almost all cases, the accuracy (margin of sample error) of a random sample is independent of the size of the population."

With small populations, you should use the finite multiplier to determine sample size.

As a general rule, a **small population** situation is one in which the sample exceeds 5% of the total population size. Notice that a small population is defined by the size of the sample under consideration. If the sample is less than 5% of the total population, you can consider the population to be of large size, and you can use the procedures described earlier in this chapter. On the other hand, if it is a small population, the sample size formula needs some adjustment with what is called a **finite multiplier**, which is an adjustment factor that is approximately equal to the square root of that proportion of the population not included in the sample. For instance, suppose our population size was considered to be 1,000 companies and we decided to take a sample of 500. That would result in a finite multiplier of about 0.71, or the square root of 0.5, which is ([1,000 − 500]/1,000). That is, we could use a sample of only 355 (or .71 times 500) companies, and it would be just as accurate as one of size 500 if we had a large population.

The formula for computation of a sample size using the finite multiplier is as follows:

Small population sample size formula

$$\text{Small Population Sample Size} = \text{Sample Size Formula} \times \sqrt{\frac{N - n}{N - 1}}$$

Here is an example using the 1,000 company population. Suppose we want to know the percentage of companies that are interested in a substance abuse counseling program for their employees offered by a local hospital. We are uncertain about the variability, so we use our 50/50 worst-case approach. We decide to use a 95% level of confidence, and the director of Counseling Services at Claremont Hospital would like the results to be accurate ±5%. The computations are as follows:

Sample size computed with $p = 50\%$, $q = 50\%$, and $e = 5\%$

$$n = \frac{1.96^2(pq)}{e^2}$$

$$= \frac{1.96^2(50 \times 50)}{5^2}$$

$$= \frac{3.84(2,500)}{25}$$

$$= \frac{9,600}{25}$$

$$= 384$$

Now, since 384 is larger than 5% of the 1000 company population, we apply the finite multiplier to adjust the sample size for a small population:

Example: Sample size formula to adjust for a small population size

$$\text{Small Size Population Sample} = n\sqrt{\frac{N - n}{N - 1}}$$

$$= 384\sqrt{\frac{1,000 - 384}{1,000 - 1}}$$

$$= 384\sqrt{\frac{616}{999}}$$

$$= 384\sqrt{.62}$$

$$= 384 \times .79$$

$$= 303$$

In other words, we need a sample size of 303, not 384, because we are working with a small population. By applying the finite multiplier, we can reduce the sample size by 81 respondents and achieve the same accuracy level. If this survey required personal interviews, we would gain a considerable cost savings.

SAMPLE SIZE USING NONPROBABILITY SAMPLING

All sample size formulas and other statistical considerations treated in this chapter assume that some form of probability sampling method has been used. In other words, the sample must be random with regard to selection, and the only sampling error present is due to sample size. Remember, sample size determines the accuracy, not the representativeness, of the sample. The sampling method determines the representativeness. All sample size formulas assume that representativeness is guaranteed with use of a random sampling procedure.

The only reasonable way of determining sample size with nonprobability sampling is to weigh the benefit or value of the information obtained with that sample against the cost of gathering that information. Ultimately, this is a subjective exercise, as the manager may place significant value on the information for a number of reasons. For instance, the information may crystallize the problem, it may open the manager's eyes to vital additional considerations, or it might even make him or her aware of previously unknown market segments. But because of the unknown bias introduced by a haphazard sample selection[25] process, it is inappropriate to apply sample size formulas. For nonprobability sampling, sample size is a judgment based

Appropriate use of the finite multiplier formula will reduce a calculated sample size and save money when performing research on small populations.

When using nonprobability sampling, sample size is unrelated to accuracy, so cost–benefit considerations must be used.

SPSS®

SPSS Student Assistant:
Coca-Cola: Sorting, Searching, and Inserting Variables and Cases

almost exclusively on the value of the biased information to the manager, rather than desired precision, relative to cost. Many managers do select nonprobability sampling plans, knowing their limitations. In these cases, the sample size question is basically, "How many people will it take for me to feel comfortable in making a decision."

 ## Synthesize Your Learning

This exercise will require you to take into consideration concepts and material from these two chapters.

Chapter 10   Determining How to Select a Sample
Chapter 11   Determining the Size of a Sample

Niagara Falls Tourism Association

One of the most popular tourist destinations in the United States is Niagara Falls, located on the U.S.–Canada border in northern New York. An estimated 10 million to 12 million visitors visit Niagara Falls each year. However, while its attractiveness has not changed, environmental factors have recently threatened to significantly decrease these numbers. At least three factors are at work: (1) high gasoline prices, (2) the substantial weakening of the U.S. economy, and (3) increased competition by beefed-up marketing efforts of other tourist attractions that are experiencing declines due to the first two factors.

A large majority of Niagara Falls visitors are Americans who drive to the location, so gasoline costs and family financial worries have the Niagara Falls Tourism Association especially concerned. The association represents all types of businesses in the greater Niagara area that rely on tourism. Among their members are 80 hotels that account for approximately 16,000 rooms. The hotels have anywhere from 20 to 600 rooms, with a large majority (about 80%, accounting for 30% of the rooms) being local and smaller, and the larger ones (the remaining 20%, accounting for 70% of the rooms) being national chains and larger. For all hotels in the area, occupancy at peak season (June 15–September 15) averages around 90%. The association wants to conduct a survey of current visitors to evaluate their overall satisfaction with their visit to the Niagara area and their intentions to tell friends, relatives, and coworkers to visit Niagara Falls. The association has designed a face-to-face interview questionnaire, and it has issued a request for proposals for sample design. It has received three bids, each of which is described below.

> *Bid #1.* The Maid of the Mist union—employees of the company that operates the boats that take tourists on the Niagara River to view and experience the falls—proposes to do the interviews with tourists who are waiting for the Maid boats to return and load up. Union employees will conduct interviews with 1,000 adult American tourists (1 per family group) during a one-week period in July at $3 per completed interview.
>
> *Bid #2.* The Simpson Research Company, a local marketing research company, proposes to take a sample of the five largest association member hotels and conduct 200 interviews in the lobbies of these hotels with American tourists (1 per family) during the months of July and August at a cost of $5 per completed interview.
>
> *Bid #3.* The SUNY-Niagara Marketing Department, an academic unit in the local university, proposes to randomly select 20 hotels from all hotels in the area (not just those belonging to the Tourism Association) and to then select a proportional random sample of rooms, using room numbers, from each selected hotel based on hotel room capacities. It will interview 750 American tourists (1 per family) in their rooms during the period of June 15–September 15 at a cost of $10 per completed interview.

Questions

1. What is the sample frame in each bid?
2. Identify the type of sample method and assess the representativeness of the sample with respect to American tourists visiting the Niagara Falls area.

3. Evaluate the accuracy (sample error) with each bid.

4. The Niagara Falls Tourism Association has budgeted $5,000 for data collection in this survey. Using information from your answers to questions 1 to 3 and further considering the total cost of data collection, which one of the proposals do you recommend that the Niagara Falls Tourist Association accept? Justify your recommendation.

Summary

Many managers adhere to the "large sample size" bias. To counter this myth, eight sample size axioms relate the size of a random sample to its accuracy, or closeness of its findings to the true population value. These axioms are the basis for the confidence interval sample size determination method, which is the most correct method because it relies on sound logic based upon the statistical concepts of variability, confidence intervals, and margin of sample error.

When estimating a percentage, marketing researchers rely on a standard sample size formula that uses variability (p and q), level of confidence (z), and acceptable margin of sample error (e) to compute the sample size, n. Confidence levels of 95% or 99% are typically applied, equating to z values of 1.96 and 2.58, respectively. For variability with percentage estimates, the researcher can fall back on a 50%/50% split, which is the greatest variability case

possible. When estimating a mean, another formula is used. The standard sample size formula is best considered a starting point for deciding the final sample size, for data collection costs must be taken into consideration. Normally, the researcher and manager will discuss the alternative sample error levels and their associated data collection costs to come to agreement on a final acceptable sample size.

Although they have limitations, there are at other methods of determining sample size: (1) designating size arbitrarily, (2) using a "conventional" size, (3) basing size on the requirements of statistical procedures to be used, and (4) letting cost determine the size. Two sampling situations raise special considerations. With a small population, the finite multiplier should be used to adjust the sample size determination formula. With nonprobability sampling, a cost–benefit analysis should take place.

Key Terms

Sample accuracy (p. 238)
Large sample size bias (p. 239)
Confidence interval approach (p. 240)
Nonsampling error (p. 240)
Margin of sampling error (p. 242)
Variability (p. 241)

Mimimum margin of sample error (p. 242)
Confidence interval (p. 243)
Central limit theorem (p. 243)
Confidence interval method (p. 245)
Acceptable margin of sample error (p. 246)

Worst-case variability (p. 249)
Arbitrary approach (p. 251)
Conventional approach (p. 252)
Statistical analysis approach (p. 252)
All you can afford approach (p. 253)
Small population (p. 254)
Finite multiplier (p. 254)

Review Questions/Applications

1. Describe each of the following methods of sample size determination and indicate a critical flaw in the use of each one.
   a. Using a "rule of thumb" percentage of the population size.
   b. Using a "conventional" sample size such as the typical size pollsters use.
   c. Using the amount in the budget allocated for data collection to determine sample size.

2. Describe and provide illustrations of each of the following notions: (a) variability, (b) confidence interval, and (c) acceptable margin of sample error.

3. What are the three fundamental considerations involved with the confidence interval approach to sample size determination?

4. When calculating sample size, how can a researcher decide on the level of accuracy to use? What about level of confidence? What about variability with a percentage?

5. Using the formula provided in your text, determine the approximate sample sizes for each of the following cases, all with precision (allowable error) of ±5%:
   a. Variability of 30%, confidence level of 95%.
   b. Variability of 60%, confidence level of 99%.
   c. Unknown variability, confidence level of 95%.

6. Indicate how a pilot study can help a researcher understand variability in the population.
7. Why is it important for the researcher and the marketing manager to discuss the accuracy level associated with the research project at hand?
8. What are the benefits to be gained by knowing that a proposed sample is more than 5% of the total population's size? In what marketing situation might this be a common occurrence?
9. A researcher knows from experience the average costs of various data collection alternatives:

Data Collection Method	Cost/Respondent
Personal interview	$50
Telephone interview	$25
Mail survey	$ 0.50 (per mailout)

If $2,500 is allocated in the research budget for data collection, what are the levels of accuracy for the sample sizes allowable for each data collection method? Based on your findings, comment on the inappropriateness of using cost as the only means of determining sample size.

10. Last year, Lipton Tea Company conducted a mall-intercept study at six regional malls around the country and found that 20% of the public preferred tea over coffee as a midafternoon hot drink. This year, Lipton wants to have a nationwide telephone survey performed with random digit dialing. What sample size should be used in this year's study to achieve an accuracy level of ±2.5% at the 99% level of confidence? What about at the 95% level of confidence?

11. Allbookstores.com has a used textbook division. It buys its books in bulk from used book buyers who set up kiosks on college campuses during final exams, and it sells the used textbooks to students who log on to the allbookstores.com website via a secured credit card transaction. The used texts are then sent by United Parcel Service to the student.

The company has conducted a survey of used book buying by college students each year for the past four years. In each survey, 1,000 randomly selected college students have been asked to indicate whether they bought a used textbook in the previous year. The results are as follows:

	Years Ago			
	1	2	3	4
Percent buying used text(s)	45%	50%	60%	70%

What are the sample size implications of these data?

12. American Ceramics, Inc. (ACI) has been developing a new form of ceramic that can withstand high temperatures and sustained use. Because of its improved properties, the project development engineer in charge of this project thinks the new ceramic will compete as a substitute for the ceramics currently used in spark plugs. She talks to ACI's marketing research director about conducting a survey of prospective buyers of the new ceramic material. During their phone conversation, the research director suggests a study using about 100 companies as a means of determining market demand. Later that day, the research director does some background using the Thomas Register as a source of names of companies manufacturing spark plugs. A total of 312 companies located in the continental United States are found in the Register. How should this finding impact the final sample size of the survey?

13. Here are some numbers you can use to sharpen your computational skills for sample size determination. Crest toothpaste is reviewing plans for its annual survey of toothpaste purchasers. With each case below, calculate the sample size pertaining to the key variable under consideration. Where information is missing, provide reasonable assumptions.

Case	Key Variable	Variability	Acceptable Error	Confidence Level
a	Market share of Crest toothpaste last year	23% share	4%	95%
b	Percent of people who brush their teeth per week	Unknown	5%	99%
c	How likely Crest buyers are to switch brands	30% switched last year	5%	95%
d	Percent of people who want tartar-control features in their toothpaste	20% two years ago; 40% one year ago	3.5%	95%
e	Willingness of people to adopt the toothpaste brand recommended by their family dentist	Unknown	6%	99%

14. Do managers really have a large sample size bias? Because you cannot survey managers easily, this exercise will use surrogates. Ask any five seniors majoring in business administration who have not taken a marketing research class the following questions. Indicate whether each of the following statements is true or false.
    a. A random sample of 500 is large enough to represent all full-time college students in the United States.
    b. A random sample of 1,000 is large enough to represent all full-time college students in the United States.
    c. A random sample of 2,000 is large enough to represent all full-time college students in the United States.
    d. A random sample of 5,000 is large enough to represent all full-time college students in the United States.

    What have you found out about sample size bias?

15. The following items pertain to determining sample size when a mean is involved. Calculate the sample size for each case.

Case	Key Variable	Standard Deviation	Acceptable Error	Confidence Level
A	Number of car rentals per year for business trip usage	10	2	95%
B	Number of songs downloaded with iTunes per month	20	2	95%
C	Number of miles driven per year to commute to work	500	50	99%
D	Use of a 9-point scale measuring satisfaction with the brand	2	0.3	95%

16. The Andrew Jergens Company markets a "spa tablet" called ActiBath, which is a carbonated moisturizing treatment for use in a bath. From previous research, Jergens management knows that 60% of all women use some form of skin moisturizer and 30% believe their skin is their most beautiful asset. There is some concern among management that women will associate the drying aspects of taking a bath with ActiBath and not believe that it can provide a skin moisturizing benefit. Can these facts about use of moisturizers and concern for skin beauty be used in determining the size of the sample in the ActiBath survey? If so, indicate how. If not, indicate why and how sample size can be determined.

17. Donald Heel is the Microwave Oven Division Manager of Sharp Products. Don proposes a $40 cash rebate program as a means of promoting Sharp's new crisp-broil-and-grill microwave oven. However, the Sharp president wants evidence that the program would increase sales by at least 25%, so Don applies some of his research budget to a survey. He uses the National Phone Systems Company to conduct a nationwide survey using random-digit dialing. National Phone Systems is a fully integrated telephone polling company, and it has the capability of providing daily tabulations. Don decides to use this option, and instead of specifying a final sample size, he chooses to have National Phone Systems perform 50 completions each day. At the end of five days of fieldwork, the daily results are as follows:

Day	1	2	3	4	5
Total sample size	50	100	150	200	250
Percentage of respondents who would consider buying a Sharp microwave with a $40 rebate	50%	40%	35%	30%	33%

For how much longer should Don continue the survey? Indicate your rationale.

CASE 10.1

Target: Deciding on the Number of Telephone Numbers

Target is a major retail store chain specializing in good quality merchandise and good values for its customers. Currently, Target operates about 1,700 stores, including more than 200 "Super Targets," in major metropolitan areas in 48 states. One of the core marketing strategies employed by Target is to ensure that shoppers have a special experience every time they shop at Target. This special shopping experience is enhanced by Target's "intuitive" department arrangements. For example, toys are next to sporting goods. Another shopping experience feature is the "racetrack" or extra wide center aisle that helps shoppers navigate the store easily and quickly. A third feature is the aesthetic appearance of its shelves, product displays, and seasonal specials. Naturally, Target continuously monitors the opinions and satisfaction levels of its customers because competitors are constantly trying to outperform Target and/or customer preferences change.

Target management has committed to an annual survey of 1,000 customers to determine these very issues and to provide for a constant tracking and forecasting system of customers' opinions. The survey will include customers of Target's competitors such as Walmart, Kmart, and Sears. In other words, the population under study is all consumers who shop in mass merchandise stores in Target's geographic markets. The marketing research project director has decided on the use of a telephone survey to be conducted by a national telephone survey data collection company, and he is currently working with Survey Sampling, Inc., to purchase the telephone numbers of consumers residing in Target's metropolitan target markets. SSI personnel have informed him of the basic formula they use to determine the number of telephone numbers needed. (You learned about this formula in the chapter-opening vignette featuring Jessica Smith.)

The formula is as follows:

Telephone numbers needed = completed Interviews/
(working phone rate
× incidence
× completion rate)

where

working phone rate = percent of telephone numbers that are "live"

incidence = percentage of those reached that will take part in the survey

completion rate = percentage of those willing to take part in the survey that actually complete the survey

As a matter of convenience, Target identifies four different regions that are roughly equal in sales volume: North, South, East, and West.

1. With a desired final sample size of 250 for each region, what is the lowest total number of telephone numbers that should be purchased for each region?
2. With a desired final sample size of 250 for each region, what is the highest total number of telephone numbers that should be purchased for each region?
3. What is the lowest and highest total number of telephone numbers to be purchased for the entire survey?

Region	North		South		East		West	
	Low	High	Low	High	Low	High	Low	High
Working Rate	70%	75%	60%	65%	65%	75%	50%	60%
Incidence	65%	70%	70%	80%	65%	75%	40%	50%
Completion Rate	50%	70%	50%	60%	80%	90%	60%	70%

CASE 10.2 INTEGRATED CASE

Global Motors

Nick Thomas, CEO of Global Motors, has agreed with Cory Rogers of CMG Research to use an online survey to assess consumer demand for new energy-efficient car models. In particular, the decision has been made to purchase panel access, meaning that the online survey will be completed by individuals who have joined the ranks of the panel data company and agreed to periodically answer surveys online. While these individuals are compensated by their panel companies, the companies claim that their panel members are highly representative of the general population. Also, because the panel members have provided extensive information about themselves such as demographics, lifestyles, and product ownership, which is stored in the panel company data banks, a client can purchase this data without the necessity of asking these questions on its survey.

Cory's CMG Research team has done some investigation and has concluded that several panel companies can provide a representative sample of American households.

Among these are Knowledge Networks, e-Rewards, and Survey Sampling International, and their costs and services seem comparable: for a "blended" online survey of about 25 questions, the cost is roughly $10 per complete response. "Blended" means a combination of stored database information and answers to online survey questions. Thus, the costs of these panel company services are based on the number of respondents, and each company will bid on the work based on the nature and size of the sample.

Cory knows his Global Motors client is operating under two constraints. First, ZEN Motors top management has agreed to a total cost for all of the research, and it is up to Nick Thomas to spend this budget prudently. If a large portion of the budget is expended on a single activity, such as paying for an online panel sample, there is less available for other research activities. Second, Cory Rogers knows from his extensive experience with clients that both Nick Thomas and ZEN Motors' top management will expect this project to have a large sample size. Of course, as a marketing researcher, Cory realizes that large sample sizes are generally not required from a sample error standpoint, but he must be prepared to respond to questions, reservations, or objections from Nick or ZEN Motors managers when the sample size is proposed. As preparation for the possible need to convince top management that CMG's recommendation is the right decision for the sample size for the Global Motors survey, Cory decides to make a table that specifies sample error and cost of the sample.

For each of the following possible sample sizes listed below, calculate the associated expected cost of the panel sample and the sample error.

1. 20,000
2. 10,000
3. 5,000
4. 2,500
5. 1,000
6. 500

Dealing with Field Work and Data Quality Issues

LEARNING OBJECTIVES

- To learn about total error and how nonsampling error is related to it
- To understand the sources of data collection errors and how to minimize them
- To learn about the various types of nonresponse error and how to calculate response rate to measure nonresponse error
- To become acquainted with data quality errors and how to handle them

"WHERE WE ARE"

1 Establish the need for marketing research.

2 Define the problem.

3 Establish research objectives.

4 Determine research design.

5 Identify information types and sources.

6 Determine methods of accessing data.

7 Design data collection forms.

8 Determine the sample plan and size.

9 Collect data.

10 Analyze data.

11 Prepare and present the final research report.

Dealing with Survey Data Quality

Steven H. Gittelman, President and CEO of Sample Source Auditors™.

Data quality is a major concern for marketing researchers, and data quality issues vary by the method of data collection. We asked Steven H. Gittelman, President and CEO of Sample Source Auditors, to provide comments on data quality.

Telephone data collection requires process rigor. Interviewers not only need to be trained on the protocols inherent in data collection, they must be supervised at several levels. Monitors listen to a percentage of respondents to verify that interviewers are capturing an accurate rendition of the information they provide. Often monitors serve as part of the validation process in that they are hearing the survey conducted live and thus can offer witness to its accuracy. However, not all interviews can be monitored in real time, and many require a phone call to the respondent in an attempt to validate 17% (one in six completes) of each interviewer's nightly work. In the event some respondents cannot pass a four- or five-question validation questionnaire, all of the interviews collected by an interviewer should be called in an attempt to validate 100% of the work he or she performs.

Clearly the emphasis on telephone quality control can be mitigated by proper training. In those cases where an interviewer fails to pass monitoring or validation quality processes, he/she should be sent back to training for a refresher. Often it is good practice to have interviewers hear their own work as recorded in real time and, when possible, to listen to the work of others so that they can become better acclimated.

Online research is another matter. The safety net that exists in telephone research, due to the probabilistic properties of random digit dialed (RDD) samples, does not exist in online. The absence of a reliable sample frame changes the protocol drastically, as does the difference in the medium. Online respondents are not supported by a live interviewer and thus cannot be corrected in real time by the presence of another human being. Instead, a large variety of tools are evolving to capture "satisficers" (those respondents who are poorly engaged and provide little thought to their answers) in real time and also post hoc. The answers of people

Text and images:
By permission, Steven H. Gittelman, Sample Source Auditors™.

who are just trying to speed through a survey so that they can collect an incentive are not only meaningless but dangerous to the data analysis process. There is a growing body of evidence that poorly engaged respondents do not enter random information but instead are directional in their responses. If this is so, then they are not only entering data that are useless but, because of its predilection to being positive in response, tend to bias the interpretation of the data at hand.

Some of the tools available to the online researcher identify speeding (either through the entire survey or in sections), straight lining, failure at trap questions, inconsistencies, and answers that are considered so rare as to be impossible. These tools may also facilitate a general analysis of outliers. All these processes capture those who are poorly engaged but fail to deal with the forces that drive respondents to become less engaged. The structure of questionnaires, too many grids, poor wording, excessive length, repetitiveness, and uninteresting subject material contribute to the loss of engagement in respondents. However, some sources of respondents, such as respondents from social media, are less engaged than others and generate different behavioral arrays in their responses.

To correct for the inconsistency of responses, some are now advocating that the differences in behavior represented between sources must be corrected in online research. Various means of creating behaviorally representative samples are being tested. In some cases, blending of different sources to achieve a behavioral mix that represents the population are being tried. At this point the challenges in obtaining a behaviorally representative sample, at least one as good as having a probabilistic sample frame like RDD, have not been resolved.

This chapter deals with data collection issues, including factors that affect the quality of data obtained by surveys. There are two kinds of errors in survey research. The first is sampling error, which arises from the fact that we have taken a sample. Those sources of error were discussed in the previous

Photo: Kurhan/Fotolia

chapter. Error also arises from a respondent who does not listen carefully to the question or from an interviewer who is almost burned out from listening to answering machines or having prospective respondents hang up. This second type of error is called *nonsampling error*. This chapter discusses the sources of nonsampling errors, along with suggestions on how marketing researchers can minimize the negative effect of each type of error. We also address how to calculate the response rate to measure the amount of nonresponse error. We relate what a researcher looks for in preliminary questionnaire screening after the survey has been completed to spot respondents whose answers may exhibit bias, such as always responding positively or negatively to questions.

Data Collection and Nonsampling Error

In the two previous chapters, you learned that the sample plan and sample size are important in predetermining the amount of sampling error you will experience. The significance of understanding sampling is that we can control sampling error.[1] The counterpart to sampling error is **nonsampling error**, which is defined as all errors in a survey *except* those attributable to the sample plan and sample size. Nonsampling error includes (1) all types of nonresponse error, (2) data gathering errors, (3) data handling errors, (4) data analysis errors, and (5) interpretation errors. It also includes errors in problem definition and question wording—everything, in fact, other than sampling error. Generally, there is great potential for large nonsampling error to occur during the data collection stage, so we discuss errors that can occur during this stage at some length. **Data collection** is the phase of the marketing research process during which respondents provide their answers or information to inquiries posed to them by the researcher. These inquiries may be direct questions asked by a live, face-to-face interviewer; they may be posed over the telephone; they may be administered by the respondent alone such as with an online survey; or they may take some other form of solicitation the researcher has decided to use. Because nonsampling error cannot be measured by a formula as sampling error can, we describe the various controls that can be imposed on the data collection process to minimize the effects of nonsampling error.[2]

Nonsampling error is defined as all errors in a survey except those due to the sample plan and sample size.

Data collection has the potential to greatly increase the amount of nonsampling error in a survey.

Possible Errors in Field Data Collection

A wide variety of nonsampling errors can occur during data collection. We divide these errors into two general types and further specify errors within each general type. The first general type is **fieldworker error**, defined as errors committed by the individuals who administer questionnaires, typically interviewers.[3] The quality of fieldworkers can vary dramatically depending on the researcher's resources and the circumstances of the survey, but it is important to keep in mind that fieldworker error can occur with professional data collection workers as well as with do-it-yourselfers. Of course, the potential for fieldworker error is less with professionals than with first-timers or part-timers. The other general type is **respondent error**, which refers to errors on the part of the respondent. These, of course, can occur regardless of the method of data collection, but some data collection methods have greater potential for respondent error than others. Within each general type, we identify two classes of error: intentional errors, or errors that are committed deliberately, and unintentional errors, or errors that occur without willful intent.[4] Table 11.1 lists the various errors/types of errors described in this section under each of the four headings. In the early sections of this chapter, we will describe these data collection errors, and, later, we will discuss the standard controls marketing researchers employ to minimize these errors.

Nonsampling errors are committed by fieldworkers and respondents.

TABLE 11.1   Data Collection Errors Can Occur with Fieldworkers or Respondents

	Fieldworker	Respondent
Intentional Errors	• Cheating	• Falsehoods
	• Leading respondents	• Nonresponse
Unintentional Errors	• Interviewer characteristics	• Misunderstanding
	• Misunderstandings	• Guessing
	• Fatigue	• Attention loss
		• Distractions
		• Fatigue

INTENTIONAL FIELDWORKER ERRORS

Intentional fieldworker errors occur whenever a data collection person willfully violates the data collection requirements set forth by the researcher. We describe two variations of intentional fieldworker errors: interviewer cheating and leading the respondent. Both are constant concerns of all researchers.

Interviewer cheating occurs when the interviewer intentionally misrepresents respondents. You might think to yourself, "What would induce an interviewer to intentionally falsify responses?" The cause is often found in the compensation system.[5] Interviewers may work by the hour, but a common compensation system is to reward them by completed interviews. That is, a telephone interviewer or a mall-intercept interviewer may be paid at a rate of $7.50 per completed interview, so at the end of an interview day, he or she simply turns in the "completed" questionnaires (or data files, if the interviewer uses a laptop, tablet, or PDA system), and the number is credited to the interviewer. Or the interviewers may cheat by interviewing someone who is convenient instead of a person designated by the sampling plan. Again, the by-completed-interview compensation may provide the incentive for this type of cheating.[6] At the same time, most interviewers are not full-time employees,[7] and their integrity may be diminished as a result.

You might ask, "Wouldn't changing the compensation system for interviewers fix this problem?" There is some defensible logic for a paid-by-completion compensation system. Interviewers do not always work like production-line workers. With mall intercepts, for instance, there are periods of inactivity, depending on mall shopper flow and respondent qualification requirements. Telephone interviewers are often instructed to call only during a small number of "prime time" hours in the evening, or they may be waiting for periods of time to satisfy the number of call-backs policy for a particular survey. Also, as you may already know, the compensation levels for fieldworkers are low, the hours are long, and the work is frustrating at times.[8] As a result, the temptation to turn in bogus completed questionnaires is certainly present, and some interviewers give in to this temptation. With marketing research in developing countries, interviewer cheating is an especially troublesome, as you will learn when you read Marketing Research Insight 11.1, which describes why interviewer cheating occurred in a study conducted in Zimbabwe.

The second error that we are categorizing as intentional on the part of the interviewer is **leading the respondent**, or attempting to influence the respondent's answers through wording, voice inflection, or body language. In the worst case, the interviewer may actually reword a question so that it is leading. For instance, consider the question, "Is conserving electricity a concern for you?" An interviewer can influence the respondent by changing the question to "Isn't conserving electricity a concern for you?"

There are other, less obvious instances of leading the respondent. One way is to subtly signal the type of response that is expected. You may want to reread Marketing Research Insight 8.3

Interviewer cheating is a concern, especially when compensation is based on a per-completion basis.

Interviewers should not influence respondents' answers.

MARKETING RESEARCH INSIGHT 11.1   *Global Application*

Interviewer Cheating in Zimbabwe

Anyone performing marketing research in developing countries soon realizes that the communication systems on which researchers in developed countries rely on heavily are not usable. In countries such as Zimbabwe, computer ownership is low, telephone systems are primitive, and even the postal system is undependable. Consequently, personal interviewers are often hired to perform the data collection function. Researchers investigating various aspects of entrepreneurs in Zimbabwe relied exclusively on hired, personal interviewers to gather their data.[9] They discovered that three out of the five interviewers turned in fabricated interviews; thus, about 60% of the collected data was bogus. The researchers were astonished at this occurrence because the interviewers had been carefully selected, and they had undergone comprehensive training. Amazingly, one interviewer turned in faked interviews even after being told that his predecessor had been caught cheating and had been sent to jail!

The researchers reflected on the special circumstances of doing marketing research in a developing country and came up with the following explanations for interviewer cheating in this situation.

1. Cheating is normative. In an impoverished country such as Zimbabwe, citizens take every opportunity to get along or ahead, and being honest can hinder one's short-run opportunities. The cheating interviewers were just doing "business as usual."
2. Cheating is the fault of the researcher. Global researchers in circumstances such as this are often aloof and culturally distant from the "hired-locally" interviewers, and the interviewers may not be informed of the nature or importance of the research. They are just given a list of do's and don'ts without any supervision in the field, so they are likely to "cut corners" with faked interviews and expenses.
3. There are monetary and psychological rewards to cheating. On the monetary side, the cheating interviewer is paid for bogus interviews and given a travel allowance that can be pocketed. On the psychological side, the cheating interviewer feels that he or she has cleverly tricked the foreign researchers, and he or she may even boast about cheating.

What about the threat of being thrown in jail? When a "good" interviewer was asked why other interviewers might have cheated, he indicated that none of them were convinced that the first cheating interviewer was ever sent to jail.

Active Learning

What Type of Cheater Are You?

Students who read about the cheating error we have just described are sometimes skeptical that such cheating goes on. However, if you are a "typical" college student, you probably have cheated to some degree in your academic experience. Surprised? Take the following test, and circle "Yes" or "No" under the "I have done this" heading for each statement.

Statement	I have done this.	
Asking about the content of an exam from someone who has taken it	Yes	No
Giving information about the content of an exam to someone who has not yet taken it	Yes	No
Before taking an exam, looking at a copy that was not supposed to be available to students	Yes	No
Allowing another to see exam answers	Yes	No
Copying off another's exam	Yes	No
Turning in work done by someone else as one's own	Yes	No
Having information programmed into a calculator during an exam	Yes	No
Using a false excuse to delay an exam or paper	Yes	No
Using exam crib notes	Yes	No
Passing answers during an exam	Yes	No
Working with others on an individual project	Yes	No
Padding a bibliography	Yes	No

If you checked circled "Yes" to more than half of these practices, you are consistent with most business students who have answered a variation of this test.[10] Now, if you and the majority of univeristy students in general are cheating on examinations and assignments, don't you think that interviewers who may be in financially tight situations are tempted to cheat on their interviews?

on page 191 that describes various ways types of leading questions. For instance, if a respondent says "yes" in response to a question, the interviewer might say, "I thought you would say 'yes' as over 90% of my respondents have agreed on this issue." A comment such as this plants a seed in the respondent's head that he or she should continue to agree with the majority.

Another area of subtle leading occurs in interviewers' cues. In personal interviews, for instance, interviewers might ever so slightly shake their heads "no" to questions they disagree with and nod "yes" to those they agree with while posing the question. Respondents may perceive these cues and begin responding in the expected manner signaled by interviewers' nonverbal cues. Over the telephone, interviewers might give verbal cues such as "unhuh" to responses they disagree with or "okay" to responses they agrees with, and this continued reaction pattern may subtly influence respondents' answers. Again, we have categorized this example as an intentional error because professional interviewers are trained to avoid them, and if they commit them, they should be aware of their violations.

UNINTENTIONAL FIELDWORKER ERRORS

An **unintentional interviewer error** occurs whenever an interviewer commits an error while believing that he or she is performing correctly.[11] There are three general sources of unintentional interviewer errors: interviewer personal characteristics, interviewer misunderstandings, and interviewer fatigue. Unintentional interviewer error is found in the interviewer's personal characteristics such as accent, sex, and demeanor. It has been shown that under some circumstances, the interviewer's voice,[12] gender,[13] or lack of experience[14] can be a source of bias. In fact, just the presence of an interviewer, regardless of personal characteristics, may be a source of bias.

Interviewer misunderstanding occurs when an interviewer believes he or she knows how to administer a survey but instead does it incorrectly. As we have described, a questionnaire may include various types of instructions for the interviewer, a variety of response scale types, directions on how to record responses, and other complicated guidelines to which the interviewer must adhere. As you can guess, there is often a considerable education gap between marketing researchers who design questionnaires and interviewers who administer them. This gap can easily become a communication problem in which the instructions on the questionnaire are confusing to the interviewer. Interviewer experience cannot overcome poor questionnaire instructions.[15] When instructions are hard to understand, the interviewer will usually struggle to comply with the researcher's wishes but may fail to do so.[16]

The third type of unintentional interviewer error pertains to **fatigue-related mistakes**, which can occur when an interviewer becomes tired. You may be surprised that fatigue can enter into asking questions and recording answers, because these tasks are not physically demanding, but interviewing is labor-intensive[17] and can become tedious and monotonous. It is repetitious at best, and it is especially demanding when respondents are uncooperative. Toward the end of a long interviewing day, the interviewer may be less mentally alert than earlier in the day, and this condition can cause slip-ups and

Unintentional interviewer errors include misunderstandings and fatigue.

Personal characteristics such as appearance, dress, or accent, although unintentional, may cause field worker errors.

Photo: Warren Goldswain/Shutterstc

mistakes to occur. The interviewer may fail to obey a skip pattern, might forget to make note of the respondent's reply to a question, might hurry through a section of the questionnaire, or might appear or sound weary to a potential respondent who refuses to take part in the survey as a result.

INTENTIONAL RESPONDENT ERRORS

Sometimes respondents do not tell the truth.

Intentional respondent errors occur when respondents willfully misrepresent themselves in surveys. There are at least two major intentional respondent errors that require discussion: falsehoods and refusals. **Falsehoods** occur when respondents fail to tell the truth in surveys. They may feel embarrassed, they might want to protect their privacy, or they may even suspect that the interviewer has a hidden agenda such as turning the interview into a sales pitch.[18] Certain topics denote greater potential for misrepresentation. For instance, personal income level is a sensitive topic for many people, marital status disclosure is a concern for women living alone, age is a delicate topic for some, and personal hygiene questions may offend some respondents. Alternatively, respondents may become bored, deem the interview process burdensome, or find the interviewer irritating. For a variety of reasons, they may want to end the interview in a hurry. Falsehoods may be motivated by a desire on the part of the respondent to deceive, or they may be mindless responses uttered just to complete the interview as quickly as possible.

Nonresponse is defined as failure on the part of a prospective respondent to take part in a survey or to answer a question.

The second type of intentional respondent error is nonresponse, which we have referred to at various times in this textbook. **Nonresponse** includes a failure on the part of a prospective respondent to take part in the survey, premature termination of the interview, or refusals to answer specific questions on the questionnaire. In fact, nonresponse of various types is probably the most common intentional respondent error that researchers encounter. Some observers believe that survey research is facing tough times ahead because of a growing distaste for survey participation, increasingly busy schedules, and a desire for privacy.[19] By one estimate, the refusal rate of U.S. consumers is almost 50%.[20] Telephone surveyors are most concerned.[21] While most agree that declining cooperation rates present a major threat to the industry,[22] some believe the problem is not as severe as many think.[23] Nonresponse in general, and refusals in particular, are encountered in virtually every survey conducted. Business-to-business (B2B) marketing research is even more challenging, presenting additional hurdles that must be cleared (such as negotiating "gatekeepers") just to find the right person to take part in the survey. We devote an entire section to nonresponse error in a following section of this chapter.

To learn about nonresponse, launch www.youtube.com, and search for "Nonresponse - AAPOR 2008: Robert Groves."

UNINTENTIONAL RESPONDENT ERRORS

Unintentional respondent errors may result from misunderstanding, guessing, attention loss, distractions, and fatigue.

An **unintentional respondent error** occurs whenever a respondent gives a response that is not valid, but that he or she believes is the truth. There are five instances of unintentional respondent errors: misunderstanding, guessing, attention loss, distractions, and fatigue. First, **respondent misunderstanding** is defined as situations in which a respondent gives an answer without comprehending the question and/or the accompanying instructions. Potential respondent misunderstandings exist in all surveys. Such misunderstandings range from simple errors, such as checking two responses to a question when only one is called for, to complex errors, such as misunderstanding terminology.[24] For example, a respondent may think in terms of net income for the past year rather than income before taxes as desired by the researcher. Any number of misunderstandings such as these can plague a survey.

Sometimes a respondent will answer without understanding the question.

Whenever a respondent guesses, error is likely.

A second form of unintentional respondent error is **guessing**, in which a respondent gives an answer when he or she is uncertain of its accuracy. Occasionally, respondents are asked about topics about which they have little knowledge or recall, but they feel compelled to provide an answer to the questions being posed. Respondents might guess the answer, and all guesses are likely to contain errors. Here is an example of guessing: If you were asked to estimate the amount of electricity in kilowatt hours you used last month, how many would you say you used?

A third unintentional respondent error occurs when a respondent's interest in the survey wanes, known as **attention loss**. The typical respondent is not as excited about the survey as is the researcher, and some respondents will find themselves less and less motivated to take part in the survey as they work their way through the questionnaire. With attention loss, respondents do not attend carefully to questions, they issue superficial and perhaps mindless answers, and they may refuse to continue taking part in the survey.

Fourth, **distractions**, such as interruptions, may occur while the questionnaire administration takes place. For example, during a mall-intercept interview, a respondent may be distracted when an acquaintance walks by and says hello. A parent answering questions on the telephone might have to attend to a fussy toddler, or an online survey respondent might be prompted that an email message has just arrived. A distraction may cause the respondent to get "off track" or otherwise not take the survey as seriously as is desired by the researcher.

Fifth, unintentional respondent error can take the form of **respondent fatigue**, in which the respondent becomes tired of participating in the survey. Whenever a respondent tires of a survey, deliberation and reflection will diminish. Exasperation will mount and cooperation will decrease. The respondent might even opt for the "no opinion" response category just as a means of quickly finishing the survey because he or she has grown tired of answering questions.

Guesses are a form of unintentional respondent error.

Photo: East/Shutterstock

 Active Learning

What Type of Error Is It?

It is sometimes confusing to students when they first read about intentional and unintentional errors and the attribution of errors to interviewers or respondents. To help you learn and remember these various types of data collection errors, see if you can correctly identify the type for each of the following data collection situations. Place an "X" in the cell that corresponds to the type of error that pertains to the situation.

Situation	Interviewer Error		Respondent Error	
	Intentional	Unintentional	Intentional	Unintentional
A respondent says "No opinion" to every question asked.				
When a mall intercept interviewer is suffering from a bad cold, few people want to take the survey.				
Because a telephone respondent has an incoming call, he asks his wife to take the phone and answer the rest of the interviewer's questions.				
A respondent grumbles about doing the survey, so an interviewer decides to skip asking the demographic questions.				
A respondent who lost her job gives her last year's income level rather than the much lower one she will earn for this year.				

SPSS®

SPSS Student Assistant: Red Lobster: Recoding and Computing Variables

Field Data Collection Quality Controls

Precautions and procedures can be implemented to minimize the effects of the various types of errors just described. Please note that we said "minimize" and not "eliminate," as the potential for error always exists. However, by instituting the following controls, a researcher can be assured that the nonsampling error factor involved with data collection will be diminished. The field data collection quality controls we describe are listed in Table 11.2.

CONTROL OF INTENTIONAL FIELDWORKER ERROR

Intentional fieldworker error can be controlled with supervision and validation procedures.

Two general strategies—supervision and validation—can be employed to guard against cases in which the interviewer might intentionally commit an error.[25] **Supervision** uses administrators to oversee the work of field data collection workers.[26] Most centralized telephone interviewing companies have a "listening in" capability that the supervisor can use to tap into and monitor any interviewer's line during an interview. (At this point you may want to reread the comments made by Steve Gittelman in the opening vignette to this chapter.) Even though they have been told that the interview "may be monitored for quality control," the respondent and the interviewer may be unaware of the monitoring, so the "listening in" samples a representative interview performed by that interviewer. The monitoring may be performed on a recording of the interview rather than in real time. If the interviewer is leading or unduly influencing respondents, this procedure will spot the violation, and the supervisor can take corrective action such as reprimanding that interviewer. With personal interviews, the supervisor might accompany an interviewer to observe that interviewer while administering a questionnaire in the field. Because "listening in" without the consent of the respondent could be considered a

TABLE 11.2 How to Control Data-Collection Errors

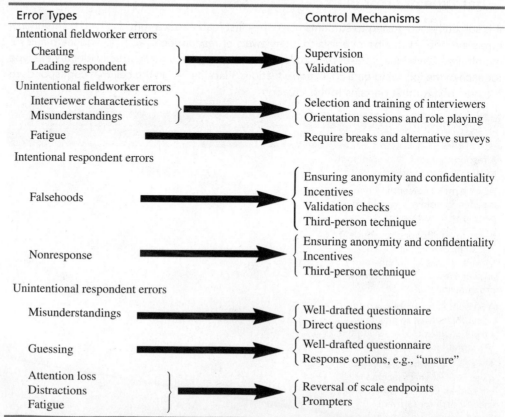

Error Types	Control Mechanisms
Intentional fieldworker errors	
Cheating Leading respondent	Supervision Validation
Unintentional fieldworker errors	
Interviewer characteristics Misunderstandings	Selection and training of interviewers Orientation sessions and role playing
Fatigue	Require breaks and alternative surveys
Intentional respondent errors	
Falsehoods	Ensuring anonymity and confidentiality Incentives Validation checks Third-person technique
Nonresponse	Ensuring anonymity and confidentiality Incentives Third-person technique
Unintentional respondent errors	
Misunderstandings	Well-drafted questionnaire Direct questions
Guessing	Well-drafted questionnaire Response options, e.g., "unsure"
Attention loss Distractions Fatigue	Reversal of scale endpoints Prompters

breach of privacy, many companies now inform respondents that all or part of the call may be monitored and/or recorded.

Validation verifies that the interviewer did the work. This strategy is aimed at the falsification/cheating problem. There are various ways to validate the work. One type of validation is for the supervisor to recontact respondents to find out whether they took part in the survey. An industry standard is to randomly select 10% of the completed surveys for purposes of making a call-back to validate that the interview was conducted. A few sample questions might even be readministered for comparison purposes. In the absence of call-back validation, a supervisor may inspect completed questionnaires, and, with a trained eye, may spot patterns in an interviewer's completions that raise suspicions of falsification. Interviewers who turn in bogus completed questionnaires are not always careful about simulating actual respondents. The supervisor might find inconsistencies, such as very young respondents with large numbers of children, that raise doubts as to a questionnaire's authenticity.

An industry standard is verification of 10% of the completed surveys.

CONTROL OF UNINTENTIONAL FIELDWORKER ERROR

As you would expect, supervision is instrumental in minimizing unintentional interviewer error. We describe four mechanisms commonly used by professional field data collection companies in this regard: selection and training, orientation sessions, role playing,[27] and methods to reduce fatigue. Interviewer personal characteristics that can cause unintentional errors are best taken care of by careful selection of interviewers. Following selection, it is important to train them well to avoid any biases resulting from manner, appearance, and so forth. **Orientation sessions** are meetings in which the supervisor introduces the survey and questionnaire administration requirements to the fieldworkers.[28] The supervisor might highlight qualification or quota requirements, note skip patterns, or go over instructions to the interviewer that are embedded throughout the questionnaire to standardize the interview across interviewers.[29] Finally, often as a means of becoming familiar with a questionnaire's administration requirements, interviewers will conduct **role-playing sessions**, which are dry runs or dress rehearsals of the questionnaire with the supervisor or some other interviewer playing the respondent's role. Successive role-playing sessions serve to familiarize interviewers with the questionnaire's special administration aspects. To control for interviewer fatigue, some researchers require interviewers to take frequent breaks and/or alternate surveys, if possible. In short, the more competent the field interverview through training, supervision, and personal skills, the lower the potential for interviewer error.[30]

Unintentional fieldworker errors can be reduced with supervised orientation sessions and role playing.

Tactics useful in minimizing intentional respondent error include anonymity, confidentiality, validation checks, and third-person technique.

Incentives sometimes compel respondents to be more truthful, and they also discourage nonresponse.

CONTROL OF INTENTIONAL RESPONDENT ERROR

To control intentional respondent error, it is important to minimize falsehoods and nonresponse tendencies on the parts of respondents. Tactics useful in minimizing intentional respondent error include anonymity, confidentiality, incentives, validation checks, and third-person technique.[31] **Anonymity** occurs when the respondent is assured that his or her name will not be associated with his or her answers. **Confidentiality** occurs when the respondent is given assurances that his or her answers will remain private. Both assurances are believed to be helpful in forestalling falsehoods. The belief here is that when respondents are guaranteed they will remain nameless, they will be more comfortable in self-disclosure and will refrain from lying or misrepresenting themselves.[32]

Another tactic for reducing falsehoods and nonresponse error is the use of **incentives**, which are cash payments, gifts, or something of value promised to respondents in return for their participation.[33] For participating in a survey, respondents may be paid cash or provided with redemption coupons. They might be given a gift such as a ballpoint pen or a T-shirt. In a sense, respondents

Confidentiality and/or anonymity may reduce refusals to take part in a survey.

Photo: Elnur/Shutterstock

are being induced to tell the truth by direct payment. Respondents may now feel morally obligated to tell the truth because they will receive compensation. Or, they may feel guilty at receiving an incentive and then not answering truthfully. Unfortunately, practitioners and academic researchers are only beginning to understand how to entice prospective respondents to take part in a survey.[34] For instance, only recently has relevance of the subject matter been documented to increase response rates.[35]

A different approach for reducing falsehoods is the use of **validation checks**, in which information provided by a respondent is confirmed during the interview. For instance, in an in-home survey on Leap Frog educational products for preschool children, the interviewer might ask to see the respondent's Leap Frog unit and modules as a verification or validation check. A more unobtrusive validation is to have the interviewer, who is trained to be alert to untrue answers, check for old-appearing respondents who say they are young, shabbily dressed respondents who say they are wealthy, and so on. A well-trained interviewer will make note of suspicious answers.[36]

Finally, there is a questionnaire design feature that a researcher can use to reduce intentional respondent errors. Sometimes the opportunity arises where a **third-person technique** can be used in a question, in which instead of directly quizzing the respondent, the question is couched in terms of a third person who is similar to the respondent. For instance, a question posed to a middle-aged man might be, "Do you think a person such as yourself uses Viagra?" Here, the respondent will most probably think in terms of his own circumstances, but because the subject of the question is some unnamed third party, the question is not seen as personal. In other words, he will not be divulging personal and private information by talking about this fictitious other person. The third-person technique may be used to reduce both falsehoods and nonresponse.

> With an embarrassing question, the third-person technique may make the situation less personal.

CONTROL OF UNINTENTIONAL RESPONDENT ERROR

The control of unintentional respondent error takes various forms as well, including well-drafted questionnaire instructions and examples, reversals of scale endpoints, and use of prompters. Well-drafted **questionnaire instructions and examples** are commonly used as a way of avoiding respondent confusion. We described these in our chapter on questionnaire design. Also, researchers sometimes resort to direct questions to assess respondent understanding. For example, after describing a 5-point agree–disagree response scale in which 1 = strongly agree, 2 = agree, 3 = neither agree nor disagree, 4 = disagree, and 5 = strongly disagree, the interviewer might be instructed to ask, "Are these instructions clear?" If the respondent answers in the negative, the instructions are repeated until the respondent understands them. Guessing may be reduced by alerting respondents to response options such as "no opinion," "do not recall," or "unsure."

> Ways to combat unintentional respondent error include well-drafted questionnaire instructions and examples, reversals of scale endpoints, use of scale endpoints, and use of prompters.

A tactic we described when we discussed the semantic differential is **reversals of scale endpoints,** in which instead of putting all of the negative adjectives on one side and all the positive ones on the other side, a researcher will switch the positions of a few items. Such reversals are intended to warn respondents that they must respond to each bipolar pair individually. With agree–disagree statements, this tactic is accomplished by negatively wording a statement every now and then to induce respondents to attend to each statement individually. Both of these tactics are intended to heighten the respondent's attention.

> Prompters are used to keep respondents on task and alert.

Finally, long questionnaires often use **prompters,** such as "We are almost finished," "That was the most difficult section of questions to answer," or other statements strategically located to encourage the respondent to remain on track. Sometimes interviewers will sense an attention lag or fatigue on the part of the respondent and provide their own prompters or comments intended to maintain the respondent's full participation in the survey. Online surveys often have a "% completed" scale or indication that informs respondents of their progress in the survey.

FINAL COMMENT ON THE CONTROL OF DATA COLLECTION ERRORS

As you can see, a wide variety of nonsampling errors can occur on the parts of both interviewers and respondents during the data collection stage of the marketing research process. Similarly, a variety of precautions and controls are used to minimize nonsampling error. Each survey is unique, of course, so we cannot provide universally applicable guidelines. We will, however, stress the importance of good questionnaire design in reducing these errors. Also, professional field data collection companies whose existence depends on how well they can control interviewer and respondent error are commonly relied on by researchers who understand the true value of these services. Finally, technology is dramatically changing data collection and helping in the control of its errors.[37]

Nonresponse Error

Although nonresponse was briefly described earlier in our discussion of mail surveys, we will now describe this issue more fully, including various types of nonresponse, how to assess the degree of this error, and some ways of adjusting or compensating for nonresponse in surveys. Nonresponse was defined earlier as a failure on the part of a prospective respondent to take part in the survey or to answer specific questions on the questionnaire. Nonresponse has been labeled the marketing research industry's biggest problem,[38,39] and it is multinational in scope.[40] Compounding the problem has been the increase in the numbers of surveys, which means the likelihood of being asked to participate in a survey has increased. Some industry observers believe that nonresponse is caused by fears of invasion of privacy, skepticism of consumers regarding the benefits of participating in research, and the use of research as a guise for telemarketing. Of course, it is unethical to force or trick people to respond. The Marketing Research Association Code of Ethics—portions of which are presented in Marketing Research Insight 11.2—clearly states that respondents have rights to refuse to participate in or withdraw from a study at any time.

The identification, control, and adjustments necessary for nonresponse are critical to the success of a survey. There are at least three different types of potential nonresponse error lurking in any survey: refusals to participate in the survey, break-offs during the interview, and refusals to answer specific questions, or item omission. Table 11.3 briefly describes each type of nonresponse.

There are three types of nonresponse error: refusals to participate in the survey, break-offs during the interview, and refusals to answer specific questions (item omissions).

MARKETING RESEARCH INSIGHT 11.2 *Ethical Consideration*

Marketing Research Association Code of Ethics: Respondent Participation

1. Will respect the respondent's right to withdraw or to refuse to cooperate at any stage of the study and will not use any procedure or technique to coerce or imply that cooperation is obligatory.

2. Will give respondents the opportunity to refuse to participate in the research when there is a possibility they may be identifiable even without the use of their name

or address (e.g., because of the size of the population being sampled).

Respondent cooperation is strictly on a voluntary basis. Respondents are entitled to withdraw from a research project. Company policies and/or interviewer instructions should state that the interviewer must give respondents the opportunity not to participate for any reason.

TABLE 11.3   **The Three Types of Nonresponses with Surveys**

Name	Description
Refusal	The prospective respondent declines to participate in the survey.
Break-off	After answering some questions in the survey, the respondent stops participating.
Item Omission	The respondent does not answer a particular question but does answer other questions.

REFUSALS TO PARTICIPATE IN THE SURVEY

Refusals to participate in surveys are increasing worldwide.

A **refusal** occurs when a potential respondent declines to take part in the survey. Refusal rates differ by area of the country as well as by demographic differences. The reasons for refusals are many and varied.[41] People may be busy or have no interest in the survey. They may be turned off by the interviewer's voice or approach. The survey topic may be overly sensitive.[42] Or refusal may just be a standard response for some people.[43] Refusals may result from negative previous survey participation experiences.[44] People may decline to participate because they do not want to take the time or regard surveys as an intrusion of their privacy. Refusals are a concern even with panels.[45]

As we previously mentioned, one way to overcome refusals is to use incentives as a token of appreciation. In a review of 15 different mail surveys, researchers found that inclusion of a small gift, such as a $1.50 rollerball pen, increased response rates by nearly 14%. A second feature that contributes to refusals is the length of the questionnaire.[46] The study previously cited found that for every minute it takes to fill out the questionnaire, the response rate drops by 0.85%. Response rates to mail surveys are also influenced by the type of appeal that is made in the cover letter. Results from one study indicated that a social utility appeal was more effective in increasing response rates when an educational institution was the sponsor. On the other hand, an egoistic appeal was more effective when the sponsor was a commercial organization. An egoistic appeal is a suggestion that the respondent's individual responses are highly important in completing the research task.[47] Of course, it is critical that well-trained interviewers be employed to carry out the surveys. Increasingly, research providers are focusing on improved training techniques and field audits.

If tired, confused, uninterested, or interrrupted, respondents may "break off" in the middle of an interview.

BREAK-OFFS DURING THE INTERVIEW

A **break-off** occurs when a respondent reaches a certain point and then decides not to answer any more questions in the survey. As you would expect, there are many reasons for break-offs. For instance, the interview may take longer than the respondent initially believed; the topic and specific questions may prove to be distasteful, too personal, or boring; the instructions may be confusing; the survey may be too complex;[48] or a sudden interruption may occur. As Marketing Research Insight 11.3 relates, break-offs are somewhat influenced by the degree of truthfulness when interviewers tell prospective respondents how long the survey will take.

REFUSALS TO ANSWER SPECIFIC QUESTIONS (ITEM OMISSION)

Even if a refusal or break-off situation does not occur, a researcher will sometimes find that specific questions have lower response rates than others. In fact, if a marketing researcher suspects ahead of time that a

A break-off may occur at any time during a survey.

Photo: Roger Costa Morera/Shutterstock

MARKETING RESEARCH INSIGHT 11.3 — *Practical Application*

Telling White Lies about the Length of a Survey: What Does It Get You?

It is well known that when asked to take part in surveys, potential respondents are less likely to participate if they think the survey will take a long time to complete. How long is too long? Some practitioners advocate keeping the survey length to 10 minutes or less. A study aimed to determine reactions of potential respondents to the stated length of the survey.[49] Researchers set up a web-based survey and invited potential respondents to take part in it. The invitation to participate included the statement "The survey lasts *x* minutes"; some invitees were told 10 minutes, some 20, and some 30. As would be expected, the participation rate dropped with the longer time interval. Specifically, 75.0% began the 10-minute survey, while only 64.9% and 62.4%, respectively, began the 20- and 30-minute survey. In other words, exceeding the 10-minute length rule caused about 10% of the invitees to decline.

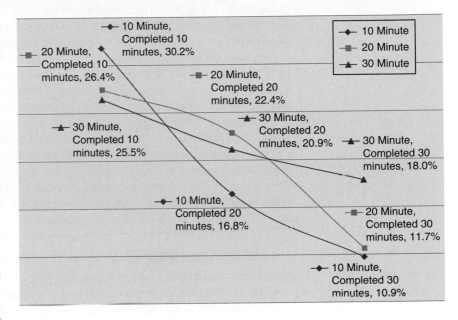

Next, the researchers tested what happens if the survey is actually longer than the stated length. In reality, the complete survey took 30 minutes. Those respondents who were told it would take 10 minutes were informed that the main part of the study was completed when they reached the 10-minute mark, but they were asked to continue and answer more questions. The 20-minute group was similarly notified at the 20-minute mark in the survey. The accompanying graph presents the break-off rates that occurred.

With respondents told the survey would take 10 minutes, 30% completed the survey, but when asked to answer more questions, about one-half exited in the next 10 minutes, and almost one-half of those remaining exited before the survey ended at 30 minutes. With the respondents told that the survey would take 20 minutes, about 22% completed the 20-minute survey, but when asked to answer more questions, about one-half broke off the survey. With respondents informed of the full 30-minute survey, the break-off trend is not as steep, and the numbers who complete the entire survey is 60% to 70% greater than the respondents who were told the "little white lies" about the survey's length. This research shows that in the recruitment of survey respondents, honesty is the best policy when it comes to informing them about the length of the survey.

---

particular question, such as the respondent's annual income for last year, will have some degree of refusals, it is appropriate to include the designation "refusal" on the questionnaire. Of course, some believe it is not wise to put these designations on self-administered questionnaires, because respondents may use this option simply as a cop-out, when they might have provided accurate answers if the designation were not there. **Item omission** is the phrase sometimes used to identify the percentage of the sample that did not answer a particular question.[50] Research has shown that sensitive questions elicit more item omissions while questions that require more mental effort garner more "don't know" responses.[51] It is useful for a researcher to offer the "don't know" option with the latter type of questions to reduce item omissions.

Occasionally, a respondent will refuse to answer a particular question that he or she considers too personal or a private matter.

WHAT IS A COMPLETED INTERVIEW?

Almost all surveys have some item omissions and break-offs. Nonetheless, these respondents did provide some information. At which point does a break-off still constitute a completed interview? At which level of item omission do we deem a survey to be incomplete? In other words, a researcher must define or specify the criteria for a "completed interview." Ultimately, it is a judgment call and will vary with each marketing research project. Only in rare cases will it be necessary that all respondents answer all of the questions. In most others, the researcher will adopt some decision rule that defines completed versus not completed interviews. For example, in most research studies, there are questions directed at the primary purpose of the study. Also, there are usually questions asked for purposes of adding insights into how respondents answered the primary questions. Such secondary questions often include a list of demographic questions. Demographics, because they are more personal in nature, are typically placed at the end of the questionnaire. Because these questions are not the primary focus of the study, a **completed interview** may be defined as one in which all the primary questions have been answered. In this way, the marketing researcher has data for primary questions and most of the data for secondary questions. Interviewers can then be given a specific statement as to what constitutes a completed survey such as, "If the respondent answers through question 18, you may count it as a completion." (The demographics begin with question 19.) Likewise, the researcher must adopt a decision rule for determining the extent of item omissions necessary to invalidate a survey or a particular question.

Marketing researchers must define a "completed" interview.

MEASURING NONRESPONSE ERROR IN SURVEYS

The marketing research industry has an accepted way to calculate a survey's response rate.

Most marketing research studies report their response rates. However, for many years there was much confusion about the calculation of response rates. There was no one universally accepted definition, and different firms used different methods to calculate response rates. In fact, there were many terms in common usage, including completion rate, cooperation rate, interview rate, at-home rate, and refusal rate, among others. In 1982, however, the Council of American Survey Research Organizations (CASRO) published a special report in an attempt to provide a uniform definition and method for calculating the response rate.[52]

According to the CASRO report, response rate is defined as the ratio of the number of completed interviews to the number of eligible units in the sample:[53]

CASRO Response Rate Formula (Simple Form)

$$\text{Response rate} = \frac{\text{Number of completed interviews}}{\text{Number of eligible units in sample}}$$

Completions are eligible people who take part in the survey.

In most surveys eligible units are respondents determined by screening or qualifying questions. For example, if we were working with a department store that was specifically concerned with its kitchenwares department, we would determine eligibility for the survey by asking prospective respondents the screening question, "Do you shop at Acme Department Store regularly?" For those who answer affirmatively, we would then ask, "Have you shopped in the kitchenwares department at any time during the last three months?" Those respondents who again answer "Yes" are eligible to take part in the survey.

Let's assume we have a sample of 1,000 shoppers, and the results of the survey are the following:

Completions = 400

Ineligible = 300

Refusals = 100

Not reached = 200

This information allows you to calculate the number of sample units that are (a) eligible, (b) ineligible, and (c) not ascertained because they were not reached. When calculating the response rate, we have the number of completions in the numerator, while in the denominator we have the number of completions plus the numbers of those who refused, whose lines were busy, and who were eligible but did not answer. Because we do not talk to those who refuse (before the screening question), don't answer, have busy signals, or are not at home, how do we determine the percentage of these people who would have been eligible? We multiply their number by the percentage of those we did talk with who are eligible. This method assumes that the same percentage of eligibles exist in the population of those we did talk with (of the 700 we talked with, 57% were eligible) as exist in the population of those we did not get to talk with (due to refusals, no answers, or busy signals). The formula for calculating the response rate for this situation is:

CASRO Response Rate Formula (Expanded Form)

$$\text{Response rate} = \frac{\text{Completions}}{\text{Completions} + \left(\dfrac{\text{Completions}}{\text{Completions} + \text{Ineligible}}\right) \times (\text{Refusals} + \text{Not reached})}$$

Here are the calculations:

Calculation of CASRO Response Rate (Expanded Form)

$$\text{Response rate} = \frac{400}{400 + \left(\dfrac{400}{400 + 300}\right)(100 + 200)}$$

$$= \frac{400}{400 + (0.57)(300)}$$

$$= 70\%$$

 Active Learning

How to Calculate a Response Rate Using the CASRO Foumula

Whereas the CASRO formulas seems simple and straightforward, questions arise as to exactly how to interpret them when dealing with individual research projects. We have created this Active Learning exercise so you can appreciate what goes into the proper calculation of a response rate.

Assume you are doing this survey as a class project and you have been assigned the task of conducting telephone interviews. You are given a list of randomly selected telephone numbers and told to fill a quota of five completions. You are instructed to make at least three contact attempts before giving up on a telephone number. Also, you are given a call record sheet where you are to write in the result of each call attempt. As you call each number, you record one of the following outcomes by the telephone number and in the column corresponding to which contact attempt pertained to that particular call. The results you can record are as follows:

Disconnected (D)—message from phone company that number is no longer in service.
Wrong Target (WT)—(ineligible) number is a business phone and you are interested only in residences.
Ineligible Respondent (IR)—no one in household has purchased an automobile within last year.
Refusal (R)—subject refuses to participate.
Terminate (T)—subject begins survey but stops before completing all questions.
Completed (C)—questionnaire is completed.
Busy (BSY)—phone line is busy; attempt call-back at later time unless this is your third attempt.
No Answer (NA)—no one anwers or you encounter a telephone answering device. You may leave a message and state that you will call back later unless this is your third attempt.
Call Back (CB)—Subject has instructed you to call back at more convenient time; record call-back time and date and return call unless this is your third attempt.

Let's assume that your list of numbers and codes looks like the following:

Telephone Number	1st Attempt	2nd Attempt	3rd Attempt
474-2892	No Answer	No Answer	Completed
474-2668	Busy	Ineligible Respondent	
488-3211	Disconnected		
488-2289	Completed		
672-8912	Wrong Target		
263-6855	Busy	Busy	Busy
265-9799	Terminate		
234-7160	Refusal		
619-6019	Call Back	Busy	Busy
619-8200	Ineligible Respondent		
474-2716	Ineligible Respondent		
774-7764	No Answer	No Answer	
474-2654	Disconnected		
488-4799	Wrong Target		
619-0015	Busy	Completed	
265-4356	No Answer	No Answer	Completed
265-4480	Wrong Target		
263-8898	No Answer	No Answer	No Answer
774-2213	Completed		

You should note that you completed your quota of 5 completed interviews with 19 telephone numbers. Look at the last code you recorded for each number and count the number of each code. Insert these numbers into the following response rate formula to determine your correctly computed response rate:

$$\text{Response rate} = \frac{C}{C + \left(\dfrac{C}{C + IR + WT}\right)(BSY + D + T + R + NA)}$$

$$= \underline{\hspace{2cm}} \%$$

Note how ineligibles were handled in the formula. Both *IR* and *WT* were counted as ineligibles. The logic is that the percentage of eligibles among those you talked with is the same as among those not talked with (*BSY, D, T, R,* and *NA*).

Dataset, Coding Data, and the Data Code Book

Because of the widespread use of computer technology, it is rare for researchers to work with printed questionnaires. Instead, the respondents' answers are typically contained in an electronic **dataset**, which is a matrix arrangement of numbers (mainly) in rows and columns similar to a Microsoft Excel or other spreadsheet. Each row pertains to the answers provided by a single respondent to the questions on the questionnaire. Each column represents a question on the questionnaire. Of course, if a question has multiple parts to it, then it would take up multiple columns. Because the answers vary from respondent to respondent, data pertaining to the questions or question parts are sometimes referred to as *variables*. Normally, the first row of a data matrix where the researcher locates a label such as "Age," "Gender," or "Satisfaction" identifies the question or question part associated with each column in the data matrix; these designations are often called *variable labels* or *variable names*.

The dataset is created by an operation called **data coding**, defined as the identification of code values that are associated with the possible responses for each question on the

A dataset is an arrangement of numbers (mainly) in rows and columns.

questionnaire. You learned about data coding in the questionnaire design chapter where we described this same operation as *precoding*. Typically, these codes are numerical because numbers are quick and easy to input, and computers work with numbers more efficiently than they do with letter or text codes. In large-scale projects, and especially in cases in which the data entry is performed by a subcontractor, researchers use a **data code book** which identifies: (1) the questions on the questionnaire, (2) the variable name or label that is associated with each question or question part, and (3) the code numbers associated with each possible response to each question. With a code book that describes the data file, any analyst can work on the dataset, regardless of whether that analyst was involved in the research project during its earlier stages. As you will soon learn, after an SPSS dataset is fully set up, the data code book is contained in the dataset.

Because precoded questionnaires have response codes associated with the various responses, it is a simple matter to create a code book. However, as we will soon point out, the researcher will no doubt encounter missing data where respondents have failed to answer a question. What code is used when a missing item is encountered? The easiest and most acceptable code for a missing response is to use a blank, meaning that nothing is entered for that respondent on the question that was not answered. Practically all statistical analysis programs treat a blank as "missing," so a blank or empty cell is the universal default code to signify missing data.

With online surveys, the data file "builds" or "grows" as respondents submit their completed online questionnaires. That is, the codes are programmed into the questionnaire file, but they do not appear as code numbers such as those customarily placed on a paper-and-pencil questionnaire. In the case of web-based surveys, the code book is vital as it is the researcher's only map to decipher the numbers found in the data file and to correlate them to the answers to the questions on the questionnaire.

With statistical analysis programs such as SPSS, it is easy to obtain the coding after the dataset has been set up. Figure 11.1 illustrates how the SPSS Variable View feature can be used to reveal the coding for each variable in an SPSS dataset. In other words, when finalized, an SPSS dataset makes the complete data code book for that dataset available to any user.

To learn about the data code book, launch www.youtube.com and search for "Code book – Lisa Dierker."

Data coding is the identification of code values associated with the possible responses for each question on the questionnaire.

Researchers use data coding when preparing and working with a computer data file.

SPSS®

SPSS Student Assistant: Noxzema Skin Cream: Selecting Cases

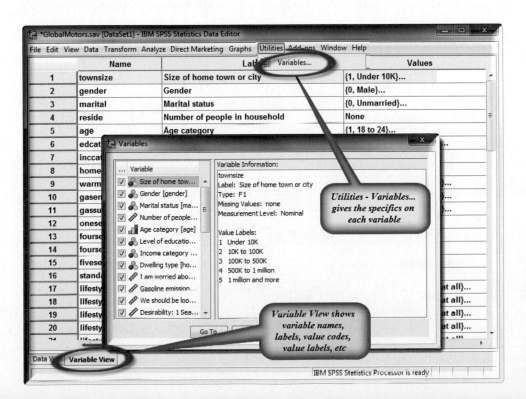

FIGURE 11.1 SPSS Variable View and Variables Command Reveals A Dataset's Code Book

Source: Reprint courtesy of International Business Machines Corporation, © SPSS, Inc., an IBM Company

Data Quality Issues

Datasets should be inspected for errors.

Nonresponses appear in practically every survey. At the same time, some respondents may provide answers that have a suspicious pattern. Both of these occurances necessitate a separate phase of the data preparation stage in the marketing research process that involves inspecting respondents' answers in the dataset. Data quality is a concern for market researchers.[54] Obviously, the researcher's goal is to work with a set of data with as few data quality issues as humanly possible. Consequently, the researcher must examine the responses for data quality problems prior to analysis.

WHAT TO LOOK FOR IN RAW DATA INSPECTION

Raw data inspection determines the presence of "bad" respondents.

The purpose of raw data inspection is to determine the presence of "bad" respondents and, as noted earlier, to throw out the ones with severe problems. Problem respondents fall into the following five categories: incomplete responses (break-offs), nonresponses to specific questions (item omissions), yea- or nay-saying patterns, and middle-of-the-road patterns. We describe each problem, and Table 11.4 illustrates an example of each one. In industry jargon, these are "exceptions," and they signal data quality errors to a researcher.

Some questionnaires may be only partially completed.

Incomplete Response An **incomplete response** is a break-off where the respondent stops answering in the middle of the questionnaire. Again, the reason the survey was not completed may never be known. In Table 11.4, Respondent A stopped answering after Question 3.

When a respondent does not answer a particular question, it is referred to as an item omission.

Nonresponses to Specific Questions (Item Omissions) For whatever reasons, a respondent sometimes leaves a question blank. In a telephone interview, he or she may decline to answer a question, and the interviewer might note this occurrence with the designation "ref" (refused) or some other code to indicate that the respondent failed to answer the question. In Table 11.4, Respondent B did not answer Questions 4 and 7.

Yea- or Nay-Saying Patterns Even when questions are answered, there can be signs of problems. A **yea-saying** pattern may be evident in the form of all "yes" or "strongly agree" answers.[55] These are identified as all "5" codes for Respondent C's Questions 5–9 in Table 11.4. The yea-sayer has a persistent tendency to respond in the affirmative regardless of the question,

TABLE 11.4 Identification of Data Quality Errors Found in Raw Data Matrix Inspection

Error Type	Q1	Q2	Q3	Q4	Q5	Q6	Q7	Q8	Q9	Description of Error
Incomplete response (Break-off)										
Respondent A	1	2	3							Questionnaire is incompletely filled out. No answers after Q3.
Nonresponse to specific question(s) (Item omission)										
Respondent B	1	2	1		4	2		4	5	The respondent refused to answer particular question(s), but answered others before and after it. Q4 and Q7 are not answered.
Yea-saying										
Respondent C	1	2	2	3	5	5	5	5	5	Respondent exhibits a persistent tendency to respond favorably (yea) regardless of the questions. Q5–Q9 are all 5, the code for "strongly agree."
Nay-saying										
Respondent D	2	1	3	1	1	1	1	1	1	Respondent exhibits a persistent tendency to respond unfavorably (nay) regardless of the questions. Q5–Q9 are all 1, the code for "strongly disagree."
Middle-of-the-road										
Respondent E	1	2	1	3	3	3	3	3	3	Respondent indicates "no opinion" to most questions Q5–Q9 are all 3, the code for "Neutral."

Code Book: Questions Q1–Q3 are 1=Yes, 2=No, 3=No opinion; Questions Q5–Q9 are 1=Strongly Disagree, 2=Disagree, 3=Neutral, 4=Agree, and 5=Strongly Agree and yea-saying implies invalid responses. The negative counterpart to the yea-saying is **nay-saying**, identifiable as persistent responses in the negative, or all "1" codes for Respondent D's Questions 5–9 in Table 11.4. Repeating the same answer on grid-type questions is a variation called "straightlining" which also signals a response quality problem.[56]

There is some research now comparing the data quality as it differs by type of respondent and/or data collection method. Marketing Research Insight 11.4 illustrates how demographic, Internet usage, and data quality differed in the case of wireless phone surveys versus those conducted with fixed or "land line" telephones.

Middle-of-the-Road Patterns The **middle-of-the-road pattern** is seen as a preponderance of "no opinion" responses or "3" codes for Respondent E's Questions 5–9 in Table 11.4. No opinion is in essence no response, and prevalent no opinions on a questionnaire may signal low interest, lack of attention, or even objections to being involved in the survey. True, a respondent may not have an opinion on a topic, but if one gives many no opinion answers, questions arise as to how useful that respondent is to the survey. It should be noted that our yea-saying, nay-saying, and middle-of-the-road examples in Table 11.4 are extreme cases; sometimes these appear as tendencies such as almost all 4s and 5s for yea-saying, almost all 1s and 2s for nay-saying, and almost all "neutral" responses for middle-of-the-road errors. Online survey respondents who yea-say, nay-say, or give excessive no opinion answers are sometimes referred to as "speeders" because they are giving rapid-fire answers without reading the questions carefully. They are also called "straightliners" because they select the same answer time and again on a scale.[57]

Other Data Quality Problems Marketing researchers may encounter other bothersome problems during questionnaire screening. For example, respondents may have checked more than one response option when only one was supposed to be checked. They may have failed

Yea-saying and nay-saying are seen as persistent tendencies on the parts of some respondents to agree or disagree, respectively, with most of the questions asked.

To learn about data quality, launch **www.youtube.com**, and search for "Survey data quality—lightspeedresearch."

Some respondents hide their opinions by indicating "no opinion" throughout the survey.

MARKETING RESEARCH INSIGHT 11.4   *Social Media Marketing*

Differences Between Wireless and Land Line Telephone Survey Respondents

It is well known that consumers who rely heavily on social media also use wireless phones almost to the exclusion of fixed or "land line" telephones. In fact, large subpopulations of social media consumers, such as college students, own only wireless phones. Whereas the land line telephone survey was the dominant data collection method in the latter decades of the 20th century, it has dramatically declined as the survey method of choice for marketing researchers. There are two complementary reasons for this decline. First, the Internet has become the dominant data collection method due to its many advantages over all other data collection methods. Second, many consumers have shifted to wireless phone communication, even if they also own a land line.

A survey in Portugal was performed with 1,000 land line respondents and 1,000 mobile phone respondents.[58] The following differences vividly depict the important differences between wireless consumers who are "into social media" consumers and land line consumers who do not use social media extensively. The mobile phone users in the Portuguese survey were:

- Younger
- Less educated (due to being younger and still in school)

- Less likely to be retired (another obvious age-related attribute)
- From larger households
- More likely to be unmarried
- More opinionated
- Less into politics
- More likely to develop friendships over the Internet

They also:

- Used the Internet more to search for job-related information
- Used the Internet for fast communication and convenience
- Completed the survey

Wireless respondents were less likely to give "don't know" or "no opinion" answers. There was no meaningful difference in acquiescence, or yea-saying, between the two groups. According to this survey, wireless phone owners do represent special concerns for marketing researchers regarding survey data quality.

to look at the back of a questionnaire page and thus missed all of the questions there. Or they may have ignored an agree–disagree scale and simply written in personal comments. Usually, detecting these errors requires physically examining the questionnaires. With online surveys, however, most such problems can usually be blocked by selecting options or requirements in the online questionnaire program that prevent such errors from occuring.

How to Handle Data Quality Issues. When a researcher encounters data quality issues such as those just described, there are three options. First, if there are several egregious errors, the researcher will most likely throw out the respondent's entire data row. Second, if the errors are minor and will not falsely sway the survey findings, the researcher will probably leave the respondent's entire data row in the dataset. Finally, if there is a combination of some obvious error-riden responses and valid responses, the researcher may opt to set the bad data items to blanks or missing data and use only the good data items in subsequent analyses.

SPSS®

SPSS Student Assistant:
Getting SPSS Help

Summary

Total error in survey research is a combination of sampling error and nonsampling error. Sampling error may be controlled by the sample plan and the sample size. Researchers must know both the sources of nonsampling error and ways to minimize the effect on total error. The data collection phase of marketing research holds great potential for nonsampling errors. Intentional and unintentional errors on the parts of both interviewers and respondents must be regulated. Dishonesty, misunderstanding, and fatigue affect fieldworkers, whereas falsehoods, refusals, misunderstanding, and fatigue affect respondents. Several controls and procedures may be used to overcome these sources of error such as supervision, validation, careful selection, and orientation sessions for interviewers. In addition, researchers use anonymity, confidentiality, incentives, validation checks, third-person technique, well-drafted questionnaires, direct questions, response options such as "unsure," reversals of scale endpoints, and prompters to minimize respondent errors.

Nonresponse errors of various types are encountered in the data collection phase, including refusals to take part in the survey, break-offs during the survey, and item omission or not answering particular questions while answering all the others. Nonresponse error can be measured by the calculation of the response rate using the CASRO response rate formula.

Responses to surveys are organized into a dataset, which is rows and columns of mostly numbers where each respondent is represented by a row and each question or question part is recorded in a column. Researchers use a data code book that indicates how the code numbers relate to the question responses on the questionnaire. Prior to data analysis, the dataset should be inspected for data quality issues such as incomplete, yea-saying, nay-saying, middle-of-the-road, and other respondents whose answers are suspect. These respondents' answers should be removed from the dataset.

Key Terms

Nonsampling error (p. 264)
Data collection (p. 264)
Fieldworker error (p. 264)
Respondent error (p. 264)
Intentional fieldworker errors (p. 265)
Interviewer cheating (p. 265)
Leading the respondent (p. 265)
Unintentional interviewer errors (p. 267)
Interviewer misunderstanding (p. 267)
Fatigue-related mistakes (p. 267)
Intentional respondent errors (p. 268)

Falsehoods (p. 268)
Nonresponse (p. 268)
Unintentional respondent error (p. 268)
Respondent misunderstanding (p. 268)
Guessing (p. 268)
Attention loss (p. 269)
Distractions (p. 269)
Respondent fatigue (p. 269)
Supervision (p. 270)
Validation (p. 271)
Orientation sessions (p. 271)

Role-playing sessions (p. 271)
Anonymity (p. 271)
Confidentiality (p. 271)
Incentives (p. 271)
Validation checks (p. 272)
Third-person technique (p. 272)
Questionnaire instructions and examples (p. 272)
Reversals of scale endpoints (p. 272)
Prompters (p. 272)
Refusals (p. 274)

Break-offs (p. 274)
Item omission (p. 275)
Completed interview (p. 276)
CASRO response rate formula (p. 276)

Dataset (p. 278)
Data coding (p. 278)
Data code book (p. 279)
Incomplete response (p. 280)

Yea-saying (p. 280)
Nay-saying (p. 281)
Middle-of-the-road pattern (p. 281)

Review Questions/Applications

1. Distinguish sampling error from nonsampling error.
2. Because we cannot easily calculate nonsampling errors, how must the prudent researcher handle nonsampling error?
3. Identify different types of intentional fieldworker error and the controls used to minimize them. Identify different types of unintentional fieldworker error and the controls used to minimize them.
4. Identify different types of intentional respondent error and the controls used to minimize them. Identify different types of unintentional respondent error and the controls used to minimize them.
5. Define *nonresponse*. List three types of nonresponse found in surveys.
6. If a survey is found to have resulted in significant nonresponse error, what should the researcher do?
7. Why is it necessary to perform preliminary screening of a dataset?
8. Identify five different problems that a researcher might find while screening a dataset.
9. What is an "exception," and what is typically done with each type of exception encountered?
10. Your church is experiencing low attendance with its Wednesday evening Bible classes. You volunteer to design a telephone questionnaire aimed at finding out why church members are not attending these classes. Because the church has limited funds, members will be used as telephone interviewers. List the steps necessary to ensure good data quality in using this do-it-yourself option of field data collection.
11. A new mall-intercept company opens its offices in a nearby discount mall, and its president calls on the insurance company where you work to solicit business. It happens that your company is about to do a study on the market reaction to a new whole life insurance policy it is considering adding to its line. Make an outline of the information you would want from the mall-intercept company president to assess the quality of its services.
12. Acme Refrigerant Reclamation Company performs large-scale reclamation of contaminated refrigerants as mandated by the U.S. Environmental Protection Agency. It wishes to determine what types of companies will have use of this service, so the marketing director designs a questionnaire intended for telephone administration. Respondents will be plant engineers, safety engineers, or directors of major companies throughout the United States. Should Acme use a professional field data collection company to gather the data? Why or why not?

13. You work part time in a telemarketing company. Your compensation is based on the number of credit card applicants you sign up. The company owner has noticed that the credit card solicitation business is slowing down, so she decides to take on some marketing research telephone interview business. When you start work on Monday, she assigns you to do telephone interviews and gives you a large stack of questionnaires to have completed. What intentional fieldworker errors are possible under the circumstances described here?
14. Indicate what specific intentional and unintentional respondent errors are likely with each of the following surveys.
    a. The Centers for Disease Control sends out a mail questionnaire on attitudes and practices concerning the prevention of AIDS.
    b. Eyemasters has a mall-intercept survey performed to determine opinions and uses of contact lenses.
    c. Boy Scouts of America sponsors a telephone survey on Americans' views on humanitarian service agencies.
15. How do you define a "completion," and how does this definition help a researcher deal with incomplete questionnaires?
16. What is nay-saying, and how does it differ from yea-saying? What should a researcher do if he or she suspects a respondent of being a nay-sayer?
17. On your first day as a student marketing intern at the O-Tay Research Company, the supervisor hands you a list of yesterday's telephone interviewer records. She tells you to analyze them and to give her a report by 5 p.m. Well, get to it!

	Ronnie	Mary	Pam	Isabelle
Completed	20	30	15	19
Refused	10	2	8	9
Ineligible	15	4	14	15
Busy	20	10	21	23
Disconnected	0	1	3	2
Break-off	5	2	7	9
No answer	3	2	4	3

CASE 11.1

Cass Corridor Food Co-Op

Founded in the 1960s, Cass Corridor Food Co-Op is a small, mostly organic or naturally grown fruits and vegetables retailer, located in Detroit, Michigan, on Cass Avenue. At one time, Cass Avenue and the "corridor" of streets parallel to it were a prestigious residential location for Detroit's wealthiest citizens, but Cass Corridor fell into hard times in the 1960s when it earned a repuation as being one of the most dangerous neighborhoods in the United States. Drug sellers and users, criminals, homeless people, and gangs roamed the area until the late 1980s when demolition and rebuilding dramatically changed the enviroment for the better. Now called "Midtown" by the new residents who are trying to revitalize it as a thriving community, the area is still referred to as "Cass Corridor" by some Detroit residents who remember its ugly past.

Cass Corridor Co-Op was founded to help the poor and unfortunate residents of this area during its worst times, so it is essentially a "bare bones" operation. Most of the new Midtown residents do not use the co-op, so its organizers and operators consulted with a marketing professor from Wayne State University, which is located directly north of the Cass Corridor area. The professor recommended that the co-op conduct a survey of the Midtown residents to see if its mission and approach fit the new consumers who are living there. Recognizing that Cass Corridor Co-Op operates on a meager budget, he suggests that it use the American Marketing Association (AMA) student chapter for data collection in a telephone survey as a means of holding costs down.

While the Cass Corridor Co-Op folks were excited about the survey, they were skeptical of the ability of students to execute this research. The professor offered to facilitate a meeting with Cass Corridor Co-Op officials and the marketing research projects director of the student AMA chapter. When he returned to campus, he informed the AMA student chapter president of the opportunity and suggested that the marketing research projects director draft a list of the quality control safeguards that would be used in a Cass Corridor Co-Op community telephone survey in which 20 Wayne State University student interviewers would be calling from their apartments or dorm rooms.

1. Take the role of the marketing research projects director, and draft all of the interviewer controls you believe are necessary to effect data collection comparable in quality to that gathered by a professional telephone interviewing company.

2. The AMA student chapter president calls the marketing research projects director and says, "I'm concerned about the questionnaire's length. It will take over 20 minutes for the typical respondent to complete over the phone. Isn't the length going to cause problems?" Again, take the role of the marketing research projects director. Indicate what nonresponse problems might result from the questionnaire's length, and recommend ways to counter each of these problems.

CASE 11.2   INTEGRATED CASE

Global Motors

Global Motors executives have decided to use an online panel company as the data collection method for a survey on consumer attitudes about energy-efficient vehicles. Among the reasons for this decision are: (1) use of an online questionnaire, (2) assurance of a random sample that represents U.S. households, (3) high response rate, (4) quick survey data collection, (5) low refusals to particular questions, (6) no need to ask about demographics, automobile ownership, and media preferences, as these attributes of online panel members are known, and (7) reasonable total cost.

Global Motors CEO Nick Thomas has agreed to leave the selection of the online panel company up to CMG

Research. Cory Rogers's team at CMG has narrowed the choice to two online panel companies, based on inspections of their website descriptions, email and telephone communications, and other factors. The costs of using these companies are comparable, so no single provider is favored at this time.

Cory's team studies the set of questions published by the European Society for Opinion and Marketing Research (ESOMAR), "26 Questions to Help Research Buyers of Online Samples."[59] The team selects five questions that are geared toward data quality. Each competing online panel company has prepared short responses to the five questions.

Question 1. *What experience does your company have with providing online samples for market research?*

Company A: We have conducted market research since 1999. We are the only panel company to take advantage of computer technology and provide a truly nationally representative U.S. sample online.

Company B: We have supplied online U.S. samples since 1990, European samples since 2000, and our Asian Panel went "live" in 2005. We have supplied approximately 5,000 online samples to our clients in the past 10 years.

Question 2. *What are the people told when they are recruited?*

Company A: Individuals volunteer for our online panel via our website, where they are informed that they will be compensated with redemption points based on the number of surveys in which they take part.

Company B: We recruit household members by asking them to join our panel, telling them they can have a say in the development of new products and services. They are rewarded with "credits" they can use to claim products.

Question 3. *If the sample comes from a panel, what is your annual panel turnover/attrition/retention rate?*

Company A: Our voluntary drop out rate is approximately 5% per month. If a panelist misses 10 consecutive surveys, he/she loses his/her panel membership.

Company B: We do a one-for-one replacement for each panel member who drops out voluntarily (about 3% per year) or who is removed due to nonparticipation (about 2% per year).

Question 4. *What profile data is kept on panel members? For how many members is this data collected and how often is this data updated?*

Company A: We maintain extensive individual-level data, in the form of about 1,000 variables, including demographics, household characteristics, financials, shopping and ownership, lifestyles, and more. All are updated every other year.

Company B: For each panelist, we have about 2,500 data points on demographics, assortment of goods and services owned, segmentation/lifestyle factors, health-related matters, political opinions, travel, financials, Internet usage, leisure activities, memberships, etc. Our updating is done annually.

Question 5. *Explain how people are invited to take part in a survey.*

Company A: Typically a survey invitation is sent via email and posted on every selected panel member's personal member page. In either case, we have a link to the online survey location: "Click here to start your survey." The email invitation is sent daily to selected panelists until the survey quota is filled.

Company B: Based on the client's sample requirements, we email selected panelists with a link to the online survey. After 48 hours, if the panelist has not participated, we send a reminder, and again 48 hours after the reminder.

Using Descriptive Analysis, Performing Population Estimates, and Testing Hypotheses

LEARNING OBJECTIVES

- To learn about the concept of data analysis and the functions it provides
- To appreciate the five basic types of statistical analysis used in marketing research
- To use measures of central tendency and dispersion customarily used in describing data
- To learn how to obtain descriptive statistics with SPSS
- To understand the concept of statistical inference
- To learn how to estimate a population mean or percentage
- To test a hypothesis about a population mean or percentage
- To learn how to perform and interpret statistical inference with SPSS

"WHERE WE ARE"

1 Establish the need for marketing research.

2 Define the problem.

3 Establish research objectives.

4 Determine research design.

5 Identify information types and sources.

6 Determine methods of accessing data.

7 Design data collection forms.

8 Determine the sample plan and size.

9 Collect data.

10 **Analyze data.**

11 Prepare and present the final research report.

Would You Say You Already Know What Basic Descriptive Statistics Are?

When asked what is meant by basic descriptive statistics, most students start trying to recall some of those concepts they learned back in the elementary statistics course. "Er, uhhh, are they *t* tests? Or, uhh, are they standard deviations?" A few of you may think you know what basic descriptive statistics are, but it may be a surprise to learn that *all* of you know what they are! That's correct. You already know. How can that be possible? Think about it this way. What is the first or second question students ask their professors when they return to class after a test and the professor is preparing to hand out the graded tests? Go ahead, give us your best guess.

"What was the average score on the test?"

You are right! That is the most common first asked question. Let's suppose your professor answers "85." Some students were likely hoping to earn much higher grade than a B, and others may be thinking, "Wow! I hope I made an 85, but I wonder how many scored below the average." Based on those reactions, what do you think the second question might be?

"What was the grade distribution? How many As, Bs, Cs and so on?"

Correct again! See, you do already know what basic descriptive statistics are. Basic descriptive statistics answer two fundamental questions: (1) How did the average person respond? and (2) How different are the others from this average? When your professor says the average grade was 85, she is answering the first question. When she gives you the number, or percentage, of letter grades (A through F), she is answering the second question. Note that it was important to you to know answers to *both* questions. Knowing only the first tells you the average performance of the class. You do know that an 85 is better than a 55 and less than a 90 average. It certainly tells you something of value, doesn't it? But by only knowing the average, you still don't know how different the other scores are. It is possible that everyone scored a 85! It is also possible that no one scored a 85; some scored very high and some scored very low! Note how different this makes the interpretation of the 85 for the professor. In the first case, everyone is doing "average." In the second case, she has some outstanding students and some who need immediate academic resuscitation. Again, we see why it is important to look at both these questions.

Let's think of a marketing research application of basic descriptive statistics. In the Global Motors case that accompanies this text, the company asks a sample of consumers many questions about their demographics, magazine readership, other media preferences, and the desirability of various fuel-efficient new automobile models that could be developed. After making certain that all the data have been correctly inputted into a computer program such as SPSS, the marketing researcher runs basic descriptive statistics. You will have the opportunity to work with

this SPSS dataset as you read and do the Active Learning and Integrated Case exercises in this chapter. For now, simply read our example. We will look at the question: "How desirable is a standard size gasoline automobile model that gets 33 mpg in the city and 50 mpg on the highway?" The answers are measured on a 1–7 scale ranging from Very undesirable (1) to Very desirable (7). Now we are ready to answer our two questions: What was the average response to the question? Since we have a scale variable, "average" may be an arithmetic mean. As you will learn in this chapter, when you want to calculate an arithmetic mean, you run the SPSS command "Descriptives," which produces the following output:

What is the first question you ask your professor just before she hands back your graded tests?

Photo: Monkey Business Images/Shutterstock

Descriptive Statistics					
	N	**Minimum**	**Maximum**	**Mean**	**Standard Deviation**
Desirability standard size Gasoline	1,000	1	7	3.21	1.453
Valid *N* (listwise)	1,000				

We see our average as 3.21 on a 7-point scale. This is akin to knowing our average test score was 85, and this knowledge alone gives us some information. We know there is some preference for this auto; we don't have a real low score, nor do we have an extremely high score. What about our second question? How different are those who didn't have this "average" score? Statisticians use the term *variance* to describe the degree to which data vary. One measure of variance is the *standard deviation*, which is reported as 1.453. The higher this number, the more people differ from the average; the lower the number, the less they differ. Another measure of variance is the *range*." We see in the table that some scored the minimum (1) and that some scored the maximum (7). If we want to know how many scored in each of the seven different scale categories, we would run another SPSS command, "Frequencies." The output follows.

Desirability Standard Size Gasoline				
	Frequency	**Percent**	**Valid Percent**	**Cumulative Percent**
Valid Very undesirable	104	10.4	10.4	10.4
Undesirable	248	24.8	24.8	35.2
Somewhat undesirable	288	28.8	28.8	64.0
Neutral	141	14.1	14.1	78.1
Somewhat desirable	150	15.0	15.0	93.1
Desirable	51	5.1	5.1	98.2
Very desirable	18	1.8	1.8	100.0
Total	1,000	100.0	100.0	

With these two tables alone, the marketing researcher has provided the client with all the basic descriptive statistics he or she needs to understand the responses to this question. In this chapter you will learn when and how to run descriptives and frequencies in SPSS. When you finish the chapter, you will be able to do more than just articulate what is meant by basic descriptive statistics. You will know how to use the powerful SPSS tool to generate them on your own. You will also learn that basic descriptive statistics are the "bread and butter" of most marketing research projects.

This chapter begins our discussion of the various statistical techniques available to the marketing researcher. As you will soon learn, these techniques are devices to convert formless data into valuable information, as illustrated in the vignette that opens this chapter. These techniques summarize and communicate patterns found in the datasets marketing researchers analyze. We preview five different types of statistical analyses commonly used by marketing researchers. Next, we define descriptive analysis and discuss descriptive measures such as the mode, median, and mean. We also discuss measures of variability, including the frequency distribution, range, and standard deviation, and the most appropriate use of each measure. In addition, we show you how to obtain the various descriptive statistics available in SPSS.

Other concepts explored in this chapter include the difference between the term *statistic*, which applies to a sample, and *parameter*, which pertains to the related population value, as well as logical inference and its relationship to statistical inference. There are two basic types of statistical inference, and we discuss both cases. First, there is parameter estimation in which a value, such as the population mean, is estimated based on a sample's mean and size. Second, there is hypothesis testing where an assessment is made as to how much of a sample's findings supports a manager's or researcher's a priori belief regarding the size of a population value. We provide formulas and numerical examples, including examples of SPSS procedures and output using survey data from our Global Motors case study.

Types of Statistical Analyses Used in Marketing Research

As you learned in the previous chapter, marketing researchers work with a dataset, which is an arrangement primarily of numbers in rows and columns. The columns represent answers to the various questions on the survey questionnaire, and each row represents a respondent. The problem confronting the marketing researcher when faced with a dataset is **data analysis**, which is defined as the process of describing a dataset by computing a small number of statistics that characterize various aspects of the data. Data analysis distills the dataset while retaining enough information so the client can mentally envision its salient characteristics.[1]

Five basic types of statistical analyses can be used by marketing researchers to reduce a dataset: descriptive analysis, inferential analysis, differences analysis, associative analysis, and predictive analysis (Table 12.1). Each one has a unique role in the data analysis process; moreover, these various methods are usually combined into a complete analysis of the information to satisfy the research objectives. These techniques are progressively more complex, but at the same time, they convert raw data into increasingly more useful information as they increase in complexity.

These introductory comments will provide a preview of the subject matter that will be covered in this and other chapters. Because this is an introduction, we use the names of statistical procedures, but we do not define or describe them here. The specific techniques are all developed later in this textbook. It is important, however, that you understand each of the various categories of analysis available to the marketing researcher and comprehend generally what each is about.

DESCRIPTIVE ANALYSIS

Certain measures such as the mean, mode, standard deviation, and range are forms of **descriptive analysis** used by marketing researchers to describe the sample dataset in such

Descriptive analysis is used to describe the variables (answers to the questions) in a dataset (all respondents' answers).

TABLE 12.1 Five Types of Statistical Analyses Used by Marketing Researchers

Type	Description	Example	Statistical Concepts
Descriptive analysis	Summarizes basic findings for the sample	Describes the typical respondent, describes how similar respondents are to the typical respondent	Mean, median, mode frequency distribution, range, standard deviation
Inference analysis	Determines population parameters, tests hypotheses	Estimates population values	Standard error, null hypothesis
Difference analysis (Chapter 13)	Determines if differences between two percentages or two or more means for groups in the sample	Evaluates the statistical significance of difference in the means of two groups in a sample	t test of differences, analysis of variance
Association analysis (Chapter 14)	Determines simple relationships	Determines if two variables are related in a systematic way	Correlation, cross-tabulation
Predictive analysis (Chapter 15)	Finds complex relationships for variables in the dataset	Determines how several independent variables influence a key dependent variable	Multiple regression

a way as to portray the "typical" respondent and to reveal the general pattern of responses. Descriptive measures are typically used early in the analysis process and become foundations for subsequent analysis.[2]

INFERENCE ANALYSIS

Inference analysis is used to generate conclusions about the population's characteristics based on the sample data.

When marketing researchers use statistical procedures to generalize the results of the sample to the target population it represents, the process is referred to as **inference analysis**. In other words, such statistical procedures allow a researcher to draw conclusions about the population based on information in the dataset provided by the sample. Inferential statistics include hypothesis testing and estimating true population values based on sample information. We describe basic statistical inference in this chapter.

DIFFERENCE ANALYSIS

Differences analysis may reveal important distinctions among various types of credit card users.

Photo: Valua Vitaly/Shutterstock

Difference analysis is used to compare the mean of the responses of one group to that of another group, such as satisfaction ratings for "heavy" users versus "light" users.

Association analysis determines the strength and direction of relationships between two or more variables (questions in the survey).

Predictive analysis allows insights into multiple relationships among variables.

Occasionally, a marketing researcher needs to determine whether two groups are different. For example, the researcher may be investigating credit card usage and want to see if high-income earners differ from moderate-income earners in how often they use American Express. The researcher may statistically compare the average annual dollar expenditures charged on American Express by high- versus moderate-income buyers. Important market segmentation information may come from this analysis. Or the researcher may run an experiment to see which of several alternative advertising themes garners the most favorable impression from a sample of target audience members. The researcher uses **difference analysis** to determine the degree to which real and generalizable differences exist in the population to help the manager make an enlightened decision on which advertising theme to use. Statistical differences analyses include the *t* test for significant differences between groups and analysis of variance. We define and describe this form of analysis in Chapter 13.

ASSOCIATION ANALYSIS

Researchers use other statistical techniques to determine systematic relationships among variables. **Association analysis** investigates if and how two variables are related. For instance, are advertising recall scores positively associated with intentions to buy the advertised brand? Are expenditures on sales force training positively associated with sales force performance? Depending on the statistic used, the analysis may indicate the strength of the association and/or the direction of the association between two questions on a questionnaire in a given study. We devote Chapter 14 to descriptions of cross-tabulations and correlations that are basic associative analysis methods used in marketing research.

PREDICTIVE ANALYSIS

Techniques are also available if the researcher is interested in determining more complex patterns of associations, but most of these procedures are beyond the scope of this textbook—with one exception. Statistical procedures and models are available to the marketing researcher to help make forecasts about future events, and these fall under the category of **predictive analysis**. The marketing researcher commonly uses regression analysis to enhance prediction capabilities. Because marketing managers are typically worried about what will happen in the future given certain conditions such as a price increase, prediction is desirable. Predictive analysis can provide valuable insight into the nature of multiple relationships among the variables in a dataset. Regression analysis is described in depth in Chapter 15.

It is not our intention to make you an expert in statistical analysis. Rather, the primary objective of our introduction to statistical analysis is to acquaint you with the basic concepts involved in each of the selected measures. You will certainly do basic statistical analysis throughout your marketing career, and it is likely that you will encounter information summarized in statistical terms. As a result, it is important for you to have a conceptual understanding of the commonly used statistical procedures. Our descriptions are intended to show when and where each measure is appropriately used and to help you interpret the meaning of the statistical result once it is reported. We also rely heavily on computer statistical program output because you will surely encounter this type of output in your company's marketing information system and/or summarized in a marketing research study report.

Understanding Data via Descriptive Analysis

SPSS®

We now turn to the several tools in descriptive analysis available to researchers to summarize the data obtained from a sample of respondents. In this chapter and in all other data analysis chapters, we will use the Global Motors survey dataset so that you can reconstruct the data analysis on your own with SPSS. To download this dataset, go to the following website (www.pearsonhighered.com/burns) and find the dataset download area.

The Global Motors questionnaire was posted online, and with the aid of a panel company, qualified respondents answered the questions and submitted their questionnaires in the time allotted for the online survey. Certain questions, such as demographics and automobile ownership, were purchased from the panel company's database. The survey and database date were combined and set up in SPSS, assigned variable names and value labels, and cleaned. The final dataset, in an SPSS data file called **GlobalMotors.sav**, has a total of 1,000 respondents and 32 variables. Download the GlobalMotors.sav file and use SPSS to examine the questions and response formats that were used in the survey. We will refer to some of these formats as we explore the use of SPSS for various types of analyses described in this and subsequent chapters.

For this introduction to data analysis, you will "watch over the shoulder" of the marketing researcher assigned to analyze this dataset. The columns in the "Data View" window are the variables that correspond to the questions and parts of questions on the questionnaire, and the individual rows represent respondents' answers to the questions.

Two sets of measures are used extensively to describe the information obtained in a sample. The first set involves measures of central tendency or measures that describe the "typical" respondent or response. The second set involves measures of variability or measures that describe how similar (dissimilar) respondents or responses are to (from) "typical" respondents or responses. Other types of descriptive measures are available, but they do not enjoy the popularity of central tendency and variability. In fact, they are rarely reported to clients.

> Commonly used descriptive analysis reveal central tendency (typical response) and variability (similarity of responses).

MEASURES OF CENTRAL TENDENCY: SUMMARIZING THE "TYPICAL" RESPONDENT

The basic data analysis goal involved in all **measures of central tendency** is to report a single piece of information that describes the most typical response to a question. The term *central tendency* applies to any statistical measure used that somehow reflects a typical or frequent response.[3] Three such measures of central tendency are commonly used as data analysis devices.[4] They are the mode, the median, and the mean. We describe each in turn.

> Three measures of central tendency are mode, median, and mean.

Mode The **mode** is a descriptive analysis measure defined as that value in a string of numbers that occurs most often. In other words, if you scanned a list of numbers constituting a field in a dataset, the mode would be that number that appeared more than any other.

The mode is a relative measure of central tendency, for it does not require that a majority of responses occurred for this value. Instead, it simply specifies the value that occurs most

> In a set of numbers, the mode is that number appearing most often.

frequently; and there is no requirement that this occurrence is 50% or more. It can take on any value as long as it is the most frequently occurring number. If a tie for the mode occurs, the distribution is considered to be "bimodal" for a two-way or "trimodal" for a three-way tie.

The median expresses the value whose occurrence lies in the middle of a set of ordered values.

Median An alternative measure of central tendency is the **median**, which expresses that value whose occurrence lies in the middle of an ordered set of values. That is, one-half of all the values is greater than the median and the other half is less than the median. Thus, the median tells us the approximate halfway point in a set or string of numbers that are arranged in ascending or descending order while taking into account the frequency of each value. With an odd number of values, the median falls on one of the values, but with an even number, the median may fall between two adjacent values.

To determine the median, the researcher creates a frequency or percentage distribution with the numbers in the string in either ascending or descending order. In addition to the raw percentages, the researcher computes cumulative percentages and, by inspecting these, finds where the 50–50 break occurs. The median supplies more information than does the mode, for a mode may occur anywhere in the string, but the median must be at the halfway point.

The mean is the arithmetic average of a set of numbers.

Mean A third measure of central tendency is the **mean**, sometimes referred to as the *average*. It differs from the mode and the median in that a computation is necessary. The mean is computed through the use of the following formula:

Formula for a mean

$$\text{Mean } (\bar{x}) = \frac{\sum_{i=1}^{n} x_i}{n}$$

where:

n = the number of cases

x_i = each individual value

Σ signifies that all the x_i values are summed

As you can see, all members in the set of n numbers, each designated by x_i, are summed, and that total is divided by the number of members in that set. The resulting number is the mean, a measure that indicates the central tendency of those values. It approximates the typical value in that set of values. Because the mean is determined by taking every member of the set of numbers into account through this formula, it is more informative than the median. Means communicate a great deal of information, and they can be plotted for quick interpretations.

MEASURES OF VARIABILITY: VISUALIZING THE DIVERSITY OF RESPONDENTS

Although they are extremely useful, measures of central tendency are incomplete descriptors of the variety of values in a particular set of numbers. That is, they do not indicate the variability of responses to a particular question or, alternatively, the diversity of respondents on some characteristic measured in our survey. To gain sensitivity for the diversity or variability of values, the marketing researcher must turn to measures of variability. All **measures of variability** are concerned with depicting the "typical" difference between the values in a set of values.

Measures of variability reveal the typical difference between the values in a set of values.

It is one matter to know the mean or some other measure of central tendency, but it is quite another matter to be aware of how close to that mean or measure of central tendency the rest of the values fall. Knowing the variability of the data could greatly influence a marketing decision based on the data because it expresses how similar the respondents are to one another on the topic under examination. There are three measures of variability: frequency distribution, range, and standard deviation. Each measure provides its own version of information that helps to describe the diversity of responses.

Measures of variability include frequency distribution, range, and standard deviation.

Frequency and Percentage Distribution A **frequency distribution** is a tabulation of the number of times that each different value appears in a particular set of values. Frequencies themselves are raw counts, and normally these frequencies are converted into percentages for ease of comparison. The conversion is accomplished simply through a quick division of the frequency for each value by the total number of observations for all values, resulting in a percent, called a **percentage distribution**. Of course, the sum of all these percent values is 100%.

To review, a frequency distribution affords an accounting of the responses to values in a set. It quickly communicates all the different values in the set, and it expresses how similar the values are. The percentage distribution is often used here because most people can easily relate to percentages. Plus, percentage distributions are easily presented as pie or bar charts,[5] which are convenient graphical representations of these distributions that researchers find very helpful in communicating findings to clients or others.

Variability indicates how different respondents are on a topic such as what model of automobile is preferred.

Photo: Kurhan/Shutterstock

Range The **range** identifies the distance between lowest value (minimum) and the highest value (maximum) in an ordered set of values. Stated somewhat differently, the range specifies the difference between the endpoints in a set of values arranged in order. The range does not provide the same amount of information supplied by a frequency distribution; however, it identifies the interval in which the set of values occurs. The range also does not tell you how often the maximum and minimum occurred, but it does provide some information on the dispersion by indicating how far apart the extremes are found.

Standard Deviation The **standard deviation** indicates the degree of variation or diversity in the values in such a way as to be translatable into a normal or bell-shaped curve distribution. Marketing researchers often rely on the standard deviation when performing basic analyses, and they usually report it in their tables. It is worthwhile to digress for a moment to describe this statistical concept.

Figure 12.1 shows the properties of a bell-shaped or normal distribution of values. The usefulness of this model is apparent in its symmetric distribution: Exactly 50% of the distribution lies on either side of the midpoint (the apex of the curve). With a normal curve, the midpoint is also the mean. Standard deviations are known units of measurement that are located on the horizontal axis. They relate directly to assumptions about the normal curve. For example, the range of 1.64 standard deviations above and 1.64 standard deviations below the midpoint includes 90% of the total area under that curve. Because the bell-shaped distribution is a theoretical or ideal concept, this property never changes. Moreover, the proportion of area under the curve and within plus or minus any number of standard deviations from the mean is perfectly known. For the purposes of this presentation, normally only two or three of these values are of interest to marketing researchers. Specifically, ±2.58 standard deviations describes the range in which 99% of the area under the curve is found, ±1.96 standard deviations is associated with 95% of the area under the curve, and ±1.64 standard deviations corresponds to 90% of the bell-shaped curve's area. Remember, we must assume that the shape of the frequency distribution of the numbers approximates a normal curve, so keep this in mind during our following examples.

Marketing Research on YouTube™ To learn about measures of central tendency, launch www.youtube.com, and search for "Measures of Central Tendency Rap."

A frequency (percentage) distribution reveals the number (percent) of occurrences of each number in a set of numbers.

The range identifies the maximum and minimum values in a set of numbers.

A standard deviation indicates the degree of variation in a way that can be translated into a bell-shaped curve distribution.

The standard deviation embodies the properties of a bell-shaped distribution of values.

It is now time to review the calculation of the standard deviation. The equation typically used for the standard deviation is as follows:

Formula for a standard deviation

$$\text{Standard deviation } (s) = \sqrt{\frac{\sum_{i-1}^{n}(x_i - \bar{x})^2}{n-1}}$$

In this equation, x_i stands for each individual observation and $\bar{x}$ stands for the mean. The standard deviation is a measure of the differences of all observations from the mean, expressed as a single number. To compute the standard deviation, you must begin with the mean, and then compare each observation to the mean by subtracting and squaring the difference. It may seem strange to square differences, add them up, divide them by $(n-1)$ and then take the square root. If we did not square the differences, we would have positive and negative values; and if we summed them, there would be a cancellation effect. That is, large negative differences would cancel out large positive differences, and the numerator would end up being close to zero. But this result is contrary to what we know is the case with large differences: There is variation, which should be expressed by the standard deviation. The formula remedies this problem by squaring the subtracted differences before they are summed. Squaring converts all negative numbers to positives and, of course, leaves the positives positive. Next, all of the squared differences are summed and divided by 1 less than the number of total observations in the string of values; 1 is subtracted from the number of observations to achieve what is typically called an "unbiased" estimate of the standard deviation. But we now have an inflation factor to worry about because every comparison has been squared. To adjust for this, the equation specifies that the square root be taken after all other operations are performed. This final step adjusts the value back down to the original measure (e.g., units rather than squared units). By the way, if you did not take the square root at the end, the value would be referred to as the **variance**. In other words, the variance is the standard deviation squared.

Now, whenever a standard deviation is reported along with a mean, a specific picture should appear in your mind. Assuming that the distribution is bell shaped, the size of the standard deviation number helps you envision how similar or dissimilar the typical responses are to the mean. If the standard deviation is small, the distribution is greatly compressed (with a high peak). On the other hand, with a large standard deviation value, the distribution is consequently flat because it is stretched out at both ends.

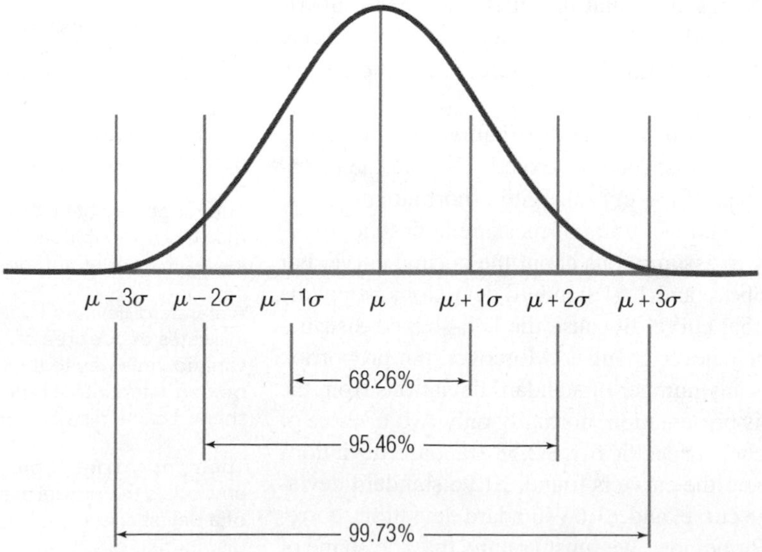

The squaring operation in the standard deviation formula is used to avoid the cancellation effect.

With a bell-shaped distribution, 95% of the values lie within ±1.96 times the standard deviation away from the mean.

FIGURE 12.1 Normal Curve Interpretation of Standard Deviation

When to Use a Particular Descriptive Measure

In Chapter 8, you learned that the level of measurement for a scale affects how it may be statistically analyzed. Remember, for instance, that nominal question forms contain much less information than do those questions with scale assumptions. Recall that in Chapter 8, we defined and gave examples of interval and ratio scales. SPSS allows users to identify scale types, and it uses "scale" as the label to refer to either an interval or a ratio scale. We will use the SPSS label from this point on. Similarly, the amount of information provided by each of the various measures of central tendency and dispersion differs. As a general rule, statistical measures that communicate the most amount of information should be used with scales that contain the most amount of information, and measures that communicate the least amount of information should be used with scales that contain the least amount of information. The level of measurement determines the appropriate measure; otherwise, the measure cannot be interpreted.

At first reading, this rule may seem confusing, but on reflection, it should become clear that the level of measurement of each question dictates the measure that should be used. It is precisely at this point that you must remember the arbitrary nature of coding schemes. For instance, if on a demographic question concerning religious affiliation, "Catholic" is assigned a 1, "Protestant" is assigned a 2, "Jewish" is assigned a 3, and so forth, a mean could be computed. But what would be the interpretation of an average religion of 2.36? It would have no practical interpretation because the mean assumes interval or ratio scaling (SPSS's "scale"), whereas the religion categories are nominal. The mode would be the appropriate central tendency measure for these responses.

Table 12.2 indicates how the level of measurement relates to each of the three measures of central tendency and measures of variation. The table should remind you that a clear understanding of the level of measurement for each question on the questionnaire is essential because the researcher must select the statistical procedure and direct the computer to perform the procedure. The computer cannot distinguish the level of measurement because we typically store and handle our data as numbers as matters of convention and convenience.

Don't monkey around! Use the guide in Table 12.2 to decide what is the appropriate descriptive analysis to use.

Photo: Vasiliy Koval/Shutterstock

Marketing Research on YouTube™ | To learn about measures of central tendency, launch **www.youtube.com**, and search for "Summarizing Distributions: Measures of Variability."

The scaling assumptions underlying a question determine which statistic is appropriate.

TABLE 12.2 What Descriptive Statistic to Use When

Example Question	Measurement Level	Central Tendency (The Most Typical Response)	Variability (How Similar the Responses Are)
What is your gender?	Nominal scale	Mode	Frequency and/or percentage distribution
Rank these five brands from your first choice to your fifth choice.	Ordinal scale	Median	Cumulative percentage distribution
On a scale of 1 to 5, how does Starbucks rate on variety of its coffee drinks?	Interval scale	Mean	Standard deviation and/or range
About how many times did you buy fast food for lunch last week?	Ratio scale	Mean	Standard deviation and/or range

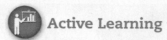 **Active Learning**

Compute Measures of Central Tendency and Variability

Thus far, the chapter has described measures of central tendency (mean, median, mode) and measures of variability (percentage distribution, range, and standard deviation). At the same time, you should realize that certain measures are appropriate for some scales, but inappropriate for other scales. The following data set is of respondents who answered questions on a survey about the propane gas grills they own.

Respondent	For how many years have you owned your gas grill?	Where did you purchase your gas grill?	About how much did your pay for your gas grill?
1	2	Department store	$200
2	7	Hardware store	$500
3	8	Department store	$300
4	4	Specialty store	$400
5	2	Specialty store	$600
6	1	Department store	$300
7	3	Department store	$400
8	4	Department store	$300
9	6	Specialty store	$500
10	8	Department store	$400
Mean	___	___	___
Standard deviation	___	___	___
Range: maximum & minimum	___	___	___
Median	___	___	___
Mode	___	___	___

Determine what measure(s) of central tendency and what measures of variability are appropriate and compute them. We have listed the relevant measures under the "Respondent" column of the dataset, and your task is to write in the proper answer (or "not appropriate") under each of the three questions in the survey.

The Global Motors Survey: Obtaining Descriptive Statistics with SPSS

INTEGRATED CASE

Beginning with this chapter and all subsequent chapters dealing with statistical analyses, we provide illustrations with the use of SPSS in two ways. First, in your textbook descriptions, we indicate step-by-step the procedures used with SPSS to obtain the statistical analyses being described. Plus, we have included examples of SPSS output in these sections. The second way is with the use of your SPSS Student Assistant. By now, you should be well acquainted with the Student Assistant. We prompt you to look at these statistical analysis sections that illustrate how to operate SPSS, as well as how to find specific statistical results in SPSS output.

Descriptive statistics are needed to see the Global Motors survey's basic findings.

OBTAINING A FREQUENCY DISTRIBUTION AND THE MODE WITH SPSS

Many questions on the Global Motors survey had categorical response options and, thus, embodied nominal scaling assumptions. With a nominal scale, the mode is the appropriate measure of central tendency, and variation must be assessed by looking at the distribution of responses across the various response categories.

To illustrate how to obtain a frequency distribution and percentage distribution and to determine the mode of our 1,000 respondent Global Motors dataset, we will use the size of home town variable as it is a nominal scale. Figure 12.2 shows the clickstream sequence to find a mode for the size of home town using the entire Global Motors survey dataset. As you can see, the primary menu sequence is ANALYZE–DESCRIPTIVE STATISTICS–FREQUENCIES. This sequence opens the variable selection window where you specify the variable(s) to be analyzed, and the Statistics … button opens the Statistics window, which has several statistical concepts as options. Because we are working only with the mode, you would click in the check mark box beside the Mode. Continue will close this window, and OK will close the variable selection and cause SPSS to create a frequency distribution and identify the mode. You can see this output in Figure 12.3, where the code number of 4 is specified as the mode response, and the frequency distribution shows that 500K to 1 million is the largest home town/city size represented with 396 respondents selecting it, or 39.6% of the total.

As you look at the output, you should notice that the variable labels and value labels were defined, and they appear on the output. The DESCRIPTIVE STATISTICS–FREQUENCIES procedure creates a frequency distribution and associated percentage distribution of the responses for each question. Its output includes a statistics table and a table for each variable that includes the variable label, value labels, frequencies, percent, valid percent, and cumulative percent.

Our Global Motors survey dataset is *not* typical because there are no missing answers. There are no missing responses because the dataset was purchased from a consumer panel company that guaranteed 100% response. However, as you learned in Chapter 11, it is not uncommon for respondents to refuse to answer a question in a survey or to be unable to answer a

SPSS®

A frequency distribution and mode are appropriate for nominal scales.

Use the ANALYZE–DESCRIPTIVE STATISTICS–FREQUENCIES procedure to produce descriptive statistics for variables with nominal or ordinal scaling.

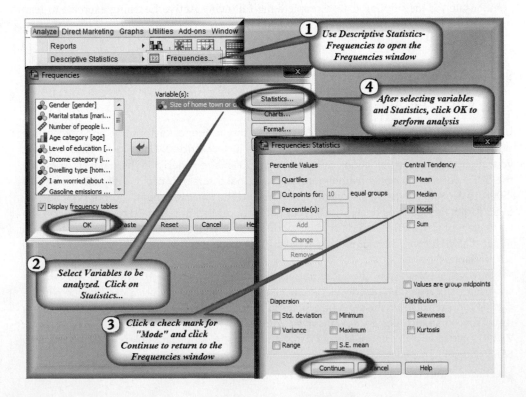

FIGURE 12.2 SPSS Clickstream to Obtain a Frequency Distribution and the Mode

Source: Reprint courtesy of International Business Machines Corporation, © SPSS, Inc., an IBM Company

FIGURE 12.3
SPSS Output for a Frequency Distribution and the Mode

Source: Reprint courtesy of International Business Machines Corporation, © SPSS, Inc., an IBM Company

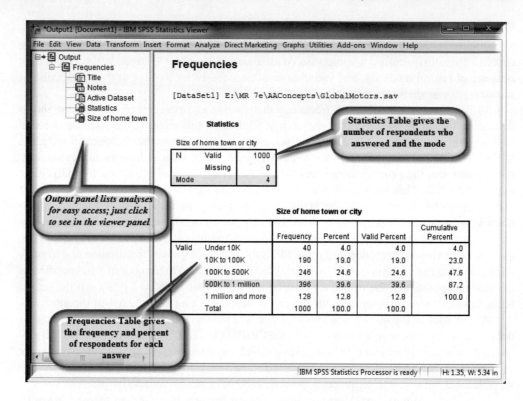

SPSS®

SPSS Student Assistant: Descriptive Statistics for Nominal Data: Frequencies, Percents, Mode.

question. Alternatively, a respondent may be directed to skip a question if his or her previous answer does not qualify him or her for the subsequent question. If any of these occurs, and the respondent is still included in the dataset, we have an instance of "missing data." This is no problem for SPSS and most other data analysis programs; the output will be adjusted to compensate for the missing data. Complete the following Active Learning exercise to learn how SPSS recognizes and handles missing data.

 Active Learning

SPSS® **How SPSS Handles Missing Data**

Use your SPSS Global Motors dataset to compute the frequency distribution and percentage distribution and to identify the mode as we have just described. Use Figure 12.2 to direct your mouse clicks and selections using the home town size variable in the dataset. Compare the SPSS output you obtain with Figure 12.3 and make sure you can identify the mode of 4 (500K to 1 million). Also, if you want to understand the "valid percent" output provided by SPSS for its Frequencies analysis, use your cursor and block the first 10 respondents on the Data View of the SPSS Data Editor. With a right-click of your mouse, use the "clear" function to set these 10 town size numbers to blanks. Then rerun the frequencies for the home town size variable.

You will now see that the SPSS frequencies table reports the 10 "Missing System" respondents because their responses were blanks. Although missing data is not a concern in the Global Motors survey dataset, you most certainly will encounter this issue if your marketing research course includes an actual survey you perform as part of the course requirements. Wait! Don't save your Global Motors dataset with the missing data unless you give it a new SPSS dataset name such as GlobalMotorswithMissingData.sav.

FINDING THE MEDIAN WITH SPSS

It is also a simple matter to determine the median using the ANALYZE–DESCRIPTIVE STATISTICS–FREQUENCIES menu sequence. As we indicated, for the median to be a sensible measure of central tendency, the values must, at minimum, have ordinal scale properties. The size of town variable uses the codes identified in Figure 12.3 (Under 100K, etc.).

The codes have ordinal properties as 1 size is smaller than a 2 size and so on through a 5 size city. It is a simple matter to use the Global Motors survey data to obtain the size of home town median from the full dataset. The procedure is similar to the mode procedure as first, the "size of home town or city" variable is selected in the variable selection window; second, the median, rather than the mode, is checked in the statistics window. Refer to Figure 12.3, and imagine that the size of home town or city is the chosen variable and that median is checked instead of mode.

The resulting SPSS output will have the frequency distribution of our town size variable, and it will show that code number 4, pertaining to "500K to 1 million," is the 50/50 location in the scale, or the median.

 Active Learning

Find a Median with SPSS

Use your SPSS Global Motors dataset to find the median size on home town variable in the Global Motors survey. Again, use Figure 12.2 as your clickstream guide, but select the "number of people in household" variable for the analysis and place a check mark in the median checkbox. If you do not find that the code number 3 is the 50/50 location in the scale, or the median, redo your work carefully to correct any errors you may have made.

FINDING THE MEAN, RANGE, AND STANDARD DEVIATION WITH SPSS

Because computer statistical programs cannot distinguish the level of measurement of various questions, it is necessary for the analyst to discern the level of measurement and to select the correct procedure(s). Some questions in the Global Motors survey asked respondents to use a 7-point Likert (very strongly disagree to very strongly agree) response scale, so we have an interval scale.

For quick data analysis of these variables, we do not want frequency tables for two reasons. First, the Likert scale variables are interval scaled. Second, the frequency tables would be full of percents of all sizes, which would make modes and medians confusing. But, we can turn to the mean and other summarization statistics for scale data for help here. Specifically, we will use the ANALYZE–DESCRIPTIVE STATISTICS–DESCRIPTIVES commands, and click on the Options button after we have selected "Gasoline emissions contribute to global warming" as the variable for analysis. In the Options panel, you can select the mean, standard deviation, range, and so forth. Refer to Figure 12.4 for the SPSS clickstream sequence.

Figure 12.5 presents the output generated from this option. In our Global Motors survey, the output reveals that the average reaction to the statement, "Gasoline emissions contribute to global warming" is 4.62. Recalling the interval scale used (1=Very strongly disagree, 2=Strongly disagree, 3=Disagree, 4=Neither disagree nor agree, 5=Agree, 6=Strongly agree, and 7=Very strongly agree), a 4.62, (about 30%) is very close to 5, meaning that, on average, our survey respondents "agree" with this statement. The standard deviation is 1.7 (rounded), meaning there was much variability, and you can also see that the lowest response (minimum) was 1, and the highest (maximum) was 7, meaning that the entire range of the scale was used by the sample of respondents.

SPSS Student Assistant: Descriptive Statistics for Scale Data: Mean, Standard Deviation, Median, Range

When using SPSS DESCRIPTIVES, always bear in mind that the variables being analyzed should be scale data.

FIGURE 12.4 SPSS Clickstream to Obtain a Mean, Standard Deviation, and Range

Source: Reprint courtesy of International Business Machines Corporation, © SPSS, Inc., an IBM Company

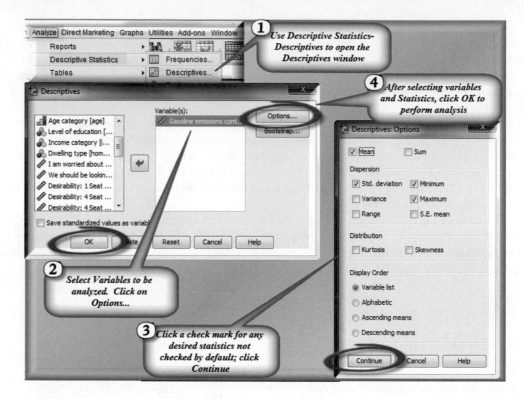

FIGURE 12.5 SPSS Output for a Mean, Standard Deviation, and Range

Source: Reprint courtesy of International Business Machines Corporation, © SPSS, Inc., an IBM Company

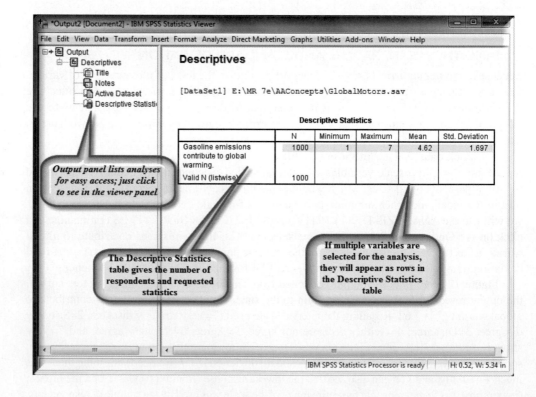

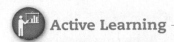 Active Learning ──────────────────────

Using SPSS for a Mean and Related Descriptive Statistics

This Active Learning exercise will let you stretch your learning a bit, for instead of simply repeating what has just been described for how to obtain the mean, range, and standard deviation with SPSS and comparing it to the SPSS output in this chapter, we want you to find the mean, range, and standard deviation for a different variable. Specifically, use the clickstream shown in Figure 12.4, but select the question that pertains to "Number of people in household" and direct SPSS to compute these descriptive statistics.

You should find that the mean is 2.61, a standard deviation of .958, and a range that has a minimum of 1 and a maximum of 6.

Reporting Descriptive Statistics to Clients

How does a marketing researcher report the findings of the various descriptive statistics used to summarize the findings of a survey? It is the researcher's responsibility to build tables, graphs, or other presentation methods to efficiently and effectively communicate the basic findings to the manager. For instance, the researcher may use a table format to show the means, standard deviations, and perhaps the ranges that have been found for a variable or a group of related variables. If percentages are computed, the researcher can develop, or "lift," a percentages table from the statistical output. Marketing Research Insight 12.1 relates guidelines and gives examples of tables for data analysis findings.

To what extent do consumers agree that fuel emissions contribute to global warming?

Photo: Taras Vyshnya/Shutterstock

Reporting Scale Data (Ratio and Interval Scales).
Scale data is summarized with the following descriptive measures: average, median, mode, standard deviation, minimum, and maximum. Typically, the researcher works with several variables or questions in the survey that are related either by the research objectives or logically. Often these questions have the same underlying response scales. For example, there may be a dozen attitude-related questions or several frequencies of product usage questions. It is often natural and efficient to combine the findings of related questions into a single table. Recommendations for what to include in standard scale variable tables are as follows:

Descriptive Measure	For a Standard Scale Variable Table . . .	Comment
Average (mean)	Absolutely include as averages are the most commonly used central tendency measure for scale data.	Place averages in a column very close to the variable descriptions and arrange variables in ascending or descending order of the averages.
Median, mode	Do not include.	Managers do not relate to medians or modes of scale data.
Standard deviation	Typically include in the table.	If most standard deviations are approximately equal, do not include as redundancy would result.
Minimum, maximum	Include if the data has several different values.	Reporting the same value several times is redundant.

MARKETING RESEARCH INSIGHT 12.1   *Practical Application*

Guidelines for the Presentation of Data Analysis

A table is the most common vehicle for presenting summarizations of data. The most useful tables facilitate a quick inspection to reveal the basic pattern(s) or the essence of the findings. Here are some table organization guidelines:[6]

- Keep tables as simple as possible.
- Use rows for the variables (scale data) or the categories (categorical data) presented in the table.
- Use columns for measures of central tendency and variability.
- Use highly descriptive and self-explanatory labels.
- Use only variables with identical response scales in a single table.

- If appropriate, arrange the variables (rows) in logical order, usually ascending or descending, based on the descriptive measure being used.
- Highlight key measures.

Beyond organization, these guidelines ensure that the table presents the data in a credible way:

- Use 1 decimal place unless convention (e.g. currency requires two decimal places for cents) demands otherwise.
- With scales, include a table footnote that describes the scale.
- Do not report measures that are largely redundant.
- Only report findings that are meaningful or useful.
- Use a conservative, professional format.

Here is an example of a scale variables table. Notice that the labels are self-explanatory, and the averages are highlighted to indicate their importance. The features are arranged in descending order of the averages so it is easy to identify the highest performing feature (assortment of breads) and the lowest performer (distinctive taste). The standard deviations are reported as they vary, but the minimum and maximum values are not reported as they are 1 or 5 in almost all cases. You should also note that an informative table footnote describes the scale used in these ratings.

Performance of the Subshop

Feature of the Subshop	Average*	Standard Deviation
Assortment of breads	**4.5**	0.5
Variety of subs	**4.3**	0.7
Variety of toppings	**4.0**	0.8
Freshness of bread	**3.9**	0.8
Freshness of toppings	**3.8**	0.7
Promptness of service	**3.7**	1.0
Cleanliness of facility	**3.7**	0.9
Value for the price	**3.6**	1.1
Generosity of toppings	**3.5**	1.0
Distinctive taste	**3.2**	1.3

*Based on a scale where 1 = "poor" and 5 = "excellent."

Reporting Nominal or Categorical Data. Nominal data is summarized with the following descriptive measures: frequencies, frequency distribution, percents, percent distribution, and mode. It is important to note that usually only one categorical variable is summarized in each table because the categories are unique to the variable (such as male and female for gender or buyer and nonbuyer for type of customer). Recommendations for what to put in standard categorical data tables are as follows:

Descriptive measure	For a Standard Categorical Variable Table...	Comment
Frequencies, Frequency distribution	Include if the researcher wants the reader to note something about the sample such as a very small sample where percents are greatly affected by a few respondents.	Place frequencies in a column very close to the variable group labels (such as male, female). If appropriate, arrange the categories in ascending or descending order of the percents. Include a total of the frequencies at the bottom.
Percents, Percent distribution	Absolutely include as percents are the most commonly used descriptive measure for nominal data.	Place percents in a column close to the variable group labels (such as male, female) and beside the frequencies, if used. If appropriate, arrange the categories in ascending or descending order of the percents. Include a 100% total at the bottom.
Mode	Highlight, but if obvious, do not report in the table.	The largest percentage group is usually readily apparent in a percent distribution and especially if ascending or descending order can be used.

Here is a sample nominal (or categorical) variable table. The frequencies are not included as a large number of respondents answered this question. Each time period is listed chronologically, and the mode is identified with the percentage in bold. The 100% total is included to indicate that all time periods are included in this table.

What Time in the Day Do You Typically Visit the Subshop?

Time Period	Percent
Before 12 p.m.	5.3%
Between 12 p.m. to 3 p.m.	**56.8%**
Between 3 p.m. to 6 p.m.	24.2%
After 6 p.m.	13.7%
Total	100.0%

Statistical Inference: Sample Statistics and Population Parameters

SPSS®

SPSS Student Assistant: Working with SPSS Output

As you have just learned, descriptive measures of central tendency and measures of variability adequately summarize the findings of a survey. However, whenever a probability sample is drawn from a population, it is not enough to simply report the sample's descriptive statistics, for these measures contain a certain degree of error due to the sampling process. Every sample provides some information about its population, but there is always some sample error that must be taken into account. Values that are computed from information provided by a sample are referred to as the sample's **statistics**, whereas values that are computed from a complete census, which are considered to be precise and valid measures of the population, are referred to as **parameters**. Statisticians use Greek letters (alpha, beta, etc.) when referring

Statistics are sample values, whereas parameters are corresponding population values.

to population parameters and Roman letters (a, b, etc.) when referring to statistics. Every sample statistic has a corresponding population parameter. For example, the notation used for a percentage is p for the statistic and π for the parameter, and the notations for the mean are $\bar{x}$ (statistic) and μ (parameter). Because a census is impractical, the sample statistic is used to estimate the population parameter. We will next describe the procedures used when estimating various population parameters.

Inference is a form of logic in which you make a general statement (a generalization) about an entire class based on what you have observed about a small set of members of that class. When you infer, you draw a conclusion from a small amount of evidence such as a sample. **Statistical inference** is a set of procedures in which the sample size and sample statistic are used to make an estimate of the corresponding population parameter. That is, statistical inference has formal steps for estimating the population parameter (the generalization) based on the evidence of the sample statistic and taking into account the sample error based on sample size. For now, let's focus on the percentage, p, as the sample statistic we are using to estimate the population percentage, π, and see how sample size enters into statistical inference. Suppose that Dodge suspected that there were some dissatisfied customers, and it commissioned two independent marketing research surveys determine the amount of dissatisfaction in its customer group. (Of course, our Dodge example is entirely fictitious. We don't mean to imply that Dodges perform in an unsatisfactory way.)

In the first survey, 100 customers who had purchased a Dodge in the last six months were surveyed, and it is found that 30 respondents (30%) are dissatisfied. This finding could be inferred to be the total population of Dodge owners who had bought one in the last six months, and we would say that there is 30% dissatisfaction. However, we know that our sample, which, by the way, was a probability sample, must contain some sample error; to reflect this error, you would have to say that there was *about 30%* dissatisfaction in the population. In other words, it might actually be more or less than 30% if we did a census because the sample provided us with only an estimate.

The second survey utilized 1,000 respondents, or 10 times more than in the first survey, and found that 35% of the respondents are "dissatisfied." Again, we know that the 35% is an estimate containing sampling error, so now we would also say that the population dissatisfaction percentage was *about* 35%. We now have two estimates of the degree of dissatisfaction with Dodges. One is *about* 30%, whereas the other is *about* 35%.

How do we translate our answers (remember they include the word "about") into more accurate numerical representations? Let's say you could translate them into "ballpark" ranges. That is, you could translate them so we could say "30 percent plus or minus x percent" for the sample of 100 and "35 percent plus or minus y percent" for the sample of 1,000. How would x and y compare? To answer this question, consider that more evidence makes for stronger inferences. With a larger sample (or more evidence), you would be more certain that the sample statistic was accurate with respect to estimating the true population value. In other words, with a larger sample size, you should expect the range used to estimate the true population value to be smaller. Actually, the range for y is smaller than the range for x because you have a larger sample and less sampling error.

With statistical inference for estimates of population parameters such as the percentage or mean, the sample statistic is used as the beginning point, and then a range is computed in which the population parameter is estimated to fall. The size of the sample, or n, plays a crucial role in this computation, as you will see in all of the statistical inference formulas we present in this chapter.

Two types of statistical inferences often used by marketing researchers are described in this chapter: parameter estimates and hypothesis tests. A **parameter estimate** is used to approximate the population value (parameter) through the use of confidence intervals. **Hypothesis testing** is used to compare the sample statistic with what is believed (hypothesized) to be the population value prior to undertaking the study.

Statistical inference takes into account that large random samples are more accurate than are small ones.

Statistical inference is based on sample size and variability, which then determine the amount of sampling error.

Two types of statistical inference are parameter estimation and hypothesis tests.

Parameter Estimation: Estimating the Population Percent or Mean

Parameter estimation is the process of using sample information to compute an interval that describes the range of a parameter such as the population mean (μ) or the population percentage (π). It involves the use of three values: the sample statistic (such as the mean or the percentage), the standard error of the statistic, and the desired level of confidence (usually 95% or 99%). A discussion of how each value is determined follows.

SAMPLE STATISTIC

The mean is the average of a set of scale variable numbers. For example, you might be working with a sample of golfers and researching the average number of golf balls they buy per month. Or you might be investigating how much high school students spend, on average, on fast foods between meals. For a percentage, you could be examining what percentage of golfers buy only Titleist balls, or you might be looking at what percentage of high school students buy from Taco Bell between meals. In either case, the mean or percentage is derived from a sample, so it is the sample statistic.

In parameter estimation, the sample statistic is usually a mean or a percentage.

STANDARD ERROR

There usually is some degree of variability in the sample. That is, our golfers do not all buy the same number of golf balls per month and they do not all buy Titleist. Not all of our high school students eat fast food between meals and not all of the ones who do go to Taco Bell. Earlier in this chapter, we introduced you to variability with a mean by describing the standard deviation, and we used the percentage distribution as a way of describing variability when percentages are being used. Also, we described how, if you theoretically took many, many samples and plotted the mean or percentage as a frequency distribution, it would approximate a bell-shaped curve called the sampling distribution. The **standard error** is a measure of the variability in the sampling distribution based on what is theoretically believed to occur were we to take a multitude of independent samples from the same population. We described the standard error formulas in Chapter 10 on sample size, but we repeat them here because they are vital to statistical inference as they tie together the sample size and its variability.

The standard error is a measure of the variability in a sampling distribution.

The formula for the standard error of the mean is as follows:

Formula for standard error of the mean

$$s_{\bar{x}} = \frac{s}{\sqrt{n}}$$

where

$s_{\bar{x}}$ = standard error of the mean

s = standard deviation

n = sample size

The formula for the standard error of the percentage is as follows:

Formula for standard error of the percentage

$$s_p = \sqrt{\frac{p \times q}{n}}$$

where

s_p = standard error of the percentage

p = the sample percentage

$q = (100 - p)$

n = sample size

The formula for mean standard error differs from a percentage standard error.

In both equations, the sample size *n* is found in the denominator. This means that the standard error will be smaller with larger sample sizes and larger with smaller sample sizes. At the same time, both of these formulas for the standard error reveal the impact of the variation found in the sample. Variation is represented by the standard deviation *s* for a mean and by $(p \times q)$ for a percentage. In either equation, the variation is in the numerator, so the greater the variability, the greater the standard error. Thus, the standard error simultaneously takes into account both the sample size and the amount of variation found in the sample. The following examples illustrate this fact.

The standard error takes into account sample size and the variability in the sample.

Suppose that a *New York Times* survey on the amount of daily time spent reading the *Times* had determined a standard deviation of 20 minutes and used a sample size of 100. The resulting standard error of the mean would be as follows:

Calculation of standard error of the mean with standard deviation = 20 and sample size = 100

$$s_{\bar{x}} = \frac{s}{\sqrt{n}}$$

$$s_{\bar{x}} = \frac{20}{\sqrt{100}}$$

$$= \frac{20}{10}$$

$$= 2 \text{ minutes}$$

Notes: Std. dev. = 20

$n = 100$

Notice how sample variability affects the standard error in these two examples.

On the other hand, if the survey had determined a standard deviation of 40 minutes, the standard error would be as follows:

Calculation of standard error of the mean with standard deviation = 40 and sample size = 100

$$s_{\bar{x}} = \frac{s}{\sqrt{n}}$$

$$s_{\bar{x}} = \frac{40}{\sqrt{100}}$$

$$= \frac{40}{10}$$

$$= 4 \text{ minutes}$$

Notes: Std. dev. = 40

$n = 100$

Statistical inference can be used to estimate how many minutes people read their daily newspaper.

Photo: Yuri Arcurs/Shutterstock

As you can see, the standard error of the mean from a sample with little variability (20 minutes) is smaller than the standard error of the mean from a sample with much variability (40 minutes), as long as both samples have the same size. In fact, you should have noticed that when the variability was doubled from 20 to 40 minutes, the standard error also doubled, given identical sample sizes. Refer to Figure 12.6.

The standard error of a percentage mirrors this logic, although the formula looks a bit different. In this case, as we indicated earlier, the degree of variability is inherent in the $(p \times q)$ aspect of the equation. Very little variability is indicated if *p* and *q* are very different in size. For example, if a survey of 100 McDonald's breakfast buyers determined that 90% of the respondents ordered coffee with their Egg McMuffin and 10% of the respondents did not, there would be very little variability because almost everybody orders coffee with breakfast. On the other hand, if the sample determined that there was a 50-50 split between those who had and those who had not ordered coffee, there would be a great deal more variability because any two customers would probably differ in their drink orders.

We can apply these two results to the standard error of percentage for a comparison. Using a 90-10 percent split, the standard error of percentage is as follows:

With a 50-50 percent split there is great variability.

Calculation of standard error of the percent with $p = 90$ and $q = 10$ and sample size = 100

$$s_p = \sqrt{\frac{p \times q}{n}}$$
$$= \sqrt{\frac{(90)(10)}{100}}$$
$$= \sqrt{\frac{900}{100}}$$
$$= \sqrt{9}$$
$$= 3\%$$

Notes: $p = 90$
$q = 10$
$n = 100$

Using 50-50 percent split, the standard error of the percentage is as follows:

Calculation of standard error of the percent with $p = 50$ and $q = 50$ and sample size = 100

$$s_p = \sqrt{\frac{p \times q}{n}}$$
$$= \sqrt{\frac{(50)(50)}{100}}$$
$$= \sqrt{\frac{2,500}{100}}$$
$$= \sqrt{25}$$
$$= 5\%$$

Notes: $p = 50$
$q = 50$
$n = 100$

A 50-50 percent split has a larger standard error than a 90-10 split when sample size is the same.

Population parameters are estimated with the use of confidence intervals.

Again, these examples show that greater variability in responses results in a larger standard error of the percentage at a given sample size.

CONFIDENCE INTERVALS

Because there is always some sampling error when a sample is taken, it is necessary to estimate the population parameter with a range. We did this in the Dodge owners' example earlier. One factor affecting the size of the range is how confident the researcher wants to be that the range includes the true population percentage (parameter). Normally, the researcher first decides on how confident he or she wants to be; that is, the researcher formally selects a level of confidence. The sample statistic is the beginning of the estimate, but because there is sample error present, a "plus" amount and an identical "minus" amount are added and subtracted from the sample statistic to determine the maximum and minimum, respectively, of the range. **Confidence intervals** are the degree of accuracy desired by the researcher and stipulated as a level of confidence in the form of a range with a lower boundary and an upper boundary.

Typically, marketing researchers rely only on the 99%, 95%, or 90% levels of confidence, which correspond to ±2.58, ±1.96, and ±1.64 standard errors, respectively. They are

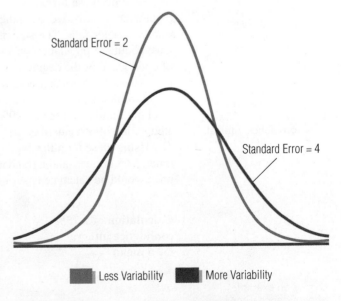

Standard Error = 2

Standard Error = 4

Less Variability   More Variability

FIGURE 12.6
Variability Found in the Sample Directly Affects the Standard Error

The range of your estimate of the population mean or percentage depends largely on the sample size and the variability found in the sample.

designated z_α, so $z_{0.99}$ is ±2.58 standard errors. By far, the **most commonly used level of confidence** in marketing research is the 95% level,[7] corresponding to 1.96 standard errors. In fact, the 95% level of confidence is usually the default level found in statistical analysis programs such as SPSS. Now that the relationship between the standard error and the measure of sample variability—be it the standard deviation or the percentage—is apparent, it is a simple matter to determine the range in which the population parameter will be estimated. We use the sample statistics, $\bar{x}$ or p, compute the standard error, and then apply our desired level of confidence. In notation form these are as follows:

Formula for confidence interval for a mean

$$\bar{x} \pm z_\alpha s_{\bar{x}}$$

where

$\bar{x}$ = sample mean

z_α = z value for 95% or 99% level of confidence

$s_{\bar{x}}$ = standard error of the mean

Formula for confidence interval for a percentage

$$p \pm z_\alpha s_p$$

Confidence intervals are estimated using these formulas.

where

p = sample percentage

z_α = z value for 95% or 99% level of confidence

s_p = standard error of the percentage

How do these formulas relate to inference? Recall that we are estimating a population parameter. That is, we are indicating a range into which it is believed that the true population parameter falls. The size of the range is determined by those pieces of information we have about the population on hand as a result of our sample. The final ingredient is our level of confidence or the degree to which we want to be correct in our estimate of the population parameter. If we are conservative and wish to assume the 99% level of confidence, then the range would be more encompassing than if we are less conservative and assume only the 95% level of confidence because 99% is associated with ±2.58 standard errors and 95% is associated with ±1.96 standard errors.

Marketing researchers typically use only 95% or 99% confidence interval.

Using these formulas for the sample of 100 *New York Times* readers with a mean reading time of 45 minutes and a standard deviation of 20 minutes, the 95% confidence interval estimate would be calculated as follows.

Calculation of a 95% confidence interval for a mean

$$\bar{x} \pm 1.96 \times s_{\bar{x}}$$

$$45 \pm 1.96 \times \frac{20}{\sqrt{100}}$$

$$45 \pm 1.96 \times 2$$

$$45 \pm 3.9$$

$$41.1 - 48.9 \text{ minutes}$$

Notes: Mean = 45
Std. dev. = 20
$z = 1.96$

Here is an example of confidence interval computation with a mean.

If 50% of the 100 Egg McMuffin eaters orders coffee, the 95% confidence interval would be computed using the percentage formula.

Calculation of a 95% confidence interval for a percentage

$$p \pm 1.96 \times s_p$$

$$p \pm 1.96 \times \sqrt{\frac{p \times q}{n}}$$

$$50 \pm 1.96 \times \sqrt{\frac{50 \times 50}{100}}$$

$$50 \pm 1.96 \times 5$$

$$50 \pm 9.8$$

$$40.2\% - 59.8\%$$

Notes: $p = 50$
$q = 50$
$n = 100$
$z = 1.96$

Here is an example of confidence interval computation with a percentage.

A 99% confidence interval is always wider than a 95% confidence interval if all other factors are equal.

Of course, if we use the 99% confidence interval, the computations would necessitate the use of 2.58. The confidence interval is always wider for 99% than it is for 95% when the sample size is the same and variability is equal. The five steps involved in computing confidence intervals for a mean or a percentage are listed in Table 12.3.

 Active Learning

Calculate Some Confidence Intervals

This Active Learning section provides some practice in calculating confidence intervals. For this set of exercises, you are working with a survey of 1,000 people who responded to questions about satellite radio. The questions, sample statistics, and other pertinent information are listed below. Compute the 95% confidence interval for the population parameter in each case. Be certain to follow the logic of the questions as it has implications for the sample size pertaining to each question.

| | | 95% Confidence Interval | |
| | | Lower Boundary | Upper Boundary |
Question	Sample Statistic(s)		
Have you heard of satellite radio?	500/1,000 = 50% responded yes		
If yes, do you own a satellite radio?	150/500 = 30% responded yes		
If you own satellite radio, about how many minutes of satellite radio did you listen to last week?	Average of 100.7 minutes; standard deviation of 25.0 minutes for the 150 satellite radio owners		

TABLE 12.3 How to Compute a Confidence Interval for a Mean or a Percentage

There are five steps to computing a confidence interval.

Step 1. Find the sample statistic, either the mean, $\bar{x}$, or the percentage, p.

Step 2. Identify the sample size, n.

Step 3. Determine the amount of variability found in the sample in the form of standard error of the mean, $s_{\bar{x}}$,

$$s_{\bar{x}} = \frac{s}{\sqrt{n}}$$

or standard error of the percentage, s_p.

$$s_p = \sqrt{\frac{p \times q}{n}}$$

Step 4. Decide on the desired level of confidence to determine the value for z:

$$z_{.95}(1.96) \text{ or } z_{.99}(2.58).$$

Step 5. Compute your (95%) confidence interval as: $\bar{x} \pm 1.96 s_{\bar{x}}$ or $p \pm 1.96 s_p$.

Marketing Research on YouTube™ To learn about confidence intervals, launch www.youtube.com, and search for "Confidence Intervals Part 1 YouTube."

HOW TO INTERPRET AN ESTIMATED POPULATION MEAN OR PERCENTAGE RANGE

How are these ranges interpreted? The interpretation is quite simple when you remember that the sampling distribution notion is the underlying theoretical concept. If we were using a 99% level of confidence, and if we repeated the sampling process and computed the sample statistic many times, the frequency distribution (the sampling distribution) would comprise a bell-shaped curve. A total of 99% of these repeated samples results would produce a range that includes the population parameter.

Obviously, a marketing researcher would take only one sample for a particular marketing research project, and this restriction explains why estimates must be used. Furthermore, the conscientious application of probability sampling techniques allows us to make use of the sampling distribution concept. Statistical inference procedures are the direct linkages between probability sample design and data analysis. Do you remember grappling with confidence levels when we determined sample size? Now we are on the other side of the table, so to speak, and we must use the sample size for our inference procedures. Confidence intervals must be used when estimating population parameters, and the size of the random sample used is always reflected in these confidence intervals.

The Global Motors Survey: How To Obtain and Use a Confidence Interval for a Mean with SPSS

OBTAINING AND INTERPRETING A CONFIDENCE INTERVAL FOR A MEAN

Fortunately, because the calculations are a bit more complicated and tedious, your SPSS program will calculate the confidence interval for a mean. To illustrate this feature, we will examine evidence that the general public agrees with the opinion that gasoline usage is detrimental. You may recall that in our descriptive analysis example of a mean (page 300), we found that the average disagree–agree response to the statement, "Gasoline emissions contribute to global warming," was 4.6, or "agree."

To determine the 95% confidence interval for this average, examine Figure 12.7, which shows the clickstream sequence to accomplish a 95% confidence interval estimate using SPSS. As you can see, the correct SPSS procedure is a "One Sample t-test," and you use the ANALYZE–COMPARE MEANS–ONE SAMPLE T TEST menu clickstream sequence to open the proper window. Refer to Figure 12.7 to see that all you need to do is to select the "Gasoline emissions contribute to global warming" variable into the Test Variables area, and then click "OK."

Figure 12.8 shows the results of ANALYZE–COMPARE MEANS–ONE SAMPLE T TEST for our "Gasoline emissions contribute to global warming" variable. As you can see, the average is 4.6, and the 95% confidence interval is 4.51–4.72. Although a 5 is the code for "Agree," this confidence interval is sufficiently close that we can claim it amounts to "Agree." Our interpretation of this finding: If we conducted a great many replications of this survey using the same sample size, we would find that 95% of the sample average agreement with the statement, "Gasoline emissions contribute to global warming" variable would be "Agree."

Active Learning

Use SPSS for a Confidence Interval for a Mean

You have just learned that the 95% confidence interval for "Gasoline emissions contribute to global warming" variable would include an average of 4.62, with a lower boundary of 4.51 and upper boundary of 4.72. What about the statement "I am worried about global warming"?

To answer this question, you must use SPSS to compute the 95% confidence interval for the mean of this variable. Use the clickstream identified in Figure 12.7 and use the annotations in Figure 12.8 to find and interpret your 95% confidence interval for the public's opinion on this topic. How do you interpret this finding, and how does this confidence interval compare to the one we found for "Gasoline emissions contribute to global warming."?

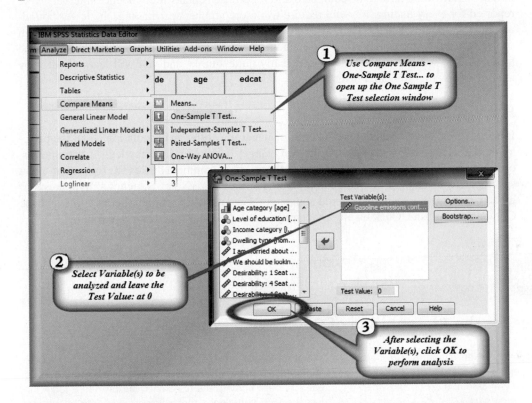

FIGURE 12.7 SPSS Clickstream to Obtain a 95% Confidence Interval for a Mean

Source: Reprint courtesy of International Business Machines Corporation, © SPSS, Inc., an IBM Company

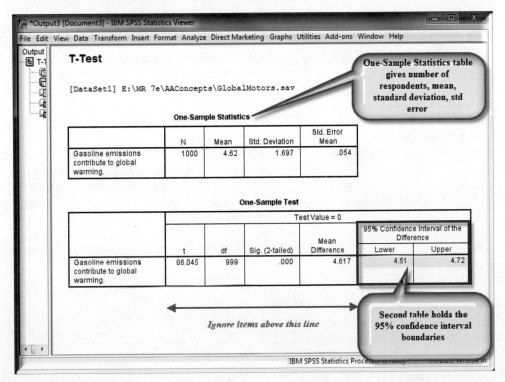

FIGURE 12.8 SPSS Output for a 95% Confidence Interval for a Mean

Source: Reprint courtesy of International Business Machines Corporation, © SPSS, Inc., an IBM Company

SPSS®   Reporting Confidence Intervals to Clients

How do marketing researchers report confidence intervals to their clients? It may surprise you to learn that detailed confidence intervals are typically not reported. Just think about all of the numbers that would have to be computed and reported to clients if confidence intervals were reported for every finding. It would require two more numbers per finding: the lower boundary and the upper boundary. That raises a dilemma: Most clients do not want to wade through so much detail, yet researchers must somehow inform clients that there is sample error in the findings. The solution to this dilemma is really quite simple, and you will learn about it by reading Marketing Research Insight 12.2.

Hypothesis Tests

A hypothesis is what the manager or researcher expects the population mean (or percentage) to be.

In some cases, the marketing researcher or manager may offer an expectation about the population parameter (either the mean or the percentage) based on prior knowledge, assumptions, or intuition. This expectation, called a **hypothesis**, most commonly takes the form of an exact specification as to what the population parameter value is. (Note: Directional hypothesis of greater than or less than are covered separately. Go to www.pearsonhighered/burns and the Companion Website. Click on any chapter and open "Online Data Analysis Modules.")

MARKETING RESEARCH INSIGHT 12.2   *Practical Application*

Guidelines for the Presentation of Confidence Intervals

Researchers have two options when it comes to reporting confidence intervals to clients or readers of their marketing research reports: (1) the general case and (2) findings-specific confidence intervals.

The General Case:

This is the industry standard; it is used almost unanimously with opinion polling, and it is by far the most popular approach used by marketing researchers. The general case is merely to state the sampling error associated with the survey sample size. For example, the report may say "findings are accurate to ±4%," or "the survey has an error of ±3.5%." This sample error, of course, is calculated using the sample error formula (refer to Chapter 10), typically at the 95% level of confidence with $p=q=50\%$, and $z=1.96$.

Sample error formula
$$\pm \text{ Sample Error\%} = 1.96 \times \sqrt{\frac{p \times q}{n}}$$

The Findings-Specific Case:

To decide whether to use the findings-specific approach, the researcher must answer the following question: "Are there findings that require more than the general case of reporting sample error?" For instance, the client may use some findings to answer critical questions or as the basis for important decisions. If the answer is no, the researcher will report the general case. If yes, the next step is to identify all of the findings he or

she believes absolutely require the reporting of findings-specific confidence intervals. To present the confidence intervals for each relevant finding, the researcher can provide a table that lists the 95% confidence interval lower and upper boundaries, which must be computed either by the researcher's statistical analysis program or the use of some other computational aid in the researcher's tool kit. The following table illustrates how a researcher can efficiently accommodate the confidence intervals for diverse variables in a single table. Most likely, these findings will have been reported elsewhere in the report with other informative summary statistics such as standard deviations and sample sizes for respondents answering various questions.

95% Confidence Intervals for Key Findings

	Sample Finding	Lower Boundary	Upper Boundary
Used the Subshop in the past 60 days.	**30%**	*26.0%*	*34.0%*
Used a Subshop coupon in the past 30 days.	**12%**	*9.2%*	*14.8%*
Number of Subshop visits in the past 60 days.	**1.5**	*1.4*	*1.6*
Overall satisfaction with the Subshop*	**5.6**	*5.4*	*5.8*

*Based on a scale where 1=very dissatisfied and 7 = Very satisfied

A **hypothesis test** is a statistical procedure used to "accept" or "reject" the hypothesis based on sample evidence.[8] With all hypothesis tests, you should keep in mind that the sample is the only source of current information about the population. Because our sample is random and representative of the population, the sample results are used to determine if the hypothesis about the population parameter is accepted or rejected.[9]

All of this might sound frightfully technical, but it is a form of inference you do every day. You just do not use the words "hypothesis" or "parameter" when you do it. Here is an example to show how hypothesis testing occurs intuitively. Your friend Bill does not use an automobile seat belt because he thinks only a few drivers actually wear them. But Bill's car breaks down, and he has to ride with his coworkers to and from work while it is being repaired. Over the course of a week, Bill rides with five different coworkers, and he notices that four out of the five buckle up. When Bill begins driving his own car the next week, he begins fastening his seat belt because he did not find support for his hypotheses that few drivers buckle up.

TEST OF THE HYPOTHESIZED POPULATION PARAMETER VALUE

The **hypothesized population parameter** value can be determined using either a percentage or a mean. The equation used to test the hypothesis of a population percentage is as follows:

Formula for test of a hypothesis about a percent

$$z = \frac{p - \pi_H}{s_{\bar{x}}}$$

where

p = the sample percentage

π_H = the hypothesized percentage

s_p = the standard error of the percentage

The equation used to test the hypothesis of a mean is identical in logic, except it uses the mean and standard error of the mean.

Formula for test of a hypothesis about a mean

$$z = \frac{\bar{x} - \mu_H}{s_{\bar{x}}}$$

where

$\bar{x}$ = the sample mean

μ_H = they hypothesized mean

$s_{\bar{x}}$ = standard error of the mean

Here are formulas used to test a hypothesized population parameter.

Tracking the logic of these equations, one can see that the sample mean ($\bar{x}$), is compared to the hypothesized population mean (μ_H). Similarly, the sample percentage (p) is compared to the hypothesized percentage (π_H). In this case, "compared" means "take the difference." This difference is divided by the standard error to determine how many standard errors away from the hypothesized parameter the sample statistic falls. The standard error, you should remember, takes into account the variability found in the sample as well as the sample size. A small sample with much variability yields a large standard error, so our sample statistic could be quite far away from the mean arithmetically but still less than one standard error away in certain circumstances. All the relevant information about the population as found by our sample is included in these computations. Knowledge of areas under the normal curve then come into play to translate this distance into a probability of support for the hypothesis: If the computed z value is greater than 1.96 or less than -1.96, we are 95% confident that the sample evidence does not support the hypothesized parameter value.

To a statistician, "compare means" amounts to "take the difference."

Here is a simple illustration using Bill's hypothesis that 10% of drivers use seat belts. Let's assume that instead of observing his friends buckling up, Bill reads that a Harris Poll finds that 80% of respondents in a national sample of 1,000 drivers wear their seat belts. The hypothesis test would be computed as follows (notice we substituted the formula for s_p in the second step):

Calculation of a test of a Bill's hypothesis that only 10% of drivers "buckle up." Sorry, Bill. No support for you.

This calculation is an example of no support for Bill's seat belt hypothesis.

$$z = \frac{p - \pi_H}{s_p}$$

$$= \frac{p - \pi_H}{\sqrt{\dfrac{p \times q}{n}}}$$

$$= \frac{80 - 10}{\sqrt{\dfrac{80 \times 20}{1{,}000}}}$$

$$= \frac{70}{\sqrt{\dfrac{1{,}600}{1{,}000}}}$$

$$= \frac{70}{\sqrt{1.6}}$$

$$= 55.3$$

Notes:

Hypothesized percent = 10
Sample percent (p) = 80
Sample q = 20
n = 1000

The sampling distribution concept holds that our sample is one of many, many theoretical samples that comprise a bell-shaped curve with the hypothesized value as the mean.

You always assume the sample information to be more accurate than any hypothesis.

The crux of statistical hypothesis testing is the **sampling distribution concept**. Our actual sample is one of the many, many theoretical samples comprising the assumed bell-shaped curve of possible sample results using the hypothesized value as the center of the bell-shaped distribution. There is a greater probability of finding a sample result close to the hypothesized mean, for example, than of finding one that is far away. However, there is a critical assumption working here. We have conditionally accepted from the outset that the person who stated the hypothesis is correct. If our sample mean turns out to be within ±1.96/±2.58 standard errors of the hypothesized mean, it supports the hypothesis maker at the 95%/99% level of confidence because it falls within 95%/99% of the area under the curve.

But what if the sample result is found to be outside this range? Which is correct—the hypothesis or the researcher's sample results? The answer to this question is always the same: Sample information is invariably more accurate than a hypothesis. Of course, the sampling procedure must adhere strictly to probability sampling requirements and ensure representativeness. As you can see, Bill was greatly mistaken because his hypothesis of 10% of drivers wearing seat belts was 55.3 standard errors away from the 80% finding of the national poll.

The following example serves to describe the hypothesis testing process with a mean. Northwestern Mutual Life Insurance Company has an internship program that allows college students to participate in training and become field agents in one academic term. Rex Reigen, district agent, hypothesizes, based on his knowledge of the program, that the typical college agent will be able to earn about $2,750 in his or her first semester of participation in the program. To check Rex's hypothesis, a survey was taken of 100 current college agents. The sample mean is determined to be $2,800, and the standard deviation is $350.

The amount of $2,800 found by the sample differs from the hypothesized amount of $2,750 by $50. Is this amount a sufficient enough difference to cast doubt on Rex's estimate? Or, in other words, is it far enough from the hypothesized mean to reject the hypothesis? To answer these questions, we compute as follows (note that we have substituted the formula for the standard error of the mean in the second step):

Bill found that his hypothesis about seat belts was not supported, so he started buckling up.

Photo: eurobanks/Shutterstock

Calculation of a test of Rex's hypothesis that Northwestern Mutual interns make an average of $2,750 in their first semester of work. Rex is supported!

$$z = \frac{\bar{x} - \mu_H}{s_{\bar{x}}}$$

$$= \frac{\bar{x} - \mu_H}{\dfrac{s}{\sqrt{n}}}$$

$$= \frac{2,800 - 2,750}{\dfrac{350}{\sqrt{100}}}$$

$$= \frac{50}{35}$$

$$= 1.43$$

Notes:

Hypothesized mean = 2,750
Sample mean = 2,800
Std. dev. = 350
n = 100

A hypothesis test provides the probability of support for your hypothesis based on your sample evidence and sample size.

Does the sample support Rex's hypothesis that student interns make $2,750 in the first semester?

The sample variability and the sample size have been used to determine the size of the standard error of the assumed sampling distribution. In this case, one standard error of the mean is equal to $35 (standard error of the mean formula: $350/\sqrt{100}$). When the difference of $50 is divided by $35 to determine the number of standard errors away from which the hypothesized mean the sample statistic lies, the result is 1.43 standard errors. As is illustrated in Figure 12.9, 1.43 standard errors is within ±1.96 standard errors of Rex's hypothesized mean. It also reveals that the hypothesis is supported because it falls in the acceptance region.

A computed of 1.43 is less than 1.96, so the hypothesis is supported.

It is handy to just recall the two numbers, 1.96 and 2.58; as we have said, these two are directly associated to the 95% and 99% confidence levels, respectively, which are the standards of the marketing research industry. Anytime the computed z value falls outside 2.58/1.96, the resulting probability of support for the hypothesis is 0.01/0.05 or less. Of course, computer statistical programs such as SPSS will provide the exact probability because they are programmed to look up the probability in the z table just as you would have to do if you did the test through your own calculations to arrive at the exact probability. The five basic steps involved in hypothesis testing are listed in Table 12.4.

Global Motors: How to Use SPSS to Test a Hypothesis for a Mean

SPSS®

We can test the hypothesized mean of any scale variable (interval or ratio scale) in our Global Motors survey. As an illustration, we will hypothesize that the general public is neutral to the statement, "I am worried about global warming." You should recall that on our scale, the neutral position corresponds to the value code of 4. Your SPSS software can be easily directed to make a mean estimation or to test a hypothesis for a mean.

To perform a mean hypothesis test, SPSS provides a Test Value box in which the hypothesized mean can be entered. As you can see in Figure 12.10, you get to this box by using the ANALYZE COMPARE MEANS–ONE SAMPLE T TEST command sequence. You then select the variable, "I am worried about global warming." Next, enter a 4 as Test Value and click on the OK button.

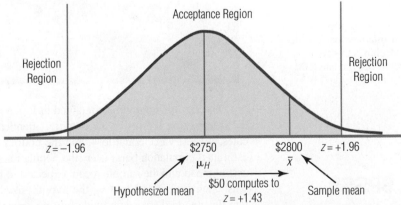

FIGURE 12.9 Sample Findings Support the Hypothesis in This Example

To test a hypothesis about a mean with SPSS, use the ANALYZE–COMPARE MEANS–ONE SAMPLE T TEST command sequence.

TABLE 12.4 The Five Basic Steps Involved in Hypothesis Testing

The Steps

Step 1. Begin with a statement about what you believe exists in the population; that is, the population mean (μ_H) or percentage (π_H).

Step 2. Draw a random sample and determine the sample mean ($\bar{x}$) or percent (p).

Step 3. Compare the statistic to the hypothesized parameter; divide by standard error to compute z.

$$z = \frac{\bar{x} - \mu_H}{s_{\bar{x}}} \qquad\qquad z = \frac{p - \pi_H}{s_p}$$

Step 4. If z is within ±1.96/±2.58 standard errors, it supports the hypothesis at the 95%/99% level of confidence. (Alternatively, the exact degree of support can be assessed on SPSS output.)

Step 5. If the sample does not support the hypothesis, revise the hypothesis to be consistent with the sample's statistic using the confidence interval formula.

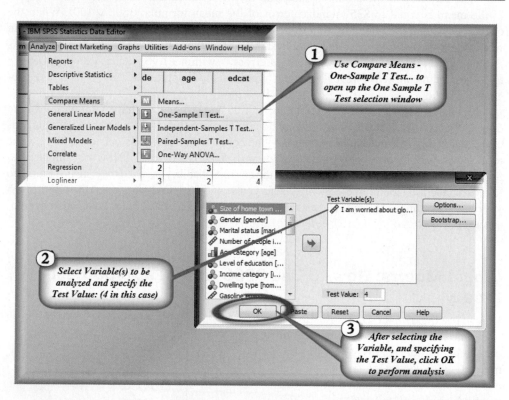

FIGURE 12.10 SPSS Clickstream to Test a Hypothesis About a Mean

Source: Reprint courtesy of International Business Machines Corporation, © SPSS, Inc., an IBM Company

SPSS®

SPSS Student Assistant:
Testing a Hypothesis for a Mean

Here are five steps in hypothesis testing.

The resulting output is contained in Figure 12.11. When you look at it, you will notice that the information layout for the output is identical to the previous output table. The output indicates our test value equal to 4, and the bottom table contains 95% confidence intervals for the estimated population parameter (the population parameter is the difference between the hypothesized mean and the sample mean, expected to be 0). There is a mean difference of .880, which was calculated by subtracting the hypothesized mean value (4) from the sample mean (4.88), and the standard error is provided in the upper half (1.329). A t value of 20.932 is determined by dividing .880 by .042. It is associated with a two-tailed significance level of 0.000. (For now, assume t value is the z value we have used in our formulas and explanations.) In other words, our Global Motors sample finding of an average of about 4.88 does not support the hypothesis of 4. Note: for tests of "directional" hypotheses, refer to the textbook website on additional and advanced statistical tests.

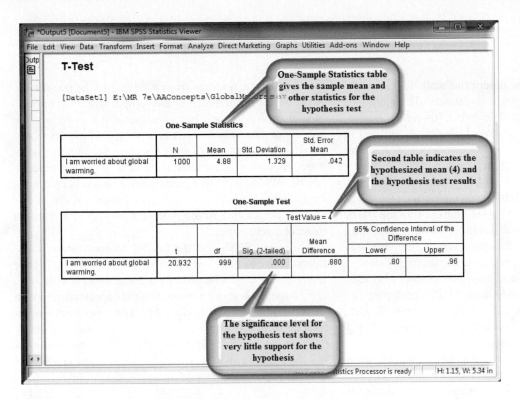

FIGURE 12.11 SPSS Output for the Test of a Hypothesis About a Mean

Source: Reprint courtesy of International Business Machines Corporation, © SPSS, Inc., an IBM Company

For tests of "directional" hypotheses, refer to the textbook website on additional and advanced statistical tests.

 To learn about hypothesis tests, launch **www.youtube.com**, and search for "Hypothesis tests, p-value - Statistics Help."

Reporting Hypothesis Tests to Clients

Explicit hypotheses are sometimes encountered by marketing researchers. When this happens, the marketing researcher performs the appropriate hypothesis test and interprets the findings. The steps involved are straightforward and listed in Marketing Research Insight 12.3.

MARKETING RESEARCH INSIGHT 12.3   *Practical Application*

Guidelines for the Presentation of Hypothesis Tests

The step-by-step approach to the presentation of hypothesis tests is as follows.

Step 1. State the hypothesis.

Step 2. Perform appropriate hypothesis test computations. That is, if the hypothesis test is stated as a percent, the percent formula should be used; if it is stated as a mean, use the mean formula.

Step 3. Determine if the hypothesis is supported by comparing the computed z value to the critical z value (normally 1.96 for a 95% level of confidence).

Step 4. If the hypothesis is not supported, compute confidence intervals to provide the client with the appropriate confidence intervals.

These steps are followed for each explicitly stated hypothesis. An example of how to present hypothesis tests in a research report follows:

Results of Hypothesis Tests

Hypothesis	Result of Test
Hypothesis 1: *60% of consumers buy from a fast-food location at least 1 time per month.*	*This hypothesis was supported at the 95% level of confidence by the findings of the survey.*
Hypothesis 2: *In a typical month, those consumers who purchase from a fast-food outlet, spend about $45 for food, drinks, snacks, etc.*	*The average was found to be $31.87, and the hypothesis of $45 was not supported. The 95% confidence intervals computations determined the range to be between $28.50 and $35.24.*

Summary

This chapter introduced the descriptive statistics researchers use to inspect basic patterns in datasets. There are five types of statistical analysis: descriptive, inferential, differences, associative, and predictive. Descriptive analysis is performed with measures of central tendency such as the mean, mode, or median, each of which portrays the typical respondent or the typical answer to the question being analyzed. Measures of variability, including the frequency distribution, range, and standard deviation, provide bases for envisioning the degree of similarity of all respondents to the typical respondent. Basically, descriptive analysis yields a profile of how respondents in the sample answered the various questions in the survey. The chapter also provided information on how to instruct SPSS to compute descriptive analyses using the Global Motors survey dataset. Both clickstream sequences for setting up the analyses and the resulting output were shown.

The chapter then distinguished a sample statistic from its associated population parameter. We introduced the concept of statistical inference, which is a set of procedures for generalizing the findings from a sample to the population. A key factor in inference is the sample size, n. It appears in statistical inference formulas because it expresses the amount of sampling error: Large samples have less sampling error than do small samples given the same variability. A population parameter, such as a mean or a percent, can be estimated by using confidence intervals computed by application of the standard error formula. A researcher can use the sample findings to test a hypothesis about a mean or a percentage.

We used SPSS and the Global Motors dataset to illustrate how to direct SPSS to calculate 95% confidence intervals for the estimation of a mean as well as how to test a hypothesis about a mean. Both are accomplished with the SPSS menu item One-Sample T Test procedure. For parameter estimation or test of a hypothesis with a percent, you can use SPSS to determine the percent, but you must use the formulas in this chapter to calculate the confidence interval or perform the significance test.

Key Terms

Data analysis (p. 289)
Descriptive analysis (p. 289)
Inference analysis (p. 290)
Difference analysis (p. 290)
Association analysis (p. 290)
Predictive analysis (p. 290)
Measures of central tendency (p. 291)
Mode (p. 291)
Median (p. 292)
Mean (p. 292)
Measures of variability (p. 292)
Frequency distribution (p. 293)
Percentage distribution (p. 293)
Range (p. 293)
Standard deviation (p. 293)

Variance (p. 294)
Statistics (p. 303)
Parameters (p. 303)
Inference (p. 304)
Statistical inference (p. 304)
Parameter estimate (p. 304)
Hypothesis testing (p. 304)
Parameter estimation (p. 305)
Hypothesis test (p. 312)
Standard error (p. 305)
Formula for standard error
 of a mean (p. 305)
Formula for standard error of a
 percentage (p. 305)
Confidence intervals (p. 307)

Most commonly used level of
 confidence (p. 308)
Formula for confidence interval of a
 mean (p. 308)
Formula for confidence interval of a
 percentage (p. 308)
Hypothesis (p. 312)
Hypothesis test (p. 313)
Hypothesized population
 parameter (p. 313)
Sampling distribution
 concept (p. 314)

Review Questions/Applications

1. Indicate what data analysis is and why it is useful.
2. Define and differentiate each of the following: (a) descriptive analysis, (b) inferential analysis, (c) associative analysis, (d) predictive analysis, and (e) differences analysis.
3. What is a measure of central tendency, and what does it describe?
4. Describe the concept of variability, and relate how it helps in the description of responses to a particular question on a questionnaire.
5. Using examples, illustrate how a frequency distribution (or a percentage distribution) reveals the variability in responses to a Likert-type question in a lifestyle study. Use two extreme examples of much variability and little variability.

6. Indicate what a range is and where it should be used as an indicator of the amount of dispersion in a sample.

7. With explicit reference to the formula for a standard deviation, show how it measures how different respondents are from one another.

8. Why is the mean an inappropriate measure of central tendency in each of the following cases: (a) gender of respondent (male or female); (b) marital status (single, married, divorced, separated, widowed, other); (c) a taste test in which subjects indicate their first, second, and third choices of Miller Lite, Bud Light, and Coors Light?

9. For each of the cases in question 8, what is the appropriate central tendency measure?

10. In a survey on magazine subscriptions, respondents write in the number of magazines they subscribe to regularly. What measures of central tendency can be used? Which is the most appropriate and why?

11. If you use the standard deviation as a measure of the variability in a sample, what statistical assumptions have you implicitly adopted?

12. What essential factors are taken into consideration when statistical inference takes place?

13. What is meant by "parameter estimation," and what function does it perform for a researcher?

14. How does parameter estimation for a mean differ from that for a percentage?

15. List the steps in statistical hypothesis testing. List the steps in "intuitive" hypothesis testing. How are they similar? How are they different?

16. What does it mean when a researcher says that a hypothesis has been supported at the 95% confidence level?

17. Here are several computation practice exercises to help you identify which formulas pertain and learn how to perform the necessary calculations. In each case, perform the necessary calculations and write your answers in the blank line provided for each case.

a. Determine confidence intervals for each of the following:

Sample Statistic	Sample Size	Confidence Level	Your Confidence Intervals?
Mean: 150 Std. Dev: 30	200	95%	_____
Percent: 67%	300	99%	_____
Mean: 5.4 Std. Dev: 0.5	250	99%	_____
Percent: 25.8%	500	99%	_____

b. Test the following hypothesis and interpret your findings:

Hypothesis	Sample Findings	Confidence Level	Your Test Results
Mean = 7.5	Mean: 8.5 Std dev: 1.2 n = 670	95%	_____
Percent = 86%	p = 95 n = 1000	99%	_____
Mean = 125	Mean: 135 Std dev: 15 n = 500	95%	_____
Percent = 33%	p = 31 n = 120	99%	_____

18. Alamo Rent-A-Car executives believe that Alamo accounts for about 50% of all Cadillacs that are rented. To test this belief, a researcher randomly identifies 20 major airports with on-site rental car lots. Observers are sent to each location and instructed to record the number of rental company Cadillacs observed in a four-hour period. About 500 are observed, and 30% are observed being returned to Alamo. What are the implications of this finding for the Alamo executives' belief?

CASE 12.1

The Hobbit's Choice Restaurant Survey Descriptive and Inference Analysis

SPSS®

In addition to the Global Motors survey, Cory Rogers of CMG Research was working with Jeff Dean, who believed there was an opportunity to build an upscale restaurant, possibly to be called The Hobbit's Choice, somewhere in the metropolitan area. The proposed restaurant was described as follows:

A restaurant with a very elegant decor, offering very personal service in a spacious, semi-private atmosphere, featuring menu items, traditional and unusual, prepared by chefs with international reputations.

The atmosphere, food, and service at this restaurant meet a standard equal to that of the finest restaurants in the world. Menu items are priced separately, known as "á la carte," and the prices are what one would expect for a restaurant meeting or surpassing the highest restaurant standards in the world.

Cory's team had designed an online questionnaire and gathered a representative sample. The code book for the SPSS dataset follows.

Question	Codes	Labels
Do you eat at an upscale restaurant at least once every two weeks?	1,2	Yes, No (If No, terminate the survey)
How many total dollars do you spend per month in restaurants (for your meals only)?	Actual dollars	No labels
How likely would it be for you to patronize this proposed new upscale restaurant?	1,2,3,4,5	Very Unlikely, … , Very Likely
What would you expect an average evening meal entrée item alone to be priced in the proposed new restaurant?	Actual dollars	No labels
Would you describe yourself as one who listens to the radio?	1,2	Yes, No
(If yes) To which type of radio programming do you most often listen?	1,2,3,4,5	Country & Western, Easy Listening, Rock, Talk/News, No Preference
Would you describe yourself as a viewer of TV local news?	1,2	Yes, No
(If yes) Which newscast do you watch most frequently?	1,2,3,4	7:00 a.m., Noon, 6:00 p.m., 10:00 p.m.
Do you read the newspaper?	1,2	Yes, No
(If yes) Which section of the local newspaper would you say you read most frequently?	1,2,3,4,5	Editorial, Business, Local, Classifieds, Life-Health-Entertainment
Do you subscribe to City Magazine?	1,2	Yes, No
In this proposed new restaurant, how much would you prefer… • Waterfront view • Drive less than 30 minutes • Formal waitstaff wearing tuxedos • Unusual desserts • Large variety of entrees • Unusual entrées • Simple décor • Elegant décor • String quartet • Jazz combo	1,2,3,4,5	Very Strongly Not Prefer, Somewhat Not Prefer, Neither Prefer Nor Not Prefer, Somewhat Prefer, Very Strongly Prefer
Year you were born	Actual year	No labels
What is your highest level of education?	1,2,3,4,5,6,7,8	Less than high school, Some high school, High school graduate, Some college, Associate degree, Bachelor's degree, Master's degree, Doctorate degree
What is your marital status?	1,2,3	Single, Married, Other
Including children under 18 living with you, what is your family size?	# children	No labels
Please check the letter that includes the ZIP code in which you live (designated by letter by combining ZIPs using the last 2 digits).	1,2,3,4	A (01 & 02), B (03, 04, & 05), C (07, 08, & 09), D (10, 11, & 12)
Which of the following categories best describes your before tax household income?	1,2,3,4,5,6,7	Under $15,000, $15,000 to $24,999, $25,000 to $49,999, $50,000 to $74,999, $75,000 to $99,999, $100,000 to $149,999, $150,000 and above
What is your gender?	1,2	Male, Female

Cory had other marketing research projects and meetings scheduled with present and prospective clients, so he called in his marketing intern, Christine Yu. Christine was a senior marketing major at Able State University, and she had taken marketing research in the previous semester. Cory called Christine into his office, and said, "Christine, it is time to do some analysis on the survey we did for Jeff Dean. For now, let's just get a feel for what the data look like. I'll leave it up to your judgment as to what basic analysis to run. Let's meet tomorrow at 2:30 p.m. and see what you have found."

Your task is to take the role of Christine Yu, marketing intern. The file name is Hobbit.sav, and it is in SPSS data file format. Your instructor will provide this SPSS data file to you or indicate how you can obtain it.

1. Determine what variables are categorical (either nominal or ordinal scales), perform the appropriate descriptive analysis, and interpret it.

2. Determine what variables are scale variables (either interval or ratio scales), perform the appropriate descriptive analysis, and interpret it.

The following day Cory says, "Christine, this is great work. Our client's name is Jeff Dean, and I am going to meet with him in an hour to show him what we have found. In the meantime, I want you to look a bit deeper into the data. I have jotted down some items that I want you to analyze. This is the next step in understanding how the sample findings generalize to the population of the greater metropolitan area."

Your task here is to again take the role of Christine Yu, marketing intern. Using The Hobbit's Choice Restaurant survey SPSS dataset, perform the proper analysis, and interpret the findings for each of the following questions specified by Cory Rogers.

3. What are the population estimates for each of the following?
   a. Preference for "easy listening" radio programming
   b. Viewing of 10 p.m. local news on TV
   c. Subscribe to *City Magazine*
   d. Average age of heads of households
   e. Average price paid of an evening meal entrée

4. Because Jeff Dean's restaurant will be upscale, it will appeal to high-income consumers. Jeff hopes that 25% of the households have an income level of $100,000 or higher. Test this hypothesis.

5. With respect to those who are "very likely" to patronize The Hobbit's Choice Restaurant, Jeff believes they will either "somewhat" or "very strongly" prefer each of the following: (a) waitstaff with tuxedos, (b) unusual desserts, (c) large variety of entrées, (d) unusual entrées, (e) elegant décor, and (f) jazz combo music. Does the survey support or refute Jeff's hypotheses? Interpret your findings.

CASE 12.2 INTEGRATED CASE

Global Motors Descriptive and Inference Analysis

SPSS®

Cory Rogers was happy to call Nick Thomas to inform him that Global Motors survey data were collected and ready for analysis. Of course, Cory had other marketing research projects and meetings scheduled with present and prospective clients, so he called in his data analyst, Celeste Brown, and said, "Celeste, it is time to do some analysis on the survey we did for Nick Thomas of Global Motors. I am going to assign you primary responsibility for all data analysis on this important project. For now, let's just get a feel for what the data look like, so do some descriptive analyses in order to reveal the basic patterns and to gain an understanding of the nature of the variability in the data. Let's meet tomorrow at 3:30 p.m. and see what you have found."

Your task in this case is to take the role of Celeste Brown, data analyst. The dataset for the Global Motors survey is now ready for descriptive analysis. The file name is GlobalMotors.sav, and it is in SPSS data file format. Your Instructor will tell you how to access this SPSS dataset. The dataset sample represents American households, and it includes owners as well as nonowners of vehicles because the market for the new vehicles to be developed and marketed by the Global Motors division of ZEN Motors will not "hit" the market for from 3 to 5 years from now.

Question Description	Codes	Value Labels
Size of home town or city	1,2,3,4,5	1 million and more, 500K to 1 million,10K to 500K,10K to 100K,Under 10K
Gender	0,1	Male, Female
Marital status	0,1	Unmarried, Married
Number of people in family	Actual number	No labels
Age category	1,2,3,4,5	18 to 24, 25 to 34, 35 to 49, 50 to 64, 65 and older
Education category	1,2,3,4,5	Less than high school, high school diploma, some college, college degree, postgraduate degree
Income category	1,2,3,4,5	Under $25K, $25K to 49K, $50K to 74K, $75K to 125K, $125K and more
Dwelling type	1,2,3,4	Single family, Multiple family, Condominium/ townhouse, Mobile home
I am worried about global warming. Gasoline emissions contribute to global warming.	1,2,3,4,5,6,7	Very strongly disagree, Strongly disagree, Disagree, Neither disagree nor agree, Agree, Strongly Agree, Very strongly agree
Desirability: 1-seat all-electric model Desirability: 4-seat all-electric model Desirability: 4-seat gasoline hybrid model Desirability: 4-seat diesel hybrid model Desirability: 5-seat standard size gasoline model	1,2,3,4,5,6,7	Very undesirable, Undesirable, Somewhat desirable, Neutral, Somewhat desirable, Desirable, Very desirable
Lifestyle: Novelist Lifestyle: Innovator Lifestyle: Trendsetter Lifestyle: Forerunner Lifestyle: Mainstreamer Lifestyle: Classic	1, … ,7	Does not describe me at all, …, Describes me perfectly
Favorite television show type	1,2,3,4,5,6,7	Comedy, Drama, Movies/mini-series, News/documentary, Reality, Science fiction, Sports
Favorite radio genre	1,2,3,4,5,6	Classic pop & rock, Country, Easy listening, Jazz & blues, Pop & chart, Talk
Favorite magazine type	1,2,3,4,5,6,7,8	Business & money, Music & entertainment, Family & parenting, Sports & outdoors, Home & garden, Cooking, food, & wine, Trucks, cars, & motorcycles, News, politics, & current events
Favorite local newspaper section	1,2,3,4,5,6,7	Editorial, Business, Local news, National news, Sports, Entertainment, Do not read
Use of online blogs Use of content communities Use of social network sites Use of online games Use of virtual worlds	1,2,3,4	Never, …, 4+ times per day

(handwritten margin notes: "nom", "ratio", "nom", "int")

For each question below, it is your task to determine the type of scale for each variable, conduct the proper descriptive analysis with SPSS, and interpret it.

1. What is the demographic composition of the sample?
2. How do respondents feel about: (1) global warming and (2) gasoline emissions?
3. What type of automobile model is the most desirable to people in the sample? What type is the least desirable?
4. Describe the "traditional" media usage of respondents in the sample.
5. Describe the social media usage of the respondents in the sample.
6. The Global Motors principals believe that the desirability on the part of the American public for each of the automobile models under consideration is the following.

Vehicle Model Type	Desirability*
1-seat all-electric	3
4-seat all-electric	4
4-seat gasoline hybrid	4
5-seat diesel hybrid	3
5-seat standard size gasoline	2

*Measured on 1-7 scale.

Test these hypotheses with the findings from the survey.

Implementing Basic Differences Tests

LEARNING OBJECTIVES

- To learn how differences are used for market segmentation decisions
- To understand when t tests or z tests are appropriate and why you do not need to worry about this issue when using SPSS
- To be able to test the differences between two percentages or means for two independent groups
- To know what a paired samples difference test is and when to use it
- To comprehend ANOVA and how to interpret ANOVA output
- To learn how to perform differences tests for means using SPSS

"WHERE WE ARE"

The Importance of Differences Analysis

Kartik Pashupati,
Research Manager,
Research Now®

Marketers often want to know if specific strategies or tactics had an impact in the marketplace in terms of "moving the needle" on key performance indicators. For example, they might want to know if consumers changed their opinions about a brand (and their willingness to consider purchasing it) based on their exposure to an ad campaign. This means market researchers need to measure the same indicators (i.e., ask the target audience the same set of questions) both before and after exposure and then examine the differences in scores to see if the ad campaign made a difference. For example, on an intentions to purchase scale, the before average might be a 3, which moves to a 4 after the ad campaign has run.

Some marketers are comfortable about using mean scores to examine changes in key performance indicators, but many others prefer to examine changes in proportions, such as changes in the percentage of survey respondents who checked the "top two boxes" in a battery of questions. (Marketers use the term "top two boxes" as a shorthand way of referring to the percentage of respondents who selected the two most positively worded items in a Likert-type question. For example, in a customer satisfaction survey, the top two boxes refer to the percentage of customers who said they were "Satisfied" or "Very Satisfied" with a product or service.) While mean scores allow for much more powerful statistical tests, they can sometimes suppress interesting results if many responses cluster around the neutral or midpoint of a scale. In such instances, marketers often find differences in proportions much more intuitive and useful for decision making, as they are most interested in making a difference among those customers who have strong positive (or negative!) opinions.

Even if the data indicate that the marketing strategy moved the needle in the desired direction, researchers need to use statistical tests to ensure that the observed changes can indeed be attributed to the marketing strategy and to rule out the possibility that the differences are due to random or chance factors.

Keeping Mr. Pashupati's comments in mind, in this chapter, we describe the logic of differences tests, and we show you how to use SPSS to conduct various types of differences tests.[1] We begin this chapter discussing why differences are important to marketing managers. Next, we introduce differences (percentages or means) between two independent groups, such as a comparison of high-speed cable versus DSL telephone Internet users on how satisfied they are with their Internet connection service. Next, we introduce ANOVA, a scary name for a simple way to compare the means of several groups simultaneously and to quickly spot patterns of significant differences. We provide numerical examples and share examples of SPSS procedures and output using the Global Motors survey data. Finally, we establish that it is possible to test for a difference between the averages of two similarly scaled questions. For instance, do buyers rate a store higher in "merchandise selection" than they rate its "good values"?

Why Differences Are Important

Perhaps one of the most useful marketing management concepts is market segmentation. Basically, market segmentation holds that different types of consumers have different requirements, and these differences can be the bases of marketing strategies. As an example, Iams, which markets pet foods, has more than 20 varieties of dry dog food geared to the dog's age (puppy, adult, senior), weight situation (small, medium, large), and activity (reduced, normal, moderate, high). Toyota Motors has 20 models, including 8 cars, 2 trucks, 7 SUVs and vans, and 3 hybrids. Even Boeing has six types of commercial jets, including the newly developed Dreamliner, plus a separate business jets division for corporate travel.

Let's look at differences from the consumer's side. Everyone washes his or her hands, but the kind of soap required differs for weekend gardeners with potting soil under their fingernails, factory workers whose hands are dirty with solvents, preschoolers who have sticky drink residue on their hands and faces, or aspiring beauty princesses who wish their hands to look absolutely flawless. The needs and requirements of each of these market segments differ greatly

Photo: © NAN/Fotolia

Market segmentation is based on differences between groups of consumers.

from the others, and an astute marketer will customize his or her marketing mix to each target market's unique situation.[2]

These differences may seem quite obvious, but as competition intensifies, prolific market segmentation and target marketing become the watchwords of most companies in an industry. Consumer marketers need to investigate differences among consumer groups, and B2B marketers seek to differentiate the needs and preferences among business establishments. One commonly used basis for market segmentation is the discovery of (1) statistically significant, (2) meaningful, (3) stable, and (4) actionable differences. We will discuss each requirement briefly. In this discussion, we will use the example of working with a pharmaceuticals company that markets cold remedies.

The differences must be significant. As you know, the notion of statistical significance underpins marketing research.[3] **Statistical significance of differences** means that the differences found in the sample(s) truly exist in the population(s) from which the random samples are drawn. Apparent differences between and among market segments must be subjected to tests that assess their statistical significance. This testing is the topic of this chapter, and we will endeavor to teach you how to perform these tests and interpret the results.

For example, we could ask cold sufferers, "How important is it that your cold remedy relieves your (insert symptom here)…" The respondents would respond using an scale of 1 = not important to 10 = very important for each cold symptom such as fever, sore throat, congestion, aching muscles, etc., and statistical tests such those described in this chapter would determine if the responses were significantly different. With those in the grip of a cold virus, we might find two groups that have statistically significant differences. *Congestion sufferers* greatly desire breathing congestion relief, whereas *muscle aches and pains sufferers* more greatly desire relief from musculoskeletal aches and pains associated with their colds.

To be potentially useful to the marketing researcher or manager, differences must, at minimum, be statistically significant.

The differences must be meaningful. A finding of statistical significance in no way guarantees "meaningful" difference. In fact, with the proliferation of data mining analysis due to scanner data with tens of thousands of records, online surveys that garner thousands of respondents, and other ways to capture very large samples, there is a real danger of finding a great deal of statistical significance that is not meaningful. The reason for this danger is that statistical significance is determined to a high degree by sample size.[4] You will see in this chapter by examining the formulas we provide that the sample size, n, is instrumental in the calculation of z, the determinant of the significance level. Large samples—those in excess of 1,000 per sample group—often yield statistically significant results when the absolute differences between the groups are quite small. A **meaningful difference** is one that the marketing manager can potentially use as a basis for marketing decisions.

In our common cold example, there are some meaningful implications that one group cannot breathe easily while the other group has aches and pains as there are cold remedy ingredients that reduce congestion and other ingredients that diminish pain. Granted, the pharmaceuticals company could include both ingredients, but the congestion sufferers do not want an ingredient that might make them drowsy due to the strong pain relief ingredient, and the aches and pains sufferers do not want their throats and nasal passages to feel dry and uncomfortable due to the decongestant ingredient. These differences are meaningful both to the customer groups and to the pharmaceuticals manufacturer.

To be useful to the marketing researcher or manager, differences must, if statistically significant, be meaningful.

The differences should be stable. Stability refers to the requirement that we are not working with a short-term or transitory set of differences. Thus, a **stable difference** is one that will be in place for the foreseeable future. The persistent problem experienced by congestion sufferers is most probably due to some respiratory weakness or condition. They may have preconditions such as allergies or breathing problems, or they may be exposed to heavy pollution or some other factor that affects their respiration in general. Muscle aches and pains sufferers may be very active people who do not have respiration weaknesses, but they

To be useful to the marketing researcher or manager, differences must, if statistically significant and meaningful, be stable.

may value active lifestyle practices, such as regular exercise, or their occupations may require a good deal of physical activity. In either case, there is a good possibility that when a cold strikes, the sufferer will experience the same discomfort, either congestion or muscle aches, time and time again. That is, the differences between the two groups are stable. The pharmaceuticals company can develop custom-designed versions of its cold relief product because managers know from experience and research that certain consumers will be consistent (stable) in seeking certain types of relief or specific product benefits when they suffer from colds.

The differences must actionable. Market segmentation requires that standard or innovative market segmentation bases are used and that these bases uniquely identify the various groups so that they can be analyzed and put in the marketer's targeting mechanisms. An **actionable difference** means that the marketer can focus various marketing strategies and tactics, such as product design or advertising, on the market segments to accentuate the differences between the segments. A great many segmentation bases are actionable, such as demographics, lifestyles, and product benefits. In our example, among the many symptoms manifest by colds sufferers, we have identified two meaningful and stable groups, so a cold remedy product line that concentrates on each one of these separately is possible. A quick glance at the cold remedies section of your local drug store will verify the actionability of these cold symptoms market segments.

You may be confused about meaningful and actionable differences. Recall that we used the words "potentially use" in our definition of a meaningful difference. With our cold remedies example, a pharmaceutical company could potentially develop and market a cold remedy that is specific to every type of cold symptom as experienced by every demographic group and further identified by lifestyle differences. For example, there could be a cold medicine to alleviate the runny noses of teenage girls who participate in high school athletics and a different one for the sniffles in teenage boys who play high school sports. But it would be economically unjustifiable to offer so many different cold medicines, so all marketers must assess actionability based on market segment size and profitability considerations. Nevertheless, the fundamental differences are based on statistical significance, meaningfulness, and stability assessments.

To be sure, the bulk of this chapter deals strictly with statistically significant differences, because it is the beginning point for market segmentation and savvy target marketing. Meaningfulness, stability, and actionability are not statistical issues; rather, they are marketing manager judgment calls.

Because cold suffers consistently have different symptoms, such as runny noses, congestion, and achy muscles, pharmaceutical companies have identified different market segments.

Photo: Andrii Oleksiienko/Shutterstock

To be useful to the manager, differences must be statistically significant, meaningful, stable and actionable.

Small Sample Sizes: The Use of a t Test or a z Test and How SPSS Eliminates the Worry

SPSS®

The t test should be used when the sample size is 30 or less.

Most of the equations related in this chapter will lead to the computation of a z value. As we pointed out in the previous chapter, computation of the z value makes the assumption that the raw data for most statistics under scrutiny have normal or bell-shaped distributions. However, statisticians have shown that this normal curve property does not occur when the sample size is 30 observations or less.[5] In this instance, a t value is computed instead of a z value. The **t test** is defined as the statistical inference test to be used with small samples sizes ($n \leq 30$). Any instance when the sample size is 30 or greater requires the use of a z **test**.

The great advantage to using statistical analysis routines on a computer is that they are programmed to compute the correct statistic. In other words, you do not need to decide whether you want the program to compute a t value, a z value, or some other value.

Most computer statistical programs report only the *t* value because it is identical to the *z* value with large samples.

With SPSS, the analyses of differences are referred to as *t tests*, but now that you realize that SPSS will always determine the correct significance level, whether it is a *t* or a *z*, you do not need to worry about which statistic to use. The talent you need to acquire is how to interpret the significance level reported by SPSS. Marketing Research Insight 13.1 introduces a "flag waving" analogy that students have told us is helpful in this regard.

MARKETING RESEARCH INSIGHT 13.1   *Practical Application*

Green Flag Signals and Significance in Statistical Analysis

The output from statistical procedures in all software programs can be envisioned as "green flag" devices. When the green signal flag is waving, statistical significance is present. Then, and only then, is it warranted to look at the findings more closely to determine the pattern of the findings; if the flag is not green, your time will be wasted by looking any further. To read statistical flags, you need to know two things. First, where is the flag located? Second, what color is it?

Where Is the Flag?

Virtually every statistical test or procedure involves the computation of some critical statistic, and that statistic is used to determine the statistical significance of the findings. The critical statistic's name changes depending on the procedure and its underlying assumptions, but usually the statistic is identified as a letter, as in *z*, *t*, or *F*. Statistical analysis computer programs automatically identify and compute the correct statistic, so although it is helpful to know ahead of time what statistic will be computed, it is not essential to know it. Moreover, the statistic is not the flag; rather it is just a computation necessary to raise the flag. You might think of the computed statistic as the flagpole.

The computer program also raises the flag on the flagpole, but its name changes a bit depending on the procedure.

The flags, called "*p* values" by statisticians, are identified on computer output by the terms *significance* or *probability*. Sometimes abbreviations such as "Sig" or "Prob" are used to economize on the output. To find the flag, locate the "Sig" or "Prob" designation in the analysis, and look at the number associated with it. The number will be a decimal, perhaps as low as 0.000 but ranging to as high as 1.000. When you locate it, you have found the statistical significance flag.

What Color Is the Flag?

In NASCAR racing, the green flag signals the start of the race. For purposes of this textbook, we have adopted the 95% level of confidence. That is, if you are 95% confident that the green flag is out, you would expect the race to be under way.

As we noted previously, the significance or probability values reported in statistical analysis output range from .0000 to 1.000, and they indicate the degree of support for the null hypothesis (no differences). If you take 1 minus the reported significance level—for example, if the sig level is .03, you would take 1 minus .03 to arrive at .97, or 97%—that is the level of confidence for our finding. Any time this value is .05 or less (95% level of confidence), you should know you have the green flag to start your interpretation of the findings.

Testing for Significant Differences Between Two Groups

Statistical tests are used when a researcher wants to compare the means or percentages of two different groups or samples.

Often, as we have done in our cold remedy example, a researcher will want to compare two groups of interest. That is, the researcher may have two independent groups such as first-time versus repeat customers, and he or she may want to compare their answers to the same question. The question may be either a nominal or an ordinal scale. Such a variable requires that the researcher compare percentages; a scale variable requires comparing means. As you know by now, the formulas differ depending on whether percentages or means are being tested.

DIFFERENCES BETWEEN PERCENTAGES WITH TWO GROUPS (INDEPENDENT SAMPLES)

Independent samples are treated as representing two potentially different populations.

When a marketing researcher is interested in making comparisons between two groups of respondents to determine whether there are statistically significant differences between them, in concept, he or she is considering them as two potentially different populations.

The question to be answered becomes whether their respective population parameters are different. (A parameter is simply a value in the population that is of interest to the researcher.) But, as always, a researcher can only work with the sample results. Therefore, the researcher must fall back on statistical significance to determine whether the difference that is found between the two sample statistics is a true population difference. You will shortly discover that the logic of differences tests is similar to the logic of hypothesis testing, which was discussed in the previous chapter.

To begin, we will refer to an intuitive approach you use every day when comparing two things to make an inference. Let's assume you have read a *Business Week* article about college recruiters that quotes a Harris poll of 100 randomly selected companies, indicating that 65% will be visiting college campuses to interview business majors. The article goes on to say that a similar poll taken last year with 300 companies found that only 40% would be recruiting at college campuses. This is great news: More companies will be coming to your campus this year with job interviews. However, you cannot be completely confident of your joyous conclusion because of sampling error. If the difference between the percentages was very large, say 80% for this year and 20% for last year, you would be more inclined to believe that a true change had occurred. But if you found out the difference was based on small sample sizes, you would be less confident with your inference that last year's and this year's college recruiting are different. Intuitively, you have taken into account two critical factors in determining whether statistically significant differences exist between a percentage or a mean compared between two samples: the magnitude of the difference between the compared statistic (65% versus 40%) and sample sizes (100 versus 300).

To test whether a true difference exists between two group percentages, we test the **null hypothesis,** or the hypothesis that the difference in their population parameters is equal to zero. The alternative hypothesis is that there is a true difference between them. To perform the test of **significance of differences between two percentages**, each representing a separate group (sample), the first step requires a comparison of the two percentages. The comparison is performed to find the arithmetic difference between them. The second step requires that this difference be translated into a number of standard errors away from the hypothesized value of zero. Once the number of standard errors is known, knowledge of the area under the normal curve will yield an assessment of the probability of support for the null hypothesis.

> With a differences test, the null hypothesis states that there is no difference between the percentages (or means) being compared.

For a difference between two percentages test, the equation is as follows:

Formula for significance of the difference between two percentages
$$z = \frac{p_1 - p_2}{s_{p_1 - p_2}}$$

Where

p_1 = percentage found in sample 1

p_2 = percentage found in sample 2

$s_{p_1 - p_2}$ = standard error of the difference between two percentages

The standard error of the difference between two percentages combines the standard error of the percentage for both samples, and it is calculated with the following formula:

Formula for the standard error of the difference between two percentages
$$s_{p_1 - p_2} = \sqrt{\frac{p_1 \times q_1}{n_1} + \frac{p_2 \times q_2}{n_2}}$$

Again, if you compare these formulas to the ones we used in hypothesis testing in Chapter 12, you will see that the logic is identical. First, in the numerator, we subtract one sample's statistic (p_2) from the other sample's statistic (p_1) just as we would subtract

> With a differences test, you test the null hypothesis that no differences exist between the two group means (or percentages).

the hypothesized percent from the sample percent in hypotheses testing. We use the subscripts 1 and 2 to refer to the two different sample statistics. Second, the sampling distribution is expressed in the denominator. However, the sampling distribution under consideration now is the assumed sampling distribution of the differences between the percentage rather than the simple standard error of a percentage used in hypothesis testing. That is, the assumption has been made that the differences have been computed for comparisons of the two sample statistics for many repeated samplings. If the null hypothesis is true, this distribution of differences follows the normal curve with a mean equal to zero and a standard error equal to one. Stated somewhat differently, the procedure requires us to accept the (null) hypothesis as true until it lacks support from the statistical test. Consequently, the differences of a multitude of comparisons of the two sample percentages generated from many, many samplings would average zero. In other words, our sampling distribution is now the distribution of the difference between one sample and the other, taken over many, many times.[6] The following example will walk you through the point we just made.

Here is how you would perform the calculations for the Harris poll on companies coming to campus to hire college seniors. Recall that last year's poll with 300 companies reported that 40% were coming to campus, while this year's poll with 100 companies reported that 65% were visiting campuses.

Computation of the significance of the difference between two percentages

$$z = \frac{p_1 - p_2}{s_{p_1 - p_2}}$$

$$= \frac{65 - 40}{\sqrt{\dfrac{65 \times 35}{100} + \dfrac{40 \times 60}{300}}}$$

$$= \frac{25}{\sqrt{22.75 + 8.0}}$$

$$= \frac{25}{5.55}$$

$$= 4.51$$

Notes:
$p_1 = 65\%$
$p_2 = 40\%$
$n_1 = 100$
$n_2 = 300$

We compare the computed z value with our standard z of 1.96 for the 95% level of confidence, and the computed z of 4.51 is larger than 1.96. A computed z value that is larger than the standard z value of 1.96 amounts to *no support* for the null hypothesis at the 95% level of confidence. There is a statistically significant difference between the two percentages, and we are confident that if we repeated this comparison many, many times with a multitude of independent samples, we would conclude that there is a significant difference in at least 95% of these replications. Of course, we would never do many, many replications, but this is the statistician's basis for the level of significance.

When z is greater than 1.96, there is little support for the null hypothesis of no difference. Therefore, there is a statistically significant difference.

We realize that it is confusing to keep in mind the null hypothesis, to understand all the equations, and to figure out how to interpret the findings. We have provided a table that describes the null hypothesis for each type of group differences test described in this chapter. Refer to Table 13.1.

It is a simple matter to apply the formulas to percentages to determine the significance of their differences, for all that is needed is the sample size of each group. Marketing Research Insight 13.2 relies on significance of the difference between percentages tests we have computed based on the information in the source. This feature highlights the significantly different profiles of grocery item impulse purchasing found for French versus Swedish supermarket customers.

TABLE 13.1   Null Hypotheses for Group Differences Tests

Null Hypothesis	What Does It Mean if the Hypothesis Is Not Supported?
Differences between two group percents	
No difference exists between the percents of the two groups (populations).	A difference does exist between the percents of the two groups (populations).
Differences between two group means	
No difference exists between the means of the two groups (populations).	A difference does exist between the means of the two groups (populations).
Differences in means among more than two groups (Note: Only differences in means can be tested here)	
No difference exists between the means of all paired groups (populations).	A difference exists between the means of at least one pair of groups (populations).

 Active Learning

Calculations to Determine Significant Differences Between Percentages

You can now perform your own tests of the differences between two percentages using the formulas we have provided and described. A local health club has just finished a media blitz (newspaper, television, radio, etc.) for new memberships. Whenever prospective members visited the health club's facilities, they were asked to fill out a short questionnaire, and one question asked them to indicate what ads they saw in the past month. Some of these prospects joined the health club, while some did not; thus, we have two populations: those who joined the health club and those who did not. At the end of the 30-day campaign, a staff member performed the following tabulations.

	Joined the Health Club	Did Not Join the Health Club
Total visitors	100	30
Recalled newspaper ads	45	15
Recalled FM radio station ads	89	20
Recalled Yellow Pages ads	16	5
Recalled local TV news ads	21	6

Use your knowledge of the formula and the test of the significance of the difference between two percentages to ascertain if there are any significant differences in this data. What are the implications of your findings with respect to the effectiveness of the various advertising media used during the membership recruitment ad blitz?

■

USING SPSS FOR DIFFERENCES BETWEEN PERCENTAGES OF TWO GROUPS

As is the case with most statistical analysis programs, SPSS does not perform tests of the significance of the difference between the percentages of two groups. You can, however, use SPSS to determine the sample percentage on your variable of interest along with its sample size. To do this you should use the SPSS command, FREQUENCIES. Repeat this descriptive analysis for the other sample, and you will have all the values required (p_1, p_2, n_1, and n_2) to perform the calculations by hand or in a spreadsheet program. (Recall that you can compute q_1 and q_2, based on the "$p + q = 100\%$" relationship.)

Marketing Research on YouTube™ To learn about proportion differences tests, launch **www.youtube.com**, and search for "Hypothesis Test Comparing Population Proportions."

 SPSS®

SPSS does not perform tests of the significance of the difference between the percentages of two groups, but you can use SPSS to generate the relevant information and perform a hand calculation.

MARKETING RESEARCH INSIGHT 13.2   *Global Application*

Impulse Purchases Differ in French Versus Swedish Consumers

It is well known that consumers buy on impulse, and supermarket purchases are commonly cited as rife with impulse purchasing. A recent study[7] addressed the question "Is impulse purchasing universal?" meaning does it exist in consumers regardless of their nationalities. If it is universal, then marketers can use similar impulse purchase strategies, such as end-of-aisle and checkout displays, to stimulate it in supermarkets. The study compared French and Swedish supermarket shoppers and found the following percentages of impulse purchases across 15 product categories.

In the figure, bars that do not have percent labels pertain to those products where no statistically significant (95% level of confidence) differences were found. It is interesting to note that while impulse buying is universal for these two nationalities, it differs by product category. Specifically, French grocery shoppers are more prone to impulse purchases of stable food items, such as crackers and biscuits, fruits, and cheese, than are Swedish grocery shoppers, while Swedish shoppers are more prone to impulse purchases of snacks such as candy and peanuts and potato chips as well as soft drinks, than are French shoppers. These differences findings reveal that marketers who seek to stimulate impulse shopping in supermarkets must vary their strategies according to the customs in each country in which they are operating.

Impulse Purchases of French and Swedish Grocery Shoppers

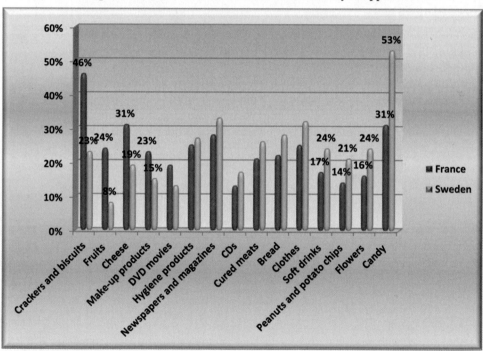

DIFFERENCES BETWEEN MEANS WITH TWO GROUPS (INDEPENDENT SAMPLES)

The procedure for testing **significance of difference between two means**, from two different groups (either two different samples or two different groups in the same sample) is identical to the procedure used in testing two percentages. However, the equations differ because a scale variable is involved.

Here is the equation for the test of difference between two sample means:

Formula for significance of the difference between two means

$$z = \frac{\bar{x}_1 - \bar{x}_2}{s_{\bar{x}_1 - \bar{x}_2}}$$

If the null hypothesis is true, when you subtract one group mean from the other, the result should be about zero.

Where

$\bar{x}_1$ = mean found in sample 1

$\bar{x}_2$ = mean found in sample 2

$s_{\bar{x}_1 - \bar{x}_2}$ = standard error of the difference between two means

Here is the formula for the standard error of the difference between 2 means and between 2 percentages.

The standard error of the difference is easy to calculate and again relies on the variability that has been found in the samples and their sizes. Because we are working with means, we use the standard deviations in the formula for the standard error of a difference between two means:

Formula for the standard error of the difference between two means

$$s_{\bar{x}_1 - \bar{x}_2} = \sqrt{\frac{s_1^2}{n_1} + \frac{s_2^2}{n_2}}$$

Where

s_1 = standard deviation in sample 1

s_2 = standard deviation in sample 2

n_1 = size of sample 1

n_2 = size of sample 2

To illustrate how significance of difference computations are made, we use the following example that answers the question "Do male teens and female teens drink different amounts of sports drinks?" In a recent survey, teenagers were asked to indicate how many 20-ounce bottles of sports drinks they consume in a typical week. The descriptive statistics revealed that males consume 9 bottles on average and that females consume 7.5 bottles of sports drinks on average. The respective standard deviations were found to be 2 and 1.2. Both samples were of size 100. Applying this information to the formula for the test of statistically significant differences, we get the following:

Is there a difference in the average number of sports drinks consumed by males versus the average number of sports drinks consumed by females?

Photo: Warren Goldswain/Shutterstock

Computation of the significance of the difference between two means

$$z = \frac{\bar{x}_1 - \bar{x}_2}{\sqrt{\frac{s_1^2}{n_1} + \frac{s_2^2}{n_2}}}$$

$$= \frac{9.0 - 7.5}{\sqrt{\frac{2^2}{100} + \frac{1.2^2}{100}}}$$

$$= \frac{1.5}{\sqrt{.04 + .0144}}$$

$$= \frac{1.5}{0.233}$$

$$= 6.43$$

Notes:

$\bar{x}_1 = 9.0$

$\bar{x}_2 = 7.5$

$s_1 = 2.0$

$s_2 = 1.2$

$n_1 = 100$

$n_2 = 100$

Here are the calculations for a test of the difference between the means of two groups.

FIGURE 13.1 A Significant Difference Exists Between the Two Means Because *z* Is Calculated to Be Greater Than 1.96 (95% Level of Confidence)

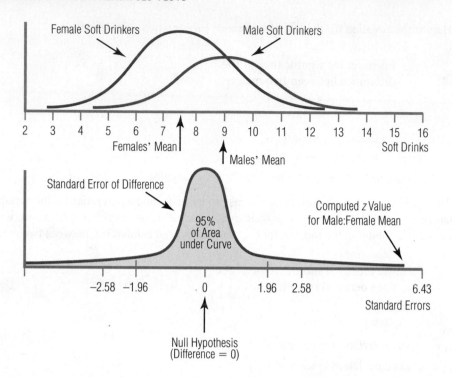

Figure 13.1 indicates how these two samples compare on the sampling distribution assumed to underlie this example. In the bottom of the figure, we have provided the standard error of the difference bell-shaped curve with 0 as its mean (the null hypothesis). By looking at computed *z*-value labeled on the graph, you can see the probability of support for the null hypothesis of no difference between the two means is less than 0.001 because the large number of standard errors (6.43) that is calculated to exist for this example is much greater than 2.58.

How do you interpret this test for significance of differences? As always, the sampling distribution concept underlies our interpretation. If the null hypothesis is true, and we draw many, many samples and do this explicit comparison each time, 95% of differences would fall within ±1.96 standard errors of zero. Of course, only one comparison can be made, and you have to rely on the sampling distribution concept and its attendant assumptions to determine whether this one particular instance of information supports or refutes the hypothesis of no significant differences found between the means of your two groups. To learn about how a researcher used differences of means to investigate Generation X versus Generation Y consumers' use of social media and e-WOM, read Marketing Research Insight 13.3.

MARKETING RESEARCH INSIGHT 13.3   *Social Media Marketing*

Gen X and Gen Y e-WOM

Marketers covet word-of-mouth (WOM) advertising because consumers very highly value personal recommendations of their friends, neighbors, relatives, and acquaintances. WOM in social media marketing (called e-WOM) is especially desirable because one-to-one communiqués can potentially become viral and reach thousands or millions of consumers in a matter of days

at practically no cost to the marketer. It is believed that the 71 million Gen Y consumers who were born between 1982 and 1995 differ from Gen X consumers who were born between 1965 and 1981 because of the two decade gap in their life experiences. Specifically, it is likely that Gen Ys embrace social media to a much greater extent than Gen Xs. A recent survey sought to identify and document these differences.[8] The following table is abstracted from the article describing the findings of the survey.

In the study, usage level was measured with a 7-point scale where 1 = Never and 7 = More than 4 times daily. The likelihood to forward items was measured with a 7-point scale where 1 = Not at all descriptive and 7 = Extremely descriptive (of me). The asterisks denote where significant differences were found between the Gen X and Gen Y group means. The significant differences found for the usage levels of the various social media reveal that while both generations use personal email at about the same level, Gen Y consumers are definitely more into the use of popular personal social media communication vehicles such as Facebook, Twitter, and YouTube. In response to receiving a message from an advertiser, the two generations are very similar; the only difference is that Gen X consumers are more likely to forward this message if it arrives on LinkedIn. With respect to receiving an ad from a personal source, the Gen Y consumer differs from the Gen X consumer only if the message arrives on Facebook, in which case the Gen Y consumer is more likely to forward it on. Thus, if a marketer wants to stimulate e-WOM among Gen Xers, the best strategy is to post an ad on LinkedIn, but if Gen Y viral e-WOM is the goal, the marketer should encourage its satisfied customers to post personal testimonials on Facebook.

Usage and Likelihood to Forward e-WOM by Source/Medium

	Usage level[a]		Likelihood to forward message from advertising source[b]		Likelihood to forward message from personal source[b]	
	Gen Y	Gen X	Gen Y	Gen X	Gen Y	Gen X
Personal email	*5.34*	*5.30*	*2.21*	*2.13*	*3.25*	*3.53*
Business email	*3.28***	*4.38***	*1.59*	*1.71*	*2.10*	*2.54*
Facebook	*4.68***	*2.91****	*2.11*	*1.49*	*3.62****	*2.13****
MySpace	*2.36**	*1.78**	*1.39*	*1.17*	*1.79*	*1.49*
LinkedIn	*1.08*	*1.13*	*1.03***	*1.22***	*1.06*	*1.13*
Twitter	*1.36**	*1.07**	*1.10*	*1.21*	*1.23*	*1.41*
YouTube	*2.84**	*2.42**	*1.49*	*1.58*	*1.80*	*1.72*

Standard deviation in parentheses.
[a]Respondents were asked 'Estimate your usage of the following communication tools on the Internet'. Responses were on 7-point Likert scale anchored by 1 ('Never') and 7 ('Four times a day').
[b]Respondents were asked 'Please estimate the extent to which you pass along information through.' Responses were on 7-point Likert scale anchored by 1 ('Never') and 7 ('Four times a day').
*Significant at 0.05.
**Significant at 0.01.
***Significant at <0.001.

INTEGRATED CASE

Global Motors: How to Perform an Independent Samples t-Test

SPSS®

Significance of Differences Between Means Test with SPSS

To demonstrate an independent samples significance test, we will take up the question of whether market segmentation is relevant to Global Motors. This example focuses on gender as a possible segmentation variable and only 4-seat standard size gasoline model. We have two groups: males and females. We can test the means of the desirability of the 4-seat standard size gasoline model, which was measured on a scale test the means of where 1 = very undesirable and 7 = very desirable.

The clickstream that directs SPSS to perform an independent samples *t* test of the significance of the difference between means is displayed in Figure 13.2. As you can see, you begin with the ANALYZE-COMPARE MEANS-INDEPENDENT SAMPLES T-TEST... menu sequence. This sequence opens up the selection menu, and the "Desirability: Standard Size Gasoline" variable is clicked into the "Test variable" area, while the "Gender" variable is clicked into the "Grouping Variable" box. Using the "Define Groups" button, a window opens to let us identify the codes of the two groups (0 = male and 1 = female). This sets up the *t* test, and a click on OK executes it.

To determine the significance of the difference in the means of two groups with SPSS, use the ANALYZE-COMPARE MEANS-INDEPENDENT SAMPLES T-TEST... menu sequence.

FIGURE 13.2 The SPSS Clickstream to Obtain an Independent Samples *t* Test

Source: Reprint courtesy of International Business Machines Corporation, © SPSS, Inc., an IBM Company

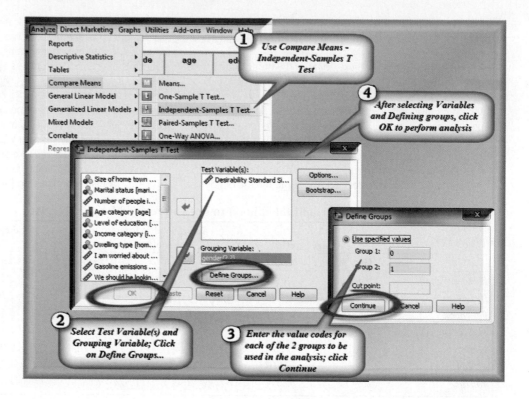

The annotated output is found in Figure 13.3. The first table reveals that the mean of the 560 males is 4.29, while the mean for the 440 females is 3.36.

The statistical test for the difference between the two means is given next. However, SPSS computes the results two different ways. One is identified as the "equal variances assumed," and the other is called the "equal variances not assumed." In our previous descriptions, we omitted a detail involved in tests for the significance of difference between two means. In some cases, the variances (standard deviations) of the two samples are about the same; that is, they are not significantly different. If so, you can use the formula pertaining to the equal variances (same variance for both samples), but if the standard deviations are statistically significant in their differences, you should use the unequal variances line on the output.

How do you know which one to use? The null hypothesis here is that there is no difference between the variances (standard deviations), and it is tested with an *F* value printed in the top row of the independent samples test table. The *F* test is just another statistical test, and it is the proper one here. (Recall that we stated earlier that SPSS will always select and compute the correct statistical test.) The *F* value is based on a procedure called "Levene's Test for Equality of Variances." In our output, the *F* value is identified as .831 with a Sig (probability) of .362. The probability reported here is the probability that the variances are equal, so anytime the probability is *greater than*, say 0.05, you would use the equal variance line on the output. If the probability associated with the *F* value is *small*, say 0.05 or less, then the variances null hypothesis is not supported, and you should use the unequal variance line. If you forget this rule, then just look at the standard deviations, and try to remember that if they are about the same size, you would use the equal variances *t* value.

Marketing Research on YouTube™ | To learn about differences between means tests, launch **www.youtube.com**, and search for "Hypothesis Test for Difference of Means."

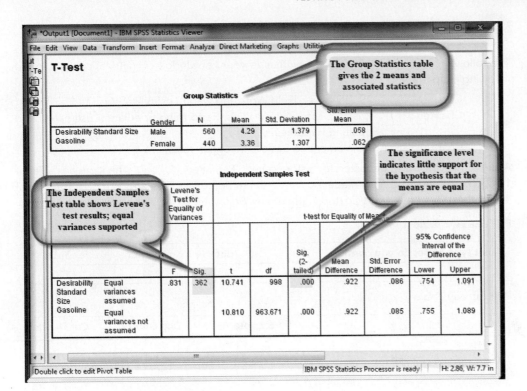

FIGURE 13.3
SPSS Output for an Independent Samples *t* Test

Source: Reprint courtesy of International Business Machines Corporation, © SPSS, Inc., an IBM Company

Using the equal variance estimate row, you will find that the computed *t* value is 10.741, and that the associated probability of support for the null hypothesis of no difference between the males' preference mean and the females' preference mean is .000. In other words, they differ significantly. Males prefer the standard-size gasoline model more than females, and Global Motors can segment this model's market using gender. However, one should bear in mind that the male mean is essentially "neutral," so perhaps other segmentation bases will derive more useful findings.

SPSS®

SPSS Student Assistant: Assessing Differences Between Means for 2 Groups (Independent)

 **Active Learning**

Perform Means Differences Analysis with SPSS

You have just observed how to perform an independent samples *t* test with SPSS using your Global Motors survey data. For this active learning exercise, determine if there is a difference in the preferences for the various possible electric or hybrid models based on gender. That is, redo the standard size gasoline model analysis just described to make sure that you can find and execute the analysis. Then use the clickstream instructions in Figure 13.2 to direct SPSS to perform this analysis for each of the four other possible models, and use the annotations on the independent samples *t* test output provided in Figure 13.3 to interpret your findings.

Synthesize Your Learning

The following case study will serve to synthesize your knowledge of material covered in the following chapters.

Chapter 11   Dealing with Field Work and Data Quality Issues
Chapter 12   Using Descriptive Analysis, Performing Population Estimates, and Testing Hypotheses
Chapter 13   Implementing Basic Differences Tests

A survey was recently conducted for a store called "Pets, Pets, & Pets." The store has a list of 10,000 customers who have made a purchase there in the last year, and a random sample of 400 of these customers participated in the survey. Below are some of the relevant findings.

PPP Survey Table 1

What type of pet do you own?	Dog	Cat	Other	Total
	45%	34%	21%	100%

PPP Survey Table 2

	Sample Yes	Dog Owner	Cat Owner
Do you use PPP quite often?	44%	50%	38%
Would recommend PPP to a friend?	82%	91%	75%
Recall a PPP newspaper ad in past month?	53%	50%	55%
Recall a PPP coupon in the past month?	47%	53%	40%

PPP Survey Table 3

Rate each of the following aspects of PPP*	Sample		Dog Owner		Cat Owner	
	Average	Std Dev	Average	Std Dev	Average	Std Dev
Assortment of merchandise	4.6	2.1	4.9	1.6	4.5	1.9
Friendliness of employees	4.6	2.1	4.7	1.3	4.5	2.2
Speed of check-out	4.4	1.9	4.6	0.9	4.2	1.8
Convenience of parking	4.1	1.9	4.5	1.6	3.8	2.4
Competitive prices	4.0	2.0	4.3	1.9	4.0	1.9
Store layout	3.8	2.1	4.3	1.6	3.6	1.6
Helpfulness of employees	3.4	1.9	3.7	1.8	3.3	2.1
Variety of cat/dog food brands	3.4	2.1	3.4	1.8	3.4	1.9
Convenient location	2.8	1.9	3.3	1.5	2.8	1.6
Overall satisfaction with PPP	4.6	1.5	4.9	1.2	4.2	2.2

*Based on a scale where 1 = very unsatisfied, ... 5 = very satisfied.

PPP Survey Table 4

What is your household income level?	Sample	Dog Owner	Cat Owner
Refused	5%	0%	25%
Between $60,000 and $80,000	10%	15%	10%
Between $80,000 and $100,000	20%	25%	10%
Greater than $100,000	65%	60%	55%
Total	100%	100%	100%

1. Do appropriate differences tests (95% level of confidence) to answer this question, "Do PPP dog owners differ from PPP cat owners with respect to their answers in PPP Table 1?" If so, how do they differ?
2. Do appropriate differences tests (95% level of confidence) to answer this question, "Do PPP dog owners differ from PPP cat owners with respect to their answers in PPP Table 2?" If so, how?
3. PPP management believes that 75% of its customers are dog owners. Test this hypothesis, and, if not supported at the 95% level of confidence, compute the confidence interval.
4. PPP management believes that all of its customers are overall "very satisfied" with PPP. Test this hypothesis, and, if not supported at the 95% level of confidence, compute the confidence interval.
5. PPP survey Table 4 suggests that if PPP targets customers with household income of greater than $100,000 per year, it should emphasize its dog merchandise. Consider the data quality information contained in the table and assess if this conclusion is correct or incorrect. Be sure to do the appropriate statistical tests at the 95% level of confidence.

Testing for Significant Differences in Means Among More Than Two Groups: Analysis of Variance

As you have learned, it is fairly easy to test for the significance of the difference between means for two groups. But sometimes a researcher may want to compare the means of three, four, five, or more different groups. Analysis of variance, sometimes called ANOVA, should be used to accomplish such multiple comparisons.[9] The use of the word *variance* is misleading, for it is not an analysis of the standard deviations of the groups. To be sure, the standard deviations are taken into consideration, and so are the sample sizes, as you just saw in all of our differences between means formulas. Fundamentally, **ANOVA (analysis of variance)** is an investigation of the differences between the group means to ascertain whether sampling errors or true population differences explain their failure to be equal.[10] That is, the word *variance* signifies for our purposes differences between two or more groups' means—do they vary from one another significantly? Although a term such as *analysis of variance* or *ANOVA* may sound frightfully technical, it is nothing more than a statistical procedure that allows you to compare the means of several groups. As we noted in our discussion on market segmentations, markets are often comprised of a number of market segments, not just two, so ANOVA is a valuable tool for discovering differences between and among multiple market segments. The following sections explain the basic concepts involved with analysis of variance and how this form of analysis can be applied to marketing research situations.

ANOVA is used when comparing the means of three or more groups.

BASICS OF ANALYSIS OF VARIANCE

In using analysis of variance there is a desire on the part of a researcher to determine whether a statistically significant difference exists between the means for *any two groups* in his or her sample with a given variable regardless of the number of groups. The end result of analysis of variance is an indication to the marketing researcher as to whether a significant difference at some chosen level of statistical significance exists between *at least* two group means. Significant differences may exist between all of the group means, but analysis of variance results alone will not communicate how many pairs of means are statistically significant in their differences.

To elaborate, ANOVA is a **green flag procedure**, meaning that if at least one pair of means has a statistically significant difference, ANOVA will signal this by indicating significance. Then, it is up to the researcher to conduct further tests (called *post hoc tests*) to determine precisely how many statistically significant differences actually exist and which ones they are. Of course, if the green signal flag does not pop up, the researcher knows that no significant differences exist.

ANOVA will "flag" when at least one pair of means has a statistically significant difference, but it does not tell which pair.

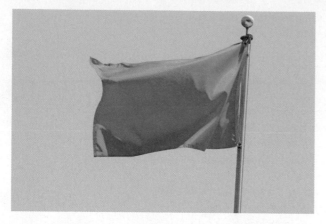

ANOVA is a "green flag waving" procedure that signals when at least one pair of means is significantly different.

Photo: L F File/Shutterstock

Let's elaborate just a bit on how ANOVA works. ANOVA uses some complicated formulas, and we have found from experience that marketing researchers do not memorize them. Instead, a researcher understands the basic purpose of ANOVA, and he or she is adept in interpreting ANOVA output. Let's assume we have three groups, A, B, and C. In concept, ANOVA performs all possible independent samples *t* tests for significant differences between the means, comparing, in our A, B, C example, A:B, A:C, and B:C. ANOVA is efficient as it makes these comparisons simultaneously, not individually as you would need to do if you were running independent samples *t* tests. ANOVA's null hypothesis is that no single pair of means is significantly different. Because multiple pairs of group means are being tested, ANOVA uses the *F* test statistic, and the significance level (sometimes referred to as the *p* value) that appears on the output in this *F* test is the probability of support for the null hypothesis.

Here is an example that will help you to understand how ANOVA works and when to use it. A major department store conducts a survey; one of the survey questions is, "In what department did you last make a purchase for over $250?" There are four departments where significant numbers of respondents made these purchases: (1) electronics, (2) home and garden, (3) sporting goods, and (4) automotive. Another question on the survey is "How likely are you to purchase another item for over $250 from that department?" The respondents indicate how likely they are to do this on a 7-point scale where 1 = very unlikely and 7 = very likely. It is easy to calculate the mean of how likely each group is to return to the department store and purchase another major item from that same department.

The researcher who is doing the analysis decides to compare these means statistically, so six different independent samples *t* tests of the significance of the differences are performed. A summary of the findings is found in Table 13.2. It may take a few minutes, but if you examine this table, you will see that the automotive department's mean is significantly different and lower than the repurchase likelihood means of the other three departments. Also, there is no significant difference in the other three department buyers' means. In other words, there is a good indication that the customers who bought an item for more than $250 from the department store's automotive department are not as satisfied with the purchase as are customers who bought large ticket items from any of the other departments.

The Sig. value in the ANOVA table indicates the level of significance.

Now, look at Table 13.3. It is an abbreviated ANOVA output. Instead of looking at several significance values as in Table 13.2, all the researcher needs to do is to look at the significance level (Sig.) for the *F* test, our signal flag. It is .000, which is less than .05, meaning that there is at least one pair of means with a significant difference so the researcher has the green flag to spend time and effort to look at the next table to find the significant difference(s). This table is arranged

TABLE 13.2 Results of 5 Independent Samples *t* Tests of How Likely Customers Are to Return to Make Their Next Major Purchase

Groups compared	Group means*	Significance	
Electronics: Home and Garden	5.1: 5.3	.873	Significant difference between the two compared groups
Electronics: Sporting Goods	5.1: 5.6	.469	
Electronics: Automotive	5.1: 2.2	.000	
Home and Garden: Sporting Goods	5.3: 5.6	.656	
Home and Garden: Automotive	5.3: 2.2	.000	
Sporting Goods: Automotive	5.6: 2.2	.000	

*Based on a scale where 1 = very unlikely and 7 = very likely.

TABLE 13.3 Results of ANOVA of How Likely Customers Are to Return to Make Their Next Major Purchase

F	Sig.	
226.991	.000	There is a significant difference between at least two groups

Department	Subsets*	
	1	2
Automotive	2.2	We have a problem with the Automotive Department!
Electronics		5.1
Home and Garden		5.3
Sporting Goods		5.6

*Means in the same column are not significantly different; means in different columns are significantly different.

so the means that are not significantly different fall in the same column, while those that are significantly different fall in separate columns, and each column is identified as a unique subset. The means are arranged in the second table from the lowest mean to the highest mean, and it is immediately apparent that the automotive department has a problem.

ANOVA has two distinct advantages over performing multiple *t* tests of the significance of the difference between means. First, it immediately notifies the researcher if there is any significant difference, because all he or she needs to do is to look at the "Sig." value, our signal flag. Second, in our example, it arranges the means so the significant differences can be located and interpreted easily.

To elaborate, this Sig(nificance) value is the flag we referenced previously. When the flag is green, the researcher is then justified at looking at the second table to find which means are significantly different. Once you learn how to read SPSS ANOVA output, it is quite easy to identify these cases. Of course, if the *F* statistic *p* value flag is not green, meaning that the *p* value is *greater than .05*, it is a waste of time to look at the differences between the pairs of means, as no difference will be statistically significant at the 95% level of confidence.

> ANOVA is much more advantageous than running multiple *t* tests of the significance of the difference between means.

POST HOC TESTS: DETECT STATISTICALLY SIGNIFICANT DIFFERENCES AMONG GROUP MEANS

As we mentioned in passing previously, **post hoc tests** are options that are available to determine where the pair(s) of statistically significant differences between the means exist(s). As you will soon see in our SPSS example, there are more than a dozen of these to choose from, including Scheffe's and Tukey's, which you may recognize from your statistics course. It is beyond the scope of this book to provide a complete delineation of the various types of tests. Consequently, only one test, Duncan's multiple range test, will be shown as an illustration of how the differences may be determined. **Duncan's multiple range test** provides output that is mostly a "picture" of what means are significantly different, and it is much less statistical than most of the other post hoc tests, so we have chosen to use it here for these reasons. The picture provided by the Duncan's post hoc test is the arrangement of the means as you saw them in Table 13.3.

> The Duncan multiple range test is our preferred post hoc test because its output is easy to interpret.

INTEGRATED CASE

Global Motors: How to Run Analysis of Variance on SPSS

In the Global Motors survey, several categorical variables have more than two groups. For example, there are five education categories: less than high school diploma, high school diploma, some college, college degree, and postgraduate degree.

FIGURE 13.4 SPSS Clickstream to Perform Analysis of Variance (ANOVA)

Source: Reprint courtesy of International Business Machines Corporation, © SPSS, Inc., an IBM Company

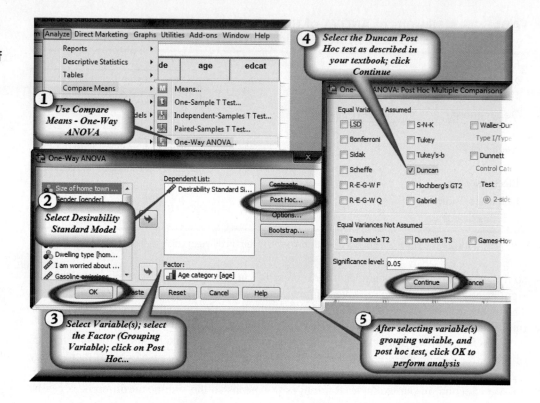

To run analysis of variance with SPSS, use the ANALYZE-COMPARE MEANS-ONE-WAY ANOVA menu command sequence.

SPSS®

SPSS Student Assistant: Applying ANOVA (Analysis of Variance)

Marketing Research on YouTube™ To learn about analysis of variance, launch **www.youtube.com**, and search for "One-Way ANOVA Using SPSS."

One-way ANOVA uses only one grouping variable, and in this case is done under the ANALYZE-COMPARE MEANS-ONE-WAY ANOVA menu command sequence illustrated in Figure 13.4. A window opens to set up the ANOVA analysis. The "Dependent list' is where you click in the variable(s) pertaining to the means, while the "Factor" variable is the grouping variable. In our example, the preference for the standard size gasoline model is our dependent variable, and the "Age category" is the grouping variable. Figure 13.4 also shows how to select the Duncan's Multiple Range option under the Post Hoc . . . Tests menu. Returning to the selection window and clicking on "OK" commences the ANOVA procedure.

Figure 13.5 is an annotated ANOVA output. The first table contains a number of intermediate and additional computational results, but our attention should be focused on the "Sig." column. Here is the support for the null hypothesis that not one pair of means is significantly different. Because the Sig. value is .000, we are assured that there is at least one significantly different pair. The next table is the Duncan's test output. Specifically, the table is arranged so that the means ascend in size from top left to right bottom, and the columns represent subsets of groups that are significantly different from groups in the other columns. We can immediately see that 25 to 34 (3.36) is the lowest group average, and it is significantly different from all the other age groups which are in separate columns. Similarly, looking at the next column, we can see three age groups with means that are not significantly different: 65 and older, 35 to 49, and 50 to 64 because they are all in the same column. Finally, we can see that the mean of the 18 to 24 age group is significantly different from all other education groups, with a mean of 6.35. Plus, since this column is the one on the far right, it is the one with the highest average. We have found that the people in the lowest age group market segment most prefer the standard size gasoline model. Now, let's think about this finding a bit. Most likely the consumers in the youngest age group are suspicious of the power of an electric or hybrid fuel vehicle and/or they don't think driving one of these automobiles would be cool. Plus, recall that these vehicles are relatively expensive.

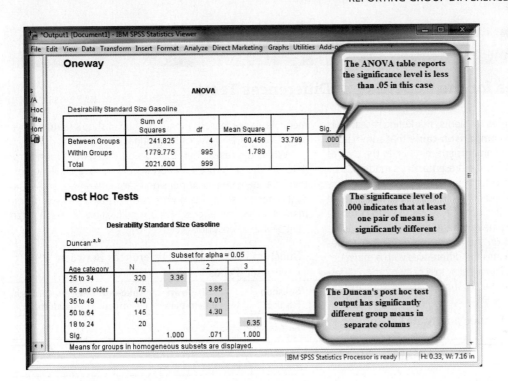

FIGURE 13.5 SPSS Output for Analysis of Variance (ANOVA)

Source: Reprint courtesy of International Business Machines Corporation, © SPSS, Inc., an IBM Company

INTERPRETING ANOVA (ANALYSIS OF VARIANCE)

How do we interpret this finding? The answer lies in understanding that if we replicated this survey hundreds of times, we would find these age group differences exactly as we have found them with this one survey. Granted, the averages' values might shift slightly up or down, but the pattern portrayed in the Duncan's multiple range test table in Figure 13.5 would appear in at least 95% of these replications. Further, we can say that we have discovered a meaningful differences finding with the "18 to 24" age group very close to the most positive end of the preference scale and quite a bit higher than the other age groups.

There are several post hoc tests with ANOVA. We have used Duncan's multiple range test as an illustration with the Global Motors survey data.

 Active Learning

Perform Analysis of Variance with SPSS

Let's investigate for age group means differences across all of the models under consideration at this time by Global Motors. We recommend that you use the GlobalMotors.sav dataset and run the ANOVA just described. Make sure that your SPSS output looks like that in Figure 13.5. Then investigate the preference mean differences for the other hybrid models by age group.

Reporting Group Differences Tests to Clients

Finding significant differences is exciting to marketing researchers because it means they will have something that is potentially useful to report to clients. Remember, market segmentation is prevalent, and whenever significant differences are found, they may represent important market segmentation implications. However, in the bowels of a long marketing research report, differences may not be obvious to the client, especially if the researcher does not take care to highlight them. Marketing Research Insight 13.4 describes how researchers can use table organization and arrangement to present differences findings in a succinct and useful manner.

MARKETING RESEARCH INSIGHT 13.4   *Practical Application*

Guidelines for the Reporting of Differences Tests

In reporting group differences to clients, marketing researchers usually construct a **group comparison table** that summarizes the significant differences in an efficient manner. In the case of two group comparison tables, the presentation is made side by side where the groups are columns and the rows are the variables where significant differences are found. Depending of the objectives of the research, it is perfectly acceptable to combine percentage differences and mean differences in the same table. Of course, it is incumbent on the marketing researcher to design a table that communicates the differences with a minimum of confusion. Study the following example of two group differences found in a survey for the Subshop.

Differences Between Female and Male Customers of the Subshop*

Item	Females	Males
Menu Items Typically Purchased		
Alcoholic beverage	14%	37%
Large size sandwich	24%	59%
Salad	53%	13%
Rating of the Subshop*		
Value for the price	5.2	6.1
Fast service	4.5	5.2
Overall satisfaction with the Subshop***	4.9	5.5
Use Subshop promotions		
Use Subshop coupons	23%	5%
Belong to Subshop frequent buyer club	33%	12%

*Statistically significant at 95% level of confidence.
**Based on a rating scale where 1 = poor and 7 = excellent.
***Based on rating scale where 1 = very unsatisfied and 7 = very satisfied.

In this group comparison table, it can be immediately seen that male and female customers of the Subshop are being compared, and that there are there four areas of comparisons:

menu items purchased, ratings of the Subshop's features, overall satisfaction, and use of promotions.

When the researcher is reporting differences found from ANOVA, the table presentation becomes more challenging as there can be overlaps of nonsignificant differences and significant differences. For the purposes of this textbook, we recommend that the researcher use a modification of the Duncan's multiple range post hoc table.

Subshop Performance Differences Between Customer Types*

Subshop feature**	Sit-down customers	Take-out customers	Drive-through customers
Fast service	5.4	6.2	
Value for the price	6.2	5.5	5.0
Friendly employees	5.1	4.0	

*Statistically significant at 95% level of confidence.
**Based on a rating scale where 1 = poor and 7 = excellent.

In this group comparison table, three types of customers are being compared, and the researcher has found significant differences for three different Subshop features. With the fast service rating, the take-out and drive-through customer groups are not different, but the sit-down customers rate the service slower than either of the other groups. With value for the price, all three group means are significantly different, while the sit-down customers' average rating for friendly employees is higher than the average for the take-out and drive-through customers, which are not significantly different. Notice that where nonsignificant differences are reported, the group cells are merged and that the average of the two groups combined is indicated so that the client will not focus on nonsignificant arithmetic differences.

The reporting of findings has a significant ethical burden for marketing researchers as they cannot choose to report only "good news" to clients. Marketing Research Insight 13.5 presents the ethical considerations from the Marketing Research Association code, which charges researchers with the responsibility of reporting "bad news" if it is discovered in the findings.

Differences Between Two Means Within the Same Sample (Paired Sample)

You can test the significance of the difference between two means for two different questions answered by the same respondents using the same scale.

The final difference test we will describe here is not used for market segmentation purposes. Occasionally, a researcher will want to test for differences between the *means for two variables* within the same sample. For example, in our pharmaceuticals company cold remedy

MARKETING RESEARCH INSIGHT 13.5   *Ethical Consideration*

 ## Marketing Research Association Code of Ethics: Reporting Findings

7. Will report research results accurately and honestly.
Describe how the research was done in enough detail that a skilled researcher could repeat the study; provide data representative of a defined population or activity and enough

data to yield projectable results; present the results understandably and fairly, including any results that may seem contradictory or unfavorable.

situation described earlier in this chapter, a survey can be used to determine "How important is it that your cold remedy relieves your..." using a scale of 1 = not important and 10 = very important for each cold symptom. The question then becomes whether any two average importance levels are significantly different. To determine the answer to this question, we must perform a **paired samples test for the difference between two means**, which is a test to determine if two means of two different questions using the same scale format and answered by the same respondents in the sample are significantly different. Of course, the variables must be measured on the same scale; otherwise, the test would be analyzing differences between variables that are logically incomparable such as the number of dollars spent versus the number of miles driven.

But the same respondents answered both questions, so you do not have two independent groups. Instead, you have two independent questions with one group. The logic and equations we have described still apply, but there must be an adjustment factor because there is only one sample involved. We do not provide the equations, but in the following SPSS section, we describe how to perform and interpret a paired samples t test.[11]

INTEGRATED CASE

The Global Motors Survey: How to Perform a Paired Samples t-Test   **SPSS®**

Significance of Differences Between Means Test with SPSS

With the paired samples test, we can test the significance of the difference between the mean of any two questions by the same respondents in our sample. Let's take a critical decision that Global Motors may have to address: Namely, are worries about global warming and gasoline emissions contributing to global warming the same? If they are not statistically significant in their differences, the difference will evaporate in the face of a single replication of the survey. In other words, if we were to do the study again, the two means could actually flip-flop. Using a paired samples difference test, one can determine the statistical significance.

The SPSS clickstream sequence to perform a paired samples t test of the significance of the difference between means is displayed in Figure 13.6. As you can see, you begin with the ANALYZE-COMPARE MEANS-PAIRED SAMPLES T-TEST... menu sequence. This sequence opens up the selection menu, and via cursor clicks, you can select "I am worried about global warming" and "Gasoline emissions contribute to global warming" as the variable pair to be tested. This sets up the t test, and a click on OK executes it.

To test the significance of difference between two means for questions answered by the same respondents, use the SPSS ANALYZE-COMPARE MEANS-PAIRED SAMPLES T-TEST... menu sequence.

FIGURE 13.6 The Clickstream to Obtain a Paired Samples *t*-Test

Source: Reprint courtesy of International Business Machines Corporation, © SPSS, Inc., an IBM Company

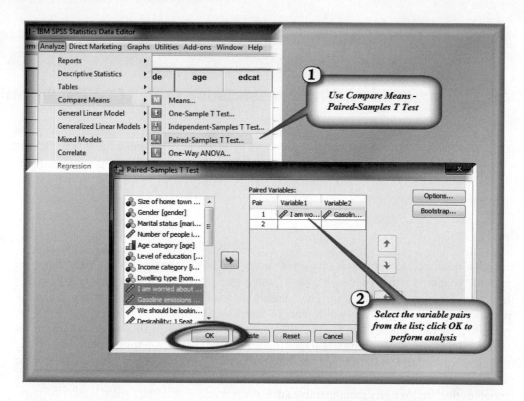

FIGURE 13.7 SPSS Output for a Paired Samples *t*-Test

Source: Reprint courtesy of International Business Machines Corporation, © SPSS, Inc., an IBM Company

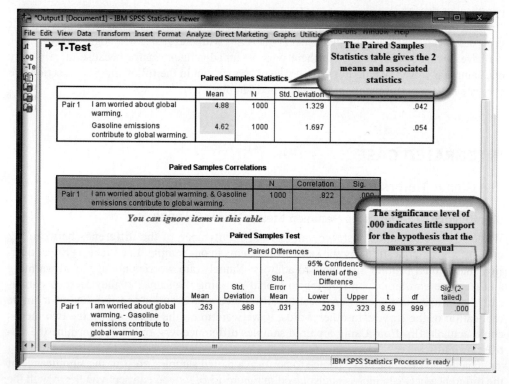

SPSS®

SPSS Student Assistant: Assessing Differences Between Means for 2 Questions (Paired)

The resulting annotated output is found in Figure 13.7. You should notice that the table is similar, but not identical, to the independent samples output. The relevant information includes: (1) 1,000 respondents gave answers to each statement and were analyzed; (2) the means for worry about global warming and gasoline emissions contributing to global warming are 4.88 and 4.62, respectively; (3) the computed *t* value is 8.59; and (4) the two-tailed significance level is 0.000. In words, the test gives almost no support for the null hypothesis that the means are equal. The worry about global warming is greater than the concern about gasoline emissions contributing to global warming.

Summary

Differences matter to marketing managers. Basically, market segmentation implications underlie most differences analyses. It is important that differences are statistically significant, but it is also vital that they are meaningful and stable and provide an actionable basis of marketing strategy.

Differences between two percentages or means in two samples can be tested for statistical significance. The chapter illustrates how to determine if two percentages drawn from two different samples are significantly different. The *t* test procedure in SPSS is used to test the significance of the difference between two means from two independent samples. This chapter presented an illustration of how to use SPSS for this analysis using the Global Motors dataset.

When a researcher has more than two groups and wishes to compare their various means, the correct procedure involves analysis of variance, or ANOVA. ANOVA is a flagging technique that tests all possible pairs of means for all the groups involved, and indicates via the Sig. (significance) value in the ANOVA table if at least one pair is statistically significant in its difference. If the Sig. value is greater than .05, the researcher will waste his or her time inspecting the means for differences. But if the Sig. value is .05 or less, the researcher can use a post hoc procedure such as Duncan's multiple range test to identify the pair or pairs of groups where the means are significantly different. This chapter also discussed the paired-samples test and how to perform and interpret it using SPSS.

Key Terms

Statistical significance of differences (p. 326)
Meaningful difference (p. 326)
Stable difference (p. 326)
Actionable difference (p. 327)
t test (p. 327)
z test (p. 327)

Null hypothesis (p. 329)
Significance of differences between two percentages (p. 329)
Significance of difference between two means (p. 332)
ANOVA (analysis of variance) (p. 339)

"Green flag" procedure (p. 339)
Post hoc tests (p. 341)
Duncan's multiple range test (p. 341)
One-way ANOVA (p. 342)
Group comparison table (p. 344)
Paired samples test for the difference between two means (p. 345)

Review Questions/Applications

1. What are differences and why should market researchers be concerned with them? Why are marketing managers concerned with them?
2. What is considered to be a "small sample," and why is this concept a concern to statisticians? To what extent do market researchers concern themselves with small samples? Why?
3. When a market researcher compares the responses of two identifiable groups with respect to their answers to the same question, what is this called?

4. With regard to differences tests, briefly define and describe each of the following:
   a. Null hypothesis
   b. Sampling distribution
   c. Significant difference
5. Relate the formula and identify each formula's components in the test of significant differences between two groups for when the question involved is
   a. a "yes/no" type.
   b. a scale variable question.

6. Are the following two sample results significantly different?

Sample One	Sample Two	Confidence Level	Your Finding?
Mean: 10.6	Mean: 11.7	95%	
Std. dev:1.5	Std. dev: 2.5		
$n = 150$	$n = 300$		
Percent: 45%	Percent: 54%	99%	
$n = 350$	$n = 250$		
Mean: 1500	Mean: 1250	95%	
Std. dev: 550	Std. dev: 500		
$n = 1200$	$n = 500$		

7. When should one-way ANOVA be used and why?
8. When a researcher finds a significant F value in analysis of variance, why can it be considered a "green flag" device?
9. What is a paired-samples test? Specifically how are the samples "paired"?
10. The Circulation Manager of the *Daily Advocate* newspaper commissions a market research study to determine what factors underlie the circulation attrition. Specifically, the survey is designed to compare current *Daily Advocate* subscribers with those who have dropped their subscriptions in the past year. A telephone survey is conducted with both sets of individuals. Below is a summary of the key findings from the study.

Item	Current Subscribers	Lost Subscribers	Significance
Length of residency in the city	20.1 yrs	5.4 yrs	.000
Length of time as a subscriber	27.2 yrs	1.3 yrs	.000
Watch local TV news program(s)	87%	85%	.372
Watch national news program(s)	72%	79%	.540
Obtain news from the Internet	13%	23%	.025
Satisfaction* with... Delivery of newspaper	5.5	4.9	.459

Item	Current Subscribers	Lost Subscribers	Significance
Coverage of local news	6.1	5.8	.248
Coverage of national news	5.5	2.3	.031
Coverage of local sports	6.3	5.9	.462
Coverage of national sports	5.7	3.2	.001
Coverage of local social news	5.8	5.2	.659
Editorial stance of the newspaper	6.1	4.0	.001
Value for subscription price	5.2	4.8	.468

*Based on a 7-point scale where 1 = very dissatisfied and 7 = very satisfied. Interpret these findings for the Circulation Manager.

11. A researcher is investigating different types of customers for a sporting goods store. In a survey, respondents have indicated how much they exercise in approximate minutes per week. These respondents have also rated the performance of the sporting goods store across 12 different characteristics such as good value for the price, convenience of location, helpfulness of the sales clerks, etc. The researcher used a 1–7 rating scale for these 12 characteristics where 1 = poor performance and 7 = excellent performance. How can the researcher investigate differences in the ratings based on the amount of exercise reported by the respondents?
12. A marketing manager of Collections, Etc., a web-based catalog sales company, uses a segmentation scheme based on the incomes of target customers. The segmentation system has four segments: (1) low income, (2) moderate income, (3) high income, and (4) wealthy. The company database holds information on every customer's purchases over the past several years, and the total dollars spent at Collections, Etc., is one of the prominent variables. Using Microsoft Excel on this database, the marketing manager finds that the average total dollar purchases for the four groups are as follows.

Market Segment	Average Total Dollar Purchases
Low income	$101
Moderate income	$120
High income	$231
Wealthy	$595

Construct a table based on the Duncan's multiple range test table concept that illustrates that the low and moderate income groups are not different from each other, but that the other groups are significantly different from one another.

CASE 13.1

The Hobbit's Choice Restaurant Survey Differences Analysis

SPSS®

(For necessary background on this case, read Case 12.1 on pages 319–321.)

Cory Rogers of CMG Research calls a meeting with Jeff Dean, who plans to open an upscale restaurant called Hobbit's Choice, and marketing intern Christine Yu sits in. At the beginning of the meeting, Cory's wife calls with news that their 5-year-old son is having a stomach ache at school, and Cory has to pick him up and take him to the doctor. Cory excuses himself, saying, "I am sorry about this, but these things happen when you are a dual-career household. Christine, sit with Jeff for a bit and find out what questions he has about the survey findings. Then take a shot at the analysis, and we'll meet about it tomorrow afternoon. I am sure that Cory Junior will be over his stomach ailment by then."

After meeting for about 20 minutes, Christine has a list of six questions from Jeff Dean. Her notes are below. Your task is to take Christine's role, using The Hobbit's Choice Restaurant survey SPSS dataset, (available at the Companion Website at www.pearsonhighered.com/burns) perform the proper analysis, and interpret the findings for each of the following questions.

1. Jeff wonders if The Hobbit's Choice Restaurant is more appealing to women than it is to men or vice versa. Perform the proper analysis, interpret it, and answer Jeff's question.
2. With respect to the location of The Hobbit's Choice Restaurant, is a waterfront view preferred more than a drive of less than 30 minutes?
3. With respect to the restaurant's atmosphere, is a string quartet preferred over a jazz combo?
4. What about unusual entrees versus unusual desserts?
5. In general, upscale establishments are appealing to higher income households, while they are less appealing to lower income households. Is this pattern the case for The Hobbit's Choice Restaurant?
6. Jeff and Cory speculated that the different geographic areas they identified by ZIP codes would have different reactions to the prospect of patronizing a new upscale restaurant. Are these anticipated differences substantiated by the survey? Perform the proper analysis and interpret your findings.

CASE 13.2 **INTEGRATED CASE**

The Global Motors Survey Differences Analysis

SPSS®

Cory Rogers also misses a meeting with Nick Thomas, so Celeste Brown steps in to talk about the survey. After meeting for about 20 minutes, Celeste understands that the Global Motors division principals are encouraged by the findings of the survey, which indicate that there is substantial demand for the various types of high-mileage automobiles under consideration. Depending on development costs, prices, and other financial considerations, it seems that any one or any combination of the new automobile models could be a viable option. The next step in their planning is to identify the target market for each automobile model type under consideration. This step is crucial to market strategy as it is known that the more precise the target market definition, the more specific and pinpointed the marketing strategy can be. For a first cut at the market segment descriptions, the survey included a number of commonly used demographic factors, which are:

- Hometown size category
- Gender
- Marital status
- Age category
- Education category
- Income category

Your task is to apply appropriate differences analysis using the survey's desirability measures in your GlobalMotors.sav SPSS dataset to determine the target market descriptions for each of the five possible automobile models.

1. 1-seat all-electric
2. 4-seat all-electric
3. 4-seat gasoline hybrid
4. 5-seat diesel hybrid
5. 5-seat standard size gasoline

Making Use of Associations Tests

LEARNING OBJECTIVES

- To learn what is meant by an "association" between two variables
- To examine various relationships that may be construed as associations
- To understand where and how cross-tabulations with Chi-square analysis are applied
- To become familiar with the use and interpretation of correlations
- To learn how to obtain and interpret cross-tabulations, Chi-square findings, and correlations with SPSS

"WHERE WE ARE"

1 Establish the need for marketing research.

2 Define the problem.

3 Establish research objectives.

4 Determine research design.

5 Identify information types and sources.

6 Determine methods of accessing data.

7 Design data collection forms.

8 Determine the sample plan and size.

9 Collect data.

10 Analyze data.

11 Prepare and present the final research report.

Significant Associations Can Help Managers Make Better Decisions

Sima Vasa,
Partner and CEO,
Paradigm Sample™

Sima Vasa is Partner and Chief Executive Officer of Paradigm Sample. She has 20 years of experience in building and growing market research businesses specifically in the technology space. Positions she has held include: Senior Partner at Momentum Market Intelligence, President of NPD Techworld at the NPD Group, Vice President of the Technology Division at NPD, and a member of the IBM Market Intelligence Group. During her tenure at NPD, Vasa spearheaded a $19 million business unit revenue increase in three years to $40 million by refocusing priorities and aggressively expanding the business portfolio.

As humans we are always searching for associations in life. What types of recreational activities give you the most enjoyment? What types of foods are tasteful to you? By knowing these associations, we can add enjoyment to our lives. Marketing managers are also searching for associations. Which advertising copy will be associated with the highest awareness level of the advertised brand? Which type of salesperson compensation and reward packages will result in the highest level of satisfaction and the lowest turnover? By understanding these associations, marketers can achieve higher sales and net profits while keeping costs low. This helps them earn a higher ROA, which gives the owners of the firm a higher RONW.

Marketing managers learn these associations through trial and error, just as you learn which activities give you the most pleasure or which foods you prefer. However, sometimes the learning process takes too long or being wrong is too costly in a business situation. Trial and error is not always the best way to learn. In these situations a manager can obtain information and examine it to see if there are associations. But, what if information collected yesterday shows there is an association, as in when ad copy B has the highest awareness scores? How do we know that pattern of association will occur if we collect the information tomorrow? Or, next month? Is that pattern of association a true pattern that exists in the population or only in the one sample of information we collected? Fortunately, the statisticians have given us ways to answer these questions. You will learn how to find significant associations by reading this chapter.

Paradigm Sample provides market research insight, through innovative data access to high-value audiences based on exclusive panels and partner panels along with proven mobile technologies. To learn about Paradigm Sample's innovative IdeaShifters and GlobalShifters panels, refer to www.paradigmsample.com.

This chapter illustrates the usefulness of statistical analyses beyond simple descriptive measures, statistical inference, and differences tests. Often, as we have described in the opening comments of this chapter, marketers are interested in relationships among variables. For example, Frito-Lay wants to know what kinds of people and under what circumstances these people choose to buy Cheetos, Fritos, Lay's potato chips, and any of the other items in the Frito-Lay line. The Chevrolet Division of General Motors wants to know what types of individuals would respond favorably to the various style changes proposed for the Cruze. A newspaper wants to understand the lifestyle characteristics of its subscribers so that it can modify or change sections in the newspaper to better suit its audience. Furthermore, the newspaper desires information about various types of subscribers so it can communicate this information to its advertisers, helping them in copy design and advertisement placement within the various newspaper sections. For all of these cases, statistical procedures called *associative analyses* are available to help identify answers to these questions. **Associative analyses** determine whether a stable relationship exists between two variables; they are the central topic of this chapter.

We begin the chapter by describing the four different types of relationships possible between two variables. Then

Associative analyses determine whether a stable relationship exists between two variables.

Photo: trekandshoot/Fotolia

we describe cross-tabulations and indicate how a cross-tabulation can be used to determine whether a statistically significant association exists between the two variables. From cross-tabulations, we move to a general discussion of correlation coefficients, and we illustrate the use of Pearson product moment correlations. As in our previous analysis chapters, we show the SPSS steps to perform these analyses and the resulting output.

Types of Relationships Between Two Variables

As you learned in Chapter 8, every scale has unique descriptors, called levels or labels, that identify the different demarcations of that scale. The term *levels* implies that the variable is either an interval or a ratio scale; while the term *labels* implies that the level of measurement is not scale, typically nominal. An example of a simple label is "yes" or "no," as in if a respondent is labeled as a buyer (yes) or nonbuyer (no) of a particular product or service. Of course, if the researcher measures how many times a respondent bought a product, the level would be the number of times, and the scale would satisfy the assumptions of a ratio scale.

> A relationship is a consistent and systematic linkage between the levels or labels for two variables.

A **relationship** is a consistent and systematic linkage between the levels for two scale variables or between the labels for two nominal variables. This linkage is statistical, not necessarily causal. A causal linkage is one in which it is certain one variable affected the other; with a statistical linkage, there is no certainty because some other variable might have had some influence. Nonetheless, statistical linkages or relationships often provide insights that lead to understanding even though we do not know it there is a cause-and-effect relationship. For example, if we found a relationship that most marathon runners purchased "Vitaminwater," we understand that the ingredients are important to marathoners. Associative analysis procedures are useful because they determine if there is a consistent and systematic relationship between the presence (label) or amount (level) of one variable and the presence (label) or amount (level) of another variable. There are four basic types of relationships between two variables: nonmonotonic, monotonic, linear, and curvilinear. A discussion of each follows.

NONMONOTONIC RELATIONSHIPS

> A nonmonotonic relationship means two variables are associated but only in a general sense.

A **nonmonotonic relationship** is one in which the presence (or absence) of the label for one variable is systematically associated with the presence (or absence) of the label for another variable. The term *nonmonotonic* means essentially that there is no discernible direction to the relationship, but a relationship exists. For example, McDonald's, Burger King, and Wendy's all know from experience that morning customers typically purchase coffee whereas noon customers typically purchase soft drinks. The relationship is in no way exclusive—there is no guarantee that a morning customer will always order coffee or that an afternoon customer will always order a soft drink. In general, though, this relationship exists, as can be seen in Figure 14.1. The nonmonotonic relationship is simply that the morning customer tends to purchase breakfast foods such as eggs, biscuits, and coffee, and the afternoon customers tend to purchase lunch items such as burgers, fries, and soft drinks. So, the "morning" label is associated with the "coffee" label while the "noon" label is associated with "soft drink" label. In other words, with a monotonic relationship, when you find the presence of one label for a variable, you tend to find the presence of another specific label of another variable: breakfast diners typically order coffee. But the association is general, and we must state each one by spelling it out verbally. In other words, we know only the general pattern of presence or nonpresence with a nonmonotonic relationship. We show you how to meaure nonmonotonic relationships using Chi-square analysis later in this chapter.

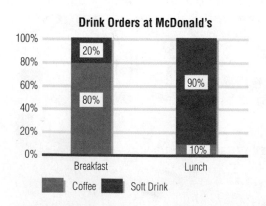

FIGURE 14.1

Example of a Non-monotonic Relationship Between Drink Orders and Meal Type at McDonald's

MONOTONIC RELATIONSHIPS

In **monotonic relationships**, the researcher can assign a general direction to the association between two variables. There are two types of monotonic relationships: increasing and decreasing. Monotonic increasing relationships are those in which one variable increases as the other variable increases. As you would guess, monotonic decreasing relationships are those in which one variable increases as the other variable decreases. You should note that in neither case is there any indication of the exact amount of change in one variable as the other changes. *Monotonic* means that the relationship can be described only in a general directional sense. Beyond this, precision in the description is lacking. For example, if a company increases its advertising, we would expect its sales to increase, but we do not know the amount of the sales increase. Monotonic relationships are not in the scope of this textbook, so we will simply mention them here.

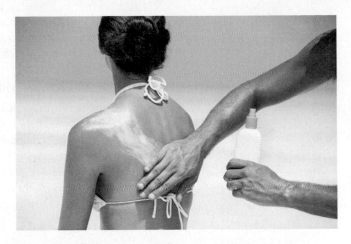

That higher SPF sunscreen blocks more ultraviolet rays is a nonmonotonic relationship, meaning that the relationship is not exact.

Photo: Yuri Arcurs/Shutterstock

LINEAR RELATIONSHIPS

Next, we turn to a more precise relationship—and one that is very easy to envision. A **linear relationship** is a "straight-line association" between two scale variables. Here, knowledge of the amount of one variable will automatically yield knowledge of the amount of the other variable as a consequence of applying the linear or straight-line formula that is known to exist between them. In its general form, a **straight-line formula** is as follows:

A monotonic relationship means you know the general direction (increasing or decreasing) of the relationship between two variables.

Formula for a straight line

$$y = a + bx$$

where

y = the dependent variable being estimated or predicted

a = the intercept

b = the slope

x = the independent variable used to predict the dependent variable

A linear relationship means the two variables have a "straight-line" relationship.

The terms *intercept* and *slope* should be familiar to you, but if they are a bit hazy, do not be concerned as we describe the straight-line formula in detail in the next chapter. We also clarify the terms *independent* and *dependent* in Chapter 15.

It should be apparent that a linear relationship is much more precise and contains a great deal more information than does a nonmontonic or a monotonic relationship. By simply substituting the values of *a* and *b*, an exact amount can be determined for *y* given any value of *x*. For example, if Jack-in-the-Box estimates that every customer will spent about $9 per lunch visit, it is easy to use a linear relationship to estimate how many dollars of revenue will be associated with the number of customers for any given location. The following equation would be used:

Straight-line formula example

$$y = 0 + 9 \text{ times number of customers}$$

In this example, *x* is the number of customers. If 100 customers come to a Jack-in-the-Box location, the associated expected total revenues would be $0 plus $9 times 100, or $900. If 200 customers are expected to visit the location, the expected total revenue would be $0 plus $9 times 200, or $1,800. To be sure, the Jack-in-the-Box location would not

Linear relationships are quite precise.

derive exactly \$1,800 for 200 customers, but the linear relationship shows what is expected to happen, on average. In subsequent sections of the textbook, we describe correlation and regression analysis, both of which rely on linear relationships.

CURVILINEAR RELATIONSHIPS

A curvilinear relationship means some smooth curve pattern describes the association.

Finally, **curvilinear relationships** are those in which one variable is associated with another variable, but the relationship is described by a curve rather than a straight line. In other words, the formula for a curved relationship is used rather than the formula for a straight line. Many curvilinear patterns are possible. The relationship may be an S-shape, a J-shape, or some other curved-shape pattern. Curvilinear relationships are beyond the scope of this text; nonetheless, it is important to list them as a type of relationship that can be investigated through the use of special-purpose statistical procedures.

Characterizing Relationships Between Variables

Depending on its type, a relationship can usually be characterized in three ways: by its presence, direction, and strength of association. We need to describe these before taking up specific statistical analyses of associations between two variables.

PRESENCE

The presence of a relationship between two variables is determined by a statistical test.

Presence refers to the finding that a systematic relationship exists between the two variables of interest in the population. Presence is a statistical issue. By this statement, we mean that the marketing researcher relies on statistical significance tests to determine if there is sufficient evidence in the sample to support the claim that a particular association is present in the population. The chapter on statistical inference introduced the concept of a null hypothesis. With associative analysis, the null hypothesis states there is no association (relationship) present in the population and the appropriate statistical test is applied to test this hypothesis. If the test results reject the null hypothesis, then we can state that an association (relationship) is present in the population (at a certain level of confidence). We describe the statistical tests used in associative analysis later in this chapter.

DIRECTION (OR PATTERN)

You have seen that in the cases of monotonic and linear relationships, associations may be described with regard to direction. For a linear relationship, if b (slope) is positive, then the linear relationship is increasing; if b is negative, then the linear relationship is decreasing. So the direction of the relationship is straightforward with linear relationships.

Direction means that you know if the relationship is positive or negative, while *pattern* means you know the general nature of the relationship.

For nonmonotonic relationships, positive or negative direction is inappropriate, because we can only describe the pattern verbally.[1] It will soon become clear to you that the scaling assumptions of variables having nonmonotonic association negate the directional aspects of the relationship. Nevertheless, we can verbally describe the pattern of the association as we have in our examples using presence or absence, and that statement substitutes for direction.

STRENGTH OF ASSOCIATION

Strength means you know how consistent the relationship is.

Finally, when present—that is, when statistically significant—the association between two variables can be envisioned as to its strength, commonly using words such as "strong," "moderate," "weak," or some similar characterization. That is, when a consistent and systematic association is found to be present between two variables, it is then up to the marketing researcher to ascertain the strength of association. Strong associations are those in which there is a high probability of the two variables exhibiting a dependable relationship, regardless of the type of relationship being analyzed. A low degree of association, on the other hand,

TABLE 14.1   Step-by-Step Procedure for Analyzing Relationships

Step	Description
1. Choose variables to analyze.	Identify which variables you think might be related.
2. Determine the scaling assumptions of the chosen variables.	For purposes of this chapter, both must be either scale (interval or ratio) or categorical (nominal) variables.
3. Use the correct relationship analysis.	For two nominal variables (distinct categories), use cross-tabulation; for two scale variables, use correlation.
4. Determine if the relationship is present.	If the analysis shows the relationship is statistically significant, it is present.
5. If present, determine the direction of the relationship.	A linear (scale variables) relationship will be either increasing or decreasing; a nonmonotonic relationship (nominal scales) will require looking for a pattern.
6. If present, assess the strength of the relationship.	With correlation, the size of the coefficient denotes strength; with cross-tabulation, the pattern is subjectively assessed.

is one in which there is a low probability of the two variables' exhibiting a dependable relationship. The relationship exists between the variables, but it is less evident.

There is an orderly procedure for determining the presence, direction, and strength of a relationship, which is outlined in Table 14.1. As can be seen in the table, you must first decide what type of relationship can exist between the two variables of interest: nonmontonic or linear. As you will learn in this chapter, the answer to this question depends on the scaling assumptions of the variables; as we illustrated earlier, nominal scales can embody only imprecise, pattern-like relationships, but scale variables (interval or ratio scales) can incorporate very precise and linear relationships. Once you identify the appropriate relationship type as either nonmonotonic or linear, the next step is to determine whether that relationship actually exists in the population you are analyzing. This step requires a statistical test, and again, we describe the proper tests beginning with the next section of this chapter.

When you determine that a true relationship does exist in the population by means of the correct statistical test, you then establish its direction or pattern. Again, the type of relationship dictates how you describe its direction. You might have to inspect the relationship in a table or graph, or you might need only to look for a positive or negative sign before the computed statistic. Finally, the strength of the relationship remains to be judged. Some associative analysis statistics, such as correlations, indicate the strength in a straightforward manner—that is, just by their absolute size. With nominal-scaled variables, however, you must inspect the pattern to judge the strength. We describe this procedure—the use of cross-tabulations—next, and we describe correlation analysis later in this chapter.

> Based on scaling assumptions, first determine the type of relationship, and then perform the appropriate statistical test.

Cross-Tabulations

Cross-tabulation and the associated Chi-square value we are about to explain are used to assess if a nonmonotonic relationship exists between two nominally scaled variables. Remember that nonmonotonic relationships are those in which the presence of the label for one nominally scaled variable coincides with the presence or absence of the label for another nominally scaled variable such as lunch buyers ordering soft drinks with their meals. (Actually, cross-tabulation can be used for any 2 variables with well-defined labels, but it is best demonstrated with nominal variables.)

CROSS-TABULATION ANALYSIS

When investigating the relationship between two nominally scaled variables, we typically use "cross-tabs," or the use of a **cross-tabulation table**, defined as a table in which data is

> A cross-tabulation consists of rows and columns defined by the categories classifying each variable.

compared using a row and column format. A cross-tabulation table is sometimes referred to as an "r × c" (or r-by-c) table because it is comprised of rows by columns. The intersection of a row and a column is called a **cross-tabulation cell**. As an example, let's take a survey where there are two types of individuals: buyers of Michelob Light beer and nonbuyers of Michelob Light beer. There are also two types of occupations: professional workers who might be called "white colar" employees and manual workers who are sometimes referred to as "blue colar" workers. There is no requirement that the number of rows and columns are equal; we are just using a 2 × 2 cross-tabulation to keep the example as simple as possible. A cross-tabulation table for our Michelob Light beer survey is presented in Table 14.2. The columns are in vertical alignment and are indicated in this table as either "Buyer" or "Nonbuyer" of Michelob Light, whereas the rows are indicated as "White Collar" or "Blue Collar" for occupation. Additionally, there is a "Totals" column and row.

TYPES OF FREQUENCIES AND PERCENTAGES IN A CROSS-TABULATION TABLE

Look at the frequencies table in Table 14.2A. It includes plus (+) and equal (=) signs to help you learn the terminology and to understand how the numbers are computed. The **frequencies table** contains the raw numbers determined from the preliminary tabulation.[2] The upper left-hand cell number is a frequency cell that counts people in the sample who are both white-collar workers and buyers of Michelob Light (152), and the cell frequency to its right identifies the number of individuals who are white-collar workers who do not buy Michelob Light (8). These cell numbers represent raw counts or frequencies—that is, the number of respondents who possess the quality indicated by the row label as well as the quality indicated by the column label. The cell frequencies can be summed to determine the row totals and column totals. For example, Buyer/White Collar (152) and Nonbuyer/White Collar (8) sum to 160, while Buyer/White Collar (152) and Buyer/Blue Collar (14) sum to 166. Similarly, the row and column totals sum to equal the grand total of 200. Take a few minutes to be familiar with the terms and computations in the frequencies table as they will be referred to in the following discussion.

Table 14.2B illustrates how at least three different sets of percentages can be computed for cells in the table. These three percentages tables are: the raw percentages table, the column percentages table, and the row percentages table.

The first table in Table 14.2B shows that the raw frequencies can be converted to raw percentages by dividing each by the grand total. The **raw percentages table** contains the percentages of the raw frequency numbers just discussed. The grand total location now has 100%

A cross-classification table can have four types of numbers in each cell: frequency, raw percentage, column percentage, and row percentage.

Raw percentages are cell frequencies divided by the grand total.

TABLE 14.2A Cross-Tabulation Frequencies Table for a Michelob Light Survey

TABLE 14.2B Cross-Tabulation Percentages Tables for a Michelob Light Survey

Raw Percentages Table

		Buyer		Nonbuyer		Totals
	White Collar	→ 76%	+	4%	=	80%
Buyer/White Collar Cell Raw Percent		(152/200)		(8/200)		(160/200)
		+		+		+
Occupational Status	Blue Collar	7%	+	13%	=	20%
		(14/200)		(26/200)		(40/200)
		=		=		=
	Totals	83%	+	17%	=	**100%**
		(166/200)		(34/200)		(200/200)

Column Percentages Table

		Buyer		Nonbuyer	Totals
	White Collar	→ 92%		24%	80%
Buyer/White Collar Column Percent		(152/166)		(8/34)	(160/200)
		+		+	+
Occupational Status	Blue Collar	8%		76%	20%
		(14/166)		(26/34)	(40/200)
		=		=	=
		100%		**100%**	**100%**
	Totals	(166/166)		(34)	(200/200)

Row Percentages Table

		Buyer		Nonbuyer		Totals
Buyer/White Collar Row Percent	White Collar	→ 95%	+	5%	=	**100%**
		(152/160)		(8/160)		(160/160)
Occupational Status	Blue Collar	35%	+	65%	=	**100%**
		(14/40)		(26/40)		(40/40)
	Totals	83%	+	17%	=	**100%**
		(166/200)		(34/200)		(200/200)

(or 200/200) of the grand total. Above it are 80% and 20% for the raw percentages of white-collar occupational respondents and blue-collar occupational respondents, respectively, in the sample. Compute a couple of the cells just to verify that you understand how they are derived. For instance $152 \div 200 = 76\%$. Our + and = signs indicate how the totals are computed.

Two additional cross-tabulation tables can be presented, and these are more valuable in revealing underlying relationships. The **column percentages table** divides the raw frequencies by its column total raw frequency. That is, the formula is as follows:

Formula for a column cell percent

$$\text{Column cell percent} = \frac{\text{Cell frequency}}{\text{Total of cell frequencies in that column}}$$

For instance, it is apparent that of the nonbuyers, 24% are white-collar and 76% are blue-collar. Note the reverse pattern for the buyers group: 92% of white-collar respondents are Michelob Light buyers and 8% are blue-collar buyers. You are beginning to see the nonmonotonic relationship; in the presence of white collar we have the presence of buying.

The **row percentages table** presents the data with the row totals as the 100% base for each. That is, a row cell percentage is computed as follows:

Formula for a row cell percent

$$\text{Row cell percent} = \frac{\text{cell frequency}}{\text{total of cell frequencies in that row}}$$

> Row (column) percentages are row (column) cell frequencies divided by the row (column) total.

Now, it is possible to see that, of the white-collar respondents, 95% are buyers and 5% are nonbuyers. As you compare the row percentages table to the column percentages table, you should detect the relationship between occupational status and Michelob Light beer preference. Can you state it at this time?

Unequal percentage concentrations of individuals in a few cells, as we have in this example, illustrates the possible presence of a nonmonotonic association. If we had found that approximately 25% of the sample had fallen in each of the four cells, no relationship would be found to exist—it would be equally probable for a white or blue collar worker to be either a buyer or nonbuyer. However, the large concentrations of individuals in two particular cells here suggests that there is a high probability that a buyer of Michelob Light beer is also a white-collar worker, and there is also a tendency for nonbuyers to work in blue-collar occupations. In other words, there is probably an association between occupational status and the beer-buying behavior of individuals in the population represented by this sample. However, as noted in step 4 of our procedure for analyzing relationships (Table 14.1), we must test the statistical significance of the apparent relationship before we can say anything more about it. The test will tell us if this pattern would occur again if we repeated the study.

Chi-Square Analysis

> Chi-square analysis assesses the statistical significance of nonmonotonic associations in cross-tabulation tables.

Chi-square (χ^2) analysis is the examination of frequencies for two nominal-scaled variables in a cross-tabulation table to determine whether the variables have a statistically significant nonmonotonic relationship.[3] The formal procedure for Chi-square analysis begins when the researcher formulates a statistical null hypothesis that the two variables under investigation are *not* associated in the population. Actually, it is not necessary for the researcher to state this hypothesis in a formal sense, for Chi-square analysis always implicitly takes this hypothesis into account. In other words, whenever we use Chi-square analysis explicitly with a cross-tabulation, we always begin with the assumption that no association exists between the two nominal-scaled variables under analysis.[4]

OBSERVED AND EXPECTED FREQUENCIES

The statistical procedure is as follows. The cross-tabulation table in Table 14.2A contains **observed frequencies**, which are the actual cell counts in the cross-tabulation table. These observed frequencies are compared to **expected frequencies**, which are defined as the theoretical frequencies that are derived from the null hypothesis of no association between the two variables. The degree to which the observed frequencies depart from the expected frequencies is expressed in a single number called the *Chi-square statistic*. The computed Chi-square statistic is then compared to a table Chi-square value (at a chosen level of significance) to determine whether the computed value is significantly different from zero.

> Expected frequencies are calculated based on the null hypothesis of no association between the two variables under investigation.

The expected frequencies are those that would be found if there were no association between the two variables. Remember, this is the null hypothesis. About the only "difficult" part of Chi-square analysis is in the computation of the expected frequencies. The computation is accomplished using the following equation:

Formula for an expected cross-tabulation cell frequency

$$\text{Expected cell frequency} = \frac{\text{cell column total} \times \text{cell row total}}{\text{grand total}}$$

The application of this equation generates a number for each cell that would occur if no association existed. Returning to our Michelob Light beer example, you were told that 160 white-collar and 40 blue-collar consumers had been sampled, and it was found that there were 166 buyers and 34 nonbuyers of Michelob Light. The expected frequency for each cell, assuming no association, calculated with the expected cell frequency is as follows:

Calculations of expected cell frequencies using the Michelob Beer example

$$\text{White-collar buyer} = \frac{160 \times 166}{200} = 132.8$$

$$\text{White-collar nonbuyer} = \frac{160 \times 34}{200} = 27.2$$

$$\text{Blue-collar buyer} = \frac{40 \times 166}{200} = 33.2$$

$$\text{Blue-collar nonbuyer} = \frac{40 \times 34}{200} = 6.8$$

Notes:
Buyers total = 166
Nonbuyers total = 34
White-collar total = 160
Blue-collar total = 40
Grand total = 200

THE COMPUTED χ^2 VALUE

Next, compare the observed frequencies to these expected frequencies. The formula for this computation is as follows:

Chi-square formula

$$\chi^2 = \sum_{i-1}^{n} \frac{(\text{Observed}_i - \text{Expected}_i)^2}{\text{Expected}_i}$$

Where
Observed$_i$ = observed frequency in cell i
Expected$_i$ = expected frequency in cell i
n = number of cells

Applied to our Michelob beer example,

Calculation of Chi-square value (Michelob example)

$$\chi^2 = \frac{(152 - 132.8)^2}{132.8} + \frac{(8 - 27.2)^2}{27.2}$$
$$+ \frac{(14 - 33.2)^2}{33.2} + \frac{(26 - 6.8)^2}{6.8} = 81.64$$

Notes:
Observed frequencies are in Table 14.2A.
Expected frequencies are computed above.

The computed Chi-square value compares observed to expected frequencies.

You can see from the equation that each expected frequency is compared (via subtraction) to the observed frequency and squared to adjust for any negative values and to avoid the cancellation effect. This value is divided by the expected frequency to adjust for cell size differences, and these amounts are summed across all of the cells. If there are many large deviations of observed frequencies from the expected frequencies, the computed Chi-square value will increase; but if there are only a few slight deviations from the expected frequencies, the computed Chi-square number will be small. In other words, the computed Chi-square value is really a summary indication of how far away from the expected frequencies the observed frequencies are found to be. As such, it expresses the departure of the sample findings from the null hypothesis of no association.

The Chi-square statistic summarizes how far away from the expected frequencies the observed cell frequencies are found to be.

THE CHI-SQUARE DISTRIBUTION

Now that you've learned how to calculate a Chi-square value, you need to know if it is statistically significant. In previous chapters, we described how the normal curve or z distribution, the F distribution, and Student's t distribution, all of which exist in tables, are used

Do these blue-collar workers want their boss to buy them a Michelob Light for doing a great job? Cross-tabulation can answer this question.

Photo: AISPIX by Image Source/Shutterstock

by a computer statistical program to determine level of significance. Chi-square analysis requires the use of a different distribution. The **Chi-square distribution** is skewed to the right, and the rejection region is always at the right-hand tail of the distribution. It differs from the normal and *t* distributions in that it changes its shape depending on the situation at hand, and it does not have negative values. Figure 14.2 shows examples of two Chi-square distributions.

The Chi-square distribution's shape is determined by the number of degrees of freedom. The figure shows that the more the degrees of freedom, the more the curve's tail is pulled to the right. In other words, the more the degrees of freedom, the larger the Chi-square value must be to fall in the rejection region for the null hypothesis.

It is a simple matter to determine the number of degrees of freedom. In a cross-tabulation table, the degrees of freedom are found through the following formula:

Formula for Chi-Square degrees of freedom

$$\text{Degrees of freedom} = (r - 1)(c - 1)$$

Where:

   r = the number of rows

   c = the number of columns

> The Chi-square distribution's shape changes depending on the number of degrees of freedom.

A table of Chi-square values contains critical points that determine the break between acceptance and rejection regions at various levels of significance. It also takes into account the numbers of degrees of freedom associated with each curve. That is, a computed Chi-square value says nothing by itself—you must consider the number of degrees of freedom in the cross-tabulation table because more degrees of freedom are indicative of higher critical Chi-square table values for the same level of significance. The logic of this situation stems from the number of cells. With more cells, there is more opportunity for departure from the

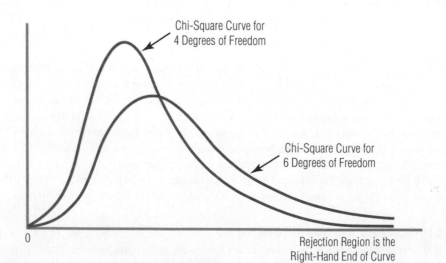

FIGURE 14.2 The Chi-Square Curve's Shape Depends on its Degrees of Freedom

expected values. The higher table values adjust for potential inflation due to chance alone. After all, we want to detect real nonmonotonic relationships, not phantom ones.

SPSS and virtually all computer statistical analysis programs have Chi-square tables in memory and print out the probability of the null hypothesis. Let us repeat this point: The program itself will take into account the number of degrees of freedom and determine the probability of support for the null hypothesis. This probability is the percentage of the area under the Chi-square curve that lies to the right of the computed Chi-square value. When rejection of the null hypothesis occurs, we have found a statistically significant nonmonotonic association existing between the two variables.

The computed Chi-square value is compared to a table value to determine statistical significance.

Computer statistical programs look up table Chi-square values and print out the probability of support for the null hypothesis.

HOW TO INTERPRET A CHI-SQUARE RESULT

How does one interpret a Chi-square result? Chi-square analysis yields the amount of support for the null hypothesis if the researcher repeated the study many, many times with independent samples. By now, you should be well acquainted with the concept of many, many independent samples. For example, if the Chi-square analysis yielded a 0.02 signficiance level for the null hypothesis, the researcher would conclude that only 2% of the time he or she would find evidence to support the null hypothesis. Since the null hypothesis is not supported, this means there is a significant association.

It must be pointed out that Chi-square analysis is simply a method to determine whether a statistically significant nonmonotonic association exists between two variables. Chi-square does not indicate the nature of the association, and it indicates only roughly the strength of association by its size. It is best interpreted as a prerequisite to looking more closely at the two variables to discern the nature of the association that exists between them. That is, the Chi-square test is another one of our "flags" that tell us whether it is worthwhile to inspect all those rows and columns percentages. Read Marketing Research Insight 14.1 to see how crosstabulation findings predict the success of a national health care initiative in Switzerland.

A significant Chi-square means the researcher should look at the cross-tabulation row and column percentages to "see" the association pattern.

INTEGRATED CASE

Global Motors: Analyzing Cross-Tabulations for Significant Associations by Performing Chi-Square Analysis with SPSS

SPSS®

Let's use our Global Motors survey data to demonstrate how to perform and interpret cross-tabulation analysis with SPSS. This dataset contains several demographic variables, including gender and marital status. We will take gender as one of the nominal variables. For the second nominal variable, we will take the preferred magazine type. Thus, we are investigating the possible association of gender (male versus female) and favorite magazine type (business and money; music and entertainment; family and parenting; sports and outdoors; home and garden; cooking, food, and wine; trucks, cars, and motorcycles; or news, politics, and current events).

The clickstream command sequence to perform a Chi-square test with SPSS is ANALYZE-DESCRIPTIVE STATISTICS-CROSSTABS, which leads to a dialog box in which you can select the variables for Chi-square analysis. In our example in Figure 14.3, we have selected gender as the column variable, and favorite magazine type as the row variable. There are three options buttons at the bottom of the box. The Cells . . . option leads to the specification of observed frequencies, expected frequencies, row percentages, column percentages, and so forth. We have opted for just the observed frequencies (raw counts) and the row percents. The Statistics . . . button opens up a menu of statistics that can be computed from cross-tabulation tables. Of course, the only one we want is the Chi-square option.

With SPSS, Chi-square is an option under the "Crosstabs" analysis routine.

MARKETING RESEARCH INSIGHT 14.1   *Global Application*

Cross-Tabulations Reveal Differences Between Swiss Users of Health E-services

Many companies are encouraging consumers to switch to the company's web-based services for good reasons. First, web-based services are largely "do it yourself," meaning that the company does not need as many service employees. Second, web-based services are available at any time, so consumers are not constrained by business hours, and third, web-based services can contain a huge storehouse of information, data, and advice that is useful and available whenever consumers want to access it. While financial institutions are prime examples of institutions that have been aggressive in encouraging customers to use e-services, health insurance providers are also promoting the use of their Internet services. In fact, eHealth Strategy is a national program in Switzerland to make online health accounts accessible to all Swiss citizens by 2015. A question addressed by a recent study of Swiss consumers was "what e-services are used by those who have online health accounts versus those

who do not?" Researchers[5] compared Swiss consumers who have an online health account to those who do not with respect to their use of nine e-services using cross-tabulations. The statistically significant findings are shown in the following graph.

It is notable that the consumers who have online health accounts are engaging in significantly more self-help behavior than those who do not. Specifically, the online health account owners are making much more use of the online health information (wiki and lifestyle information); they are using the online health care providers rating tools more; they are participating in online forums more; and they are using live chats with health coaches somewhat more than the nonowners. It appears that when the eHealth Strategy Switzerland program is fully implemented, Swiss citizens will use these tools to make healthier lifestyle choices as well as to tap into all of the health-related online information.

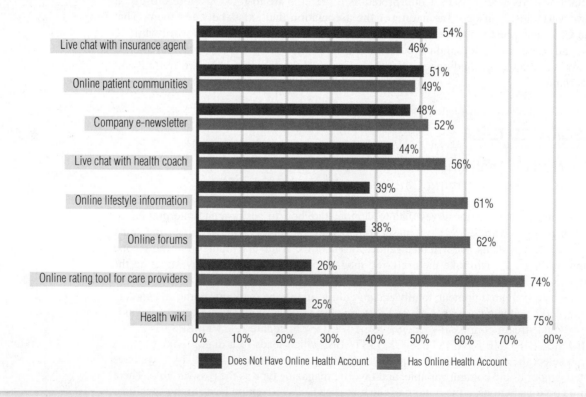

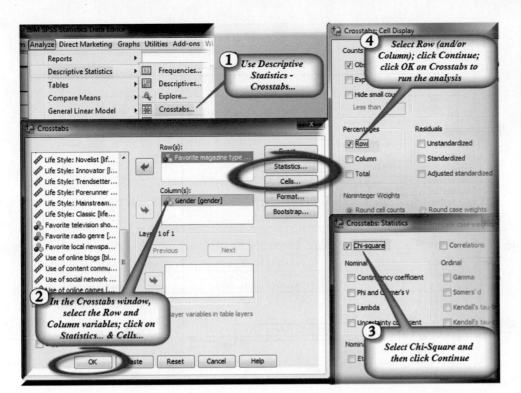

FIGURE 14.3 SPSS Clickstream to Create Cross-Tabulations with Chi-Square Analysis

Source: Reprint courtesy of International Business Machines Corporation, © SPSS, Inc., an IBM Company.

The resulting output is found in Figure 14.4. In the top table, you can see that we have variable and value labels, and the table contains the raw frequency as the first entry in each cell. Also, the row percentages are reported along with each row and column total. In the second table, there is information on the Chi-square analysis result. For our purposes, the only relevant statistic is the "Pearson Chi-square," which you can see has been computed to be 16.671. The df column pertains to the number of degrees of freedom, which is 7; and the Asymp. Sig. corresponds to the probability of support for the null hypothesis. Significance in this example is .020, which means that there is practically no support for the null hypothesis that gender and favorite magazine type are not associated. In other words, they are related.

SPSS has effected the first step in determining a nonmonotonic association. Through Chi-square analysis it has signaled that a statistically significant association is present. The next step is to fathom the nature of the association. Remember that with a nonmonotonic relationship, you must inspect the pattern and describe it verbally. We can ask the question, "Which gender is reading what magazine type?" Remember that the pattern is a matter of degree, not "on versus off." Look at the row percents in Figure 14.4, and you will see some magazine types that garner proportionally more male readers: trucks, cars, and motorcyles; cooking, food, and wine, and sports and outdoors. The other magazine types have somewhat balanced readership profiles with respect to gender. You can interpret this finding in the following way: If Global Motors wants to communicate to prospective male automobile buyers, it should use the magazine types they prefer, and if it desires to communicate to prospective female buyers, it should not use these types as women do not prefer to read them.

In other words, because the significance was less than .05, it was worthwhile to inspect and interpret the percentages in the cross-tabulation table. By doing this, we can discern the pattern or nature of the association, and the percentages indicate its relative strength. More importantly, because the relationship was determined to be statistically significant, you can be assured that this association and the relationship you have observed will hold for the population this sample represents.

SPSS®

SPSS Student Assistant: Setting Up and Analyzing Cross-Tabulations

With Chi-square analysis, interpret the SPSS significance level as the amount of support for *no* association between the two variables being analyzed.

FIGURE 14.4 SPSS Output for Cross-Tabulations with Chi-Square Analysis

Source: Reprint courtesy of International Business Machines Corporation, © SPSS, Inc., an IBM Company.

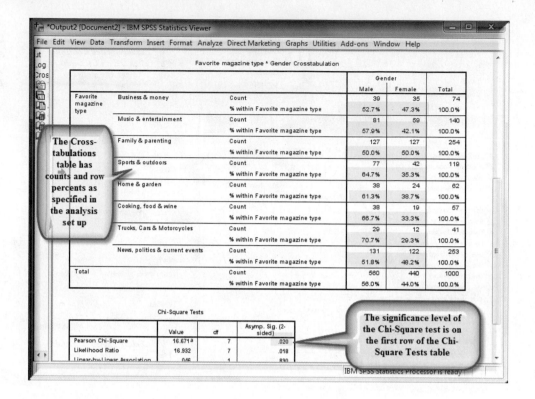

The Cross-tabulations table has counts and row percents as specified in the analysis set up

The significance level of the Chi-Square test is on the first row of the Chi-Square Tests table

 Active Learning ―――――――――――――

Practice Crosstabulation Analysis with SPSS

To make certain you can perform SPSS cross-tabulation with Chi-square analysis, use the Global Motors SPSS dataset and replicate the Gender-Favorite magazine type analysis just described. When you are convinced that you can do this analysis correctly and interpret the output, use it to see if there is an association between marital status and favorite magazine type. What about marital status and newspaper reading habits?

Marketing Research on YouTube™ To learn about cross-tabulation and chi square analysis, launch www.youtube.com, and search for "Interpreting the SPSS Output for a Chi Square Analysis."

Bar charts can be used to "see" a nonmonotonic relationship.

Reporting Cross-Tabulation Findings to Clients

Whenever the researcher finds a statistically significant cross-tabulation relationship, he or she moves to the presentation phase. When we introduced the notion of relationship or association analysis, we noted that characterizing the direction and strength of nonmonotonic relationships are not possible because nominal scales are involved. Nominal scales do not have the characteristics of order or origin; they are simply categories or labels that uniquely identify the data. As you have learned in our descriptions of the various tables possible with cross-tabulations, percents are easily prepared, and percents can usually depict nonmonotonic relationships quite well. In addition, to reveal the nonmonotonic relationships found significant in cross-tabulation tables, researchers often turn to graphical presentations as pictures will show the relationships adequately. Marketing Research Insight 14.2 describes alternative ways to present the findings of cross-tabulation relationships analyses to clients.

MARKETING RESEARCH INSIGHT 14.2 · *Practical Application*

Guidelines for Reporting Cross-Tabulation Findings

Using Column and Row Percents

A question that quickly arises whenever a researcher finds a statistically significant relationship in a cross-tabulation analysis is "Should I report the row percents or the column percents?" The answer to this question depends on the research objective that fostered the nominal questions on the survey. Take, for instance, the following significant cross-tabulation finding for the Subshop.

Column Percents Table

Size of Sandwich Ordered	Males	Females
Jumbo Size	**50%**	5%
Large Size	**40%**	20%
Regular Size	10%	**75%**
Total	100%	100%

Rows Percents Table

Size of Sandwich Ordered	Males	Females	Total
Jumbo Size	**90%**	10%	100%
Large Size	**67%**	33%	100%
Regular Size	13%	**87%**	100%

If the research question is "Who orders what size of sandwich?" the rows percents table is appropriate as it indicates that males tend to order the Jumbo size and the Large size (90% and 67%, respectively), while females tend to be the ones who order the Regular size (87%). On the other hand,

if the research question is "What do males versus females order?" then the column percents table is appropriate as it indicates that males order Jumbo and Large sizes (50% and 40%), while females order the Regular size (75%). You should remember that we described a nonmonotonic relationship as an identifiable association where the presence of one variable is paired with the presence (or absence of another) so the relationships are not 100% versus 0%; rather, it is a degree or relative presence that exists in the population. Study our two presentation tables, and you will notice that we have used shading to help the reader understand how the percents are computed. That is, the males and females columns are different shades as they express percents within each gender. Similarly, the sandwich size rows are different shades as they represent percents within each sandwich size. We have also used bold font to emphasize where the percents reveal especially strong relationships.

Using Stacked Bar Charts

A handy graphical tool that illustrates a nonmonotonic relationship is a stacked bar chart. With a stacked bar chart, two variables are accommodated simultaneously in the same bar graph. Each bar in the stacked bar chart stands for 100%, and it is divided proportionately by the amount of relationship that one variable shares with the other variables. Thus, a stacked bar chart is an excellent visual display of row or column percents in a cross-tabulation table. For instance, you can see in the following figures that the two Subshop cross-tabulation percents tables have been used to create the visual displays.

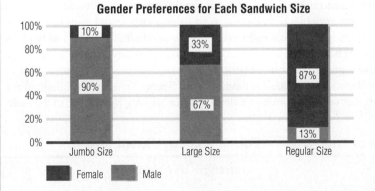

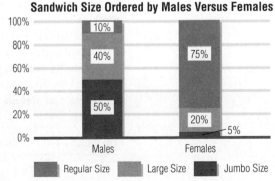

Correlation Coefficients and Covariation

We now move to the relationship between two scale variables. The **correlation coefficient** is an index number, constrained to fall between the range of −1.0 and +1.0, that communicates both the strength and the direction of a linear relationship between two metric variables.

A correlation coefficient translates the covariation between two scale variables into a number ranging from −1.0 to +1.0.

The strength of association between two variables is communicated by the absolute size of the correlation coefficient, whereas its sign communicates the direction of the association. Stated in a slightly different manner, a correlation coefficient indicates the degree of covariation between two variables. **Covariation** is defined as the amount of change in one variable systematically associated with a change in another variable. The greater the absolute size of the correlation coefficient, the greater is the covariation between the two variables, or the stronger is their relationship.[6]

To use a correlation, you must first determine that it is statistically significant from zero.

Let's take up the statistical significance of a correlation coefficient first. Regardless of its absolute value, a correlation that is not statistically significant has no meaning at all. This is because of the null hypothesis, which states that the population correlation coefficient is equal to zero. If this null hypothesis is rejected (statistically significant correlation), then you can be assured that a correlation other than zero will be found in the population. But if the sample correlation is found to be not significant, the population correlation will be zero. If you can answer the following question correctly, you understand the statistical significance of a correlation: If you repeated a correlational survey many, many times and computed the average for a correlation that was not significant across all of these surveys, what would be the result? (The answer is zero because if the correlation is not significant, the null hypothesis is true, and the population correlation is zero.)

Step 4, "Determine if the relationship is present," in our "Procedure for Analyzing Relationships" in Table 14.1, requires a statistical test, but how do you determine the statistical significance of a correlation coefficient? While tables exist that give the lowest value of the significant correlation coefficients for given sample sizes, most computer statistical programs will indicate the statistical significance level of the computed correlation coefficient. SPSS provides the significance in the form of the probability that the null hypothesis is supported. We will focus on the "Sig." value when we examine SPSS correlation output.

RULES OF THUMB FOR CORRELATION STRENGTH

Rules of thumb exist concerning the strength of a correlation based on its absolute size.

After we have established that a correlation coefficient is statistically significant, we can talk about some general rules of thumb concerning the strength of association. Correlation coefficients that fall between the absolute values of 1.00 and .81 are generally considered to be "strong." Those correlations that fall between the absolute values of .80 and .61 are generally indicate a "moderate" association. Those that fall between the absolute values of .60 and .41 are typically considered to be "low," and they denote a weak association. Any correlation that falls between the absolute value range of .21 and .40 is usually considered indicative of a very weak association between the variables. Finally, any correlation that is equal to or less than the absolute value of .20 is typically uninteresting to marketing researchers because it rarely identifies a meaningful association between two variables. Table 14.3 offers a reference on these rules of thumb. As you use these guidelines, remember two things: First, we are assuming that the statistical significance of the correlation has been established. Second, researchers adapt rules of thumb, so you may encounter someone whose guidelines differ slightly from those in the table.[7]

TABLE 14.3 Rules of Thumb about Correlation Coefficient Size*

Coefficient Range	Strength of Association*
+.81 to +1.00; −.81 to −1.00	Strong
+.61 to +.80; −.61 to −.80	Moderate
+.41 to +.60; −.41 to −.60	Weak
+.21 to +.40; −.21 to −.40	Very weak
+.20 to −.20	None

*Assuming the correlation coefficient is statistically significant

In any case, it is helpful to think in terms of the closeness of the correlation coefficient to 0 or to ±1.00. Statistically significant correlation coefficients that are close to 0 show that there is no systematic association between the two variables, whereas those that are closer to +1.00 or −1.00 express that there is some systematic association between the variables.

THE CORRELATION SIGN: THE DIRECTION OF THE RELATIONSHIP

But what about the sign of the correlation coefficient? The sign indicates the direction of the relationship. A positive sign indicates a positive direction; a negative sign indicates a negative direction. For instance, if you found a significant correlation of .83 between years of education and hours spent reading *National Geographic* magazine, it would mean that people with more education spend more hours reading this magazine; that is a positive relationship. If you found a significant negative correlation between years of education and frequency of cigarette smoking, it would mean that more educated people smoke less; that is, a negative relationship.

A correlation indicates the strength of association between two variables by its size. The sign indicates the direction of the association.

GRAPHING COVARIATION USING SCATTER DIAGRAMS

We addressed the concept of covariation between two variables in our introductory comments on correlations. It is now time to present covariation in a slightly different manner. Here is an example: A marketing researcher is investigating the possible relationship between total company sales for Novartis, a leading pharmaceuticals sales company, in a particular territory and the number of salespeople assigned to that territory. At the researcher's fingertips are the sales figures and number of salespeople assigned for each of 20 different Novartis territories in the United States.

It is possible to depict the raw data for these two variables on a scatter diagram such as the one in Figure 14.5. A **scatter diagram** plots the points corresponding to each matched pair of *X* and *Y* variables. In this figure, the vertical axis is Novartis sales for the territory and the horizontal axis contains the number of salespeople in that territory. The arrangement or scatter of points appears to fall in a long ellipse. Any two variables that exhibit systematic covariation will form an ellipse-like pattern on a scatter diagram. Of course, this particular scatter diagram portrays the information gathered by the marketing researcher on sales and the number of salespeople in each territory and only that information. In actuality, the scatter diagram could have taken any shape, depending on the relationship between the points plotted for the two variables concerned.[8]

Covariation can be examined with the use of a scatter diagram.

Different types of scatter diagram results are portrayed in Figure 14.6. Each of these scatter diagram results is indicative of a different degree of covariation. For instance,

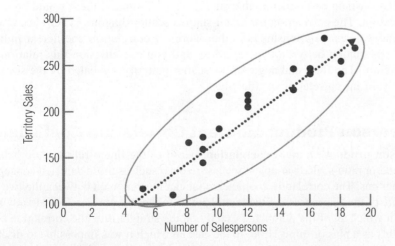

FIGURE 14.5 A Scatter Diagram Showing Covariation

FIGURE 14.6 Scatter Diagrams Illustrating Various Relationships

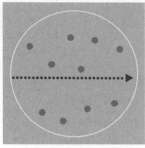

(a) No Association

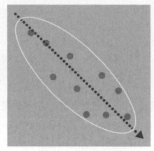

(b) Negative Association

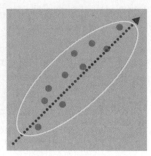

(c) Positive Association

The success of a prescription drug pharmaceutical company may be related to how many salespersons it has in the field to talk with doctors.

Photo: Andresr/Shutterstock

Two highly correlated variables will appear on a scatter diagram as a tight ellipse pattern.

you can see that the scatter diagram depicted in Figure 14.6(a) is one in which there is no apparent association or relationship between the two variables; the points fail to create any identifiable pattern. Instead, they are clumped into a large, formless shape. Those points in Figure 14.6(b) indicate a negative relationship between variable x and variable y; higher values of x tend to be associated with lower values of y. Those points in Figure 14.6(c) are fairly similar to those in Figure 14.6(b), but the angle or the slope of the ellipse is different. This slope indicates a positive relationship between x and y, because larger values of x tend to be associated with larger values of y.

What is the connection between scatter diagrams and correlation coefficients? The answer to these questions lies in the linear relationship described earlier in this chapter. Look at Figures 14.6(b) and 14.6(c). Both form ellipses. Imagine taking an ellipse and pulling on both ends. It would stretch out and become thinner until all of its points fall on a straight line. If you happened to find some data that formed an ellipse with all of its points falling on the axis line and you computed a correlation, you would find it to be exactly 1.0 (+1.0 if the ellipse went up to the right and −1.0 if it went down to the right). Now imagine pushing the ends of the ellipse until it became the pattern in Figure 14.6(a). There would be no identifiable straight line. Similarly, there would be no systematic covariation. The correlation for a ball-shaped scatter diagram is zero because there is no discernable linear relationship. In other words, a correlation coefficient indicates the degree of covariation between two variables, and you can envision this relationship as a scatter diagram. The form and angle of the scatter pattern is revealed by the size and sign, respectively, of the correlation coefficient.

The Pearson Product Moment Correlation Coefficient

The **Pearson product moment correlation** measures the linear relationship between two interval- and/or ratio-scaled variables (scale variables) such as those depicted conceptually by scatter diagrams. The correlation coefficient that can be computed between the two variables is a measure of the "closeness" of the scatter points to the straight line. You already know that in a case in which all of the points fall exactly on the straight line, the correlation coefficient indicates this as a plus or minus 1.00. In the case in which it was impossible to discern an ellipse such as in scatter diagram Figure 14.6(a), the correlation coefficient approximates zero.

Of course, it is extremely unlikely that you will find perfect 1.00 or 0 correlations. Usually, you will find some value in between that, if statistically significant, can be interpreted as high, moderate, or low correlation using the rules of thumb given earlier.

The computational formula for Pearson product moment correlations is as follows:

Formula for Pearson product moment correlation

$$r_{xy} = \frac{\sum\limits_{n}^{i=1}(x_i - \overline{x})(y_i - \overline{y})}{ns_x s_y}$$

Where

x_i = each x value

x = mean of the x values

y_i = each y value

$\overline{y}$ = mean of the y values

n = number of paired cases

s_x, s_y = standard deviations of x and y, respectively

We briefly describe the components of this formula to help you see how the concepts we just discussed fit in. In the statistician's terminology, the numerator represents the cross-products sum and indicates the covariation or "covariance" between x and y. The cross-products sum is divided by n to scale it down to an average per pair of x and y values. This average covariation is then divided by both standard deviations to adjust for differences in units. The result constrains rxy to fall between -1.0 and $+1.0$.

Here is a simple computational example. You have some data on population and retail sales by county for 10 counties in your state. Is there a relationship between population and retail sales? You do a quick calculation and find the average number of people per county is 690,000, and the average retail sales is $9.54 million. The standard deviations are 384.3 and 7.8, respectively, and the cross-products sum is 25,154. The computations to find the correlation are:

Calculation of a correlation coefficient

$$r_{xy} = \frac{\sum\limits_{i-1}^{n}(x_i - \overline{x})(y_i - \overline{y})}{ns_x s_y}$$

$$= \frac{25,154}{10 \times 7.8 \times 384.4}$$

$$= \frac{25,154}{29,975.4}$$

$$= .84$$

Notes:

Cross-products sum = 25,154

$n = 10$

Std dev of x = 7.8

Std dev of y = 384.3

The Pearson product moment correlation coefficient measures the degree of linear association between two variables.

A correlation of .84 is a high positive correlation coefficient for the relationship. This value reveals that the greater the number of citizens living in a county, the greater the county's retail sales.

To summarize, Pearson product moment correlation and other linear association correlation coefficients indicate not only the degree of association but the direction as well because as we described in our introductory comments on correlations, the sign of the correlation coefficient indicates the direction of the relationship. Negative correlation coefficients reveal that the relationship is opposite: As one variable increases, the other variable decreases. Positive correlation coefficients reveal that the relationship is increasing: Larger quantities of one variable are associated with larger quantities of another variable. It is important to note that the angle or the slope of the ellipse has nothing to do with the size of correlation coefficient. Everything hinges on the width of the ellipse. (The slope will be considered in Chapter 15 under regression analysis.) To learn how correlations were used to discover the relationships among certain personality traits and self-promotion on Facebook, read Marketing Research Insight 14.3.

A positive correlation signals an increasing linear relationship, whereas a negative correlation signals a decreasing one.

MARKETING RESEARCH INSIGHT 14.3   *Social Media Marketing*

Correlations Offer Insight on the Use of Facebook

A researcher who was curious about consumers' use of Facebook as a new method of self-presentation recently investigated the relationship of certain personality traits with individuals' postings on Facebook.[9] She rated five aspects of individuals' Facebook pages: (1) the "About Me" section, (2) the first 20 pictures on the View Photos of Me, (3) the Main Photo, (4) the Notes section, and (5) the Status Updates Section. Specifically, any descriptive or photo information that appeared to be attempting to persuade the reader of the positive qualities of the Facebook user were tallied. These included positive adjectives about oneself, facial expresssions, photo editing, self-promoting mottos and quotes, and so forth. The 5-point rating scale ranged from *not at all* (1) to *very much* (5). At the same time, the researcher administered pyschological tests that measured self-esteem and narcissism. Self-esteem is the degree to which a person is satisfied or happy with one's current situation and self.

Narcissism is essentially the degree to which a person thinks he or she is better than most other people. Other measures included how many times per day the person checked Facebook and the amount of time spent on Facebook per session.

Using correlations, the researcher found significant positive correlations between narcissism and the number of times and the amount of time on Facebook. On the other hand, the researcher found significant negative correlations between self-esteem and the number of times and the amount of time on Facebook. Similarly, significant positive correlations were found between narcissism and most of the five aspects of Facebook, whereas significant negative correlations were discovered between self-esteeem and most of the five aspects of Facebook. It appears from this exploratory study that narcissistic individuals are using Facebook for active self-promotion, while indivduals with high self-esteem do not find it necessary to use Facebook for self-promotion.

 Active Learning

Date.net: Male Users' Chat Room Phobia

Date.net is an online meeting service. It operates a virtual meeting place for men seeking women and women seeking men. Date.net's public chat room is where its members first become aquainted, and, if a couple moves into a private chat room, Date.net creates one and assesses a fee for each minute the couple is chatting in this private area. Recent internal analysis has revealed that women chat room users are considerably less satisfied with Date.net's public chat room than are its male chat room users. This is frustrating to Date.net principals as they know that disappointing public chats will not lead to private chats.

They commission an online marketing research company to design a questionnaire that is posted on the Date.net website. The survey asks a number of demographic, online chatting, Date.net services usage, and personal satisfaction questions; more than 5,000 Date.net users fill it out. Date.net executives request a separate analysis of male members who use the public chat room. The research company reports all correlations that are significant at the 0.01 level. Here is a summary of the correlation analysis findings.

Correlation with Factor	Amount of Date.net	Chat Room Use
Demographics:	Age	−.68
	Income	−.76
	Education	−.78
	Number of years divorced	+.57
	Number of children	+.68
	Years at present address	−.90
	Years at present job	−.85

Correlation with Factor	Amount of Date.net	Chat Room Use
Satisfaction with:	Relationships	−.76
	Job/career	−.86
	Personal appearance	−.72
	Life in general	−.50
Online behavior:	Minutes online daily	+.90
	Online purchases	−.65
	Other chatting time/month	+.86
	Number of email accounts	+.77
Use of Date.net (where 1 = not important and 5 = very important)	Meet new people	+.38
	Only way to talk to women	+.68
	Looking for a life partner	−.72
	Not much else to do	+.59

For each factor, use your knowledge of correlations and provide a statement of how it characterizes the typical Date.net male chat room user. Given your findings, what tactics do you recommend to Date.net to address the low satisfaction with Date.net's public chat room that has been expressed by its female members?

INTEGRATED CASE

Global Motors: How to Obtain Pearson Product Moment Correlation(s) with SPSS

SPSS®

With SPSS, it takes only a few clicks to compute correlation coefficients. Once again, we will use the Global Motors survey case study. The survey measured preferences for each of the five possible automobile models on a 7-point interval scale. CMG Research also purchased the lifestyle measures of the respondents, represented by six categories: Novelist, Innovator, Trendsetter, Forerunner, Mainstreamer, and Classic. Each lifestyle type is measured with a 7-point interval scale where 1 = "does not describe me at all" and 7 = "describes me perfectly." Correlation analysis can be used to find out what lifestyle profile is associated with what automobile model preference. That is, high positive correlations would indicate that they wanted that model and that they scored high on the lifestyle type. Conversely, low or negative correlations would signal that they did not match up well at all. We'll only do one of the model preferences here, and you can do the rest in your SPSS integrated case analysis work specified at the end of the chapter.

We need to perform correlation analysis with the preference for the large, standard gasoline automobile model and the six lifestyle types to determine which, if any, lifestyle type is associated with preference for this hybrid model. The clickstream sequence is ANALYZE-CORRELATE BIVARIATE that leads, as can be seen in Figure 14.7, to a selection box to specify which variables are to be correlated. Note that we have selected the desirability of the standard model and all six lifestyle types. Different types of correlations are optional, so we have selected Pearson's, and the two-tailed test of significance is the default.

The output generated by this command is provided in Figure 14.8. Whenever you instruct SPSS to compute correlations, its output is a symmetric correlation matrix composed of rows

With SPSS, correlations are computed with the CORRELATE-BIVARIATE feature.

FIGURE 14.7 SPSS Clickstream to Obtain Correlations

Source: Reprint courtesy of International Business Machines Corporation, © SPSS, Inc., an IBM Company.

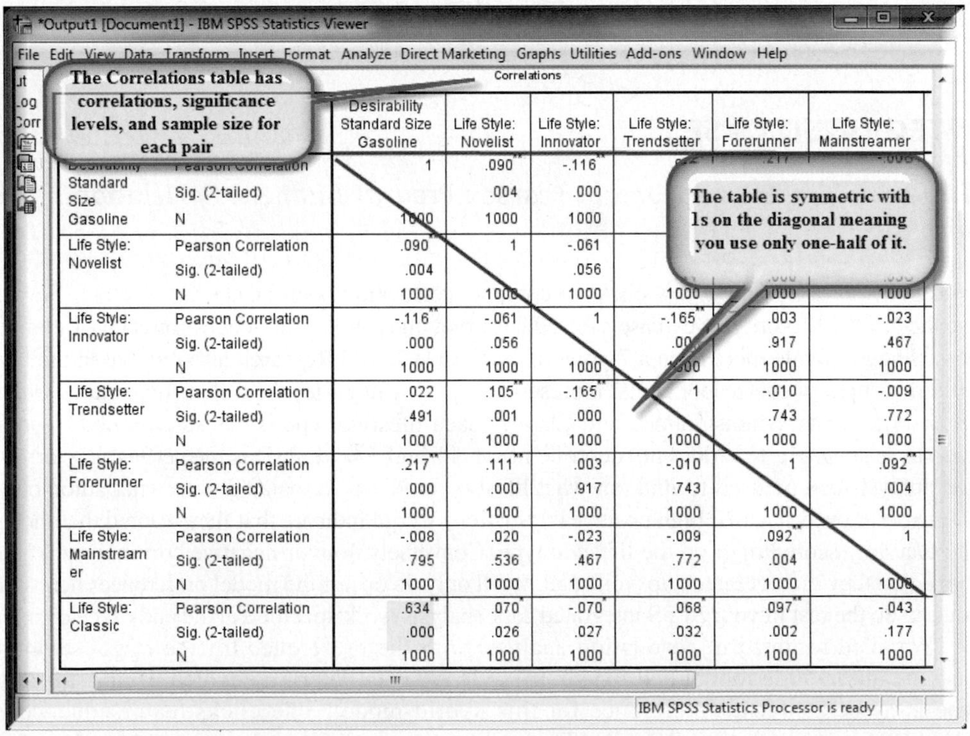

FIGURE 14.8 SPSS Output for Correlations

Source: Reprint courtesy of International Business Machines Corporation, © SPSS, Inc., an IBM Company.

Correlations

		Desirability Standard Size Gasoline	Life Style: Novelist	Life Style: Innovator	Life Style: Trendsetter	Life Style: Forerunner	Life Style: Mainstreamer
Desirability Standard Size Gasoline	Pearson Correlation	1	.090**	-.116**	[illegible]	[illegible]	[illegible]
	Sig. (2-tailed)		.004	.000	[illegible]	[illegible]	[illegible]
	N	1000	1000	1000	[illegible]	[illegible]	[illegible]
Life Style: Novelist	Pearson Correlation	.090**	1	-.061	[illegible]	[illegible]	[illegible]
	Sig. (2-tailed)	.004		.056	[illegible]	[illegible]	[illegible]
	N	1000	1000	1000	1000	1000	1000
Life Style: Innovator	Pearson Correlation	-.116**	-.061	1	-.165**	.003	-.023
	Sig. (2-tailed)	.000	.056		[illegible]	.917	.467
	N	1000	1000	1000	1000	1000	1000
Life Style: Trendsetter	Pearson Correlation	.022	.105**	-.165**	1	-.010	-.009
	Sig. (2-tailed)	.491	.001	.000		.743	.772
	N	1000	1000	1000	1000	1000	1000
Life Style: Forerunner	Pearson Correlation	.217**	.111**	.003	-.010	1	.092**
	Sig. (2-tailed)	.000	.000	.917	.743		.004
	N	1000	1000	1000	1000	1000	1000
Life Style: Mainstreamer	Pearson Correlation	-.008	.020	-.023	-.009	.092**	1
	Sig. (2-tailed)	.795	.536	.467	.772	.004	
	N	1000	1000	1000	1000	1000	1000
Life Style: Classic	Pearson Correlation	.634**	.070*	-.070*	.068*	.097**	-.043
	Sig. (2-tailed)	.000	.026	.027	.032	.002	.177
	N	1000	1000	1000	1000	1000	1000

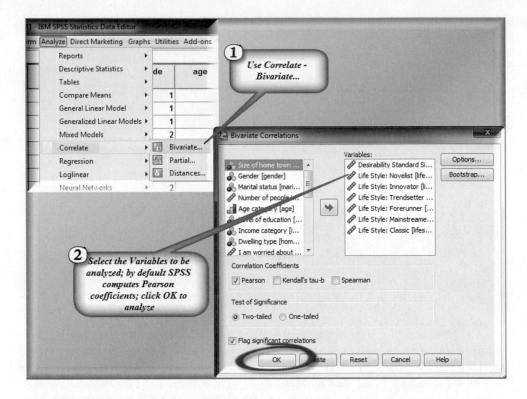

and columns that pertain to each of the variables. Each cell in the matrix contains three items: (1) the correlation coefficient, (2) the significance level, and (3) the sample size. Figure 14.8 sets out the computed correlations between "Desirability: Standard Size Gasoline" and the six lifestyles of Novelist, Innovator, Trendsetter, Forerunner, Mainstreamer, and Classic.

If you look at our correlation printout, you will notice that a correlation of 1.000 is reported where a variable is correlated with itself. This reporting may seem strange, but it serves the purpose of reminding you that the correlation matrix that is generated with this procedure is symmetric. In other words, the correlations in the matrix above the diagonal 1s are identical to those correlations below the diagonal. With only a few variables, this fact is obvious; however, sometimes several variables are compared in a single run, and the 1s on the diagonal are handy reference points. Notice that all the off-diagonal cells, have a "Sig" value of .000 that translates into a .001 or less probability that the null hypothesis of zero correlation is supported.

Now that we know the correlations are statistically significant, or significantly different from zero, we can assess their strengths. Searching the first column of statistics, we find only one correlation of appreciable size. It is .634 for Classic. In other words, we only have one lifestyle type relationship that is stable and moderately strong. The interpretation of this finding is that those who prefer the standard size gasoline model are people who tend to be traditional and are reluctant to change their ways.

> A correlation matrix is symmetric with 1s on the diagonal.
>
> With correlation analysis, each correlation has a unique significance level.

SPSS®

SPSS Student Assistant: Working with Correlations

SPECIAL CONSIDERATIONS IN LINEAR CORRELATION PROCEDURES

Perhaps because the word *correlation* is used in everyday language, statistical correlations are sometimes misunderstood by clients.[10] We will discuss each of four cautions to keep in mind when working with correlations. To begin, we will reiterate that the correlation coefficient discussed in this section assumes that both variables share interval-scaling assumptions at minimum. If the two variables have nominal scaling assumptions, the researcher would use cross-tabulation analysis. Next, the correlation coefficient takes into consideration only the relationship between two variables. It does not take into consideration interactions with any other variables. In fact, it explicitly assumes that they do not have any bearing on the relationship with the two variables of interest. All other factors are considered to be constant or "frozen" in their bearing on the two variables under analysis.

Third, the correlation coefficient explicity does not assume a **cause and effect relationship**, which is a condition of one variable bringing about the other variable. Although you might be tempted to believe that more company salespeople cause more company sales or that an increase in the competitor's salesforce in a territory takes away sales, correlation should not be interpreted to demonstrate such cause-and-effect relationships. Just think of all of the other factors that affect sales: price, product quality, service policies, population, advertising, and more. It would be a mistake to assume that just one factor causes sales. Instead, a correlation coefficient merely investigates the presence, strength, and direction of a linear relationship between two variables.

> Correlation does not demonstrate cause and effect.

Finally, the Pearson product moment correlation expresses only linear relationships. Consequently, a correlation coefficient result of approximately zero does not necessarily mean that the scatter diagram that could be drawn from the two variables defines a formless ball of points. Instead, it means that the points do not fall in a well-defined elliptical pattern. Any number of alternative, curvilinear patterns such as an S-shape or a J-shape pattern are possible, and the linear correlation coefficient would not be able to communicate the existence of these patterns to the marketing researcher. Only those cases of linear or straight-line relationships between two variables are identified by the Pearson product moment correlation. In fact, when a researcher does not find a significant or strong correlation, but still believes some relationship exists between two variables, he or she may resort to running a scatter plot. This procedure allows the researcher to visually inspect the plotted points and possibly spot a systematic nonlinear relationship. You probably already know that your SPSS program has a scatter plot option that will provide a scatter diagram you can use to obtain a sense of the relationship, if any, between two variables. Last, the Pearson product moment correlation coefficient is calculated from standardized data. Therefore, it is not necessary that the scales of the two variables be identical.

> Correlation will not detect nonlinear relationships between variables.

Marketing Research on YouTube™ To learn how to compute a Pearson Product Moment Correlation, launch www.youtube.com, and search for "Product Moment Correlation Coefficient: ExamSolutions."

Reporting Correlation Findings to Clients

We remind you of the importance of step 4 of the procedure for analyzing relationships outlined in Table 14.1: The researcher must test to determine that a significant correlation has been found before reporting it. Losing sight of this step is entirely possible when a statistical analysis program issues a great many correlations often in a layout that is confusing to first-time data analysts. To our knowledge, there is no marketing research industry standard on how to report statistically significant correlations to clients. We recommend an approach that takes into account correlation signs and sizes. Our recommendation is in Marketing Research Insight 14.4.

MARKETING RESEARCH INSIGHT 14.4 *Practical Application*

Guidelines for Reporting Correlation Findings

To begin, marketing researchers usually have a "target" or a "focal" variable in mind, and they look at correlations of other variables of interest with this target variable. As an illustration, in our fictitious Subshop survey, the researcher decides that the target variable is the number of times Subshop customers used the Subshop in the past two months. This is a scale variable (ratio scale) where respondents have given a number such as 0, 3, 10, and so on. The researcher has found six other variables with statistically significant correlations with the target in the analysis of the Subshop survey data. Naturally, some of these have negative correlations, and the correlations range in size or strength. Study how these findings are arranged in the following table.

Notice in the table that the target variable is clearly indicated, and the positive and negative correlations are identified and separated. Also, in each case, the correlations are reported in descending order based on the absolute size. In this way, the client's attention is drawn first to the positively related variables, and he or she can see the pattern from strong to weak positive correlations. Next, the client's attention is drawn to the negatively associated variables, and, again, he or she can see the pattern from strong to weak negative correlations. If the researcher thinks it appropriate, a third column can be added

Variables Correlated with Subshop Patronage

Variable	Correlation
Variables positively correlated with patronage: *	
I tend to use the same sandwich shop. **	.76
I worry about calories. **	.65
Age	.55
Number of years with present company	.40
Variables negatively correlated with patronage: *	
I "do" lunch at the place closest to my work. **	−.71
Years of education	−.51

*Subshop Patronage (number of times used in past 2 months)

** Based on a 7-point scale where 1 = strongly disagree and 7 = strongly agree

to the table, and the designations of "Strong," "Moderate," "Weak," and so on can be placed beside each correlation according to the rules of thumb strength labels listed in Table 14.3. Alternatively, these designations can be specified as asterisks linking to table footnotes or otherwise noted in the text that describes the findings verbally.

Summary

This chapter dealt with instances in which a marketing researcher seeks to determine if there is a relationship between the responses to one question and the responses to another question in the same survey. Four different types of relationship are possible. First, a nonmonotonic relationship indicates that the presence (or absence) of a label for one nominal variable is systematically associated with the presence (or absence) of a label for another nominal variable. Second, a monotonic relationship indicates the direction of one variable relative to the direction of the other variable. Third, a linear relationship is characterized by a straight-line appearance if the variables are plotted against one other on a graph. Fourth, curvilinear relationship refers to a pattern with a definite curved shape. Associative analyses are used to assess these relationships statistically.

Associations can be characterized by presence, direction, and strength, depending on the scaling assumptions of the questions being compared. With Chi-square analysis, a cross-tabulation table is prepared for two nominal-scaled questions, and the Chi-square statistic is computed to determine whether the observed frequencies (those found in the survey) differ significantly from what would be expected if there were no nonmonotonic relationship between the two. If the null hypothesis of no relationship is rejected, the researcher then looks at the cell percentages to identify the underlying pattern of association.

A correlation coefficient is an index number, constrained to fall between the range of +1.0 to −1.0, that communicates both the strength and the direction of association between two scale variables. The sign indicates the direction of the relationship, and the absolute size indicates the strength of the association. Normally, correlations in excess of ±.8 are considered high. With two questions that are interval and/or ratio in their scaling assumptions (scale variables), the Pearson product moment correlation coefficient is appropriate as the means of determining the underlying linear relationship. A scatter diagram can be used to inspect the pattern.

Key Terms

Associative analyses (p. 351)
Relationship (p. 352)
Nonmonotonic relationship (p. 352)
Monotonic relationships (p. 353)
Linear relationship (p. 353)
Straight-line formula (p. 353)
Curvilinear relationship (p. 354)
Cross-tabulation table (p. 355)
Cross-tabulation cell (p. 356)

Frequencies table (p. 356)
Raw percentages table (p. 356)
Column percentages table (p. 357)
Row percentages table (p. 358)
Chi-square χ^2 analysis (p. 358)
Observed frequencies (p. 358)
Expected frequencies (p. 358)
Chi-square formula (p. 359)
Chi-square distribution (p. 360)

Correlation coefficient (p. 365)
Covariation (p. 366)
Scatter diagram (p. 367)
Pearson product moment correlation (p. 368)
Cause and effect relationship (p. 373)

Review Questions/Applications

1. Explain the distinction between a statistical relationship and a causal relationship.
2. Define and provide an example for each of the following types of relationship: (a) nonmonotonic, (b) monotonic, (c) linear, and (d) curvilinear.
3. Relate the three different aspects of a relationship between two variables.
4. What is a cross-tabulation? Give an example.
5. With respect to Chi-square analysis, describe or identify each of the following: (a) r-by-c table, (b) frequencies table, (c) observed frequencies, (d) expected frequencies, (e) Chi-square distribution, (f) significant association, (g) scaling assumptions, (h) row percentages versus column percentages, and (i) degrees of freedom.
6. What is meant by the term *significant correlation*?
7. Briefly describe the connections among the following: covariation, scatter diagram, correlation, and linear relationship.
8. Indicate, with the use of a scatter diagram, the general shape of the scatter of data points in each of the following cases: (a) a strong positive correlation, (b) a weak negative correlation, (c) no correlation, (d) a correlation of −.98.
9. What are the scaling assumptions assumed by Pearson product moment correlation?
10. Listed below are various factors that may have relationships that are interesting to marketing managers. With each one, (1) identify the type of relationship, (2) indicate its nature or direction, and (3) specify how knowledge of the relationship could help a marketing manager in designing marketing strategy.
    a. Readership of certain sections of the Sunday newspaper and age of the reader for a sporting goods retail store
    b. Ownership of a telephone answering machine and household income for a telemarketing service being used by a public television broadcasting station soliciting funds
    c. Number of miles driven in company cars and need for service such as oil changes, tune-ups, or filter changes for a quick auto service chain attempting to market fleet discounts to companies
    d. Plans to take a five-day vacation to Jamaica and the exchange rate of the Jamaican dollar to that of other countries for Sandals, an all-inclusive resort located in Montego Bay
    e. Amount of do-it-yourself home repairs and declining state of the economy (for example, a recession) for Ace Hardware stores
11. Indicate the presence, nature, and strength of the relationship involving purchases of intermediate size automobiles and each of the following factors: (a) price, (b) fabric versus leather interior, (c) exterior color, and (d) size of rebate.
12. With each of the following examples, compose a reasonable statement of an association you would expect to find existing between the factors involved,

and construct a stacked bar chart expressing that association.

a. Wearing of braces to straighten teeth by children attending expensive private schools versus those attending public schools

b. Having a Doberman pinscher as a guard dog, use of a home security alarm system, and ownership of rare pieces of art

c. Adherence to the "diet pyramid" recommended by the Surgeon General of the United States for healthful living and family history of heart disease

d. Purchases of toys as gifts during the Christmas buying season versus other seasons of the year by parents of preschool-aged children

13. Below is some information about 10 respondents to a survey concerning candy purchasing. Use SPSS to construct the four different types of cross-tabulation tables that are possible. Label each table, and indicate what you perceive to be the general relationship apparent in the data.

Respondent	Buy Plain M&Ms	Buy Peanut M&Ms
1	Yes	No
2	Yes	No
3	No	Yes
4	Yes	No
5	No	No
6	No	Yes
7	No	No
8	Yes	No
9	Yes	No
10	No	Yes

14. Morton O'Dell is the owner of Mort's Diner, which is located in downtown Atlanta, Georgia. Mort's opened up about 12 months ago, and it has experienced success, but Mort is always worried about what food items to order as inventory on a weekly basis. Mort's daughter, Mary, is an engineering student at Georgia Tech, and she offers to help her father. She asks him to provide sales data for the past 10 weeks in terms of total pounds of food bought by customers. With some difficulty, Mort comes up with the following list.

Week	Meat	Fish	Fowl	Vegetables	Desserts
1	100	50	150	195	50
2	91	55	182	200	64
3	82	60	194	209	70
4	75	68	211	215	82
5	66	53	235	225	73
6	53	61	253	234	53
7	64	57	237	230	68
8	76	64	208	221	58
9	94	68	193	229	62
10	105	58	181	214	62

Mary uses these sales figures to construct scatter diagrams that illustrate the basic relationships among the various types of food items purchased at Mort's Diner over the past 10 weeks. She tells her father that the diagrams provide some help in his weekly inventory ordering problem. Construct Mary's scatter diagrams with SPSS to indicate what assistance they are to Mort. Perform the appropriate associated analysis with SPSS and interpret your findings.

CASE 14.1

The Hobbit's Choice Restaurant Survey Associative Analysis

SPSS®

(For necessary background, read Case 12.1 on pages 319–321 and Case 13.1 on pages 349.)

Cory Junior's stomach ailment turns out to be much worse than Cory Rogers expected, so Cory Senior calls to inform Christine Yu, his marketing intern at CMG Research, that it might be several days before he can get back to the office. Cory says to Christine, "I know you might feel a bit lost with The Hobbit's Choice Restaurant project, but why don't you take a look at the proposal and see if there is any further analysis that you can do while I am out. Have Tonya pull the proposal from the file."

As Christine studies the research proposal, she jots down some notes on research questions that need to be addressed. Her notes are below and numbered 1-4.

Your task is to use The Hobbit's Choice Restaurant SPSS dataset and perform the proper analysis. You will also need to interpret the findings.

1. Perform the correct analysis and interpret your findings with regard to The Hobbit's Choice Restaurant menu, décor, and atmosphere for those people who prefer to drive less than 30 minutes to get to the restaurant.

2. Do older or younger people want unusual desserts and/or unusual entrees?

3. Use the variable that distinguishes the "Probable patrons" (likely to patronize Hobbit's Choice responses 1 or 2) for the "Not probable patrons" (likely to patronize Hobbit's Choice responses 3, 4, or 5). If the probable patrons constitute The Hobbit's Choice Restaurant target market, what is the demographic makeup of this target market? Use the demographics of household income, education level, gender, and zip code.

4. Is the *City Magazine* a viable advertising medium for Jeff Dean to use? Apart from this question, are there other viable promotion vehicles that Jeff should know about?

CASE 14.2 INTEGRATED CASE

The Global Motors Survey Associative Analysis

SPSS®

Cory Rogers is very pleased with the way the Global Motors project is shaping up. Celeste Brown, the CMG data analyst, applied differences analysis using the desirability measures for the various alternaive automobile models that might be developed, and she found a unique demographic target market profile for each model. Celeste summarized her findings into a professional PowerPoint presentation that Cory and Celeste presented to Nick Thomas and his assembled managers just yesterday. The presentation was one of the smoothest possible, and Nick's development team members became very excited and animated when they realized that Global Motors had a possibility of five "winner" model vehicles to work with. In fact, at the end of the meeting, Nick decided to go ahead with a preliminary marketing plan for each model.

Nick informed Cory and Celeste that ZEN Motors places a huge amount of emphasis on its communications, investing millions of dollars every year in many different types of advertising to convince prospective customers that its models are the best possible choices. Nick explained, "ZEN does not shotgun its advertising. Everything is based on solid marketing research that reveals the media usage characteristics of each target market. That is why I insisted on including the media usage information in our Global Motors survey. ZEN corporate will most certainly shoot us down if we come to it with any preliminary marketing plan for any proposed automobile model that does not have advertising recommendations based on media usage research. I did not realize at the time that we would be working on all five models, but each of my development teams will need whatever media usage findings you can come up with for its particular model."

Cory and Celeste talk the following day to discuss further analysis for the Global Motors project. Cory says, "I recall that we have a lot of detail on the media habits of the survey respondents. Let's see, it includes favorite television show type, radio genre, magazine type, local newspaper section, and four different types of social marketing media. Nick Thomas called this morning and asked if we could have our findings to him inside of a week, so I guess he and his teams are moving very fast. Nick also told me that he spoke to the ZEN Motors advertising group, and they have strong preferences as to what demographic factors should be used for what media. Nick says that for radio, they prefer to use age; for newspaper and television, they prefer to use education; and for magazines, they prefer to use income. Social media is new to ZEN, so if you could find distinct profiles for these, it would be like icing on the cake."

Celeste says, "Needs it yesterday, so what else is new? Seriously, I can get to it by the end of this week and have it ready to present early next week, assuming no glitches." Cory concludes the meeting with, "Great, just let me know on Friday morning how it is coming, as I told Nick I will call him on that day to set up the presentation."

Your task in this case is to revisit Case 13.2 where you used differences analyses to find the unique demographic profiles for each of the five possible new models.

- 1-seat all-electric
- 4-seat all-electric
- 4-seat gasoline hybrid
- 5-seat diesel hybrid
- 5-seat standard size gasoline

1. Use each unique automobile model demographic profile to determine whether statistically significant associations exist, and if they do, to recommend the specific media vehicles for radio, newspaper, television, and magazines. Use the ZEN Motors advertising division's preferred demographic for each medium.

2. What is the social media profile of each of the possible target markets, and what are the implications of this finding for the placement of advertising messages that would "speak" to this market segment when the automobile model is introduced?

15

Understanding Regression Analysis Basics

LEARNING OBJECTIVES

- To understand the basic concept of prediction
- To learn how marketing researchers use regression analysis
- To learn how marketing researchers use bivariate regression analysis
- To see how multiple regression differs from bivariate regression
- To learn how to obtain and interpret multiple regression analyses with SPSS

"WHERE WE ARE"

1 Establish the need for marketing research.

2 Define the problem.

3 Establish research objectives.

4 Determine research design.

5 Identify information types and sources.

6 Determine methods of accessing data.

7 Design data collection forms.

8 Determine the sample plan and size.

9 Collect data.

10 Analyze data.

11 Prepare and present the final research report.

A Marketing Research Practitioner's Comments on Multiple Regression Analysis

William D. Neal,
Founder and Senior Partner,
SDR Consulting

Marketing research practitioners have two basic missions: describe the current state of the marketplace and predict how the marketplace will react to changes in current product offerings or the introduction of new offerings. Prediction is the more difficult of these two missions simply because so many variables must be measured. Consider the introduction of a new type of yogurt. To predict sales among regular yogurt purchasers, one would need to initially measure awareness of the new offering, consumer importance of differing product attributes (e.g., taste, calories, claimed benefits, package size), relative price, availability, and so forth. Some of these product attributes may be important predictors of sales, and some may not. But it is obvious that it is highly unlikely one single attribute will adequately predict sales. Rather it is most likely it will require a combination of measures to provide an acceptable sales prediction model.

One of the best tools for unraveling this prediction complexity is linear regression. Executed correctly, regression can help you understand whether the variables you have measured can aid in predicting sales (or consideration, or the likelihood of choice). Linear regression is one of the fundamental and most important tools in the researcher's toolbox.

When I first studied regression in graduate school, we were required to do the analysis manually using only a simple hand calculator. That was a great learning experience and taught me how to analyze residuals to understand whether the data was truly linear and whether the data was a good fit to the model I developed. In this age, we have powerful computers and sophisticated software to do all those things. However, since the advent of these new tools, I have also seen too many instances where researchers who lack a deep understanding of regression analysis produce a regression-based model they represented to be a good predictor when it is not, leading to erroneous conclusions. Thus, a note of caution is in order: Test it, test it, and test it again.

Text and Images: By permission, William D. Neal, Founder and Senior Partner, SDR Consulting.

As you can surmise from reading the opening vignette, this chapter takes up the subject of multiple regression analysis. Undoubtedly, your reading of William Neal's description has left you with more questions than answers. For example, what is a residual? Truly linear? Good fit? Your questions should alert you to the fact that we are going to describe a complex analytical technique. We will endeavor to describe regression analysis in a slow and methodical manner, and when we end our description, we will warn you that, while you have learned to run it and interpret its findings, we have barely scratched the surface of this complicated analysis.

Bivariate Linear Regression Analysis

In this chapter, we will deal exclusively with linear regression analysis, a predictive model technique often used by marketing researchers. However, regression analysis is a complex statistical technique with a large number of requirements and nuances.[1] You must understand that this chapter offers only a basic introduction to this area, and as we will warn you toward the end of the material, a great many aspects of regression analysis are beyond the scope of this textbook.

We define **regression analysis** as a predictive analysis technique in which one or more variables are used to predict the level of another by use of the straight-line formula. **Bivariate regression** means only two variables are being analyzed, and researchers sometimes refer to this case as *simple regression*. We will review the equation for a straight line and introduce basic terms used in regression. We also describe some basic computations and significance with bivariate regression.

With bivariate regression, one variable is used to predict another variable using the straight-line formula.

A straight-line relationship underlies regression, and it is a powerful predictive model. Figure 15.1 illustrates a straight-line relationship, and you should refer to it as we describe the elements in a general straight-line formula. The formula for a straight line is:

Formula for a straight-line relationship $y = a + bx$

where

  y = the predicted variable

  x = the variable used to predict y

  a = the **intercept**, or point where the line cuts the y axis when $x = 0$

  b = the **slope**, or the change in y for any 1 unit change in x

Photo: Eisenhans/Fotolia

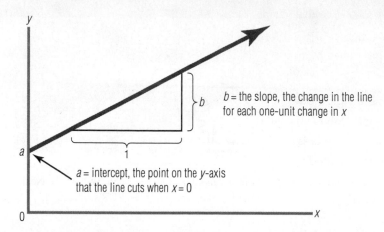

FIGURE 15.1
General Equation for a Straight Line in Graph Form

The straight-line equation is the basis of regression analysis.

Regression is directly related to correlation by the underlying straight-line relationship.

In regression, the independent variable is used to predict the dependent variable.

You should recall the straight-line relationship we described underlying the correlation coefficient: When the scatter diagram for two variables appears as a thin ellipse, there is a high correlation between them. Regression is directly related to correlation.

BASIC CONCEPTS IN REGRESSION ANALYSIS

We now define the variables and show how the intercept and slope are computed.

Independent and Dependent Variables As we indicated, bivariate regression analysis is a case in which only two variables are involved in the predictive model. When we use only two variables, one is termed dependent and the other is termed independent. The **dependent variable** is that which is predicted, and it is customarily termed y in the regression straight-line equation. The **independent variable** is that which is used to predict the dependent variable, and it is the x in the regression formula. We must quickly point out that the terms *dependent* and *independent* are arbitrary designations and are customary to regression analysis. There is no cause-and-effect relationship or true dependence between the dependent and the independent variable. It is strictly a statistical relationship, not causal, that may be found between these two variables.

Computing the Slope and the Intercept To compute a (intercept) and b (slope), you must work with a number of observations of the various levels of the dependent variable paired with different levels of the independent variable, identical to the scatter diagrams we illustrated previously when we were demonstrating how to perform correlation analysis.

The formulas for calculating the slope (b) and the intercept (a) are rather complicated, but some instructors are in favor of their students learning these formulas, so we have included them in Marketing Research Insight 15.1.

When SPSS or any other statistical analysis program computes the intercept and the slope in a regression analysis, it does so on the basis of the least squares criterion. The **least squares criterion** is a way of guaranteeing that the straight line that runs through the points on the scatter diagram is positioned to minimize the vertical distances away from the line of the various points. In other words, if you draw a line where the regression line is calculated and calculate the distances of all the points away from that line (called *residuals*), it would be impossible to draw any other line that would result in a lower sum of all of those distances. The least squares criterion guarantees that the line is the one with the lowest total squared residuals. Each residual is squared to avoid a cancellation effect of positive and negative residuals.

The least squares criterion used in regression analysis guarantees that the "best" straight-line slope and intercept will be calculated.

HOW TO IMPROVE A REGRESSION ANALYSIS FINDING

When a researcher would wants to improve a regression analysis, the researcher can use a scatter diagram to identify outlier pairs of points. An **outlier**[2] is a data point that is substantially outside the normal range of the data points being analyzed. As one author has noted, outliers "stick out like sore thumbs."[3] When using a scatter diagram to identify outliers,[4] the researcher draws an ellipse that encompasses most of the points that appear to be in an elliptical pattern.[5] He or she then eliminates outliers from the data and reruns the regression analysis. Generally, this approach will improve the regression analysis results.

Marketing Research on YouTube™ To learn about linear regression, launch **www.youtube.com**, and search for "Intro to Linear Regression."

How to Calculate the Intercept and Slope of a Bivariate Regression

In this example, we are using the Novartis pharmaceuticals company sales territory and number of salespersons data found in Table 15.1. Intermediate regression calculations are included in Table 15.2.

TABLE 15.1   Bivariate Regression Analysis Data and Intermediate Calculations

Territory (*I*)	Sales ($ millions) (*y*)	Number of Salespersons (*x*)	*xy*	x^2
1	102	7	714	49
2	125	5	625	25
3	150	9	1,350	81
4	155	9	1,395	81
5	160	9	1,440	81
6	168	8	1,344	64
7	180	10	1,800	100
8	220	10	2,200	100
9	210	12	2,520	144
10	205	12	2,460	144
11	230	12	2,760	144
12	255	15	3,825	225
13	250	14	3,500	196
14	260	15	3,900	225
15	250	16	4,320	256
16	275	16	4,400	256
17	280	17	4,760	289
18	240	18	4,320	324
19	300	18	5,400	324
20	310	19	5,890	361
Sums	**4,325**	**251**	**58,603**	**3,469**
	(Average = 216.25)	(Average = 12.55)		

The formula for computing the regression parameter *b* is:

Formula for *b*, the slope, in bivariate regression

$$b = \frac{n \sum_{i=1}^{n} x_i y_i - \left(\sum_{i=1}^{n} x_i \right)\left(\sum_{i=1}^{n} y_i \right)}{n \sum_{i=1}^{n} x_i^2 - \left(\sum_{i=1}^{n} x_i \right)^2}$$

where

x_i = an *x* variable value
y_i = a *y* value paired with each x_i value
n = the number of pairs

The calculations for b, the slope, are as follows:

Calculation of b, the slope, in bivariate regression using Novartis sales territory data

$$b = \frac{n\sum_{i=1}^{n} x_i y_i - \left(\sum_{i=1}^{n} x_i\right)\left(\sum_{i=1}^{n} y_i\right)}{n\sum_{i=1}^{n} x_i^2 - \left(\sum_{i=1}^{n} x_i\right)^2}$$

$$= \frac{20 \times 58603 - 251 \times 4325}{20 \times 3469 - 251^2}$$

$$= \frac{1172060 - 1085575}{69380 - 63001}$$

$$= \frac{86485}{6379}$$

$$= 13.56$$

Notes:

$n = 20$
Sum $xy = 58603$
Sum of $x = 251$
Sum of $y = 4325$
Sum of $x^2 = 3469$

The formula for computing the intercept is:

Formula for a, the intercept, in bivariate regression

$$a = \bar{y} - b\bar{x}$$

The computations for a, the intercept, are as follows:

Calculation of a, the intercept, in bivariate regression using Novartis sales territory data

$$a = \bar{y} - b\bar{x}$$

$$= 216.25 - 13.56 \times 12.55$$

$$= 216.25 - 170.178$$

$$= 46.07$$

Notes:

$\bar{y} = 216.25$
$\bar{x} = 12.55$

In other words, the bivariate regression equation has been found to be:

Novartis sales regression equation

$$y = 46.07 + 13.56x$$

The interpretation of this equation is as follows. Annual sales in the average Novartis sales territory are $46.07 million, and sales increase $13.56 million annually with each additional salesperson.

Multiple Regression Analysis

We follow up our introduction to bivariate regression analysis by discussing multiple regression analysis. You will find that all of the concepts in bivariate regression apply to multiple regression analysis, except you will be working with multiple independent variables.

AN UNDERLYING CONCEPTUAL MODEL

A *model* as a structure that ties together various constructs and their relationships. It is beneficial for the marketing manager and the market researcher to have some sort of model in mind when designing the research plan. The bivariate regression equation is a model that ties together an independent variable and its dependent variable. The dependent variables that interest market researchers are typically sales, potential sales, or some attitude held by those who make up the market. For example, in the Novartis example, the dependent variable was territory sales. If Dell Computers commissioned a survey, it might want information on those who intend to purchase a Dell computer, or it might want information on those who intend to buy a competing brand as a means of understanding these consumers and perhaps dissuading them. The dependent variable would be purchase intentions for Dell computers. If Maxwell House Coffee were considering a brand of gourmet iced coffee, it would want to know how coffee drinkers feel about gourmet iced coffee; attitudes toward buying, preparing, and drinking iced coffee would be the dependent variable.

There is an underlying general conceptual model in multiple regression analysis.

Figure 15.2 provides a general conceptual model that fits many marketing research situations, particularly those that are investigating consumer behavior. A **general conceptual model** identifies independent and dependent variables and shows their expected basic relationships to one another. In Figure 15.2, you can see that purchases, intentions to purchase, and preferences are in the center, meaning they are dependent. The surrounding concepts are possible independent variables. That is, any one could be used to predict any dependent variable. For example, one's intentions to purchase an expensive automobile like a Lexus could depend on one's income. It could also depend on the friends' recommendations (word of mouth), one's opinions about how a Lexus would enhance one's self-image, or experiences riding in or driving a Lexus.

In truth, consumers' preferences, intentions, and actions are potentially influenced by a great number of factors as would be evident if you listed all of the subconcepts that make up each concept in Figure 15.2. For example, there are probably a dozen demographic variables; there could be dozens of lifestyle dimensions, and a person is exposed to a great many types of advertising media every day. Of course, in the problem definition stage, the researcher and manager reduce the myriad of independent variables down to a manageable number to be included on the questionnaire. That is, they have the general model structure in Figure 15.2 in mind, but they identify and measure specific variables that pertain to the problem at hand. Because bivariate regression analysis treats only one dependent–independent pair, it would take a great many bivariate regression analyses to account for all possible relevant dependent–independent pairs of variables in a general model such as Figure 15.2. Fortunately, there is no need to perform a great many bivariate regressions, as *multiple regression analysis* is a much better tool, and a technique we are about to describe in some detail.

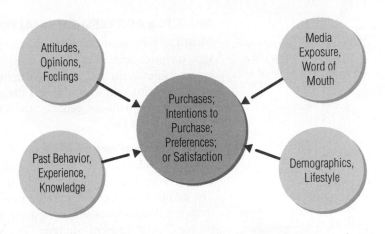

FIGURE 15.2 A General Conceptual Model for Multiple Regression Analysis

The researcher and manager identify, measure, and analyze specific variables that pertain to the general conceptual model in mind.

 Active Learning

The General Conceptual Model for Global Motors

Understandably, Nick Thomas, CEO of Global Motors, a new division of a large automobile manufacturer, ZEN Motors, wants everyone to intend to purchase a new gasoline alternative technology automobile; however, this will not be the case due to different beliefs and predispositions in the driving public. Regression analysis will assist Nick by revealing what variables are good predictors of intentions to buy the various new technology automobile models under consideration at Global Motors. What is the general conceptual model apparent in the Global Motors survey dataset?

In order to answer this question and to portray the general conceptual model in the format of Figure 15.2, you must inspect the several variables in this SPSS dataset or otherwise come up with a list of the variables in the survey. Using any "Desirability" variable as the dependent variable, diagram the general types of independent or predictor variables that are apparent in this study. Comment on the usefulness of this general conceptual model to Nick Thomas; that is, assuming that the regression results are significant, what marketing strategy implications will become apparent?

MULTIPLE REGRESSION ANALYSIS DESCRIBED

Multiple regression means you have more than one independent variable to predict a single dependent variable.

Multiple regression analysis is an expansion of bivariate regression analysis in that more than one independent variable is used in the regression equation. The addition of independent variables complicates the conceptualization by adding more dimensions or axes to the regression situation. But it makes the regression model more realistic because, as we have just explained with our general model discussion, predictions normally depend on multiple factors, not just one.

With multiple regression, you work with a regression plane rather than a line.

Basic Assumptions in Multiple Regression Consider our Novartis example with the number of salespeople as the independent variable and territory sales as the dependent variable. A second independent variable, such as advertising levels, can be added to the equation. The addition of a second variable turns the regression line into a regression plane because there are three dimensions if we were to try to graph it: territory sales (Y), number of sales people (X_1), and advertising level (X_2). A **regression plane** is the shape of the dependent variable in multiple regression analysis. If other independent variables are added to the regression analysis, it would be necessary to envision each one as a new and separate axis existing at right angles to all other axes. Obviously, it is impossible to draw more than three dimensions at right angles. In fact, it is difficult to even conceive of a multiple dimension diagram, but the assumptions of multiple regression analysis require this conceptualization.

Everything about multiple regression is largely equivalent to bivariate regression except you are working with more than one independent variable. The terminology is slightly different in places, and some statistics are modified to take into account the multiple aspect, but for the most part, concepts in multiple regression are analogous to those in the simple bivariate case. We note these similarities in our description of multiple regression.

The equation in multiple regression has the following form:

A multiple regression equation has two or more independent variables (x's).

Multiple regression equation $\quad y = a + b_1x_1 + b_2x_2 + b_3x_3 + \cdots + b_mx_m$

Where

y = the dependent, or predicted, variable

x_i = independent variable i

a = the intercept

b_i = the slope for independent variable i

m = the number of independent variables in the equation

As you can see, the addition of other independent variables has done nothing more than to add b_ix_i's to the equation. We have retained the basic $y = a + bx$ straight-line formula, except now we have multiple x variables, and each one is added to the equation, changing y by its individual slope. The inclusion of each independent variable in this manner preserves the straight-line assumptions of multiple regression analysis. This is sometimes known as **additivity** because each new independent variable is added to the regression equation.

Let's look at a multiple regression analysis result so you can better understand the multiple regression equation. Here is a possible result using our Lexus example:

Lexus purchase intention multiple regression equation example

Intention to purchase a Lexus = 2
+ 1.0 × attitude toward Lexus (1–5 scale)
− .5 × attitude toward current auto (1–5 scale)
+ 1.0 × income level (1–10 scale)

Notes:
$a = 2$
$b_1 = 1.0$
$b_2 = -.5$
$b_3 = 1.0$

This multiple regression equation says that you can predict a consumer's intention to buy a Lexus level if you know three variables: (1) attitude toward the Lexus brand, (2) attitude toward the automobile he/she owns now, and (3) income level using a scale with 10 income levels. Further, we can see the impact of each of these variables on Lexus purchase intentions. Here is how to interpret the equation. First, the average person has a 2 intention level, or some small propensity to want to buy a Lexus. Attitude toward Lexus is measured on a 1–5 scale; with each attitude scale point, intention goes up one point. That is, an individual with a strong positive attitude of 5 will have a greater intention than one with a strong negative attitude of 1. With attitude toward the current automobile he/she owns (for example, a potential Lexus buyer may currently own a Cadillac or a BMW), the intention *decreases* by .5 for each level on the 5-point scale. Of course we are assuming that these potential buyers own automobile makes other than a Lexus. Finally, the intention increases by 1 with each increasing income level.

Here is a numerical example for a potential Lexus buyer whose Lexus attitude is 4, current automobile make attitude is 3, and income is 5:

Calculation of Lexus purchase intention using the multiple regression equation

Intention to purchase a Lexus $= 2$
$+ 1.0 \times 4$
$- .5 \times 3$
$+ 1.0 \times 5$
$= 9.5$

Notes:
Intercept $= 2$
Attitude toward Lexus $(x_1) = 4$
Attitude toward current auto $(x_2) = 3$
Income level $(x_3) = 5$

Multiple regression is a powerful tool, because it tells us what factors are related to the dependent variable, how (the sign) each factor influences the dependent variable, and how much (the size of b_i) each factor influences it.

While you have yet not learned how to run multiple regression analysis on SPSS, you have sufficient knowledge to realize that this analysis can provide interesting insights into consumer behavior. Marketing Research Insight 15.2 presents an application of multiple regression analysis in the social media marketing research arena.

As with bivariate regression analysis in which we alluded to the correlation between y and x, it is possible to inspect the strength of the linear relationship between the independent variables and the dependent variable with multiple regression. Multiple R, also called the **coefficient of determination**, is a handy measure of the strength of the overall linear relationship. As with bivariate regression analysis, the multiple regression analysis model assumes that a straight-line (plane) relationship exists among the variables. Multiple R ranges from 0 to +1.0 and represents the amount of the dependent variable "explained," or accounted for, by the combined independent variables. High multiple R values indicate that the regression plane applies well to the scatter of points, whereas low values signal that the straight-line model does not apply well. At the same time, a multiple regression result is an estimate of the population multiple regression equation, and, as was the case with other estimated population parameters, it is necessary to test for statistical significance.

> Multiple R indicates how well the independent variables can predict the dependent variable in multiple regression.

Multiple R is like a lead indicator of the multiple regression analysis findings. As you will see soon, it is one of the first pieces of information provided in a multiple regression output. Many researchers mentally convert the multiple R value into a percentage. For example a multiple R of .75 means that the regression findings will explain 75% of the dependent variable. The greater the explanatory power of the multiple regression finding, the better and more useful it is for the researcher.

Before we show you how to run a multiple regression analysis using SPSS, consider this caution: The **independence assumption** stipulates that the independent variables must be statistically independent and uncorrelated with one another. The independence assumption is crucial because if it is violated, the multiple regression findings are untrue. The presence of moderate or stronger correlations among the independent variables is termed **multicollinearity**, which will violate the independence assumption of multiple regression analysis results when it occurs.[6] It is up to the researcher to test for and remove multicollinearity if it is present.

> With multiple regression, the independent variables should have low correlations with one another.

MARKETING RESEARCH INSIGHT 15.2   *Social Media Marketing*

Multiple Regression Analysis Gives Insights into Students' Use of Twitter and Facebook

Two researchers recently took note of the widespread adoption of Twitter and Facebook by university students.[7] They pondered the possible factors and reasons why these two social media tools are so popular. Using adoptions of innovations theory, they identified several independent variables that might be related to the use of one or both vehicles. Drawing samples of undergraduate students from both a large Midwest university and a large Southeastern university, they used an online survey to obtain information about some demographic variables (such as gender), several behavioral variables (such as amount of mobile phone usage), and a number of other variables (such as popularity or degree to which friends use Twitter/Facebook).

The researchers then used multiple regression analysis with these items treated as independent variables, and the degree of use of Twitter/Facebook as the dependent variables. As reported by the researchers, the statistically significant independent variables for amount of use of Twitter and Facebook are summarized in the following table by "Yes." A "No" means that no statistically significant relationship was found.

Variable	Twitter Use	Facebook Use
Amount of mobile phone usage	*Yes*	*No*
How long used account	*No*	*Yes*
Friends expect me to use	*Yes*	*Yes*
Attitude toward Twitter/Facebook	*Yes*	*No*
To pass the time	*No*	*Yes*
Substitute for face-to-face	*Yes*	*No*
My friends use it	*No*	*Yes*

The findings reveal that university students use Twitter if: (1) they are heavy mobile users, (2) they believe their friends expect to tweet, (3) they have a positive attitude toward Twitter, and (4) they prefer to use Twitter in place of face-to-face meetings with their friends. On the other hand, university students use Facebook if: (1) they are established users of Facebook, (2) they have a positive attitude toward Facebook, (3) they are bored and want to do something to pass the time, and (4) many of their friends use it. It is interesting to note that gender and age were not found to be significantly related to either the use of Twitter or Facebook.

Multicollinearity can be assessed and eliminated in multiple regression with the VIF statistic.

The way to avoid multicollinearity is to use warning statistics issued by most statistical analysis programs to identify this problem. One commonly used method is the **variance inflation factor (VIF)**. The VIF is a single number, and a rule of thumb is that as long as the VIF is less than 10, multicollinearity is not a concern. With a VIF of greater than 10 associated with any independent variable in the multiple regression equation, it is prudent to remove that variable from consideration or to otherwise reconstitute the set of independent variables.[8] In other words, when examining the output of any multiple regression, the researcher should inspect the VIF number associated with each independent variable that is retained in the final multiple regression equation by the procedure. If the VIF is greater than 10, the researcher should remove that variable from the independent variable set and rerun the multiple regression.[9] This iterative process is used until only independent variables that are statistically significant and that have acceptable VIFs are in the final multiple regression equation.

INTEGRATED CASE

Global Motors: How to Run and Interpret Multiple Regression Analysis on SPSS

Running multiple regression first requires specification of the dependent and independent variables. Let's select the desirability of the standard size gasoline automobile model as the dependent variable, and think about a general conceptual model that might pertain to Global Motors. We already know from basic marketing strategy that demographics are often used for target marketing, and we have hometown size, age, income, education, and household size. Also, beliefs are often useful for predicting market segments, and we have some variables that pertain to beliefs about the gasoline emissions and global warming. To summarize, we have determined our conceptual model: the desirability of a standard-size gasoline automobile related to (1) household demographics and (2) beliefs about global warming. Where appropriate, we have recoded the ordinal demographic variables with midpoints to convert them to ratio scales.

The ANALYZE-REGRESSION-LINEAR command sequence is used to run a multiple regression analysis, and the variable, Desirability: standard size gasoline model, is selected as the dependent variable, while the other nine are specified as the independent variables. You will find this annotated SPSS clickstream in Figure 15.3.

As the computer output in Figure 15.4 shows, the multiple R value (Adjusted R Square in the Model Summary table) indicating the strength of relationship between the independent variables and the dependent variable is .235, signifying that there is some linear relationship present. Next, the printout reveals that the ANOVA F is significant, signaling that the null hypothesis of no linear relationship is rejected, and it is justifiable to use a straight-line relationship to model the variables in this case.

It is necessary in multiple regression analysis to test for statistical significance of the b_i (beta) determined for the each independent variable. In other words, you must determine whether sampling error is influencing the results and giving a false reading. One must test for significance from zero (the null hypothesis) through the use of separate t tests for each b_i. The SPSS output in Figure 15.4 indicates the levels of statistical significance in the Coefficients table in the column labeled "Sig."; we have highlighted in yellow the cases where the significance level is .05 or less (95% level of confidence). It is apparent that size of hometown, gender, number of people in the household, age, income, and the two attitude variables are statistically significant. The other independent variables fail this test, meaning that their computed betas must be treated as zeros. No VIF value is greater than 10, so multicollinearity is not a concern here.

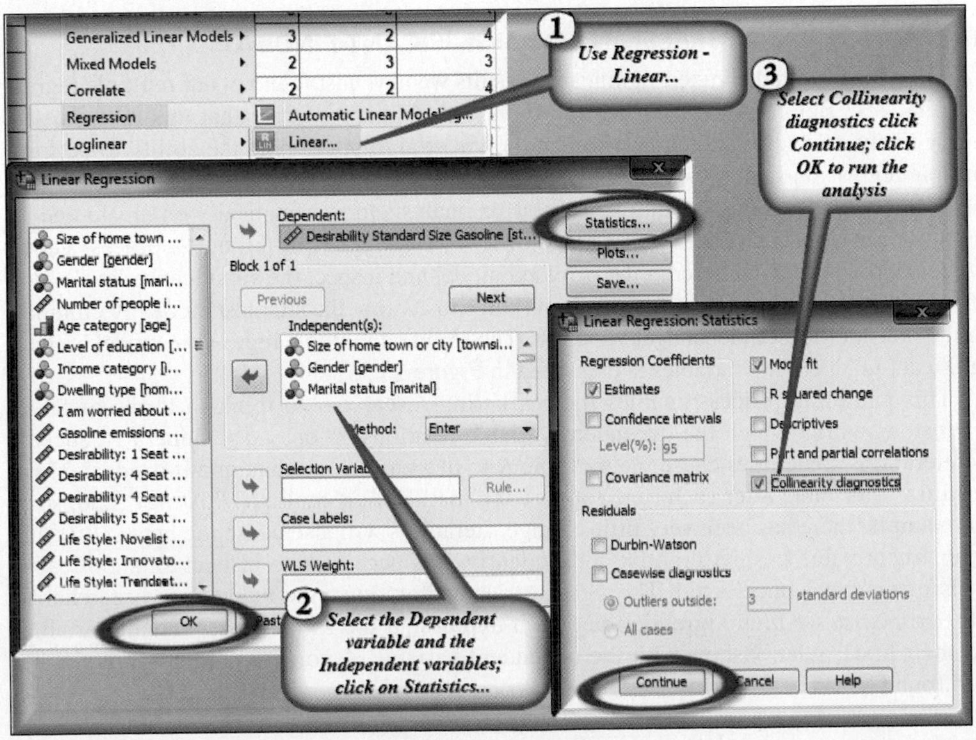

The SPSS ANALYZE-REGRESSION-LINEAR command is used to run multiple regression.

With multiple regression, look at the significance level of each calculated beta.

FIGURE 15.3 SPSS Clickstream for Multiple Regression Analysis

Source: Reprint courtesy of International Business Machines Corporation, © SPSS, Inc., an IBM Company.

FIGURE 15.4 SPSS Output for Multiple Regression Analysis

Source: Reprint courtesy of International Business Machines Corporation, © SPSS, Inc., an IBM Company.

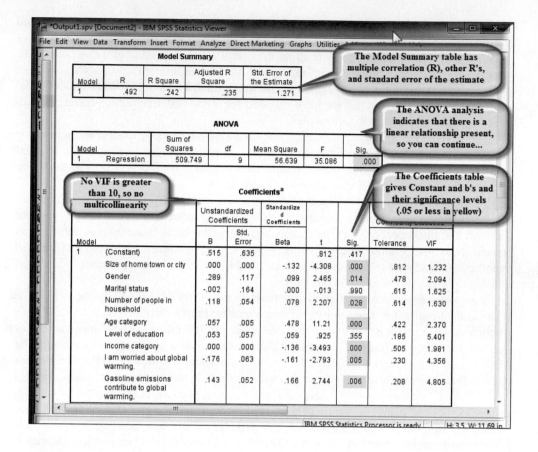

"TRIMMING" THE REGRESSION FOR SIGNIFICANT FINDINGS

What do you do with the mixed significance results we have just found in our multiple regression analysis? Before we answer this question, you should be aware that this mixed result is very likely, so understanding how to handle it is vital to developing the ability to perform multiple regression analysis successfully.

A trimmed regression means that you eliminate the nonsignificant independent variables and rerun the regression.

It is standard practice in multiple regression analysis to systematically eliminate one by one those independent variables that are shown to be insignificant through a process called *trimming*. You successively rerun the trimmed model and inspect the significance levels each time. This series of eliminations or iterations helps to achieve the simplest model by eliminating the nonsignificant independent variables. The trimmed multiple regression model with all significant independent variables is presented in Figure 15.5.

Run trimmed regressions iteratively until all betas are significant.

This trimming process enables the marketing researcher to think in terms of fewer dimensions within which the dependent variable relationship operates. Generally, successive iterations sometimes cause the multiple *R* to decrease somewhat, and it is advisable to scrutinize this value after each run. You can see that the new multiple *R* is now .236, so in our example, there has been very little change. Iterations will also cause the beta values and the intercept value to shift slightly; consequently, it is necessary to inspect all significance levels of the betas once again. Through a series of iterations, the marketing researcher finally arrives at the final regression equation expressing the salient independent variables and their linear relationships with the dependent variable. A concise predictive model has been found.

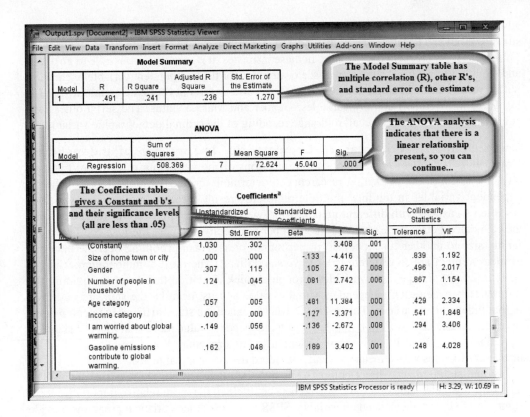

FIGURE 15.5 SPSS Output for Trimmed Multiple Regression Analysis

Source: Reprint courtesy of International Business Machines Corporation, © SPSS, Inc., an IBM Company.

SPSS®

SPSS Student Assistant: Running and Interpreting Multiple Regression

SPECIAL USES OF MULTIPLE REGRESSION ANALYSIS

We will return to our findings in Figure 15.5 shortly, but first we need to describe some special uses and considerations to keep in mind when running multiple regression analysis. These include using a "dummy" independent variable, examining standardized betas to compare the importance of independent variables, and using multiple regression as a screening device.

Using a "Dummy" Independent Variable A **dummy independent variable** is defined as one that is scaled with a nominal 0-versus-1 coding scheme. The 0-versus-1 code is traditional, but any two adjacent numbers might be used such as 1-versus-2. The scaling assumptions that normally underlie multiple regression analysis require that the independent and dependent variables be at least interval scaled. However, there are instances in which a marketing researcher may want to use an independent variable that does not embody interval-scaling assumptions. It is not unusual, for instance, for the marketing researcher to wish to use a dichotomous or two-level nominal variable as an independent variable in a multiple regression analysis. Some commonly used dummy variables are: gender (males versus female), purchasing (buyer versus nonbuyer),

Gender can be used as a dummy variable in multiple regression analysis.

Photo: Jakrit Jiraratwaro/Shutterstock

The interval-at-minimum scaling assumption requirement of multiple regression may be relaxed by use of a dummy variable.

advertising exposure (recalled versus not recalled), or purchase history (first-time buyer versus repeat buyer). For instance, with gender, a researcher may want to use a 0 for male and 1 for female as an independent variable. In these instances, it is usually permissible to go ahead and slightly violate the assumption of scale variables for the independent variable to come up with a result that is in some degree interpretable. In our Global Motors multiple regression example, we used two dummy variables: Gender and Marital status. The seven other variables were scale variables (recall midrange recoding of the ordinal demographic variables).

Using Standardized Betas to Compare the Importance of Independent Variables

Regardless of the application intentions of the marketing researcher, it is usually of interest to the marketing researcher to determine the relative importance of the independent variables in the final multiple regression result. Because independent variables are often measured with different units, it is erroneous to make direct comparisons between the calculated betas. For example, it is improper to directly compare the beta coefficient for family size to another for money spent per month on personal grooming because the units of measurement are so different (people versus dollars). The most common approach is to standardize the independent variables through a quick operation that involves dividing the difference between each independent variable value and its mean by the standard deviation of that independent variable. This results in what is called the **standardized beta coefficient**. In other words, standardization translates each independent value into the number of standard deviations away from its own mean. Essentially, this procedure transforms these variables into a set of values with a mean of 0 and a standard deviation equal to 1.0.

The researcher can compare standardized beta coefficients' sizes directly, but comparing nonstandardized betas is like comparing apples and oranges.

When standardized, direct comparisons may be made among the resulting betas. The larger the absolute value of a standardized beta coefficient, the more relative importance it assumes in predicting the dependent variable. SPSS and most other statistical programs provide the standardized betas automatically. In Figure 15.5, we have highlighted the standardized betas with light blue, and we will discuss how to interpret them shortly. To further your exposure to standardized beta coefficients, read Marketing Research Insight 15.3.

Using Multiple Regression as a Screening Device

A final important application of multiple regression analysis is as an identifying or **screening device**. That is, the marketing researcher may be faced with a large number and variety of prospective independent variables in his or her general conceptual model, and he or she may use multiple regression as a way of spotting the salient (statistically significant) independent variables for the dependent variable at hand. In this instance, the intent is *not* to determine some sort of a prediction of the dependent variable; rather, it may be to search for clues as to what factors help the researcher understand the behavior of this particular dependent variable. For instance, the researcher might be seeking market segmentation bases and could use regression to spot which demographic variables are related to the consumer behavior variable under study. For example, if the true purpose is to identify segments of the car-buying public that are more likely to purchase various vehicle models in the future, then this goal is usually well served when multiple regression is used as a screening device to identify the salient segmentation factors. Marketing Research Insight 15.4 illustrates the use of multiple regression analysis as a screening device.

Used as a screen device, multiple regression analysis identifies independent variables that do not qualify to be part of the final equation.

Photo silver-john Shutterstock

Interpreting the Findings of Multiple Regression Analysis

By now, you probably realize that our Global Motors multiple regression analysis example is the use of multiple regression analysis to identify the significant demographic and/or attitudinal independent variables.

MARKETING RESEARCH INSIGHT 15.3   *Global Application*

Standardized Betas Reveal Reasons Why Thai Customers Are Satisfied with Their Mobile Phone Service

In Thailand, it has been noted that the penetration of mobile phones is almost 100%, accounting for 63 million mobile phone subscribers. Three mobile phone companies account for almost all subscribers, and because the market is in its maturity, these companies strive to maintain their respective market shares by emphasizing customer satisfaction, which begets loyalty to the company. Researchers[10] consulted prior customer satisfaction studies and identified eight factors that have been found to variously contribute to customer satisfaction in other industries. These factors are: quality of service, promotions by the company, innovativeness of the company, social status of the company brand, customer service quality, call center quality,

emotional value or the customer's enjoyment and happiness of using the network, and company image with respect to fairness, reliability, adaptability, and responsibility to society.

A total of 400 Thai mobile phone users who represented all of the major Thai mobile phone companies were interviewed and asked to respond to scales measuring overall satisfaction with their mobile phone company and its performance of each of the eight factors. The researchers applied multiple regression analysis using overall satisfaction as the dependent variable and the eight other measures as independent variables. The findings, including the standardized beta coefficients, are displayed below.

Independent Variable	Beta	Standardized Beta	Significant?
Quality of service	.145	.139	*Yes*
Promotions by the company	.153	.158	*Yes*
Innovativeness of the company	.055	.060	*No*
Social status of the company brand	−.013	−.015	*No*
Customer service quality	.150	.155	*Yes*
Call center quality	.112	.129	*Yes*
Emotional value or the customer's enjoyment and happiness of using the network	.117	.114	*Yes*
Company image with respect to fairness, reliability, adaptability, and responsibility to society	.168	.150	*Yes*

Source: Based on Table 2 from "Factors that Impact Customer Satisfaction: Evidence from the Thailand Mobile Cellular Network Industry" by Orose Leelakulthanit and Boonchai Hongcharu, from *International Journal of Management & Marketing Research*, 2011, Volume 4(2). The Institute for Business & Finance Research.

Of the six statistically significant independent variables, three have standard betas in the .150+ range. Namely, promotions by the company, customer service quality, and company image are the most important performance facets of a Thai mobile phone company with respect to "driving" overall customer satisfaction. Service quality falls closely behind these three aspects, with call center quality just a step behind.

How does one interpret these findings? The top three facets are the most important, so in order to be competitive, a

Thai mobile phone company absolutely must endeavor to be at the top if its game with each one. Service quality and call center quality are also important, although the company might relax just a tiny bit in its demands for employee excellence on these two dimensions. The remaining statistically significant performance dimensions are not unimportant, but the company should prioritize improving them somewhat less than improving the five top facets according to the standardized beta coefficients.

That is, it was used as a screening device. Now, let's look at the standardized beta values (blue highlight in Figure 15.5) to interpret our findings. Interpretation is facilitated by the relative sizes of the standardized beta and their signs. A positive value means that there is a positive relationship, so people who are desirous of the standard-size gasoline automobile model are males (dummy coded with 0 = female and 1 = male), have more people in their households, are older, and tend to believe that gasoline emissions contribute to global warming. A negative sign means that there is a negative relationship, so desire for the standard-size gasoline automobile model tends to be higher for individuals living in smaller hometowns, with lower income, and

Standardized betas indicate the relative importance of alternative predictor variables.

MARKETING RESEARCH INSIGHT 15.4 *Practical Application*

Using Multiple Regression Analysis as a Screening Device Simplifies Marketing Competition in the Optical Centers Industry

According to the Vision Council of America, about 75% of adults use some sort of vision correction. Not all, but a great many of these individuals use optical or vision centers for eye testing, diagnoses, and purchases. Eyeglass purchasing is a unique phenomenon. Often vision is directly affected by age. That is, young people with 20/20 vision almost invariably experience deterioration in vision, normally farsightedness, as they age. It is quite common for individuals in their 40s and 50s to realize that reading regular-sized print becomes difficult, so they turn to optical centers or other eye testing alternatives for diagnosis and prescriptions for reading glasses. However, the decision to wear eyeglasses or contact lens is subject to a number of considerations. For instance, there are social influence factors, such as the advice of opinion leaders, family members, coworkers, or other acquaintances. There are psychological factors, such as motivations, perceptions, and self-concept. Last, there are individual differences, such as gender or financial well-being.

Researchers[11] listed 13 possible competitive factors that might affect a consumer's decision to adopt eyeglasses and used multiple regression analysis to determine which ones were significantly related to the age-related eyeglass purchase decision. These factors included:

- Design of the frame
- Lens brand
- Price
- Weight of the frame
- Warranty
- Treatment of the lens (such as scratch-resistance, etc.)
- Materials making up the lens (glass, plastic, etc.)
- Lens type (such as polarized, bifocals, etc.)
- Lens accessories
- Purchase promotion
- Eye exam
- Point-of-sale service
- Advertising

Due to the several independent variables identified, the researchers used multiple regression analysis as a screening device to identify the statistically significant ones. Three variables were found to be significant at the 95% level of confidence, while a fourth was significant at the 90% level of confidence. To be more precise, price, warranty, and advertising comprise the first three statistically significant independent variables, and point-of-sale service was the fourth. Interestingly, advertising was found to have a negative beta coefficient, whereas the other three exhibited positive relationships.

Interpretation of these findings gives marketing strategy recommendations for optical centers: (1) offer competitive prices, (2) incorporate attractive warranties, (3) ensure that point-of-sale purchase employees and systems are top-notch, and (4) do not engage in advertising battles with other optical centers.

with people who are less worried about global warming. Because it has the highest absolute standardized beta (.418), age is the most important variable in identifying people desiring the standard-size gasoline model, and belief that gasoline emissions contribute to global warming falls into second place. When you examine the standardized betas and take into consideration their relative sizes and signs, you can develop a mental market segment picture of the kind of individual who would be the target market if Global Motors develops a standard-size gasoline automobile model. You can also begin to understand these consumers' desires for a gasoline-powered automobile: They are not worried about global warming.

 Active Learning

Segmentation Associates, Inc.

Segmentation Associates, Inc., is a marketing research company that specializes in market segmentation studies. It has access to large and detailed databases on demographics, lifestyles, asset ownership, consumer values, and a number of other consumer descriptors. It has developed a reputation for reducing these large databases into findings that are managerially relevant to its clients. That is, Segmentation Associates is known for its ability to translate its findings into market segmentation variables for clients to use in their marketing strategies.

In the past year, Segmentation Associates has conducted a great many market segmentation studies for automobile manufacturers. The company has agreed to provide disguised findings of some of its work. In the following table, segmentation variables are identified, and each of three different types of automobile buyer types is identified. For each segmentation variable, Segmentation Associates has provided the results of its multiple regression findings. The values are the standardized beta coefficients of those segmentation variables found to be statistically significant. Where "—" appears, that regression coefficient was not statically significant.

Segmentation Variable	Economy Automobile Buyer	Sports Car Buyer	Luxury Automobile Buyer
Demographics			
Age	−.28	−.15	+.59
Education	−.12	+.38	—
Family Size	+.39	−.35	—
Income	−.15	+.25	+.68
Lifestyle/Values			
Active	—	+.59	−.39
American Pride	+.30	—	+.24
Bargain Hunter	+.45	−.33	—
Conservative	—	−.38	+.54
Cosmopolitan	−.40	+.68	—
Embraces Change	−.30	+.65	—
Family Values	+.69	—	+.21
Financially Secure	−.28	+.21	+.52
Optimistic	—	+.71	+.37

Here are some questions to answer.

1. What is the underlying conceptual model used by Segmentation Associates that is apparent in these three sets of findings?
2. What are the segmentation variables that distinguish economy automobile buyers and in what ways?
3. What are the segmentation variables that distinguish sports car buyers and in what ways?
4. What are the segmentation variables that distinguish luxury automobile buyers and in what ways?

Stepwise Multiple Regression

When the researcher is using multiple regression as a screening tool or he/she is otherwise faced with a large number of independent variables in the conceptual model that are to be tested by multiple regression, it can become tedious to narrow down the independent variables by successive manual trimming. Fortunately, there is a type of multiple regression that does the trimming operation automatically, called *stepwise multiple regression*.

Here is a simple explanation. With **stepwise multiple regression**, the one independent variable that is statistically significant and explains the most variance in the dependent variable

Stepwise regression is useful if a researcher has many independent variables and wants to narrow the set down to a smaller number of statistically significant variables.

is determined and entered into the multiple regression equation. Then the statistically significant independent variable that contributes most to explaining the remaining unexplained variance in the dependent variable is determined and entered. This process is continued until all statistically significant independent variables have been entered into the multiple regression equation.[12] In other words, all of the insignificant independent variables are eliminated from the final multiple regression equation based on the level of significance stipulated by the researcher in the multiple regression options. The final output contains only statistically significant independent variables. Stepwise regression is used by researchers when they are confronted with a large number of competing independent variables and they want to narrow down the analysis to a set of statistically significant independent variables in a single regression analysis. With stepwise multiple regression, there is no need to trim and rerun the regression analysis because SPSS does the trimming automatically based on the stepwise method selected by the researcher.

SPSS® HOW TO DO STEPWISE MULTIPLE REGRESSION WITH SPSS

A researcher executes stepwise multiple regression by using the ANALYZE-REGRESSION-LINEAR command sequence precisely as was described for multiple regression. The dependent variable and many independent variables are selected into their respective windows as before. To direct SPSS to perform stepwise multiple regression, use the "Method:" drop-down menu to select "Backward." The findings will be the same as those for a researcher who uses iterative trimmed multiple regressions, which we described earlier. Of course, with stepwise multiple regression output, information on those independent variables is taken out of the multiple regression equation based on nonsignificance; if you wish, SPSS stepwise multiple regression will also take into account the VIF statistic to ensure that multicollinearity is not an issue.

We do not have screenshots of stepwise multiple regression, as this technique is quite advanced. In fact, there are four different stepwise regression methods available on SPSS. We do not recommend that you use stepwise multiple regression unless you gain a good deal more background on multiple regression, as you may encounter findings that are difficult to understand or even counterintuitive.[13]

Marketing Research on YouTube™ | To learn about performing stepwise multiple regression with SPSS, launch **www.youtube.com**, and search for "Multiple Regression – SPSS (Brief)."

STEP-BY-STEP SUMMARY OF HOW TO PERFORM MULTIPLE REGRESSION ANALYSIS

While we have attempted to move slowly, you are no doubt overwhelmed by all the facets of multiple regression analysis that we have covered. Nonetheless, it is important to emphasize that every statistical analysis beyond simple descriptive ones involves some sort of statistical test, and the complexity of regression analysis requires multiple tests. These tests are considered in a step-by-step manner by the marketing researcher, and we have listed and described these steps in Table 15.2 as a way of summarizing how to perform multiple regression analysis.

Warnings Regarding Multiple Regression Analysis

Before leaving our description of multiple regression analysis, we must issue warnings about your interpretation of regression. First, we all have a natural tendency to think in terms of causes and effects, and regression analysis invites us to think in terms of a dependent variable resulting or being caused by the actions of an independent variable. This line of thinking is absolutely incorrect: Regression analysis is nothing more than a statistical tool that assumes a linear relationship between two variables. It springs from correlation analysis, which is, as you will recall, a measure of the linear association and not the causal relationship between two variables. Consequently, even though two variables, such as sales

Regression is a statistical tool, not a cause-and-effect statement.

TABLE 15.2   Step-by-Step Procedure for Multiple Regression Analysis Using SPSS

Step	Description
1. **Choose the dependent variable and independent variables to analyze.**	The dependent variable (y) is the predicted variable, and the independent variables (x_i's) are used to predict y. Typically, both y and x variables are scale variables (interval or ratio scales), although some dummy independent variables are allowable.
2. **Determine whether a linear relationship exists in the population (using 95% level of confidence).**	From the initial SPSS output, the ANOVA table reports a computed F value and associated Sig level. a. If the Sig value is .05 or less, there is a linear relationship among the chosen variables in the population. Go to Step 3. b. If the Sig value is more than .05, there is no linear relationship among the chosen variables in the population. Return to Step 1 with a new set of variables, or stop.
3. **Determine whether the chosen independent variables are statistically significant (using 95% level of confidence).**	Also look at the Sig level for the computed beta coefficient for the each associated independent variable. a. If the Sig level is .05 or less, it is permissible to use the associated independent variable to predict the dependent variable with the $y = a + bx$ linear equation. b. If the Sig level is more than .05, it is not permissible to use the associated independent variable to predict the dependent variable. c. If you find a mixture of a and b, you should do "trimmed" or stepwise multiple regression analysis (see the text on these techniques).
4. **Determine the strength of the relationship(s) in the linear model.**	In the SPSS output Model Summary table, R Square is the square of the correlation coefficient; the Adjusted R Square reduces the R^2 by taking into account the sample size and number of parameters estimated. Use Adjusted R Square as a measure of the "percent variance explained" in the y variable using the linear equation to predict y.
5. **Interpret the findings.**	With a result where only statistically significant independent variables are used in the analysis, use the magnitudes and signs of the standardized betas to assess each independent variable's relative importance and relationship direction with the dependent variable.

and advertising, are logically connected, a regression analysis does not permit the marketing researcher to make cause-and-effect statements because other independent variables are not controlled.

Our other warning is that the introduction to multiple regression analysis presented in this chapter is indeed rudimentary. There is a great deal more to multiple regression analysis that is beyond the scope of this textbook. Our coverage introduces regression analysis and provides enough information for you to run uncomplicated regression analyses on SPSS, identify the relevant aspects of the SPSS output, and interpret the findings. As you will see when you work with the SPSS regression analysis procedures, we have only scratched the surface of this topic.[14] There are many more options, statistics, and considerations involved.[15] In fact, there is so much material that whole textbooks on regression exist. Our purpose has been to teach you the basic concepts and to help you interpret the statistics associated with these concepts as you encounter them as statistical analysis program output. Our descriptions are merely an introduction to multiple regression analysis to help you comprehend the basic notions, common uses, and interpretations involved with this predictive technique.[16]

Despite our simple treatment of it, we fully realize that even simplified regression analysis is complicated and difficult to learn and that we have showered you with a great many regression statistical terms and concepts in this chapter. Seasoned researchers are intimately knowledgeable with them and comfortable in using them. However, as a student encountering

TABLE 15.3 Regression Analysis Concepts

Concept	Explanation
Regression analysis	A predictive model using the straight-line relationship of $y = a + bx$
Intercept	The constant, or a, in the straight-line relationship that is the value of y when $x = 0$
Slope	The b, or the amount of change in y for a 1 unit change in x
Dependent variable	Y, the variable that is being predicted by the x(s) or independent variable(s)
Independent variable(s)	The x variable(s) used in the straight-line equation to predict y
Least squares criterion	A statistical procedure that ensures that the computed regression equation is the best one possible
R Square	A number ranging from 0 to 1.0 that reveals how well the straight-line model fits the scatter of points; the higher, the better
Multiple regression analysis	A powerful form of regression where more than one x variable is in the regression equation
Additivity	A statistical assumption that allows the use of more than one x variable in a multiple regression equation: $y = a + b_1 x_1 + b_2 x_2 \ldots + b_m x_m$
Independence assumption	A statistical requirement that when more than one x variable is used, no pair of x variables has a high correlation
Multiple R	Also called the coefficient of determination, a number that ranges from 0 to 1.0 that indicates the strength of the overall linear relationship in a multiple regression; the higher the better
Multicollinearity	The term used to denote a violation of the independence assumption that causes regression results to be in error
Variance inflation factor (VIF)	A statistical value that identifies what x variable(s) contribute to multicollinearity and should be removed from the analysis to eliminate multicollinearity; any variable with VIF of greater than 10 should be removed
Trimming	Removing an x variable in multiple regression because it is not statistically significant, rerunning the regression, and repeating until all remaining x variables are significant
Beta coefficients and standardized beta coefficients	Slopes (b values) determined by multiple regression for each independent variable, x; these are normalized to be in the range of .00 to .99 so they can be compared directly to determine their relative importance in y's prediction
Dummy independent variable	Use of an x variable that has a 0,1 or similar coding, used sparingly when nominal variables must be in the independent variables set
Stepwise multiple regression	A specialized multiple regression that is appropriate when there is a large number of independent variables that need to be trimmed to a small, significant set and the researcher wishes the statistical program to do this automatically

them for the first time, you undoubtedly feel intimidated. While we may not be able to reduce your anxiety, we have created Table 15.3 that lists and explains all of the regression analysis concepts described in this chapter. At least, you will not need to search through the chapter to find these concepts when you are trying to learn or use them.

Reporting Regression Findings to Clients

The objective of a screening mechanism is to identify the relevant or meaningful variables as they relate to some dependent variable of interest. For most clients, the dependent variable of interest is sales, purchases, intentions to purchase, satisfaction, or some other variable that translates in some way how customers regard or behave toward the company or brand. Normally, the researcher is faced with a large number of possible factors, any combination of which might relate to the dependent variable. When regression is used as a screening device, the items to report are: (1) dependent variable, (2) statistically significant independent variables, (3) signs of beta coefficients, and (4) standardized beta coefficients for the significant variables. Here is a table that reports the use of regression analysis to determine the target market profile of the Subshop.

Factors Related to Number of Visits to the Subshop (Stepwise Regression Analysis Results)

Dependent Variable		
How many times have you eaten at the Subshop in the past 30 days?	288 Total Cases	
Independent Variable(s)	**Coefficient***	**Standardized**
Demographic Factors		
Gender**	−3.02	−.43
Age	4.71	.35
Education	−7.28	−.12
*Lifestyle Factors***		
I typically go to restaurants that have good prices	0.32	0.35
Eating at restaurants is a large part of my diet.	−0.21	−0.27
I usually buy the "special of the day" at lunch.	−0.17	−0.20
Intercept	2.10	

* 95% level of confidence.
**(Dummy variable coded 0 = female and 1 = male).
***Based on a scale where 1 = strongly disagree and 7 = strongly agree.

This presentation table features several nuances. First, the method of multiple regression (stepwise) is reported. Second, only the statistically significant (95% level of confidence) independent variables are reported. Third, the types of independent variables (demographics and lifestyle, here) are separated. Fourth, within each type, the independent variables are arranged in descending order according to the absolute values of their standardized beta coefficients. Fifth, where the coding of the independent variable is pertinent to proper interpretation, the measurement scale is reported as a footnote to the table. Note, in particular, that gender was used as a dummy variable, so it is important that the reader know the code in order to realize that the finding denotes that the Subshop's target market is skewed toward women.

 Synthesize Your Learning

This exercise will require you to take into consideration concepts and material from these three chapters:

Chapter 13	Implementing Basic Differences Tests
Chapter 14	Making Use of Associations Tests
Chapter 15	Understanding Regression Analysis Basics

Alpha Airlines At the beginning of the second decade of the 21st century, many airlines found themselves in an unfortunate situation. On the supply side, prices rose at an unusually high rate. Aviation fuel costs, in particular, rose at an alarming pace, and other expenses, including employee wages and salaries, supplies, services, rent, and repairs, increased faster than ever before. Unable to counter these cost increases, most airlines slowly instituted price increases and unbundled some of their services, such as charging $15 per checked-in bag.

Alpha Airlines uses marketing research to decide on service improvements.

Photo: Monika Wisniewska/Shutterstock

On the demand side, as the result of a long recession and rising costs of many goods and services, business flyers reduced their flying and consumers cut back on their travel plans or turned to less expensive travel methods such as going by train or personal automobile. Reports by ticket sales agencies confirmed that many international vacationers and tourists had cancelled or indefinitely postponed their plans.

Alpha Airlines, a major international airline, felt the squeeze of both sides of the equation during this time as passenger miles and revenues began to fall in what some airline industry analysts characterized as a "death spiral." However, marketing executives at Alpha Airlines vowed to not give up, and they designed a questionnaire to obtain some baseline data and to assess the reactions of Alpha Airlines customers to possible changes in the airline's services and prices. An abbreviated version of the questionnaire follows.

1. Approximately how many of the following trips have you taken on Alpha Airlines this year?
   a. Domestic business _____
   b. Domestic tourist _____
   c. International business _____
   d. International tourist _____

2. Do you … (check all that apply)
   _____ Belong to Alpha Airlines frequent-flyer program?
   _____ Belong to Alpha Airlines Prestige Club (private lounge areas in some airports)?
   _____ Use Alpha Airlines website to book most of your flights?
   _____ Usually travel business class (including first class) on Alpha Airlines?

3. Indicate from 1 to 7, where 1 = do not want at all and 7 = desire very much, how desirable each of the following potential new Alpha Airline services is to you.
   _____ Double Alpha Airlines frequent-flyer miles for any trips after you have earned 25,000 miles in that year
   _____ From 33% to 50% savings airfare for a second family member on any international flight with you
   _____ No $15 checked-in bag charge if you belong to the Alpha Airlines Prestige Club
   _____ Priority boarding on international Alpha Airlines flights if you belong to the Alpha Airlines Frequent Flyer program
   _____ Free wireless Internet service while in flight

In addition to the answers to these questions, the questionnaire also gathered information on the following: gender, education level (highest level in years), income level (in $10,000 increments), age (actual years), marital status, approximate number of air flight (any airline) trips taken for each of the past three years, and some lifestyle dimensions.[17] (From my experience, I have found that the larger the airline company, the lower the actual cost of travel has been; I generally call several airlines or travel agents to get price quotes and routing before I decide on a particular airline; The price I pay for my ticket is more important to me than the service I receive prior to and during the flight; I choose to travel by airline because my time is very valuable to me; I feel that the services

I receive during the flight are good; I feel that the pre-flight services (e.g., baggage handling, ticket processing) are good; and Normally, I fly with one particular airline company.)

The self-administered questionnaire is handed out by flight attendants to all Alpha Airlines passengers traveling on domestic or international flights during the first week of the month, resulting in more than 20,000 completed and usable questionnaires. The Alpha Airlines marketing executives have a number of questions they hope will be answered by this survey.

For each of the following questions, indicate the specific questions or variables in the survey that should be analyzed, paying close attention to the scale properties of each variable. Specify the type of statistical analysis that is appropriate and how SPSS output would indicate whether statistically significant findings are present.

1. What is the target market profile each of the following types of Alpha Airlines traveler? That is, what demographic and lifestyle factors are related to the number of miles traveled on Alpha Airlines for each of the following types?

   a. Domestic business traveler?
   b. Domestic tourist traveler?
   c. International business traveler?
   d. International tourist traveler?

2. Are there differences in the desirabilities of each of the five potential new Alpha Airlines services with respect to:

   a. Gender?
   b. Belonging (or not) to Alpha Airlines frequent-flyer program?
   c. Belonging (or not) to Alpha Airlines Prestige Club (private lounge areas in some airports)?
   d. Use or nonuse of Alpha Airlines website to book most flights?
   e. Usual class of seating (business versus economy class) on Alpha Airlines?

3. Do relationships exist for estimated number of flights in each of the past three years on any airline with:

   a. Age?
   b. Income?
   c. Education?
   d. Any of the lifestyle dimensions?

4. Do associations exist for: (1) participating or not in Alpha Airlines frequent-flyer program, (2) membership or not to Alpha Airlines Prestige Club (private lounge areas in some airports), and/or (3) use or not of Alpha Airlines website to book most flights with:

   a. Gender?
   b. Marital status?
   c. Usual class of seating (business versus economy class) on Alpha Airlines?

Summary

Market researchers use regression analysis to make predictions. The basis of this technique is an assumed straight-line relationship existing between the variables. With bivariate regression, one independent variable, x, is used to predict the dependent variable, y, using the straight-line formula of $y = a + bx$. A high R^2 and a statistically significant slope indicate that the linear model is a good fit. With multiple regression analysis, the underlying conceptual model specifies that several independent variables are to be used, and it is necessary to determine which ones are significant. Multiple regression analysis allows for the use of several independent variables (additivity) that are not highly correlated with one another. Multicollinearity, or the condition of high correlations among the independent variables, violates this necessary condition. Statistical analysis programs can be programmed to report variance inflation factors (VIFs) that will warn the researcher of this violation and prompt him or her to eliminate some of the offending independent variables.

By systematically eliminating the nonsignificant independent variables in an iterative manner, a process called *trimming*, a researcher will ultimately derive a set of significant independent variables that yield a significant predictive model. While the dependent and independent variables should be scale variables (interval or ratio scales), it is permissible to use a few dummy independent variables, which are nominally coded for two categories such as male/female. With surveys, it is common for market researchers to use multiple regression analysis as a screening device to determine the statistically significant independent variables that emerge from a large set of possible independent variables. Interpretation on a multiple regression analysis finding is facilitated by examining the standardized beta coefficients that indicate the relative importance and the direction of the relationship of the variables.

Because the process of trimming nonsignificant independent variables is tedious and time consuming, seasoned researchers may opt to use stepwise multiple regression analysis if faced with a large number of candidate independent variables, such as several demographic, lifestyle, and buyer behavior characteristics. With stepwise multiple regression, independent variables are entered by the statistical analysis program until the multiple regression equation contains only statistically significant independent variables define the regression findings.

Key Terms

Regression analysis (p. 379)
Bivariate regression (p. 379)
Intercept (p. 379)
Slope (p. 379)
Dependent variable (p. 380)
Independent variable (p. 380)
Least squares criterion (p. 380)

Outlier (p. 380)
General conceptual model (p. 383)
Multiple regression analysis (p. 384)
Regression plane (p. 384)
Additivity (p. 384)
Independence assumption (p. 385)
Multicollinearity (p. 385)

Variance inflation factor
   (VIF) (p. 385)
Dummy independent variable (p. 389)
Standardized beta coefficient (p. 390)
Screening device (p. 390)
Stepwise multiple regression (p. 393)

Review Questions/Applications

1. Use an x-y graph to construct and explain a reasonably simple linear model for each of the following cases:
   a. What is the relationship between gasoline prices and distance traveled for family automobile touring vacations?
   b. How do hurricane-force warnings relate to purchases of flashlight batteries in the expected landfall area?
   c. What is the relationship between carry-on luggage and charges for checking luggage on airlines?

2. Indicate what the scatter diagram and probable regression line would look like for two variables that are correlated in each of the following ways (in each instance, assume a negative intercept): (a) −0.89, (b) +0.48, and (c) −0.10.

3. Circle K runs a contest, inviting customers to fill out a registration card. In exchange, they are eligible for a grand prize drawing of a trip to Alaska. The card asks for the customer's age, education, gender, estimated weekly purchases (in dollars) at that Circle K, and approximate distance the Circle K is from his or

her home. Identify each of the following if a multiple regression analysis were to be performed: (a) independent variable, (b) dependent variable, (c) dummy variable.

4. Explain what is meant by the independence assumption in multiple regression. How can you examine your data for independence, and what statistic is issued by most statistical analysis programs? How is this statistic interpreted? That is, what would indicate the presence of multicollinearity, and what would you do to eliminate it?

5. What is multiple regression? Specifically, what is "multiple" about it, and how does the formula for multiple regression appear? In your indication of the formula, identify the various terms and the signs (positive or negative) they may take on.

6. If one uses the "enter" method for multiple regression analysis, what statistics on an SPSS output should be examined to assess the result? Indicate how you would determine each of the following:
   a. Variance explained in the dependent variable by the independent variables
   b. Statistical significance of each of the independent variables
   c. Relative importance of the independent variables in predicting the dependent variable

7. Explain what is meant by the notion of "trimming" a multiple regression result. Use the following example to illustrate your understanding of this concept.

   A bicycle manufacturer maintains records over 20 years of the following data: retail price in dollars, cooperative advertising amount in dollars, competitors' average retail price in dollars, number of retail locations selling the bicycle manufacturer's brand, and an indication whether the winner of the Tour de France was riding the manufacturer's brand (coded as a dummy variable where 0 = no and 1 = yes).

   The initial multiple regression result determines the following:

Variable	Significance Level
Average retail price in dollars	.001
Cooperative advertising amount in dollars	.202
Competitors' average retail price in dollars	.028
Number of retail locations	.591
Tour de France winner	.032

Using the "enter" method in SPSS, what would be the trimming steps you would expect to undertake to identify the significant multiple regression result? Explain your reasoning.

8. Using the bicycle example in question 7, what do you expect would be the elimination of variables sequence using stepwise multiple regression? Explain your reasoning with respect to the operation of each step of this technique.

9. Using SPSS graphical capabilities, diagram the regression plane for the following variables.

Number of Gallons of Gasoline Used per Week	Miles Computed for Work per Week	Number of Riders in Carpool
5	50	4
10	125	3
15	175	2
20	250	0
25	300	0

10. The Maximum Amount is a company that specializes in making fashionable clothes in large sizes for plus-size people. A survey was performed for the Maximum Amount, and a regression analysis was run on some of the data. Of interest in this analysis was the possible relationship between self-esteem (dependent variable) and number of Maximum Amount articles purchased last year (independent variables). Self-esteem was measured on a 7-point scale in which 1 signifies very low and 7 indicates very high self-esteem. Below are some items that have been taken from the output.

    Pearson product moment correlation = +0.63
    Intercept = 3.5
    Slope = +0.2

    All statistical tests are significant at the 0.01 level or less. What is the correct interpretation of these findings?

11. Wayne LaTorte is a safety engineer who works for the U.S. Postal Service. For most of his life, Wayne has been fascinated by UFOs. He has kept records of UFO sightings in the desert areas of Arizona, California, and New Mexico over the past 15 years, and he has correlated them with earthquake tremors. A fellow engineer suggests that Wayne use regression analysis as a means of determining the relationship. Wayne does this and finds a "constant" of 30 separate earth tremor events and a slope of 5 events per UFO sighting. Wayne then writes an article for the *UFO Observer*, claiming that earthquakes are largely caused by the subsonic vibrations emitted by UFOs as they enter the Earth's atmosphere. What is your reaction to Wayne's article?

CASE 15.1

The Hobbit's Choice Restaurant Survey Predictive Analysis   **SPSS®**

(For necessary background, refer to Case 12.1 on pages 319, Case 13.1 on pages 349, and Case 14.1 on pages 376.)

Aspiring restaurant owner Jeff Dean was pleased to learn that his dream of opening The Hobbit's Choice could be a reality. Through the research conducted under Cory Rogers's expert supervision and Christine Yu's SPSS analysis, Jeff had a good idea of what features were desired, where it should be located, and even what advertising media to use to promote the new restaurant. He believed he had all the information he needed to obtain the financing necessary to design and build The Hobbit's Choice Restaurant.

Jeff called Cory on Friday morning and said, "Cory, I am very excited about everything your work has found about the good prospects of The Hobbit's Choice Restaurant. I want to set up a meeting with my banker next week to pitch it to him for the funding. Can you get me the final report by then?"

Cory was silent for a moment. Then he said, "Christine is doing the final figures and dressing up the tables so we can paste them into the report document. But I think you

have forgotten about the last research objective. We still need to address the target market definition with a final set of analyses. I know Christine just finished some exams at school, and she has been asking if there is any work she can do over the weekend. I'll give her this task. Why don't you plan on coming over at 11 a.m. on Monday? Christine and I will show you what we have found, and then we can take Christine to lunch for giving up her weekend."

Your task in this case is to take Christine's role, use The Hobbit's Choice Restaurant SPSS data set, and perform the proper analysis. You will also need to interpret the findings.

1. What is the demographic target market definition for The Hobbit's Choice Restaurant?
2. What is the restaurant spending behavior target market definition for The Hobbit's Choice Restaurant?
3. Develop a general conceptual model of market segmentation for The Hobbit's Choice Restaurant. Test it using multiple regression analysis and interpret your findings for Jeff Dean.

CASE 15.2 **INTEGRATED CASE**

Global Motors Segmentation Analysis   **SPSS®**

It is Monday, the first day in your new marketing internship. After a rigorous application and review process including two grueling interviews with Cory Rogers and Celeste Brown, you have been hired by CMG Research.

It is 9 a.m., and you are in Cory Rogers's office along with. Cory says, "We know it is just your first day as the CMG Research marketing intern, but we are getting bogged down with a lot of work that must be completed very quickly, or our clients will be unhappy. As I indicated to you a few days ago when I let you know that we chose you to be this year's marketing intern, Celeste and I were very impressed with your command of SPSS and your understanding of more advanced statistical analyses such as regression and analysis of variance. So, we are going to let you show us your stuff right away."

Cory continues, "We are in the final stages of a major survey that we conducted for Global Motors. The company has five automobile models under consideration for multi-million-dollar development. We have provided the

managers with a great deal of analysis, and they are in the process of narrowing down the development list. I would like to give them one more set of findings. Specifically, I would like to give them target market definitions for each of the possible models. That is, using multiple regression analysis as a screening device, we need to identify the significant demographic and attitudes about global warming that uniquely define these preference segments."

Celeste then says, "I can give you a copy of the SPSS data set, and, as you know, you can use SPSS Variable View or Utilities-Variables to see the code book for this survey." Cory ends the meeting with a concluding comment: "Great. I am sure that you will do a fantastic job with this assignment. Celeste and I have to catch a flight in a couple hours, and we will be out of town for the next three days. But, you can call, text, or email. Let's set a meeting for 9 a.m. on Thursday, and you can show us what you have found."

Your task as the new CMG marketing intern: use the GlobalMotors.Recorded.sav data file. Perform the proper analyses to identify the salient demographic and/or attitude factors that are related to preferences for each of the five automobile models under consideration. With each automobile model, prepare a summary that:

1. Lists the statistically significant independent variables (use 95% level of confidence).
2. Interprets the directional of the relationship of each statistically significant independent variable with respect to the preference for the automobile model concerned.
3. Identifies or distinguishes the relative importance of each of the statistically significant independent variables.
4. Assesses the strength of the statistically significant independent variables as they join to predict the preferences for the automobile model concerned.

16

The Research Report

LEARNING OBJECTIVES

- To appreciate the importance of the marketing research report
- To examine new tools marketing researchers are using to make report writing more efficient, including online digital dashboards
- To know how to position the report for the audience and to learn the elements that should be included in the marketing research report
- To learn what plagiarism is, why it is a serious problem, and how to properly reference sources
- To learn the basic guidelines for writing effective marketing research reports
- To know how to use visuals, such as figures, tables, charts, and graphs
- To learn how to make visuals, such as tables and charts, using SPSS
- To learn to be ethically sensitive when making visuals in a report or presentation
- To learn the basic principles for presenting your report orally
- To learn how to access and use an online report writing tool, the *iReportWriting Assistant*, that will help you write better reports

Are Today's Research Reports and Presentations Yesterday's CDs?

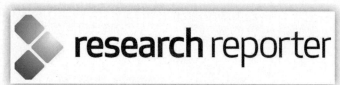

Visit Research Reporter at www.insightmarketing.com.

Text and logo: **By permission, Chris Forbes, Research Reporter.**

Technology has changed the way we do many things. Just a few years ago I would go to the record store and buy a CD and put it in my disc player and sit down to read and enjoy the music. If a tune came on I really didn't like, I would just wait for it to be over and hope I liked the next one. Fast-forward to today. I don't need to drive to the record store to buy my music. I can purchase it online—right from my chair. I can preview tracks and only buy the ones I like. After I download, I can create my own playlists, and I can skip tracks easily if I happen to be bored. So today, instead of having the pre-packaged, somewhat rigid music product, current technology has changed all this to a more personalized music presentation.

How has research changed since the 1990s in terms of how we access it and consume it? We have seemed to master PowerPoint, but we haven't seemed to have perfected research's equivalent of the change in the way we access and consume music. Yet, there are reasons we need to change. The presentations of the past are difficult, as it is nearly impossible to get everyone together. We solve this by sending out research findings in a stack of slides via email. But this separates the report from the presenter, so the research loses its value as readers speed-read and flip through slides. Moreover, we are not confined to the dimly lit slide projection room. Access of secondary information through the browser opens the opportunity to access and compile information from multiple sources, creating "playlists" of information applications such as new product releases or annual market planning. But rarely does that primary data, stored away in one file of PowerPoints, find its way into a playlist.

IT teams have developed browser-based, searchable, online research libraries. Still, once a file is found, users have to muddle through the entire file in hopes of finding some relevant information. A solution? Why not create multiproject research summaries, collecting numerous projects and combining them all into a new file? This creates a "best of" album that relies on more use and reuse of past research. By storing research outputs into separate categories, the entries can be searched and displayed using any criteria the users need, similar to how music tracks are stored by artist, genre, etc. Outputs can be searched by words or phrases, allowing users to identify insights quickly. One company already doing this makes greater use of research by reviewing research findings against key growth drivers and identifies whether the finding represents a strength, weakness, opportunity, or threat (SWOT). This results in research findings having direct input into building strategic plans. Another firm tags research findings to specific responsibilities, enabling someone new to learn from past studies about their brand or task responsibility. The research team may have to put in more time to create this type of compilation, but they save time by not having to educate newcomers in terms of what is already known. This keeps the investment in past research alive.

I predict that an emerging core skill among researchers will be the capacity to quickly combine research findings to business problems—creating insights from playlists on the fly. Will all these possibilities replace the stack of slides sent out via email or the dimly lit projector room with many absentees? It may be too early to tell, but researchers need to understand how the impact of changes affects our reports and presentations just as it did the music industry.

In this chapter you will read about the basics of writing a research report and making a presentation. No matter how the reports will be delivered in the future, you will need to know these basic skills.

—*Chris Forbes*

Forbes is cofounder of Research Reporter, a Melbourne, Australia, research software company. We asked him to summarize his thoughts for you after reading an article he wrote on this topic.[1]

"WHERE WE ARE"

1 Establish the need for marketing research.
2 Define the problem.
3 Establish research objectives.
4 Determine research design.
5 Identify information types and sources.
6 Determine methods of accessing data.
7 Design data collection forms.
8 Determine the sample plan and size.
9 Collect data.
10 Analyze data.
11 Prepare and present the final research report.

Photo: Ionescu Bogdan/Fotolia

We included the opening vignette by Chris Forbes because it represents some creative thinking about the future for report writing and presentations. Like Forbes, we don't know when report writing will go the way of the CD, but we know it has already changed and will likely change more in the future. In this chapter we will introduce a concept that has been growing in terms of its use, that of digital dashboards. Also, tools like SPSS are constantly changing and making improvements in report writing, presentation, and distribution. We will provide keystroke instructions for making tables and graphs using SPSS. Still, the basics of good report writing haven't changed. Technology will continue to impact how reports are produced, but nothing will replace the need for a well-written report with enlightening, ethical graphics that communicate the intended message to the client/reader. This chapter will provide you with the tools you will need in order to write a good research report and make a good research presentation.

The **marketing research report** is a factual message that transmits research results, vital recommendations, conclusions, and other important information to the client, who in turn bases his or her decision making on the contents of the report. This chapter deals with the essentials of writing and presenting the marketing research report. To help you in writing a marketing research report, we have created an online tool called the *iReportWriting Assistant*. Where appropriate, we will refer to it in this chapter, and we provide a detailed overview at the end of this chapter of the contents of the *iReportWriting Assistant*. Finally, we offer some good examples from others on report writing and presentations, which appear on YouTube.

The Importance of the Marketing Research Report

The importance of the research report was addressed by the marketing research director at Kodak, who stated that even the best research will not drive the appropriate action unless the audience understands the outcomes and implications.[2] Recently, marketing researcher James A. Rohde noted that the presentation is important in demonstrating that the findings are relevant to the decision maker client because these decision makers base their judgments on what they can accomplish with the information in the final report. They are less concerned about the method and analytical tools used by the researcher.[3] This places greater importance on writing a report that is relevant to the decisions the client must make. Good communications means that you must be able to transfer exactly what is in your mind to the mind of the receiver of your message. The ultimate result of all the work on the research project is communication with the client.

The marketing research report is the product that represents the efforts of the marketing research team, and it may be the only part of the project the client will see. If the report is poorly written, riddled with grammatical errors, sloppy, or inferior in any way, the quality of the research (including its analysis and information) becomes suspect and its credibility is reduced. If organization and presentation are faulty, the reader may never reach the intended conclusions. The time and effort expended in the research process are wasted if the report does not communicate effectively.

If, on the other hand, all aspects of the report are done well, the report will not only communicate properly, but it will also serve to build credibility. Marketing research users[4] and suppliers[5] agree that reporting the research results is one of the most important aspects of the marketing research process. Many managers will not be involved in any aspect of the research process but will use the report to make business decisions. Effective reporting is essential, and all of the principles of organization, formatting, good writing, and good grammar must be used.

Improving the Efficiency of Report Writing

Assuming you have written a term paper (or several!), you realize that report writing is not easy. As we noted previously, technology has affected report writing. Word processing software now typically includes many features that increase writing efficiency. Features such

The marketing research report is a factual message that transmits research results, vital recommendations, conclusions, and other important information to the client, who in turn bases his or her decision making on the contents of the report.

To see a description of business reports, go to www.youtube.com and type in "The Key Forms of Business Writing: Reports."

To help you in writing a marketing research report, we have created an online tool called the *iReportWriting Assistant*. We will refer to it in this chapter and provide a detailed overview of its contents. Go to: http://www.pearsonhighered.com/burns/. Click on Companion Website and open any chapter. Look in the left margin and you will see a link for the iReportWriting Assistant.

The time and effort expended in the research process are wasted if the report does not communicate effectively.

as automatic referencing coupled with automated citation formatting, available on many of today's online databases, have reduced much of the tedious time spent on report writing. Most of today's statistical analysis packages, such as SPSS, include sophisticated tools that allow for ease of presentation in tables, pie charts, bar graphs, and so on that allow for customization to suit the writer's purpose.

Much of what Mr. Forbes talks about in our opening vignette, however, deals with the distribution side of reports. How can users more easily access and interact with the reports? One significant trend in this area in recent years has been the use of dashboards of information made available to users online.

Dashboards provide digital interfaces that allow users to quickly and easily see information that is presented in a simplified manner. Marketing Research Insight 16.1 provides an example illustrating how SKOPOS uses a dashboard to report findings from its service that monitors online social media buzz about a company and/or its brands.

> Technology has improved the efficiency of report writing.
>
> One significant trend in distribution to users and their interaction with reports in recent years has been the use of dashboards of information made available to users online.

MARKETING RESEARCH INSIGHT 16.1   *Social Media Marketing*

Reporting Social Media Buzz Using Digital Dashboards

Visit SKOPOS at www.skopos.info.

The earliest pilots of aircraft needed information critical to the performance and safety of the plane reported in an easy-to-access and easy-to-interpret manner. Dashboards containing such critical information were designed to fill this need. While there have been improvements, today's dashboards have a lot in common with their early cousins. With the evolution of computer technology and digital displays, the dashboard concept has been adopted as a way to make critical information easy to access and easy to interpret by managers.

SKOPOS has a service that monitors online social media buzz about a company and/or its brands. Billions of minutes are spent on Facebook each day, 13 hours of video are loaded onto YouTube every minute, more than 3 million Tweets are sent every day, and over 4 billion photos shared on Flickr. When we add over a million blogs to the mix, we can easily understand why companies need to know what is being said about them and their brands. SKOPOS' ChatBack™ service offers firms the ability to monitor opinion, sentiment, comments,

and associations made anywhere in the social media. ChatBack also offers clients the ability to monitor these critical components using a digital dashboard as shown below.

As shown in the ChatBack Dashboard, managers can easily see how often their brands are mentioned over time; the source of the information (influencers), such as Bloomberg or Facebook; the platform (a blog, the news, a forum); sentiment measured on stacked bar charts with height indicating the frequency and color indicating positive, negative, or indeterminate comments; and other useful information. Key words may be entered and monitored. In this case a drug, Priligy, is being monitored.

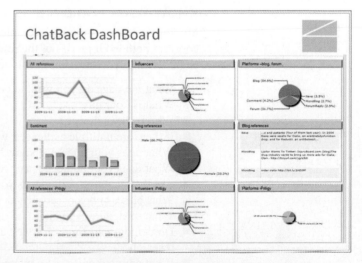

Text and Images: Copyright © 2012 by SKOPOS. Reprinted with permission.

Online reporting software electronically distributes marketing research reports to selected managers in an interactive format that allows each user to conduct his or her own analyses.

Marketing Research Insight 16.2 and an Active Learning exercise offer a "close encounter" with Burke's dashboard concept.

Other research firms, such as Burke, Inc., provide their clients with access to online reporting tools. These services allow clients to watch data come in as they are being collected and organizes data into presentation-quality tables. Readers can examine total results or conduct their own subgroup analysis, even down to examining the results of individual respondents. Because the reports are available online, different client users can access the reports and conduct analyses that are important to their unit or division. **Online reporting software** electronically distributes marketing research reports to selected managers in an interactive format that allows each user to conduct his or her own analyses. To give you a "close encounter" with Burke's dashboard concept, we provide an Active Learning exercise followed by Marketing Research Insight 16.2.

 Active Learning

Take a Tour of an Online Marketing Research Report Service

To take a closer look at Burke's online reporting writing software, Digital Dashboard, go to www.digitaldashboard.com. Click on "About Digital Dashboard®." Read about the features and take a look at the example output pages. (Don't run the demonstration yet!) Note the features of "In the Customer's Words," "Individual Reports," and "Data Collection Status Report." When you have read all the features, it is time to take the tour, noted at the bottom of the screen. (The program will run automatically—just give it a few seconds.) Watch for features such as the data filter, executive summary, trends over time, and comparison of the results of significant subgroups; the ability to filter to examine any subgroup results desired; the option to search for verbatim comments; the ability to conduct statistical testing using the report software; and the utility to create your own charts and titles and transfer data to spreadsheets. Can you see how such tools can make the reporting process more efficient and the report more usable for clients?

Writing the Report

KNOW YOUR AUDIENCE

Marketing research reports are tailored to specific audiences and purposes, and you must consider both in all phases of the research process, including planning the report. Before you begin writing, you must answer some questions:

- What message do you want to communicate?
- What is your purpose?
- Who is the audience?
- If there are multiple audiences, who is your primary audience? Your secondary audience?
- What does your audience know?
- What does your audience need to know?
- Are there cultural differences you need to consider?
- What biases or preconceived notions of the audience might serve as barriers to your message?
- What strategies can you use to overcome these negative attitudes?
- Do demographic and lifestyle variables of your audience affect their perspective of your research?
- What are your audience's interests, values, and concerns?

These and other questions must be addressed before you can determine how best to structure your report.

MARKETING RESEARCH INSIGHT 16.2 *Practical Application*

Moving Beyond the Traditional Research Report: Digital Dashboard from Burke, Inc.

Mike Webster
Senior Vice President,
Research Solutions

Burke, Inc., has developed an online reporting tool that allows clients to access and create reports that are being updated in near real time as data are being collected in the field. The Digital Dashboard® is a web-based application that can be accessed worldwide and enables users to create custom views of their data as well as access predefined reports. The flexibility of this application allows users to analyze data themselves to help them make better decisions and ensure that everyone involved in the research project can interact with the data. Traditionally, the client did not see any data until all data were collected and analyzed and the final written report was prepared. Additionally, the traditional printed research report was not interactive. The manager needing to examine the data differently than reported had to make a special request and wait for further processing. In many cases, the manager would forgo the additional work. The Digital Dashboard is an evolution in reporting that removes the barriers to further analyzing data that are present in traditional reporting methods. Like a driver

Visit Burke, Inc., at www.burke.com.

monitoring a vehicle's dashboard for important information, clients using the Digital Dashboard can monitor the entire research project and input custom changes to make sure project results take them to the right destination—making the correct decision.

The Digital Dashboard is comprised of modules that allow the user to interact with data in multiple ways. The Report Builder module enables a user to create multiple charts and tables by following a guided wizard and to analyze the data and display it in a most meaningful way. These custom reports can then be shared with other users in the organization. Once shared, a user can continue to work with the report to meet his or her needs. The Catalog Builder module enables a user to view respondent level data. The user takes advantage of the same guided wizard available in the Report Builder to create views in this module as well. Data can be exported or scheduled to be delivered at regular intervals by email from this portion of the tool. The Project Background module provides a place for the client to communicate important details about the project and offer guidelines for interpreting the results. The Digital Dashboard can be used for online surveys as well as other data collection modes, such as telephone and mail surveys and mall-intercept surveys.

Mike Webster has played a leading role bringing Burke Interactive to the forefront of Internet research. A key developer of Burke's Digital Dashboard, Webster has designed online reporting solutions for leading-edge clients in a wide variety of industries, including information technology, telecommunications, financial services, and consumer goods. He serves as Burke's resident expert on data collection and online reporting software, working with a variety of languages and platforms. His title is Senior Vice President, Research Solutions.

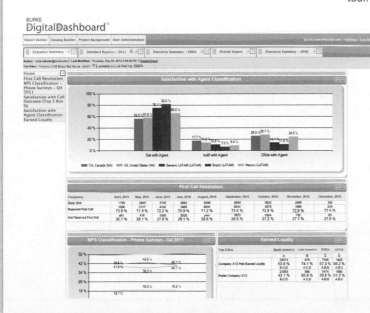

Text and images: Copyright © 2012 by Burke, Inc. Reprinted with permission.

When you are preparing the final report, it is often helpful "to get on the other side of the desk." Assume you are the reader instead of the writer.

When you are preparing the final report, it is often helpful "to get on the other side of the desk." Assume you are the reader instead of the writer. Doing so will help you see things through the eyes of your audience and increase the success of your communication. This is your opportunity to ask that basic (and critical) question from the reader's point of view: "What's in it for me?" Once you have answered these questions, you need to organize your report.

Elements of the Report

Reports are organized in sections, or elements. If the organization for which you are conducting the research has specific guidelines for preparing the document, you should follow them. If no specific guidelines are provided, certain elements must be considered when you are preparing the report. These elements can be grouped in three sections: front matter, body, and end matter. Table 16.1 depicts these three sections as well as elements covered in each section.

FRONT MATTER

Front matter consists of all pages that precede the first page of the report.

The **front matter** consists of all pages that precede the first page of the report: the title page, letter of authorization (optional), letter/memo of transmittal, table of contents, list of illustrations, and abstract/executive summary.

Title Page The **title page** (Figure 16.1) contains four major items of information: (1) the title of the document, (2) the organization/person(s) for whom the report was prepared, (3) the organization/person(s) who prepared the report, and (4) the date of submission. If names of individuals appear on the title page, they may be in either alphabetical order or some other agreed-upon order; each individual should also be given a designation or descriptive title.

The document title should be as informative as possible. It should include the purpose and content of the report, such as "An Analysis of the Demand for a Branch Office of the Law Firm of Dewey, Cheatam, and Howe" or "Alternative Advertising Copy to Introduce the New M&M/Mars Low-Fat Candy Bar." The title should be centered and printed in all uppercase (capital) letters. Other items of information on the title page should be centered and printed in uppercase and lowercase letters. The title page is counted as page i of the front matter;

iReportWriting Assistant: Visit the online report writing guide for a discussion of the elements of the marketing research report. Templates for many of the report parts are provided.

TABLE 16.1 The Elements of a Marketing Research Report

A. Front Matter
1. Title Page
2. Letter of Authorization
3. Letter/Memo of Transmittal
4. Table of Contents
5. List of Illustrations
6. Abstract/Executive Summary

B. Body
1. Introduction
2. Research Objectives
3. Method
4. Results
5. Limitations
6. Conclusions or Conclusions and Recommendations

C. End Matter
1. Appendices
2. Endnotes

FIGURE 16.1
Title Page

GLOBAL MOTORS DIVISION

OF ZEN MOTORS:

A MARKETING RESEARCH STUDY OF
U.S. POTENTIAL AUTO BUYERS' PREFERENCES
FOR SELECTED MODELS AND A PROFILE OF
MODELS' TARGET MARKETS

Prepared for
Mr. Nick Thomas, CEO

Prepared by
Cory Rogers, Vice President
CMG Research, Inc.

July, 2013

however, no page number is printed on it. See Figure 16.1. On the page following the title page, the printed page number will be ii.

Some experts recommend that you change the title to be brief and understandable if you are making a presentation on the survey results.[6] For example, "An Analysis of the Demand for a Branch Office of the CPA Firm of Dean and Allen" would be simplified to "Demand for a Branch Office of Dean and Allen." Some additional insights on preparing for an oral presentation are provided later in the chapter.

Letter of Authorization The **letter of authorization** is the marketing research firm's certification to do the project. This element is optional. It includes the name and title of the persons authorizing the research to be performed, and it may also include a general description of the nature of the research project, completion date, terms of payment, and any special conditions of the research project requested by the client or research user. If you allude to the conditions of your authorization in the letter/memo of transmittal, the letter of authorization is not necessary in the report. However, if your reader may not know the conditions of authorization, inclusion of this document is helpful.

Letter/Memo of Transmittal Use a **letter of transmittal** to release or deliver the document to an organization for which you are not a regular employee. Use a **memo of transmittal** to deliver the document within your organization. The letter/memo of transmittal describes the general nature of the research in a sentence or two and identifies the individual who is releasing the report. The primary purpose of the letter/memo of transmittal is to orient the reader to the report and to build a positive image of the report. It should establish rapport between the writer and receiver. It gives the receiver a person to contact if questions arise.

> Use a letter for transmittal outside your organization and a memo within your organization.

Writing style in the letter/memo of transmittal should be personal and slightly informal. Some general elements that may appear in the letter/memo of transmittal are a brief identification of the nature of the research, a review of the conditions of the authorization to do the research (if no letter or authorization is included), comments on findings, suggestions for further research, and an expression of interest in the project and further research. It should end with an expression of appreciation for the assignment, acknowledgment of assistance from others, and suggestions for following up. Personal observations, unsupported by the data, are appropriate. Figure 16.2 presents an example of a letter of transmittal.

Table of Contents The **table of contents** helps the reader locate information in the research report. The table of contents (Figure 16.3) should list all sections of the report that follow; each heading should read exactly as it appears in the text and should identify the number of the page on which it appears. If a section is longer than one page, list the page on which it begins. Indent subheadings under headings. All items except the title page and the table of contents are listed with page numbers in the table of contents. Front-matter pages are numbered with lowercase Roman numerals: i, ii, iii, iv, and so on. Arabic numerals (1, 2, 3) begin with the introduction section of the body of the report.

List of Illustrations If the report contains tables and/or figures, include in the table of contents a **list of illustrations** with page numbers on which they appear. All tables and figures should be included in this list, which helps the reader find specific illustrations that graphically portray the information. **Tables** are words and/or numbers arranged in rows and columns; **figures** are graphs, charts, maps, pictures, and so on. Because tables and figures are numbered independently, you may have both a Figure 1 and a Table 1 in your list of illustrations. Give each a name, and list each in the order in which it appears in the report.

Abstract/Executive Summary Your report may have many readers. Some of them will need to know the details of your research, such as the supporting data on which you base your conclusions and recommendations. Others will not need as many details but will want to read the conclusions and recommendations. Still others with a general need to know may read only the executive summary. Therefore, the **abstract** or **executive summary** is a "skeleton" of your report. It serves as a summary for the busy executive or a preview for the in-depth reader. It provides an overview of the most useful information, including the conclusions and recommendations. The abstract or executive summary should be very carefully written, conveying the information as concisely as possible. It should be single-spaced and should briefly cover the general subject of the research, the scope of the research (what the research covers/ does not cover), identification of the methods used (i.e., a mail survey of 1,000 homeowners), conclusions, and recommendations.

> Abstracts are "skeletons" of reports.

BODY

The **body** is the bulk of the report. It contains an introduction to the report, an explanation of your method, a discussion of your results, a statement of limitations, and a list of conclusions

FIGURE 16.2
Letter of
Transmittal

CMG Research, Inc.
1100 St. Louis Place
St. Louis, MO

July 21, 2013

Mr. Nick Thomas
Global Motors Division
Zen Motors
Motortown, USA 00000

Dear Mr. Thomas:

With your letter of authorization, dated February 25, 2013, you authorized CMG to conduct a research project for Global Motors. With this letter, I am hereby transmitting to you the report of that project, entitled "A MARKETING RESEARCH STUDY OF U.S. POTENTIAL AUTO BUYERS PREFERENCES FOR SELECTED MODELS AND A PROFILE OF MODELS' TARGET MARKETS."

The method used to generate the findings of this report is described in detail in the report. Moreover, the method follows that described in our proposal to you. We believe the report accomplishes the research objectives we set out at the beginning of this process and therefore, you should be able to use the information contained herein to make the important decisions needed for Global Motors.

My colleagues and I have been pleased to work with you on this project. We are prepared to make a presentation of the report at your convenience. Do not hesitate to call me (877) 492-2891 should you have any questions.

Sincerely,

Cory Rogers

Cory Rogers

and recommendations. Do not be alarmed by the repetition that may appear in your report. Only a few people will read it in its entirety. Most will read the executive summary, conclusions, and recommendations. Therefore, formal reports are repetitious. For example, you may specify the research objectives in the executive summary and refer to them again in the findings section as well as in the conclusions section. Also, do not be concerned that you use the same terminology to introduce the tables and/or figures. In many lengthy reports, repetition actually enhances reader comprehension.

The first page of the body contains the title, such as "Introduction." Whatever title you select should be centered on the top of the page; this page is counted as page 1, but no page number is printed on it. All other pages throughout the document are numbered consecutively.

Introduction The **introduction** to the marketing research report orients the reader to its contents. It may contain a statement of the background situation leading to the problem, the

Table of Contents

statement of the problem, and a summary description of how the research process was initiated. It should contain a statement of the general purpose of the report and also the specific objectives for the research.

Listing of research objectives should follow the statement of the problem.

    Research objectives may be listed either as a separate section or within the introduction section. The listing of research objectives should follow the statement of the problem, since the two concepts are closely related. The list of specific research objectives often serves as a good framework for organizing the results section of the report.

Method The **method** describes, in as much detail as necessary, how you conducted the research, who (or what) your subjects were, and what tools or methods were used to achieve your objectives. In most cases, the method section does not need to be long. It should, however, provide the essential information your reader needs to understand how the data were collected and how the results were achieved. It should be detailed enough that the data collection could be replicated by others for purposes of reliability. In other words, the method section should be clear enough that other researchers could conduct a similar study. In some cases, the needs of the research user may dictate an extensive method section. A client may, for example, want the researcher to not only thoroughly describe the method that was used but also discuss why other methods were not selected. For example, in situations in which research information will be provided in litigation, where there is certain to be an adversary, a researcher may be asked to provide an exhaustive description of the methods used in conducting the study and the methods that were not chosen.

Method or Methodology?   You will note that we have named the section of the research report that describes the details of the procedures and tools used the *method* section. Some reports may instead use *methodology* as the title for this section, but we recommend sticking with *method*. Why? The two terms have different meanings. Because so many people use them interchangeably does not mean that such usage is correct. **Methodology** refers to the science of determining appropriate methods to conduct research. It has been defined as the theoretical analysis of the methods appropriate to a field of study or to the body of methods and principles particular to a branch of knowledge.[7] Therefore, it would be appropriate to say that there are *objections to the methodology of a consumer survey* (that is, objections dealing with the appropriateness of the methods used in the survey) or to say the *methodology of modern marketing research* (that is, the principles and practices that underlie research in the field of marketing research).[8] Consequently, there is an important conceptual distinction between methodology and method. *Method* refers to the tools of scientific investigation (and the tools used in a marketing research project are described in detail in the method section of the report). *Methodology* refers to the principles that *determine how* such tools are deployed and interpreted. Marketing research *methodology* prescribes, for example, that we must use probability samples if we desire to have a sample that is representative of some population. Researchers would describe their use of their probability sample for a particular study in the *method* section of their paper. In short, use *method* not *methodology*.

Supplementary information should be placed in the appendix. If you used secondary information, you will need to document your sources (provide enough information so that your sources can be located).[9] You do not need to document facts that are common knowledge or can be easily verified. But if you are in doubt, document! **Plagiarism** refers to representing the work of others as your own. Citing the work of others not only allows you to avoid charges of plagiarism, but a well-referenced paper adds credibility to your message.

Students often underestimate just how seriously society takes plagiarism. It is a serious offense; it can cost you your job. Take the opportunity to learn more about plagiarism by watching the YouTube video cited in the following feature. You can also explore the Internet for examples of how serious plagiarism is; students have lost their college degrees, top-level professionals have lost their jobs, and well-known celebrity writers have been defamed. Marketing Research Insight 16.3 offers more information about this important topic.

Results   The **results** section is the most important portion of your report. Some researchers prefer to use the term *findings*. This section should logically present the findings of your research and may be organized around the research objectives for the study. The results should be presented in narrative form and accompanied by tables, charts, figures, and other appropriate visuals that support and enhance the explanation of results. Tables and figures are supportive material; they should not be overused or used as filler. Each should contain a number and title and should be referred to in the narrative.

Outline your results section before you write the report. The survey questionnaire itself can serve as a useful aid in organizing your results because the questions are often grouped in

The method describes in detail how the research was conducted, who (or what) the subjects were, and what tools or methods were used to achieve the objectives.

The section in the report in which you describe the details of the procedures and tools used in the research project should be called the *method* section, not *methodology*.

Make sure you understand what plagiarism means. If in doubt, provide a reference to the source and put the citation in the proper format.

Citing the work of others not only allows you to avoid charges of plagiarism, but a well-referenced paper adds credibility to your message.

Students often underestimate just how seriously society takes plagiarism. It is a serious offense; it can cost you your job. To learn more, read Marketing Research Insight 16.3.

Marketing Research on YouTube™   To learn more about the perils of plagiarism, go to www.youtube.com and type in "Diagnosis: Plagiarism."

iReportWriting Assistant: See the online report writing guide for more information on plagiarism.

The results section is the most important portion of your report and should logically present the findings of the research.

MARKETING RESEARCH INSIGHT 16.3   *Ethical Consideration*

Properly Reference Your Sources

Referencing sources is essential in the business world.

Photo: © Volker Witt/Fotolia

Plagiarism is derived from a Latin word for kidnapping a Roman citizen's slave.[10] Words can be thought of as property. Avoiding plagiarism involves respect for the original author's work and respect for your audience's needs or desire to trace data and learn more from the source.

Just as all printed sources must be documented, so must information found online. In a letter to the *New York Times*, Marilyn Bergman, the president of the American Society of Composers, Authors, and Publishers, expressed a disturbing trend of online theft of words when she said that Americans are prompted by a "free for the taking" feeling of information on the Web.[11] The Internet is not public domain. Proper documentation of all sources helps a writer avoid public humiliation and maintain professional integrity.

APA (American Psychological Association) and MLA (Modern Language Association) are two styles that offer formats for citation. Many online databases offer a "Cite This" option that automatically gives you the reference in a format of your choice. In terms of formats, APA is used in business fields, and MLA is used in the humanities. Style books and university websites offer examples on documentation for a range of sources, including electronic formats.

For example, much of the preceding information was found on the library services website of the University of Maryland University College (UMUC). The source citation and format follow.

> University of Maryland University College. (1998). Citing Internet resources: APA style. Retrieved from http://www.umuc.edu/.

Format:

> Author, I., Author, I., & Author, I. (Year, month date). Title, [Type of medium]. Available: Site/Path/File [Access date].

You can learn more about proper citing formats on the library services Web site of the University of Maryland University College (UMUC). Examples of source citation and formatting follow.

> *Author*—The creator or compiler of the information on the web page. This can be the webmaster or the name of the organization that is responsible for the page.
> *Year, month date*—The date that the web page was put online; it should be the same as the "last updated" date, if available.
> *Title*—The title of the document. Often, this can be found at the top of the web page.
> *Type of medium*—The way the document was accessed. If the document was found on the web or through another Internet service, this field should read "Online."
> *Site/Path/File*—The address or URL of the Web site.
> *Access date*—The date that you viewed the Web page or accessed the information.

---

a logical order or in purposeful sections. Another useful method for organizing your results is to individually print all tables and figures and arrange them in a logical sequence. Once you have the results outlined properly, you are ready to write the introductory sentences, definitions (if necessary), review of the findings (often referring to tables and figures), and transition sentences to lead into the next topic.

Limitations Do not attempt to hide or disguise problems in your research; no research is faultless. Always be above board and open regarding all aspects of your research. Avoiding discussion of limitations may render suspect your integrity and your research. To not report research results accurately and honestly is against the Marketing Research Association's Code of Marketing Research Standards.[12] Suggest what the limitations are or may be and what impact they have on the results.

> Do not attempt to hide or disguise problems in your research. Suggest what the limitations are or may be and what impact they have on the results.
>
> Avoiding discussion of limitations may render suspect your integrity and your research.

You might also suggest opportunities for further study based on the limitations. Typical **limitations** in research reports often focus on but are not limited to factors such as constraints of time, money, size of sample, and personnel. Consider the following example: "The reader should note that this study was based on a survey of graduating students at a midsized public university in the Southeast United States. Budget constraints limited the sample to this university and this region of the country. Care should be exercised in generalizing these findings to other populations."

Conclusions and Recommendations Conclusions and recommendations may be listed together or in separate sections, depending on the amount of material you have to report. In any case, you should note that conclusions are not the same as recommendations. **Conclusions** are the outcomes and decisions you have reached based on your research results. For example, if the data show the order of preference for five car models, a conclusion would be: "Model C had the highest preference." **Recommendations** are suggestions for how to proceed based on the conclusions. For example, "The company should produce and market Model C." Unlike conclusions, recommendations may require knowledge beyond the scope of the research findings themselves—that is, information on conditions within the company or industry, for example. Therefore, researchers should exercise caution in making recommendations. The researcher and the client should determine prior to the study whether the report is to contain recommendations. A clear understanding of the researcher's role will result in a smoother process and will help avoid conflict. Although a research user may desire the researcher to provide specific recommendations, both parties must realize that the researcher's recommendations are based solely on the knowledge gained from the research report, not familiarity with the client. Other information, if made known to the researcher, could change the researcher's recommendations.

> Conclusions are the outcomes and decisions you have reached based on your research results. Recommendations are suggestions for how to proceed based on the conclusions.

> Because researchers do not understand all the conditions within the client company, they should exercise caution in making recommendations. The researcher and the client should determine prior to the study whether the report is to contain recommendations.

If recommendations are required and if a report is intended to initiate further action, however, recommendations are the important map to the next step. Writing recommendations in a bulleted list and beginning each with an action verb help to direct the reader to the logical next step.

END MATTER

The **end matter** comprises the **appendices**, which contain additional information to which the reader may refer for further reading but that is not essential to reporting the data; references list; and endnotes. Appendices contain the "nice to know" information, not the "need to know." Therefore, that information should not clutter the body of the report but should instead be inserted at the end for the reader who desires or requires additional information. Tables, figures, additional reading, technical descriptions, data collection forms, and appropriate computer printouts are some elements that may appear in an appendix. (If they are critical to the reader, however, they may be included in the report itself.) Each appendix should be labeled with both a letter and a title, and each should appear in the table of contents.

> End matter contains additional information to which the reader may refer for further reading but that is not essential to reporting the data.

A reference page or endnotes (if appropriate) should precede the appendix. A **reference list** contains all of the sources from which information was collected for the report. The references should be complete so that a reader could retrieve the source if needed. **Endnotes** are notes at the end of a document that provide supplementary information or comments on ideas provided in the body of the report.

Guidelines and Principles for the Written Report

In addition to understanding the purpose of the parts of the research report, you should also consider their form, format, and style.

FORM AND FORMAT

Form and format concerns include headings, subheadings, and visuals.

Headings and subheadings act as signals and signposts to serve as a road map for a long report.

iReportWriting Assistant: The online report writer provides examples of proper heading and subheading formats.

A well-organized report, with appropriate headings and subheadings, will substantially improve readability. Learn how to use headings and subheadings, and you will improve your writing skills.

Visuals can dramatically and concisely present information that might otherwise be difficult to comprehend.

iReportWriting Assistant: For an in-depth discussion of the construction of visuals, see the online report writing guide.

Stylistic devices can make the difference in whether your reader gets the message as you intended it.

Headings and Subheadings In a long report, your reader needs signals and signposts that serve as a road map. Headings and subheadings perform this function. **Headings** indicate the topic of each section. All information under a specific heading should relate to that heading, and **subheadings** should divide that information into segments. A new heading should introduce a change of topic. Choose the kind of heading that fits your purpose—single word, phrase, sentence, question—and consistently use that form throughout the report. If you use subheadings within the divisions, the subheadings must be parallel to one another but not to the main headings.

You should begin by organizing your report into sections. This requires time on the front end of the process, but it is time well spent. A well-organized report, with appropriate headings and subheadings, will substantially improve readability. Then find any communications book and organize your headings using one of the standard formats. For example, a Level 1 heading is centered and all caps, and a Level 2 heading is left justified with upper- and lowercase. Alternatively, use the professional format contained in a word-processing program such as Microsoft Word. Learn how to use headings and subheadings, and you will improve your writing skills.

VISUALS

Visuals are tables, figures, charts, diagrams, graphs, and other graphic aids. Used properly, they can dramatically and concisely present information that might otherwise be difficult to comprehend. Tables systematically present numerical data or words in columns and rows. Figures translate numbers into visual displays so that relationships and trends become comprehensible. Examples of figures are graphs, pie charts, and bar charts.

Visuals should tell a story; they should be uncluttered and self-explanatory. Even though they are self-explanatory, the key points of all visuals should be explained in the text. Refer to visuals by number: " . . . as shown in Figure 1." Each visual should be titled and numbered. If possible, place the visual immediately below the paragraph in which its first reference appears. Or, if sufficient space is not available, continue the text and place the visual on the next page. Visuals can also be placed in an appendix. Additional information on preparing visuals in SPSS is presented later in this chapter.

STYLE

Consider stylistic devices when you are writing the sentences and paragraphs in your report. These can make the difference in whether your reader gets the message as you intended it. Consider the following tips as you begin your report writing.

Proper grammar and sentence construction are essential in report writing. Sentences should be constructed for the reader's ease of reading and understanding, and the rules of grammar should be observed. Readers will make assumptions about your knowledge of other subjects based on your knowledge of grammar.

Good paragraph construction is essential to a well-written report. A good paragraph has one main idea, and a **topic sentence** should state that main idea. For example: "To assess whether residents would patronize an upscale restaurant, respondents were asked their likelihood of patronizing an upscale restaurant." Next, the **body of the paragraph** provides the main idea of the topic sentence by giving more information, analysis, or examples. For example, continuing from the topic sentence example: "A description of an upscale restaurant was read to all respondents. The description was as follows: . . . The respondents were then asked to indicate their likelihood of patronizing an upscale restaurant by selecting a choice on a 5-point response rating scale ranging from 'Very likely to patronize' to 'Very unlikely to patronize.' The actual scale was as follows: . . . "

Paragraphs should close with a sentence that signals the end of the topic and indicates where the reader is headed. For example: "How respondents answered the likelihood-to-patronize scale is discussed in the following two paragraphs." Note this last sentence is a **transitional sentence**, which tells readers where they are headed. This helps readers' comprehension.

Controlling for the **length of paragraphs** should encourage good communication. As a rule, paragraphs should be short. Business communication experts believe most paragraphs should be under or around the 100-word range.[13] This is long enough for the topic sentence and three or four sentences in the body of the paragraph. The paragraph should never cover more than one main topic. Complex topics should be broken into several paragraphs.

Other guidelines for improving the style of your report are: use jargon sparingly; use strong verbs (say "recommend" instead of "making a recommendation"); use active voice (the subject of the verb is doing the action); remove extra words; avoid changes in tense; keep the subject and the verb close together; and edit and proofread carefully!

Using Visuals: Tables and Figures

Visuals assist in the effective presentation of numerical data. The key to a successful visual is a clear and concise presentation that conveys the message of the report. The selection of the visual should match the presentation purpose for the data. Common visuals include the following:[14]

Tables, which identify exact values (see Marketing Research Insight 16.4)

Graphs and *charts*, which illustrate relationships among items

> *Pie charts*, which compare a specific part of the whole to the whole (see Marketing Research Insight 16.5)
> *Bar charts* (see Marketing Research Insight 16.6) and *line graphs*, which compare items over time or show correlations among items

Flow diagrams, which introduce a set of topics and illustrate their relationships (useful when the sequence of events or topics is important)

Maps, which define geographical locations

Photographs, which present an aura of legitimacy because they are not "created" in the sense that other visuals are created (i.e., they depict factual content)

Drawings, which focus on visual details

A discussion of some of these visuals follows.

TABLES

Tables allow the reader to compare numerical data. Effective table guidelines are as follows:

Tables allow the reader to compare numerical data.

1. Do not allow computer analysis to imply a level of accuracy that is not achieved. Limit your use of decimal places (12% or 12.2% instead of 12.223%).
2. Place items you want the reader to compare in the same column, not the same row.
3. If you have many rows, darken alternating entries or double-space after every few (five) entries to assist the reader in accurately lining up items.
4. Total columns and rows when relevant.

In practice, researchers commonly report the first two scores (or the bottom two scores) in a table. They call this **top-two box scores**.[15] For example, instead of showing an entire table, only the "Very Likely" and "Somewhat Likely" scores are shown. Top-two box scores refer to the sum of percentages in the top two boxes (e.g., Agree and Strongly Agree) on a 5-point or 7-point scale.

Instead of showing an entire table, only the "Very Likely" and "Somewhat Likely" score are shown as the top-two box scores.

Clients often request (and tab programs such as SPSS's *Quantum* routinely provide) top-two box, top box, and (sometimes) bottom-two box scores. They find these easier to interpret than mean scores. Marketing Research Insight 16.4 lists the necessary keystroke instructions to create tables using SPSS.

MARKETING RESEARCH INSIGHT 16.4   *Practical Application*

How to Create a Table Using SPSS

We will use the integrated case Global Motors dataset (GlobalMotors.sav), which we have used for statistical analysis examples in previous chapters, to demonstrate creating a table with SPSS. Let's say we want to find out education levels of respondents. To do this, we create a simple frequency table for responses to the question in our SPSS dataset, "Level of education." Refer to Figure 16.4.

1. Create a frequency table for responses to the question on the questionnaire: "Level of education" After opening the data file, use ANALYZE-DESCRIPTIVE STATISTICS-FREQUENCIES and select the variable corresponding to education level. The resulting frequency table is displayed in the SPSS output Viewer.
2. To edit the table, put the cursor anywhere on the table and double-click. This activates the table editor, which is indicated by a black table label and a red arrow pointing to the selected table.
3. Right click on the table, and select "TableLooks" from the drop-down menu that appears.
4. To select a particular table format, browse through the directory and select one that suits your need. In this case,

we used AvantGarde format. However, because we want to change the fonts, we have to edit the format we had selected.

5. To edit an already available format, click "Edit Look" while in TABLELOOKS. To change the fonts, alignment, margins, and so on, click on Cell Formats. Change the fonts, size, style, and so on to suit your needs. To change borders, click on Borders and select appropriate borders. You can hide categories by shading all the data in a column, right-clicking, and selecting CLEAR. You can also do this by moving your cursor to the right side of the border of a column and dragging the border to close the column.
6. After adjusting the table properties for the attributes you want, save your customized table format by clicking on SAVE AS within the TABLELOOKS dialog box and saving the table under a new file name.
7. You are now back in the table edit mode. The next step is to change the text in specific cells if you so desire. To do this, double-click on the cell in which you want to change the text. The selected text will be highlighted. Simply type over and press Enter when you are done.

FIGURE 16.4 How to Use SPSS Table-Looks Feature to Create an Impressive Table

Source: Reprint courtesy of International Business Machines Corporation, © SPSS, Inc., an IBM Company.

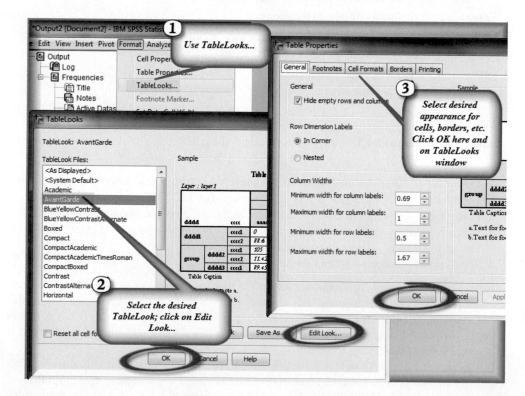

PIE CHARTS

When you want to illustrate the *relative* sizes or *proportions* of one component versus others, pie charts are useful. For example, if you wanted to illustrate the proportions of consumers that prefer different types of radio programming, a pie chart would be an excellent tool for showing the relative sizes of each type of programming preference. The **pie chart** is a circle divided into sections. Each section represents a percentage of the total area of the circle associated with one component. Today's data analysis programs easily and quickly make pie charts. Your SPSS program, for example, allows you to build customized pie charts.

Most experts agree that the pie chart should have a limited number of segments (four to eight, at most). If your data have many small segments, consider combining the smallest or the least important into an "other" or "miscellaneous" category. Because internal labels are difficult to read for small sections, labels for the sections should be placed outside the circle.

Marketing Research Insight 16.5 lists the keystroke instructions for creating pie charts using SPSS.

> When you want to illustrate the relative sizes or proportions of one component versus others, pie charts are useful.
>
> The pie chart is a circle divided into sections. Each section represents a percentage of the total area of the circle associated with one component.

MARKETING RESEARCH INSIGHT 16.5   *Practical Application*

How to Create a Pie Chart Using SPSS

We again use data from the Global Motors survey (GlobalMotors.sav) to demonstrate the creation of a simple pie graph using SPSS. Let's say we want to show responses to the question, "Level of education" in the form of a pie chart.

1. Create a pie chart for responses to the question on the questionnaire: "Level of education."

   As Figure 16.5 demonstrates, use the Command sequence of GRAPHS- LEGACY DIALOGS-PIE. Click Summaries for Groups of Cases and then Define.

   The next screen allows you to choose the variable you want to graph. Select the variable corresponding to the question on the questionnaire; click the button for Define Slices By, and the variable will be entered. You can choose what you want your slices to represent. In this case, we selected the slices to represent % of cases.

2. Enter the titles and footnotes for the chart by clicking on TITLES and entering the appropriate labels. Using the command OPTIONS, you can decide how you want missing values to be treated. Click OK and the resulting pie chart will appear in the SPSS Viewer. SPSS displays a legend with the pie chart. You are now ready to edit the chart.

   (If you have an existing template of a pie graph, you can request the output to be formatted according to template specifications by double-clicking anywhere on the chart; go to FILE-APPLY CHART TEMPLATE and select the saved file name.)

3. Scroll down to the pie chart. To edit the chart, double-click anywhere on the chart. This takes you to the SPSS Chart Editor screen. You will do all your editing in this screen. Refer to Figure 16.6.

4. In the Chart Editor screen, click on the area you wish to edit. This puts a border around the area to be edited. It also changes the editing tools available to you in Chart Editor. Click once on the title. You can now edit the font. Right-click once on the pie. Go to SHOW DATA LABELS. A Properties prompt screen will appear. To place a descriptive label on each slice as well as the value, click on the description under Not Displayed and click the green upward arrow. Click Apply and Close. This places values and corresponding descriptive labels within each slice. Click once on any slice so that only that slice is highlighted with a border. Right-click and go to EXPLODE SLICE.

5. Still in Chart Editor, right-click on the pie chart, as shown in Figure 16.6. Choose PROPERTIES WINDOW. Select DEPTH & ANGLE-3-D for EFFECT, move the slide bar down to –60 for ANGLE, 3 for DISTANCE. apply & close.

6. You can add text *anywhere* on the chart in SPSS. Click the TEXT icon in Chart Editor (or go OPTIONS-TEXT BOX).

7. After making all the changes, save your customized chart by using command options FILE-SAVE CHART TEMPLATE. For future charts, you can call up the customized template, saving the need for you to edit every pie chart you create.

8. The chart is now ready to be transferred to a word processing document.

FIGURE 16.5 How to Make a Pie Chart with SPSS

Source: Reprint courtesy of International Business Machines Corporation, © SPSS, Inc., an IBM Company.

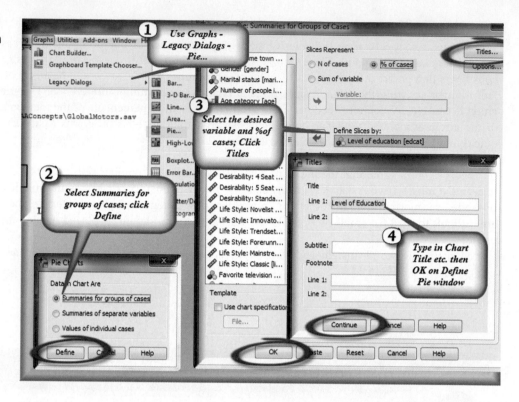

FIGURE 16.6 Use the SPSS Chart Editor to Improve your Pie Chart's Appearance

Source: Reprint courtesy of International Business Machines Corporation, © SPSS, Inc., an IBM Company.

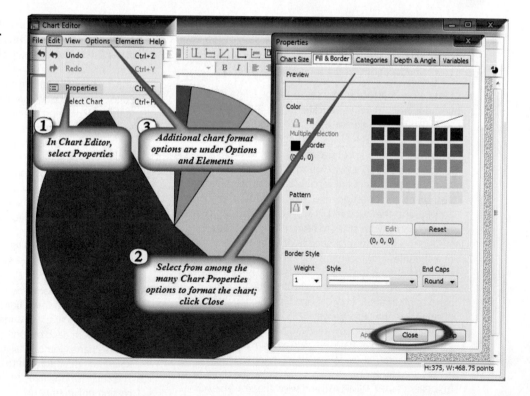

BAR CHARTS

Bar charts are used often in reporting survey data because they are easy to interpret. They are useful to report the magnitude of response or to show magnitude or response comparisons between groups. They are also useful for illustrating change over time. Several types of bar charts can be used. Marketing Research Insight 16.6 lists the keystroke instructions for creating bar charts of various types using SPSS. Study the types of bar charts available to you in SPSS. Your selection of the type of bar chart will depend on what you are trying to communicate to your readers.

Bar charts are useful to report the magnitude of response, to show magnitude or response comparisons between groups, and to illustrate change over time.

LINE GRAPHS

Line graphs are easy to interpret if they are designed properly. Line graphs may be drawn in SPSS using the *graphs* option. You will notice there are several options in types of line graphs.

Flow diagrams introduce a set of topics and illustrate their relationships. Flow diagrams are particularly useful to illustrate topics that are sequential, for example, step 1, step 2, and so on.

Flow diagrams introduce a set of topics and illustrate their relationships.

MARKETING RESEARCH INSIGHT 16.6   *Practical Application*

How to Create a Bar Chart Using SPSS

We use data from the Global Motors dataset (GlobalMotors.sav) to demonstrate the creation of a simple bar graph using SPSS. Let's say we want to show graphically the frequency distribution of the level of education.

1. Create a bar chart for responses for "Level of Education." As you can see in Figure 16.7, after opening the data file, use the Command GRAPHS-LEGACY DIALOGS-BAR. You have the option of choosing from three different styles of bar charts. In this case, we used the Simple chart. Click Summaries for Groups of Cases and then Define.

    The next screen allows you to choose the variable you want to graph. Enter "Level of Education" in Category Axis. You can choose what you want your bars to represent. In this case, we selected the bars to represent % of cases because we want to know the percentages of respondents' level of education.

2. At this stage, you can also enter the titles and footnotes for the chart by clicking on TITLES.

    Click OK and the bar chart will appear in the SPSS Viewer. You are now ready to edit the chart.

    (If you have an existing template of a bar graph while in the Define Simple Bar Summaries for Groups of Cases box, you can request the output to be formatted according to template specifications by clicking on Use Chart Specifications From, and selecting the saved file name.)

3. To edit the chart, double-click anywhere on the chart. This opens the SPSS Chart Editor screen. You will do all your editing in this screen. Figure 16.8 shows the operation of the SPSS Chart Editor screen with our bar chart.

4. In the Chart Editor screen, right-click and select Properties Window. This window allows size, fill and border, 3-D elements, and Variables selections.

5. Click once on one of the bars. All the bars should now be highlighted with a border around them. Notice the tools available to you on the menu bar. Go to the PROPERTIES icon (or go EDIT-PROPERTIES). Select DEPTH & ANGLE, choose SHADOW for EFFECT, and set OFFSET to +15 by moving the slide bar. APPLY. Again, click on a bar and then the PROPERTIES icon. Select FILL & BORDER and select a pattern and fill color for your bars. APPLY. *Note:* Click the fill button to change the color of the bars. The border button allows you to change the color of the border line of the bars.

6. Still in Chart Editor, click anywhere other than a bar. Select PROPERTIES WINDOW-FILL & BORDER. Change the color of the background. APPLY

7. To edit the textual content of the chart, select the TEXT icon in Chart Editor (or go to OPTIONS-TEXT BOX). A box and a set of markers will appear. Insert your text and then drag the box where you want the text to appear.

8. After making all the changes, you can save your customized chart by using the command FILE-SAVE CHART TEMPLATE. For future charts, you can call up the customized template, saving the need for you to edit every bar chart you create.

9. The chart is now ready to be transferred to a word processing document.

FIGURE 16.7
How to Make a Pie Chart with SPSS

Source: Reprint courtesy of International Business Machines Corporation, © SPSS, Inc., an IBM Company.

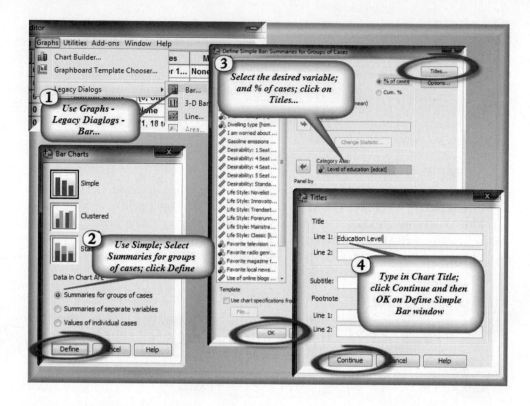

FIGURE 16.8 Use the SPSS Chart Editor to Improve your Pie Chart's Appearance

Source: Reprint courtesy of International Business Machines Corporation, © SPSS, Inc., an IBM Company.

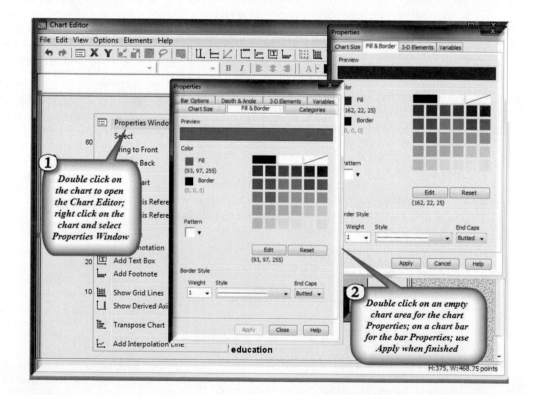

Producing an Accurate and Ethical Visual

A marketing researcher should always follow the doctrine of full disclosure. An **ethical visual** is totally objective in terms of how information is presented in the research report. Sometimes misrepresenting information is intentional (as when a client asks a researcher to misrepresent the data to promote his or her "pet project") or it may be unintentional. In the latter case, those preparing a visual are sometimes so familiar with the material being presented that they falsely assume the graphic message is apparent to all who view it.

There are many ways a visual may be created to lead to reader misinterpretation. Changing the scale on a graph is a common method used to create an unethical visual. It is unethical to change the scale within the body of the report without informing the reader and making sure the reader understands the reason for and the effect of the change. SPSS will automatically assign a range for your scale. Unless there is some justifiable reason for doing so, it's best to not change the scales. Other methods of creating an unethical visual include omission of data and understating or overstating the meaning of the data.

To ensure that you have objectively and ethically prepared, your visuals you should do the following:

1. Double- and triple-check all labels, numbers, and visual shapes. A faulty or misleading visual discredits your report and work.
2. Exercise caution if you use three-dimensional figures. They may distort the data by multiplying the value by the width and the height.
3. Make sure all parts of the scales are presented. Truncated graphs (having breaks in the scaled values on either axis) are acceptable only if the audience is familiar with the data.

> An ethical visual is totally objective in terms of how information is presented in the research report.

Presenting Your Research Orally

You may be asked to present an oral summary of the recommendations and conclusions of your research. The purpose of the **oral presentation** is to succinctly present the information and to provide an opportunity for questions and discussion. The presentation may be accomplished through a simple conference with the client, or it may be a formal presentation to a roomful of people. In any case, says Jerry W. Thomas, CEO of Decision Analyst, research reports should "be presented orally to all key people in the same room at the same time." He believes this is important because many people do not read the research report, and others may not understand all the details of the report. "An oral presentation ensures that everyone can ask questions to allow the researchers to clear up any confusion."[16] It also ensures that everyone hears the same thing.

To be adequately prepared when you present your research orally, follow these steps:

> The purpose of the oral presentation is to succinctly present the recommendations and conclusions of research and to provide an opportunity for questions and discussion.

1. Identify and analyze your audience. Consider the same questions you addressed at the beginning of the research process and at the beginning of this chapter.
2. Find out the expectations your audience has for your presentation. Is the presentation formal or informal? Does your audience expect a graphical presentation?
3. Determine the key points your audience needs to hear.
4. Outline the key points, preferably on 3-by-5 cards or in presentation software "notes" areas to which you can easily refer.
5. Present your points succinctly and clearly. The written report will serve as a reference for further reading.
6. Make sure your visuals graphically and ethically portray your key points.
7. Practice your presentation. Be comfortable with what you are going to say and how you look. The more prepared you are and the better you feel about yourself, the less you will need to worry about jitters.
8. Check out the room and media equipment prior to the presentation.
9. Arrive early.

10. Be positive and confident. You are the authority; you know more about your subject than anyone else.
11. Speak loudly enough for all in the room to hear. Enunciate clearly. Maintain eye contact and good posture. Dress appropriately.

The iReportWriting Assistant

As we stated at the beginning of this chapter, we prepared the online *iReportWriting Assistant* to help you write your research report. We have directed you to the program in several places, where appropriate, in the chapter. This concluding section summarizes the contents of the *iReportWriting Assistant*.

WHERE TO FIND THE *iReportWriting ASSISTANT*

Before we list the contents of this online tool, we should tell you where to find it! Go to the companion website for this book: www.pearsonhighered.com/burns/. Select the seventh edition and click on Companion Website. Once you open the seventh edition's website, when you open any chapter, you will see a menu. The menu will contain a link to the *iReportWriting Assistant*. Open that link.

WHAT TO DO PRIOR TO WRITING

Because report preparation is so critical to the marketing researcher, you have been provided with a tool to guide you through the marketing research report writing process. This tool, the *iReportWriting Assistant*, provides an overall discussion of the research report from the pre-writing step (analyzing your purpose, anticipating your audience, and adapting the message to the audience) through the research step (which includes research, which you have learned about in this text, organization of your information into a workable outline, and composition of your first draft) and finally to the revision step (revision, proofreading, and evaluation of whether your report will accomplish your purpose).

TEMPLATES TO HELP YOU GET STARTED

Knowledge of the writing process will prepare you to publish reports, but the actual course of action can be a bit more daunting. For example, what should the title page look like? How do you construct a list of illustrations? The *iReportWriting Assistant* helps solve these concerns by providing templates for the title page and list of illustrations, along with letters of authorization and transmittal, table of contents, research objectives, and method. Headings and subheadings are also explained so that the information you provide in a report is clear and flows well.

HELP WITH GRAMMAR

Two other areas are of great concern in ensuring the quality of your report: grammar and citations. Despite the statistical accuracy and thorough coverage you may provide in your report, if your grammar is lacking, readers may question your ability, dedication, and effectiveness. Online grammar aid is also provided with the *iReportWriting Assistant*.

PROPER CITATIONS

Finally, though you have done much research for your report, chances are that you have used information from other sources. Proper citation is not only polite, it is a requirement to avoid plagiarism (also discussed on the *iReportWriting Assistant*). You will probably be using one of two citation styles: APA (from the American Psychological Association) or MLA (from the Modern Language Association). Either is an acceptable citation form, but the forms differ in rules of formatting. After determining which style you should use for your report (whether required by a professor, organization, client, etc.), you must follow the rules of the chosen style. Some report writers find this part of the report a bit confusing, but never fear. The *iReportWriting Assistant* will guide you in the information needed for citing sources, including online sources.

AN EXAMPLE REPORT

As a final help to budding research report writers, an example of a proper marketing research report is supplied. Check it out before writing or compare your own report to it during the revision step. In either case, good luck and happy report writing!

Summary

Technology has changed the way we do many things, and it has also affected report writing and presentations. The marketing research report is a factual message that transmits research results, vital recommendations, conclusions, and other important information to the client, who in turn bases his or her decision making on the contents of the report. The client's decisions may hinge on how well the report communicates the research results. Regardless of the care in the design and execution of the research project itself, if the report does not adequately communicate the project to the client, all is lost.

We have prepared an online tool to aid in your report writing. You can access the *iReportWriting Assistant* at www.pearsonhighered.com/burns; click on the Companion Website link for this text. Open any chapter and look for the link.

While preparing and writing the report may be time consuming, advances are being made to make report writing more efficient. Online reporting software is an efficient tool that assists marketing researchers in monitoring data collection and disseminating research results. It also allows data users to interact with the reports and to massage data. The Digital Dashboard from Burke, Inc., is a good example of an online reporting system that allows clients to interact with the report. Word processing software has many features to enhance efficiency in report writing. Tools are available that automatically provide citations for sources of information used in a report. Statistical packages, such as SPSS, have features that allow for ease of preparation of tables and visuals such as bar charts and pie charts. Technology will continue to improve report writing, presentation preparation, and distribution of reports.

Marketing research reports should be tailored to their audiences. They are typically organized into the elements of front matter, body, and end matter. Each of these elements has subparts, each serving a specific purpose.

Plagiarism refers to representing the work of others as your own. It is a serious offense in the real world to plagiarize; people lose their jobs due to this ethical lapse. Proper referencing of source materials not only allows writers to avoid charges of plagiarism but offers other advantages.

Conclusions are based on the results of the research, and recommendations are suggestions on how to proceed based on conclusions. Not all clients wish to have the researcher prepare recommendations in the report.

Guidelines for writing the marketing research report include proper use of headings and subheadings, which serve as signposts and signals to the reader, and proper use of visuals, such as tables and figures. Style considerations include beginning paragraphs with topic sentences, using transitional sentences, and keeping paragraphs short. Style also includes spare use of jargon, strong verbs, active voice, consistent tense, and proofreading.

Care should be taken to ensure that all presentations are clear and objective to the reader. Many visual aids may be distorted so that they have a different meaning to the reader. Researchers must adhere to ethical guidelines when preparing research reports. Reports rely on tables, figures, and graphical displays of various types. SPSS includes routines for creating report tables and graphs. We describe step-by-step commands on how to use SPSS to make professional-appearing tables and graphs.

In some cases, marketing researchers are required to present the findings of their research project to the client orally. Guidelines for making an oral presentation include knowing the audience and their expectations and the key points you wish to make; correctly preparing visuals; practicing; checking out presentation facilities and equipment prior to the presentation; and being positive.

The chapter ends with a detailed description of the contents of the *iReportWriting Assistant*, which provides prewriting guidance, templates to show you how to start writing sections of the report, links to help with grammar, proper citation styles, and an example of a finished marketing research report.

Key Terms

Marketing research report (p. 406)
Dashboards (p. 407)
Online reporting software (p. 408)
Front matter (p. 410)
Title page (p. 410)
Letter of authorization (p. 411)
Letter of transmittal (p. 412)
Memo of transmittal (p. 412)
Table of contents (p. 412)
List of illustrations (p. 412)
Tables (p. 412)
Figures (p. 412)
Abstract/executive summary (p. 412)
Body (p. 412)
Introduction (p. 413)

Research objectives (p. 414)
Method (p. 414)
Methodology (p. 415)
Plagiarism (p. 415)
Results (p. 415)
Limitations (p. 417)
Conclusions (p. 417)
Recommendations (p. 417)
End matter (p. 417)
Appendices (p. 417)
Reference list (p. 417)
Endnotes (p. 417)
Headings (p. 418)
Subheadings (p. 418)
Visuals (p. 418)

Topic sentence (p. 418)
Body of the paragraph (p. 418)
Transitional sentence (p. 418)
Length of the paragraph (p. 419)
Tables (p. 419)
Top-two box scores (p. 419)
Pie charts (p. 420)
Bar charts (p. 422)
Line graphs (p. 422)
Flow diagrams (p. 422)
Ethical visual (p. 422)
Oral presentation (p. 422)
iReportWriting Assistant (p. 426)

Review Questions/Applications

1. Describe what may be in the future for report writing, based on the perspectives shared by Chris Forbes in the opening vignette.
2. Discuss the relative importance of the marketing research report to the other stages in the marketing research process.
3. What is the *iReportWriting Assistant*?
4. What are the main functions provided by the *iReportWriting Assistant*?
5. How can you access the *iReportWriting Assistant*?
6. What are the components of the marketing research report?
7. When should you include or omit a letter of authorization?
8. When should you write a memo? When should you write a letter?
9. What is the derivation of the word *plagiarism*?
10. Should you use *method* or *methodology* to describe how the research was conducted? Why?
11. Distinguish among results, conclusions, and recommendations.
12. When should you acknowledge you have a limitation/s in your report?
13. When should you use a subheading?
14. What are the components of a readable, logical paragraph?
15. What are some elements of good style in report writing?

16. What makes a table a table?
17. What are the first few keystrokes in making a table using SPSS?
18. What are the first few keystrokes in making a pie chart using SPSS?
19. What visual would be the best at displaying the relative changes in spending between four promotion mix variables over time?
20. What kind of visual would you create if you wanted to use images of people to illustrate the differences in employment levels among three industries?
21. Why do you think we included a discussion of ethics in preparing visuals? Can you illustrate how a visual could present data in an unethical fashion?
22. Go online and search for examples of marketing research reports. Or, visit your library and ask your reference librarian if he or she is aware of any marketing research reports that have been placed in the library. Chances are good that you will be able to find several reports of various kinds. Examine the reports. What commonalities do they have in terms of the sections the authors have created? Look at the sections carefully. What types of issues were addressed in the introduction section? The method section? How did the authors organize all of the information reported in the results section? Are recommendations different from conclusions?

CASE 16.1 INTEGRATED CASE

Global Motors: Using iReportWriting Assistant

Cory Rogers is ready to write the first draft of the final report for Global Motors. He decides to go to the online report writing module he learned when he took his first marketing research course in college. Since the *iReportWriting Assistant* is constantly updated, Cory knows he will have access to the latest links and information to assist him in writing his report. Nick Thomas of Global Motors has told Cory that ZEN Motors has its own marketing research department and that researchers there are eager to read his report. Cory knows they will be particularly interested in technical issues such as determination of sample size and margin of error. Cory has also had a frank discussion with Nick about conclusions and recommendations. Nick told him:

> "Cory, I want to know what the numbers say. What are the conclusions based on those numbers? In terms of how to proceed, I will meet with my top staff members, and we will make those decisions. We have to factor in many constraints to make final decisions."

As an experienced marketing researcher, Cory is very familiar with the steps in the marketing research process. Knowledge of these steps is useful in writing the method section of his marketing research reports. For example, Cory knows he should address the types and sources of information used in the report; he should also address the research design and why it was chosen over other designs. The sampling plan and sample size should also be included in this section. Cory makes a list of topics he should cover and starts organizing these topics in terms of headings and subheadings that will be used in the final report.

Cory reminds himself, "I have to properly cite every source I have used in this report." He dreads this step. As many times as he has written reports, remembering every detail that goes in a reference is just something that will not stay in Cory's memory bank. Still, he understands how important it is to use the proper form for his reference list.

Before you start on the questions that follow, access the *iReportWriting Assistant* by going to www.pearson-highered.com/burns and click on the Companion Website link for this text. Click on any chapter for the link to the *iReportWriting Assistant*. Now read over the major topics covered before you read the following questions. Once you are finished reviewing the contents of the *iReportWriting Assistant,* you should be ready to answer the following questions.

1. What should Cory consider doing with the information in this case before he actually begins to write the report? Name some specific issues Cory should address.
2. Should Cory include the standard "Conclusions and Recommendations" section of the report? Why or why not?
3. We are told that Cory has made a list of issues to include in the method section of the report. What, if anything, is included in the *iReportWriting Assistant* that could help Cory ensure that he has included all necessary information?
4. What section of the *iReportWriting Assistant* should Cory seek out to help him with properly citing the secondary sources used in the marketing research report?

CASE 16.2 INTEGRATED CASE

Global Motors: Making a PowerPoint Presentation

Cory Rogers completes the report for Global Motors and decides to make some PowerPoint slides to use in his presentation of the findings. Working in Microsoft Word, he writes a title to his presentation: *Global Motors: A Marketing Research Study to Determine Car Model Preferences and Profile Market Segments.* Then he writes several other comments he wants to include in the beginning of his presentation, such as the research objectives and several

issues dealing with the method used, including the sample plan and sample size. After Cory writes a number of the statements that he thinks might help him communicate the purpose and method of the study, he turns his attention to presenting the findings.

Cory decides to begin his presentation of the study with a description of the sample, often referred to as a "profile of the sample." He notices that for gender and marital status, there are only two categories (male, female and married, unmarried) for each question. He decides to orally report the percentages of these categories. However, for some of the other variables, there are several categories of response, and he decides the best way to communicate the results is by showing the frequency distribution table. He prepares a frequency distribution of the responses to these questions using SPSS and then continues to make several key analyses of the data using SPSS.

1. Using a word processing program, write several of the statements you think would be appropriate to present to the client in an oral presentation.

2. Import the statements you prepared in question 1 into PowerPoint using copy and paste. Experiment with different color text and font sizes and styles.

3. For each statement, using SPSS, run the appropriate frequency distribution. Using tablelooks, select the format you like. Copy and paste your tables into PowerPoint.

4. Using SPSS, make a bar chart of the answers to the question regarding the variable "I am worried about global warming." Experiment with the different options of bar charts available to you in SPSS. Select a bar chart and copy and paste that chart into PowerPoint using copy and paste. Experiment with making edits on your slide.

Endnotes

Chapter 1

1. Poynter, R. (2010). *The handbook of online and social media research: Tools and techniques for market researchers.* West Sussex, UK: Wiley, p. 405.

2. Wasserstrom, J. (2011, February 24). Media and Revolution 2.0: From Tiananmen to Tahrir. Retrieved from Miller-McCune, http://www.miller-mccune.com/media/media-and-revolution-2-0-tiananmen-to-tahrir-28595/

3. Kotler, P., & Keller, K. L. (2006). *Marketing management* (12th ed.). Upper Saddle River, NJ: Prentice Hall, p. 5.

4. "Kindle Fire is the most successful product we've ever launched." (2011, December 11). *Time Techland.* Retrieved from http://techland.time.com/2011/12/15/amazon-kindle-fire-is-the-most-successful-product-weve-ever-launched

5. American Marketing Association. (2007, October). Definition of marketing. Retrieved from http://mpdev.marketingpower.com/AboutAMA/Pages/DefinitionofMarketing.aspx

6. Vargo, S. L., & Lusch, R. F. (2004). Evolving to a new dominant logic for marketing. *Journal of Marketing, 68*(1), 1–17.

7. Shostack, G. L. (1977). Breaking free from product marketing. *Journal of Marketing, 41*(2), 74. Shostack's original example used General Motors.

8. Schneider, J., & Hall, J. (2011, April). Why most product launches fail. *Harvard Business Review,* 21–23.

9. 25 biggest product flops of all time. *Daily Finance.* Retrieved from http://www.dailyfinance.com/photos/top-25-biggest-product-flops-of-all-time/, accessed January 21, 2012.

10. Retrieved from Cadbury.co.UK/press centre/brands/wispa, accessed February 5, 2012.

11. Poynter, R. (2008). Viewpoint: Facebook: The future of networking with consumers. *International Journal of Market Research, 50*(1), 11-12.

12. Retrieved from Cadbury website.

13. These philosophies epitomize the product concept and the selling concept. See Kotler, P., & Armstrong, G. (2001). *Principles of marketing* (9th ed.). Upper Saddle River, NJ: Prentice Hall, p. 18.

14. Kotler, P. (2003). *Marketing management* (11th ed.). Upper Saddle River, NJ: Prentice Hall, p. 19.

15. Some scholars have added the concept of holistic marketing, which includes four components: relationship marketing, integrated marketing, internal marketing, and social responsibility marketing. For additional reading on this topic, see Kotler & Keller, Marketing management, pp. 15–23.

16. Bennett, P. D. (Ed.) (1995). *Dictionary of marketing terms* (2nd ed.). Chicago: American Marketing Association, p. 169.

17. See the Marketing Research Association website for a glossary of these and other terms used in the marketing and opinion research industry. Retrieved from http://www.marketingresearch.org/glossary, accessed June 29, 2012.

18. Pimley, S. (2008, August). Looking to increase their (s)miles per gallon. *Quirk's Marketing Research Review,* 32.

19. Berstell, G. (2011, December) "Listen and learn—and sell. *Quirk's Marketing Research Review,* 48.

20. Segbers, R. (2006, June). Research lays foundation for hospital's non-traditional ad campaign. *Quirk's Marketing Research Review,* 30.

21. Dahab, D., O'Gara, L., & Vermass, J. (2007, October). As banks strive to build relationships, a national tracking study finds that good service is still key for customers. *Quirk's Marketing Research Review,* 52.

22. Janakiraman, N., Meyer, R., & Hoch, S. (2011). The psychology of decisions to abandon waits for service. *Journal of Marketing Research, 48*(6), 970. Retrieved from ABI/INFORM Global (Document ID: 2548456281).

23. Personal communication with the authors from Vincent P. Barabba, General Motors Corp, 1997.

24. Market research: Pre-testing helps ad effectiveness. (2003, May 8). *Marketing,* 27.

25. Tracy, K. (1998). *Jerry Seinfeld: The entire domain.* Secaucus, NJ: Carol, pp. 64–65.

26. Hodock, C. L. (2007). *Why smart companies do dumb things.* Amherst, NY: Prometheus, p. 157.

27. The description of MIS is adapted from Kotler & Keller, *Marketing management.*

Chapter 2

1. Lockley, L. C. (1950). Notes on the history of marketing research. *Journal of Marketing, 14*(5), 733–736.

2. Gallup, G., & Rae, S. F. (1940). *The pulse of democracy.* New York: Simon & Schuster, p. 35.

3. Hower, R. M. (1939). *The history of an advertising agency.* Cambridge, MA: Harvard University Press. pp. 88–90.

4. You can see a list of past Parlin Award winners going back to 1945 at: http://themarketingfoundation.org/parlin_recipients.html

5. Hardy, H. (1990). *The politz papers: Science and truth in marketing research.* Chicago: American Marketing Association.

6. Bartels, *The history of marketing thought,* p. 125.

7. Much of this section was excerpted from Honomichl, J. (2006). Jack J. Honomichl on the marketing research industry. In A. C. Burns & R. F. Bush, *Marketing Research* (5th ed., pp. 40–41). Upper Saddle River, NJ: Pearson/Prentice Hall.

8. Honomichl, J. Jack J. Honomichl on the marketing research industry.

9. Poynter, R. (2010). *The handbook of online and social media research: Tools and techniques for market researchers.* West Sussex, UK: Wiley, p. xix.

10. Murphy, L. F. (2012, Spring). Market research: An industry in transition. *GreenBook research industry trends report* New York: AMA Communications Services.

11. Klein, K. E. (2007, November 19). Do-it-yourself market research. *BloombergBusiness.* Retrieved from www.Businessweek.com, accessed February 25, 2012.
12. Poynter, *The handbook of online and social media research.*
13. ESOMAR Industry Report. (2011). *Global market research 2011.* Amsterdam, The Netherlands: ESOMAR, p. 6.
14. Honomichl, J. (2011, August 30). 2011 Honomichl global top 25 research report. *Marketing News, 13.*
15. Honomichl, 2011 Honomichl global top 25 research report, 13.
16. Honomichl, J. (2012). The 2012 Honomichl top 50 report. *Marketing News*, June 30, 2012, 19.
17. ESOMAR Industry Report, *Global market research 2011*, p. 7.
18. ESOMAR Industry Report, *Global market research 2011*, p. 9.
19. ESOMAR Industry Report, *Global market research 2011*, p. 10.
20. ESOMAR Industry Report, *Global market research 2011*, p. 11.
21. Poynter, *The handbook of online and social media research,* pp. xiv–xix.
22. Kaplan, A. M., & Haenien, M. (2010). Users of the world, unite! The challenges and opportunities of social media. *Business Horizons, 59,* 59–68.
23. ESOMAR Industry Report, *Global market research 2011,* pp. 22–29.
24. Wilson, S., & Macer, T. (2007). *The 2007 Confirmit annual market research software survey.* London: Meaning, Ltd., p. 19.
25. How can we increase our email marketing response rates? (2002, December 9). *CRM Magazine.* Retrieved from http://www.destinationcrm.com/Articles/ReadArticle.aspx?ArticleID=48059
26. Braunsberger, K., Wybenga, H., & Gates, R. (2007). A comparison of reliability between telephone and web-based surveys. *Journal of Business Research, 60,* 758–764.
27. ESOMAR Industry Report, *Global market research 2011, p. 24.* (See comments by Sanja Burns, Head of Consumer Understanding, APAC, Flavours, with Givaudan in Singapore.)
28. Schultz, D. E. (2005, February 15). MR deserves blame for marketing's decline. *Marketing News,* 7; Schultz, D. E., Schultz, H. F., & Haigh, D. (2004, September). *A roadmap for developing an integrated, audience-focused, market research-driven organization.* ESOMAR World Congress. Readers seeking more information on Schultz's suggested remedy are encouraged to read the ESOMAR paper.
29. Mahajan, V., & Wind, J. (1999, Fall). Rx for marketing research: A diagnosis of and prescriptions for recovery of an ailing discipline in the business world. *Marketing Research,* 7–13.
30. The following paragraphs are based on: Mahajan & Wind, Rx for marketing research.
31. Honomichl, J. (2003). *The marketing research industry: As old order crumbles a new vision takes shape.* Marketing Aid Center; Krum, J. R. (1978, October). B for marketing research departments. *Journal of Marketing, 42,* 8–12; Krum, J. R., Rau, P. A., & Keiser, S. K. (1987, December–1988, January). The marketing research process: Role perceptions of researchers and users. *Journal of Advertising Research, 27,* 9–21; Dawson, S., Bush, R. F., & Stern, B. (1994, October). An evaluation of services provided by the marketing research industry. *Service Industries Journal, 14*(4), 515–526; also see Austin, J. R. (1991). An exploratory examination of the development of marketing research service relationships: An assessment of exchange evaluation dimensions. In M. C. Gilly et al. (Eds.), *Enhancing knowledge development in marketing,* (pp. 133–141). 1991 AMA Educators' Conference Proceedings; Swan, J. E., Trawick, I. F., & Carroll, M. G. (1981, August). Effect of participation in marketing research on consumer attitudes toward research and satisfaction with a service. *Journal of*

Marketing Research, 356–363; Malholtra, N. K., Peterson, M., & Kleiser, S. B. (1999, Spring). Marketing research: A state-of-the-art review and directions for the 21st century. *Journal of the Academy of Marketing Science, 27*(2), 160–183.
32. What is a push poll? AAPOR defines it as a form of negative campaigning disguised as a political poll. "Push polls" are actually political telemarketing—phone calls disguised as research that aim to persuade large numbers of voters and affect election outcomes, rather than measure opinions. Retrieved from http://www.aapor.org/What_is_a_Push_Poll_1.htm, accessed March 10, 2012.
33. Council of American Survey Research Organizations. (n.d.). *Surveys and you.* Retrieved from http://www.casro.org/survandyou.cfm, accessed July 2, 2012.
34. American Association for Public Opinion Research. (2012, June). *Transparency Initiative.* Retrieved from http://www.aapor.org/Transparency_Initiative.htm
35. Donnelly, T. (2012, February). Evolution of the PRC: The next chapter. *Alert! 52*(2), 40–42.
36. ESOMAR Industry Report, *Global market research 2011*, pp. 40–41.

Chapter 3

1. Moore-Mezler, C. (2012). Quote excerpted from Burns, A. C., & Bush, R. F. (2012). *Basic marketing research: Using Microsoft® Excel data analysis.* Upper Saddle River, NJ: Pearson/Prentice-Hall, pp. 46–47.
2. Others have broken the marketing research process down into different numbers of steps. Regardless, there is widespread agreement that using a step process approach is a useful tool for learning marketing research.
3. For some insights on marketing research during hard economic times, see: What is the best way to conduct research during a difficult economy? (2010, February). *PRweek* (U.S. ed.), *13*(2), 51–52.
4. Goodman, J., & Beinhacker, D. (2003, October). By the numbers: Stop wasting money! *Quirk's Marketing Research Review.*
5. Malhotra, N. (2010). *Marketing research: An applied orientation* (6th ed.). Upper Saddle River, NJ: Pearson/Prentice Hall, p. 14.
6. Hagins, B. (2010, May). The ROI on calculating research's ROI. *Quirk's Marketing Research Review, 14,* 52–58.
7. Adapted from Adler, L. (1979, September 17). Secrets of when, and when not to embark on a marketing research project. *Sales & Marketing Management Magazine,* 123, 108.
8. Wilson, S., & Macer, T. (2007). *The 2007 Confirmit annual market research software survey.* London: Meaning, p. 6. Retrieved from http://www.meaning.uk.com/resources/reports/2007-confirmit-mr-software-survey.pdf
9. Murphy, L. F. (2012, Spring). *Market research: An industry in transition.* GreenBook Research Industry Trends Report, p. 6.
10. Marketing Research and Intelligence Association. (2011, June). *MRIA industry financial survey 2010.* Mississauga, Ontario: Author.
11. ESOMAR Industry Report. (2011). *Global market research 2011.* Amsterdam, The Netherlands: ESOMAR, p. 70.
12. These data are consistent with data reported in 2007 in that online data collection was the most popular. See Wilson & Macer, *2007 Confirmit Annual Market Research Software Survey*, p. 6.
13. This example was provided by Doss Struse, former Director of Marketing Research for Betty Crocker, to one of the authors.
14. Personal communication with Lawrence D. Gibson, 2000. Also see Gibson, L. D. (1998, Spring). Defining marketing problems: Don't spin your wheels solving the wrong puzzle. *Marketing Research, 10*(4), 5–12.

15. Einstein, A., & Infield, L. (1938). *The evolution of physics.* New York: Simon & Schuster, p. 92.
16. Raiffa, H. (1968). *Decision analysis.* Reading, MA: Addison-Wesley.
17. Gibson, Defining marketing problems.
18. Gibson, Defining marketing problems, 7.
19. Retrieved from www.dictionary.com, accessed November 13, 2003.
20. Kotler, P. (2003). *Marketing management: Analysis, planning, implementing, and control* (11th ed.). Upper Saddle River, NJ: Prentice Hall, p. 102.
21. For example, see Gordon, G. L., Schoenbachler, D. D., Kaminski, P. F., & Brouchous, K. A. (1997). New product development: Using the salesforce to identify opportunities. *Business and Industrial Marketing, 12*(1), 33; Ardjchvilj, A., Cardozo, R., & Ray, S. (2003, January). A theory of entrepreneurial opportunity identification and development. *Journal of Business Venturing, 18*(1), 105.
22. Kotler, *Marketing management*, p. 103.
23. Nachay, K. (2010, January). Mintel predicts 2010 flavor trends. *Food Technology, 64*(1), 10. Retrieved March 30, 2010, from Research Library (Document ID: 1966978711).
24. Muthalyan, S. (2011, November 15). Maximizing retail promotions using smart alerts. *Marketing News*, 13.
25. Personal communication with Gibson; Gibson, Defining marketing problems.
26. Semon, T. (1999, June 7). Make sure the research will answer the right question. *Marketing News, 33*(12), H30.
27. Adapted from Merriam-Webster online at http://www.merriam-webster.com/dictionary/hypothesis and dictionary.com/hypothesis.
28. "Students may be surprised to learn that there is little agreement in the advertising industry as to what constitutes a 'better' advertising claim at the testing stage. The researcher is often saddled with the task of measuring the quality of the claims and with defining what a better claim should be. It would be helpful if the firm has a history of testing claims and has reached agreement on what constitutes a 'better' claim. In the end the definition of 'better' must be based on consensus or the decision cannot be made." Quote provided to the authors by Ron Tatham, Ph.D.
29. Adapted from www.dictionary.com, accessed November 15, 2003. Also see Bagozzi, R. P., & Phillips, L. W. (1982, September). Representing and testing organizational theories: A holistic construal. *Administrative Science Quarterly, 27*(3), 459.
30. Smith, S. M., & Albaum, G. S. (2005). *Fundamentals of marketing research.* Thousand Oaks, CA: Sage, p. 349.
31. American Marketing Association. (n.d.). Dictionary. Retrieved from www. marketingpower.com, accessed December 10, 2003.
32. Bearden, W. O., Netemeyer, R. G., & Mobley, M. F. (1993). *Handbook of marketing scales.* Newberry Park, CA: Sage; Bearden, W. O., & Netemeyer, R. G. (1999). *Handbook of marketing scales: Multi-item measures for marketing and consumer behavior research.* Thousand Oaks, CA: Sage; and Bruner, G. C., Hensel, P. J., & James, K. E. (2005). *Marketing scales handbook: A compilation of multi-item measures for consumer behavior and advertising.* Chicago: American Marketing Association.
33. Moser, A. (2005). Take steps to avoid misused research pitfall. *Marketing News, 39*(15), 27.
34. See Burns, A. C., & Bush, R. F. (2006). Insights based on 30 years of defining the problem and research objectives, *Marketing research* (5th ed.). Upper Saddle River, NJ: Pearson/Prentice Hall, pp. 92–93.
35. Jones, S. (1985). Problem-definition in marketing research: Facilitating dialog between clients and researchers. *Psychology and Marketing, 2*(2), 83.
36. Kane, C. (1994, November 28). New product killer: The research gap. *Brandweek, 35*(46), 12.
37. Mariampolski, H. (2000, December). A guide to writing and evaluating qualitative research proposals. *Quirk's Marketing Research Review.*
38. Mariampolski, A guide to writing and evaluating qualitative research proposals.

Chapter 4

1. Singleton, D. (2003, November 24). Basics of good research involve understanding six simple rules. *Marketing News*, 22–23.
2. For an excellent in-depth treatment of research design issues, see Creswell, J. (2003). *Research design: Qualitative, quantitative, and mixed methods approaches.* Thousand Oaks, CA: Sage.
3. Personal communication with Holly McLennan, Marketing Director, 1-800-GOT-JUNK? on April 27, 2005; Martin, J. (2003, October 27). Cash from trash: 1-800-Got Junk? *Fortune, 148*, 196.
4. Company test marketing water bottle kiosks at WVU. (2012, April 9). *The Marietta Times.* Retrieved from www.mariettatimes.com.
5. For one example, see Parasuraman, A., Berry, L. L., & Zeithaml, V. A. (1991, Winter). Refinement and reassessment of the SERVQUAL scale. *Journal of Retailing, 67*(4), 420ff. A small effort of exploratory research on this topic will find many references on measuring service quality.
6. Stewart, D. W. (1984). *Secondary research: Information sources and methods.* Newbury Park, CA: Sage; Davidson, J. P. (1985, April). Low cost research sources. *Journal of Small Business Management, 23*, 73–77.
7. Malhotra, N. K. (2010). *Marketing research: An applied orientation* (6th ed.). Upper Saddle River, NJ: Pearson Prentice Hall, p. 40.
8. Knox, N. (2003, December 16). Volvo teams up to build what women want. *USA Today*, 1B.
9. Bonoma, T. V. (1984). Case research in marketing: Opportunities, problems, and a process. *Journal of Marketing Research, 21*, 199–208.
10. Kinnear, T. C., & Taylor, J. R. (1991). *Marketing research: An applied approach.* New York: McGraw-Hill, p. 142.
11. Sudman, S., & Wansink, B. (2002). *Consumer panels* (2nd ed.). Chicago: American Marketing Association. This book is recognized as an authoritative source on panels.
12. Lohse, G. L., & Rosen, D. L. (2002, Summer). Signaling quality and credibility in Yellow Pages advertising: The influence of color and graphics on choice. *Journal of Advertising, 30*(2), 73–85.
13. Wyner, G. (2000, Fall). Learn and earn through testing on the Internet: The Web provides new opportunities for experimentation. *Marketing Research, 12*(3), 37–38.
14. In fact, the Affordable Care Act signed into law in March 2010 by President Obama requires the FDA to develop standards requiring restaurant chains with 20 or more outlets to provide food labeling.
15. See, for example: Montgomery, D. (2001). *Design and analysis of experiments.* New York: Wiley; Kerlinger, F. N. (1986). *Foundations of behavioral research* (3rd ed.). New York: Holt, Rinehart, and Winston.
16. Campbell, D. T., & Stanley, J. C. (1963). *Experimental and quasi-experimental designs for research.* Chicago: Rand McNally.
17. Calder, B. J., Phillips, L. W., & Tybout, A. M. (1992, December). The concept of external validity. *Journal of Consumer Research, 9*, 240–244.
18. Gray, L. R., & Diehl, P. L. (1992). *Research methods for business and management.* New York: Macmillan, pp. 387–390.
19. Brennan, L. (1988, March). Test marketing. *Sales Marketing Management Magazine, 140*, 50–62.
20. Miles, S. (2001, January 17). MyTurn is cutting back in unusual way. *Wall Street Journal*, Eastern edition.

21. Churchill, G. A., Jr. (2001). *Basic marketing research* (4th ed.). Fort Worth, TX: Dryden Press, pp. 144–145.
22. Dog TV launches a canine cable network. (2012, April). Retrieved from www.baywoof.com, accessed May 18, 2012.
23. Missouri seeks to market pain-free dental tool. (2011, December 31). *BusinessWeek.* Retrieved from http://www.businessweek.com/ap/financialnews
24. White Castle testing alcohol in Indiana. (2011, December 22). *Business First.* Retrieved from www.bizjournals.com/columbus/morning_call/2011/12/white-castle-testing-alcohol-drinks
25. Ziobro, P. (2011, December 3). Dr. Pepper slims down five more of its sodas. *The Wall Street Journal.* Retrieved from online.wsj.com
26. Spethmann, B. (1985, May 8). Test market USA. *Brandweek, 36,* 40–43.
27. Melvin, P. (1992, September). Choosing simulated test marketing systems. *Marketing Research, 4*(3), 14–16.
28. Ibid. Also see Turner, J., & Brandt, J. (1978, Winter). Development and validation of a simulated market to test children for selected consumer skills. *Journal of Consumer Affairs,* 266–276.
29. Greene, S. (1996, May 4). Chattanooga chosen as test market for smokeless cigarette. *Knight-Ridder/Tribune Business News.* Retrieved from Lexis-Nexis.
30. Power, C. (1992, August 10). Will it sell in Podunk? Hard to say. *Business Week,* 46–47.
31. Murphy, P., & Laczniak, G. (1992, June). Emerging ethical issues facing marketing researchers. *Marketing Research,* 6.
32. Much of the content of this case was taken from a discussion with marketing researcher Doss Struse.

Chapter 5

1. For an example of using secondary data for a marketing research project, see Castleberry, S. B. (2001, December). Using secondary data in marketing research: A project that melds web and off-web sources. *Journal of Marketing Education, 23*(3), 195–203.
2. Survey monitor: Boomers and gen X the most spend-happy; Millennials buy more per trip. (2010, May). *Quirk's Marketing Research Review, 14,* pp. 10, 59.
3. Weiss, M. J. (2003, September 1). To be or not to be. *American Demographics.* Retrieved from LexisNexis.
4. Tootelian, D. H., & Varshney, S. B. (2010). The grandparent consumer: A financial "goldmine" with gray hair? *The Journal of Consumer Marketing, 27*(1), 57–63. Retrieved May 5, 2010, from ABI/INFORM Global (Document ID: 1945854611).
5. Kotler, P., & Keller, K. L. (2009). *Marketing management* (13th ed.). Upper Saddle River, NJ: Pearson Prentice Hall, p. 143.
6. Senn, J. A. (1988). *Information technology in business: Principles, practice, and opportunities.* Upper Saddle River, NJ: Prentice Hall, p. 66.
7. Grisaffe, D. (2002, January 21). See about linking CRM and MR systems. *Marketing News, 36*(2), 13.
8. Drozdenko, R. G., and Drake, P. D. (2002). *Optimal database marketing.* Thousand Oaks, CA: Sage.
9. Berman, B., & Evans, J. R. (2010). *Retail management: A strategic approach.* Upper Saddle River, NJ: Pearson Prentice Hall, p. 235.
10. Kotler & Keller, *Marketing management,* pp. 143–145.
11. McKim, R. (2001, September). Privacy notices: What they mean and how marketers can prepare for them. *Journal of Database Marketing, 9*(1), 79–84.
12. For a discussion of these and other similar situations, see Crosen, C. (1994). *Tainted truth: The manipulation of fact in America.* New York: Simon & Schuster, p. 140.

13. America's experience with Census 2000. (2000, August). *Direct Marketing, 63*(4), 46–51.
14. Accuracy of the census is measured by Census Coverage Measurement (CCM). CCM for the 2010 Census showed that it had an error of .01 percent overcount, meaning that an estimated 36,000 extra people were counted. Retrieved from http://www.census.gov on May 24, 2012.
15. Lange, K. E. (2009, November). The big idea: Electric cars. *National Geographic,* p. 24.
16. Database of personalities (living and dead). (n.d.). Retrieved from http://www.qscores.com/Web/personalities.aspx, accessed May 30, 2012.
17. Based on information provided to the authors by Marketing Evaluations, Inc., on May 31, 2012. These were the top two celebrities in the 2012 Performer Q study.
18. Television measurement. (2012). Retrieved from http://www.nielsen.com/us/en/measurement/television-measurement.html, accessed May 30, 2012.
19. Lifestyles-Esri Tapestry Segmentation. (n.d.). Retrieved from http://www.esri.com/data/esri_data/tapestry.html, accessed May 30, 2012.
20. Actually, virtually all these firms offer some customization of data analysis, and many offer varying methods of collecting data. Still, while customization is possible, these same companies provide standardized processes and data.

Chapter 6

1. Ezzy, D. (2001, August). Are qualitative methods misunderstood? *Australian and New Zealand Journal of Public Health, 25*(4), 294–297.
2. Clark, A. (2001, September 13). Research takes an inventive approach. *Marketing,* 25–26.
3. DeNicola, N. (2002, March 4). Casting finer net not necessary. *Marketing News, 36*(5), 46.
4. Venkatraman, M., & Nelson, T. (2008). From servicescape to consumptionscape: A photo-elicitation study of Starbucks in the New China. *Journal of International Business Studies, 39,* 1010–1026.
5. Cusumano, L. (2010, April). How big pharma is misusing qualitative marketing research. *Quirks Marketing Research Review, 24*(4), 18–20.
6. Rydholm, J. (2011, May). A clearer picture. *Quirks Marketing Research Review, 25*(5), 30–33.
7. Smith, S. M., & Whitlark, D. B. (2001, Summer). Men and women online: What makes them click? *Marketing Research, 13*(2), 20–25.
8. Piirto, R. (1991, September). Socks, ties and videotape. *American Demographics,* 6.
9. Fellman, M. W. (1999, Fall). Breaking tradition. *Marketing Research, 11*(3), 20–34.
10. Modified from Tull, D. S., & Hawkins, D. I. (1987). *Marketing research* (4th ed.). New York: Macmillan, p. 331.
11. Rust, L. (1993, November/December). How to reach children in stores: Marketing tactics grounded in observational research. *Journal of Advertising Research, 33*(6), 67–72; Rust, L. (1993, July/August). Parents and children shopping together: A new approach to the qualitative analysis of observational data. *Journal of Advertising Research, 33*(4), 65–70.
12. Rydholm, J. (2010, May). Steering in the right direction. *Quirks Marketing Research Review, 24*(5), 26–32.
13. Bean, C. Where can we make a difference? (2010, June). *Quirks Marketing Research Review, 24*(6), 30–35.
14. Viles, P. (1992, August 24). Company measures listenership in cars. *Broadcasting, 122*(35), 27.

15. Mariampolski, H. (1988, January 4). Ethnography makes come-back as research tool. *Marketing News, 22*(1), 32, 44; Peñaloza, L. (1994, June). Atravesando Fronteras/Border Crossings: A critical ethnographic study of the consumer acculturation of Mexican immigrants. *Journal of Consumer Research, 21*, 32–53; Peñaloza, L. (2006). Researching ethnicity and consumption. In Russell W. Belk (Ed.), *Handbook of qualitative research techniques in marketing.* Cheltenham, England: Edward Elgar, 547–549; Carlon, M. (2008, April). Evolving ethnography. *Quirk's Marketing Research Review, 22*(4), 18, 20.

16. Kephart, P. (1996, May). The spy in aisle 3. *American Demographics Marketing Tools.* Retrieved from www.marketingtools.com/Publications/MT/96_mt/9605MD04.htm

17. Del Vecchio, E. (1988, Spring). Generating marketing ideas when formal research is not available. *Journal of Services Marketing, 2*(2), 71–74.

18. Hellebursch, S. J. (2000, September 11). Don't read research by the numbers. *Marketing News, 34*(19), 25.

19. Greenbaum, T. I. (1988). *The practical handbook and guide in focus group research.* Lexington, MA: D. C. Heath.

20. Stoltman, J. J., & Gentry, J. W. (1992). Using focus groups to study household decision processes and choices. In R. P. Leone and V. Kumar (Eds.), *AMA Educator's Conference Proceedings*, Vol. 3. Enhancing knowledge development in marketing (pp. 257–263). Chicago: American Marketing Association.

21. Last, J., & Langer, J. (2003, December). Still a valuable tool. *Quirk's Marketing Research Review, 17*(11), 30.

22. Kahn, A. (1996, September 6). Focus groups alter decisions made in business, politics. *Knight-Ridder/Tribune Business News*, 916.

23. Wellner, A. (2003, March). The new science of focus groups. *American Demographics, 25*(2), 29ff.

24. Greenbaum, T. L. (1993, March 1). Focus group research is not a commodity business. *Marketing News, 27*(5), 4.

25. Greenbaum, T. L. (1991, May 27). Answer to moderator problems starts with asking right questions. *Marketing News, 25*(11), 8–9; Fern, E. F. (1982, February). The use of focus groups for idea generation: The effects of group size, acquaintanceship, and moderator on response quantity and quality. *Journal of Marketing Research*, 1–13.

26. Greenbaum, T. L. (1991). Do you have the right moderator for your focus groups? Here are 10 questions to ask yourself. *Bank Marketing, 23*(1), 43.

27. For guidelines for "backroom observers," see Langer, J. (2001, September 24). Get more out of focus group research. *Marketing News, 35*(20), 19–20.

28. Grinchunas, R., & Siciliano, T. (1993, January 4). Focus groups produce verbatims, not facts. *Marketing News, 27*(1), FG-19.

29. Lonnie, K. (2001, November 19). Combine phone, Web for focus groups. *Marketing News, 35*(24), 15–16.

30. For interesting comments, see DeNicola, N., & Kennedy, S. (2001, November 19). Quality Inter(net)action. *Marketing News, 35*(24), 14.

31. Jarvis, S., & Szynal, D. (2001, November 19). Show and tell. *Marketing News, 35*(24), 1, 13.

32. Based on a table in Goon, E. (2011, May). Need research? Won't travel. *Quirks Marketing Research Review, 25*(5), 22–28.

33. Langer, J. (2001). The mirrored window: Focus groups from a moderator's viewpoint. New York: Paramount Market, 11.

34. Quinlan, P. (2000, December). Insights on a new site. *Quirk's Marketing Research Review, 15*(11), 36–39.

35. Hines, T. (2000). An evaluation of two qualitative methods (focus group interviews and cognitive maps) for conducting research into entrepreneurial decision making. *Qualitative Market Research,*

3(1), 7–16; Quinlan, P. (2008, June). Let the maps be your guide. *Quirk's Marketing Research Review, 22*(6), 74, 76, 77.

36. Berlamino, C. (1989, December/January). Designing the qualitative research project: Addressing the process issues. *Journal of Advertising Research, 29*(6), S7–S9; Johnston, G. (2008, June). Qualitatively speaking. *Quirk's Marketing Research Review, 22*(6), 18, 20; *Alert! Magazine.* (2007, September). Special expanded qualitative research issue, *45*(9); Brownell, L. (2008, April). Chief executive column. *Alert! Magazine, 46*(4): 11, 23.

37. Perez, R. (2010, May). Shaping the Ddscussion. *Quirk's Marketing Research Review, 24*(5):34–40.

38. See for example, Seidler, Sharon. (2010, May). Qualitative research panels: A new spin on traditional focus groups. *Quirks Marketing Research Review, 25*(5), 18–20.

39. Flores Letelier, M., Spinosa, C., & Calder, B. (2000, Winter). Taking an expanded view of customers' needs: Qualitative research for aiding innovation. *Marketing Research, 12*(4), 4–11.

40. Grapentine, T. (2010, December). Does more time equal more insights? *Quirks Marketing Research Review, 24*(10), 34–37.

41. Donnely, T. (2011, May). Marrying phone and web. *Quirks Marketing Research Review, 25*(5), 42–46.

42. Kahan, H. (1990, September 3). One-on-ones should sparkle like the gems they are. *Marketing News, 24*(18), 8–9.

43. Roller, M. R. (1987, August 28). A real in-depth interview wades into the stream of consciousness. *Marketing News, 21*(18), 14.

44. Kahan, One-on-ones should sparkle like the gems they are.

45. An interesting article on developments in in-depth interviewing is Wansink, B. (2000, Summer). New techniques to generate key marketing insights. *Marketing Research, 12*(2), 28–36.

46. Kates, B. (2000, April). Go in-depth with depth interviews. *Quirk's Marketing Research Review, 14*(4), 36–40.

47. Mitchell, V. (1993, First Quarter). Getting the most from in-depth interviews. *Business Marketing Digest, 18*(1), 63–70.

48. Reynolds, T. J., & Gutman, J. (1988). Laddering, method, analysis, and interpretation. *Journal of Advertising Research, 28*(1), 11–21.

49. Qualitative Research Services. (n.d.). Word association tests. Retrieved from www.decisionanalyst.com May 20, 2005.

50. Qualitative Research Services. (n.d.). Sentence completion tests. Retrieved from www.decisionanalyst.com May 20, 2005.

51. An example is Piirto, R. (1990, December). Measuring minds in the 1990s. *American Demographics, 12*(12), 30–35.

52. American Marketing Association. (n.d.). Dictionary. Retrieved from www.marketingpower.com.

53. Taylor, C. (2003, December). What's all the fuss about? *Quirk's Marketing Research Review, 17*(11), 40–45.

54. These techniques are provided by Holly M. O'Neill, President, Talking Business™.

55. Brogdon, T. (2011, February). A bit more personal. *Quirks' Marketing Research Review, 25*(2), 50–53.

56. Elwood, M. (2010, May). Of stovetops and laptops. *Quirks Marketing Research Revew, 24*(5), 42–45.

57. Burns, A. and Bush, R. (2010). Marketing Research, 6th ed. Upper Saddle River, NJ: Prentice Hall, 231.

58. Green, P., Wind, Y., Krieger, A., & Saatsoglou, P. (2000, Spring). Applying qualitative data. *Marketing Research, 12*(1), 17–25.

59. Rellis, C. (2010, December). Picture this. *Quirks Marketing Research Review, 24*(12), 30–33.

60. Leiman, B. (2010, December). Is TMI the new normal? *Quirks Marketing Research Review, 24*(12), 44–48.

61. Marshall, S., Drapeau, T., & DiSciullo, M. (2001, July/August). An eye on usability. *Quirk's Marketing Research Review, 15*(7), 20–21, 90–92.

62. Zapata, C. (2012). What caught their eye? *Quirk's Marketing Research Review, 26*(5), 32–37.

63. Singer, N. (2010, November 12). Making ads that whisper to the brain. *The New York Times.* Retrieved from http://www.nytimes.com.

64. Thompson, C. (2003, October 26). There's a sucker born in every medial prefrontal cortex. *The New York Times.* Retrieved from http://www.nytimes.com.

65. McClure, S., Li, J., Tomlin, D., Cypert, K., Montague, L., & Montague, P. R. (2004). Neural correlates of behavioral preference for culturally familiar drinks. *Neuron, 44*(2), 379–387. Retrieved from http://ac.els-cdn.com.

66. Green, S., & Holbert, N. (2012). Neuroimaging and marketing research. In R. Kaden, G. Linda, & M. Prince (Eds.), *Leading edge marketing research: 21st-century tools and practices* (pp. 252–272). London, England: Sage.

67. Green, & Holbert, Neuroimaging and marketing research.

68. Allmon, D. E. (1988). Voice stress and likert scales: A paired comparison. In D. L. Moore (Ed.), Marketing: Forward motion, *Proceedings of the Atlantic Marketing Association,* 710–714.

69. Rydholm, J.. (2011, May). FAQ: Neuromarketing research. *Quirks Marketing Research Review, 25*(5), 56–59.

70. This section was contributed by Courtney Murphy, Masters of Marketing Research Candidate. Southern Illinois University, Edwardsville, 2011. Other references on neuroimagery include: Green, & Holbert, Neuroimaging and marketing research; McClure et al., Neural correlates of behavioral preference for culturally familiar drinks.

Chapter 7

1. Malhotra, N. (1999). *Marketing research: An applied orientation* (3rd ed.). Upper Saddle River, NJ: Prentice Hall, p. 125.

2. Tourangeau, R. (2004). Survey research and societal change. *Annual Review of Psychology, 55*(1), 775–802.

3. Snider, M. (2011, April 21). More people ditching home phone for mobile. *USA Today.* Retrieved from www.usatoday.com.

4. Blyth, B. (2008). Mixed mode: The only 'fitness' regime. *International Journal of Market Research, 50*(2), 241–266.

5. Curtin, R., Presser, S., & Singer, E. (2005, Spring). Changes in telephone survey nonresponse over the past quarter century. *Public Opinion Quarterly, 69*(1), 87–98.

6. See Oishi, S. M. (2003). *How to conduct in-person interviews for surveys.* Thousand Oaks, CA: Sage, p. 6.

7. Tourangeau, Survey research and societal change.

8. Tourangeau, Survey research and societal change.

9. See Macer, T. (2002, December). CAVI from OpinionOne. *Quirk's Marketing Research Review.*

10. Bourque, L., & Fielder, E. (2003*). How to conduct self-administered and mail surveys* (2nd ed.). Thousand Oaks, CA: Sage.

11. Jang, H., Lee, B., Park, M., & Stokowski, P. A. (2000, February). Measuring underlying meanings of gambling from the perspective of enduring involvement. *Journal of Travel Research, 38*(3), 230–238.

12. Ericson, P. I., & Kaplan, C. P. (2000, November). Maximizing qualitative responses about smoking in structured interviews. *Qualitative Health Research, 10*(6), 829–840.

13. See, for example, Dudley, D. (2001, January)., The name collector. *New Media Age,* 18–20; Kent, R., & Brandal, H. (2003). Improving email response in a permission marketing context. *International Journal of Market Research, 45*(4), 489–540; Agrawal, A., Basak, J., Jain, V., Kothari, R., Kumar, M., Mittal, P. A., et al. (2004,

September/October). Online marketing research. *IBM Journal of Research & Development, 48*(5/6), 671–677.

14. Bronner, F., & Kuijlen, T. (2007). The live or digital interviewer. *International Journal of Market Research, 49*(2), 167–190.

15. Haynes, D. (February 2005). Respondent goodwill is a cooperative activity. *Quirk's Marketing Research Review, 19*(2), 30–32.

16. Macer, T., & Wilson, S. (February 2007). Online makes more inroads. *Quirk's Marketing Research Review, 23*(2), 50–55; Westergaard, J. (2005, November). Your survey, our needs. *Quirk's Marketing Research Review, 19*(10), 64–66.

17. Some authors restrict the definition to only cases where two or more data collection methods are used in the same phase of the study. See Hogg, A. (2002, July). Multi-mode research dos and don'ts, *Quirk's Marketing Research Review.* Retrieved from http://www.quirks.com

18. Cuneo, A. Z. (2004, November).Researchers flail as public cuts the cord. *Advertising Age, 75,* (46), 3.

19. Townsend, L. (2010, November). Hit 'em where they surf. *Quirks Marketing Research Review, 24*(11), 40–43.

20. Katz, M., & Mackey, P. (2010, April). Positive, negative, or neutral. *Quirks Marketing Research Review,* 24(4), 26–31.

21. See, for example, www.uwf.edu/panel.

22. Fricker, S., Galesic, M., Tourangeau, R., & Ting, Y. (2005, Fall). An experimental comparison of web and telephone surveys. *Public Opinion Quarterly, 69*(3), 370–392.

23. See Roy, A. (2003). Further issues and factors affecting the response rates of e-mail and mixed-mode studies. In M. Barone et al. (Eds.), *Enhancing knowledge development in marketing.* Proceedings of the American Marketing Association Educators' Conference, Chicago, pp. 338–339; Bachmann, D., Elfrink, J., & Vazzana, G. (1999). E-mail and snail mail face off in rematch. *Marketing Research, 11*(4), 11–15.

24. Hogg, Multi-mode research dos and don'ts.

25. Based on Pferdekaemper, T. (2010, June). On-the-go and in-the-moment. *Quirks Marketing Research Review, 24*(6), 52–59.

26. Roy, S. (2004, July). The littlest consumers. *Display & Design Ideas, 16*(7), 18–21.

27. See Jacobs, H. (1989, Second Quarter). Entering the 1990s: The state of data collection–From a mall perspective. *Applied Marketing Research, 30*(2), 24–26; Lysaker, R. L. (1989, October). Data collection methods in the U.S. *Journal of the Market Research Society, 31*(4), 477–488; Gates, R., & Solomon, P. J. (1982, August/September). Research using the mall intercept: State of the art. *Journal of Advertising Research,* 43–50; Bush, A. J., Bush, R. F., & Chen, H. C. (1991). Method of administration effects in mall intercept interviews. *Journal of the Market Research Society, 33*(4), 309–319.

28. See, for example, Ghazali, E., Mutum, A. D., & Mahbob, N. A. (2006). Attitude towards online purchase of fish in urban Malaysia: An ethnic comparison. *Journal of Food Products Marketing, 12*(4), 109–128; Yun, W., & Heitmeyer, J. (2006, January). Consumer attitude toward US versus domestic apparel in Taiwan, *International Journal of Consumer Studies, 30*(1), 64–74.

29. Frost-Norton, T. (2005, June). The future of mall research: Current trends affecting the future of marketing research in malls. *Journal of Consumer Behaviour, 4*(4), 293–301.

30. Hornik, J., & Eilis, S. (1989, Winter). Strategies to secure compliance for a mall intercept interview. *Public Opinion Quarterly, 52*(4), 539–551.

31. At least one study refutes the concern about shopping frequency. See DuPont, T. D. (1987, August/September). Do frequent mall shoppers distort mall-intercept results? *Journal of Advertising Research, 27*(4), 45–51.

32. Bush, A. J., & Grant, E. S. (1995, Fall). The potential impact of recreational shoppers on mall intercept interviewing: An exploratory study. *The Journal of Marketing Theory and Practice, 3*(4), 73–83.

33. Bourque, L., & Fielder, E. (2003). *How to conduct telephone interviews* (2nd ed.). Thousand Oaks, CA: Sage.

34. Bush, A. J., & Hair, J. F. (1983, May). An assessment of the mall intercept as a data collection method. *Journal of Marketing Research, 22,* 158–167.

35. Holbrook, A. L., Green, M. C., Krosnick, J. A. (2003, Spring). Telephone versus face-to-face interviewing of national probability samples with long questionnaires. *Public Opinion Quarterly, 67*(1), 79–126.

36. Sheppard, J. (2000, April). Half-empty or half-full? *Quirk's Marketing Research Review, 14*(4), 42–45.

37. See, for example, Xu, M., Bates, B. J., & Schweitzer, J. C. (1993). The impact of messages on survey participation in answering machine households. *Public Opinion Quarterly, 57,* 232–237; Meinert, D. B., Festervand, T. A., & Lumpkin, J. R. (1992). Computerized questionnaires: Pros and cons, in Robert L. King (Ed.), *Marketing: Perspectives for the 1990s, Proceedings of the Southern Marketing Association,* 201–206.

38. Remington, T. D. (1993). Telemarketing and declining survey response rates. *Journal of Advertising Research, 32*(3), RC-6–RC-7.

39. Brennan, M., Benson, S., & Kearns, Z. (2005). The effect of introductions on telephone survey participation rates. *International Journal of Market Research, 47*(1), 65–75.

40. At the extreme, it is reported that Chinese research companies monitor at least 50% of all telephone interviews; see Harrison, M. (2006, Winter). Learning the language. *Marketing Research, 18*(4), 10–16.

41. Bos, R. (1999, November). A new era in data collection, *Quirk's Marketing Research Review, 12*(10), 32–40.

42. Fletcher, K. (1995, June 15). Jump on the omnibus. *Marketing,* 25–28.

43. DePaulo, P. J., & Weitzer, R. (1994, January 3). Interactive phone technology delivers survey data quickly. *Marketing News, 28,* 1, 15.

44. Jones, P., & Palk, J. (1993). Computer-based personal interviewing: State-of-the-art and future prospects. *Journal of the Market Research Society, 35*(3), 221–233.

45. For a "speed" comparison, see Cobanouglu, C., Warde, B., & Moeo, P. J. (2001). A comparison of mail, fax and Web-based survey methods. *International Journal of Market Research, 43*(3), 441–452.

46. Not all observers agree that this trend is positive. See Lauer, H. (2005, July/August). You say evolution, I say devolution. *Quirk's Marketing Research Review, 19*(7), 82–88.

47. Miles, L. (2004, June 16). Online market research panels offer clients high response rates at low prices. *Marketing,* 39.

48. Grecco, C. (2000, July/August). Research non-stop. *Quirk's Marketing Research Review, 14*(7), 70–73.

49. Greenberg, D. (2000, July/August). Internet economy gives rise to real-time research. *Quirk's Marketing Research Review, 14*(7), 88–90.

50. Frazier, D. & Rohmund, I. (2007, July/August). The real-time benefits of online surveys, *Electric Perspectives, 32*(4), 88–91.

51. See, for example, Deutskens, E., Jong, A., Ruyter, K., & Wetzels, M. (2006, April). Comparing the generalizability of online and mail surveys in cross-national service quality research. *Marketing Letters, 17*(2), 119–136; Coderre, F., St-Laurent, N., & Mathieu, A. (2004). Comparison of the quality of qualitative data obtained through telephone, postal and email surveys. *International Journal of Market Research, 46*(3), 347–357; Kaplowitz, M. D., Hadlock, T. D., & Levine, R. (2004, Spring). A comparison of eeb and mail survey response rates. *Public Opinion Quarterly, 68*(1), 94–101;

Sparrow, N., & Curtice, J. (2004). Measuring the attitudes of the general public versus Internet polls: An evaluation. *International Journal of Market Research, 46*(1), 23–44.

52. Macer, T., & Wilson, S. (2011, February). *Globalpark annual market research software survey 2010.* Retrieved from http://www.meaning.uk.com

53. Brown, S. (1987). Drop and collect surveys: A neglected research technique? *Journal of the Market Research Society, 5*(1), 19–23.

54. See Ibeh, K. I. & Brock, J. K. (2004). Conducting survey research among organisational populations in developing countries. *International Journal of Market Research,* (3), 375–383, Ibeh, K. I., Brock, J. K., & Zhou, Y. J. (2004, February). The drop and collect survey among industrial populations: Theory and empirical evidence. *Industrial Marketing Management, 33*(2), 155–165.

55. Bourque, & Fielder, *How to conduct self-administered and mail surveys.*

56. American Statistical Association. (1997). More about mail surveys. *ASA Series: What is a survey?* Alexandria, VA: Author.

57. Nonresponse is a concern with any survey, and our understanding of refusals is minimal. See, for example, Groves, R. M., Cialdini, R. B., & Couper, M. P. (1992). Understanding the decision to participate in a survey. *Public Opinion Quarterly, 56,* 475–495.

58. Anderson, R. C., Fell, D., Smith, R. L., Hansen, E. N., & Gomon, S. (2005, January). Current consumer behavior research in forest products. *Forest Products Journal, 55*(1), 21–27.

59. Grandcolas, U., Rettie, R., & Marusenko, K. (2003). Web survey Bias: sample or mode effect? *Journal of Marketing Management, 19,* 541–561.

60. See, for example, McDaniel, S. W., & Verille, P. (1987, January). Do topic differences affect survey nonresponse? *Journal of the Market Research Society, 29*(1), 55–66; Whitehead, J. C. (1991, Winter). Environmental interest group behavior and self-selection bias in contingent valuation mail surveys. *Growth & Change, 22*(1), 10–21.

61. An industry study identified effectiveness, demand for a specific modality, cost, speed of data collection, and available resources as the top five selection criteria when selecting a data collection modality. Pioneer Marketing Research. (2004, April). *Research industry trends: 2004 report.*Retrieved from Dialtek L.P. Web site, http://www.dialtek.com.

62. For an example of a new data collection method, see Wentz, L. (2004, April 12). Mindshare to read 20,000 media minds. *Advertising Age, 75*(15), 1.

63. Philpott, G. (2005, February). Get the most from Net-based panel research. *Marketing News, 39*(2), 58.

64. Gerlotto, C. (2003, November). Learning on the go: Tips on getting international research right. *Quirk's Marketing Research Review,* 44.

65. Weiss, L. (2002, November). Research in Canada. *Quirk's Marketing Research Review,* 40.

66. Morgan, R., Myers, J., Quigley, A., & Zivin, S. (2011, April). The rules of engagement. *Quirks Marketing Research Review, 25*(4), 24–28.

67. Smedley, C., & Abraham, A. (2010). The 8095 Exchange: Millennials, their actions surrounding brands, and the dynamics of reverberation. Retrieved from http://www.strategyone.com/portfolio_item/the-8095-exchange/

Chapter 8

1. For an example of scale development using college students as respondents, see Blankson, C. (2008, April). Measuring college students' choice of credit cards: Scale development and validation. *Journal of Marketing Management, 24*(3–4), 317–344.

2. See for example, Yoon, S., & Kim, J. (2001, November/December). Is the Internet more effective than traditional media? Factors affecting the choice of media. *Journal of Advertising Research, 41*(6), 53–60; Donthu, N. (2001, November/December). Does your web site measure up? *Marketing Management, 10*(4), 29–32; Finn, A., McFadyen, S., Hoskins, C., & Hupfer, M. (2001, Fall). Quantifying the sources of value of a public service. *Journal of Public Policy & Marketing, 20*(2), 225–239.

3. See, for example, Wellner, A. S. (2002, February). The female persuasion. *American Demographics, 24*(2), 24–29; Wasserman, T. (2002, January 7). Color me bad. *Brandweek, 43*(1), 2; Wilke, M., & Applebaum, M. (2001, November 5). Peering out of the closet. *Brandweek, 42*(41), 26–32.

4. Kaplanidou, K., & Vogt, C. (2010, September). The meaning and measurement of a sport event experience among active sport tourists. *Journal of Sport Management, 24*(5), 544–566.

5. Other methods of brand image measurement have been been found to be comparable. See Driesener, C., & Romaniuk, J. (2006). Comparing methods of brand image measurement. *International Journal of Market Research, 48*(6), 681–698.

6. Another way to avoid the halo effect is to have subjects rate each stimulus on the same attribute and then move to the next attribute. See Wu, B. T. W., & Petroshius, S. (1987). The halo effect in store image management. *Journal of the Academy of Marketing Science, 15*(1), 44–51.

7. The halo effect is real and used by companies to good advantage. See, for example, Moukheiber, Z., & Langreth, R. (2001, December 10). The halo effect. *Forbes, 168*(15), 66; Sites seeking advertising (the paid kind). (2002, March 11). *Advertising Age, 73*(10), 38.

8. Some authors recommend using negatively worded statements with Likert scales to avoid the halo effect; however, recent evidence argues convincingly against this recommendation. See Swain, S. D., Weathers, D., & Niedrich, R. W. (2007, February). Assessing three sources of misresponse to reversed Likert items. *Journal of Marketing Research, 45*(1), 116–131.

9. Garg, R. K. (1996, July). The influence of positive and negative wording and issue involvement on responses to Likert scales in marketing research. *Journal of the Marketing Research Society, 38*(3), 235–246.

10. See, for example, Bishop, G. F. (1985, Summer). Experiments with the middle response alternative in survey questions. *Public Opinion Quarterly, 51*, 220–232; Schertizer, C. B., & Kernan, J. B. (1985, October). More on the robustness of response scales. *Journal of the Marketing Research Society, 27*, 262–282.

11. See also Duncan, O. D. & Stenbeck, M. (1988, Winter). No opinion or not sure? *Public Opinion Quarterly, 52*, 513–525; Durand, R. M., & Lambert, Z. V. (1988, March). Don't know responses in survey: Analyses and interpretational consequences. *Journal of Business Research, 16*, 533–543.

12. Semon, T. T. (2001, October 8). Symmetry shouldn't be goal for scales. *Marketing News, 35*(21), 9.

13. Semon, Symmetry shouldn't be goal for scales.

14. Elms. P. (2000, April). Using decision criteria anchors to measure importance among Hispanics. *Quirk's Marketing Research Review, 15*(4), 44–51.

15. Ashley, D. (2003, February). The questionnaire that launched a thousand responses. *Quirk's Marketing Research Review*. Retrieved from www.quirks.com

16. Scale development requires rigorous research. See, for example, Churchill, G. A. (1979, February). A paradigm for developing better measures of marketing constructs. *Journal of Marketing Research, 16*, 64–73; Ram, S., & Jung, H. S. (1990). The conceptualization

and measurement of product usage. *Journal of the Academy of Marketing Science, 18*(1), 67–76.

17. Cavallaro, K. (2011, January). Are global scales as easy as 1-2-3 or A-B-C? *Quirks Marketing Research Review, 25*(1), 18–22.

18. The topic of internal consistency of multiple item measures is too advanced for this basic textbook. Also, recent research touts single-item measures in certain instances. See Bergkvist, L., & Rossiter, J. (2007, May). The predictive validity of multiple-item versus single-item measures of the same constructs. *Journal of Marketing Research, 44*(2), 175–184.

19. For example, bogus recall was found negatively related to education, income, and age, but positively related to "yea-saying" and attitude toward the slogan. See Glassman, M., Ford, J. B. (1988, Fall). An empirical investigation of bogus recall. *Journal of the Academy of Marketing Science, 16*(3–4), 38–41; Singh, R. (1991). Reliability and validity of survey research in marketing: The state of the art, in R. L. King (Ed.), *Marketing: Toward the twenty-first century, Proceedings of the Southern Marketing Association* (pp. 210–213); Pressley, M. M., Strutton, H. D. & Dunn, M. G. (1991). Demographic sample reliability among selected telephone sampling replacement techniques, in R. L. King (Ed.), *Marketing: Toward the twenty-first century, Proceedings of the Southern Marketing Association* (pp. 214–219); Babin, B. J., Darden, W. R., & Griffin, M. (1992). A note on demand artifacts in marketing research, in R. L. King (Ed.), *Marketing: Perspectives for the 1990s, Proceedings of the Southern Marketing Association* (pp. 227–230); Dunipace, R. A., Mix, R. A., & Poole, R. R. (1993). Overcoming the failure to replicate research in marketing: A chaotic explanation, in Tom K. Massey, Jr. (Ed.), *Marketing: Satisfying a diverse customerplace, Proceedings of the Southern Marketing Association* (pp. 194–197); Malawian, K. P., & Butler, D. D. (1994). The semantic differential: Is it being misused in marketing research? in R. Achrol & A. Mitchell (Eds.), *Enhancing knowledge development in marketing, A.M.A. Educators' Conference Proceedings*, 19.

20. Susan, C. (1994). Questionnaire design affects response rate. *Marketing News, 28*, H25; Sanchez, M. E. (1992). Effects of questionnaire design on the quality of survey data. *Public Opinion Quarterly, 56*, 206–217.

21. For a more comprehensive coverage of this topic, see Baker, M. J. (2003, Summer). Data collection: Questionnaire design. *Marketing Review, 3*(3), 343– 370.

22. Babble, E. (1990). *Survey research methods* (2nd ed.). Belmont, CA: Wadsworth, pp. 131–132.

23. Hunt, S. D., Sparkman, R. D., & Wilcox, J. (1982, May). The pretest in survey research: Issues and preliminary findings. *Journal of Marketing Research, 26*(4), 269–273.

24. Dillman, D. A. (1978). *Mail telephone surveys: The total design method.* New York: Wiley.

25. Interested readers may wish to read: Wood, R. T., & Williams, R. J. (2007, February). 'How much money do you spend on gambling?' The comparative validity of question wordings used to assess gambling expenditure. *International Journal of Social Research Methodology, 10*(1), 63–77.

26. Loftus, E., & Zanni, G. (1975). Eyewitness testimony: The influence of the wording of a question. *Bulletin of the Psychonomic Society, 5*, 86–88.

27. For an alternative set of guidelines, see Webb, J. (2000, Winter). Questionnaires and their design. *The Marketing Review, 1*(2), 197–218.

28. Several other marketing research textbooks advocate question focus. See Baker, Data collection: Questionnaire design;Do's and Don'ts. (2008, February). *CRM Magazine, 12*(2), Special section, 13.

29. Webb, Questionnaires and their design.
30. Ibid.
31. Question clarity must be achieved for respondents of different education levels, ages, socioeconomic strata, and even intelligence; see Noelle-Neumann, E. (1970, Summer). Wanted: Rules for wording structured questionnaires. *Public Opinion Quarterly, 34*(2), 191–201.
32. Webb, Questionnaires and their design.
33. For memory questions, it is advisable to have respondents recontruct specific events. See, for example, Cook, W. A. (1987, February–March). Telescoping and memory's other tricks. *Journal of Advertising Research, 27*(1), RC5–RC8.
34. Baker, Data collection: Questionnaire design.
35. Ibid.
36. Peterson, R. A. (2000). *Constructing effective questionnaires.* Thousand Oaks, CA: Sage, p. 58.
37. Henderson, N. (2011, Spring). The a*ha* moment for moderators. *Marketing Research, 23*(1), 29–30.
38. Webb, Questionnaires and their design.
39. Baker, Data collection: Questionnaire design.
40. Webb, Questionnaires and their design.
41. See, for example, More ways to build a better survey. (2008, May). *HR Focus, 85*(5), 13–14.
42. Plummer, B. (2010, October). Ask and you shall receive. *Quirks Marketing Research Review, 24*(10), 66–70.
43. Raimondi, V. (2011, May). Best practices for well-differentiated questionnaire data. *Quirks Marketing Research Review, 25*(5), 16–20; Mora, M. (2010, July). Intelligent (survey) design. *Quirks Marketing Research Review, 24*(7), 42–48.
44. Brennan, M., Benson, S., & Kearns, Z. (2005). The effect of introductions on telephone survey participation rates. *International Journal of Market Research, 47*(1), 65–74.
45. There is some evidence that mention of confidentiality has a negative effect on response rates, so the researcher should consider not mentioning it in the introduction even if confidentiality is in place. See Brennan, Benson, & Kearns, The effect of introductions on telephone survey participation rates.
46. Screens can be used to quickly identify respondents who will not answer honestly. See Waters, K. M. (1991, Spring–Summer). Designing screening questionnaires to minimize dishonest answers. *Applied Marketing Research, 31*(1), 51–53.
47. The Marketing Research Association offers recommendations and model introduction, closing, and validation scripts on its website (http://cmor.org/resp_coop_tools.htm).
48. For recommended guidelines for introductions in B2B surveys, see Durkee, A. (2005, March). First impressions are everything in b-to-b telephone surveys. *Quirk's Marketing Research Review, 19*(3), 30–32.
49. While we advocate common sense, researchers are mindful of question order effects. See, for instance, Laflin, L., & Hansen, M. (2006, October). A slight change in the route. *Quirk's Marketing Research Review, 20*(9), 40–44.
50. Smith, R., Olah, D., Hansen, B., & Cumbo, D. (2003, November/December). The effect of questionnaire length on participant response rate: A case study in the U.S. cabinet industry. *Forest Products Journal, 53*(11/12), 33–36.
51. Webb, Questionnaires and their design.
52. Bethlehem, J. (1999/2000, Winter). The routing structure of questionnaires. *International Journal of Market Research, 42*(1), 95–110.
53. Baker, Data collection: Questionnaire design.
54. At least one group-administered survey found that question sequence had no effect on cooperation rate. See Roose, H., De Lange, D., Agneessens, F., & Waege, H. (2002, May). Theatre audience on stage: Three experiments analysing the effects of survey design features on survey response in audience research. *Marketing Bulletin, 13*, 1–10.
55. They also represent new presentation and format considerations that need to be researched. See, for example, Healey, B., Macpherson, T., & Kuijten, B., (2005, May). An empirical evaluation of three web survey design principles. *Marketing Bulletin, 16*, 1–9; Christian, L. M., Dillman, D. A., & Smyth, J. D. (2007, Spring). Helping respondents get it right the first time: The influence of words, symbols, and graphics in web surveys. *Public Opinion Quarterly, 71*(1), 113–125.
56. Highly sophisticated questionnaire design systems have a great many question formats and types in their libraries, and they sometimes have algorithms built into them to arrange the questions into a logical format. See Jenkins, S., & Solomonides, T. (1999/2000, Winter). Automating questionnaire design and construction. *International Journal of Market Research, 42*(1), 79–95.
57. While very effective, "check all that apply" questions have recently been found to be slighly less effectivne than forced choice or yes/no question formats. See Smyth, J. D., Christian, L. M., & Dillman, D. A. (2008). Does yes or no on the telephone mean the same as check-all-that-apply on the web? *Public Opinion Quarterly, 72*(1), 103–113.
58. At least one author says to not pretest is foolhardy; see Webb, Questionnaires and their design.
59. Some authors refer to pretesting as piloting the questionnaire, meaning pilot testing the questionniare. See Baker, Data collection: Questionnaire design.
60. Normally pretests are done individually, but a focus group could be used. See Long, S. A. (1991, May 27). Pretesting questionnaires minimizes measurement error. *Marketing News, 25*(11), 12.
61. For a detailed description of the goals and procedures used in pretesting, see Czaja, R. (1998, May). Questionnaire pretesting comes of age. *Marketing Bulletin, 9*, 52–64.
62. For a comprehensive article on pretesting, see Presser, S., Couper, M. P., Lessler, J. T., Martin, E., Martin, J., Rothgeb, J. M., & Singer, E. (2004, Spring). Methods for testing and evaluating survey questions. *Public Opinion Quarterly, 68*(1), 109–130.

Chapter 9

1. Statement by deputy U.S. commerce secretary Rebecca Blank on release of data measuring 2010 census accuracy. (2012). Lanham, United States, Lanham: Retrieved from http://ezproxy.lib.uwf.edu/login?url=http://search.proquest.com/docview/1015154014?accountid=14787.
2. Wyner, G. A. (2001, Fall). Representation, randomization, and realism. *Marketing Research, 13*(3), 4–5.
3. Sample frame error is especially a concern in business samples. See, for example, Macfarlene, P. (2002). Structuring and measuring the size of business markets. *International Journal of Market Research, 44*(1), 7–30.
4. Gittelman, S., & Trimarchi, E. (2009). Variance between purchasing behavior profiles in a wide spectrum of online sample sources. Retrieved from http://www.mktginc.com/pdf/Short_%20Variance.pdf
5. Wyner, G. A. (2007, Spring). Survey errors. *Marketing Research, 19*(1), 6–8.
6. Bradley, N. (1999, October). Sampling for Internet surveys: An examination of respondent selection for Internet research. *Journal of the Market Research Society, 41*(4), 387.

7. Hall, T. W., Herron, T. L., & Pierce, B. J. (2006, January). How reliable is haphazard sampling? *CPA Journal, 76*(1), 26–27.

8. The Excel cell entry is ROUND(RAND()*30,1), which produces a random number from 0 to .9999 times 30, rounded to no decimal, generating random numbers from 0 to 30.

9. Burton, S., & Soboleva, A. (2011), Interactive or reactive? Marketing with Twitter, Journal of Consumer Marketing, 28(7), 491–499.

10. Foreman, J., & Collins, M. (1991, July). The viability of random digit dialing in the UK. *Journal of the Market Research Society, 33*(3), 219–227; Hekmat, F., & Segal, M. (1984). Random digit dialing: Some additional empirical observations, in D. M. Klein & A. E. Smith (Eds.), *Marketing Comes of Age: Proceedings of the Southern Marketing Association* (pp. 176–180).

11. A recent change in the British telephone system has greatly increased the ability of RDD to access a representative sample. See Nicolaas, G., & Lynn, P. (2002, August). Random-digit dialing in the UK: Viability revisited. *Journal of the Royal Statistical Society, 165*(2), 297–316.

12. See Tucker, C., Brick, J. M., & Meekins, B. (2007, Spring). Household telephone service and usage patterns in the United Stated in 2004: Implications for telephone samples. *Public Opinion Quarterly, 71*(1), 3–22; Link, M. W., Battaglia, M. P., Frankel, M. R., Osborn, L., & Mokdad, A. H. (2008, Spring). A comparison of address-based sampling (ABS) versus random-digit dialing (RDD) for general population surveys. *Public Opinion Quarterly, 72*(1), 6–27.

13. Random digit dialing is used by the major web traffic monitoring companies. See Fatth, H. (2000, November 13). The metrics system. *Adweek, 41*(46), 98–102.

14. Tucker, C., Lepkowski, J. M., & Piekarski, L. (2002). The current efficiency of list-assisted telephone sampling designs. *Public Opinion Quarterly, 66*(3), 321–338.

15. Economy is dependent on the number of clusters. See Zelin, A., & Stubbs, R. (2005). Cluster sampling: A false economy? *International Journal of Market Research, 47*(5), 503–524.

16. See also Sudman, S. (1985, February). Efficient screening methods for the sampling of geographically clustered special populations. *Journal of Marketing Research, 22,* 20–29.

17. Cronish, P. (1989, January). Geodemographic sampling in readership surveys. *Journal of the Market Research Society, 31*(1), 45–51.

18. For a somewhat more technical description of cluster sampling, see Carlin, J. B., & Hocking, J. (1999, October). Design of cross-sectional surveys using cluster sampling: An overview with Australian case studies. *Australian and New Zealand Journal of Public Health, 23*(5), 546–551.

19. Academic global business researchers often use nonprobability samples for cost savings. See Yang, Z., Wang, X., & Su, C. (2006, December). A review of research methodologies in international business. *International Business Review, 15*(6), 601–617.

20. Thomas, J. S., Reinartz, W., & Kumar, V. (2004, July/August). Getting the most out of all your customers. *Harvard Business Review, 82*(7/8), 116–124.

21. Academic marketing researchers often use convenience samples of college students. See Peterson, R. A. (2001, December). On the use of college students in social science research: Insights from a second-order meta-analysis. *Journal of Consumer Research, 28*(3), 450–461.

22. Wyner, G. A. (2001, Fall). Representation, randomization, and realism. *Marketing Research, 13*(3), 4–5.

23. A variation of the snowball sample is found in Eaton, J., & Struthers, C. W. (2002, August). Using the Internet for organizational research: A study of cynicism in the workplace. *CyberPsychology & Behavior, 5*(4), 305–313; university students were required to return surveys completed by family, friends, or coworkers.

24. Browne, K. (2005, February). Snowball sampling: Using social networks to research non-heterosexual women. *Journal of Social Research Methodology, 8*(1), 47–60.

25. For an application of referral sampling, see Moriarity, R. T., Jr., & Spekman, R. E. (1984, May). An empirical investigation of the information sources used during the industrial buying process. *Journal of Marketing Research, 21,* 137–147.

26. Sharma, S. K., Sharma, K., & Makshud, K. (2011). A study and analysis of customer satisfaction of Tata Motors in Jaipur, Rajasthan. *International Journal of Business Management and Economic Research, 3*(4), 250–257.

27. Personal communication from Jerry W. Thomas, President/CEO, Decision Analyst, Inc.

28. For an historical perspective and prediction about online sampling, see Sudman, S., & Blair, E. (1999, Spring). Sampling in the twenty-first century. *Academy of Marketing Science, 27*(2), 269–277.

29. Internet surveys can access hard-to-reach groups. See Pro and con: Internet interviewing. (1999, Summer). *Marketing Research, 11*(2), 33–36.

30. Sample plans are useful wherever someone desires to draw a representative group from a population. For an auditing example, see Martin, J. (2004, August). Sampling made Simple. *The Internal Auditor, 61*(4), 21–23.

Chapter 10

1. One author refers to these attributes as "quality" and "quantity." See Hellebusch, S. J. (2006, September). Know sample quantity for clearer results. *Marketing News, 40*(15), 23–26.

2. Lenth, R. (2001, August). Some practical guidelines for effective sample size determination. *The American Statistician, 55*(3), 187–193.

3. Williams, G. (1999, April). What size sample do I need? *Australian and New Zealand Journal of Public Health, 23*(2), 215–217.

4. Cesana, B. M., Reina, G., & Marubini, E. (2001, November). Sample size for testing a proportion in clinical trials: A "two-step" procedure combining power and confidence interval expected width, *The American Statistician, 55*(4), 288–292.

5. This chapter simplifies a complex topic. See, for example, Williams, What size sample do I need?

6. This chapter pertains to quantitative marketing research samples. For qualitative research situations, see, for example, Christy, R., & Wood, M. (1999). Researching possibilities in marketing. *Qualitative Market Research, 2*(3), 189–196.

7. Frendberg, N. (1992, June). Increasing survey accuracy. *Quirk's Marketing Research Review*. Retrieved from http://www.quirks.com

8. Frendburg (1992) states it simply: "Sampling error has the unique distinction of being a measurable source of error in survey research."

9. We realize that some researchers prefer to always use the sample size formula that includes N; however, since N does not affect sample size unless N is small (or n is large relative to N), we have opted for simplicity in using the sample size formula without N.

10. Xu, G. (1999, June). Estimating sample size for a descriptive study in quantitative research. *Quirk's Marketing Research Review*. Retrieved from http://www.quirks.com

11. For a similar, but slightly different treatment, see Sangren, S. (1999, January). A simple solution to nagging questions about survey, sample size and validity. *Quirk's Marketing Research Review*. Retrieved from http://www.quirks.com

12. For a different formula that uses the difference between two means, see Minchow, D. (2000, June). How large did you say the sample has to be? *Quirk's Marketing Research Review*. Retrieved from http://www.quirks.com

13. For a caution on this approach, see Browne, R. H. (2001, November). Using the sample range as a basis for calculating sample size in power calculations. *The American Statistician, 55*(4), 293–298.

14. See Shiffler, R. E., & Adams, A. J. (1987, August). A correction for biasing effects of pilot sample size on sample size determination. *Journal of Marketing Research, 24*(3), 319–321.

15. For more information, see Lenth, Some practical guidelines for effective sample size determination.

16. Other factors affect the final sample size; see, for example, Sangren, S. (2000, April). Survey and sampling in an imperfect world. *Quirk's Marketing Research Review*. Retrieved from http://www .quirks.com

17. See, for example Cesana, Reina, & Marubini, Sample size for testing a proportion in clinical trials.

18. To see how simple cross-tabulations can increase the required sample size, see Sangren, Survey and sampling in an imperfect world.

19. Kupper, L. L., & Hafner, K. B. (1989, May). How appropriate are popular sample size formulas? *American Statistician, 43*(2), 101–195.

20. Bartlett, J., Kotrlik, J., & Higgins, C. (2001, Spring). Organizational research: Determining appropriate sample size in survey research. *Information Technology, Learning, and Performance Journal, 19*(1), 43–50.

21. Hunter, J. E. (2001, June). The desperate need for replications. *Journal of Consumer Research, 28*(1), 149–158.

22. A different statistical analysis determination of sample size is through use of estimated effect sizes. See, for example, Semon, T. T. (1994). Save a few bucks on sample size, risk millions in opportunity cost. *Marketing News, 28*(1), 19.

23. Ball, J. (2004, February). Simple rules shape proper sample size. *Marketing News, 38*(2), 38.

24. Ibid.

25. See, for example, Hall, T. W., Herron, T. L., Pierce, B. J., & Witt, T. J. (2001, March). The effectiveness of increasing sample size to mitigate the influence of population characteristics in haphazard sampling. *Auditing, 20*(1), 169–185.

Chapter 11

1. In Chapter 10 you learned how to control sampling error by using a sample size formula that determines the sample size required to control for the amount of sample error (e) you are willing to accept.

2. For a breakdown of the types of nonsampling errors encountered in business-to-business marketing research studies, see Lilien, G., Brown, R., & Searls, K. (1991, January 7). Cut errors, improve estimates to bridge biz-to-biz info gap. *Marketing News, 25*(1), 20–22.

3. Interviewer errors have been around for a long time. See Snead, R. (1942). Problems of field interviewers. *Journal of Marketing, 7*(2), 139–145.

4. Intentional errors are especially likely when data is supplied by competitors. See Croft, R. (1992). How to minimize the problem of untruthful response. *Business Marketing Digest, 17*(3), 17–23.

5. To better understand this area, see Barker, R. A. (1987, July). A demographic profile of marketing research interviewers. *Journal of the Market Research Society, 29*, 279–292.

6. For some interesting theories on interviewer cheating, see Harrison, D. E., & Krauss, S. I. (2002, October). Interviewer cheating: Implications for research on entrepreneurship in Africa. *Journal of Developmental Entrepreneurship, 7*(3), 319–330.

7. Peterson, B. (1994, Fall). Insight into consumer cooperation. *Marketing Research, 6*(4), 52–53.

8. These problems are international in scope. For an example from the United Kingdom, see Kreitzman, L. (1990, February 22). Market research: Virgins and groupies. *Marketing*, 35–38.

9. Harrison & Krauss, Interviewer cheating.

10. Brown, B. S., & McInerney, M. (2008, December). Changes in academic dishonesty among business students in the United States. *International Journal of Management, 25*(4), 621–632.

11. Collins, M. (1997, January). Interviewer variability: A review of the problem. *Journal of the Market Research Society, 39*(1), 67–84.

12. See Flores-Macias, F., & Lawson, C. (2008, Spring). Effects of interviewer gender on survey responses: Findings from a household survey in Mexico. *International Journal of Public Opinion Research, 20*(1), 100–110; Oksenberg, L., Coleman, L., & Cannell, C. F. (1986, Spring). Interviewers' voices and refusal rates in telephone surveys. *Public Opinion Quarterly, 50*(1), 97–111.

13. Pol, L. G., & Ponzurick, T. G. (1989, Spring). Gender of interviewer/gender of respondent bias in telephone surveys. *Applied Marketing Research, 29*(2), 9–13.

14. See Hansen, K. M. (2007, Spring). The effects of incentive, interview length, and interviewer characteristics on response rates in a CATI study. *International Journal of Public Opinion Research, 19*(1), 112–121; Olson, K., & Peytchev, A. (2007, Summer). Effect of interviewer experience on interview pace and interviewer attitudes. *Public Opinion Quarterly, 71*(2), 273–286.

15. Sanchez, M. E. (1992, Summer). Effects of questionnaire design on the quality of survey data. *Public Opinion Quarterly, 56*(2), 206–217.

16. Kiecker, P., Nelson, J/ E. (1996, April). Do interviewers follow telephone survey instructions? *Journal of the Market Research Society, 38*(2), 161–173.

17. Loosveldt, G., Carton, A., & Billiet, J. (2004). Assessment of survey data quality: A pragmatic approach focused on interviewer tasks. *International Journal of Market Research, 46*(1), 65–82.

18. Epstein, W. M. (2006, January). Response bias in opinion polls and American social welfare. *Social Science Journal, 43*(1), 99–110.

19. Honomichl, J. (1991, June 24). Legislation threatens research by phone. *Marketing News, 25*(13), 4; Webster, C. (1991). Consumers' attitudes toward data collection methods, in R. L. King (Ed.), *Marketing: Toward the twenty-first century, Proceedings of the Southern Marketing Association*, 220–224.

20. Jarvis, S. (2002, February 4). CMOR finds survey refusal rate still rising. *Marketing News, 36*(3), 4.

21. See, for example, Honomichl, J. (1991, May 27). Making a point—again—for an 'industry identifier.' *Marketing News, 25*(11), 1135; Spethmann, B. (1991, June 10). Cautious consumers have surveyors wary. *Advertising Age, 62*(24), 34.

22. Arnett, R. (1990). Mail panel research in the 1990s. *Applied Marketing Research, 30*(2), 8–10.

23. Not all observers share this view. See Schlossberg, H. (1991, January 7). Research's image better than many think. *Marketing News, 25*(1), 24–25.

24. One author refers to responses to questions on a survey as "hearsay," which includes potential for misunderstanding. See Semon, T. (2003). Settle for personal truth vs. facts in surveys. *Marketing News, 37*(2), 17.

25. Of course, eliminating the interviewer entirely may be an option. See Horton, K. (1990, February). Disk-based surveys: New way to pick your brain. *Software Magazine, 10*(2), 76–77.

26. For early articles on interviewers and supervision, see Clarkson, E. P. (1949, January). Some suggestions for field research supervisors. *Journal of Marketing, 13*(3), 321–329; Reed, V. D., Parker, K. G., & Vitriol, H. A. (1948, January). Selection, training, and supervision

of field interviewers in marketing research. *Journal of Marketing, 12*(3), 365–378.

27. Se Fowler, F., & Mangione, T. (1990). *Standardized survey interviewing: Minimizing interviewer-related error.* Newbury Park, CA: Sage.

28. There are advocates for interviewer certification in the United Kingdom. See Hemsley, S. (2000, August 17). Acting the part. *Marketing Week, 23*(28), 37–40.

29. For an argument against interviewer standardization, see Gobo, G. (2006, October). Set them free: Improving data quality by broadening the interviewer's tasks. *International Journal of Social Research Methodology, 9*(4), 279–301.

30. Tucker, C. (1983, Spring). Interviewer effects in telephone surveys. *Public Opinion Quarterly, 47*(1), 84–95.

31. See Childers, T., & Skinner, S. (1985, January). Theoretical and empirical issues in the identification survey Respondents. *Journal of the Market Research Society, 27,* 39–53; Finlay, J. L., & Seyyet, F. J. (1988). The impact of sponsorship and respondent attitudes on response rate to telephone surveys: An exploratory investigation, in David L. Moore (Ed.), *Marketing: Forward motion, Proceedings of the Atlantic Marketing Association,* 715–721; Goldsmith, R. E. (1987). Spurious response error in a new product survey, in J. J. Cronin, Jr., & M. T. Stith (Eds.), *Marketing: Meeting the Challenges of the 1990s, Proceedings of the Southern Marketing Association,* 172–175; Downs, P. E., & Kerr, J. R. (1982). Recent evidence on the relationship between anonymity and response variables, in J. H. Summey, B. J. Bergiel, & C. H. Anderson (Eds.), *A spectrum of contemporary marketing ideas, Proceedings of the Southern Marketing Association,* 258–264; Glisan, G., & Grimm, J. L. (1982). Improving response rates in an industrial setting: Will traditional variables work? in J. H. Summey, B. J. Bergiel, & C. H. Anderson (Eds.), *A spectrum of contemporary marketing ideas, Proceedings of the Southern Marketing Association,* 265–268; Taylor, R. D., Beisel, J., & Blakney, V. (1984). The effect of advanced notification by mail of a forthcoming mail survey on the response rates, item omission rates, and response speed, in D. M. Klein & A. E. Smith (Eds.), *Marketing comes of age, Proceedings of the Southern Marketing Association,* 184–187; Friedman, H. H. (1979, Spring). The effects of a monetary incentive and the ethnicity of the sponsor's signature on the rate and quality of response to a mall survey. *Journal of the Academy of Marketing Science,* 95–100; Goldstein, L., & Friedman, H. H. (1975, April). A case for double postcards in surveys. *Journal of Advertising Research,* 43–49; Hubbard, R., & Little, E. L. (1988, Fall). Cash prizes and mail response rates: A threshold analysis. *Journal of the Academy of Marketing Science,* 42–44; Childers, T. L., & Ferrell, O. C. (1979, August). Response rates and perceived questionnaire length in mail surveys. *Journal of Marketing Research,* 429–431; Childers, T. L., Pride, W. M., & Ferrell, O. C. (1980, August). A reassessment of the effects of appeals on response to mail surveys. *Journal of Marketing Research,* 365–370; Steele, T., Schwendig, W., & Kilpatrick, J. (1992, March/April). Duplicate responses to multiple survey mailings: A problem? *Journal of Advertising Research,* 26–33; Wilcox, J. B. (1977, November). The interaction of refusal and not-at-home sources of nonresponse bias. *Journal of Marketing Research,* 592–597.

32. An opposite view is expressed by Pruden and Vavra, who contend it is important to identify participants and provide some sort of follow-up acknowledgement of their participation in the survey. Pruden, D. R., & Vavra, T. G. (2000, Summer). Customer research, not marketing research. *Marketing Research, 12*(2), 14–19.

33. See, for example, Lynn, P. (2002, Autumn). The impact of incentives on response rates to personal interview surveys: Role and perceptions of interviewers. *International Journal of Public Opinion Research, 13*(3), 326–336.

34. A comparison on nonresponse errors under different incentives is offered by Barsky, J. K., & Huxley, S. J. (1992, December). A customer-survey tool: Using the 'quality sample.' *The Cornell Hotel and Restaurant Administration Quarterly, 33*(6), 18–25.

35. Derham, P. (2006, October). Increase response rates by increasing relevance. *Quirk's Marketing Research Review, 20*(9), 26–30.

36. Screening questionnaires can also be used. See Waters, K. M. (1991, Spring/Summer). designing screening questionnaires to minimize dishonest answers. *Applied Marketing Research, 31*(1), 51–53.

37. For examples, see Prete, D. D. (1991, September 2). Clients want more specific research—and faster. *Marketing News, 25*(18), 18; Hawk, K. (1992, November 12). More marketers going online for decision support. *Marketing News, 24*(23), 14; Riche, M. F. (1990). Look before leaping. *American Demographics, 12*(2), 18–20; Wolfe, M. J. (1989, September 11). New way to use scanner data and demographics aids local marketers. *Marketing News, 23*(19), 8–9.

38. Coleman, L. G. (1991, January 7). Researchers say nonresponse is single biggest problem. *Marketing News, 25*(1), 32–33.

39. Landler, M. (1991, February 11). The 'bloodbath' in market research. *Business Week, 72,* 74.

40. Baim, J. (1991, June). Response rates: A multinational perspective. *Marketing & Research Today, 19*(2), 114–119.

41. Groves, R. M., Couper, M. P., Presser, S., Singer, E., Tourangeau, R., Acosta, G. P., & Nelson, L. (2006). Experiments in producing nonresponse bias. *Public Opinion Quarterly, 70*(5), 720–736.

42. Tourangeau, R., & Yan, T. (2007, September). Sensitive questions in surveys. *Psychological Bulletin, 133*(5), 859–883.

43. For an interesting attempt to explain participation in surveys, see Heerwegh, D., & Loosveldt, G. (2009, July). Explaining the intention to participate in a web survey: A test of the theory of planned behaviour. *International Journal of Social Research Methodology, 12*(3), 181–195.

44. Eisenfeld, B. (2011, January). Play it forward. *Quirks Marketing Research Review, 25*(1), 58–61.

45. Vogt, C. A., Stewart, S. I. (2001). Response problems in a vacation panel study. *Journal of Leisure Research, 33*(1), 91–105.

46. Farrell, B., & Elken, T. (1994, August 29). Adjust five variables for better mail surveys. *Marketing News,* 20.

47. Tyagi, P. K. (1989, Summer). The effects of appeals, anonymity, and feedback on mail survey response patterns from salespeople. *Journal of the Academy of Marketing Science, 17*(3), 235–241.

48. Suresh, N., & Conklin, M. (2009, July). Designed to engage. *Quirks Marketing Research Review, 24*(7), 34–41.

49. Galesic, M., & Bosnjak, M. (2009, Summer). Effects of questionnaire length on participation and indicators of response quality in a web survey. *Public Opinion Quarterly, 73*(2), 349–360.

50. Some authors use the term *unit nonresponse* to refer to item omissions. See, for example, Hudson, D., Seah, L., Hite, D., & Haab, T. (2004). Telephone presurveys, self-selection, and non-response bias to mail and Internet surveys in economic research. *Applied Economics Letters, 11*(4), 237–240.

51. Shoemaker, P. J., Eichholz, M., & Skewes, E. A. (2002, Summer). Item nonresponse: Distinguishing between don't know and refuse. *International Journal of Public Opinion Research, 14*(2), 193–201.

52. Frankel, L. R. (1982). *Special report on the definition of response rates.* Port Jefferson, NY: Council of American Survey Research Organizations.

53. The CASRO formula pertains to telephone surveys. For web-based surveys, see Bowling, J. M., Rimer, B. K., Lyons, E. J., Golin, C. E., Frydman, G., & Ribisl, K. M. (2006, November). Methodologic

challenges of e-health research. *Evaluation and Program Planning, 29*(4), 390–396.

54. Data quality issues endemic in marketing. (2007, October). *Data Strategy, 3*(8), 10.

55. For yea-saying and nay-saying, see Bachman, J. G., & O'Malley, P. M. (1985, Summer). Yea-saying, nay-saying, and going to extremes: Black–white differences in response styles. *Public Opinion Quarterly, 48,* 491–509; Greenleaf, E. A. (1992, May). Improving rating scale measures by detecting and correcting bias components in some response styles. *Journal of Marketing Research, 29*(2), 176–188.

56. Fisher, S. (2007). How to spot a fake. *Quirk's Marketing Research Review, 21*(1), 44.

57. Speeders are not necessarily straightliners. See Professional test takers. (2008, Spring). *Marketing Research, 20*(1), 4.

58. Vicente, P., Reis, E., & Santos, M. (2009). Using mobile phones for survey research. *International Journal of Market Research, 51*(5), 613–633.

59. ESOMAR. (2012). 26 questions to help research buyers of online samples. Retrieved from http://www.esomar.org/index.php/26-questions.html

Chapter 12

1. It is important for the researcher and client to have a partnership during data analysis. See, for example, Fitzpatrick, M. (2001, August). Statistical analysis for direct marketers—in plain English. *Direct Marketing, 64*(4), 54–56.

2. The use of descriptive statistics is sometimes called *data reduction*, although some authors use this term for any appropriate analysis that makes sense of data. See Vondruska, R. (1995, April). The fine art of data reduction, *Quirk's Marketing Research Review.* Retrieved from www.quirks.com

3. Some authors argue that central tendency measures are too sterile. See, for example, Pruden, D. R., & Vavra, T. G. (2000, Summer). Customer research, not marketing research. *Marketing Research, 12*(2), 14–19.

4. For an illustrative article on central tendency measures used in business valuation, see Sellers, K., Yingping, H., & Campbell, S. (2008, January/February). Measures of central tendency in business valuation. *Value Examiner,* 7–18.

5. Gutsche, A. (2001, September 24). Visuals make the case. *Marketing News, 35*(20), 21–23.

6. Some guidelines are drawn from Ehrenberg, A. (2001, Winter). Data, but no information, *Marketing Research, 13*(2), 36–39.

7. The 95% level is standard in academic research and commonly adopted by practitioners; however, some authors prefer to use the "probability" or 1 minus the discovered significance level of a finding being true. See Zucker, H. (1994). What is significance? *Quirk's Marketing Research Review.* Retrieved from www.quirks.com

8. The frequent misuse of tests of statistical significance in the social sciences, including the field of marketing research, has been well documented. Critics note that researchers endow the tests with more capabilities than they actually have and rely on them as the sole approach for analyzing data (Sawyer & Peter, 1983). Other critics note that combining p values with alpha levels in the often-used model $p \leq \alpha$ = significance is inappropriate, as the two concepts arise from incompatible philosophies (Hubbard & Bayarri, 2003). Users of statistical tests should be familiar with these arguments and other writings noting misinterpretations of statistical significance testing (Carver, 1978). See: Sawyer, A. G., & Peter, J. P. (1983, May). The significance of statistical significance tests in marketing research. *Journal of Marketing Research, 20,* 122–133; Hubbard, R., & Bayarri, M. J. (2003, August). Confusion over measures of

evidence (p's) versus errors (a's) in classical statistical testing (with comments). *The American Statistician, 57,* 171–182; Carver, R. P. (1978, August). The case against statistical significance testing. *Harvard Educational Review, 48,* 278–399.

9. Some disciplines, such as psychology and medicine, encourage their researchers to refrain from performing hypothesis and to report confidence intervals instead. See Fidler, F., Cumming, G., Burgman, M., & Thomason, N. (2004, November). Statistical reform in medicine, psychology and ecology. *Journal of Socio-Economics, 33*(5), 615–630; Fidler, F., Thomason, N., Cumming, G., Finch, S., & Leeman, J. (2004, February). Research article editors can lead researchers to confidence intervals, but can't make them think: Statistical reform lessons from medicine. *Psychological Science, 15*(2), 119–126.

Chapter 13

1. One author considers t tests (differences tests) to be one of the most important statistical procedures used by marketing researchers. See Migliore, V. T. (1996). If you hate statistics . . . *Quirk's Marketing Research Review.* Retrieved from http://www.quirks.com

2. For a contrary view, see Mazur, L. (2000, June 8). The only truism in marketing is they don't exist. *Marketing,* 20.

3. Unfortunately, there is no common agreement on the nature of statistical significance. See Hubbard, R., & Armstrong, J. S. (2006). Why we don't really know what statistical significance means: Implications for educators. *Journal of Marketing Education, 28*(2), 114–120.

4. Meaningful difference is sometimes called "practical significance." See Thompson, B. (2002, Winter). "Statistical," "practical," and "clinical": How many kinds of significance do counselors need to consider? *Journal of Counseling and Development, 30*(1), 64–71.

5. This is common, but controversial. See Ozgur, C., & Strasser, S. (2004). A study of the statistical inference criteria: Can we agree on when to use z versus t? *Decision Sciences Journal of Innovative Education, 2*(2), 177–192.

6. For some cautions about differences tests, see Helgeson, N. (1999). The insignificance of significance testing. *Quirk's Marketing Research Review.* Retrieved from http://www.quirks.com

7. Hulten, P., & Vanyushyn, V. (2011). Impulse purchases of groceries in France and Sweden. *Journal of Consumer Marketing, 28*(5), 376–384.

8. Strutton, D., Taylor, D., & Thompson, K. (2011). Investigating generational differences in e-WOM behaviors. *International Journal of Advertising, 30*(4), 559–586.

9. Hellebusch, S. J. (2001, June 4). One chi square beats two z tests. *Marketing News, 35*(12), 11, 13.

10. For illumination, see Burdick, R. K. (1983, August). Statement of hypotheses in the analysis of variance. *Journal of Marketing Research, 20,* 320–324.

11. For an example of the use of paired samples t tests, see Ryan, C., & Mo, X. (2001, December). Chinese visitors to New Zealand: demographics and perceptions. *Journal of Vacation Marketing, 8*(1), 13–27.

Chapter 14

1. For elaboration and an example, see Semon, T. (1999, August). Use your brain when using a Chi-square *Marketing News, 33*(16), 6.

2. It is not advisable to use cross-tabulations analysis with Chi-square when there are cases of expected cell frequencies of less than 5. See Migliore, V. (1998). Ten research industry secrets and how to handle them *Quirk's Marketing Research Review.* Retrieved from http:///www.quirks.com

3. For advice on when to use Chi-square analysis, see Hellebush, S. J. (2001, June 4). One Chi square beats two Z tests. *Marketing News, 35*(12), 11, 13.

4. An alternative view is that the researcher is testing multiple cases of percentage differences (analogous to multiple independent group means tests), in a cross-tabulation table, and use of the Chi-square test compensates for Type I error that reduces the confidence level. See Neal, W. (1989, March). The problem with multiple paired comparisons in crosstabs. *Marketing Research, 1*(1), 52–54.

5. Muhdi, L., & Boutellier, R. (2010). Diffusion of potential health-related e-services: An analysis of Swiss health customer perspectives. *Journal of Management and Marketing in Healthcare, 3*(1), 60–72.

6. Garee, M. (1997, September). Statistics don't lie if you know what they're really saying. *Marketing News, 31*(9), 11.

7. Correlation is sensitive to the number of scale points, especially in instances when variables have less than 10 scale points. See Martin, W. (1973, August. Effects of scaling on the correlation coefficient: Additional considerations, *Journal of Marketing Research, 15*(2), 304–308.

8. For a more advanced treatment of scatter diagrams, see Goddard, B. L. (2000, April). The power of computer graphics for comparative analysis. *The Appraisal Journal, 68*(2), 134–141.

9. Mehdizadeh, S. (2010). Self-presentation 2.0: Narcissism and self-esteem on Facebook. *Cyberpsychology, Behavior, and Social Networking, 13*(4), 357–364.

10. See also Gibson, L. (2007). Irreverent thoughts: Just what are correlation and regression? *Marketing Research, 19*(2), 30–33.

Chapter 15

1. At least one marketing researcher thinks regression analysis is so complex that it actually clouds reality. See Semon, T. T. (2006). Complex analysis masks real meaning. *Marketing News, 40*(12), 7.

2. There are, of course, other and more acceptable ways of identifying outliers. However, our approach relates to the graphical presentation we have used for visualizing linear relationships existing in correlations and regression. At best, our approach simply introduces students to outlier analysis and helps them identify the most obvious cases.

3. Semon, T. (1999, June 23). Outlier problem has no practical solution *Marketing News, 31*(16), 2.

4. A marketing academic has recommended graphing to researchers: Zinkhan, G. (1993). Statistical inference in advertising research. *Journal of Advertising, 22*(3), 1.

5. For more sophisticated handling of outliers, see Clark, T. (1989, June). Managing outliers: Qualitative issues in the handling of extreme observations in marketing research. *Marketing Research, 2*(2), 31–48.

6. For more information, see, for example, Grapentine, T. (1997, Fall). Managing multicollinearity. *Marketing Research, 9*(3), 11–21; Mason, R. L., Gunst, R. F., & Webster, J. T. (1986). Regression analysis and problems of multicollinearity in marketing models: Diagnostics and remedial measures. *International Journal of Research in Marketing, 3*(3), 181–205.

7. Lee, S., & Moonhee, C. (2011, December). Social media use in a mobile broadband environment: Examination of determinants of Twitter and Facebook use. *International Journal of Mobile Marketing, 6*(2), 71–87.

8. For a graphical presentation, see Stine, R. (1995, February). Graphical interpretation of variance inflation factors. *The American Statistician, 49*(1), 53–56.

9. For alternatives, see Wang, G. (1996, Spring). How to handle multicollinearity in regression modeling. *The Journal of Business Forecasting, 14*(4), 23–27.

10. Leelakulthanit, O., & Boonchai, H. (2011). Factors that impact customer satisfaction: Evidence from the Thailand mobile cellular network industry. *International Journal of Management and Marketing Research, 4*(2), 67–76.

11. Cano, L. Z., Sandoval, E. C., & Olivares Urbina, M. A. (2012). Proposals for marketing strategies for optical centers based on the consumer. *Global Conference on Business and Finance Proceedings, 7*(1), 601–606.

12. Our description pertains to "forward" stepwise regression. We admit that this is a simplification of stepwise multiple regression.

13. See, for example, Kennedy, P. (2005, Winter). Oh no! I got the wrong sign! What should I do? *Journal of Economic Education, 36*(1), 77–92.

14. Our description of regression is introductory. Two books that expand this description are Lewis-Beck, M. S. (1980). *Applied regression: An introduction.* Newbury Park, CA: Sage; Schroeder, L. D., Sjoffquist, D. L., & Stephan, P. E. (1986). *Understanding regression analysis: An introductory guide.* Newbury Park, CA: Sage.

15. For readable treatments of problems encountered in multiple regression applied to marketing research, see Mullet, G. (1994, October). Regression, regression. *Quirk's Marketing Research Review.* Retrieved from http://www.quirks.com; Mullet, G. (1998, June). Have you ever wondered… *Quirk's Marketing Research Review.* Retrieved from http://www.quirks.com; Mullet, G. (2003, February). Data abuse, *Quirk's Marketing Research Review.* Retrieved from http://www.quirks.com.

16. Regression analysis is commonly used in academic marketing research. Here are some examples: Callahan, F. X. (1982, April/May). Advertising and profits 1969–1978. *Journal of Advertising Research, 22,* 17–22; Dubinsky, A. J., & Levy, M. (1989, Summer). Influence of organizational fairness on work outcomes of retail salespeople. *Journal of Retailing, 65,* 221–252; Frieden, J. B., & Downs, P. E. (1986, Fall). Testing the social involvement model in an energy conservation context. *Journal of the Academy of Marketing Science, 14,* 13–20; and Tellis, G. J., & Fornell, C. (1988, February). The relationship between advertising and product quality over the product life cycle: A contingency theory. *Journal of Marketing Research, 25,* 64–71.

17. Taken from: Bruning, E. R., Kovacic, M. L., & Oberdick, L. E. (1985). Segmentation analysis of domestic airline passenger markets. *Journal of the Academy of Marketing Science, 13*(1), 17–31.

Chapter 16

1. Forbes, C. (2012, April). Staying in tune with today: How technology can improve the access and consumption of research presentations. *Quirk's Marketing Research Review,* 52–55.

2. Based on personal communications with the authors and Michael Lotti. Originally published in: Burns, A., & Bush, R. (2005). *Marketing research: Online research applications* (4th ed.). Upper Saddle River, NJ: Prentice Hall, 580.

3. Rohde, J. A. (2012, May). Three steps to better research presentations. Retrieved from Quirk's e-newsletter at http://www.quirks.com

4. Deshpande, R., & Zaltman, G. (1982, February). Factors affecting the use of market research information: A path analysis. *Journal of Marketing Research, 19,* 14–31.

5. Deshpande, R., & Zaltman, G. (1984, February). A comparison of factors affecting researcher and manager perceptions of market research use. *Journal of Marketing Research, 21,* 32–38.

6. Fink, A. (2003). *How to report on surveys* (2nd ed.). Thousand Oaks, CA: Sage, 35.

7. *The American Heritage Dictionary of the English Language* (4th ed.) (2000). Boston: Houghton-Mifflin. Retrieved from http://www.dictionary.com, accessed May 24, 2005.

8. *American Heritage Dictionary.* Retrieved from http://www.dictionary.com, accessed May 24, 2005.

9. To properly cite your sources, see Modern Language Association of America. (2001). *MLA handbook for writers of research papers* (5th ed.). New York: Author; American Psychological Association. (2010). *Publication manual of the American Psychological Association* (6th ed.). Washington, DC: Author.

10. Jameson, D. A. (1993, June). The ethics of plagiarism: How genre affects writers' use of source materials. *The Bulletin, 2,* 18–27.

11. Imperiled copyrights. (1998, April 15). *New York Times*, A24.

12. See Section A.7, Marketing Research Association's Code of Marketing Research Standards. Retrieved from http://www.marketing research.org/standards, accessed June 7, 2012.

13. Ober, S. (1998). *Contemporary business communication* (3rd ed.). Boston: Houghton Mifflin, 121.

14. Tufte, E. R. (1983). *The visual display of quantitative information.* Cheshire, CT: Graphics Press.

15. Based on personal conversation with the authors and *Research Now's* Kartik Pashupati following a discussion of terms used by marketing research practitioners on March 9, 2012.

16. Thomas, J. (2001, November). Executive excellence. *Marketing Research, 13,* 11–12.

Name Index

Subject Index

Selected Formulas

Chapter 10 Determining the Size of a Sample

p. 237: Survey Sampling, International Formula for Determining the Number of Telephone Numbers Needed

$$\frac{\text{Number of Telephone}}{\text{Numbers Needed}} = \frac{\text{Completed Interviews}}{\text{Working Phone Rate} \times \text{Incidence} \times \text{Completion Rate}}$$

$$\pm \text{ Sample Error Percent} = 1.96 \sqrt{\frac{pq}{n}}$$

p. 245: Standard sample size formula for a proportion

$$n = \frac{z^2(pq)}{e^2}$$

Where

  n = the sample size
  z = standard error associated with the chosen level of confidence (typically, 1.96)
  p = estimated percent in the population
  $q = 100 - p$
  e = acceptable sample error

p. 248: Sample size formula for a mean

$$n = \frac{z^2 s^2}{e^2}$$

Where

  n = the sample size
  z = standard error associated with the chosen level of confidence (typically, 1.96)
  s = variability indicated by an estimated standard deviation
  e = the amount of precision or allowable error in the sample estimate of the population

Chapter 12 Using Basic Descriptive Analysis, Performing Population Estimates, and Testing Hypotheses

p. 292: Formula for a sample mean

$$\text{Mean } (\bar{x}) = \frac{\sum\limits_{i=1}^{n} x_i}{n}$$

Where

  n = the number of cases
  x_i = each individual value

  $\sum$ signifies that all the x_i values are summed

p. 294: Formula for a sample standard deviation

$$\text{Standard deviation } (s) = \sqrt{\frac{\sum\limits_{i-1}^{n}(x_i - \bar{x})^2}{n-1}}$$

Where

  x_i — each individual observation
  $\bar{x}$ = the sample mean

p. 305: Formula for standard error of the mean

$$s_{\bar{x}} = \frac{s}{\sqrt{n}}$$

Where

  $s_{\bar{x}}$ = standard error of the mean
  s = sample standard deviation
  n = sample size

p. 305: Formula for standard error of the percentage

$$s_p = \sqrt{\frac{pq}{n}}$$

Where

  s_p = standard error of the percentage
  p = the sample percentage
  $q = (100 - p)$
  n = sample size

p. 308: Formula for confidence interval for a Mean

$$\bar{x} \pm z_\alpha s_{\bar{x}}$$

Where

  $\bar{x}$ = sample mean
  z_α = z value for 95% or 99% level of confidence
  $s_{\bar{x}}$ = standard error of the mean

p. 308: Formula for confidence interval for a Percentage

$$p \pm z_\alpha s_p$$

Where

  p = sample percentage
  z_α = z value for 95% or 99% level of confidence
  s_p = standard error of the percentage

p. 313: Formula for test of a hypothesis about a percent

$$z = \frac{p - \pi_H}{s_{\bar{x}}}$$

Where

  p = the sample percentage
  π_H = the hypothesized population percentage
  s_p = the standard error of the percentage

p. 313: Formula for test of a hypothesis about a mean

$$z = \frac{\bar{x} - \mu_H}{s_{\bar{x}}}$$

Where

  $\bar{x}$ = the sample mean
  μ_H = the hypothesized population mean
  $s_{\bar{x}}$ = standard error of the mean

Chapter 13 Implementing Basic Differences Tests

p. 329: Formula for significance of the difference between two percentages

$$z = \frac{p_1 - p_2}{s_{p_1 - p_2}}$$

Where

  p_1 = percentage found in sample 1
  p_2 = percentage found in sample 2